20,4

THE HUMAN SPECIES
Its Nature, Evolution, and Ecology

THE
HUMAN SPECIES
ITS NATURE, EVOLUTION, AND ECOLOGY

RICHARD M. TULLAR

Professor Emeritus of Zoology, Los Angeles Pierce College

McGRAW-HILL BOOK COMPANY New York St. Louis San Francisco Auckland Bogotá Düsseldorf Johannesburg London Madrid Mexico Montreal New Delhi Panama Paris São Paulo Singapore Sydney Tokyo Toronto

This book was set in Garamond
by Ruttle, Shaw & Wetherill, Inc.
The editors were William J. Willey,
Thomas A. P. Adams, and Richard S. Laufer;
the designer was Barbara Ellwood;
the production supervisor was Charles Hess.
The drawings were done
by E. H. Technical Services.
Von Hoffmann Press, Inc., was
printer and binder.

THE HUMAN SPECIES
Its Nature, Evolution, and Ecology

Library of Congress Cataloging in Publication Data

Tullar, Richard M   date
  The human species.

  Includes index.
    1.   Physical anthropology. 2. Human biology.
3. Human ecology. I. Title.
GN60.T84   573   76-27295
ISBN 0-07-065423-9

1 2 3 4 5 6 7 8 9 0 VHVH 7 8 3 2 1 0 9 8 7 6

To Gric with love

CONTENTS

PREFACE

This book is an outgrowth of a life-long preoccupation with things biological, of which nearly thirty years have been spent teaching college courses in human biology, physical anthropology, human evolution, and ecology. I believe that the kind of knowledge embodied in these courses, and conceptualized in this text, is of inherent interest and value to everyone pursuing a college education. It was with this conviction foremost in mind that I undertook to write about the biological nature, evolution, and ecology of the human species.

The Human Species: Its Nature, Evolution, and Ecology asks and attempts to answer three questions: What are we? Where did we come from (and how)? What problems confront us as a species for the foreseeable future? They are the central themes of the three sections into which the book is divided.

The first section, The Human Species, addresses the question of our biological nature. Evidence is presented to substantiate the biological relationship of humankind to nonhuman primates, with particular stress on the behavior and ecology of the latter, to give perspective to our biological kinship. Two chapters are devoted exclusively to the human animal and its distinctive anatomical, physiological, psychosocial, and cultural features.

The second section, Human Evolution, investigates our evolutionary history and the processes involved in evolutionary change. In tracing the course of human evolution to the present, particular attention is given to the importance of paleoecology in directing that course and to the kinds of life-style followed by various members of the hominid lineage. The process of evolution is examined in three chapters. The first deals with the hereditary basis of biological change; the second carries evolutionary mechanisms to the populational and ecological levels and discusses the nature and course of evolutionary change; the third investigates the consequences of evolution—extinction or adaptation—and ends with a discussion of the adaptiveness of *Homo sapiens.*

The final section, Human Ecology, is concerned with the ecological problems of the human species and possible solutions. After an introduction to the principles of general ecology, the remaining chapters are devoted to the human population and environment: the structure, distribution, and growth of human populations; the means by which population size can be held within the environmental capacity of our planet; resource depletion, waste, and pollution; and a number of remedial measures. The book ends with matters at the forefront of current discussion: how our ecological crises may be resolved by changing from a growth to a stable economy based upon ecological land-use and urban planning.

Annotated suggested readings appear at the end of each chapter along with review questions, which are intended as a multi-purpose chapter summary, student review, list of learning objectives, and as problems for stimulating class discussion. The glossary is separate from the index and should serve as a convenient reference.

The thrust of the book is functional throughout. I have avoided scientific minutiae and nomenclature except where I felt they were essential to an understanding of a concept or process. The details of anatomic structure and physiological mechanisms are considered only when they contribute to a better comprehension of the whole organism, its origin, its behavior, or the ecological niche it fills. Behavior, ecological setting, and evolutionary process are recurring themes of emphasis in every section.

Primarily, the book is written for students who have little or no training in the sciences. Treatment of the subject is narrative in style: concept follows concept in a logical succession both in and between chapters. Every effort has been made to make the writing flow in an easily readable manner while providing good solid background for those planning to pursue human biology, anthropology, or human ecology in greater depth.

This text is unusual because it interrelates human biology, human evolution, and human ecology into one integrated whole. Introductory works in physical anthropology little more than mention human ecology, and they fail to describe the social behavior of man with the same vigor that appears in their discussion of other primates. Texts in human ecology are weak in human evolution, evolutionary process and human behavior. And general texts in human biology are often prodigious tomes of biologic detail which lack adequate treatment of human evolution, human behavior, or the environmental aspects of human ecology. *The Human Species* is of sufficient depth and comprehensivenesss to serve as a sound introductory text in all three fields.

During the long process of bringing this book to its present form I have received much valuable assistance which I gratefully acknowledge. Many former colleagues at Los Angeles Pierce College encouraged and advised me at various stages. Among them, William R. Madden and Carole S. Kalionzes of the library staff were especially helpful. Other acknowledgments must include Edward S. Tarvyd, Roberta A. Beatty, and my several reviewers who critically read and commented on part or all of the manuscript, especially Naomi Bishop, University of Massachusetts, Boston; Philip G. Grant, University of Texas at Austin; Eldra Soloman, Hillsborough Community College; and Curtis A. Williams, State University of New York, Purchase. Richard F. Firenze offered invaluable service by not only reviewing the entire manuscript but also testing a preliminary version of the text at Broome Community College, Binghamton, New York. And I am equally indebted to Paul B. Weisz of Brown University whose witty and acidulous criticisms raised not only my blood pressure but the quality of my writing as well.

I would also like to extend my appreciation to the staff of McGraw-Hill and particularly to my editors, William J. Willey, Thomas A. P. Adams, and Richard Laufer. John Hendry's perceptive and comprehensive editorial comments were of inestimable value during the preparation of the final draft.

But above all, to her who shielded me from the work-a-day world, created an atmosphere for writing, corrected manuscript, cajoled, inspired, criticized but always empathized, profound gratitude is due my good friend and wife, Shirley Scott Tullar.

RICHARD M. TULLAR

What walks on four feet in the morning,
on two at noon,
and on three in the evening?

SECTION I

In Greek mythology, there lived near the ancient city of Thebes a sphinx that put a certain riddle to any traveler unfortunate enough to come too close to this monster. Those who could not solve the riddle died. The Sphinx itself was destroyed when the riddle was finally answered by Oedipus: "Man crawls on all fours as a baby, walks upright in the prime of life, and uses a staff in old age."

But what is this creature that walks on four legs, then on two, and finally on three? Through more than two thousand years, the answers have been as varied and numerous as one might expect. To Aristotle, this creature was a "political animal." According to Mark Twain the principal difference between a dog and a man is that, "If you pick up a starving dog and make him prosperous, he will not bite you." The French philosopher Blaise Pascal called this creature "the glory and shame of the universe." And perhaps the most famous description of all comes from a source unknown: "Man is the only animal that eats when he is not hungry, drinks when he is not thirsty, and makes love in all seasons." None of these descriptions, of course, tells us much about the creature itself, a species that has left its footprints in the surface of the earth and the dust of the moon.

This first section attempts to clarify our biological identification in five stages. Chapter 1 examines our status as a living organism and identifies us as *primates,* indicating what that term means. Chapter 2 critically inspects the evidence by which this classification has been determined and concludes that our relationship to other primates is based on common descent. Chapter 3 discusses the primate heritage which we share, insofar as it is reflected in the lives of our living primate relatives. Chapters 4 and 5 focus on the human animal—first from the standpoint of its distinguishing anatomical and physiological characteristics; and then from the standpoint of its psychosocial and cultural features. It is in the latter area that we have the greatest difficulty defining our nature, particularly in the sense of understanding why we behave as we do. Man remains, in large measure, an enigma to man.

THE HUMAN SPECIES

ONE

OUR STATUS AS A LIVING ORGANISM

WHAT ARE WE?

The human species is an enigma unto itself. Self-appraisal and self-identification are entirely different endeavors from the challenge of classifying seashells or wildflowers. It is not that the living world around us lacks wonder or mystery, but rather that often we tend to be overwhelmed by our mental ability and symbolic language, and the cultural products they generate. In short, it is difficult for us to be objective about ourselves.

That we are living creatures scarcely can be argued. Furthermore, our characteristics are animallike rather than plantlike: we have muscles, nerves, and a digestive tract; we cannot manufacture food by using the sun's energy in photosynthesis, but we can eat it. These and other characteristics indicate clearly that we are animals. What other animal can pass great bodies of knowledge from generation to generation, or develop complex cultural systems? Are we not more than an animal, or at least a very special kind?

We build jet aircraft, moon rockets, sky-scrapers, and nuclear reactors. We compose symphonies, write poetry, worship gods, sculpt statues, care for the sick and elderly, and assist the poverty-stricken. But these do not make us more than an animal. Neither do rape, robbery, embezzlement, pollution, homicide, suicide, genocide, and wars to end war make us less than one. They may indicate our capacity for committing excesses, but they are the excesses of animals nonetheless. To say that we are more than mere animals because of our culture is like saying that bats are more than mere mammals because of their flight. The whole issue is clouded by the assumption that a mere animal could not possibly become cultured. This implies an abysmal ignorance of both animal nature and human nature. Desmond Morris clarifies this matter when he writes:

> [Man is an] unusual and highly successful species [who] spends a great deal of time examining his higher motives and an equal amount of time studiously ignoring his fundamental ones. He is proud that he has the biggest brain of all the primates, but attempts to conceal the fact that he also has the biggest penis. . . . He is an intensely vocal, acutely exploratory, over-crowded [creature] . . . ; in acquiring lofty new motives, he has lost none of the earthy old ones.[1]

Every animal species[2] is unique. More than one million different species of animals have been identified, each one distinct from all others and singularly adapted to its particular role in the community of living things. We humans count as one species among this million. Our species, however, is a rather exceptional one, ranking with many other exceptional species that have left their mark in the long evolutionary history of life. Like the first backboned animals to survive in a land environment some 400 million years ago, man also is unusual in that he is a pioneer in a new kind of evolution. In the past, all animals have necessarily become adapted to their environment in order to survive. Through culture, however, man has found ways to reverse this process and modify the environment to suit himself.

We surround ourselves in an environment of our own making and go deep into the sea in diving chambers, into flaming infernos in asbestos suits, and into space in rocket ships. From the highest mountain tops to the ocean's depths, from the desert to the Antarctic, and from the planet of our birth to its moon in space, the human species has the widest distribution of any living thing and has indeed ventured where no living being exists. Few, if any, organisms on earth today have not been affected either directly or indirectly by human activity. Certainly no region of any size has escaped the effects of our enormous energies. Because of our near-universal presence and influence, we would be regarded as unusual even if biology books could be written by oysters or centipedes.

It should not be assumed that our environmental manipulations are always well-advised. Our efforts at environmental management often have had serious consequences for other forms of life and even for ourselves, as we will see in the discussions on the human population and environment in Section III.

By any biological standards we are exceptional specimens among the citizenry of nature. But citizens of nature we are. Although unique, we are a product of natural processes that have been in operation for hundreds of millions of years. We are consequently an integral part of nature, a fact that all too often slips our mind.

The variety and diversity of living species attest to the adaptability of living things to a multitude of living conditions and ways of life. More than $1\frac{1}{2}$ million different species of microorganisms, plants, and animals have been identified, each a unique biological specialist. Of this enormous aggregation of organisms,

---

[1] D. Morris, *The Naked Ape*, New York: McGraw-Hill Book Company, 1967, p. 9.

[2] The species is the basic unit of biologic classification. It is a population of interbreeding individuals which do not interbreed with other species (populations).

animals clearly are the most complex, from the standpoint both of architectural form and of adaptive behavior. This is particularly apparent in the so-called higher animals, represented by octopuses, insects, fishes, reptiles, birds, and mammals. Elegant and sophisticated behavioral responses are the rule here, not the exception. Certain untrained nonhuman representatives of this group can fashion as well as use a variety of tools, will share their food with others, are capable of reasoning, and have demonstrated a competence in learning language skills.[3] Others are capable of behavioral feats quite beyond our capabilities. They can navigate a migratory journey of hundreds and thousands of kilometers through water or air without prior training or experience. Some can clock the position of the sun in the heavens without seeing it and can communicate that information to others. To say that man is an animal, then, is not to debase him.

Having assigned our species to the kingdom of animals, we can now inquire further into our biological relationships to ascertain what kind of an animal we are. This determination can be made by comparing our basic biological characteristics with the qualifications required for inclusion in some one of two dozen or so major animal groups, or *phyla,* that constitute the animal kingdom. Fundamentally, we are bilaterally symmetrical animals. That is, we have right and left sides, front and hind ends, and bellies and backs. We are also segmented; that is, many of our organs are a repeated series of structures; our vertebrae have nerves and blood vessels aligned with them; our ribs have muscles that lie be-between them. Possessing vertebrae qualifies us as one of the many and varied *vertebrate* animals. Like them, our vertebrae interconnect with one another to form a *backbone.* It not only supports our body but also encloses and protects our spinal cord. Because we are vertebrates, we belong in the phylum of animals known as the *chordates* (Fig. 1-1), which includes fishes, amphibians, reptiles, birds, and mammals, as well as their invertebrate relatives, the sea squirts and lancelets.

WHAT IT MEANS TO BE A MAMMAL

Of the several major groups, or *classes,* of vertebrates, we are clearly mammals (Fig. 1-2). More specifically, as explained in Fig. 1-2, we belong among the *placental* mammals rather than the pouch-bearing mammals such as the kangaroo and opossum or egg-laying mammals such as the duckbill platypus. The placental mammals are distinguished from other types in that their young reach an advanced stage of development within the uterus (womb) before they are born. The embryo is nourished by a structure, the *placenta,* which is formed by the union of the uterine lining with the outermost membrane of the embryo. These mammals have been preeminently successful the world over because of a number of characteristics which have increased enormously their capacity for survival in many different environments. Consequently, these animals have diversified over their 100-million-year history into a great variety of species. The biological attributes largely responsible for their expansion are (1) warm-bloodedness, (2) increased nutritional efficiency, (3) new reproductive strategies, and (4) behavioral adaptations.

Warm-bloodedness

Whether an organism is as simple as a bacterium or as complex as a mammal, all the basic physiological processes which support it consist of elaborate and elegantly coordinated sequences of chemical reactions. Chemical energy is responsible for the discharge of nerve impulses in a brain, their transmission to a pair of legs, and the brisk walk down the street that results. All biological activity, whether it be muscular, glandular, or nervous, is ultimately chemical at its source.

[3] R. S. Fouts, "Language: Origins, Definitions and Chimpanzees," *Journal of Human Evolution,* vol. 3, no. 6, November 1974, p. 480.

A

B

FIGURE 1-1
The chordate phylum. Chordates are those animals that possess a notochord (a skeletal rod running along the back) at some time in their lives. The notochord of vertebrates (*B, C, D, E,* and *F*) is partially or completely replaced during larval or embryonic development by vertebrae made of cartilage or bone. The lancelets (*A*) lack vertebrae and are therefore invertebrate (nonvertebrate) chordates. Vertebrates consist of five classes: *B*, fishes (perch); *C*, amphibians (bullfrog); *D*, reptiles (alligator); *E*, birds (robin); *F*, mammals (fox). [*B, Los Angeles County Museum of Natural History; C–F, San Diego Zoo Photos, all but robin by Ron Garrison.*]

C

The speed of these activities—their metabolic rate—is dependent upon the body temperature at which chemical reactions take place. Within the temperature range tolerated by living processes, it is generally true that the rate of chemical reaction is doubled for every 10°C increase in temperature. The importance of temperature to biological activity is clearly demonstrated by cold-blooded vertebrates such as lizards and snakes, which are unable to control their body temperature. Their rapid movements during warm weather contrast sharply with the sluggish muscular responses they make when they are cold. Daily, as well as

D

E

F

seasonal, changes in air temperature greatly affect the level of activity in cold-blooded vertebrates. Except in tropical areas, the essential activities of hunting, feeding, defense, and reproduction must be carried out mainly in daylight hours and during nonwinter months. Mammals and birds can control their body temperature and are not so restricted. Being warm-blooded, they gain a significant advantage over their cold-blooded relatives in that they can maintain a steady level of activity regardless

A

FIGURE 1-2
Mammals are warm-blooded verte-brates that have hair and nourish their young with milk secreted from mammary glands. The class Mammalia consists of three subclasses: *A*, the egg-laying mammals (duck-bill platypus); *B*, the pouch-bearing mammals (kangaroo and opossum above); and *C*, the placental mammals (orangutan and impala above). In placental mammals, the young (embryo, fetus) undergoes complete development within the uterus (womb), nourished by a structure, the placenta, which is formed by the union of the uterine lining with the outermost membrane of the embryo. [*A, Courtesy of Sol Karlin, Los Angeles Pierce College; B and C, San Diego Zoo Photos, all but orangutan by Ron Garrison.*]

B

C

of changes in external temperature. Consequently, in the temperate zones of the world, mammals and birds are not only more actively competitive with other creatures than are reptiles and amphibians, but they are also capable of thriving in vast polar and subpolar regions where cold-blooded vertebrates have failed to become established.

The internal body temperature of a mammal is maintained at a level that permits optimal metabolic efficiency for that particular mammalian species and the "life style" to which it is adapted. The extent to which this temperature varies is under the control of a heat-regulating center in the mammalian brain.

A warm-blooded animal must expend considerable energy just to maintain a constant body temperature. This means the mammal has an energy requirement the cold-blooded animal does not have: it is committed to eating larger quantities of food as well as to utilizing that food as efficiently as possible.

An added energy requirement cannot be met without improving both the rate of consumption and the distribution of oxygen. Mammals have increased oxygen intake by means of a *diaphragm,* a muscular partition unique to mammals which separates the chest from the abdominal cavity (Fig. 1-3). When the dome-like diaphragm is flattened through muscular contraction, the chest cavity is enlarged and air is thereby sucked into the lungs. Air intake may be augmented by the contraction of a set of muscles between adjacent ribs which enlarges the chest cavity at its apex below the neck. With these two mechanisms—diaphragm and rib muscles—in operation, the ventilation of the lungs can be exceedingly rapid and efficient. By way of contrast, cold-blooded vertebrates, such as lizards and snakes, lack a diaphragm and must rely solely on their rib muscles for air intake.

The distribution of oxygen via the bloodstream to all parts of the body also has been greatly improved in mammals. Oxygen-depleted blood returning from the body to the heart is not mixed with blood going from the

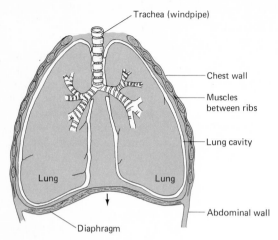

Trachea (windpipe)

Chest wall

Muscles
between ribs

Lung cavity

Lung   Lung

Abdominal wall

Diaphragm

FIGURE 1-3
Human lungs and diaphragm. When muscles of the dia-
phragm contract, the domelike structure flattens (arrow).
This enlarges the chest cavity and air is sucked into the
lungs. [*Modified from B. A. Schottelius and D. D. Schottelius,
Textbook of Physiology, 17th ed., Mosby, St. Louis, 1973.*]

heart to the body, as it is in amphibians and
reptiles. The four-chambered heart maintains
this separation of oxygen-rich and oxygen-poor
blood by providing a separate pump for each
kind of blood: the two chambers on the right
side pump unoxygenated blood to the lungs for
oxygenation while the two chambers on the left
side pump oxygenated blood that has returned
from the lungs to the rest of the body (Fig. 1-4).

The heat energy needed to maintain normal body temperature comes essentially from
contracting muscles. As much as 80 percent of
the energy used in muscle contraction is lib-
erated as heat. Even a relaxed mammal produces heat in this way because many of the
voluntary muscles are continuously in a state of
mild contraction, a condition known as *muscle
tone*. A resting person will radiate as much heat
as a 60-watt light bulb in this manner. During
cold weather, muscle tension increases and we,
like other mammals, may start to shiver, our
teeth may chatter, and our legs may quiver.
Hair erector muscles all over our body con-

tract, producing gooseflesh. In other mammals, hair erector muscles elevate the hair to
create insulating dead-air spaces in their furry
coats. As a result of these responses to cold,
heat production may be augmented by as much
as 400 percent.

The heat produced by muscular tension
in the mammalian body not only must be
regulated in accordance with external temperatures but also must be effectively used.
During cold weather only minimal amounts of
heat can be lost to the surroundings. During
hot weather, when the external temperature is
higher than normal body heat, maximal
amounts of heat should be released to the
environment if body temperature is to be kept
constant.

To control heat loss, mammals have a
number of unique and effective adaptations at
their disposal. As previously stated, the mammalian coat of hair may act as an insulating
blanket, restricting heat loss. Lying beneath
the skin is another insulating blanket in the
form of a layer of subcutaneous fat (*sub*, "beneath"; *cutaneous*, "skin"). In the skin itself, and
external to the subcutaneous fat, many mammals possess innumerable sweat glands and a
rich network of small blood vessels. Sweat
(mainly water) secreted onto the skin surface
releases large amounts of heat as it evaporates.[4]
Many mammals, for example, dogs and even
man on occasion, lose heat in a similar fashion
by panting: moisture is evaporated from the
lining of respiratory passages. The small
cutaneous blood vessels may act either to conserve or lose heat by regulating the amount of
blood in the skin. During hot weather these
blood vessels are dilated and carry relatively
large amounts of blood close to the body surface, where heat can easily radiate away. In
cold weather these same vessels are constricted, allowing substantially less heat to be
lost in this way.

[4] When a fluid evaporates, it absorbs heat from its surroundings.
Humans lose about 600 kilocalories (diet calories) per liter of
sweat evaporated from the body.

Nutritional efficiency

Mammals have evolved a number of significant adaptations insofar as the exploitation of food energy is concerned. Many of these trace their origins back 250 million years, before the first primitive mammals had yet evolved from their ancestors, the mammallike reptiles. At first glance, these adaptive features appear to be a hodgepodge of seemingly unrelated attributes. But under closer scrutiny they clearly involve certain aspects of increased nutritional efficiency, specifically (1) more effective mobilization of the energy derived from food, (2) greater capacity for food intake, and (3) more rapid and complete digestion of food.

Mammals, unlike cold-blooded vertebrates, carry their legs beneath them rather than extended to the side. Positioning the limbs vertically rather than laterally affords leg muscles a much better mechanical advantage, reducing the energy necessary to keep the body off the ground.[5] This makes running not only easier but also swifter.

Compared to reptiles, mammals have a greatly simplified, yet highly functional, skeleton. Neck ribs and abdominal ribs, primitive structures still found in reptiles, are wanting in mammals. The loss of ribs in the neck permits freer neck movements. This in turn enhances the potential not only for increased food intake but also for increased efficiency of food intake per unit of energy expended. The effectiveness of a pair of jaws can be greatly improved when manipulated from the end of a supple neck. The absence of abdominal ribs similarly allows greater flexibility in the lower trunk and less restricted movement of the hind legs directly below. This increased flexibility has made possible a type of running found only in mammals in which the hind feet can be extended between the front legs by a forward bending (flexing) of the abdominal trunk.

Members of the dog and cat families are particularly expert at back-flexing and include the fastest terrestrial animals on earth.

Structural simplification also has occurred in the mammalian skull and jaw. The crocodile, a representative reptile, has 44 bones in its skull and 12 in its lower jaw. Man, by contrast, has 28 bones in the skull and 2 in the lower jaw (1 on each side, not 6 like the crocodile). In the evolution of mammals there has been a significant reduction in the number of bones through both loss and fusion. A comparison of the lower jaws of a modern mammal and an ancient mammalian ancestor illustrates this clearly (Fig. 1-5). These economies have been made at the same time that the functional effectiveness of the upper and lower jaws have been improved.

FIGURE 1-4
Schematic diagrams of blood circulation in a mammal. *A,* Purely schematic; *B,* less schematic, showing relationship of the four heart chambers to blood flow. Color denotes oxygenated blood; black, unoxygenated blood.

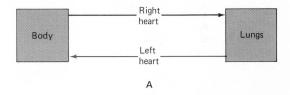

A

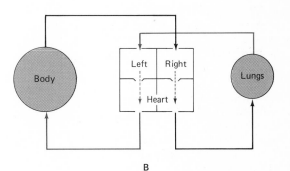

B

[5] A. S. Romer, *The Vertebrate Body, Shorter Version*, Philadelphia: W. B. Saunders Company, 1962, p. 163.

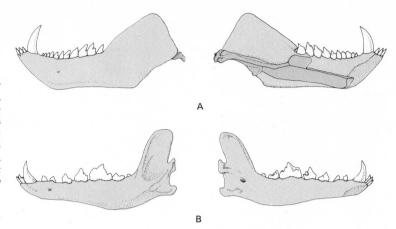

FIGURE 1-5
Reduction in number of lower jaw bones during mammalian evolution. *A*, Advanced mammallike reptile (*Cynognathus*); *B*, modern dog. Dog's jaw is one bone (dentary) while some mammalian ancestors had six bones (colored) in addition to dentary. *Left*, outer view; *right*, inner view of left lower jaws. [*After A. S. Romer, The Vertebrate Body, W. B. Saunders, Philadelphia, 1962.*]

FIGURE 1-6
Section through the head of a mammal (man) illustrating the separation of the nasal and oral cavities by the hard (bony) and soft palate.

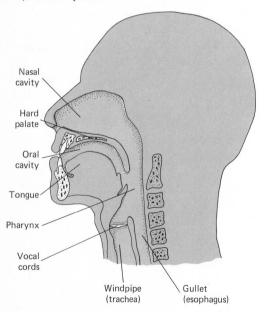

Nasal cavity

Hard palate

Oral cavity

Tongue

Pharynx

Vocal cords

Windpipe (trachea)

Gullet (esophagus)

The teeth of mammals, unlike those of any other vertebrate, are structurally and functionally differentiated into specific types called *incisors, canines, premolars,* and *molars* (Figs. 1-12 and 1-16). The incisors in front act as knives or chisels, whereas the canines next to them pierce or tear and may be used for grasping and holding prey. Alongside the cheeks are the premolars and molars for pulverizing and grinding. A mobile tongue shunts food to the appropriate teeth for thorough mastication at the same time that it mixes the chewed mass with a moistening and lubricating saliva. The saliva itself contains a distinctly mammalian digestive enzyme,[6] *ptyalin,* which initiates the chemical digestion of starches. The mechanical pulverization of the food into tiny particles and the warmth of the body greatly speed chemical digestion in the mouth as well as later on in the stomach and intestine.

The elaborate processes of mastication and insalivation could not take place were it not for the long palate separating the oral and nasal cavities (Fig. 1-6). This partition enables the mammal to continue breathing during the act of chewing and even allows for the option of eating on the run.[7]

[6] An enzyme is a protein substance which serves as a catalyst, that is, a substance which speeds a chemical reaction.
[7] Ibid., p. 190.

The entire mechanism of oral digestion in mammals is revolutionary. It occurs in no other group of vertebrates. It not only adds to the efficiency of the digestive process in mammals but also enlarges the inventory of items that can be effectively consumed. A great variety of foods can be exploited which if left to chemical digestion alone would only be partly used, if at all. As a consequence, a variety of foods is used more efficiently by mammals than by reptiles, including plant materials, such as leaves, stems, tubers, roots, and seeds, and animal materials, ranging from bone to the nutriment encased in the tough covering of many insects.

Reproductive strategies

The placental mammals also are distinguished by reproductive adaptations that greatly reduce egg production. The laying of hundreds or thousands of unguarded eggs by one female is typical of fish and amphibians. Even among reptiles it is common for one female, depending on the species, to lay 10 to 50 or more eggs. After she has buried or otherwise hidden them, she leaves the nest and never returns. The unattended eggs incubate without parental assistance or protection, and the young which ultimately hatch must fend for themselves. Obviously many embryos and young are lost to predators and accident.

In other reptiles — some snakes, for instance — the fertilized eggs are retained in the body of the mother and the young are born alive. These reptilian infants receive no parental care or protection. The egg-laying alligator is the sole exception. But even here the mother looks after her young but not the eggs.

In placental mammals, as well as in reptiles, eggs are fertilized within the body of the female. The range in number of fertilized eggs, however, is considerably smaller than among reptiles. Few wild mammals give birth to more than 10 young; most of them do not bear more than 5 or 6, and many bear only 1 or 2. Further,

each fertilized egg is microscopic in size since it contains little, if any, nutrient yolk. This reduction both in egg production and the manufacture of energy-rich yolk material is made possible by the distinctive manner in which the egg is retained and nourished within the mammalian reproductive tract.

In the female reproductive system, very tiny eggs, produced in a pair of *ovaries,* are swept into a corresponding pair of tubelike *oviducts.* If copulation has occurred shortly before, these eggs will be met and fertilized by sperm in the upper oviducts, and the fertilized eggs will start to pass on down the oviducts towards the womb, or *uterus,* into which the oviducts empty (Fig. 1-7). The journey to the uterus usually takes a few days, during which each of the fertilized eggs, nurtured by nutrient secretions from the oviduct walls, becomes a many-celled embryo. Each tiny embryo develops special membranes, the outermost one of which unites with the lining of the uterus and its rich supply of maternal blood to form the placenta, as mentioned previously. By means of the placenta, the embryo is nourished with nutrients from the mother's bloodstream. Within the warm, safe confines of the mother's womb, the young develops to a relatively advanced stage before it is finally born.

A given number of offspring can result from fewer and much smaller eggs when these eggs are protected and nurtured in the mother's reproductive tract during the entire period of embryonic development. A number of mammalian adaptations have made this possible: (1) the development of the uterus from a portion of the vertebrate oviduct; (2) the formation of a placenta; and (3) an elaborate system controlled by the brain and hormone-secreting (*endocrine*) glands to coordinate the entire process of development from sex-cell formation to birth and the period of nursing and parental care which follows.

In other words, mammalian involvement in the reproductive process does not stop at

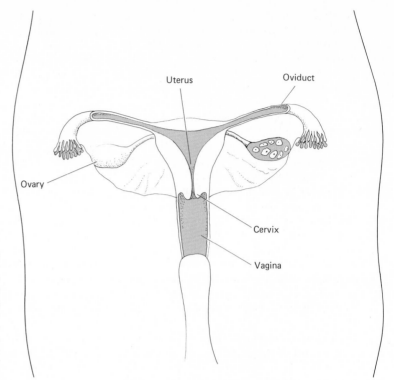

FIGURE 1-7
Human female reproductive system, front view. Egg produced in ovary is swept into the funnellike openings of the oviduct (the fingerlike projections around each opening usually cover the ovary but are displaced here for clarity). During copulation, sperm are deposited deep in the vagina at the mouth of the cervix; union of sperm and egg usually occurs in upper third of oviduct.

birth. Once born, the mammalian infant continues to be fed and protected by its mother for some time. Milk secreted from special mammary glands provides all the substances required for normal growth and development of the young. Comparative safety results from a strong infant-mother bond which keeps the young close to its mother. Consequently the chances for postnatal as well as prenatal (embryonic) survival are greatly increased, and the number of offspring required per birth to maintain a given population is minimized.

Behavioral adaptations

The intimate bond between young mammals and their parents makes possible not only a reduction in infant mortality but also a substantial decrease in mortality in all age groups in the population. This far-reaching development is an outgrowth of the greatly expanded opportunities for learning behavior within the strong bond that unites mother and infant.

Learning may be defined as any relatively permanent change in behavior as a result of practice or experience.[8] Reptiles, amphibians, fishes, and indeed many invertebrates develop behaviors which are learned by trial and error. The primary drives of hunger, self-preservation, and sex provide the motivation for this learning, as they do in most animals. Learning comes

[8] C. T. Morgan and R. A. King, *Introduction to Psychology*, 4th ed., New York: McGraw-Hill Book Company, 1975, p. 97.

directly from experience. When learning occurs, it is a relatively simple behavior pattern that is never conveyed by the learner to the unlearned. It is an "every man for himself" education in which each generation must repeat the timeworn mistakes of the previous one.

In mammals, and also in birds, learning is quite a different matter. The intimate relationship between parents and their young makes possible the transmission of learned behavior by imitation. It is characteristic of mammals (and birds) that their young have a natural inclination to imitate the actions of their parents. This is an effective means by which the younger generation can assimilate behavioral responses which adults have acquired through trial-and-error learning or by imitating *their* parents. As generation succeeds generation, learning acquired by adults becomes cumulative, and the repertory of those behaviors which contribute to survival grows larger and more comprehensive.

The result of learning by imitation is to reduce the necessity for trial-and-error learning since the lessons of the previous generation need not be learned anew. Much of the learning motivated by the three primary biological drives — hunger, self-preservation, and sex — can be achieved through imitation. Mammals, however, have added a fourth dimension to behavioral motivation that does not involve these three drives. This additional element is seen in the play and exploratory activity which so clearly distinguishes the behavior of young mammals from that of almost all other creatures.[9] This *explorative drive* generates a form of trial-and-error learning by the young while under the watchful eye and protective presence of an adult. Exploration of the many components of a complex environment, reinforced by the zest and vigor of play, gradually builds a keener awareness of the kinds of consequences that follow certain actions. As a result, the maturing mammal may develop a vast catalog of alterna-

[9] Play behavior has been reported also in a few species of birds, notably members of the crow family. See E. O. Wilson, *Sociobiology*, Cambridge, Mass.: Harvard University Press, 1975, pp. 164–166.

tive behaviors and learns to respond more and more effectively to the world it inhabits.

Mammalian evolution has produced a number of adaptations which make these sophisticated behavioral activities possible. That part of the brain known as the *cerebrum* (or *cerebral hemispheres*) has undergone much greater development in mammals than in other vertebrates (Fig. 1-8). The cerebrum is known to be the part of the brain most directly involved in memory storage and problem-solving. It may be likened, in a sense, to a computer with its memory bank. The brain's output is dependent, at least in part, upon the input it receives. Input in the case of the mammal is provided by highly developed sense organs which furnish the information content for charging memory storage. Cerebral output yields new patterns of adaptive behavior. For example, when a mammal is confronted with a novel situation in which survival may be at stake, the mammalian brain may forecast the possible course of events by recalling past experiences which bear some similarity to the existing predicament. From such analyses, highly adaptive, intelligent behavior may result in response to unfamiliar circumstances.

It is just this kind of phenomenon that is involved in the act of thinking, a facility the human species so often reserves solely for itself. It is, of course, true that our expertise in the "art" of thinking and in the transmission of learning from generation to generation far surpasses that of any other mammal. Human language and the culture it generates are unique. At the same time it must be emphasized that the foundation on which human culture rests is the transmission of behavior by imitation (reinforced by teaching) in the parent-infant relationship. Beyond this, our culture is, in large part, an outgrowth of the mammalian drive to explore and to investigate.

The human species has exploited certain elements of its mammalian inheritance. Characteristically, we bear only one child at a time. This is efficient to the extent that it concentrates parental care on one individual rather than diluting it among several. The period of infant dependency, moreover, has been prolonged to the point where it greatly exceeds that of any other organism. As a result of this delayed maturation, human young have a longer time in which to learn and to assimilate the knowledge and culture handed down from the past. Finally, these additional opportunities for learning are further enhanced by the exceptional development of the human cerebrum. In all these instances, we are a genuine product of the mammalian heritage. We differ from our

FIGURE 1-8
Brains of representative vertebrates. The cerebrum is colored, the cerebellum shaded. Note the increase in the relative size of the cerebrum from fishes to man. [*Modified from T. I. Storer et al General Zoology, 5th ed., McGraw-Hill, New York, 1972.*]

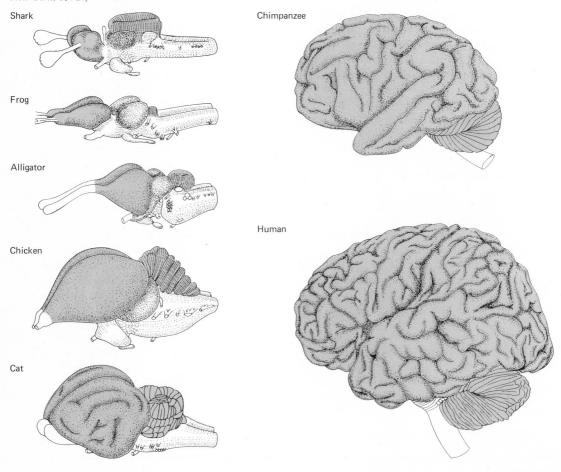

Shark

Frog

Alligator

Chicken

Cat

Chimpanzee

Human

nonhuman relatives only in the degree to which certain mammalian features have been developed.

OUR PRIMATE HERITAGE

Many of the special features that distinguish the human species from other mammals are shared in varying degrees by 149 species of monkeys and apes. The monkeys and apes, together with their relatives, the lemurs, lorises, and tarsiers, make up a subgroup *(order)* of mammals known as the *Primates* (Fig. 1-9). It will be obvious from a review of the characteristics that distinguish this order (Fig. 1-10) that the human species belongs in this group also. The biological classification of man illustrated in Figure 1-11 shows that we are members of the suborder Anthropoidea (monkeys, apes, and man).

The primates trace their origin back 70 or more million years, when the Age of Dinosaurs was coming to an end. The primate order evolved from the earliest stock of placental mammals, probably of the order Insectivora, represented today by shrews, moles, and hedgehogs. The limb structure of early primate fossils suggests the animals were arboreal (tree-dwelling), a habit which the primate order has adopted as its characteristic life style. The evolutionary history of the order has been a complex one, however, and will be described in some detail in the discussion on primate evolution in Section II. Certainly most of the living primates today are tree-dwelling creatures, and the few that are not have arboreal ancestors in their past.

Living in trees poses complications the ground-dweller seldom, if ever, faces. Locomotion, for example, is a problem because there is no firm, continuous dependable surface on which to move. Instead there are only vertical trunks and horizontal branches that are often obscured by leaves, made slippery by rain, and moved by the wind. Faulty judgment or a clumsy movement may plunge an arboreal ani-

mal to the ground below. One cannot follow the scent left behind by members of the troop as they jump or swing from tree to tree, nor can food or predators be located in this way. Rarely is there room to lie down or sprawl, although there are ample opportunities for sitting. Curtains of foliage in any direction can restrict an animal's vision, making it easy prey for a concealed predator, such as a snake.

There are compensations. The arboreal environment, particularly in the subtropical and tropical forests where primates are common, contains a great variety of leafy vegetation, flowers, fruits, nuts, insects, and other small animals, both invertebrate and vertebrate. The food supply is abundant, varied, and accessible. Although competition is keen, the opportunities for herbivorous, frugivorous (fruit-eating), insectivorous, or omnivorous creatures are excellent.

Primate adaptations for arboreal living are numerous and varied. Although there is variation in the number, kinds, and arrangement of teeth *(dentition)* throughout the order, dental adaptations generally are those of an omnivore. Most primates live on leaves, fruits, insects, and even meat when they can get it. The dentition of all Old World anthropoids in Asia and Africa (Fig. 1-9) is similar to man's, consisting of two pairs of upper and lower incisors, one pair of upper and lower canines, two pairs of upper and lower premolars, and three pairs of upper and lower molars (Fig. 1-12).[10]

In general the order has retained many ancient vertebrate characteristics, such as five fingers and five toes, and two bones in the lower arm and lower leg. These have contributed to the ability of the group as a whole to adapt to diverse ecological opportunities and even to modify and manipulate environments. This order has, in fact, produced an unusual creature

---

[10] Dentition often is expressed in a *dental formula*. The formula for Old World anthropoids is $\frac{2.1.2.3}{2.1.2.3}$, indicating that one half of the upper and lower jaws contains two incisors, one canine, two premolars, and three molars.

A

B

whose ecological niche and mode of life re-volve around culture. The human species can live in environments to which it is not biologi-cally adapted because it can modify and even create environments as a result of cultural be-havior. Even in this capacity we do not stand entirely alone. As we will see in Chap. 3, simple forms of cultural behavior (protoculture) have been reported in several anthropoids. We are what we are, in large part, because we have been the beneficiaries of a primate heritage of arboreal adaptations. These adaptations con-veniently fall into four interrelated categories: (1) locomotor adaptations, (2) sensory and ex-ploratory adaptations, (3) reproductive adapta-tions, and (4) behavioral adaptations.

Locomotor adaptations

The substrate on which the tree-dweller is sup-ported and on which it moves consists of tree trunks and branches extending in every direc-tion. Primates have evolved a considerable number of locomotor adaptations to this pre-carious substrate that rank them among the more expert of arboreal mammals. Both fore-legs and hind legs are capable of a wide range of movements. They can support the body re-gardless of the relative position of the nearest hand- or foothold. This is particularly true of the arms in hominoids (apes and man). The ability to hang suspended by one or both fore-limbs is made possible by well-developed collar

C

FIGURE 1-9
The class of mammals is composed of many subgroups (*orders*). The order man belongs in is the Primates, consisting of two *suborders,* the Prosimii, represented by the sifaka (*A*), and the Anthropoidea, represented by the squirrel monkey (*B*) and gibbon (*C*). The names and distributions of a number of prosimians and anthropoids are listed in D. [*San Diego Zoo Photos, by Ron Garrison.*]

REPRESENTATIVE PROSIMIANS

Lemurs of Madagascar
Sifakas of Madagascar
Lorises of Southeast Asia
Galagos (bushbabies) of Africa
Tarsiers of Southeast Asia

REPRESENTATIVE ANTHROPOIDS

New World monkeys
  Spider monkeys of Mexico, Central America, and South America
  Squirrel monkeys of Central America and South America

Old World monkeys and apes (includes man)
  Macaque monkeys of Asia and Africa
  Baboons of Asia and Africa
  Gibbons (lesser apes) of Southeast Asia
  Orangutan (great ape) of Borneo and Sumatra
  Chimpanzees (great apes) of Africa
  Gorilla (great ape) of Equatorial Africa

D

bones *(clavicles)* which prevent undue twisting of the shoulder blades *(scapulas)* when the arms pull directly from above. The overall dexterity of the arm is further increased by the extent to which the hand can be rotated through 180° from *pronated* (palm down) to *supinated* (palm up). This was brought about by a retention of the early vertebrate condition of two bones in the forearm *(radius and ulna),* in which one of the bones *(radius)* rotates around the other (Fig. 1-13).

Retaining the ancient vertebrate trait of five fingers and five toes permitted the development of grasping hands and feet. Prehensile efficiency resulted not only from this but also from several additional features. Five highly

A

Hands and/or feet prehensile (grasping); fingers mobile; thumb and/or big toe opposable

Some or all digits (fingers and toes) with flattened nails rather than claws

Well-developed clavicles (collar bones)

Mammary glands usually two, pectorally placed (on chest)

Compared to most mammals olfactory (smell) apparatus reduced, including snout or muzzle and olfactory lobes in brain

Vision excellent, usually binocular

Sense of movement and sense of balance very well developed

Brain large relative to body size

B

Cerebrum expanded to the rear, covering cerebellum, and with increased surface convolutions

Depth perception and color vision well developed

Tactile (touch) sense well developed in fingers

High degree of manual dexterity

Upper and lower lips mobile; variety of facial expressions

Period of postnatal dependency and development prolonged

Extreme dependence on social learning; highly intelligent

FIGURE 1-10
Characteristics of the Primate order. *A*, Primates in general; *B*, additional traits found in anthropoids (monkeys, apes, and man).

FIGURE 1-11
The biological classification of man. Just as a class consists of one or more orders, so does an order consist of one or more families, a family of one or more genera (plural of genus), and a genus of one or more species. Today the family Hominidae contains only one genus (*Homo*) and that genus has only one species (*Homo sapiens*). In prehistoric times there was at least one other species of *Homo* (*H. erectus*) and at least one other genus of hominid (*Australopithecus*).

Kingdom: *Animalia*
  Phylum: *Chordata*
    Class: *Mammalia*
      Order: *Primates*
        Suborder: *Anthropoidea* (monkeys, apes, man)
          Superfamily: *Hominoidea* (apes, man)
            Family: *Hominidae* (manlike creatures)
              Genus: *Homo*
                Species: *Homo sapiens*
                (human species today)

mobile fingers and five toes can cling more effectively to an irregular surface than fewer less mobile digits. Having an opposable thumb or big toe, or both, converts a fingerhold into a viselike grip. Both the palms of the hands and the soles of the feet, as well as the fingers and toes, have a hairless grasping surface of minutely ridged friction skin which hinders slippage of anything held in the grasp. Finally, each of the fingers and toes in most primates and in all Old World anthropoids terminates in a fleshy pad supported by a flattened nail. Consequently a compressive grip can be maintained to the tip of every digit. Lacking claws that penetrate and hold, the grip can be released as quickly as it was made (Fig. 1-14).

Rapid locomotion high above the ground in the complex three-dimensional world of branches and vines demands a keen sense of movement. Responses must be quick and precise. Estimates of the distances to various branches, the relative amount and direction of

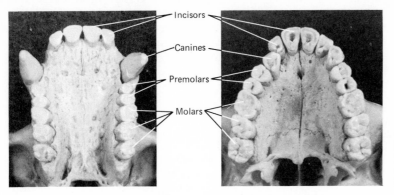

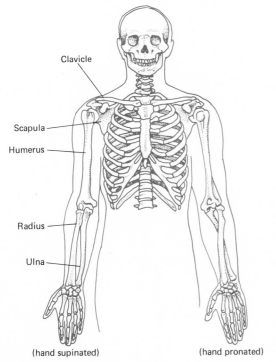

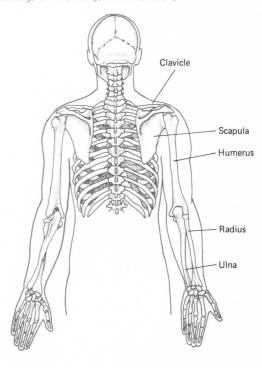

FIGURE 1-12
The upper jaw dentitions of two anthropoids, chimpanzee (*left*) and human (*right*). Chimp jaw is a cast.

FIGURE 1-13
Skeleton of the upper body of man. *A,* Front view; *B,* rear view. [*Modified from C. C. Francis, Introduction to Human Anatomy, 6th ed., Mosby, St. Louis, 1973.*]

movement between them, if any, and their size, shape, and strength, must be made reliably and swiftly. Sense organs, nerves, brain, and muscles must work as a smoothly efficient unit in reaching rapid, accurate decisions and in effecting immediate and appropriate responses.

Locomotor patterns

The actual mode of locomotion utilized by primates depends upon the primate and whether the individual is in the trees or on the ground. Again the generalized physical structure of the order makes it possible to employ a variety of locomotor patterns suitable to the occasion. By far the most characteristic are (1) vertical clinging and leaping, (2) brachiation, (3) quadrupedalism, and (4) bipedalism (Fig. 1-15).

Vertical clinging and leaping is a type of arboreal behavior seen among certain prosimians. At rest the animal clings to a branch, keeping its body (trunk) erect. Moving to another branch is accomplished by a froglike leap. When on the ground these primates may move about by kangaroolike bipedal hopping, quadrupedal walking, or even bipedal walking.

Brachiation is a pattern of arboreal locomotion in which the body is vertically suspended from above by the arms. The animal is propelled from branch to branch by hand-over-hand arm-swinging. All apes, except adult gorillas, can travel through trees in this way. When on the ground these species walk or run quadrupedally or bipedally.

Quadrupedalism, or moving about on all fours, is employed both in trees and on the ground. It is widely used in both places by a variety of primates that walk, run, jump, and climb quadrupedally. The great apes are essentially semierect quadrupeds because their front legs are much longer than those behind, an adaptation for brachiation. The chimpanzee and gorilla are called *knuckle-walkers* because the weight on the forelegs is borne on the knuckles rather than on the palm.

Bipedalism is reserved almost exclusively for the terrestrial environment, although some primates occasionally may walk along branches bipedally. In bipedal walking or running, the body is supported on one foot and then the other by alternate leg-swinging. From bipedal hopping to human striding, erect bipedal locomotion is practiced widely throughout the

FIGURE 1-14
The grasping surfaces of the hands and feet of anthropoids. *A,* Hands of (1) baboon, (2) orangutan, (3) gorilla, and (4) man. *B,* The sole of the feet of (1) gorilla and (2) man. [*After S. Washburn (ed.), Classification and Human Evolution, Aldine, Chicago, 1963.*]

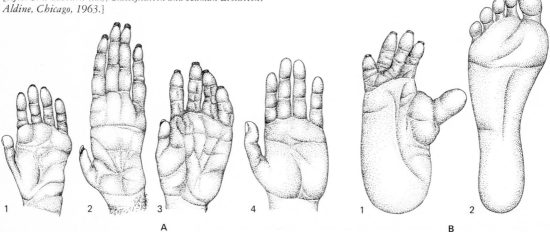

A   B

order. Only in man, however, is bipedalism the sole method of locomotion.

It is clear from this brief résumé that the order has a diversified repertory of locomotor patterns. It also is clear that the primate body spends a lot of its time during travel in an erect position. If one considers that when primates are not moving they usually are sitting erect on their haunches or bottoms, it must be concluded that the primate body in general spends a preponderant amount of time either seated, supported, or suspended erectly.

FIGURE 1-15
Locomotor patterns in primates. *A,* Vertical clinging and leaping in a lemur; *B,* brachiation in the gibbon; quadrupedal walking in (*C*) an Old World monkey and (*D*) a chimpanzee (knuckle-walking); *E,* bipedal hopping in a galago; and *F,* walking in man. *A* and *E* are tracings from a motion-picture film. [*A and E after J. Biegert (ed.), Folia Primatologica, vol. 6, S. Karger AG, Basel, 1967; C and D after M. Hildebrand, American Journal of Physical Anthropology, vol. 26, 1968.*]

Cranial modifications for body erectness

Erect posture requires that the skull be set at an angle to the vertebral column so that the eyes look directly forward. This means that the vertebral column must join the underside of the skull at a point forward to the corresponding joint in a four-legged animal like the dog (Fig. 1-16). This bending or flexion of the cranium on the vertebral column is typical of all primates, but reaches its greatest development in apes and, more especially, man. The human vertebral column connects almost directly in the center of the underside of the skull. In a dog this connection is at the rear of the skull.

There is a further flexion of the face with respect to the cranium. In a dog, or any other fully quadrupedal animal, the face is immediately in front of the braincase, but in a primate it is forward of and slightly below the braincase. This has not been an adaptation related directly to erect posture but is associated with the space requirements of a large brain. The diminished importance of the sense of smell in arboreal living has brought about a reduction in the amount of space required for a snout. This in turn results in a smaller, flatter face. A skull can accommodate a relatively large brain if the face is small and displaced downward. This smaller, somewhat lower face is a primate characteristic and again is most pronounced in apes and man.

Sensory and exploratory adaptations

The emancipation of the forelimb

It is not surprising that body (trunk) erectness is a characteristic feature of primate posture because a vertical body alignment utilizes space most economically in an arboreal setting where supporting surfaces are small, irregular, widely spaced, and often precarious. The typical resting postures of vertical clinging and sitting also free one or both of the forelimbs to test prospective hand- and footholds and to explore the immediate surroundings in a variety of ways. Emancipated from operating solely in locomotion and support, the primate forelimb is used widely, especially in the anthropoids, as an exploratory device. The sense of touch, localized primarily in the muzzle of other mammals, is most acutely developed in the fingertips of anthropoids. A grasping hand can be a very effective tactile organ when the fingers end—as they do in primates—in sensitive fleshy pads backed by flattened nails. It also can serve other senses by bringing objects close to the eyes, nose, and mouth for a closer examination as well as additional manipulative functions, such as gathering

FIGURE 1-16
Cranial adaptations for erect posture in primates, showing the angle the skull makes with the vertebral column (angle *a*) and the angle the face makes with the skull (angle *b*) in (*A*) a typical nonprimate (dog), (*B*) a New World monkey, and (*C*) man. The colored lines are parallel to the alignments of the vertebral column, skull, and face. The shaded portion indicates the area of the face.

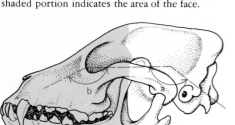

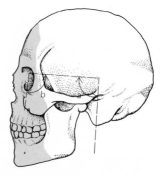

A   B   C

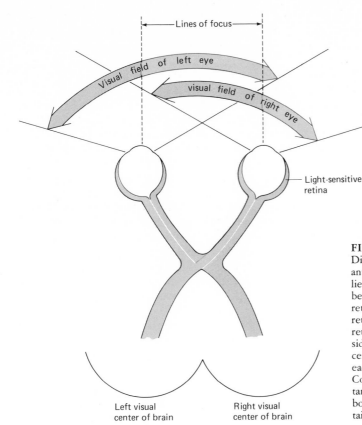

FIGURE 1-17
Distance perception (stereoscopic vision) in anthropoids. That part of the visual field which lies between the lines of focus of both eyes will be viewed by the left half of the light-sensitive retina of the left eye and the right half of the retina of the right eye. Nerve fibers from the retina are so arranged that those from the left side of each eye pass to the left visual brain center, whereas those from the right side of each eye pass to the right visual brain center. Consequently the brain can "compute" the distance of objects within the lines of focus of both eyes by comparing visual information obtained from two different angles.

food and holding it while it is being eaten. There can be little doubt that the tactile sensitivity and manipulative dexterity of the human hand trace their origin back to the emancipation of the forelimb as an arboreal adaptation in the primate order.

Perceiving a world of depth and color
The three-dimensional world of a tropical or subtropical tree-dweller is a multistoried habitat that abounds in a richness of colors as well as in numerous shades of green. For active mammals, keenness of vision is essential in gauging distances precisely and in judging the strength of

branches and vines. It also is necessary in identifying which of innumerable plant and small animal species are good to eat and which are not.

Primates, and anthropoids in particular, have responded to these environmental demands through a number of adaptations by which vision has become the dominant sensory mode for perceiving the outside world. The eyes are relatively large, which increases the size of the visual field and the amount of light received. They are placed well forward in the skull so that the two visual fields overlap, resulting in binocular vision. In anthropoids depth perception reaches its fullest development. The eyes are completely forward so that each eye shares most of what it sees with the other, except that the two images are received from slightly different angles. Furthermore, the nerve fibers from the eyes to the brain are so arranged that those from the left side of *each* eye pass to the left side of the brain whereas those from the right side of *each* eye pass to the right side of the brain. By comparing this visual information, the brain can judge distances quite accurately (Fig. 1-17).

The anthropoid eye also is well fitted to the task of discriminating colors, the fine details of form, and the detection of movement. The inner sensory layer of the eye *(retina)* contains two kinds of light-sensitive cells, the *rods* and the *cones*. The rods are sensitive to the low levels of illumination experienced at twilight and dawn, when they appear to function in detecting movement of objects. They are much more numerous than cones and are the only light-sensitive cells in the outer portions of the retina. The cones predominate almost to the exclusion of the rods, however, at and near the center of the retina, where the center of focus and the area of sharpest vision is located. Cones are stimulated by higher levels of illumination, such as are experienced during the day, and serve two functions. They make it possible to distinguish fine details of form and to discriminate between the almost endless gradations of colors that lie between the violet and red extremes of the visible spectrum.

Reproductive adaptations

Primates generally have no more than two or three offspring at a time, and anthropoids seldom have more than one. In fact many species have single births only once every one to three years. This tendency for most primates to have single births has been accompanied by the development of a number of reproductive innovations of far-reaching significance.

In those mammals characterized by multiple births, there is competition between embryos during pregnancy, in which the rapidly developing individuals have an advantage over the more slowly developing ones. When only one embryo is carried at a time, the selective advantage of rapid growth is eased, if not eliminated. As a consequence the period of embryonic development can be extended, allowing for improvements in the uterine environment which might further reduce the risks of premature birth or defective young. That this has occurred is evidenced by the fact that among mammals, on a pound-for-pound basis, the primates have an exceptionally long gestation period. There is, moreover, a definite trend in the primate order toward longer pregnancies as one progresses from lemurs through monkeys and apes to man (see Fig. 1-18).

In tarsiers and anthropoids there is an unusually intimate union between the embryos and mother during intrauterine development. When the tiny embryo reaches the uterus, it does not remain in the cavity of the uterus, as in other mammals, but actively bores into the uterine wall as if it were a parasite. There it resides through the balance of term, firmly bound by the rootlike processes of its embryonic membranes to the uterine wall in which it is buried (Fig. 1-19). This clearly affords an added measure of security for the embryo; it also incurs an added obligation. The uterine wall must be prepared for its anticipated guest. It must become engorged with blood. It would, of course, be physiologically expensive to maintain the uterus perpetually in such a state until fertilization happened to occur. As a consequence the estrous cycle of mammals was modified to a menstrual cycle in which the lining of the uterus as well as its engorged blood is periodically discharged when fertilization fails to take place. The process of menstruation is unique to primates, occurring only in tarsiers, monkeys, apes, and ourselves.

The lack of any selective advantage for

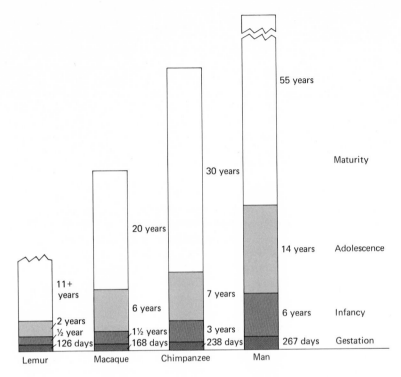

FIGURE 1-18
The time intervals for gestation, infancy, adolescence, and maturity in representative primates. The macaque is an Old World monkey. [*After Alison Jolly, The Evolution of Primate Behavior, Macmillan, New York, 1972.*]

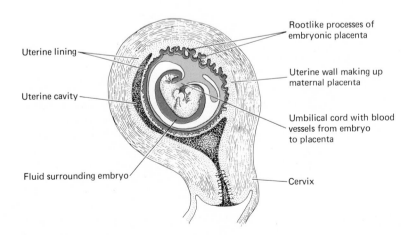

FIGURE 1-19
Human uterus and embryo at about the fifth week of pregnancy, side view. Compare with Fig. 1-7.

rapid development also carries over into the postnatal period, when the young are dependent upon maternal care for survival. Competition between fast- and slower-growing litter mates is avoided with single births. The postnatal period of parental dependency consequently may be lengthened since it would result in greater assurances for the survival of the newborn to maturity. That this is the case is reflected in the unusually long periods of infant and juvenile dependency in primates compared to other mammals. There is, moreover, an unmistakable trend toward longer periods of postnatal dependency, as is indicated by the duration of infancy in lemurs, monkeys, apes, and man (Fig. 1-18).

Finally, in addition to longer pregnancies and postnatal periods, primates show a marked increase in life span over other mammals of comparable size. Even tiny mouse lemurs that weigh 76 grams (1/6 pound) live eight years or more. As with gestation and infancy, there is a progressive increase in longevity from lemurs through monkeys and apes to man (Fig. 1-18). Since most species average one or fewer offspring per female per year, an increase in longevity and the total span of the reproductive period tend to ensure the birth and survival of sufficient offspring to maintain the species. In fact, one anthropoid—man—has a problem with excessive numbers, to which we will give close attention in the discussion on human population in Section III. The presence of older, more experienced, and wiser members in a social unit (such as a monkey troop) also can prove advantageous to the survival of the entire group, especially among species that are as communicative, responsive, and socially gregarious as the anthropoids.

Behavioral adaptations

The long period of postnatal dependency with its powerful parent-infant bond and the adolescent period of maturation in a peer group which

follows provide many opportunities for an anthropoid to learn complex social behaviors. The specific behaviors learned vary from species to species, but the social systems themselves tend to serve four fundamental functions: (1) training the young to be self-sufficient in obtaining the necessities of life, such as food, water, and shelter; (2) the control of intragroup strife and the maintenance of order through a hierarchy; (3) the protection and defense of the group against predators; and (4) the control of group size with respect to food sources and other environmental conditions. All of these matters will be covered at some length in our discussion of anthropoid behavior in Chap. 3.

Almost all social behavior in anthropoids is learned. In this they contrast sharply with creatures like honeybees whose social behavior is largely a product of inherited mechanisms and responses. Few animals, if any, with the possible exception of the social Canidae (dog family), appear to rely upon memory and learning to the extent that anthropoids do.[11]

The brain centers responsible for memory and learning are apparently well developed in anthropoids, which would account in part for the large brains of these animals with respect to their body size. Acquiring communication skills, so necessary to primate social organization, is an important part of learning. Such skills are complex learned behaviors involving the use of a great many facial expressions, bodily postures, and vocalizations in a variety of social situations.

The anthropoid cerebrum also is involved in many other functions. For example, the emancipation of the forelimb entails manual dexterity, eye-hand coordination, and great tactile discrimination. Various forms of locomotion, each capable of functioning with speed and precision, require excellent muscular control, balance, and a sense of movement. All these abilities are controlled by the brain, which means that brain

[11] Ibid., p. 152.

tissue must be available for the job. Hearing, touch, and especially vision involve extensive perceptual areas in the brain. Only in the case of smell has there been a reduction in a sensory area of the cerebrum.

Another portion of the brain lying behind the cerebrum also is enlarged in primates. This structure, the *cerebellum,* is responsible for muscle coordination and maintaining balance (Fig. 1-8).

To all these brain functions — social learning; tactile, auditory, and visual perception; muscle response and coordination — must be added the processes of prediction- and decision-making which are so vital in the complex physical and social environment of every anthropoid. Judgments must be made accurately and often swiftly on the basis of instantaneous sensory appraisals of intricate situations. Indeed, it is not surprising that monkeys, apes, and man have large complicated brains compared to other vertebrates (Fig. 1-8).

From this brief survey, it is clear that the human species is a primate that is most closely related to the monkeys and apes. Biologists believe that these primate affiliations represent a true biologic (evolutionary) relationship. In the following chapter various lines of scientific evidence will be presented which indicate that man indeed has a real biologic kinship with other anthropoids.

Our primate heritage of arboreal adaptations has been modified through evolution for a life on the ground. The constitutional requirements for a successful life in the trees are remarkably suited to life on the ground, with a few minor modifications. Complete emancipation of the forelimb through total bipedalism, manual dexterity, tactile discrimination, an omnivorous diet, a long period of postnatal dependency, and a highly developed brain constitute most of the requirements for toolmaking and a terrestrial life. Communication through vocalizations and facial expressions within the framework of a complex social structure provides the foundation on which language could

develop, especially in an exclusively terrestrial species whose survival as a hunter-gatherer was tied to toolmaking.

The phenomenon of language leads us to one final consideration in this preliminary examination of our status as a living organism: our *specifically human* attributes.

WHAT IT MEANS TO BE HUMAN

We have said that we are living creatures, and we have examined some of the attributes we share with most animals. We also have seen what it means to be a particular kind of animal — a mammal — and we have narrowed the focus even further in considering our primate heritage.

Now we must ask: what attributes, if any, are ours alone? In other words, what does it mean to be human, as distinct from being any other kind of animal? In answering this question we must bear in mind that no species, not even our own, has an exclusive claim on a particular biologic trait. Species differ, especially closely related ones, by a combination of traits, each of which has been developed and modified in varying ways and degrees. Every species is unique not because it possesses unique characteristics but because those characteristics it has have been modified as a *complex of traits* that are found in no other creature.

Of the various traits that distinguish *Homo sapiens,* one in particular is preeminent: the extent to which human life is dependent on learned behavior and culture. Earlier we listed a few of the things humans do. They included acts — the building of moon rockets, the composing of symphonies, the committing of embezzlement, the waging of war — which are human activities that we do not share with other animals. All these activities and innumerable others we engage in are products of what is called *culture.* Culture refers to the process of transmitting information — *learned* behavior —

from individual to individual and from generation to generation. As we shall see in Chap. 3, our species does not have a total monopoly to transmit learned behavior in such a fashion; anthropoids possess it to some degree.

But human culture differs from these simple forms of "protoculture" in its almost total dependence on the manipulation of *symbols,* or *language.* Even here it appears that human beings cannot make exclusive claims: chimpanzees can be taught to use symbols (language) in a rudimentary way. There is no evidence, however, that chimps or any other animal besides ourselves have devised their own symbol system and learned to use it. Chimps have had to be taught by man to use symbols devised by man.

As far as we know, we are the only animals who transmit, store, and recombine information by means of a symbol system. Symbol-using gives our mode of information transmission and its products—which we call culture—two great advantages over the modes used by other animals. (1) We can transmit or exchange much greater amounts of information and much more complex information among ourselves (for instance, powerful mathematical equations and detailed instructions for assembling airplane engines). And (2) we can *store* truly enormous amounts of information in the form of visual symbols (written language, pictures, drawings and sketches on wood, clay, stone, paper, and film), oral symbols (oral tradition, legend,

spoken language on magnetic tape), and even tactile symbols in the form of Braille. In nonhuman animals, on the other hand, the transmission and storage of acquired knowledge occurs only through imitative behavior and memory. This means that their potential for culture is rudimentary indeed compared to our own.

We may say, then, that man's ability to invent and manipulate symbols—and thereby develop complex symbol-based cultures—is for all practical purposes an attribute that is man's alone. We might even say that the possession of this ability, more than anything else, is "what it means to be human."

This book is not an inquiry into the cultural aspects of man's nature. That is the province of cultural anthropologists, historians, philosophers, and others. But because human culture is rooted in human biology and because cultural evolution is an integral part of human evolution, culture and its basic building block, the symbol, cannot be ignored here. We shall have more to say later about symbols, language, and culture as we pursue the question of what it means to be human in Chaps. 4 and 5 and probe into our evolutionary origins in Section II.

Before doing so, however, we will first turn our attention to the bases for believing that we humans do have a primate heritage. We will then consider what that heritage is insofar as it is reflected in the lives of living primates.

SUGGESTED READINGS

CAMPBELL, BERNARD G.: *Human Evolution: An Introduction to Man's Adaptations,* 2d ed., Chicago: Aldine Publishing Company, 1974. A very readable text dealing at length with the major anatomical, physiological, and behavioral adaptations of mammals, primates, and man.

DUBOS, R.: *So Human An Animal,* New York: Charles Scribner's Sons, 1968. A clearly written account of the human species as both an animal and a human being.

MAYR, ERNST: *Principles of Systematic Zoology,* New York: McGraw-Hill Book Company, 1969. This and Simpson's text are excellent technical sources of the basic principles of animal classification.

ROMER, A. S.: *The Vertebrate Story,* Chicago: University of Chicago Press, 1959. An interesting, nontechnical account of the evolution of fishes, amphibians, reptiles, birds, and mammals.

SIMPSON, G. G.: *Principles of Animal Taxonomy,* New York: Columbia University Press, 1961.

REVIEW QUESTIONS

1 To what phylum, class, and subclass of animals does the human species belong? List at least four characteristics which place us in these categories.

2 Mammals possess many adaptations which contribute to warm-bloodedness. Briefly describe six such adaptations.

3 Reproduction among placental mammals is quite efficient despite the fact that they produce far fewer and much smaller eggs than other vertebrates, such as reptiles. What mammalian characteristics make this possible?

4 Mammals have a much greater capacity for learning than do any of the cold-blooded vertebrates. What behavioral traits are primarily responsible for this?

5 Cite five anatomical or physiological features shared by man and primates in general. Show how each of these presumably evolved originally as an adaptation for arboreal life.

6 What is meant by "the emancipation of the forelimb," and of what adaptive significance is it to anthropoids?

7 Among primates what trends can be observed in duration of gestation, length of infancy and adolescence, and life span? Indicate the significance of these trends to species survival.

8 The anthropoid cerebrum is involved in many physiological and behavioral functions. List ten of them.

9 What is culture? To what extent is human culture unique in the animal kingdom, and what are its major advantages insofar as information transfer is concerned?

TWO

OUR BIOLOGICAL KINSHIPS:
Real Versus Coincidental

We have considered our status as organisms according to the classificational system used by biologists. Living things are classified under this system in a hierarchy of groups and subgroups depending largely on the degree to which they do or do not share certain structural (anatomical) and functional (physiological) traits. On these bases we have established that we belong, along with 149 species of monkeys and apes, to a subgroup of primates called the *anthropoids*.

It is our purpose now to investigate the meaning of our biological status. Is classification basically a matter of convenience wherein diverse organisms are placed in groups and subgroups so they can be named and cataloged? Although that is an important function, biologists believe that classification is more than that. They believe that classificational status is a reflection of genuine biological relationship based on kinship. Various species are placed in a group because they descended from a common ancestral stock that lived millions of years ago (Fig. 2-1). New species arise through adaptive modifications in older ones, a process biologists call *organic evolution*. Biologists believe in the principle of organic evolution because that principle has met the standards for scientific acceptance.

Whenever scientists, including biologists, attempt to explain natural processes they are guided by evidence. Demonstrable evidence is the foundation on which scientific judgments are based. In testing which of several plausible explanations *(hypotheses)* is most likely to be true, evidence is gathered through observation and experimentation. That hypothesis which has the most evidence to support it, and which has withstood repeated scientific attempts to disprove it, is called a *theory*. The principle of organic evolution is a theory just as the "law" of universal gravitation is a theory. Both are supported by an overwhelming body of evidence and both have withstood all scientific attempts to disprove them.

By its very nature, however, evidence never can be complete. There is always a tomorrow and evidence continues to accumulate. As a result scientific theory, no matter how well documented, is always subject to whatever modifications may be necessary in the light of future study.

The theory of organic evolution—like most well-documented scientific theories—has proved to be immensely useful. The principle of organic evolution unites all branches of biological science because it provides a common theme capable of explaining all kinds of biological phenomena. As a result it has thrown new light on old problems that resisted solution and has added fresh insights into all manner of living processes and relationships.

The balance of this chapter will be devoted to some of the evidence that supports the idea that living creatures are related in varying degrees through common descent. We will confine ourselves to a sampling from six biological sciences and will especially emphasize our own biological kinships.

COMPARATIVE EMBRYOLOGY AND ANATOMY

We will consider these two sciences as one because both are concerned with comparing the bodily structures of different animals. One, embryology, deals with the progressive changes in the earliest stages of development of an animal—the larval or embryonic stages. The other, anatomy, deals with the bodily structures of both the growing and the mature animal.

Comparative embryology

When tracing the embryonic development of vertebrates, we find that all vertebrate embryos look remarkably alike at corresponding stages in their development. All have embryonic gill pouches and arches (Fig. 2-2), yet none of the reptiles, birds, and mammals has aquatic larvae and the adults breathe by lungs alone. These nonfunctional gill elements assume significance, however, when vertebrates are viewed as an evolutionary series that began with fish hundreds of millions of years ago. They successively diverged into amphibians, reptiles, and finally, from the latter, birds and mammals. The record of fossils preserved in rocks gives ample evidence of such an evolutionary line of descent. New forms appear to have arisen by modification and divergence in older lines. For example, embryonic structures like gill arches and pouches give rise to gills in fishes. In land vertebrates certain gill arches are modified to form the skeletal supports of the voice box *(larynx)* and windpipe *(trachea)*; one pair of gill pouches develops into the eustachian tubes connecting the middle ear cavity and the throat *(pharynx)*. Lungs themselves develop as an outpocketing in the structure (pharynx) that bears

FIGURE 2-1
The major animal phyla (capital letters in color) and some of their representatives, showing probable biological relationships based on common descent through time. Groups now living are in color, others (black) became extinct at about the time indicated by X. [*Modified from T. I. Storer et al., General Zoology, 5th ed., McGraw-Hill, New York, 1972.*] (See also Fig. 2-13.)

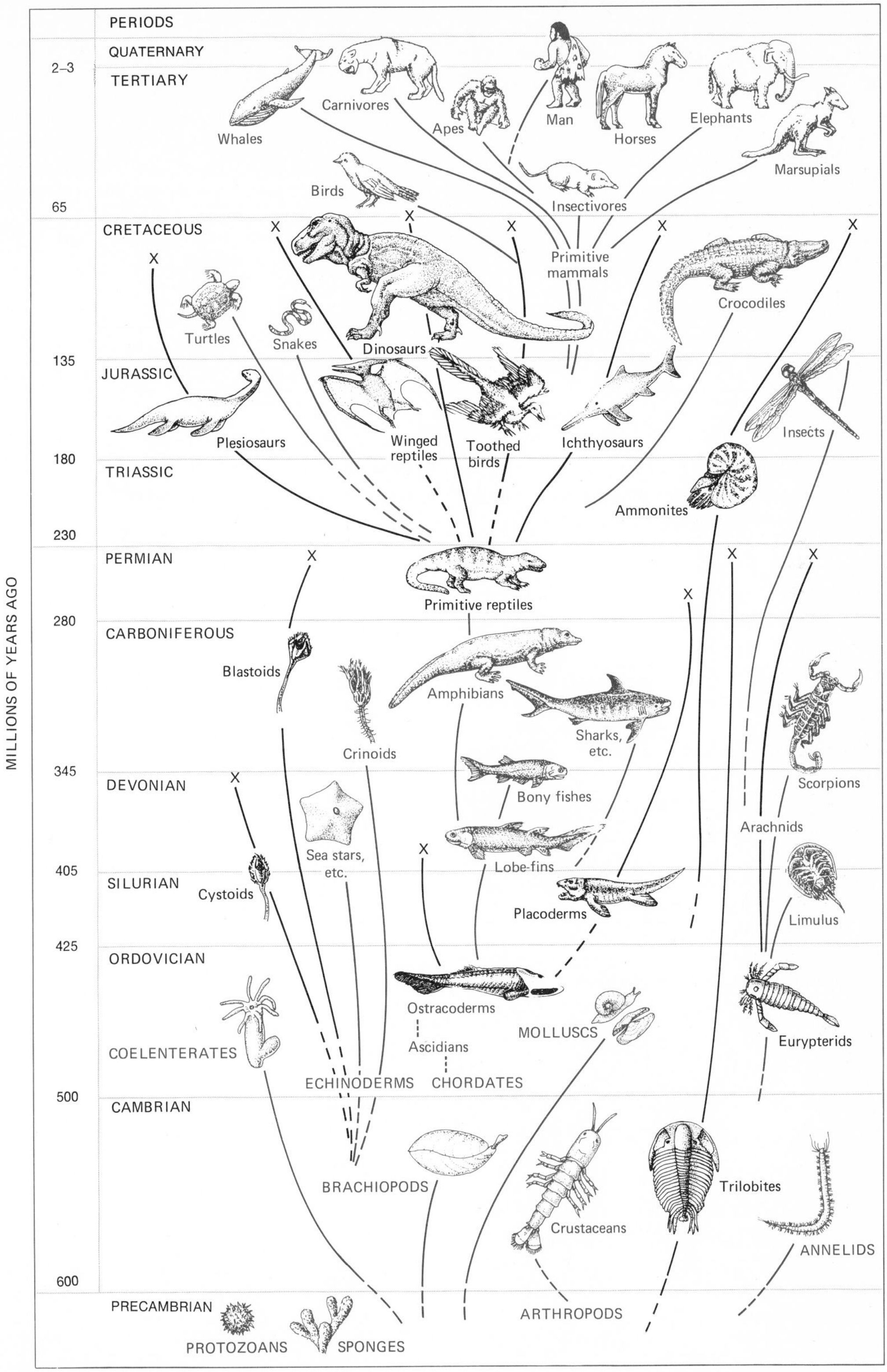

PERIODS

MILLIONS OF YEARS AGO

2–3 QUATERNARY
      TERTIARY

65

CRETACEOUS

135

JURASSIC

180

TRIASSIC

230

PERMIAN

280

CARBONIFEROUS

345

DEVONIAN

405

SILURIAN

425

ORDOVICIAN

500

COELENTERATES

CAMBRIAN

600

PRECAMBRIAN

Whales
Carnivores
Apes
Man
Horses
Elephants
Marsupials
Birds
Insectivores
Primitive mammals
Crocodiles
Turtles
Snakes
Dinosaurs
Plesiosaurs
Winged reptiles
Toothed birds
Ichthyosaurs
Insects
Ammonites
Primitive reptiles
Blastoids
Amphibians
Crinoids
Sharks, etc.
Scorpions
Bony fishes
Sea stars, etc.
Arachnids
Cystoids
Lobe-fins
Placoderms
Limulus
Ostracoderms
Ascidians
MOLLUSCS
Eurypterids
ECHINODERMS
CHORDATES
BRACHIOPODS
Crustaceans
Trilobites
ANNELIDS
ARTHROPODS
PROTOZOANS
SPONGES

gill arches and pouches in the embryo.

It is also noteworthy that the embryos of a fish, salamander, turtle, chicken, cow, pig, rabbit, and man (Fig. 2-2) possess, at comparable stages in their early development, structural characteristics found in the most primitive fish, such as lamprey eels. Some of the many embryonic similarities include (1) the absence of paired appendages, (2) a well-developed tail, (3) a two-chambered heart, and (4) similar brain

development through the differentiation of a foremid-, and hindbrain.

The circulatory system of a human embryo 3 millimeters long resembles that of an adult shark (Fig. 2-3). Both have a two-chambered heart that receives blood from the body in similar (cardinal) veins and delivers blood to a series of paired arteries (aortic arches, see Fig. 2-3) which, in the shark, carry blood to the gills. In the human adult, the heart is four-chambered. The cardinal veins have been modified to drain blood only from the heart and chest walls, and the aortic arches have become arteries supplying blood to the lungs and body tissues.

These similarities between the embryos

FIGURE 2-2
The embryos of representative vertebrates at comparable stages in development: early stage (*top*), intermediate stage (*middle*), and late stage (*bottom*). Note gill pouches and arches (labeled) in early stage of all embryos. [*After Haeckel, 1891.*]

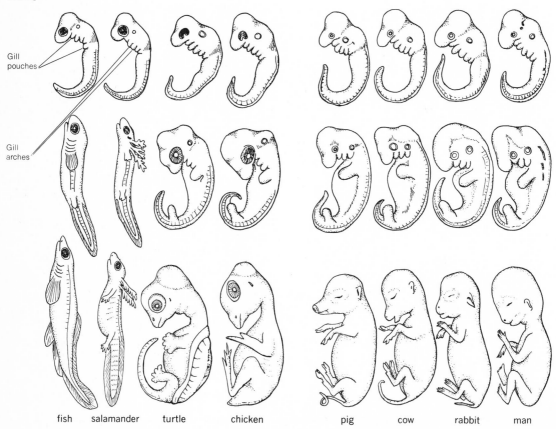

Gill pouches

Gill arches

fish   salamander   turtle   chicken   pig   cow   rabbit   man

and adults of various vertebrate classes cease to be puzzling when viewed as a natural consequence of evolutionary change. Like all mammals, we are a product of a vertebrate lineage that goes back to ancient fishes. In the long evolutionary development from fishes to land vertebrates, lungs evolved as a modification of the respiratory apparatus. In amphibians one more chamber was added to the two-chambered heart of fishes, followed by the addition of a fourth chamber in some of the reptiles and in all the birds and mammals. The basic elements of these alterations and modifications are preserved during the embryonic development of land vertebrates because they are simple and economical means by which lungs and hearts can be built from the ancient vertebrate heritage which all of them share.

Comparative anatomy

The degree of structural similarity among different vertebrates is notable and is particularly impressive among those animals that are adapted to widely diverse modes of life. If we were to select amphibious, aerial, aquatic, and terrestrial species, we would not expect any one structural pattern to meet the needs of such

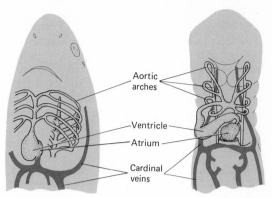

FIGURE 2-3
Similarities in the circulatory system of an adult shark (*left*) and a 3-millimeter-long human embryo (*right*). Both have a two-chambered heart (atrium and ventricle), several paired aortic arches (arteries), and cardinal veins that carry blood from the body to the heart. [*Modified from T. I. Storer et al., General Zoology, 5th. ed., McGraw-Hill, New York. 1972.*]

functionally different life styles, especially where appendages are concerned. Yet when the front appendages of salamanders, birds, bats, whales, and man are compared, one basic skeletal structure appears throughout (Fig. 2-4). It would seem that all of these appendages had

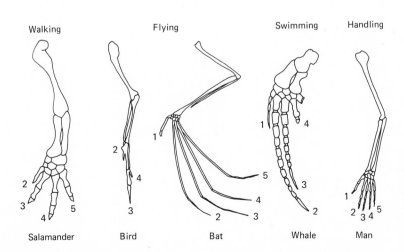

FIGURE 2-4
The left front leg bones of five vertebrates. Numbers indicate fingers. Note similarity in structure despite varying uses. [*Modified from T. I. Storer et al., General Zoology, 5th ed., McGraw-Hill, New York, 1972.*]

evolved, through adaptive modification, from the foreleg of a common ancestor. Vertebrate fossils, in fact, lend support to the belief that this common ancestor was not greatly unlike modern salamanders.

Among anthropoids, anatomical resemblances are especially pronounced, both in the degree of similarity between shared traits and in the number of traits shared. This remarkable correspondence occurs despite the fact that many of the animals are exclusively arboreal, some are both terrestrial and arboreal in vary-

ing degrees, and one, man, is exclusively terrestrial.

The great similarity of general structure between the gorilla and man is evident in their skeletons (Fig. 2-5). More detailed resemblances between man and other primates are observable in a comparison of the general form of anthropoid skulls and the interrelationships of their component bones (Fig. 2-6). A comparative study of the bones of the feet shows a rather striking correspondence in specific characteristics, even when our nongrasping

FIGURE 2-5
A comparison of the skeletons of the gorilla (*left*) and human (*right*). [*Human skeleton after C. C. Francis, Introduction to Human Anatomy, 6th ed., Mosby, St. Louis, 1973.*]

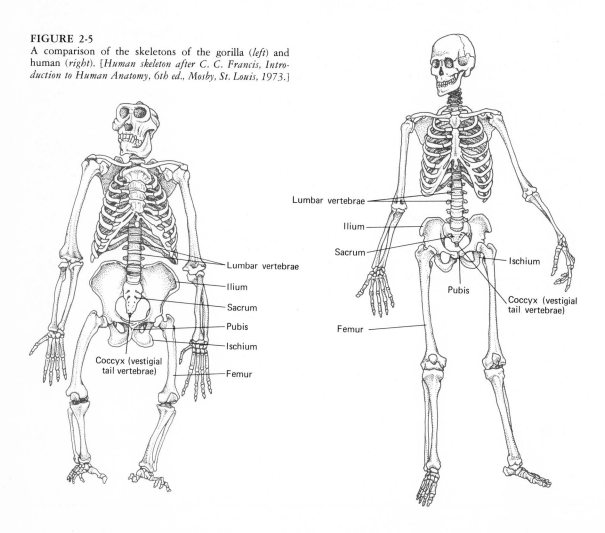

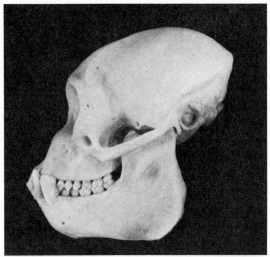

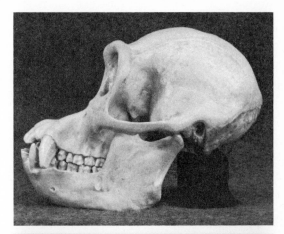

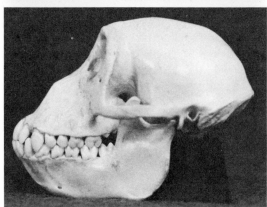

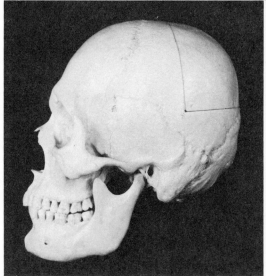

foot is compared to those with opposable toes (Fig. 2-7).

Since anthropoids share so many specific as well as general skeletal features, it should not be surprising that the situation would be much the same insofar as the skeletal musculature is concerned. A study of the leg muscles of man and the gorilla clearly indicates this is the case (Fig. 2-8). There are obvious differences in the relative proportions of certain muscles since the gorilla is essentially a quadrupedal animal. For example, the *biceps femoris* muscle in Fig.

FIGURE 2-6
A comparison of the skulls of a New World (woolly) monkey, *upper left*; Old World (rhesus) monkey, *lower left*; chimpanzee (cast), *upper right*; and man, *lower right*.

2-8 (4) is relatively larger in the gorilla because of its importance in extending the leg during walking. The *gluteus maximus* muscle (3) is relatively larger in man because of its importance in keeping the trunk erect.

Similar comparisons could be made al-

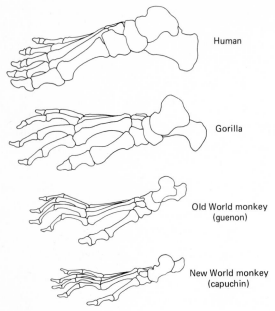

most without end of digestive, respiratory, circulatory, excretory, reproductive, and neural anatomy. Such comparisons would only belabor the point. One more example will suffice: a comparison of the vertebrate brains shown in Fig. 1-8 and the anthropoid cerebrums illustrated in Fig. 2-9. The evidence does indeed suggest that not only are we a product of the vertebrate lineage, but we also share a close common ancestry with the anthropoids in particular.

Vestigial organs

One of the most intriguing aspects of comparative anatomy is the presence of structures of reduced size that seem to have no function. Such *vestigial structures* are common among vertebrates. Both python snakes and whales possess useless remnants of hip bones that usually support hind legs. Two functionless splint bones are found in the lower leg of a horse which, in other animals, connect to the second

FIGURE 2-7
The skeletons of the right foot of four anthropoids. [*From G. A. Harrison et al., Human Biology, Oxford University Press, Oxford, 1964, after W. E. Gregory, Memoirs of the American Museum of Natural History, 1920.*]

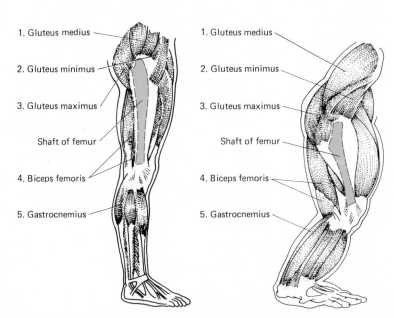

FIGURE 2-8
A comparison of the musculature of the right leg of man (*left*) and a gorilla (*right*). [*Modified from J. Buettner-Janusch, Origins of Man, Wiley, New York, 1966.*]

and fourth toes. Man possesses perhaps as many as 90 such parts.

A few of our many vestigial features are illustrated in Fig. 2-10. A pinkish membrane is found at the inner corner of each eye which represents the transparent third eyelid *(nictitating membrane)* seen in cats, birds, frogs, and other vertebrates. The muscles that move the external ears of many mammals are so reduced in man that they will not move the ears at all in many individuals. Our wisdom teeth, or third molars, usually erupt abnormally and cannot be used in mastication; they are commonly a painful hindrance which must be removed. Almost one-fifth of us are spared this misery, however, and never develop a third molar. The *pyramidalis muscle,* which lies just above the external sex organs, also is absent in about one-fifth of the population, but its presence in the other four-fifths is neither harmful nor beneficial. Muscular performance is unaffected by its presence or absence.

The existence of such structures can be explained through evolutionary mechanisms. Such organs are interpreted as relics of those that were functional in ancestral forms. As environmental changes occurred over long periods of time, certain organs no longer were essential to survival and were reduced to vestigial remnants. The presence of a useful biological structure in a species depends upon the hereditary material *(genes)* responsible for its development (see Chap. 8). Changes in this hereditary material *(mutations)* may be damaging, if not lethal, to the individual that inherits the change. As a result, such harmful changes tend to be eliminated from the population. On the other hand, if a structure is no longer essential to survival, mutations which impair the development of that structure will not be eliminated. In fact, they confer a certain advantage because it is biologically extravagant—wasteful of energy—to develop and maintain useless structures. Consequently, these mutations will accumulate and, in time, the structure will be reduced to a nonfunctional remnant or vestige.

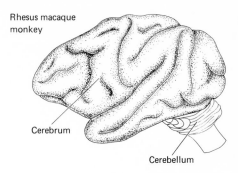

Rhesus macaque monkey

Cerebrum

Cerebellum

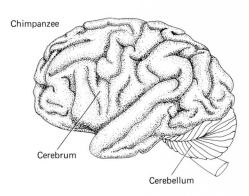

Chimpanzee

Cerebrum

Cerebellum

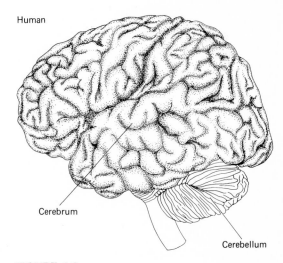

Human

Cerebrum

Cerebellum

FIGURE 2-9
The brains of three anthropoids. (Compare with Figure 1-8.)

COMPARATIVE BIOCHEMISTRY

Comparative biochemistry, like comparative anatomy, involves comparisons between different organisms. In biochemistry comparisons are made of the chemistry of biological processes rather than of anatomical structure.

Comparative biochemistry reveals chemical similarities in vertebrates that parallel those of a structural nature. If animals originally had been classified on the basis of their biochemistry rather than their anatomical structure, the classification would have been essentially the same.

Vertebrates, for example, produce similar hormones. *Thyroid hormone* from cattle is effective in the treatment of people whose thyroxine secretion is below normal; it is equally effective in tadpoles that have had their thyroid glands

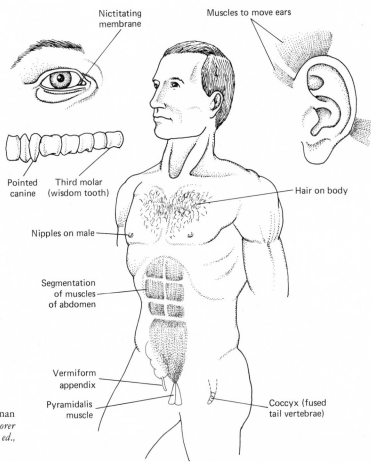

Nictitating membrane

Muscles to move ears

Pointed canine

Third molar (wisdom tooth)

Hair on body

Nipples on male

Segmentation of muscles of abdomen

Vermiform appendix

Pyramidalis muscle

Coccyx (fused tail vertebrae)

FIGURE 2-10
Some vestigial features of the human species. [*Modified from T. I. Storer et al., General Zoology, 5th ed., McGraw-Hill. New York, 1972.*]

removed. Although a given hormone may be found in all vertebrate classes, its function varies. In mammals, thyroxine is involved in regulating metabolic rate. In amphibians it is also necessary, along with *lactogenic hormone,* for the transformation *(metamorphosis)* of tadpoles into frogs. Lactogenic hormone, from the pituitary gland below the brain, is involved in the control of sodium levels in migrating fishes, metamorphosis in amphibians, growth in lizards, broodiness in birds, and milk secretion in mammals. Here at the functional level we see the same phenomenon we saw at the structural level in Fig. 2-4. In this case a hormone, rather than the structure of front leg bones, apparently has been inherited from a common ancestor, and its function has been modified in such a way as to be useful to each of its different owners.

Blood-group substances similar to our own have been found in a variety of primates. The A and B blood-group substances *(antigens)* have been identified in apes, monkeys, and lemurs. The human antigens, however, seem to be more like their counterparts in the apes than those in monkeys and lemurs. The Rh factors (antigens) got their name from the rhesus monkey in whom they first were discovered. It appears, however, that the Rh antigens of the chimpanzee are closest of any primate tested to the human antigens.

Comparative protein chemistry

Some of the most compelling evidence of man's close kinship with the great apes lies in the protein molecules produced by living systems. A protein is a giant molecule, or *macromolecule,* composed of a long chain of smaller molecules, called *amino acids.* A given protein may consist of thousands of amino acid units. Since there are 20 different kinds of amino acids which can be incorporated into these chains, the number of different kinds of proteins is truly astronomical.[1] Albumin, for example, is not one specific kind of protein. It is a group of protein

molecules that have similar, but not identical, amino acid sequences; as a group they share certain biochemical properties.

Serum albumin is the principal protein in the blood plasma of vertebrates and consists of about 570 amino acid units. This sequence of 570 units (of some 20 different kinds) varies from species to species throughout the vertebrate classes. A convenient way to determine the degree of similarity in the serum albumin of various vertebrates is to use a technique employed by immunologists.

Serum albumin is taken from a human subject, purified, and injected into a number of rabbits. Although rabbits have their own albumin, it is not the same molecule as that in man. As a consequence, human albumin is a foreign substance to rabbits, and they respond to it by making antibodies which react specifically with it. These antibodies can now be used as a test indicator (reagent) because they reflect the structure of the injected foreign protein.

If blood serum is taken from these immunized rabbits and mixed with human serum albumin, the antibodies combine with our albumin and form insoluble solids that settle out as a visible precipitate. The strength of the reaction can be measured by determining the amount of precipitate formed. This immunized rabbit serum also can be mixed with serum albumin from animals other than man, and the amount of precipitate, if any, similarly measured. In this way it is possible to determine the degree of similarity between the serum albumin proteins of various vertebrates and that of man.

The albumin of chimpanzees and gorillas shows only a 1 percent immunologic difference from our own. The orangutan is not far behind, followed by the gibbon. It is interesting to note that this close resemblance is quite comparable to the degree of similarity between other well-known look-alikes: horse-donkey, horse-zebra,

---

[1] For example, a chain of 500 amino acid units could occur in 20^{500} (20 multiplied by itself 500 times) different sequences.

dog-fox, sheep-goat, and cat-lion. The remaining primates fall within the same rank of kinship that is reflected in their comparative anatomy: Old World monkeys, New World monkeys, and lemurs.

Comparisons of this nature can be measured even more accurately by techniques of modern analytical biochemistry in which the actual sequence of amino acids has been determined for a considerable number of protein molecules. Normal human adult hemoglobin is one of these; it consists of a specific sequence of 574 amino acid units arranged in four interconnected chains. Vertebrates as well as a great many other organisms also possess their own particular form of hemoglobin. The detailed molecular structure of some of these has been similarly established. Of the wide diversity of hemoglobin types known to occur in nature — some even produced by leguminous plants — there is one organism whose hemoglobin is identical to ours, the chimpanzee. The hemoglobins of Old World monkeys differ on the average in 15 amino acid units (2.6 percent of 574) from their human counterpart.

Evidence of this kind clearly suggests that man is related to all living things in varying degree. We share serum albumins with all vertebrates, and hemoglobins with vertebrates as well as some invertebrates and plants. But we also share almost the same albumin and the identical hemoglobin with our closest relative, the chimpanzee.

APPLIED, CELLULAR, AND CHEMICAL GENETICS

Direct evidence of evolution as an ongoing biologic process is provided by the great diversity of crop plants, ornamental plants, farm animals, and animal pets which man has created, and continues to create, through selective breeding and the application of genetic (hereditary) principles. Many of these organisms have not been assigned to separate species because

(1) they are known to be the products of selective breeding, and (2) related types are usually interfertile with one another. The vast majority of natural species, however, have been defined on the basis of structural characteristics alone, without regard to the possibility of cross-fertility between them. In several instances different natural species have been shown to be interfertile when the barrier normally separating them has been removed.

It seems highly unlikely that botanists would have placed turnips, brussels sprouts, cauliflower, cabbage, kohlrabi, kale, and collards in the same species if these plants had been discovered first in a wild state. All these plants, nonetheless, have been developed through selective breeding from one wild species in the mustard family. It is equally unlikely that zoologists, under similar circumstances, would have classified Great Danes, bulldogs, German shepherds, Afghan hounds, and Chihuahuas in the same species.

Genetics is considered in some detail in Chap. 8. There we will discuss the close relationship between man and anthropoids at the level of both cellular and chemical genetics.

In the meantime we should be aware of the remarkable consistency of a variety of lines of evidence thus far. Whether it be comparative anatomy, the blood-group factors, serum albumin, hemoglobin, or genetics, in every case our closest relatives are the African apes, and in most instances it is the chimpanzee in particular.

COMPARATIVE PSYCHOLOGY AND BEHAVIOR

In zoos, the popularity of monkeys and apes is due in large part to the humanlike quality of their gestures, facial expressions, manipulative ability, intelligence, and social deportment in general. In fact, it was as a result of field studies on the behavior of wild chimpanzees that the definition of man as the only toolmaking animal had to be abandoned. Laboratory studies of chimpanzees have even challenged our status as the only animal capable of expressing ideas in symbolic language.

Jane van Lawick-Goodall was the first to discover that wild chimpanzees in Tanzania make, as well as use, several kinds of tools. They crush leaves in their mouth and use them as sponges to soak up water in crevices for drinking. After sucking the water from the leaves, the process is repeated several times with the same "sponges." Leaves also are used as toilet paper or towels. Chimps commonly throw sticks and stones at potential aggressors, and will tear off tree branches to throw or wield as clubs. Twigs from a branch or stalks of grass are used as raw stock for the making of insect probes. The insects in this case are termites and ants. The twig or grass stalk is broken to the appropriate length (the tool for ant collecting is longer than that for termites) and any lateral branches or leaves are trimmed off. The pruned twig or stalk is then inserted into an opened insect nest and held there for a moment (Fig. 3-11). The tool is then withdrawn, and the insects clinging to it are eaten promptly. Young chimps learn to "termite" by watching their elders. Baboons will observe this procedure, but they never attempt to duplicate it, even though the insects are a delicacy to them.

An incident involving manual dexterity with a seemingly altruistic motive has been observed in an outdoor enclosure at the Yerkes Laboratories of Primate Biology.[2] The enclosure harbored a pair of chimps who were long-time companions. On this particular occasion, the male chimp was observed removing a foreign body from the eye of his female partner. In answer to her whimperings he had crouched in front of her and peered into her left eye at close range. His two forefingers peeled back the eyelid, exposing the pink mucous membrane and the offending particle, which he removed.

In laboratorylike situations, the manual skill and intellectual capacity of chimpanzees is well known. Caged chimps can obtain bananas beyond their reach by piling boxes on top of one another or by making a long pole from short lengths of bamboo fitted into one another. In one such demonstration, a chimp led its human attendant by the hand to a spot below the banana, at which point one primate completely surprised the other by climbing on his shoulders to retrieve the delicious morsel.[3]

Chimpanzees, orangutans, and gorillas will paint or draw, using several different techniques and a variety of materials. If they are equipped with paper, brushes, and poster paints they will work with concentrated attention and become extremely angry when their efforts are interrupted. They appear to know when they have finished and will tear off the completed page to begin on a clean sheet.[4] Some individuals will even execute variations on a particular geometric theme and attempt to complete or balance a geometric pattern.

Perhaps the greatest expertise among apes in manipulative skills has been shown by a chimp named Julia who was studied and trained by B. Rench and J. Dohl.[5] Julia first was taught to open boxes secured by 14 different kinds of fastening devices. From this, she learned to open unfamiliar boxes that required the insertion of miniature keys into miniature padlocks or the unscrewing of minute screws with tiny screwdrivers, which she had to guide along a thumbnail in order to engage the screwdriver into the slot of the screw. She even learned to open new and unfamiliar fastening devices.

Julia also solved complex mazes. When six biology students were given the same mazes to solve, they required about half the time, on the average, that Julia did. Their scores overlapped,

[2] W. R. Miles, "Chimpanzee Behavior: Removal of Foreign Body From Companion's Eye," *Science*, vol. 140, April 26, 1963, p. 383.

[3] Wolfgang Kohler, *The Mentality of Apes*, London: Routledge & Kegan Paul, Ltd., 1927, pp. 48–49.

[4] Alison Jolly, *The Evolution of Primate Behavior*, New York: The Macmillan Company, 1972, pp. 287–288.

[5] Ibid., pp. 284–287.

however; in some cases, Julia was faster than the students.

The use of language

We tend to assume that the human species is unique in its ability to communicate ideas, to make statements about the past and the future, and to express new ideas through a system of abstract symbols called *language.* A dozen or more young chimpanzees, however, have cast considerable doubt upon this assumption; we may not be quite as unusual as we sometimes think.

The first of these chimps, called Washoe, was taught the American Sign Language for the Deaf (ASL) under the care and tutelage of B. T. Gardner and R. A. Gardner.[6] The ASL is a formal set of symbolic gestures that must be learned like a spoken language. Washoe began her training in June 1966, when she was about a year old. At the age of seven she could use 175 words. Her responses during the learning process were remarkably similar to those of human children. She "talked" to herself, sometimes in front of a mirror, repeating again and again some newly learned "words" or grammatical constructions. She would name pictures to herself that she saw in a picture book. On one occasion she even gave the sign for "hurry" on her way to her potty chair.

Although Washoe's remarks do not exceed four words in length, they demonstrate understanding and imagination in the use of language. She invented her own name for ducks, calling them "water birds." Once at dinner she was asked to name her bib. Having forgotten the sign she was taught, she responded by drawing the outline of a bib on her chest with the index finger of both hands. In another instance, a research assistant named Susan purposely stepped on Washoe's rubber

doll to observe the reaction. Washoe's response was both imaginative and appropriate: "Up Susan, Susan up, mine please up, gimme baby, please shoe, more mine, up please, please up, more up, baby down, shoe up, baby up, please more up, and you up."

Another infant chimpanzee named Sarah has been taught a different kind of language by Ann James Premack and David Premack.[7] This language consists of words which are variously shaped and colored pieces of plastic with a metal backing. These "words" are placed vertically, Chinese-fashion, on a magnetized board (Fig. 2-11). Sarah had a vocabulary of about 130 words which she used correctly 75 to 80 percent of the time.

Sarah was able not only to learn the names of objects such as chocolate candy or various kinds of fruits, but also was capable of discerning class concepts like the color brown or green. As a case in point, she was shown the two sentences, "Brown [is the] color of chocolate" and "Green [is the] color of grape." Only *brown* and *green* were new words for her at this point. Later, she was presented with four disks, only one of which was brown, and was instructed to "take brown." She chose the brown disk. In doing so, Sarah apparently conceived of the property of brownness from the original sentence, "Brown [is the] color of chocolate."

Still another young chimp named Lana has been taught to read and construct sentences by using a computer.[8] The computer is equipped with a display panel for Lana to observe and a typewriterlike keyboard of 50 keys for her to operate. Different geometric shapes on the keys represent words in a special language. If Lana constructs a sentence that is grammatically correct, she is rewarded. If incorrect, her sentence is automatically erased. Over

[6] B. T. Gardner and R. A. Gardner, "Two-way Communication with an Infant Chimpanzee," in *Behavior of Nonhuman Primates,* vol. 4, A. Schrier and F. Stollnitz (eds.), New York: Academic Press, Inc., 1971, pp. 117–184.

[7] David Premack and Ann James Premack, "Teaching Language to An Ape," *Scientific American,* October 1972, pp. 92–99.

[8] D. M. Rumbaugh et al., "Reading and Sentence Completion by a Chimpanzee (Pan)," *Science,* vol. 182, 1973, pp. 731–733; J. D. Fleming, "The State of the Apes," *Psychology Today,* January 1974, p. 46.

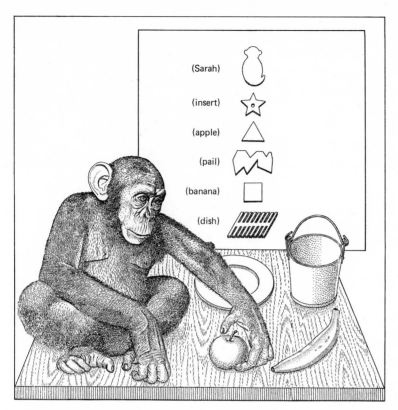

FIGURE 2-11
Sarah and her vertical language of plastic shapes. The message reads "Sarah insert apple pail banana dish." She put apple in the pail and banana in the dish. [*After A. J. Premack and D. Premack, Scientific American, October, 1972.*]

a six-month training period Lana learned to ask for all her food and drink, as well as such extra rewards as a look outside, toys, music, movies, and human companionship. She also complies with instructions which experimenters project on the display panel. In fact, when experimenters display both correctly and incorrectly worded sentences, it appears that Lana can distinguish between them.

From this brief account, it would seem that the achievements of chimpanzees in manipulation, language, and possibly even in thought itself are comparable, if not at times identical, to those of very young children. Although our performance in these skills as adults vastly exceeds that of any ape, our claim to distinction in these areas is not entirely uncontested. At the same time we should stress

that chimps have to be taught to use symbols that were designed by people, and they cannot be taught to speak. Only the human species, so far as we know, has the capacity to develop symbol systems and to use verbal language. We must still consider the use of language as an essentially human attribute.

PALEONTOLOGY

The study of the remains or traces, called *fossils,* of ancient organisms preserved in the rocks is called *paleontology.* The basic aim of this science is to reconstruct the history of life as it is reflected in the fossil record. Paleontology, then, affords a direct approach to the ques-

FIGURE 2-12
The Grand Canyon of the Colorado River in Arizona. Some 1,600 meters (a vertical mile) of geologic formations are exposed, the youngest of which, at the canyon rim, were laid down before dinosaurs had evolved, 230 to 280 million years ago. [*U.S. Geological Survey, photograph by N. W. Carkhuff.*]

tion of whether evolution did in fact occur.

As one descends into the Grand Canyon of the Colorado River in Arizona (Fig. 2-12), layer upon layer of increasingly older rock formations come into view. Ages ago, many of these rocks were uncompacted sediments laid down by wind, rivers, lakes, and coastal waters. Others originated as volcanic ash coughed from the throats of active volcanoes. Some of these sediments contained the skeletal remains of organisms, which became fossilized as the loose sediments were converted into hard sandstones, shales, and other forms of sedimentary rock. Examining these layers and their fossils is almost like scanning the pages of a great book backwards. As one proceeds to the bottom of the canyon and the earlier chapters in the book, a history of life unfolds: both the diversity and complexity of fossil organisms decrease as one goes farther back in time. The lowest section harboring abundant fossils does not contain vertebrates. But it has large numbers of invertebrate types, some of which have been extinct for hundreds of millions of years. The ancient altered sediments which form the riverbed were laid down 2 billion or more years ago. A vertical mile above the river, the canyon rim is edged with geologic formations 230 to 280 million years old, which contain the footprints of early reptiles that lived long before the first dinosaurs.

A sketch of some of the major landmarks in the history of life is outlined in Fig. 2-13. Geologic history is divided into eras, periods, and epochs based upon notable geologic changes that have occurred during the 4.8 billion years since our planet was born. The ages of these historical divisions have been determined by geologic methods of radioactive dating such as the potassium-argon and uranium-lead techniques.

The fossils which make up this comprehensive paleontological record constitute a vast and diverse assemblage housed in museums and universities all over the world. They demonstrate beyond any doubt whatever that living things in ages past were quite different

Era	Period	Epoch	Life
Cenozoic (65)	Quaternary (2–3)	Recent (0.025) Pleistocene (2–3)	Rapid expansion of mammals and birds. Rise of grasses. Glaciation. Establishment of primate lineage leading to *Homo* in Pleistocene. Dominance of man and extinction of many large mammals.
	Tertiary (65)	Pliocene (12) Miocene (25) Oligocene (36) Eocene (58) Paleocene (65)	
Mesozoic (230)	Cretaceous (135)		Extinction of many reptilian forms. First modern birds. Mammals begin to diversify.
	Jurassic (180)		The appearance of birds. First flowering plants. The age of reptiles.
	Triassic (230)		Extinction of early amphibians. Many reptilian types. First dinosaurs and mammals.
Paleozoic (600)	Permian (280)		Reptiles diversify, displacing amphibians as dominant group. Increasing aridity and glaciation with extinction of many early Paleozoic organisms.
	Carboniferous (345)		The age of coal-forming forests and amphibians. The first reptiles.
	Devonian (405)		The age of sharklike and bony fishes. The first forests. The rise of amphibians.
	Silurian (425)		Plants and invertebrates invaded land. First insects and scorpions.
	Ordovician (500)		First vertebrates (primitive fish) appeared. No land animals or plants.
	Cambrian (600)		Appearance of all major invertebrate groups, including some no longer living today. No land animals or plants.
Pre-Cambrian ↓ Birth of Planet (4800)			Algae and/or bacteria up to 3.5 billion years ago or more. Relatively simple invertebrates like jellyfish 0.6 to 0.9 billion years ago. The planet was probably lifeless the first billion years.

FIGURE 2-13
Some major episodes in the history of life preserved in the fossil record, with approximate time to beginning of each in millions of years.

from those with which we are familiar. No species on earth today has a fossil record of itself from 20 million years ago; yet that same fossil record testifies to the existence of innumerable species that do not exist today, some

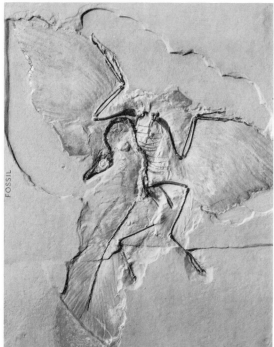

FOSSIL

FIGURE 2-14
The Jurassic fossil bird *Archaeopteryx* (*left*) and its restoration (*right*). [*Courtesy of The American Museum of Natural History.*]

of which left voluminous remains of themselves. If we eliminate the lineages that have become extinct, however, the remainder were *similar* to modern species and indicate the lines of descent that led to present-day forms.

An excellent example of this is provided by the fossil remains of the ancient toothed bird, *Archaeopteryx* (Fig. 2-14). One individual left clear impressions of its feathers that have endured some 160 million years after its death. The fossilized skeleton left unmistakable evidence of three claws on the ends of its wing fingers as well as the claws on its toes. Many other reptilian features, not seen in modern birds, also are in evidence, such as the presence of teeth, the poorly developed breastbone, and the large number of vertebrae in the tail. Other reptilian fossils, specifically those comprising the lineage that led to dinosaurs and crocodiles, leave little doubt that birds did, in fact, evolve

from reptiles. This is further corroborated by the relatively high degree of correspondence in the serum albumins of modern birds, crocodiles, and alligators. Crocodiles and alligators, moreover, are the only reptiles that have, like birds and mammals, a completely four-chambered heart, and alligators are the only reptiles known to care for their young.

The human species is likewise not without fossil evidence of its primate heritage. The primate order, like all orders, is composed of a number of subgroups called *families*. One of these families, the Pongidae, embraces the great apes: chimpanzees, gorillas, and orangutans. Another, the Hominidae, is the family to which man belongs; it is represented today by only one species. In early to mid-Miocene time,

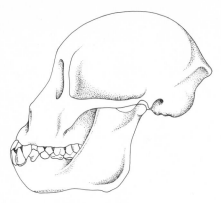

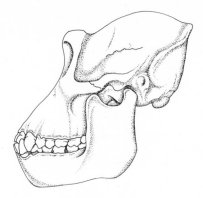

Dryopithecus africanus
(18 million B.P.)

Female gorilla
(present)

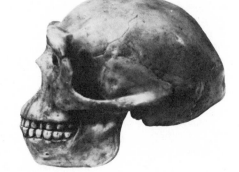

Australopithecus africanus
(2 million B.P.)

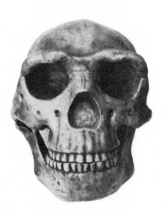

Homo erectus
(500,000 B.P.)

some 18 to 23 million years ago (see Fig. 2-13), the fossil record reveals a considerable variety of ancient pongid species. Not until later in the Miocene, perhaps 15 million years ago, do we find the earliest hominid fossils and these show a remarkable resemblance to some of their pongid contemporaries. These similarities can be seen in Fig. 2-15 by comparing the skulls of a Miocene ape *(Dryopithecus),* an early hominid *(Australopithecus),* and a modern female gorilla.

The paleontological record of our family indicates that our species clearly is the current end product of a gradual series of modifications in ancestral forms which extend back at least 15 million years. Although these early ancestors were similar to apes which lived at, and prior to, that time, the consensus among authorities competent to judge is that they were more hominid than pongid.[9] Paleontological discoveries in East Africa have shown that by 2.6 million years ago early hominids *(Australopithecus)* were already making primitive pebble tools. From that time to the present,

[9] E. L. Simons, *Primate Evolution.* New York: The Macmillan Company, 1972, pp. 266–277; David Pilbeam, *The Ascent of Man.* New York: The Macmillan Company, 1972, pp. 91–99.

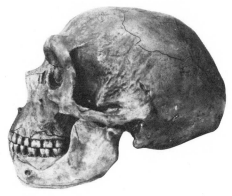

Early *Homo sapiens*
(90,000 B.P.)

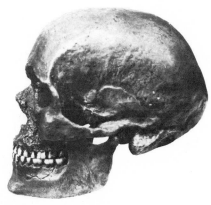

Late *Homo sapiens*
(25,000 B.P.)

FIGURE 2-15
A chronological series of fossil hominid skulls. The skulls of a modern female gorilla and the Miocene ape *Dryopithecus* are for comparative purposes. B.P. is years before the present. Photographs are of casts. [*Dryopithecus from LeGros Clark, History of the Primates, University of Chicago Press, Chicago, 1965; gorilla from LeGros Clark, The Fossil Evidence for Human Evolution, University of Chicago Press, Chicago, 1955.*]

the fossil evidence supports the origin of modern man through gradual evolutionary change (Fig. 2-15). The many fossil remains of early and late *Homo erectus,* followed by those of early and late *Homo sapiens,* give mute testimony to the nature and course of human evolution.

BIOGEOGRAPHY

The distribution of living things over the earth (biogeography) presents many puzzling patterns. For example, the plants and animals in the deserts of North America and Australia are quiet different although the environments are comparable. Unlike other large land masses, most of the native mammals of Australia are not placentals; they consist largely of primitive egg-laying types, such as the spiny anteaters, and a great variety of pouch-bearing marsupials, such as kangaroos and wallabies.

On the other hand, the Galápagos Islands lying 1,000 kilometers (600 miles) off the coast of Ecuador are the home of 23 species of land birds found nowhere else in the world. Yet all 23 resemble birds on the mainland where the climates and environments are quite different. Why should similar species be found in dissimilar environments?

Biogeographic examples of this kind are legion and are the natural consequence of organic evolution. Insofar as Australia is concerned, there is growing geologic evidence that this subcontinent was in contact with, and part of, a huge continental land mass that embraced what is now South America, Africa, Antarctica, and India during the Mesozoic era. At the time of its separation from this supercontinent, probably during the Cretaceous period some 100 million years ago, placental mammals had not yet evolved. As a consequence, Australia was populated with primitive mammals. By the time placental mammals had evolved on the continental land masses, the subcontinent had become totally isolated.

In the case of the Galápagos Islands, this archipelago was formed by volcanic activity somewhat over 2 million years ago. Its bird population probably traces its ancestry back to early migrants from the South American mainland. Colonization of this kind has been observed to occur on oceanic islands of recent volcanic origin, and 2 million years would appear to be an adequate period for the evolution of new species.

Every species has a center of origin from which it disperses into areas available to it. As it does so, it undergoes modifications imposed by the environment. The end result of this process often is a discontinuous distribution, such as is shown by the camel family. The camels of Africa, the Near East, and Asia are a long way removed from the remaining members of their family, the llamas of South America. The paleontological record shows that millions of years ago fossil members of the family had a continuous distribution between the regions now occupied. The oldest of these early types lived in North America and was the common ancestor of both camels and llamas. As this ancestral group dispersed from its place of origin, it gradually split into separate lineages. One succeeded in moving southward over the land bridge between the Americas and became South American llamas. The other migrated north and west into Eurasia over the land bridge that existed during much of Tertiary times (now the Bering Straits); this lineage ultimately became camels. Extinction over much of the Old World, and in all of North and Central America, has left two isolated remnants of a family that once inhabited most of the globe.

If we turn to the distribution of our own species, it would seem that quite a different situation prevails. Man inhabits, or visits, essentially every region on earth. Unlike the camel family, man has so far steadily increased his range of distribution. The species to which modern man belongs, *Homo sapiens,* was a relative latecomer to both Australia and the Western Hemisphere. Fossil remains and artifacts indicate that our species inhabited Australia approximately 30,000 years ago. The oldest records for man's presence in the New World are currently set by radioactive (radiocarbon) dating at 25,000 to 29,000 years ago on the basis of skeletal remains and bone artifacts. Contrasted with this, there is fossil evidence of the existence of early (archaic) forms of modern man in England and Germany as long ago as 150,000 to 200,000 years. There is, in fact, paleontological justification for the belief that the populations of Europe, North and East Africa, and the adjacent portions of Western Asia were a mosaic of relatively archaic and more advanced forms of *Homo sapiens* 100,000 years ago or more. This general region, it would seem, encompasses the place of origin of our species.

Such a place of origin would be a logical one because it corresponds to the distribution of our hominid ancestors. *Ramapithecus,* a fossil of late Miocene to early Pliocene age, is considered to be the earliest known hominid. *Ramapithecus* left its remains in East Africa, Asia, and Europe. Miocene apes like *Dryopithecus* resembled *Ramapithecus* in many ways and left fossils in Europe, Africa, and Asia. *Australopithecus* occupied Africa and perhaps Asia in the late Pliocene and early Pleistocene, followed later by *Homo erectus,* whose remains occur in Europe as well as in Africa and Asia.

Like the ancestral members of the camel family in North America, the hominid family has dispersed from its center of origin. Unlike the camel family, only one species of hominids remains alive today, but that one species has never been eliminated from any area it formerly occupied. Advanced forms of *Homo sapiens,* presumably having originated in East Africa, Arabia, Western Asia, and India, gradually spread throughout Eurasia and Africa. Dispersal into Australia and the Western Hemisphere apparently did not take place for some time because of formidable water barriers and adverse climatic conditions.

The Pleistocene epoch, during which these events were taking place, was marked by a series of major glacial advances and recessions, each of which spanned thousands of years. A major glacial advance was the result of tremendous snowpack accumulations in the northerly latitudes. The snowpack recrystallized as ice, forming continental glaciers up to a kilometer or more in thickness over an area of millions of square kilometers. Such immense accumulations of water in its solid state lowered sea levels over the world as much as 150 meters (500 feet). (See Fig. 2-16.) Conversely, as these continental glaciers began to melt and recede, sea levels rose.

The occupation of Australia by modern man would have been facilitated during a glacial advance by reducing the size of the deep-water channels among the Indonesian Islands that separate Australia from the mainland. That alone would probably not have been sufficient to lure a primitive people on even a short marine voyage, however, unless they had a very good reason for making one. It is reasonable to suppose, therefore, that the first people to populate Australia were tempted into the area because they were fishermen, and made use of rafts or canoes to ply their skills. This degree of Paleolithic technology did not occur until quite late in the Pleistocene, perhaps not much earlier than 30,000 years ago.

The entrance of man into the Western Hemisphere was via a route across the Bering Strait between Alaska and Siberia. Inasmuch as the waters of the Bering Strait are only about 50 meters (175 feet) deep, periods of glacial advance converted the strait into a broad land bridge connecting North America and Asia (Fig. 2-16). Ancestral camels used this bridge in gaining access to Asia. Ancestral bison, reindeer, and the elephantlike mastodons and mammoths that had their centers of origin in Eurasia crossed the same bridge in the opposite direction as they entered the New World. It is believed that man crossed this bridge also in the normal course of hunting large animals for which he had developed an apparent preference. These animals included bison, reindeer, mastodon, and mammoth. During the last

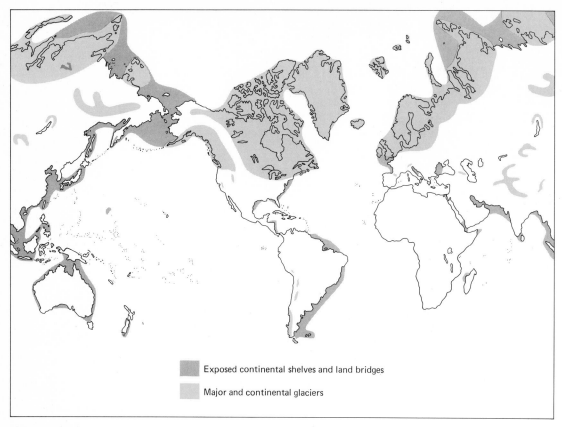

FIGURE 2-16
The world during the last major glacial advance. Major and continental glaciers colored; exposed continental shelves and land bridges shaded.

major glacial advance, there was an ice-free corridor from Alaska to the Great Plains along the eastern flank of the Rocky Mountains (see Fig. 2-16). By this time, man's technology had reached a point where human populations could, and did, live under arctic conditions. Tailored garments made of animal hides have been discovered in Arctic Asia, preserved through freezing for many thousands of years.

Biogeography, then, joins the other five biological sciences we have examined in sup-port of the principle that biological kinships are real. Animals are said to be related if they have evolved from a common ancestral stock. Six biological sciences—comparative embryology and anatomy, comparative biochemistry, genetics, comparative psychology and behavior, paleontology, and biogeography—demonstrate our kinship with other living things. More importantly, they all point to the pongids as our closest relatives.

We should now inquire into the nature of the biologic lineage of which we are a part. In the next chapter we will examine the primate heritage insofar as it is reflected in the lives of our living relatives, the nonhuman primates.

SUGGESTED READINGS

CLARK, W. E. LEGROS: *The Antecedents of Man,* Edinburgh: Edinburgh University Press, 1959. A comprehensive but moderately technical general introduction to the comparative anatomy of primates based upon living species and fossil evidence.

COLBERT, E. H.: *Evolution of the Vertebrates,* New York: John Wiley & Sons, Inc., 1969. An account of the lives and times of ancestral vertebrates as revealed by their fossil remains and the geologic record.

DARWIN, CHARLES: *Voyage of the Beagle,* Garden City, N. Y., Doubleday & Company, Inc., 1962. Notes and observations of Charles Darwin on the geology and natural history of various countries visited during the voyage of H.M.S. Beagle from 1832 to 1836.

DICKERSON, R. E.: "The Structure and History of Ancient Protein," *Scientific American,* April 1972. The chemical structure of an enzyme (cytochrome *c*) found in almost all living things suggests the same evolutionary relationships as those revealed by comparative anatomy and the fossil record.

SARICH, V.: "A Molecular Approach to the Question of Human Origins," in *Background for Man,* eds. P. Dalhinow and V. Sarich. Boston: Little, Brown and Company, 1971. How an analysis of blood serums may reveal evolutionary origins and relationships.

WALLACE, B.: *Chromosomes, Giant Molecules, and Evolution,* New York, W. W. Norton & Company, Inc., 1966. Evidence for evolution from modern genetics.

REVIEW QUESTIONS

1 What is a scientific hypothesis? How may such an hypothesis become a scientific theory? Why is scientific knowledge always subject to modification?

2 Cite three anatomical similarities between the embryo and adult of various vertebrate classes. How does evolutionary theory explain these similarities?

3 What logical explanation is there for the structural similarity in the appendages of amphibious, aerial, aquatic, and terrestrial vertebrates?

4 Name five vestigial structures possessed by the human species. How do biologists explain the existence of such structures?

5 What is the function of lactogenic hormone in fishes, amphibians, reptiles, birds, and mammals?

6 The protein molecule hemoglobin has precisely the same molecular structure in both humans and chimpanzees. Why is this fact considered so remarkable?

7 Why have domesticated varieties of plants and animals not been placed in different species from their wild ancestors?

8 Referring to studies on the use of language by the chimps Washoe, Sarah, and Lana, cite a case in which the ape *(a)* invented its own name for an object, *(b)* discerned an abstract class concept, and *(c)* distinguished between grammatically correct and incorrect sentences.

9 The fossil record often indicates the probable lines of descent of present-day species. Trace the probable line of descent of modern man, giving the scientific name and approximate geologic age of each fossil form.

10 Fossil evidence points to what general region as the center of origin of the human species? What is the nature of that evidence? What kind of conditions theoretically prevailed to provide *Homo sapiens* with the opportunity for entry into the Western Hemisphere?

THREE

OUR LIVING RELATIVES

We have established that the human species has a biological kinship with the primates based upon common descent. We next inquire into our living relatives. Who are they? What kind of lives do they lead? By addressing these questions, we gain a fuller understanding of the primate heritage which we share. Such an understanding will be most useful when we undertake to examine our own species in a similar vein.

The order Primates is most closely related to the order Insectivora. The biological ties between the two orders are clearly illus-

trated by a family of animals known as the tree shrews (Tupaiidae) of India and Southeast Asia (Fig. 3-2A). The classificational status of these little creatures has shifted a number of times. They have been considered the most primitive of primates. They have been classified, with equal persuasion, as primatelike insectivores. Tree shrews do resemble insectivores, such as moles and shrews, by their generally rodentlike appearance. They have long bodies and tails, relatively short legs, and their toes are equipped with claws. Their faces are prolonged into long narrow snouts that termi-

Suborder	Infraorder	Superfamily	Family
Prosimii	Lemuriformes	Lemuroidea	Lemuridae
			Indriidae
		Daubentonioidea	Daubentoniidae
	Lorisiformes	Lorisoidea	Lorisidae
	Tarsiiformes	Tarsiioidea	Tarsiidae
Anthropoidea		Ceboidea	Callithricidae
			Cebidae
		Cercopithecoidea	Cercopithecidae
		Hominoidea	Hylobatidae
			Pongidae
			Hominidae

FIGURE 3-1
A classification of living primates. Examples list both common and scientific names. The scientific name is composed of two terms; the first term is the *generic name* (name of the *genus*) and the second is the *species name*. A family consists of one or more *genera* (plural of genus) and a genus consists of one or more species. A species is the fundamental category of classification and refers to a population of organisms that is reproductively isolated from—does not interbreed with—other species. The abbreviation spp. represents the plural of species. (Refer to Figs. 1-9 and 1-11.)

nate in muzzles with jutting tactile bristles. On the other hand, they are primatelike in that their digits are quite mobile, the visual centers of their brain are enlarged, and their olfactory centers are reduced. They are also similar to prosimians in their protein chemistry. In sum, they appear to be good examples of animals intermediate between prosimians and insectivores. Indeed, their controversial status lends support to the belief that primates evolved from early insectivores.

Figure 3-1 shows that the primate order consists of two *suborders,* the Prosimii (Greek *pro,* "before"; Latin *simi,* "ape"), including lemurs, lorises, and tarsiers, and the Anthropoidea (Greek *anthropus,* "man"),[1] including

monkeys, apes, and humans. Each suborder is composed of smaller categories (*infraorders* and *superfamilies*) which in turn are comprised of one or more *families* of living primates. Examples are listed for each of these families, giving both their common and scientific names. The scientific name consists of two terms, *genus* and *species,* which represent the two lowermost categories in the hierarchy of classification. (The full hierarchy of classification is presented in Fig. 1-11.) Genus and species are explained more fully in the caption of Fig. 3-1. Photographs of species representing most of the

---

[1] The term primate (Latin *primus,* "first") implies that the group in which man belongs is first in rank.

EXAMPLES

Genus	Species	Common name
Lemur	*catta*	Ring-tailed lemur
Propithecus	spp.	Sifaka
Daubentonia	*madagascariensis*	Aye-aye
Loris	*tardigradus*	Slender loris
Galago	spp.	Bushbaby
Tarsius	spp.	Tarsier
Callithrix	spp.	Marmoset
Cebus	spp.	Capuchin monkey
Ateles	spp.	Spider monkey
Macaca	spp.	Macaque monkey
Colobus	spp.	Colobus monkey
Hylobates	spp.	Gibbon
Symphalangus	*syndactylus*	Siamang
Pongo	*pygmaeus*	Orangutan
Pan	*troglodytes*	Chimpanzee
Gorilla	*gorilla*	Gorilla
Homo	*sapiens*	Man

superfamilies are shown in Fig. 3-2*A* to *L*.

In developing a fuller understanding of our biological cousins, we will stress the interrelationships which they have with their total environment (ecology) and the behavior which they exhibit in it (ethology).

THE PROSIMIANS

Ranging generally from the size of mice to very large domestic cats, most prosimians are relatively small animals. Aside from the Tarsiiformes (Fig. 3-1), the remaining prosimians represent a fairly homogeneous group.

Both the Lemuriformes and Lorisiformes have snouts and muzzles like the tree shrews, although they are not nearly as long and narrow. Their eyes are placed forward and the fields of vision overlap, but color vision is lacking. The hands are well developed for grasping with thumbs and first toes that are opposable or nearly so, but the independent control of individual fingers is slight. The hands are used for locomotion, holding food, grooming, playing, and fighting. With the exception of the second toe, which bears a claw that is used primarily in grooming, their fingers and toes typically are equipped with nails. The lower incisors and canines are adapted almost exclusively for grooming. They are slender, closely placed, and forwardly directed to form a *dental comb*. This is a cosmetic device with which one animal can remove dried skin, seeds, and so on from the body of another.[2]

Greater dependence is placed on smell than in any other group of primates. Olfaction is important in the location of food. In fact, like members of the dog family, these prosimians mark off their territories[3] by urine- or scent-marking. Learned behavior is significantly less developed than among the anthropoids. Facial expression is also less varied; common expressions include the staring open-mouth threat and the defensive, bared-teeth "grin" (Fig. 3-2*E*). Both expressions are widespread among anthropoids and generally signify aggression or threat, and submission or defense, respectively.

The bushbabies and lorises (Lorisiformes)

The true lorises (Fig. 3-2*C*) are nocturnal arboreal animals found in the tropical forests

---

[2] Tree shrews also have a dental comb.

[3] A *territory* is a specific area of a habitat occupied by an individual, a pair of individuals, or a group belonging to the same species. The area is actively defended by the resident species against intrusion by nonresident members of the same species. If the area is not actively defended, it is referred to as a *home range* rather than a territory.

A Tree shrew (*Tupaia glis*)   **B** Ringtailed lemur (*Lemur catta*)   **C** Slender loris (*Loris tardigradus*)

D Bushbaby (*Galago senegalensis*)   **E** Mindanao tarsier (*Tarsius syricta*)   **F** Goeldi's marmoset (*Callimico goeldii*)

FIGURE 3-2
Representative primates. [*San Diego Zoo Photos, D and I by Ron Garrison. L by F. D. Schmidt.*]

and woodlands of Africa and Asia, where they subsist on a diet of insects, small lizards, and birds. They are distinguished by large eyes, small ears, and very short tails. In some species the tail is lacking entirely. Both the thumb and the big toes are set wide apart from the other digits, resulting in a powerful, viselike grip.

Locomotion is quadrupedal and absurdly slow and deliberate. Apparently this is an adap-

G Spider monkey (*Ateles sp.*)

I Whitehanded gibbon (*Hylobates lar*)

H Pigtailed macaque (*Macaca nemestrina*)

J Female and male orangutans (*Pongo pygmaeus*)

K Western chimpanzee (*Pan troglodytes*)

L Lowland gorilla (*Gorilla gorilla*)

tation by which lorises remain inconspicuous both to their predators and their animal prey. Their noctural habit also reduces their chances of being preyed upon and provides the added bonus of restricting competition from the more intelligent anthropoids that are usually diurnal (active in daylight). Generally they are believed to be solitary animals, but relatively little is known of their social behavior in the wild.

The galagos, or bushbabies (Fig. 3-2D), are found only in the tropical forests and savannas (grasslands) of Africa. They are arboreal and nocturnal, although some are active at dawn and at dusk. Their natural bill of fare includes fruits, insects, and even small vertebrates. Unlike the lorises, they have large, highly mobile ears and long bushy tails, which presumably serve as organs of balance. Their hind legs are long, especially in the region of the ankle *(tarsus),* which enables them to make unusual leaps. A bushbaby only 15 centimeters (6 inches) long is capable of a vertical jump of 2 meters (about 6½ feet).

In contrast with the slow-moving lorises, galagos move quickly. Arboreal locomotion is by vertical clinging and leaping. During such leaps they are capable of capturing insects in midair. On the ground they move either quadrupedally or by kangaroolike hops. They are not strictly solitary animals but form sleeping nests harboring as many as nine individuals among whom mutual grooming occurs.

The lemurs and their relatives (Lemuriformes)

The lemurs and their relatives are confined entirely to the island of Madagascar (Malagasy Republic). In Eocene time, 45 million years ago, however, ancient lemuroids ranged widely, leaving fossil remains in Europe and North America. Madagascar probably was colonized originally by a relatively small number of prosimians who arrived accidentally aboard natural rafts of trees and floating debris on which they had become stranded along the coast of Africa. It is unlikely that they could have arrived otherwise because the Mozambique Channel separating the island from its mainland is both wide and deep. It has been a barrier to terrestrial migration since Cretaceous, if not Jurassic, times (see geologic time

periods in Fig. 2-13). Because of its isolated nature, Madagascar lacks the rich variety of animal types native to the mainland. There are no monkeys or apes and only a few carnivores. As a result of minimal competition and freedom from serious predation, the lemuroids have prospered in Madagascar.

Under the protective cloak of isolation, the Lemuriformes have become quite diversified and have filled the ecologic roles, or niches, of monkeys and apes. Although many are strictly arboreal, some are partially terrestrial. There are both diurnal and nocturnal species. Diet runs the gamut from insectivorous to herbivorous to omnivorous. One highly specialized species, the unusual aye-aye, lives on fruit and the larvae of wood-boring beetles. This exceptional primate has rodentlike incisors, claws on all digits except for the nail on the big toe, and a long thin middle finger that looks, and functions, more like a wire probe than a digit.

Many of the lemuroid species have a complex social organization of the kind seen in anthropoids. This is particularly true in diurnal semiterrestrial species like the ring-tailed lemur (*Lemur catta,* Fig. 3-2B) but also is the case to a lesser degree in arboreal diurnal types like the white sifaka (*Propithecus verreauxi,* Fig. 1-9A). Both these lemurs group themselves into social units or *troops* which are anthropoidlike in structure: unlike most nonprimate mammals, an infant is born into a troop in which it will remain the rest of its life. A lemur troop, consequently, is composed of animals of all ages and is organized around several adults of both sexes. In the sifaka, a large troop will consist of 10 individuals; ring-tailed lemur troops are bigger, numbering up to about 24.

The puzzling tarsiers (Tarsiiformes)

The infraorder Tarsiiformes is represented today by only three species and these are members of the one genus, *Tarsius* (Fig. 3-2E). All are native to various islands in the East Indies, where they are found as arboreal inhabitants of the tropical rain forest. They are nocturnal in habit and appear to live on an animal diet of insects, spiders, and lizards. Very little is known of their behavior under natural conditions, although some observations have been made of zoo specimens. The study of captive animals, however, does not necessarily throw much light on natural behavior.

In some ways, the tarsiers resemble other prosimians. They are quite small, ranging from 90 to 150 grams (1/5 to 1/3 pound), and are similar to galagos in several respects, not the least of which is that they fill almost the same ecologic niche. They have long, although not bushy, tails. They have short forelimbs and very long hind limbs, especially the tarsal portion, from which they get their name. Like the bush-babies, they are expert at vertical clinging and leaping and can jump very high to catch insects on the wing. Their enormous forward-looking eyes are adapted to nocturnal life and are incapable of color vision. The ears are large and mobile. They have large pads on the end of each digit, somewhat like the galagos, but are unlike them and other prosimians in having grooming claws on the third as well as the second toe.

The tarsiers are unusual primates in that they possess a number of traits which are not present in other prosimians but are typical of anthropoids. The face of a tarsier is relatively flat and lacks both a snout and a muzzle. The nose is small and lies above a hairy mobile upper lip. Despite an anthropoidlike upper lip, the tarsier still drinks by lapping water with its tongue. The lower incisors and canines are not specialized as a dental comb. The huge eyes are similar to those of anthropoids in that they are set in essentially complete bony sockets. The eyes, however, are entirely immobile. As a compensatory measure, the animal can rotate its head so as to look directly backward like an owl. The brain is expanded considerably, especially the visual center at the rear. Because of this, there is increased flexion of the cranium on the vertebral column. This flexure further serves to adapt the animal to its characteristic

posture; whether sitting, hopping, or leaping, its body usually is erect. The tarsier's world is primarily a visual one. While the senses of touch and hearing also are of undoubted importance, reliance upon olfaction must be relatively minor because of significant reductions both in the olfactory center of the brain and in its facial accessory, the snout. Finally, it is notable that, although the uterus is divided as in other prosimians, the tarsier placenta is anthropoidlike. Unlike any loris, galago, or lemur, these little creatures menstruate just as monkeys, apes, and people do.

Most of the characteristics just described are found only in anthropoids. At the same time, tarsiers demonstrate many points of similarity with prosimians also. Consequently, insofar as their classificational status is concerned, the tarsiers share a similar fate with the tree shrews: they are commonly classified with the prosimians (as done here). Others place them with the anthropoids. Still others consider them as a separate group between prosimians and anthropoids. As with the tree shrews, this lack of agreement does not indicate ignorance on the part of biologists but merely affirms the intermediate character of a transitional type. Evolution is a gradual process and often lacks clearly defined boundaries and divisions. In Eocene times, tarsiioids were distributed widely over the world. Many genera have left fossil remains both in North America and in Europe. It was once thought that some of these early tarsiioids may have been the ancestral groups from which both the Ceboidea in the New World and the Cercopithecoidea in the Old World evolved. Certainly the intermediate position of the tarsiers between prosimians and anthropoids would suggest such an evolutionary event, just as the intermediate position of tree shrews corroborates the presumed origin of primates from insectivores. However, there is no hard evidence to support either of these speculations. Primate biologists today consider modern tarsiers as representatives of an ancient family of specialized primates.

THE HUMANLIKE PRIMATES (ANTHROPOIDEA)

Whatever common ancestry the Ceboidea (New World monkeys) and Cercopithecoidea (Old World monkeys) may have had, both groups have followed separate evolutionary courses since their origins in the Eocene or Oligocene epochs. The New World monkeys evolved in isolation from Old World anthropoids. The environments inhabited by them in the Western Hemisphere are restricted to the forested areas of Central and South America, including the Amazon basin. This region has been blanketed continuously by forests since the Eocene, so that the Ceboidea have enjoyed a long period of fairly uniform environments. The Cercopithecoidea and the Hominoidea (apes and man), on the other hand, have been perennial residents of a much vaster area in Asia and Africa where the environments are not only much more diverse but also have undergone many changes during that same period of time. As a result, the Old World anthropoids have been subjected to great ecologic (environmental) challenges to which they have responded by producing a profuse variety of primate forms, the most notable and notorious of which is man himself.

The New World monkeys (Ceboidea)

The monkeys of the Western Hemisphere are entirely arboreal. They consist of two families, one of which comprises the marmosets and their allies (Fig. 3-2F). The marmosets are the smallest and most distinctive of monkeys. They possess claws rather than nails on all digits except the big toe. On the other hand, they are also monogamous, which represents the highest development of sexual bonding. The remaining members of this superfamily constitute a rather diverse family represented by the capuchin, night, howler, and spider monkeys (Fig. 3-2G). The Ceboidea in general vary in size from about 150 grams (1/3 pound) to 7,500 grams (16 pounds).

The New World monkeys differ structurally from those of the Old World in a number of respects. The nostrils open to the side, are far apart, and are separated by a broad nasal partition. Such broad noses contrast sharply with the downward- or forward-facing nostrils of the narrow-nosed Old World monkeys. The character of their teeth (dentition) is different: they have three pairs of upper and lower premolars rather than two. Their thumbs are not fully opposable although the big toe is.[4] Spider monkeys do not have a thumb. However, the spider monkey and a number of other New World species possess a distinctive appendage in the form of a prehensile (grasping) tail. The terminal portion of this tail is naked on the underside, and its bare skin is minutely ridged, like fingerprints. The tail can be used to grasp small objects, such as morsels of food. Although these monkeys are basically quadrupedal, some species often move through the trees by brachiation. When traveling in this fashion, the tail is used as an extra appendage and often is the animal's sole support.

Except for the night monkey, all the Ceboidea are diurnal. Some small species like the marmosets are mainly insectivorous and live in family units. The larger species subsist essentially on fruits and leaves. They form troops of from 10 to 40 or more individuals. New World monkeys are alert and intelligent. Apparently they are quite as capable of problem-solving under laboratory conditions as are Old World monkeys.

The Old World monkeys (Cercopithecoidea)

The Old World monkeys resemble both man and the apes with their narrow noses, dental formula, and opposable thumbs. They consist of two groups (subfamilies), one of which is essen-

---

[4] A thumb or big toe is fully opposable if its fleshy tip can squarely meet the corresponding tips of the other four digits.

tially arboreal and lives primarily on leaves and shoots. The other is omnivorous and contains a number of species which, except for their arboreal sleeping habits, are almost as terrestrial as man. Since our early hominid ancestors also made the transition from an arboreal to a terrestrial life, we will confine our attention to the latter group. This group includes the grassland macaque monkeys and baboons (Figs. 3-2H and 3-4). A study of creatures of this kind may throw some light on the behavior of early hominids.

The social behavior of macaques and baboons is their principal adaptation for survival. Terrestrial or semiterrestrial life for primates in open woodlands, grassy savannas, and sparse arid environments requires a high degree of social organization as a means of protection from predators. Before proceeding further we must stress that there are great behavioral differences not only between species but also between different populations within a species. This discussion is intended only to be a summary.[5]

The social unit: size and range

Group size among grassland macaques and baboons varies from species to species and habitat to habitat. Baboons inhabiting the tropical forests of Uganda form smaller troops than those living in open grassland (savanna). In general, troop size in macaques and baboons ranges from 20 to 80 individuals, with variations both below and above these figures.

Two species, the hamadryas and gelada baboons *(Papio hamadryas* and *Theropithecus gelada),* are exceptions to the above. These monkeys are native to sparse arid habitats and live in *harem groups* and *herds* rather than troops. A harem group includes a male and the one or more females that make up his harem, plus their offspring. A harem may consist of 5 to 30 individuals. During the day the harem

groups often feed separately. At night the harem units join in huge herds numbering up to 400 or more animals. Although other baboons usually sleep in trees, these two species spend the night on the ground, sleeping on rock ledges or along the edges of cliffs.

The largest home range occupied by a single baboon group is about 40 square kilometers (15 square miles); the maximum for macaque species is about 8 kilometers (3 square miles). Only in exceptional cases is this range defended as a territory. The home ranges of different troops of the same species may overlap extensively (Fig. 3-3), but rarely do neighboring troops engage in conflict over their ranges. A home range contains certain areas, called *core areas,* where members of the group spend most of their time. A core area usually has a water hole, a good feeding and resting area, or a group of "sleeping trees." Members of neighboring monkey groups tend to avoid core areas other than their own (Fig. 3-3). Among hamadryas and gelada baboons a male usually will not fight for the harem female of another male.

Some monkeys will defend a territory, however. Troops of chacma baboons *(Papio ursinus)* living in a desert canyon habitat displace one another at critical resource areas, such as concentrated food trees and limited water holes. Troops of this species inhabiting a swamp environment will also defend their home-range boundaries. In all cases males predominate in the defensive action.[6]

The social unit: structure and integration

A macaque or baboon group can be divided into six classes: adult males, adult females, adolescent males, adolescent females, juveniles, and infants. Within a troop the members generally are ranked in a complex hierarchy of social status ("dominance hierarchy") according to their class and their position within that class. There usually is a hierarchy among adult

[5] Much of the source material comes from Alison Jolly, *The Evolution of Primate Behavior,* New York: The Macmillan Company, 1972, pp. 102–267.

[6] W. J. Hamilton III et al., "Chacma Baboon Tactics During Intertroop Encounters," *Journal of Mammalogy,* 1975, in press.

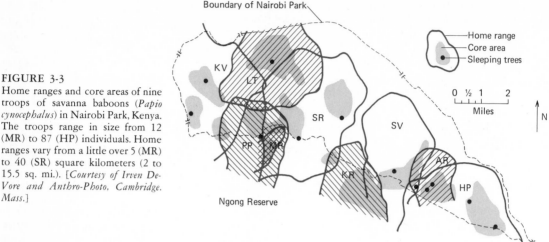

FIGURE 3-3
Home ranges and core areas of nine troops of savanna baboons (*Papio cynocephalus*) in Nairobi Park, Kenya. The troops range in size from 12 (MR) to 87 (HP) individuals. Home ranges vary from a little over 5 (MR) to 40 (SR) square kilometers (2 to 15.5 sq. mi.). [*Courtesy of Irven De-Vore and Anthro-Photo, Cambridge, Mass.*]

females as well as among adult males, and males are generally dominant over females. Males are more aggressive and much larger than females, particularly in baboons, and possess longer canine teeth. High-ranking or dominant males protect the troop from predators and break up fights among troop members.

The relative social status of animals can be measured in many ways. An animal will give way to one of higher status over food, a watering site, or a preferred resting place. If more than one male is interested at any one time in a receptive female in estrus ("heat") the less dominant male will yield to the more dominant. Among rhesus macaques, however, females play an important role in mate selection. Furthermore, their choice of mate is not necessarily related to the social rank of the male.[7] Specific order of rank may be reflected during *redirected aggression*. This kind of behavior occurs among baboons, for example, when the number one male has a brief spat with the number two male. Male number two then threatens another male of lower rank, who in turn may challenge another male of lower rank still. This has its human counterpart in the man who yells at his wife, who then scolds her

[7] Donald G. Lindburg, "Mate Selection in the Rhesus Monkey, *Macaca mulatta*," *American Journal of Physical Anthropology*, vol. 42, 1975, p. 315 (abstract).

child, who in turn ends the affair by kicking the cat.

Actual fighting over rank is uncommon. Social status is expressed by ritualized gestures and vocalizations which indicate submission or assertion. Lower-ranking individuals "present" their genital area to a more dominant animal or show the appeasement grin so common among primates (Fig. 3-4). A higher-ranking individual will pretend to mount a "presenting" subordinate. A dominant male baboon will threaten by yawning with bared teeth (Fig. 3-5).

Although male dominance is determined to some extent by individual strength, personality usually is more important. Aggressiveness and the ability to obtain the support of other males are the marks of the most dominant individuals. Such animals tend to retain a "privileged" status even after their physical condition begins to decline through age. This in turn can be an advantage to the troop. Aging individuals can contribute to troop wisdom and survival through their unusual store of experience, as mentioned in the first chapter.

The role of females in maintaining troop stability is subtle but of great significance. Females have close social ties with more indi-

FIGURE 3-4
A female savanna baboon bares her teeth in the "appeasement grin" or "fear gimace," accompanied by a yakking vocalization. [*Courtesy of Irven DeVore and Anthro-Photo, Cambridge, Mass.*]

viduals than do males because they not only have the sole responsibility of rearing the young but also perform most of the grooming in a troop. The mother's rank to a large extent determines the rank of her offspring. Male and female young learn through imitation the submissive or assertive behaviors of their mother. Since young animals maintain a close relationship with their mothers into adult life, the importance of high-ranking females to troop stability and organization can scarcely be overstated. Among Japanese macaques, kinship groups spanning two or more generations move, feed, and groom together as a unit. Infants are groomed and protected not only by their mothers but also by their aunts, uncles, older cousins, and sibs (brothers and sisters).

General group attraction to a mother-infant pair also is a powerful unifying force in most cases. The mother and her young are the

FIGURE 3-5
Adult male savanna baboon, showing yawn threat. [*Courtesy of Irven DeVore and Anthro-Photo. Cambridge, Mass.*]

focus of attention throughout the troop during the rearing period. Adult males, adult females, and even juveniles gather around the pair to hold the infant or to groom the mother and her offspring.

Males of baboon and macaque species not uncommonly change troops, often to attempt matings with females in neighboring groups. Such transfers may be associated with severe changes in the male hierarchy. In the face of such changes in male dominance and the membership of the troop itself, it is the females that are largely responsible for troop cohesion. The stabilizing influence of maternal kinship groups and the generally unifying stimulus of the mother-infant pair binds the troop into an integrated whole.

The social development of the young

The newborn infant is a center of attraction, particularly for adult, near-adult, and adolescent females. Females other than the mother may hold or groom the baby. Failing in this, they will groom the mother until they have an opportunity to handle the infant. This "aunt behavior," as it is called, with the baby's intimate relationship with its mother, provides a rich environment for the early social development of the offspring. Adolescent and near-adult females also get their first training in being mothers.

Differences are shown in the maternal treatment of monkey infants, depending upon the sex of the young. This differential treatment has interesting parallels in the handling of human children. Among rhesus macaques, for example, mothers treat their infant sons more roughly and restrain them less than their infant daughters. Mothers are more protective of their female young and cuddle them closer. It is possible that this difference in treatment may strongly influence the development of adult sex roles. It is known that aggression increases in rhesus monkeys if they are treated roughly; such treatment may in part be responsible for the more aggressive behavior of males.

As the macaque or baboon infant grows it begins to associate with other infants and older offspring—its peers. Progressively more time is spent in such peer play activity. As in all mammals, play is first and foremost an educational affair. Through social interaction with their peers, young monkeys practice and refine the gestures used in communication. They also gradually become aware of their social rank in the group. Play in a peer group probably has a major role in molding adult behavior. Friendships and friendship groups established during this stage may last throughout life.

The exploratory drive and inquisitiveness of young monkeys also may result in the development of new behavior patterns in a troop. A good example of this occurred on Koshima Island, Japan, where a troop of Japanese macaques were introduced to a new food (sweet potatoes). Monkeys commonly clean their food by rubbing it with their hands. A 16-month-old female started cleaning her potatoes by washing them in a stream. The practice gradually spread among juveniles and then among adults. Within 10 years the new habit had spread to almost every member in the troop. Bipedal walking also became more frequent because in taking the food to water the monkeys commonly carried the potatoes in their hands, walking on their hind legs (Fig. 3-6).[8]

Laboratory experiments with rhesus monkeys have demonstrated the critical importance of the mother-infant and play-group

relationships to the normal social development of the young. Babies have been taken from their mothers at 6 to 12 hours after birth and reared in isolation. Although the physical development of these isolated, motherless youngsters appeared normal, they displayed a variety of behavioral abnormalities that persisted into adulthood. At sexual maturity the males did not know how to copulate with normal sexually excited females. Motherless females were similarly incapable in the presence of normal males. When motherless females became pregnant through the sheer persistence of normal males, either they were indifferent to their infants and rejected them, or they attacked them viciously. Maternal instinct obviously is undeveloped in the absence of necessary social background. There can be little doubt that the role of the mother is to provide some of this background and to prepare her young for normal social interaction.

Of particular interest to human development is the finding that rhesus infants may show

[8] John E. Frisch, "Individual Behavior and Intertroop Variability in Japanese Macaques," in *Primates*, ed. P. C. Jay, New York: Holt, Rinehart and Winston, Inc., 1968, p. 249.

A

FIGURE 3-6
Japanese magaques wash sweet potatoes before eating them (*A*). In carrying potatoes to water, they commonly walk erect (*B*). [*Courtesy of Dr. Masao Kawai, Primate Research Institute, Kyoto University, Japan.*]

B

long-term effects even when they are separated from their mothers for a few days. Infants from five to eight months old have been separated from their mothers for six days. During the period of separation each was allowed to remain with the same animals it had been living with (an adult male, two to four females, and their offspring). The effects of their brief separation included decreased locomotor and play activities. These symptoms were observed to persist for as long as two years.[9]

The social interaction between infants and other young juveniles also is of great importance to normal behavioral development. Monkeys reared in laboratory cages by their mothers but isolated from other monkeys develop abnormalities in sociosexual behavior. On the other hand, infants that have been reared for the first 6 months (or even 12 months) of their lives in *total* isolation can apparently be rehabilitated, in time, through social interaction with normal monkeys. Infants that have been so isolated have been permitted to react with three-month-old socially normal monkeys ("therapists") for eight hours per week over a six-month period. Each isolate was placed in a cage with a single therapist. Three-month-old therapists were used because aggression has not yet developed at this age, but simple play patterns are starting to emerge. At the end of the six-month period, isolates and therapists were scarcely distinguishable in social behavior. Isolates at three and a half years of age appeared to be interacting appropriately with nonisolates even in group situations, forming stable dominance relationships and engaging in normal sexual behavior.[10]

[9] R. A. Hinde and Yvette Spencer-Booth, "Effects of Brief Separation from Mother on Rhesus Monkeys," *Science*, vol. 173, 1971, pp. 111–118.

[10] S. J. Suomi et al., "Reversal of Social Deficit Produced by Isolation Rearing in Monkeys," *Journal of Human Evolution*, vol. 3, no. 6, 1974, pp. 527–534.

Our nearest living relatives: the nonhuman Hominoidea

The lesser apes, or Hylobatidae (gibbons and siamangs), and the great apes, or Pongidae (orangutans, chimpanzees, and gorillas), make up this group. The great apes are giants, as primates go, ranging from 45 to 275 kilograms (100 to 600 pounds). These two families differ from other anthropoids in a number of respects. Their forelimbs are longer than their hind limbs. Their chests, like man's, are broad and shallow rather than narrow and deep, as in monkeys and dogs. Both these attributes are adaptations for brachiation, although the manner in which the broad chest serves this function is not at first obvious. Since muscles contract about one-third of their length, a long muscle shortens more during contraction than a short one. The muscles that move the arms at the shoulder joint are essentially flat sheets spreading across the front of the chest (*pectoralis major*), across the back (*latissimus dorsi*) and over the lateral surface of the shoulder joint itself (*deltoid*). A broad chest allows for long muscles and great arm mobility. The hominoids, unlike most primates, lack an external tail; this taillessness is believed to be an adaptation for brachiation. Despite the absence of this appendage, the tail musculature has been preserved in the form of a muscular sheet that spans the lower pelvic opening. This muscular pelvic floor supports the abdominal organs, an essential service in a large animal that characteristically assumes an erect posture while brachiating, walking bipedally, and sitting. Even when walking quadrupedally, a great ape is partially erect because of the shortness of the hind limbs.

In these ways and in many others, the hominoids are distinct from other anthropoids. As we saw in Chap. 2, nonhuman hominoids are more closely related to the human species anatomically, embryologically, biochemically, genetically, and psychologically than any other primate group.

The lesser apes (Figs. 1-9C and 3-2I) live in the East Indies and Southeast Asia. Orangutans (Fig. 3-2J) once ranged into China and India but now are a vanishing species confined to the islands of Borneo and Sumatra. Chimpanzees and gorillas (Fig. 3-2K, L) are native to equatorial Africa. It is with the African apes that man has the closest kinship, and, of the two of them, the chimpanzee is by all odds our closest living nonhuman relative.

Chimpanzees inhabit forests and open woodlands. Since the family to which we belong (Hominidae) may well have originated in the open woodlands of Africa, we should take a close look at the life of this creature that resembles us so strikingly in so many different ways. Of the two living species of chimpanzees, the common and the pygmy, we will confine our remarks to the common chimpanzee, *Pan troglodytes*.

A case study of the common chimpanzee

By being specialized as brachiators, chimpanzees are adapted to a forest or open (grassy) woodland environment. They rarely inhabit the open savanna so commonly frequented by baboons. This fundamental difference in ecologic adaptation between the two species is reflected in their social organization. The structured order of many baboon troops has its direct opposite in a chimpanzee community. Rigid dominance hierarchies are lacking. At any one time, the community itself is invisible because it is fragmented into small nomadic bands whose membership is changing continuously from day to day. It is interesting that baboons living in the relative safety of Ugandan forests do not have tight hierarchies either, and their social structure is much looser. On the other hand, chimpanzees crossing over open mountain ridges between forests have been observed moving in structured, almost baboonlike groups. Such variations in social behavior demonstrate the adaptive flexibility of anthropoid species.

Much of what is known about the life of

wild chimpanzees has come from the studies of Jane Goodall at the Gombe Stream Reserve in Tanzania.[11] A chimpanzee community of some 150 individuals resides here, ranging over an open woodland habitat of about 80 square kilometers (30 square miles) in small groups or bands. Although one may see as many as 20 or more individuals in one band, most possess fewer than 10, and it is not unusual to find a single animal traveling alone. The size and composition of a given band may change from day to day. Commonly encountered bands contain (1) males, females, and young; (2) females and young only; (3) adult and subadult males and females; or (4) males only. Mutual attraction and friendship are important factors in bringing animals together. A mother with her offspring, both young and old, is probably the only stable group in the entire community (Fig. 3-7).

During the course of a day, a chimpanzee band seeks out its favorite feeding sites. In so doing, it roams over a considerable area. Fruit is the predominant dietary source and fruit-bearing trees are rather widely scattered in both woodland and forest. Different species of fruits are, of course, commonly ready for consumption during different seasons, and this seasonal restriction in availability is further complicated by an annual variation in the relative productivity of each of the palatable species. Because of these factors, and the 45-kilogram (100-pound) bulk of the consumer, it is understandable that a mature chimp annually will range over an area of 50 to 80 square kilometers (20 to 30 square miles) in the Gombe Reserve.

The chimpanzee menu is by no means limited to fruit. On the Gombe Reserve over three dozen species of fruit are consumed, to which are added a lesser variety of leaves and leaf buds, as well as several kinds of blossoms, seeds, stems, and even two species of bark.

[11] Jane Goodall, "Chimpanzees of the Gombe Stream Reserve," in *Primate Behavior*, I. DeVore (ed.), New York: Holt, Rinehart and Winston, Inc., 1965, pp. 425–473.

FIGURE 3-7
A chimpanzee family group. The mother, called Flo by Jane Goodall, is over 30 years old. Fifi, the 4-year-old daughter of Flo, is kissing her 4-month-old brother, Flint. Flo's 7-year-old son Figan and 11-year-old son Faben commonly join the family group. [*National Geographic Society.*]

About 90 percent of this bill of fare grows in trees. However, not all the diet is vegetarian since certain insects are considered a delicacy, notably termites, ants, and gall insects. Small mammals also are killed and consumed.

In the morning of a typical day, a chimpanzee band may start to feed while they are still in their sleeping trees, or they may descend to the ground and leisurely walk for 3 or 4 kilometers before stopping to eat. Usually they walk quadrupedally but occasionally will stop to stand erect to get a better view of their surroundings. Sometimes they walk or run bipedally for as far as 30 meters (100 feet). Only during rainy weather is arboreal travel used to any appreciable extent, and then only for short distances. As they move about, mature individuals exhibit no apparent fear of predators. Despite the fact that a leopard could kill a fully grown individual, adults have been seen walking placidly by one of these big cats when it was in plain view.

Once chimps have found satisfactory feeding trees, they will climb aloft and begin to eat. After consuming one kind of food for two or three hours, they usually move on to another source. Particularly favorable and productive feeding sites tend to be revisited on successive days. The band normally rests for

about two hours during the morning, of which perhaps 30 minutes is spent in sleep. The remaining time is devoted to grooming and relaxation. Altogether, 50 to 70 percent of their waking day is given to feeding and resting, most of which occurs in trees. Day nests are built in the fork of a limb or between two parallel limbs by bending leafy branches back on themselves as crosspieces between the two supports (Fig. 3-8). When the animals are on the ground, periods of relaxation also occur (Fig. 3-7) and play activities commonly take place among juveniles and between mother and young (Fig. 3-9).

A typical chimpanzee day commonly ends in a feeding area. The members of the band

FIGURE 3-8
A male chimp in his day nest. [*National Geographic Society.*]

prepare their tree nests for the night, none of which is less than 4.5 meters (15 feet) from the ground. Sometimes more than one band will finish the day in the same area. The animals usually sleep in groups of two to six individuals; infants sleep with their mothers. Adult males often sleep alone at some distance from these slumber groups. Upon awakening, the animals may regroup themselves for a new day's activities with little apparent compulsion to include their companions of the previous day, save that infants go with their mothers. The groups that leave probably will differ in composition or number from those that arrived the evening before. And of those that leave, they too may change before a new day is done.

FIGURE 3-9
A chimpanzee mother playing with her son. [*National Geographic Society.*]

Group and feeding behavior The informal structure, the constantly changing composition, and the often fleeting existence of these nomadic bands are characteristic features of the wild chimpanzee community. One may wonder where leadership exists and what form it takes. In small groups a dominant individual usually acts as the leader, signaling when and in what direction the group will move on to another area. The signal is more of a suggestion than a command, however, and may even be disregarded, at least temporarily. There is a ranking of social status, but it rarely reveals itself in aggressive or threatening behavior. The Gombe community of some 150 chimps is headed by a single adult male. The male hierarchy under him generally is dominant over adult females, adolescents, and juveniles. There is an independent hierarchy among mature females as well, and these individuals in most cases outrank adolescent males. Usually they are not subordinate to their sons, even when the latter are mature. Dominant males normally are quite tolerant and easygoing with their subordinates, a trait that is not as commonly shared among females. The few dominance interactions that do occur are more often between dominant males, and these are relatively rare. Vernon Reynolds recorded only 17 quarrels involving threats or fights, none of which lasted over a few seconds, in 300 hours of observation.[12] A threatening male may exhibit any one or a combination of behaviors, all of which usually are accompanied by hair erection on the shoulders, arms, and back; high-pitched screaming, glaring with mouth tensed, slapping the ground, shaking branches, hitting tree trunks, slapping motions toward the threatened victim or object, arm-swinging while walking or running erect, and brandishing a broken branch in the air or dragging it along the ground are all familiar examples (Fig. 3-10). Only seldom is an actual attack observed. Jane Goodall witnessed one

in which the attacker, a chimp named Huxley, bit the shoulder and hit the scrotum of the victim, William, who had taken a bite of meat on which Huxley had been feeding. William screamed but made no attempt to escape or to retaliate. No evidence of injury was visible after the attack, even though Huxley was assisted at one point by another male.[13] Signs of submission given by subordinate animals include the appeasement grin (lowering the lower lip, revealing teeth and gums), touching the lips, thigh, or genital area of the dominant animal, giving way to a dominant animal on a tree branch, running away, or, as in the case of William, screaming. A female may present.

When traveling in a small group of 6 or fewer individuals, chimpanzees are quiet, sedate, and almost listless. A larger group of 10 or more is more active, engages in considerable vocalization, and covers more ground. When two bands, each with one or more adult males, come together, the general mood instantly changes to one of noisy excitement and exuberance. Males drum with hands and feet on tree trunks, shake branches, slap the ground, and call loudly. Females and juveniles usually take to the trees to observe the affair from balcony seats. The display may last for 5 minutes before relative quiet is restored. During rains, Goodall has observed similar behavior by one or more males in a band. This "rain dance" often begins at the top of a hill with excited males running down the slope, sometimes bipedally, tearing off branches and dragging them behind or waving them in the air. Once at the bottom, they walk up the slope to repeat the performance, perhaps altering the routine by branch-bending, ground-slapping, and trunk-hitting to the accompaniment of low-pitched screams. This behavior may continue for as long as 30 minutes.

In the Budongo Forest of Uganda, to the north of the Gombe Reserve, chimpanzees hold what have been called "carnivals." These noisy gatherings occur either at night or during

[12] Vernon Reynolds and Frances Reynolds, "Chimpanzees of the Budongo Forest," in *Primate Behavior*, I. DeVore (ed.), p. 416.

[13] Goodall, op. cit., p. 466.

the day and last for several hours. The plank buttresses at the base of the ironwood trees are drummed upon so forcefully that the ground vibrates and the sound carries up to 3 kilometers (2 miles). Prolonged drumming rolls, coupled with hoots, howls, screams, and the sound of stamping and running feet in every direction, produce a thunderous din that brings a tense moment or two to the most stalwart of observers who have witnessed the affair. The reasons for such carnivals are obscure, but on at least two occasions they appeared to be associated with two chimpanzee bands that were relatively unfamiliar with one another and who came together at a common food source. Outbursts of calls and drumming occur normally throughout the day in the Budongo Forest, lasting only one to three minutes. According to Vernon and Frances Reynolds, who have studied these chimps, such noisy episodes

FIGURE 3-10
Chimpanzee threat behavior: glaring with mouth tensed while walking erect, swinging arms. Note bristling hair over arms and shoulders. [*Photograph by Baron Hugo van Lawick.*]

usually are associated with group excitement and an abundance of food.[14] Chimpanzees definitely are attracted to the noise. It has been suggested that a large fruit-eating animal like the chimpanzee could not find adequate amounts of food if it roamed its forested habitat in one compact community. Dispersal of the population in small nomadic bands enhances the likelihood of locating food sources. Community survival would then depend upon some sort of communication between bands when good feeding areas were discovered. Drumming may indeed be a means of signaling over distances that are too great for vocalization.

[14] Vernon Reynolds and Frances Reynolds, op. cit., pp. 368–425.

The manner in which the nutritional needs of a community are met varies with the habitat, but in any case the adaptability and ingenuity of the species always are evident. Chimpanzees in the Budongo Forest do not "fish" for ants and termites like their neighbors to the south. On the Gombe Reserve, where colonies of ants and termites comprise an abundant and accessible resource, the opportunity is exploited. As described in Chap. 2, twigs, grass stems, or vines are pruned as probes to be inserted into the opened passages of ant or termite nests (Fig. 3-11). After a moment, the utensil is withdrawn and the insects clinging to it are eaten. If the end of the tool becomes bent, the diner switches ends or

FIGURE 3-11
A chimpanzee using a grass stalk trimmed as a tool for collecting insects. It is inserted here into an opened passage in a termite nest. [*National Geographic Society, photograph by Baron Hugo van Lawick.*]

breaks off the tip and continues its use until the stick becomes too short, at which point a new utensil is fashioned. Ant and termite hills are worked just before the time that the winged reproductive forms emerge, when the covering layer of the nest is thin and the insects are relatively close to the surface. Often a chimpanzee will prepare a termite stick in advance and carry it around in its mouth while it looks for a termite hill that is ready for working. South of the Gombe Reserve in western Tanzania, chimpanzees use sticks to scoop honey out of honeycombs, and employ stones as hammers to crack the shells of hard fruit.

The ingenious capacity of these animals to manipulate objects and to make tools is shown in many ways. These "technologies" vary, as we have just seen, from habitat to habitat, depending upon environmental conditions, necessity, and the unpredictable occurrence of local discovery. We have already seen in Chap. 2 how the Gombe animals utilize leaves as towels and as toilet paper and how they will crumple leaves as sponges to soak water from a crevice in the crotch of a tree. The usefulness of leaf sponges apparently has not occurred to the Budongo chimpanzees; they follow a simpler but less efficient practice of merely dipping their fingers into the watery contents of these natural hollows.

Adriaan Kortlandt conducted an interesting comparative study of aggressive behavior that throws light on the role necessity plays in manual dexterity and tool use. He rigged a stuffed leopard with a mechanism that would move its head and tail. The mock leopard was so mounted that it could be pulled from some shrubbery into full view of a group of chimpanzees that was being observed. One of the two groups studied was native to a savanna-woodland habitat in Guinea where attack by predators is likely. The response of these animals was immediate and effective. Amidst a pandemonium of hooting and yelling, they attacked the leopard with well-aimed heavy blows, using big sticks and clubs made from broken branches. Innumerable objects were

thrown both overhand and underhand with variable accuracy. When a similar dummy was exposed to chimps living in a forested habitat of the Congo, the results were different. Here, where predatory attacks are relatively infrequent, the animals either ignored the dummy or took to the trees. When aggressive action was taken, it was more like a noisy harassment than a skillfully directed attack. Branches and sticks were brandished and hurled, but none found their mark.[15] Jane Goodall has observed similar behavior when baboons approached too closely to a group of feeding chimpanzees. The apes commonly threatened the interlopers by throwing large rocks at them. Although their throwing was usually unaimed, a few rocks found their mark when thrown at close range.[16]

The interrelationships between baboons and chimpanzees on the Gombe Reserve are puzzling and complex. The two species are in frequent contact. They travel many of the same trails and engage in numerous contests over the same preferred feeding sites. Familiarity has bred a kind of tolerance for one another, almost as though they were members of a common species. A mature female baboon, for example, has been observed approaching an adult male chimpanzee that was eating bananas. She presented to him, expressed an appeasement grin, and scampered away with a banana skin. Sometimes the interactions between adults and subadults of these two species appear almost like play, and they will take turns chasing one another. The young commonly engage in play and grooming, and often become good friends. Interestingly enough, when the chimpanzees hunt, they commonly seek out young baboons for the kill because of their ready accessibility. An adult male may charge into the midst of a baboon troop and seize a juvenile. Even though he may be leaped upon

---

[15] Adriaan Kortlandt, "How Do Chimpanzees Use Weapons When Fighting Leopards?" *Yearbook of American Philosophical Society,* 1965, pp. 327–332.

[16] Jane van Lawick-Goodall, *In the Shadow of Man,* New York: Dell Publishing Co., Inc., 1972, p. 215.

by adult male baboons, he emerges unscathed, except for a few scratches, with his prey in hand. The attacker is treated almost as if he were another baboon. And yet the reverse also is true. A group of chimpanzees were observed watching an unusually savage fight between two male baboons, in which one of the contestants was killed. Rather than claiming the carcass for meat, some of the chimpanzees began grooming the dead body. This same behavior has been observed when chimpanzees encounter a dead companion.[17]

Hunting for meat occurs perhaps once a month, often after the consumption of large quantities of vegetable food. Hunting is performed predominantly by mature males acting singly or in hunting packs of two to five or more individuals. Lizards, bird eggs and fledgling birds, the young of antelopes (bushbuck) and wild pigs (bushpig), three species

of monkey, and young baboons are known prey species, of which the primates constitute the biggest share. No animal over 10 kilograms (22 pounds) is sought. Other than by simple seizure, animals are captured by chasing or stalking. When several hunters are involved, pursuit clearly suggests cooperative behavior in a hunting strategy, despite the fact that it is done in silence. When the prey is caught, it is usually killed by breaking its neck or smashing its body against the ground or a tree trunk. The instant that capture occurs there is an outburst of loud vocalization to summon chimpanzees within earshot to the food that is available. If there is more than one hunter, the hunters divide the carcass between them. Other chimpanzees attracted to the spot gather in one or more sharing clusters around the hunter(s) to request a portion of meat. Meat is requested by peering intently into the face of the possessor, by touching his mouth, or by touching the meat. A request also can be made by extending the hand, palm up (Fig. 3-12). Most of those

[17] G. Teleki, "The Omnivorous Chimpanzee," *Scientific American,* January 1973, pp. 34-35.

FIGURE 3-12
A young chimpanzee gestures with outstretched hand for some of the leaf wad its mother is chewing. [*Courtesy of Geza Teleki.*]

present eventually obtain some meat, even when there are as many as 17 sharing the carcass of a small monkey. The meat is eaten slowly and thoroughly savored. According to Geza Teleki, on the average about four hours is spent in consuming a carcass and every vestige is eaten, hair and teeth included. At no point in the entire procedure from pursuit to consumption has fighting among the apes ever been observed over the possession of the carcass or any of its parts. Moreover, social rank or status carries no special privilege, whether it be during the chase, when the victim is being divided, or when the meat is being shared by all. Teleki observed the number one male of the Gombe community request meat for several hours from a subordinate male. The head man "received nothing for his pains."[18] The hunter apparently shares his meat primarily with those with whom he has some social tie through kinship, friendship, or as a mating consort.[19]

Sexual behavior   Although there is insufficient evidence to define a fixed mating season, most copulations in the Gombe Reserve occur between August and November when the apes move about in larger groups. Whether sexual excitement brings more apes together or the social activities of bigger groups is more sexually stimulating is a question that has not been resolved. The estrous cycle is about 35 days, during which there is a gradual increase in genital swelling which enhances the female's attractiveness to males. This swelling reaches its climax in the middle of the cycle for a period of about a week, when ovulation (egg release) occurs and sexual receptiveness is highest. Females generally have their first menstruation between 8 and 10 years of age. They usually do not begin to breed until they are about 10. Once pregnant, the gestation period lasts for seven and a half months. If this pregnancy is successful and the infant lives, the next birth will not occur in less than three years—occur-

ring, on the average, in five and a half years. This wide interval between births occurs because the infant is nursed until it is between four and five years of age, and lactation (milk secretion) generally suppresses the estrous cycle.[20]

Copulation can be initiated by either sex. When the female solicits, she crouches near a male and looks back at him. Male courtship is variable and may include vigorous swinging from branch to branch, or rocking from foot to foot while standing erect. Sometimes such preliminaries are dispensed with entirely, and the parties merely copulate. The copulating male usually places one hand on the back of the female and squats with his rump close to the ground. Copulation usually consists of four to eight slow pelvic thrusts, commonly accompanied by lip smacking. The female may emit short high-pitched screams. Mutual grooming often follows completion of the act.

Young captive chimps who have not had sexual experience are unable to copulate. Wild infants two to three years old watch their mother very carefully when she copulates, often peering closely and touching the lips of her vulva near the inserted penis.

Although sexual activity may occur with the onset of sexual swelling in mature females, copulations are most frequent when the genital swelling has reached its peak. At no time during the mating period is there any evidence of aggressive or threatening behavior. The animals are quite promiscuous. On one occasion seven males were observed patiently awaiting their turn to mount one female. One of them, a model of patience, if not capacity, was rewarded twice.

Mothers apparently do not mate with their sons and sexual interactions between brothers and sisters occur only rarely. In the Gombe Reserve Figan and Faben were never observed mating with their mother, Flo (Fig. 3-7). When they tried to mate with their sister,

---

[18] Ibid., pp. 33–42.

[19] G. Teleki, "Chimpanzee Subsistence Technology," *Journal of Human Evolution*, vol. 3, no. 6, 1973, p. 592.

[20] E. E. Hunt, G. Teleki, and J. H. Pfifferling, "Demographic Studies of Wild Chimpanzees in the Gombe National Park, Tanzania, 1963–1973" (in preparation).

Fifi, she protested vigorously.[21] Incest presumably does occur in father-daughter matings, however. Fathers do not know which females are their daughters nor do females know which males are their fathers.

Care of the young   Births usually are single and labor is short. Infant weight is less than half that of a human infant.[22] Unlike macaques and baboons, the newborn must be supported by the mother for the first month before it is able to cling to the hair on the underside of her belly. The ape infant also matures more slowly than its monkey counterpart. For the first four to six months, the chimp infant is completely dependent on its mother for food, protection, and transport. Although the mother may "hang it up" on a branch at her side for a few moments while she feeds, she never allows it to be more than 60 centimeters (2 feet) away. Toward the end of this first few months, the youngster begins to eat solid food that has been half-chewed by its mother and starts to ride on its mother's back. During the ensuing two to two and a half years, the infant gradually becomes more active, venturing farther from its mother, but rarely out of her sight. Now the infant begins to ride its mother "cowboy style," except when she climbs into trees or goes into underbrush. The mother no longer helps her charge with every little problem. If, for example, the infant fails to make a difficult jump after several attempts, it may hit a branch, scream, or jump up and down in what may become a temper tantrum. The mother, however, does not respond, and the youngster soon calms down and solves its own problem by taking some alternate route. Punishment is seldom resorted to. In over 2,000 hours of observation, Goodall has witnessed a punishing response on only 10 occasions, and reassurance followed all of these, by an immediate embrace. Mothers play with their infants often, gently sparring with them or tickling them. They also permit a juvenile or adolescent daughter to look after and play with them (Fig. 3-7). Infants commonly play with objects by swinging or jumping from branch to branch, pushing broken branches back and forth, breaking off twigs and poking them into holes, or making small nests. Most play, however, is with other infants—peer play —in tugs-of-war with sticks and gentle wrestling. Peer play becomes more vigorous in late infancy and entails active wrestling, chasing, and tickling. Whenever such activities involve juveniles and adolescents, the older animals are always gentle, tolerant, and helpful when the infant gets into trouble. This requires patience and understanding when a resting adolescent is jumped upon by a biting, kicking, hair-pulling infant without warning. At this point, the youngster is eating solid food almost entirely. It suckles intermittently during late infancy and apparently initiates its own weaning at two to two and a half years.

A young chimpanzee is referred to as a juvenile from the approximate time of its weaning until it is seven or eight years old. It is now independent of its mother for feeding, sleeping, and transportation, but not for protection. Although the juvenile continues to associate with its peers, it retains a close relationship with its mother for at least a year after the birth of her next infant. It may then join other juveniles and adolescents who move about with one or two mature females in a kind of nursery group, or it may affiliate with another mother and its offspring, as if it were being farmed out to a baby-sitter. In any case, these associations are only temporary arrangements for a portion of the day, and the juvenile still remains with its mother. Play even at this age continues to be quiet, broken only by a soft panting which is the equivalent of human laughter. Often a juvenile may burst out laughing in the midst of play, ostensibly in anticipation of being tickled.

Adolescence begins at puberty and extends roughly from 8 to 10 or 11 years of age. Play activities begin to decrease at puberty

---

[21] van Lawick-Goodall, *In the Shadow of Man*, p. 188.
[22] A. H. Schultz, *The Life of Primates*, New York: Universe Books, Inc., 1969, p. 152.

while more time is spent on social grooming and resting. Females develop sexual swellings and menstruate at this time, but often they do not copulate until they reach maturity between 10 and 11. Adolescent males do copulate; in fact one of their number was included in the seven males, mentioned earlier, who patiently waited for a chance to do so. The adolescent may remain with its mother even though it may also be seen alone or with other groups. Family ties apparently can last through life. A family studied by Goodall included a mother named Flo, over 30 years old; her infant son, Flint, aged 3 months; a 4-year-old daughter, Fifi; a 7-year-old son, Figan; and an 11-year-old son, Faben (Fig. 3-7). These animals commonly were seen together and formed a persistent grooming group. Flo later gave birth to a daughter, Flame, when Flint was 5 years old.[23] Family resemblances between chimps are as striking as those among humans. Many grooming groups include animals that appear to be sibs (brother or sister), in the company of an older female who looks like one or more of them.

Most mutual grooming occurs between adults, followed by grooming between adults and adolescents, mothers grooming their young, and grooming between adolescents. As many as six individuals of any age and sex have been observed in one grooming cluster (Fig. 3-13). Juveniles, and especially infants, participate in very little grooming activity. Between adults, a grooming session may last as long as two hours. Among adolescents it is considerably briefer. During long grooming sessions, periods of intense concentration, accompanied by lip smacking, are broken by lapses of drowsy euphoria as each chimp sits with eyes half closed, idly moving an index finger through the hair of its partner in lazy circles. On occasion, grooming is elevated to the status of medical care, as described in Chap. 2 when one chimp

[23] van Lawick-Goodall, *In the Shadow of Man*, pp. 111–121; 238–240.

removed a foreign body from the eye of another. Small wounds or sores may be scrutinized closely and cleaned by licking. Splinters may be removed by carefully pinching the patient's skin between two forefingers.

The long period of development from infancy through adolescence provides rich opportunities for learning, especially in a species that is as intelligent as the chimpanzee. Signs of this intelligence are seen early in life when chimp infants play with inanimate objects. Animal psychologists believe that such behavior shows unusual awareness and great sensitivity to surroundings. The recognition of self also is thought to be characteristic of a superior intelligence. If chimpanzees see themselves in a mirror, they soon realize they are looking at themselves and will begin to pick their teeth or to make wry faces at themselves. A monkey never learns—nor does a dog, cat, or other nonprimate—to associate the image it sees with itself. The chimpanzee with its high intelligence and 10 years of infancy and adolescence in which to observe, play, and explore, is well endowed with the potential and the opportunity of developing a multitude of behaviors to serve a multitude of situations. It learns how to "fish" for termites and ants, how to soak water from crevices, how to crack open hard fruits, how to build a nest, how to hunt, how to groom, and how to copulate. These and many more "hows" as well as some "whys" are learned through observation, trial and error, and insight. Teaching has not been observed. The young evidently learn from their elders only through imitation. Learning to communicate is no exception.

Communication Chimpanzees communicate by vocalizations, gestures, facial expressions, and bodily postures. Jane Goodall has described 23 different vocalizations heard on the Gombe Reserve during a variety of social interactions. Some of these are listed in Fig. 3-14 in terms of the situation in which they generally were employed. Some of the vocalizations, gestures,

FIGURE 3-13
A grooming cluster of five adult males. The second chimp from the left was the number one male of the Gombe chimpanzee community at the time the picture was taken. [*Courtesy of Geza Teleki.*]

1 Threat

2 Social excitement

3 Before chasing another chimp

4 Fleeing from another chimp

5 Rage

6 Uneasiness with an observer

7 When crossing an open ridge

8 By a subordinate to a dominant animal

9 By a dominant animal for reassurance

10 When startled

11 When refused bananas and forced to resort to less preferred food

12 When male moves off and looks back at others

13 Between nearby groups

14 When two groups join

15 When eating desirable food

16 Greeting between chimps

17 During play

18 When two chimps begin to groom one another

FIGURE 3-14
Some chimpanzee vocalizations described by Jane Goodall in terms of the situations in which they were usually employed. [*By permission of Jane Goodall.*]

facial expressions, and bodily postures used in threat, submission, general excitement, food-sharing, courtship, copulation, play, and grooming have already been described. The "rain dance," if not an example of redirected aggression, is probably at least a related activity.

Communicative behavior among these apes often is quite humanlike. They scratch their heads or their arms when they are perplexed. Irrelevant behavior of this kind, known as *displacement activity,* is not uncommon.

Chimpanzees also will swat at flying insects with the back of their hands. Alarm at a sudden noise or movement sometimes is expressed by flinging an arm across the face. When two males have been surprised in this way, one or both may place a hand on the arm, shoulder, or scrotum of the other. Or they may reach out and touch hands. Similar responses may be made to the sharp alarm call of a monkey, antelope, or bird.

A variety of gestures and bodily postures are utilized as signs of affection or greeting. A common display of affection is kissing (Fig. 3-15). A female in estrus usually is greeted by being touched on her sexual swelling. A male

FIGURE 3-15
A young female (*right*) greets a young male (Figan) with a kiss. [*National Geographic Society, photograph by Baron Hugo van Lawick.*]

who greets her often places his face close to the genital area as if he were smelling. Standing erect and swaying from one foot to the other is used as a greeting and also in male courtship. Two animals who have just met commonly make grooming movements with one hand on the shoulder of the other. When two individuals approach, they may nod or bow to one another. They also may touch the hands, head, shoulder, thigh, groin, or genital area of the other. The human handshake and our custom of placing a hand on the shoulder or thigh of a fellow male are remarkably similar behaviors. An adult male chimp commonly greets an infant with a fatherly pat on the back. The greeting of two individuals who have not seen one another for some time may have all the drama of the closing scene in a low-budget movie. As one stands tall with arm upraised, the other rushes forward. With soft, panting laughter, they throw their arms around one another in an affectionate embrace (Fig. 3-16).[24]

Cultural behavior in anthropoids

We have seen a number of instances in which anthropoid behavior has a humanlike quality. Redirected aggression, displacement activity, and various facial expressions, gestures, and bodily postures are notable examples. It is therefore reasonable to ask whether anthropoids exhibit to any degree a kind of behavior that often is considered to be exclusively human, namely, *cultural behavior*. Cultural behavior was described in Chap. 1 as learned behavior that is transmitted from individual to individual and from generation to generation.

A number of cases already have been cited which demonstrate that cultural behavior is shown, at least at a very basic level, in monkeys and especially apes. The practice of washing sweet potatoes among Japanese macaques, for example, would seem to be a better way of

cleaning food than the customary hand-rubbing method. The behavior, first started by a young female, was observed by other juveniles who gradually adopted the practice. The mothers of these juveniles also learned through observation to wash their potatoes. Within 10 years this cultural behavior was transmitted to almost every member of the troop.

Cultural traditions often can be identified by behavioral differences in troops of the same species. A troop of chacma baboons *(Papio ursinus),* for example, had a unique method of obtaining drinking water. The only water source they could use was a hot spring. The water was too hot to drink and it could not be followed downstream because the water flowed dangerously close to a farmhouse. To obtain water, about a third of the troop would line up along the watercourse and scoop out ditches in the mud at right angles to the water flow. When the furrows filled with water, the baboons moved away and waited with the rest of the troop for the water to cool. After about an hour the entire troop approached the ditches and began to drink.[25]

Learned traditions vary greatly between wild chimpanzee populations. As will be recalled, the Budongo Forest chimpanzees obtained water from bowls and crevices in trees by dipping their fingers into the water whereas the Gombe Stream chimps had adopted the more efficient practice of using leaf sponges.

Although the Gombe chimpanzees fish for ants in subterranean nests with long sticks, they rarely fish for arboreal ants. A chimpanzee community in the Mahali Mountains to the south, however, commonly fishes for ants in arboreal nests but seldom fishes for subterranean ants and termites.[26]

Differences in the learned traditions of various chimpanzee communities apparently

[24] Goodall, "Chimpanzees of the Gombe Stream Reserve," pp. 471–472.

[25] Eugene Marais, *The Soul of the Ape,* New York: Atheneum Press, 1969, pp. 74–76.

[26] T. Nishida, "The Ant-gathering Behavior by the Use of Tools Among Wild Chimpanzees of the Mahali Mountains," *Journal of Human Evolution,* vol. 2, 1973, pp. 357–370.

FIGURE 3-16
Four male chimps embrace with great excitement. [*Courtesy of Geza Teleki.*]

result in large measure from environmental differences and the geographic isolation of each community. Such variations in tool behavior indicate the importance of learning through observation in the establishment of cultural traditions among these apes.

Novel types of tool behavior may be discovered almost as readily by a baboon as a chimpanzee. The ability of baboons to acquire information by observational learning, however, is much less developed than that of chimps.[27] As a result, discovery is much less likely to be

[27] B. B. Beck, "Baboons, Chimpanzees, and Tools," *Journal of Human Evolution*, vol. 3, 1974, pp. 509–516.

transmitted among a troop of baboons than a community of the apes. It is therefore no coincidence that varied forms of tool behavior are common among chimps but relatively rare among baboons.

The significance of observational learning to the development of cultural behavior among chimps may be relevant to the evolution of human culture. One may assume that the beginnings of hominid toolmaking were related to a high capacity for observational learning. Since observational learning is greatly enhanced by language, one might even infer that early hominid cultures were dependent upon a facility for language also. Our closest living nonhuman relative may throw some light on the nature of this early hominid heritage. It may be no coincidence that chimpanzees are noted not only for a high level of observational learning and a variety of tool behaviors but a rather unusual talent for symbol-using as well.[28]

PRIMATES, PEOPLE, AND BEHAVIOR: A SUMMARY NOTE

The earlier discussion of primates in Chap. 1 particularly emphasized structural features. This chapter has been primarily concerned with the more functional aspects of primate life. We have especially focused on social behavior, with particular reference to macaques, baboons, and chimpanzees. From time to time we have noted parallels in the social behavior of these monkeys and apes and the social responses of people. No attempt has been made to point out all the similarities; many are obvious. Some are so obvious that their full significance can be easily missed. Chief among the latter is the complex social organization of primates, especially anthropoids.

An anthropoid social unit, whether it be a macaque troop, a gelada baboon herd, or a chimpanzee community, is a highly organized and immensely complicated society that is established and maintained through learned behavior. We learned, for example, that a troop of Japanese macaques is composed in large part of separate kinship groups, each spanning two or more generations. The social interactions between members of one kinship group are complicated enough, but many other types of social interaction can also take place. For instance, there can be interaction between individuals of different kinship groups, between individuals of different social rank, between individuals of different friendship groups, between individuals of a friendship group whose members cross kinship lines, and between individuals who belong to different troops. An enormous amount of social learning takes place

to organize interrelationships of this complexity into a stable, integrated society (troop).

A prolonged period of infancy and adolescence (Fig. 1-18), however, provides a rich opportunity for social learning under the stimulus of the mother-infant bond and peer play. An impressive battery of ritualized communications are learned in the form of facial expressions, gestures, bodily postures, and vocalizations (Fig. 3-14). Cultural behavior is acquired through observational learning, particularly among chimpanzees. The number of learned behavioral responses gradually becomes so diversified that the near-adult anthropoid has a great storehouse of potential behaviors. We say its behavior is flexible and adaptable. But learning does not stop when adulthood is reached. Formerly dominant animals tend to be "respected" even in their old age. Elderly individuals have an unusual store of experience and may contribute much to the social wisdom of anthropoid society. Social knowledge of this sort is particularly noticeable in large troops or communities where collective wisdom far exceeds that of any individual.

In short, learning plays a major role in the lives of anthropoids. That role is larger in a chimpanzee community than it is in a macaque or baboon troop. In Chaps. 4 and 5 when we examine those traits which distinguish our own species, we shall see that learning plays an even larger role in the behavior of people than it does in the behavior of chimpanzees. And in Section II we shall see that learning must have played an ever-growing role in the evolutionary history of our hominid ancestors.

SUGGESTED READINGS

ALTMANN, S. A., and JEANNE ALTMANN: *Baboon Ecology: African Field Research,* Chicago: University of Chicago Press, 1970. This book, Schaller's book, and Goodall's book (on chimpanzees) are out-

[28] Ibid., p. 515.

standing examples of a number of books written by authors with extensive field experience with a particular primate species.

EIMERL, S., and I. DE VORE: *The Primates,* New York: Time-Life Books, 1965. A richly illustrated general introduction to the primates.

JOLLY, ALISON: *The Evolution of Primate Behavior,* New York: The Macmillan Company, 1972. An excellent account of a wide range of behaviors in all kinds of primates.

NAPIER, J. R., and P. H. A. NAPIER: *A Handbook of Living Primates,* New York: Academic Press, Inc., 1967. A beautifully illustrated handbook of all primate genera, with discussions on their anatomy, ecology, and behavior.

SCHALLER, G.: *The Year of the Gorilla,* Chicago: University of Chicago Press, 1964.

SCHULTZ, A. H.: *The Life of Primates,* New York: Universe Books, Inc., 1969. The life and behavior of primates including their origins, anatomical features, growth and development, reproduction, diseases, distribution, and evolutionary trends.

VAN LAWICK-GOODALL, JANE: *In the Shadow of Man,* Boston: Houghton Mifflin Company, 1971. This book and Schaller's book are nontechnical.

REVIEW QUESTIONS

1 Lemuriform and lorisiform prosimians represent a fairly homogeneous group. List five anatomical, physiological, and/or behavioral traits which all of them share. (Do not include generalized characteristics found in all mammals.) Give two examples of the Lemuriformes and two examples of the Lorisiformes.

2 Tarsiers are unusual primates in possessing traits some of which are common to prosimians and some of which are typical of anthropoids. Cite four anatomical, physiological, and/or behavioral traits which tarsiers share with other prosimians and four which they share with anthropoids.

3 Briefly describe three ways in which New World monkeys differ structurally from Old World monkeys.

4 Baboon and macaque troops are generally relatively peaceful. Discuss the role of adult females in maintaining troop stability and cohesion.

5 Laboratory experiments have shown that mother-infant and play-group relationships are of critical importance to the normal social development of young rhesus monkeys. Outline the procedures used in one such experiment and summarize the results.

6 Elaborate on the complex social organization of a macaque troop by listing five different types or levels of social interaction other than sexual relationships.

7 Hominoids differ anatomically from other anthropoids in a number of ways. Give three major differences other than size.

8 What are chimpanzee "carnivals"? What explanation has been suggested to account for such behavior?

9 Toolmaking and tool-using behaviors by chimpanzees vary in different habitats and chimp communities. Document this by at least one example from each of three chimp communities. Can chimp tool behavior be called cultural behavior, and can differences in tool behavior be called cultural differences? Support your answer.

10 The human species is often said to be the only primate who regularly hunts other mammals for food and shares the kill with its fellows. Is this true, partially true, or false? Support your answer.

11 Describe in some detail the nature of grooming groups and of grooming activities among chimpanzees.

12 A variety of gestures and bodily postures are used by chimps as signs of affection or greeting. Cite six examples. Give two additional examples of behaviors, one of redirected aggression and the other of displacement activity.

FOUR

THE HUMAN SPECIES I:
Anatomical and Physiological Features

A common primate heritage links the human species with its closest living relatives. This heritage is the base on which our structural adaptations were developed. It gives vent to the fundamental urges which determine the quality of our behavior. We have much in common with our primate "cousins." On the other hand, we are also unique just as each of them is unique. It is the purpose of this chapter to explore the human animal and some of its distinctive anatomical and physiological charac-

teristics. In doing so, occasionally we will examine the extent to which these characteristics deviate from those of other primates, especially macaques, baboons, and chimpanzees.

It is commonly believed that man's cleverness is so great that it has enabled him to survive for countless generations as a biological weakling and a mechanical misfit. At best, this belief is only half true. Clever we are; misfits we are not. We are bigger and stronger than most mammals. We can climb, swim, jump, kick, and throw. We can run faster than most mammals and can outwalk any of them, including the horse. In all-around physical prowess, we rank high among the animals.

One of the most distinctive features of our species, cleverness aside, is that we are terrestrial hominoids who have adopted the life style of carnivores. We have evolved as a bipedal hunting hominoid. We will follow the course of this evolution in Section II, but there is ample evidence today of our predatory origins still to be found among peoples who have a technologically simple culture.

The aboriginal population of southern Africa, the Bushmen of the Kalahari Desert, have followed a simple hunter-gatherer technology for at least the past 15,000 years. Recent generations, however, have begun to adopt more advanced agricultural practices from surrounding cultures.

The Ngatatjara people of Western Australia are hunter-gatherers whose material culture apparently is identical to that of their Stone Age forebears 30,000 years ago. Simple stone tools used by these aborigines are identical in form, workmanship, and microscopic wear patterns to archaeological artifacts in the same area dating from 10,000 to 30,000 years ago. Archaeological remnants of ancient hunting blinds, earth-oven trenches, wells, and living sites are similarly indistinguishable from their modern counterparts. One two-family living site at the foot of a steep cliff has been in more or less continuous use for the past 10,000 years. As practitioners of a primitive hunter-gatherer economy, the Ngatatjara throw considerable light on the kind of biological life style to which our species became adapted. This is particularly true of a small 13-member group, studied by Richard Gould, which is one of the last remnants of a Stone Age society uncontaminated by alien cultures.[1]

Because of the relative scarcity of food, the Ngatatjara are widely dispersed in small groups. The group studied by Gould, for example, was a two-family unit consisting of three women, two men, and eight children ranging from 4 to 15 years of age. Each group has a hunting territory with a home base, which may be separated from the nearest neighboring group, and its home base, by 160 kilometers (100 miles) or more. A home base is necessary because of the prolonged period of dependency of the young. A human mother cannot be expected to rear her child and to engage in protracted hunting forays as well; nor can she and her helpless infant lead the nomadic life of a chimpanzee.

All-male hunting expeditions require a center of operations from which to depart and return. Although this operating base may change from time to time, it is the site where the women and children are found. Ngatatjara women are responsible for gathering fruits and seeds and for obtaining edible roots with their digging sticks. A nursing child of up to three or more years is carried on its mother's hip or slung over her back while older children tag along. Men go off together to hunt. Although they are excellent trackers and stalkers of game, usually they try to ambush their prey, particularly in the heat of summer. Favored prey is the ostrichlike emu, kangaroo, and wallaby. These are brought down by spears hurled from a spear-thrower, a wooden device which adds to the length of the throwing arm and bears a hook for holding the spear at its butt end (Fig. 4-1). Large animals are not common, however, and most of the game caught consists of lizards, snakes, birds and their eggs, rabbits, and other small animals, all of which comprise about 30 to 40 percent of the total diet. Here then, stripped of the embellishments of civilization, standing naked in the Australian sun, is the kind of creature we are.

The Ngatatjara differ from those of us in the so-called civilized world in the direction in which they have plied their productive energies. In an attempt to preserve the past and

[1] R. A. Gould, *Yiwara: Foragers of the Australian Desert,* New York: Charles Scribner's Sons, 1969, pp. 3–44, 54–165.

A

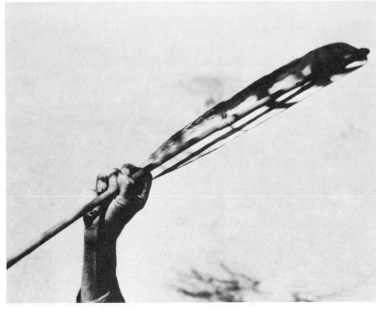

B

FIGURE 4-1
Australian aboriginal throwing spear with spear-thrower. *A,* An Ngatatjara man at the instant the spear is to be thrust forward (pants were acquired from an Australian Mission); *B,* close-up view of the way the spear and spearthrower are held. Spearthrower is wooden device about 75 centimeters (30 inches) long and 10 centimeters (4 inches) wide, with a knob at one end for a handle and a hook at the other to hold butt end of spear. Device is also used for other purposes, e.g., as a mixing tray, a musical percussion instrument, a shovel, and a woodworking tool. [*From R. A. Gould, Yiwara: Foragers of the Australian Desert. Scribner, New York, 1969.*]

prevent change, their creative efforts have been expended in formulating and perpetuating a complex socioreligious system. Their technology is very primitive and they live simple lives in what they call their "dreamtime" world.

Aside from such cultural distinctions, human beings the world over live out their lives as predatory primates of one form or another. Beyond that, we are unique anthropoids in many other ways. We are fully erect, wholly terrestrial, and zealously protective of our territorial hunting ground and its home base. We are the most intelligent, hairless, sweaty, not to mention sexy, primate on earth. And—a sure first in the animal kingdom—we are the only organism with a symbolic language, an elaborate technology, and an enormous cultural inheritance.

These facets of our biological nature will be discussed both separately and correlatively because they are interrelated in one fashion or another, often in subtle, if not unexpected, ways.

ADAPTATIONS OF THE TRUNK AND APPENDAGES

We are the only mammalian species that stands fully erect with our heads directly above our feet, and our trunks and legs aligned along an unbroken vertical plane between them. When we stride, this posture is maintained except for the oppositely swinging legs below. Locomotor techniques of whatever variety have disadvantageous, as well as advantageous, features; the mode used invariably is that which serves the survival of a given species, considering the locomotor opportunities that were open to its ancestral stock. This certainly is the case with our own species. Bipedal walking and erect posture are not without risks and complications. Compared to quadrupedal walking, some stability is sacrificed. Because of locomotor modifications in the bony pelvis, we are afflicted with prolonged labor during birth. We also

complain of varicose veins, hemorrhoids, ruptured vertebral disks, torn knee cartilages, and a variety of foot disorders (not all due to badly designed or poorly fitted shoes). On the other hand, there are overriding benefits which tip the scales decidedly in favor of erect posture. When facing a potential adversary, we stand taller than animals which, in terms of weight and muscle, are much bigger. Large *apparent* size may have protective value because it poses a threat to potential enemies. The range of vision is increased, particularly for a terrestrial species living on grassy savannas and plains. Hands, freed from locomotor functions, can carry food or infants, throw objects, and above all, make and use tools. The complete freeing of the forelimb is possible only through bipedal locomotion. This total emancipation set the stage for the mutual feedback by which toolmaking and intelligence promoted one another during the course of human evolution. We are what we are, in large measure, because of erect posture. Prolonged childbirth and a few other relatively minor complaints are unavoidable consequences of locomotor modifications required for bipedal walking. They are a small price to pay for the success our species has achieved.

We have seen that the great apes and man are giants among primates. The advantages of large size are at least twofold. Within a group of related mammals, the period needed for the young to grow to maturity tends to increase with the size of the species; large species tend to mature more slowly than smaller species. This is an asset to intelligent animals like pongids and hominids because it allows more time for the learning process during maturation. Size and strength also are useful to animals who spend much of their time on the ground, where they can be in constant danger from predators.

The trunk

We saw in Chap. 3 that in hominoids a muscular sheet supports the pelvic floor on which the visceral organs rest. This muscular sheet is especially important to man because he is not only large but fully erect as well. As a consequence of our weight and posture, we require an additional trunk modification not found in other hominoids. This involves the portion of the vertebral column which lies behind the abdomen: the *lumbar segment* (Fig. 4-2). In pongids, the entire series of trunk vertebrae form an open rounded arch which is an ideal structure for supporting body weight in a quadrupedal animal, just as it is for supporting a bridge. In man, however, the rounded arch of the rib, or thoracic, vertebrae is reversed at the lumbar segment, resulting in an open S-shaped alignment. The short reverse curve of the lumbar segment accommodates large vertical stresses pulling downward along the trunk axis. Had we retained the long pongid arch, great muscular effort would be necessary to prevent the arch from collapsing on itself as we stand erect.

Immediately below the lumbar segment are five stout vertebrae which are fused into a single structure called the *sacrum,* to which the pelvic girdle attaches (Fig. 2-5). Since the sacrum must support the weight that rests upon it, it is to be expected that the human sacrum is especially massive, broad, and wedge-shaped compared to that of quadrupedal, brachiating hominoids.

The appendages

The pelvic girdle, or pelvis, consists of three fused bones on each side, the *ilium, ischium,* and *pubis* (Figs. 2-5 and 4-2). Together with the

FIGURE 4-2
Comparison of the posture and skeleton of a gorilla and man. Note that trunk vertebrae of gorilla form an open, rounded arch whereas in man they form an open S curve (colored dashed lines). Axis of pelvic opening is indicated by colored dashed lines. (See also Fig. 2-5.)

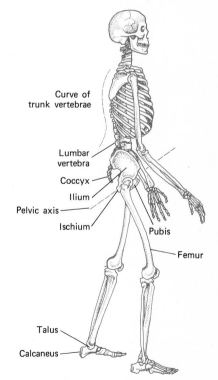

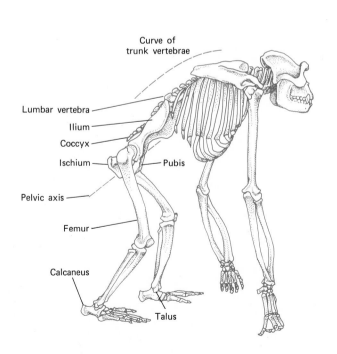

sacrum to which the two ilia attach at the sacro-iliac joint, this assembly comprises a bony ring through which the birth canal passes. The human pelvis differs from that of other hominoids in that it is adapted for erect posture. Overlying abdominal organs are supported by two ilia that are shortened and broadened into a shallow basinlike bowl. The pelvis has tipped forward about 45°, providing ample bony abutments against the vertical thrust of the femurs (thighbones). Although this forward rotation restricts the dimensions of the birth canal, the pelvis and its opening are larger in women than in men. A large pelvis partially compensates for the restriction at the cost of some loss in locomotor efficiency.

Surprisingly enough, long legs serve to lower the center of gravity for greater stability. Only about one-third of an ape's total height is in leg length, whereas our legs are almost one-half of our total height. What this means is that the ape carries relatively more of its weight *higher* than a human does. The center of gravity in an erect gibbon, for example, is just below its last rib; ours is at the sacrum. Our legs are close together rather than separated as in apes (Fig. 4-3*A*). Consequently, our weight is balanced over the supporting foot as we walk, rather than being shifted from side to side in the rocking fashion characteristic of a bipedal chimpanzee. At each step, our pelvis is tilted downward slightly on one side to center the body's weight directly over the supporting foot. The gluteus medius and gluteus minimus muscles are responsible for this pelvic tilting or wobble (Fig. 2-8). They are much more powerfully developed in the ape because they are used to extend the leg. The gluteus maximus muscle, on the other hand, is primarily, although not exclusively, responsible for both leg extension and trunk erectness in man. Consequently, as is reflected in our protruding buttocks, it is a very prominent muscle. The buttocks are particularly well developed in females because of their relatively larger pelvises and because of the greater amounts of subcutaneous fat around the hips. As a result, women have a character-istic pelvic wobble when they walk, a feature which is also generally considered to increase their sexual attractiveness.

The human foot has been modified from a mobile, grasping structure to one that is stable and supportive (Figs. 1-14, 2-7, and 4-2). The great toe is long, strongly built, and parallel to the others. The second through fifth toes are very short and largely incapable of grasping. An arch runs along the inside and outside of the foot from the heel bone, or *calcaneus,* to the base of the great and little toes, respectively; a third arch extends across the foot between the bases of the toes. These arches all serve to absorb shock when we walk, run, and jump. Two ankle bones are especially well developed. One of them, the *talus,* is relatively massive; it supports the entire weight of the body during walking. The other, the calcaneus, also is enlarged and extends backward as a lever to which the calf muscles (e.g., *gastrocnemius,* Fig. 2-8) are attached.

Man alone walks in a way that has been defined as a *stride.*[2] Minimal energy output is required, which enables man the hunter to follow his quarry for 12 hours or more, sometimes for days on end, with great economy of effort. As a locomotor technique, striding may be described as beginning when the heel strikes the ground. The weight is supported progressively forward on the foot as the body passes over, and slightly beyond, the ball of the foot. This is called the *stance phase* (see Fig. 4-3*B*). At this point, the body is propelled by a push-off from the great toe through the contracting calf muscles; the leg enters a *swing phase* in preparation for the next heel strike as the opposite leg enters its stance phase. During normal walking, each leg is in the stance phase about 60 percent of the time and in the swing phase about 40 percent of the time. Both feet are on the ground about 25 percent of the time, but this figure decreases with the speed of

[2] John Napier, *The Roots of Mankind,* Washington: The Smithsonian Institution Press, 1970, pp. 168–172.

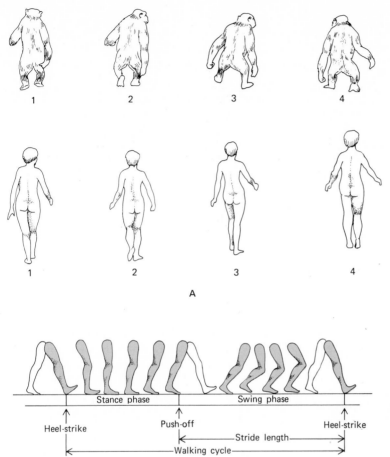

FIGURE 4-3
The striding gait of man. *A,* Comparison of bipedal walking between chimpanzee (*top*) and human (*bottom*), rear view; *B,* phases of the striding gait in man. (See also Fig. 1-15.) [*B, After John Napier, The Roots of Mankind, Smithsonian Institution Press, Washington, D.C., 1970.*]

walking. When a person is running, there is a period when both feet are off the ground.

The arm and hand

Although the human arm has been emancipated from direct involvement in locomotion, it does perform an accessory locomotor function. As we walk, the pelvis rotates clockwise and counterclockwise as the legs alternate between swing and stance phases. The rotation of the pelvis in one direction puts a twist into the trunk which is compensated by a forward swing of the arm on the opposite side. The left arm swings forward with the right leg; the right arm, with the left leg. Compensatory arm-swinging reduces the energy needed to reverse the trunk twist of alternating strides. With arm-swinging, the shoulders are at right angles to the direction of travel; without it, the entire trunk must pivot on the pelvis.

Our arms, of course, perform a variety of other functions, all of which depend to a large degree on the arm's extensive mobility. The previous chapter referred to the broad chest of hominoids and how it served the brachiator by increasing the amount of arm movement. In man, this mobility has been exploited toward different ends. The arm and hand are used extensively in communication through gestures. The hand as an organ of touch is second in importance only to our eyes in providing us with sensory information about our environment. Moreover, it is capable of responding in an elaborate, rapid, and precise manner by reason of its extreme manipulability. It is in the latter category that the human hand is unique, both in structure and in function.

The hands of apes are long, with short, weak thumbs; they serve well as grasping hooks during brachiation (Figs. 1-14*A* and 4-2). Our hands are short and broad, and our thumbs are both long and strong. Our fingers are shorter and straighter than those of apes. The human thumb has great freedom of movement and can readily oppose each of the other digits, thumbtip to fingertip. Of all the muscles in the hand, 39 percent are devoted to controlling the thumb; in apes this figure is only 24 percent.

Many forms of hand grip are possible, such as the hook grip used in strap-hanging on a bus, the "cigarette grip" between the second and third fingers, and so on. Most grasping movements, however, naturally fall into two categories: the power grip and the precision grip. In the power grip, an object is held between the undersurfaces of the fingers and the palm. In a precision grip, the object is held between the tip of a finger, usually the index finger, and the tip of the thumb. A great variety of manual movements are possible beyond these. To list them would be a herculean, if not impossible, task. The manual dexterity, precision, and coordination necessary for a mastery of the piano, violin, or harp defy description. The difference between man and ape in these areas does not rest solely in the anatomy of the hand and the arm. The motor cortex of the brain devoted to fine manual control is more extensively developed in man than in his hominoid relatives.

CRANIAL ADAPTATIONS

The skull and face

The evolutionary changes that produced the human head are good examples of the principle that one thing leads to another. As discussed in Chap. 1, body erectness and a large brain have resulted in the vertebral column attaching to the skull almost in the center of its lower surface (Fig. 1-16). As a consequence, the head is relatively well balanced. Unlike the gorilla, strong bony ridges and flanges for the attachment of powerful neck muscles are not needed to hold the human head in position (Fig. 4-4). Having a large brain requires a large braincase, and more of the skull is given over to housing the brain. As a result, the size of the face is correspondingly reduced. There has also been a reduction in the size of the snout, resulting in a very flat face. And since a small, flat face can only accommodate a jaw of matching size, such a jaw would indeed be ill-suited for any other than small teeth (Fig. 1-12). What enabled man to survive with small jaws and teeth was his technology: tools facilitate the capture, collection, preparation, and eating of food while cooking tenderizes the animal and plant products we consume. Our survival does not depend on projecting canine teeth, either for aggression or for threat. The canines do have long roots which may be an adaptation for occasional heavy-duty chewing of tough foods. Projecting canines also would interlock the jaws and prevent the lateral and rotary chewing of these tougher morsels.[3] Neither do we have powerful jaw muscles. Our expanded braincase offers ample attaching surface for the muscles used to chew our soft foods. Unlike gorillas, who eat coarse tropical vegetation, we lack a *sagittal crest* and *supraorbital ridge* to se-

[3] It is believed that our early ancestors 10 million and more years ago lived in large part on the tough grass seeds, stems, and roots of the open savanna and woodland. We will discuss this in greater detail in Section II.

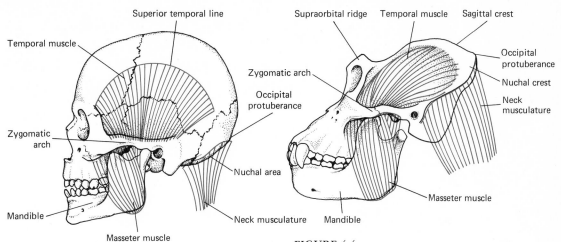

FIGURE 4-4
The skull of man and a male gorilla. Because of better head balance, strong bony ridges (*occipital protuberance* and *nuchal crest*) for the attachment of powerful neck muscles are not developed in man. Gorilla also has a prominent *sagittal crest, supraorbital ridge,* and powerful *zygomatic arch* for the attachment of chewing muscles (*temporal* and *masseter*). Small braincase provides limited area for muscle attachment considering coarse food the ape eats. Both *temporal* and *masseter* muscles (color) attach to *mandible* (lower jaw).

cure a temporal muscle, and such a stout *zygomatic arch* to anchor the *masseter muscle* (Fig. 4-4).

The forward position of our vertebral column relative to the skull, coupled with erect posture and a short jaw, have had interesting consequences within the mouth and throat (Fig. 4-5). A short jaw restricts the fore and aft dimensions for tongue attachment. Substituting a *chin eminence* for the *simian shelf* of our hominoid relatives not only provides an adequate buttress for our jaws in front but also makes possible a more forward attachment for certain tongue muscles. The result is greater freedom of tongue movement in the forepart of the mouth—with great implications for our ability to communicate by vocal language. This freedom is further increased at the base of the tongue to the rear of the mouth cavity. The human jaw is considerably broader at the rear than it is in front because it joins or *articulates* with a laterally expanded braincase. Again, because of erect posture and a small jaw, the voice box, or *larynx,* lies directly below and at some distance from, the tongue and soft palate. Given these structural interrelationships, the vocal cords in the larynx are well situated for

producing sounds which can be modulated in diverse ways by a highly mobile tongue acting in concert with hard and soft palate, teeth, thick everted lips, and the nasal cavities directly above. It should not be assumed, of course, that oral anatomy alone makes speech possible. Our ability to speak, to write, and to understand the written and spoken word are essentially products of the human brain. That portion of the cerebrum devoted to the muscles of speech is greater than that allotted to the entire body musculature, *except for the muscles of the hand.* Nevertheless, it is true that human oral anatomy undoubtedly has facilitated articulate speech.

As one final consequence of body erectness, the human face has attained unusual significance as a sexually sensitive as well as a

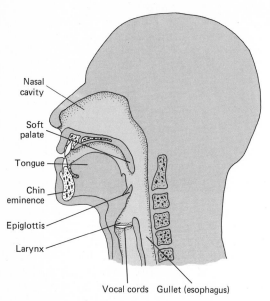
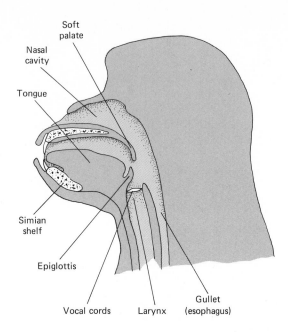

FIGURE 4-5
The mouth, nasal cavity, and larynx of the chimpanzee and man. In man the base of the tongue projects into the throat and lies directly above the larynx; the distance from the soft palate to the larynx is also greater than in the ape. (See also Fig. 1-6.)

sexually responsive area. Body erectness restricts social encounters to face-to-face contacts. The communicative techniques of facial expression, gesturing, and speaking usually occur between individuals looking at one another, so that each technique reinforces the others. It is no coincidence, therefore, that human copulation takes place most commonly in a horizontal face-to-face position. This will be discussed in greater detail later, but suffice it to say our signaling devices are located in front. The thick, everted lips of our species are unlike the thin lips of our hominoid relatives. During sexual excitement our lips become swollen be-

cause of the dilation of blood vessels within them. Furthermore, they are capable of arousing sexual desire as a result of mouth-to-mouth stimulation. There is reason to believe that lips may act visually to excite sex interest. Desmond Morris hypothesizes that this may account for the strongly everted lips of dark-skinned people.[4] If, according to Morris, the contrast of full red lips against a light skin is a sexual signal, then the lips of dark-skinned people would have to be even fuller to sustain the contrast. The human earlobe constitutes another facial feature that also becomes swollen during sexual arousal. It, too, is erotically sensitive to oral stimulation. In fact orgasm has been achieved in both male and female through earlobe stimulation.[5]

[4] Desmond Morris, *The Naked Ape*, New York: McGraw-Hill Book Company, 1967, pp. 67–69.
[5] A. C. Kinsey et al., *Sexual Behavior in the Human Female*, Philadelphia: W. B. Saunders Company, 1953, p. 589.

The human brain

Our most elegant cranial adaptation is the large organ housed on the premises. It is not as large as the brain of a whale, or even the brain of an elephant, but there is no animal approaching our size that has a brain nearly as big. The tiny marmoset monkeys have larger brains with respect to their size, but smaller mammals generally have a higher brain-weight to body-weight proportion. Wild adult gorillas weigh up to 180 kilograms (400 pounds) and have cranial capacities (brain volumes) ranging from 340 to 685 cubic centimeters. Wild adult chimpanzees weigh approximately 45 kilograms (100 pounds) and their cranial capacities vary between 290 and 500 cubic centimeters. The brains of human adults range between 900 and 2,200 cubic centimeters, with an average of about 1,350.

The human skull is large primarily because of its expansive braincase. The act of birth would be impossible in view of the restricted human birth canal were it not for certain modifications in the growth of the skull and the brain within. When an infant is born, its brain is 23 percent of adult size. Its brain is over two and a half times larger than that of a newborn chimpanzee.[6] The separate bones of the fetal braincase are separated by spaces (fontanels) which not only allow for change in skull shape during and after birth but also permit further postnatal skull and brain growth. Human brain growth is rapid for the first 6 years or more and actually does not cease until we are about 23 years old. By contrast, a young chimpanzee attains full brain growth in its first postnatal year. In short, brain growth is completed about 10 years after puberty in man and 6 to 7 years before puberty in chimps.

Our brain is not merely an enlarged version of some pongid counterpart (Fig. 2-9). The

[6] A. H. Schultz, *The Life of Primates*, New York: Universe Books, Inc., 1969, pp. 127–128.

human cerebrum, as in all vertebrates, is divided by a longitudinal fissure into two interconnected halves, the *left and right hemispheres.* The outer mantle, or *cortex,* of these hemispheres is a layer about 2 to 4 millimeters thick in man, consisting of countless branching nerve cells *(neurons).* The human cortex is the most extensively folded, or *convoluted,* of any primate, to the degree that the cortical surface has been increased at least 50 percent over what it would be were it not convoluted. It encompasses an area of 1,300 or more square centimeters (200 or more square inches) and contains more than 7 billion neurons. From the standpoint of brain circuitry, the potential number of different interconnections within a neuron population of this magnitude could be represented by the number 1 followed by 15 million zeros. The cortex of each hemisphere is divided by conspicuous fissures into four lobes: the *frontal, parietal, occipital,* and *temporal* (Fig. 4-6). The frontal lobe is the largest of the four, taking up 47 percent of the cortical surface. It comprises only about 33 percent of the cortical surface in pongids.

Some of the functional areas of the cerebral cortex are shown in Fig. 4-6. These areas commonly are grouped under three categories: motor, sensory, and association. Motor areas are involved with routing, discharging, or suppressing nerve impulses to particular muscles, or groups of muscles, and glands. Sensory areas receive nerve impulses from the various sense organs and sensory cells *(receptors)* of the body. Since nerve impulses generated in a stimulated eye are the same as those generated in a stimulated ear or touch corpuscle, the psychic sensation that these respective impulses produce depends upon their destination in a specific sensory area in the cortex. If the sensory nerve tracts to the cortical centers of vision and hearing were switched, we would see thunder and hear lightning. In short, it is actually the brain that is the information processor enabling us to hear, see, feel, and so on.

The neurons in association areas link sensory and motor areas together. In man, the association areas are larger and their component neurons more complex than in any other animal. One neuron may have as many as 10,000 incoming connections (*synapses*) from other neurons, some of them associative, some of them from sensory areas, and some of them from motor areas. Each and every neuron in the vast cellular assemblage of the associative cortex has been modified and molded through the accumulation of memory stores and knowledge acquired by the system. The functioning of any one of these neurons is intimately interwoven with all of its fellows as well as the entire sensory input from the body. Brain cells, unlike transistors in a computer system, are living units with a kind of "memory"; they will discharge impulses, depending upon their past neural experience, even when isolated from all incoming sensory stimulation. The human brain, in collaboration with eyes, ears, nerves, muscles, etc., is capable of processing enormous amounts of raw data. These raw data are interpreted, classified, and interrelated, and predictive assessments are made about them before they are finally acted upon in what usually turns out to be an adaptive response.

The frontal lobe of the cortex contains the motor area, a large portion of which controls the muscles of speech (the lowermost portion) and the muscles of the hand (the middle portion). As is typical of cerebral function, the left cortical area controls the right side of the body and vice versa; the muscles of speech, however, appear to be controlled predominantly by the left side. Most of the remaining portion of the frontal cortex is associative. The frontal lobe has undergone considerable expansion during human evolution. It contains several inhibitory or suppressor centers which, by enabling us to screen out distracting stimuli, may have contributed powerfully to our prolonged attention span. The parietal lobe includes a body-sense (*somesthetic*) area which gives us an awareness of the position of our various body parts as well as the sensations of touch, temperature, and degree of muscle tension. As a result, this sensory area enables us to determine the size, shape, weight, and texture of objects. The remaining

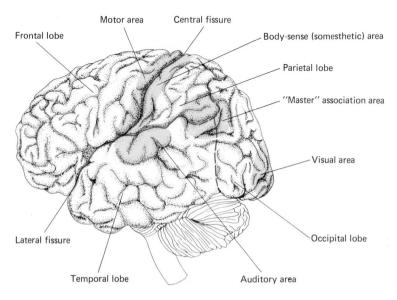

FIGURE 4-6
The human brain (cerebrum) and its functional areas. Body-sense area, through sensibility to body and arm positions, muscle tension, tactility, and temperature, gives us awareness of size, shape, weight, and texture of objects. The "master" association area is thought to be associated with the human capacity for language. (See also Fig. 2-9.)

Frontal lobe

Motor area

Central fissure

Body-sense (somesthetic) area

Parietal lobe

"Master" association area

Visual area

Lateral fissure

Occipital lobe

Temporal lobe

Auditory area

parietal cortex is largely associative. The visual cortex is located in the occipital lobe and the auditory cortex in the temporal lobe. Except for their sensory areas, the remainder of both these lobes is predominantly associative.

An association area of particular interest borders, and overlaps, the temporal, occipital, and parietal lobes (Fig. 4-6). This "master" association area may be involved in the development of language.[7] It is absent, or nearly so, in monkeys, but is developed to some extent in chimpanzees, which may account for the symbol-using performances of Sarah, Washoe, Lana, et al. In man, the master association area encompasses a region about an inch or more across. It is strategically located near the body-sense, visual, and auditory areas, and therefore is well situated as a center for cross-indexing and correlating the sound of a word with the feel, shape, size, weight, and image of an object. It may equally well associate the image of a word with the sound, feel, and image of the object. These processes underlie the elementary aspects of learning a language. Intelligent thought entails classifying objects and ascertaining some sort of order or interrelationship between them. Language not only serves as the communicative vehicle for such thought but also functions as a powerful expeditor of the intellectual process itself. By the use of verbal and written symbols which represent objects (nouns), processes (verbs), and qualifying attributes for each (adjectives and adverbs), one not only communicates but also records a chain of thought. Whether that which is expressed is descriptive or logical, the communicated message serves as a kind of road map, especially if written, of an intellectual itinerary. It can be checked, rechecked, corrected, and added to, and in the end has enabled our species to express ideas based upon countless millions of hours of observation and contemplation. Without language, such an accomplishment would

have been out of the question.

In the evolution of man the hunter, language presumably played an important role. All-male hunting expeditions might last for several days. Such forays would be more fruitful if they were planned in advance. What should be the strategy of attack? If an ambush is planned, where and how should it be set up? Should a pitfall be dug? Could hunters be deployed to stampede the game over a cliff? And so on. When and how language first evolved is a moot point. Before they had a language, our ancestors presumably communicated by ape-like gestures and calls (vocalizations). As their technology grew and they began to hunt big game, greater collaborative effort would be required on the hunt. Uniquely human kinds of social groups would begin to emerge, made up of smaller bands held together by a kinship system. A communication system based on gestures and calls would rapidly become overloaded during such a transition. Only symbolic language could accommodate the complexities of societal man. We cannot be certain when our lineage began to speak and write. It would seem virtually certain, however, that the development of man's biological adaptations for language — vocal apparatus, master association area, etc. — was an integral part of the evolution of societal man.

HAIR AND SKIN

One of our most conspicuous distinctions is that of being almost hairless hominoids. Although we are technically as hairy as a gorilla, the hairs over most of our body are so fine that we are little better than naked except for the scalp, axillary (armpit), and pubic areas. Mature males also have hair on their faces, arms, legs, usually chests, and occasionally backs; the density of chest hair can, in some individuals, approach that of an ape. The relatively sparse body hair that we do have is unique in that it does not start to grow until we reach puberty.

[7] Norman Geshwind, "The Development of the Brain and the Evolution of Language," in Monograph Series on Languages and Linguistics, no. 17, Georgetown University Press, 1964, pp. 155–169.

The baldness of some of us is not unique, however, because it is shared with certain species of monkeys, orangutans, and chimpanzees. Wherever it occurs, it is a natural process associated with maturity, and in fact may begin to appear in chimpanzees of both sexes during adolescence.

It was Charles Darwin who first suggested that the relative hairlessness of man probably was a cooling device. Man the hunter is an unusual predator. He hunts by day, not by night. He has preferred large game such as bison and various members of the elephant family when he could get them. Big-game species are not readily brought to earth by a few men equipped with nothing but their wits and some primitive weapons. The hunt often entailed many hours of pursuit across the plain or savanna during the heat of the day (Fig. 4-7). Adequate protection against overheating meant the difference between success and failure, survival and starvation. Hairlessness may have been an answer to the problem, but, if so, it was only an accessory one in that it facilitated the evaporation of sweat.[8]

From the standpoint of the number of sweat (eccrine) glands per unit area, and the total area over which they are distributed, we are an unusual mammal. Certainly no other primate remotely approaches our ability to perspire. No significant portion of our body surface is without sweat glands, although they reach their highest concentration on the scalp, forehead, palm of the hand, and sole of the foot. We are equipped with about 133 sweat glands per square centimeter of body surface, on the average, with the total number lying somewhere between 2 and 5 million. As mentioned early in Chap. 1, the most effective methods by which mammals lose heat is through evaporation of moisture from respiratory surfaces or of sweat from the body surface. In man the latter technique is used through copious sweat secreted over a relatively hairless, evaporative

surface. A furry insulative coat may have been sacrificed in the process; if so, it was partially compensated for by a well-developed layer of subcutaneous fat to help keep us warm when the temperature drops and we are inactive.

Skin color

Human skin varies in almost indefinite gradations from very light to very dark. These extremes of skin pigmentation differ in a number of respects, especially insofar as their consequences are concerned. One of these is the amount of heat absorption. Dark-colored bodies absorb more heat from solar radiation than light-colored bodies. This could be a definite advantage to a dark-colored mammal or bird living in a cold climate, since less metabolic energy would be required to keep the body warm. Many dark-skinned African peoples do live where the temperatures at dawn and dusk are cool enough that they might benefit from maximal absorption of solar radiation during those periods. Solar radiation during the day, however, is usually so intense as to pose the greater disadvantage of excessive heat absorption and overheating. Furthermore, many peoples who are native to cold regions are not dark-skinned; many Arctic birds and mammals have plumages and pelages that are white, not dark.

Perhaps another reason should be sought for differences in the degree of pigmentation, such as protective coloration. The white snowy owl and the Arctic hare are difficult to see against a background of snow. The black Congo pygmy is equally difficult to see as he stalks his prey in the jungle. On the other hand, the dark skins of the Ngatatjara and the Bushmen stand out against the light sands of the Gibson and Kalahari Deserts.

It may be that heat absorption and camouflage are involved to some extent in the determination of human skin color, but current evidence suggests other factors of possibly greater significance. Contrary to what might be expected if heat absorption were an important

[8] C. L. Brace and M. F. Montagu, *Man's Evolution*, New York: The Macmillan Company, 1965, pp. 220-221.

FIGURE 4-7
Three African Bushmen about to kill a large antelope (gemsbok). [*Courtesy of Marjorie Shostak and Anthro-Photo. Cambridge, Mass.*]

determinant, black heat-absorbing skin is found among native peoples near the equator and white reflective skin commonly occurs in those inhabiting higher latitudes. There is reason to believe that these differences may relate, at least in part, to vitamin D synthesis by the skin.[9]

[9] W. F. Loomis, "Skin-Pigment Regulation of Vitamin-D Biosynthesis in Man," *Science,* vol. 157, August 4, 1967, pp. 501–506.

Before the advent of dietary supplements of vitamin D or the use of fish-liver oils, the human diet usually contained only small amounts of this vitamin in the summer and practically none in the winter.

For all practical purposes, man's sole

source of vitamin D was through its synthesis by the skin. Within the living layers of skin, a provitamin D substance is found which is derived from cholesterol. When this provitamin D is irradiated by the ultraviolet radiation in sunlight, it is converted to vitamin D. At this point, it is carried by the bloodstream to the rest of the body, where it regulates the metabolism of calcium and phosphorus. If inadequate amounts of vitamin D are synthesized because of low levels of solar radiation, a disease known as *rickets* may result. If excessive amounts of vitamin D are synthesized because of overexposure to solar radiation, a toxic hypervitaminosis D may ensue. The latter disease is characterized by the hardening of soft tissues through deposits of insoluble calcium salts, kidney stones, and ultimately death from diseased kidneys. Vitamin D synthesis is supposedly regulated within these extremes (0.01 to 2.5 milligrams per day) by modifying ultraviolet penetration through skin pigmentation or keratinization.[10] People native to the higher latitudes presumably have adapted to the reduced solar radiation by maximizing ultraviolet penetration through reduced pigmentation. People native to equatorial regions have, in turn, adapted to high solar intensities by minimizing ultraviolet penetration with maximal pigmentation. In support of this hypothesis, it has been known for some time that dark-skinned people living in the temperate zone are highly susceptible to rickets unless their diet is fortified with vitamin D. On the other hand, white Europeans who expose their bodies for six hours to the equatorial sun synthesize eight times the amount of vitamin D required to induce a hypervitaminosis (20 milligrams). Black Africans, under the same conditions, synthesize 5 to 10 percent of this amount, well within the normal range.

An interesting recent study suggests that cold injury could have been a contributing factor in the evolution of "white" skin.[11] An analysis of the occurrence of frostbite among soldiers in two world wars and the Korean War showed that susceptibility to cold injury was directly related to the degree of skin pigmentation — the darker the skin, the greater the susceptibility to frostbite. Laboratory experiments and observations seem to support the same conclusion.

Sexual and erotic features

The sexual significance of what little body hair our species has is suggested by the fact that body hair does not start to grow until puberty. The secondary sexual characteristics that distinguish males and females, such as the heavier musculature in males and the broadening of the hips and development of breasts in females, begin at this time. These differences in body form between the two sexes *(sexual dimorphism)* indicate the different biological roles played by each sex. They also serve as sexual signals proclaiming the advent of sexual maturity, and as sexual attractants serving the establishment and perpetuation of the all-important pair bond. It is in the latter sense that human body hair may play a significant role.

The axillary and pubic hair common to both sexes possibly functions in a signaling role that is both visual and olfactory. In the latter case, its function would be indirect in that it contributes to the dispersal of aromatic substances contained in the secretions of scent *(apocrine)* glands.

Human scent glands are concentrated in the armpits and around the genitals. The female has 75 percent more of these glands than the male. Males presumably tend to be stimulated by these secretions, especially during precopulatory behavior. During late precopulatory and copulatory activity, the female herself may be erotically affected by them. Axillary and pubic hair help to retain these secretions and thereby would extend their effectiveness in both sexes.

We again note that these erotic areas are located on the front of the body where they may encourage the face-to-face copulatory posi-

---

[10] Keratin is the predominant protein in fingernails and hair; in the skin, it imparts a characteristic yellow color.

[11] Peter W. Post et al., "Cold Injury and the Evolution of 'White' Skin," *Human Biology,* vol. 47, no. 1, 1975, pp. 65–80.

tion. Each partner's nose is assured of being close to a scent-producing area during both copulatory and precopulatory activity. And, as a final feature, the sensuous contact between two almost hairless bodies enhances the excitement of sexual union thereby adding to the strength of the pair bond.

SEXUAL ADAPTATIONS

Men and women are distinguished by a number of features not directly related to reproduction. This sexual dimorphism is moderate when compared to other primates[12] and encompasses a number of secondary sex characteristics (Fig. 4-8). To hairiness and body musculature in the male, already mentioned, can be added a more protruding Adam's apple *(larynx)* and a lower voice, as well as broader shoulders and 10 to 15 percent greater height and weight. Females are characterized by having broader hips and well-developed bosoms, and are usually shorter and lighter. The degree to which these distinguishing features are contrasted indicates a difference between the two sexes in their traditional biological roles. The degree of this contrast is subject to cultural factors as we will see later. But most males today still are biologically outfitted for their ancient hunting role just as most females are equipped for childbearing and rearing. Interestingly enough, these two roles, coupled with some other human traits, have interacted to produce the world's sexiest primate, if not vertebrate.

In those vertebrates where the task of rearing young is especially burdensome for one parent, a strong pair bond commonly develops between male and female parent that endures at least throughout the period of dependency of the young. In certain species of birds, for example, the male and female alternate sitting on the eggs, and both forage food for the hatch-

lings. No animal produces offspring that are dependent as long or demand as much attention as our own. The appearance of a pair bond in the human species would seem to be a natural development. Man also is a predatory species that has hunted in all-male groups; each male leaves his mate and offspring at a home base. Not only are females burdened with children but, as mentioned previously, their wider pelvises also reduce their locomotor efficiency. Such circumstances require a strong pair bond for a number of reasons. In the first place, the female is dependent upon male support of the family unit just as the male is dependent upon the plant foods his mate gathers. Furthermore, the possibility of two or more males competing for the same female could seriously interfere with the productiveness of a hunting party. Last, and by no means least, the long-dependent offspring must be assured of the stability and parental cooperation required to attain effective adulthood. Our species has established a bond capable of meeting these demands through intensified sexual attraction, a perennial sexual appetite, and highly motivating copulatory rewards. Most of our sexual activities apparently serve the establishment and perpetuation of the pair bond and are in no direct way related to reproduction.

Sexual attraction

The erotic surfaces and structures of the human body are located in front, presumably as an adaptation for face-to-face copulation in a horizontal position. Studies of a wide variety of cultures over the world have shown that face-to-face copulation is almost universally the favored position.[13] This position is a natural one because the human *vagina,* unlike that of other primates, is directed forward (Fig. 4-9). The face-to-face position also allows for maximum stimulation of the highly sensitive *clitoris,* the

---

[12] For example, in humans and chimpanzees the weight of females is about 89 percent that of males; in gorillas and orangutans this figure is just under 50 percent.

[13] C. S. Ford, and F. A. Beach, *Patterns of Sexual Behavior,* New York: Paul B. Hoeber, Inc., 1951.

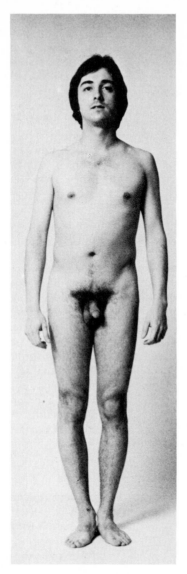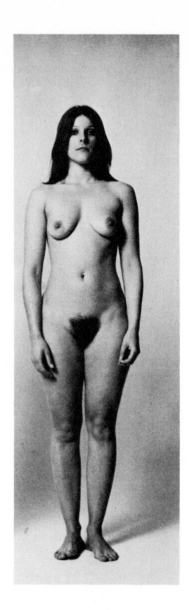

FIGURE 4-8
Sexual dimorphism in the human species. [*From E. T. Pengelley, Sex and Human Life, Addison-Wesley, Reading, Mass., 1974.*]

female counterpart of the penis, during the deep thrusts of the penis and the rhythmic pressure of the male's pubic area.

Frontally placed lips, earlobes, scent glands, body hair, and genitals would seem to compose an effective battery of strategically located sexual attractants. To these we should add the hemispherical breasts and the broad, fat-padded buttocks of the female. The nipples and the breasts are erotically sensitive to stimulation and both of these structures swell noticeably during sexual arousal. The human female breast has no counterpart among primates either for size or for conspicuousness. Both the

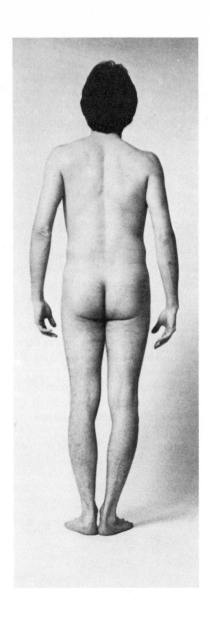 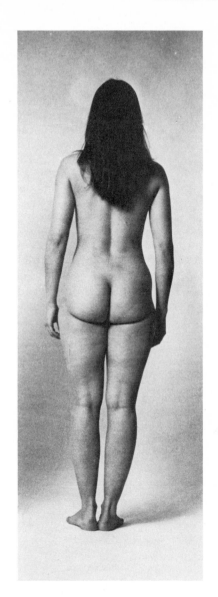

nipple and the circular area (*areola*) around it are pigmented, contrasting sharply with the surrounding prominence. The nipple is short compared to that on a baby bottle or that with which a chimpanzee mother is naturally endowed. The human baby must insert both nipple and areola into its mouth so that the nipple reaches the palate and the top of the tongue to activate the sucking reflex. In so doing, the nose may become buried in the mother's breast, resulting in suffocation, and a child that is said to "fight the breast." This reaction, which can have unfortunate emotional consequences for both if the mother does not recognize its cause quickly and accommodate the infant accordingly, appears paradoxical from an evolutionary point of view. It would seem that the human female breast has been adapted for an erotic function as well as a maternal one.[14]

[14] R. J. Andrew, "The Displays of the Primates," in *Evolutionary and Genetic Biology of Primates*, J. Buettner-Janusch (ed.), New York: Academic Press, Inc., 1964, p. 227.

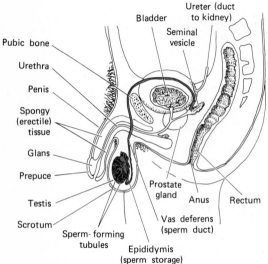

FIGURE 4-9
Human reproductive organs. Above is a male side sectional view, to the right, a female side sectional view and a view from below (facing page).

Sexual appetite

The environment appears to have some effect on the period in which most conceptions occur; there are more births in the Northern Hemisphere during the first six months of the year and more in the Southern Hemisphere during the last six months. This should not be construed, however, as evidence for a human breeding season. A female may copulate at any time during her 28-day menstrual cycle, although there may be greater sexual desire in some individuals either during the middle of the cycle or just prior to menstruation. The only time when human females do not copulate is a relatively short interval before and after birth. Since sex interest in the human male is continuous, we have a much greater sexual appetite than baboons, chimpanzees, or any other primate.

By the age of 14, most girls in this country begin to menstruate and most boys have had an ejaculation. The maximum capacity for achieving orgasm in males is reached at about age 19 or 20. In females, this maximum is attained usually between 25 and 30. Most females begin to engage in sexual activity—all

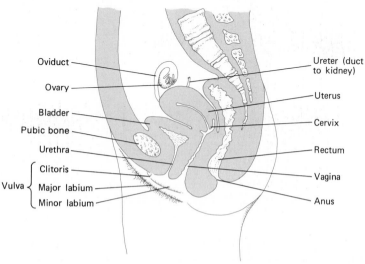

forms of sex behavior considered — at an older age than males. They reach their sexual peak at about 30 years of age, some 10 years later than most males. There may be a distinct biological advantage in this difference. The female should have some protection against the occurrence of a pregnancy where the pair bond would stand little chance of enduring. Initial sex encounters would best not be engaged in with any haste until the female is at least reasonably sure that a pair bond can develop.

Essentially all of our scientific knowledge of human sexual habits and capabilities stems from the work of Alfred C. Kinsey, and from the studies of William H. Masters and Virginia E. Johnson.[15] These investigations have been limited to an examination of sexual behavior in the United States. Such studies have shown that practically all men and about 90 percent of all women experience orgasm. A few women, how-

ever, may not achieve their first orgasm until they are 30 to 40 years old. On the other hand, women greatly surpass men in the number of orgasms they can achieve in a given time and in the duration of a single orgasm. Kinsey reported that married men had intercourse on an average of 2.8 times a week, and women 2.6 times a week, when they were 20 years old. At age 40, the frequency was 1.5 times a week, and by age 60 the rate was 0.6 times weekly. The onset of menopause at about age 50 does not materially affect sexual responsiveness. At the age of 70 and beyond, both sexes continue to retain a capacity and an interest in sexual activity.

Courtship and sexual intercourse

The act of human copulation and the events that lead up to it have no counterpart among mammals insofar as their character, duration, and intensity are concerned. The orgasmic response which usually climaxes copulation is a total-body reaction in both sexes; it does not occur in any other mammal. It not only adds a powerful reward for copulation but also en-

[15] A. C. Kinsey et al., *Sexual Behavior in the Human Male*, Philadelphia: W. B. Saunders Company, 1948; *Sexual Behavior in the Human Female*, Philadelphia: W. B. Saunders Company, 1953; W. H. Masters and V. E. Johnson, *Human Sexual Response*, Boston: Little, Brown and Company, 1966; *Human Sexual Inadequacy*, Boston: Little, Brown and Company, 1970.

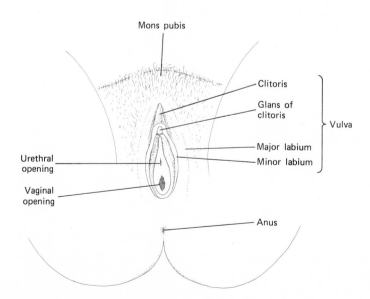

hances fertility by leaving the female temporarily relaxed and prone. To describe these events, we will divide them into two stages: (1) courtship and precopulatory behavior, and (2) sexual intercourse. We will restrict ourselves to sexual behavior in the United States.

Courtship and precopulatory behavior

Courtship usually lasts for several weeks or months, depending upon the individuals and the circumstances.

As intimacy develops and sexual intercourse is approached, there is a marked increase in the frequency and intensity of tactile stimulation. Visual and vocal communication are largely replaced by tactile stimuli. More and more body contact occurs in a prone or near-prone position. Mouth-to-mouth contacts become more frequent and prolonged. Each partner kisses various parts of the other's body, but oral stimulation is particularly concentrated on the erotic areas. The mouth also may be used to bite the arm, leg, or some other portion of the body gently. Accompanying these oral stimulations, extensive manual caressing of the body occurs, especially of the face, buttocks, and genital area of both sexes, and the breasts of the female. Tactile stimulation is further heightened as arms, legs, and particularly thighs become intertwined in a writhing, clinging embrace of strong muscular contractions.

At this point a level of sexual excitement has been reached which is usually followed by the insertion of the penis into the vagina, and copulation takes place.

Sexual intercourse

The entire process of sexual intercourse, including the physiologic changes that accompany it, has been called "the sexual response cycle" by Masters and Johnson. They have divided the sexual response cycles of both sexes into four phases: (1) the excitement phase, (2) the plateau phase, (3) the orgasmic phase, and (4) the resolution phase.

This sexual cycle is the result of two basic physiological responses to sexual stimulation. The first of these is widespread congestion of the blood vessels (*vasocongestion*); the affected body parts enlarge because the rate of blood supply to the part exceeds the rate of removal. The other is a general increase in muscle tension.[16]

These basic responses bring about a variety of bodily changes in both sexes. The magnitude of these changes reflects the intensity of human sexual behavior. This is clearly demonstrated by the physiological responses that occur in the four phases of the sexual cycle.

The *excitement phase* may last from a few minutes to several hours. During this interval there is a quickening of the heartbeat, a rise in blood pressure, and an increase in muscle tension in both sexes. A measleslike rash known as the *sex flush* develops in most women and in some men. This flush begins on the abdomen and extends over the breasts.

In females this phase is marked by the lubrication of the vagina with fluids coming directly from the vaginal walls. This accommodates the entrance and pistonlike movements of the penis. Muscles encircling the vagina may contract, tightening the vaginal walls against the penis and sometimes expelling some of the vaginal lubricant. The *minor labia* (Fig. 4-9) swell, increasing the effective length of the vaginal tube. The inner two-thirds of the vagina increases in size, adding further to the length of the vaginal tube as well as to its diameter where it joins the *cervix*. The breasts enlarge and the nipples become erect.

In males, vasocongestion of the penis marks the first response of this phase and results in partial to complete penile erection. This involves an increase in both the length and diameter of the penis. The testes and the scrotum become elevated and the scrotal skin thickens. The nipples may swell, but this response is less common than among females.

As sexual tensions rise, the *plateau phase* is entered, lasting for about one-half to three minutes or more. Both sexes experience mounting muscular tension. The neck may become

---

[16] Masters and Johnson, *Human Sexual Response,* pp. 3–8.

rigid, the back arched, and the thighs and buttocks tensed. The nostrils often are flared and the face may be contorted by the spastic contraction of facial muscles. Breathing becomes heavier, and there is a marked increase in blood pressure and pulse rate. If a sexual flush has developed, it may spread to the head, arms, back, and thighs.

In females, vasocongestion continues to mount in the minor labia and the outer third of the vagina. As a result, the minor labia increases even more in size, and the diameter of the outer third of the vaginal cavity is reduced. The inner two-thirds of the vaginal tube undergoes further increase in width and depth. The breasts become larger and the nipples fully erect.

In males, the testes become elevated in the scrotum to the point where they lie close against the body. Vasocongestion causes some additional enlargement of the glans penis (Fig. 4-9), and the size of the testes is increased by 50 percent or more.

The *orgasmic phase* is an explosive psychological and physiological release of the sexual tensions that have built up during the excitement and plateau phases. Although it is of brief duration in both sexes (3 to 10 seconds), it may sometimes continue for as long as a minute in women. It is the sensory peak of the sexual cycle. A feeling of intensely sensual pleasure focuses in the pelvic region and radiates throughout the body. All other sensory awareness is usually dampened, if not lost. The center of focus in females is the area of the clitoris, vagina, uterus, and muscles of the pelvic floor. In males it is the area of the penis, prostate, seminal vesicles (Fig. 4-9), and pelvic floor musculature.

Physiological responses include involuntary and spasmodic muscular contractions in many parts of the body. The rate of breathing and the pulse rate may be double or triple that of normal. Blood pressure may be 30 percent to 80 percent above normal.

In females, orgasm begins simultaneously with strong contractions of muscles in the lower pelvis, forcing blood out of the congested veins in that region. The outer third of the vagina undergoes 5 to 12 rhythmic contractions, the first 3 to 6 of which occur at about 0.8-second intervals. The uterus contracts irregularly.

In males, orgasm is associated with ejaculation. The process of ejaculation is a progressive series of contractions that begins in the testes and passes successively to the *epididymis, vas deferens, seminal vesicles,* and *prostate gland* (Fig. 4-9). The latter two organs eject the main bulk of seminal fluid. It is during these preliminary contractions that the male has a feeling that ejaculation is about to occur. At this point, strong contractions of muscles at the base of the penis and those in the muscular floor of the pelvis cause the seminal fluid to squirt from the penis. Ejaculation is a rhythmic series of contractions, the first three or four of which occur at about 0.8-second intervals, as in females. It is accompanied by the all-absorbing sensation of orgasm.

The orgasmic experience of females shows much greater variation both in intensity and duration than that of males (Fig. 4-10). A single orgasm may last considerably longer in a woman than in a man, as mentioned previously. Some women also are capable of having three or more orgasms without loss of sexual excitement below plateau-phase levels. The later orgasms often are more satisfying than the first. Men, on the other hand, are almost always slower to respond to restimulation than women. After each orgasm the male enters a "refractory period" in which he is both resistant and unresponsive to sexual stimulation. If a second orgasm follows closely after this refractory period, it is not as intense as the first.

The final *resolution phase* is a period during which the individual is gradually returned through plateau and excitement levels of physiological tension to the sexually unstimulated state. Following orgasm, this may take from 10 minutes to 2 hours, depending upon the individual and the level of stimulation. At the close of this phase, both males and females commonly perspire. Each sexual partner is left relaxed and

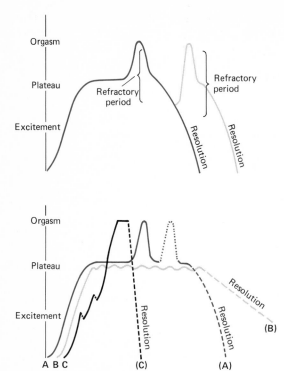

FIGURE 4-10
The sexual response cycle of the human male (*top*) and female (*bottom*). Unlike the female, the male has a sexually unresponsive "refractory period," which results in loss of sexual excitement below plateau level. Female response is more variable in both intensity and duration: may have two or more orgasms without loss of sexual excitement below plateau level (*A*), a prolonged period at plateau level (*B*), or a prolonged orgasm (*C*). [*After W. H. Masters and V. E. Johnson, Human Sexual Response, Little, Brown, Boston, 1966.*]

with a strong desire to sleep. If orgasm did not occur, the resolution phase may last for 12 hours or more.

BIRTH AND GROWING UP

Women generally have a childbearing period of about 30 years, between the ages of about 20 and 50. The gestation period is 9 months (267 days). Human birth is complicated by pelvic modifications for erect posture and by the size of the relatively large-headed fetus. A newborn gorilla weighs 2.6 percent, and a newborn chimpanzee 4 percent, of its mother's weight; human birthweights average 5.5 percent. The period of labor during which the fetus is delivered usually lasts a number of hours. Several adults ordinarily are in attendance at this time to render assistance, a practice which probably extends far back into our biologic history. Soon after birth, the mother's breasts begin to secrete milk and the infant suckles for about six to nine months — at least among the breast-fed babies of modern society. While lactating, the mother usually does not menstruate or ovulate (release eggs), thereby reducing the likelihood of conception. Among aboriginal people like the Ngatatjara, breast-feeding ordinarily goes on for three years or more. This serves a two-fold purpose in that it not only compensates for a lack of suitable infant food from other sources but also reduces the birth rate. Their harsh environment places severe restrictions on the number of people that can be adequately fed (Fig. 4-11). Birth control is an absolute necessity for survival. When twins are born to a Ngatatjara woman, she is unable to carry and nurse both of them, so one is killed. Sometimes single infants are also sacrificed. Killing the infant is the responsibility of the mother, and generally she performs her function within an hour after birth. The only consolation she or her group has is their religious conviction that the soul of the infant will enter the body of another infant yet unborn. In times past, at least 15 percent to as many as 50 percent of the infants have been killed, according to Joseph Birdsell, a longtime student of these people.[17]

Human mothers, like mothers of certain other mammalian species, have low-protein, low-fat milk. The infants of these species are

[17] J. B. Birdsell, "Some Environmental and Cultural Factors Influencing the Structuring of Australian Aboriginal Populations," *The American Naturalist*, vol. 87, no. 834, 1953, pp. 171–207.

FIGURE 4-11
The winter camp of a Ngatatjara family. Its chief accommodations are hearths and a brush windbreak. [*From R. A. Gould, Yiwara: Foragers of the Australian Desert, Scribner, New York, 1969.*]

characteristically frequent feeders. The young which feed frequently also tend to suck slowly, and the human infant sucks very slowly. It is significant in this regard that the infants of Bushmen mothers are carried most of the time and have free access to the breast. It appears that these infants feed at least every half hour for 30 seconds to 10 minutes. Such an arrangement tends to develop a close bond between mother and infant. The frequent occurrence of hunger and its quick satisfaction would tend to assure that the baby remains with its mother. If such is the natural character of infant nursing behavior, and it appears that it is, the great variety of feeding schedules that infants adapt to is a commentary on man's flexibility even in his earliest hours.

Lee Salk has studied and made some intriguing observations about how the human infant is held.[18] He noted, for example, that among 466 works of art from all over the world which show an infant being held by a woman, 80 percent (373) had the child on the woman's left side. A clinical study of mothers and their newborn indicated the same side preference for holding the young infant, whether the

[18] L. Salk, "The Role of Heartbeat in the Relations Between Mother and Infant," *Scientific American.* May 1973, pp. 24–27.

mothers were left-handed or right-handed. Why the preference for the left side? Is it because the baby can hear and feel the mother's heartbeat better, the sensations of which are associated with the tension-free state of life in the womb? To test this suggestion, Salk subjected 102 infants in a hospital nursery to the recorded sound of the human heartbeat during their first four days after birth. Another group of 112 infants in the same nursery were not exposed to the heartbeat sound. Although there was no significant difference in food consumption between the two groups, the heartbeat group cried much less and gained significantly more weight, both on the basis of average weight gain (40 grams per child versus 20) and the number of individuals that gained weight (70 percent versus 33 percent). It would seem that the sound of the human heartbeat has a beneficial effect. One might even go further: the rhythm of music, whether from the rituals of aboriginal tribes or from the works of Beethoven, shows some similarities to the heartbeat. The universal appeal of music may well be lodged in the primal sense of well-being associated with the sound and force of the mother's heart as we lay secure within her uterine walls. We may indeed speculate that these considerations, unconscious as they no doubt were, have been relevant to the choice of the heart as the seat of love in both song and poetry.

A human infant is the image of physical helplessness and dependency. It must be held to the breast with its mouth at the nipple. For the first few days, it averages almost 17 hours of sleep daily, an average that will diminish gradually to about 8 hours by the time puberty is reached. At the end of its first month, it can raise its chin when in a belly-prone position. By 6 months, it can sit up and grasp objects. At 10 months, it is able to crawl on its hands and knees and can stand erect if there is something to hang on to. Not until 15 months of age or more are most children able to walk unaided. Motor control is acquired very slowly during these early months. The benefits of a close mother-infant bond are not quickly realized in our species; there is much to develop and nourish in the infant both physically and psychologically. Prolonging the period of dependency provides the opportunities for this development.

It is no coincidence that an important part of the emotional development of the child (or lack of it) occurs during these first months of life. We shall trace some of the elements of this progress in the following chapter, where we will concentrate our attention on the psychological, sociological, and cultural dimensions of the human species.

SUGGESTED READINGS

CAMPBELL, BERNARD G.: *Human Evolution: An Introduction to Man's Adaptations,* 2d ed., Chicago: Aldine Publishing Company, 1974. A very readable text on human biological adaptations in relationship to corresponding adaptations in other primates both living and extinct.

GROLLMAN, S.: *The Human Body: Its Structure and Physiology,* New York: The Macmillan Company, 1974. A clearly and interestingly written text on human anatomy and physiology.

HARRISON, G. A., et al.: *Human Biology,* New York: Oxford University Press, 1964. This and the book by Young are encyclopedic works covering, among other things, growth, mental development, and aging.

PENGELLEY, E. T.: *Sex and Human Life,* Reading, Mass.: Addison-Wesley Publishing Company, Inc., 1974. An excellent little book on the biological, psychological, social, and political aspects of human sexuality written by an experienced teacher in the field.

YOUNG J. Z.: *An Introduction to the Study of Man,* New York: Oxford University Press, 1971.

REVIEW QUESTIONS

1 Cite five advantages and five disadvantages of erect posture and bipedal locomotion.

2 The human species possesses numerous skeletal adaptations for erect posture. Briefly describe six of these that involve the trunk and legs. Explain how two of the gluteal muscles are involved in erect posture and striding.

3 How does the human hand differ from that of a pongid? List five differences.

4 Man possesses a number of structural adaptations that make speech possible. Identify five and indicate how each facilitates speech.

5 Describe the functional areas of the frontal lobe of the human cerebrum. What is the "master" association area and how is it thought to be related to the learning of language?

6 Theoretically what is the adaptive significance to the human species of having a relatively hairless body and large numbers of sweat glands?

7 Offer two theories backed by clinical and laboratory evidence which might explain differences in human skin pigmentation among peoples throughout the world.

8 The sexual bond between the human male and female is powerfully reinforced in three different ways. What are they? Discuss one of them in some detail.

9 What is the sexual response cycle? How does the orgasmic experience of women differ from that of men?

10 Human mothers have low-protein, low-fat milk. What, presumably, is the adaptive significance of this?

11 Why are most infants held on their mothers' left side? Give experimental evidence to support your answer.

FIVE

THE HUMAN SPECIES II:
Psychosocial and Cultural Features

The human species is distinguished even more by its psychological, sociological, and cultural dimensions than it is by its anatomical and physiological features. This chapter will discuss learning, language, social behavior, social organization, and culture. It is logical that we begin with the behavioral development of the infant.

THE BEHAVIORAL DEVELOPMENT OF THE INFANT

Despite its physical helplessness, the infant is able to communicate by facial expressions and vocalizations, and is also able to respond to such communications from others. It is an active participant in its own behavioral development and is much more perceptive than it is often given credit. The mother who forces a superficial smile for her five-month-old child probably does not reassure it as much as she confuses it. The infant is born into the world with many behavioral biases or predispositions. It has a predisposition to explore, to learn in a certain way, and to use symbolic language. It also has a predisposition, regardless of the culture in which it is reared, to vocalize by crying, gurgling, laughing, shouting, screaming, whimpering, and moaning. To these are added a number of facial expressions of equally universal occurrence: the smile, frown, stare, crying face, panic face, and angry face.

The baby gurgle of contentment appears very early in life. Crying first occurs even earlier, when the baby is born. It is a signal of pain, discomfort, or insecurity, and it usually brings a quick response on the part of an attending adult. The crying face is a reddened one with tearful eyes, an open mouth, and retracted lips. It is accompanied by muscular tension, heavy breathing, and rasping, if not shrieklike, vocalizations. During the first three months, crying habits depend on the individual infant rather than the character of the maternal response. Some infants cry 20 minutes out of every hour they are awake; at the other extreme are those who scarcely cry at all. By the end of 12 months, however, there is less crying among those infants whose mothers respond quickly than among those in which the response is delayed or lacking entirely. Prompt response to an infant's request is all-important because it reinforces the elements of dependability and order which every human imposes upon its surroundings. Making sense out of the world is a very large chore, especially at this stage of life.

Temper tantrums and crying from anger are special cases in which failure to respond may be indicated. Crying from anger begins to appear between three and four months of age and is the first sign of aggressive behavior. As the child gains muscular control and coordination, these emotions become mobilized as attack, with its attendant trademarks of the tight-lipped glare, the frown, and clenched fists. Displays of stylized threat and redirected ag-

gression are added to these later and include shaking the fist, slamming the fist on a table, stamping the feet, and throwing objects to the ground.

Quite the opposite of aggressive behavior is a much more commonly expressed display which reveals the predisposition of infants to attract others and to bring them closer, rather than to turn them away. This display is the *smile*. It is possible that the smile may appear first in an undeveloped form two months or more before birth. Usually it is seen first *as a response to a specific stimulus* between the ages of four to six weeks. The specific stimulus to which the child directs its first smile is a pair of human eyes or some likeness of them, such as two black dots on a sheet of paper. By measuring the time periods an infant fixes its eyes on various kinds of visual forms and configurations (triangles, squares, circles, ovals, and the like), it has been found that the infant is born with a bias for giving special attention to the kinds of rounded contours and configurations which are found in the human face.[1] The visual image that the infant first develops of its mother's face, and the soothing sounds and warm touch associated with it, is a pair of round, glistening eyes. The moment of recognition of this visual symbol of its mother apparently is signaled by a baby's smile. As time passes, nose, lips, teeth, hair, and so on are added. At three to four months of age, the child has filled in most of the details. Now, usually the only face that will bring a smile is the one face that meets the child's refined standards of recognition, that of its mother.[2]

At this point, the infant begins to watch its mother move about, smiling all the while. It is almost as if the fixed gaze and smile of the child were a substitute for physical contact with its mother; visual tracking nearly becomes

[1] R. L. Fantz, "The Origin of Form Perception," *Scientific American*, May 1961, pp. 66–72.
[2] J. A. Ambrose, "The Concept of a Critical Period for the Development of Social Responsiveness," in *Determinants of Infant Behavior II*, B. M. Foss (ed.); London: Methuen Company, 1963, pp. 201–226.

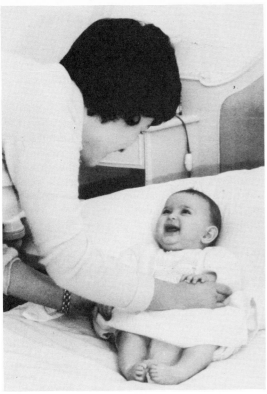

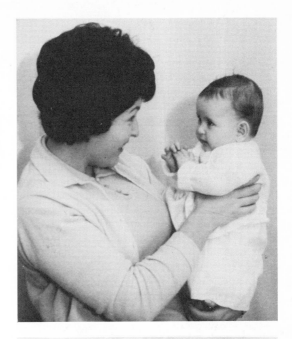

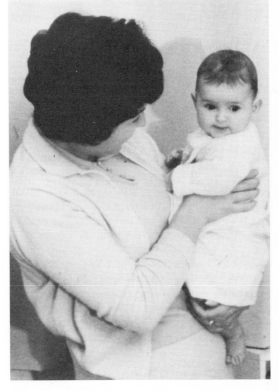

FIGURE 5-1
The infant's smile as a request to explore. Smiling infant attracts mother (*above*). Once in mother's arms, infant stops smiling (*right above*) and begins to explore world around it (*right*). [*Courtesy of J. A. Ambrose.*]

a form of following or accompanying. There is, in fact, some reason to believe that the infant's smile may have evolved as a substitute clinging response, to compensate for the immobility of the infant and its inability to cling to a hairless body. When the baby smiles, it commonly reacts with random body movements as though it were trying to make body contact with the mother. The mother's usual response is to smile in return and to fondle the child or pick it up. Crying might accomplish the same contact, but crying is a demand that is reserved for distress. The infant's smile, on the other hand, is a request to explore. The smiling child stops smiling almost the instant it is picked up (Fig. 5-1). There is no point in continuing a request that has already been met, and there is every reason to take advantage of the opportunity for mobility, adventure, and exploration while it lasts.

Ultimately, the smile is employed in several ways. It plays a powerful role in keeping interpersonal relationships friendly and tension-free. A baby who has tried the patience of its mother may relieve her displeasure with a smile, even though it may do so unknowingly. The broad beaming smile is a universal signal of greeting, usually accompanied by a handshake. On the other hand, the smile also is used as a grin of submission and becomes the appeasement grin so widespread among primates; it is cold rather than warm; it conveys humiliation rather than congeniality. It contains certain elements of the fear face which essentially is a face with wrinkled forehead and raised eyebrows to which an exaggerated appeasement grin has been added.

There has been considerable speculation about the evolutionary origin of smiling and its presumably related display, laughter. One hypothesis, that of van Hooff, is backed by substantial evidence and holds that smiling and laughter involve a continuous series of intergrading displays that can be described in terms of two common anthropoid behaviors.[3] These two behaviors are the bared-teeth display or appeasement grin (Fig. 3-4) and the relaxed open-mouth display or play face (Fig. 3-9). Although the bared-teeth display is commonly used by anthropoids as a defensive or submissive behavior, it is also used on occasion as a signal of nonhostility and friendliness. In a similar vein, the relaxed open-mouth display resembles the staring open-mouth expression given during aggression. The former, however, lacks evidence of tension and is used during episodes of play. Van Hooff suggests that human smiling and laughing have evolved from the bared-teeth and relaxed open-mouth displays of nonhuman anthropoids.

[3] J. A. R. A. M. van Hooff, "A Comparative Approach to the Phylogeny of Laughter and Smiling," in *Non-verbal Communication,* R. A. Hinde (ed.), New York and London: Cambridge University Press, 1972, pp. 209–241.

It is believed that laughter may be the result of the unusual mixing of fear and enjoyment. The child does not laugh until it is three to four months of age, the same age at which it first recognizes its mother as the individual responsible for its well-being and security. The mother is the symbol of protection and contentment, the opposite of danger and hurt. A startling or fearful stimulus coming from the infant's protector would suggest that the danger was not real. The startle of a peekaboo or the shock of being lifted high are not the genuine thing when mother is the culprit. The response is that delightful blend of gurgling with contentment and crying from fear which we know as a *laugh.* The facial expression, reddened face, tearful eyes, heavier breathing, and muscular tension are remarkably similar to crying. But the vocalizations are neither shrieky nor raspy; they are lower-pitched, softer, shorter, more rapidly repeated, and more musically connected.

As the child grows older, it learns that the laugh can be very degrading when it is directed at someone because it asserts that the person is both surprisingly odd as well as unworthy of being considered seriously. As we mature, we also learn to become quite expert at exploiting the merriment of humor. We startle ourselves into peals of laughter on endless occasions over the unexpected consequences of contrived or ridiculous situations.

LEARNING, SYMBOLS, AND LANGUAGE

We learn many things in many ways (Fig. 5-2), and much of our learning is helped (although it is sometimes hindered, too) by the uniquely human invention of teaching. Our potential for retaining that which is learned is enormous. It has been estimated that we are born with a brain that can store, catalog, cross-index, and retrieve enough information to fill 1,000 twenty-four volume sets of the *Encyclopaedia*

FIGURE 5-2
Social learning by direct imitation. Older brother is observed and copied by younger sibling. [*Courtesy of J. A. Thompson.*]

Britannica. We also are born with a drive to explore that is unmatched by any other creature. We carry this exploratory urge throughout our lives so that we retain the option for change despite the traditional (imitative) nature of much of our learning. This has made possible one of man's main strengths, the great flexibility of his behavior.

The urge to explore can be observed in a newborn infant when it is confronted by a plain dark background. It keeps looking in various directions as if it were trying to find something interesting. It seems predisposed,

even on its first day, to follow an object in motion with its eyes and, as time goes on, to distinguish different objects from one another. These exploratory activities are by no means random and unbiased. The child comes into the world with a bias to learn in a certain way and with an inborn, or *innate,* awareness of certain sensory interrelationships. It has been demonstrated experimentally, for example, that a newborn infant expects an object which it sees to be capable of being touched and grasped.[4] When confronted with a three-dimensional (stereoscopic) image of an object, the child expresses vocal surprise when it cannot touch the illusion. Predispositions of this nature are clearly illustrated when we first begin to speak in our native tongue.

The evidence indicates that the child not only takes the initiative when it learns a language but that it is also virtually impossible (short of drastic measures) to prevent that child from acquiring a language. Young children have a ready capacity for subject-verb and verb-object relationships. Continually they surprise their parents with original and meaningful phrases such as "my's all through" and "all-gone milk." During these early years we teach our child to speak much as we make its body grow: we provide the food, the child assimilates it and produces more child; we provide the word sounds and their inflections, the child imitates them and creates for itself a spoken language.

The infant utters a few simple words when it is about one year old. Within six months it forms simple sentences, and by two years of age it has a vocabulary of some 300 words. At the age of four, it has a speaking vocabulary of about 1,500 words, but it probably comprehends 3 to 4 times this number. At this point, the child already can be said to have a good command of its native language. Most adults have a speaking vocabulary of approximately 10,000 words and comprehend about 10 times that number.

Our capacity for learning a language, or for learning anything, is truly remarkable. We should therefore examine this unusual talent in greater detail.

Learning

As implied, if not stated, there are two basic types of behavior: innate and learned. Innate,

or inborn, behavior is determined for the most part by hereditary mechanisms. A newborn infant innately expects to be able to touch something it sees. Infants blind from birth not only smile at voices but also turn their eyes toward the sound. In contrast, learned behavior, although dependent upon inherited structures like sense organs and a brain, is essentially the result of experience.

All animals learn. Learning plays a larger role in the behavior—and survival—of some organisms than it does in others. In primates, learning plays a very large role; in man, almost all behavior beyond early infancy is powerfully influenced by it. Man far surpasses any other animal in the number, kinds, and complexity of the behaviors he learns—and in his near-total dependency, from morning to night and from birth to death, on these learned behaviors. The human animal is a learning animal *par excellence*.

Since learning plays such a critically important role in our lives, we should take a closer look at the nature of learning, the different kinds of learning, and the drives or motives that initiate learning.

The nature of learning

As stated in Chap. 1, learning can be defined as any relatively permanent change in behavior which occurs as a result of experience.[5] This definition stresses three elements. First, learning results in a change in behavior. Second, regardless of the nature of the change, it must last a relatively long time; short-lived behavioral changes due, for example, to fatigue would be ruled out. And third, the change must result primarily from practice and experience, and must not be a consequence of innate behavior alone.

Sometimes it is difficult to determine what is learned and what is innate in a given behavior. For example, we know that the general pattern of the birdsong of a given species is innate, yet its exact pattern depends in part

---

[4] T. G. R. Bower, "The Object in the World of the Infant," *Scientific American,* October 1971, p. 31.

[5] C. T. Morgan and R. A. King, *Introduction to Psychology,* 4th ed., New York: McGraw-Hill Book Company, 1975, p. 97.

on each bird's opportunity to hear other birds of the same species sing "their" song. So we say that such a bird's song is partly learned behavior.

To take a different example, and one that may at first glance seem absurd: we human beings do not have to learn to wake up in the morning, but we do have to learn to roll over and shut off the alarm clock when its ring wakes us. And before that, we have to learn how to set the alarm clock. And before that, to learn how to tell time; before that, to learn numbers and the concepts of "number" and "time"; and so on.

These two examples illustrate three important points about learning and behavior. First, it is not always immediately apparent what is learned and what is not, particularly in our own behavior. Do we learn emotional responses such as smiling and crying? Does an aggressive child learn to be aggressive, as opposed to just being "born that way" (Fig. 5-3)? Is neurotic behavior learned? We now know that the answer to each of these questions is, "In part, yes."

The alarm-clock example illustrates two additional features of human learning, namely, just how much of our behavior is learned and how much of what is learned depends on previous learning. We learn uncountable numbers of things and, having learned them, never give them a second thought.

Types of learning

Three basic types of learning are generally recognized by biologists and psychologists: (1) classical conditioning, also called type I learning; (2) operant conditioning, also called type II learning; and (3) cognitive learning. We may consider the word *conditioning* to be just another word for *learning*. All primates, including man, learn by all three types.

In classical conditioning, or type I learning, new associations are established in reactions involving a specific stimulus and a specific response to that stimulus. For example, if light is shined into a person's eye, the pupils

FIGURE 5-3
An example of learned aggression. The boy on the ground is having a temper tantrum. [*Bacchus, Design Photographers International, Inc.*]

contract. If this light is accompanied by the sound of a bell, the two stimuli become associated and eventually the pupils will contract at the sound of the bell alone. A more realistic example is the mother who teaches her child to fear fire by holding its hand near a flame.

Operant conditioning, or type II learning, occurs as a result of an organism's own activity. Also called *trial-and-error learning,* reward (*reinforcement*) is essential to the process. If reinforcement depends on making a particular response, that response is more likely to occur. For example, a child who wants to get out of the yard first looks at the gate and perhaps whines. It may then shake the gate, accidentally bumping the latch, and the gate swings open. Soon the child is able to open the gate quickly and easily; gate-opening is learned because it is rewarded by the opportunity to cross the street and play.

Cognitive learning is distinguished by the storing of new information and by modifying the meanings and associations of old information. It involves a change in the way learned information is processed. And it also involves relatively permanent changes in behavior in situations where immediate reinforcement (reward) is lacking.[6] For example, rats will learn to find their way through a maze. They will go through it a second, third, and fourth time—each time a little more quickly than the last—even though there is no food or other reward at the end of the maze. Animals in the wild doubtlessly "learn their way around" in much the same way: no immediate reward, such as a meal or a safe haven from a predator, is involved in much of it. Such cognitive learning is sometimes called *latent learning* because the new information that is learned, or the old information that is given new meanings and associations, often is not put to use; that is, it does not appear in behavior until later when there is some occasion to employ it.

Reading this book is a peculiarly human form of cognitive learning in which new information is stored and old information gains new meanings and associations. It is clear that the label, *latent learning,* describes much of what is going on when one reads a book.

There is another type of cognitive learning that is particularly important to man: so-called *imitation learning,* or *modeling.* Children imitate (model) the behavior of adults and other children (Fig. 5-2). The process of *socialization* by which children learn the attitudes, beliefs, and behaviors appropriate to their culture is heavily dependent on imitation learning.

Social learning—developing appropriate behavior toward others and meeting the demands of society—is not a kind of learning in the same sense as are the classical, operant, and cognitive types. However, all three, especially

cognitive and one of its subtypes, imitation learning, are involved in social learning.

An important part of human life, being *taught,* is not a kind of learning, but rather it is an activity which may involve one or more of the basic kinds of learning. Teaching seems to be a uniquely human invention; chimpanzee mothers sometimes appear to encourage certain behaviors in their children, such as walking and following, but it cannot really be said that they teach these or any other activities to their offspring.[7]

Motivation and learning

Finally, it should be noted that most learning does not occur in a vacuum. It must be *motivated. Drive* and *motivation* mean much the same thing. Biologists, and some psychologists, use the first term in discussing basic biological "needs." As we saw in Chap. 1, the basic drives of hunger, self-preservation, sex, and (in mammals) exploration are satisfied by behaviors that are in large part learned. The word *motivation* is more often used when considering complex social situations; in these instances the term *social motives* is commonly used.

All learning need not be initiated by a particular motivated state, or drive. The child might be idly jiggling the gatelatch one day when suddenly it pops open. But the next day, the child's trial-and-error behavior *is* motivated: it is directed toward opening the latch. When the child is able to open that latch whenever it tries, we say that it has *learned* to open the latch, and we also say that its learning behavior was *motivated.*

A great deal of our own behavior is motivated, even if we cannot always define our motivation. Why does one go to college? We may not be entirely sure, but we can probably list several possible motives. We must be aware, however, that many of these social motives are themselves learned. There is, for example, no

[6] Ibid., p. 120.

[7] R. A. Hinde, *Biological Bases of Human Social Behavior,* New York: McGraw-Hill Book Company, 1974, p. 244.

basic biological drive, or motive, to earn money, go to college, or become a doctor, artist, or historian.

This section has dwelt at some length with the nature and kinds of learning because learning plays such an important role in almost everything we do. One of the important things we do—indeed, one of the things that *only we* do—is talk. All three types of learning discussed—classical, operant, and cognitive—play a role in language learning. Conversely, *language, through the human invention of teaching, plays a powerful role in learning.* Any consideration of the human species requires a careful look at that feature which most clearly distinguishes us from other creatures: our use of symbols and language.

Symbols and language

All animals communicate in the sense that one animal transmits information to another in some fashion. The information transmitted may simply indicate an animal's presence; it might also signal alarm, threat, fear, playfulness, sexual interest, etc. Many such signals used by primates were described in Chap. 3; they included gestures, bodily postures, facial expressions, and calls or vocalizations (Fig. 3-14).

Language is a particular kind of communication. It can be defined as a distinctly human system of communicative behavior based on arbitrary vocal symbols. The term "vocal" in this definition asserts the importance of speech in human language. All available evidence confirms the belief that writing is based on speaking. The language of aboriginal peoples is unwritten (Fig. 5-4). All the four to five thousand languages in the world today are spoken. Of those which have a system of writing, that system dates back to relatively recent times (Bronze and Iron Ages).[8] The manner in which children learn their native tongue further supports the belief that the written language of

any people represents an attempt to translate spoken symbols into visual ones.

The word *symbol* in the definition refers to a sound (e.g., a spoken word), a visual form (e.g., a note on a musical score), or a tactile surface (e.g., a word in Braille) that represents something else. The connection between symbol and what the symbol refers to is arbitrary; rarely does the symbol bear any likeness to that which it represents (Fig. 5-5). The words *book, livre,* and книга bear no resemblance either in their sound or their appearance to the object before you. They are arbitrary designations in the English, French, and Russian languages which refer to the same thing.

The design features of language

The linguist Charles F. Hockett has pointed out that human language has certain characteristics, or *design features,* some of which are not found in any other form of animal communication, including that of hominoids. One of these design features, *arbitrariness,* was just discussed. Seven others are particularly significant: (1) discreteness, (2) specialization, (3) duality of patterning, (4) information redistribution, (5) reflexiveness, (6) openness, and (7) displacement.[9]

Discreteness refers to the distinctiveness of word sounds in a language. Word sounds do not blend one into another; "glad" is distinct from "sad." When a contented gibbon is suddenly alarmed, one call grades into the next. The discreteness of language makes communication much more precise.

Specialization refers to the ability of animals to communicate without being totally involved in the physical act of communication. A baboon, for example, can express an appeasement grin as it reaches for food. In man, this feature is particularly well-developed. Two people busily at work can talk about subjects totally unrelated to what they are doing.

Duality of patterning relates to the two

[8] E. A. Hoebel, *Anthropology: The Study of Man,* 4th ed., New York: McGraw-Hill Book Company, 1972, p. 601.

[9] C. F. Hockett, *Man's Place in Nature.* New York: McGraw-Hill Book Company, 1973, pp. 101–115.

FIGURE 5-4
In some cultures there are no books to consult. People must rely on their memory to store the history of their tribe and its culture. Here a Bushman elder passes along information to a group of boys. This knowledge will become part of the memory stores of his listeners, who in turn will pass it on to others. [*Reprinted with permission of Hill and Wang, a division of Farrar, Straus & Giroux, Inc., from Kalahari by Jens Bjerre.*]

subsystems contained in every language. One subsystem consists of meaningless sounds, indicated in written English by single letters of the alphabet or simple combinations of letters such as "th" and "ng." The other subsystem consists of meaningful sounds, indicated in written English by whole words or phrases. Language therefore achieves an enormous richness of expression with great economy of signaling units. A finite number of sounds can be combined and recombined into units of meaning (words), and these units of meaning can be combined and recombined into an infinite variety of sentences, paragraphs, pages, and so on.[10] Duality is an exclusive feature of human language.

Information redistribution is a major biologic function of talking in a human community. The degree to which information is constantly distributed throughout a community by means of language is quite unmatched in any other species. Because of this communicational efficiency, human groups are capable of highly complex cooperative behaviors as well as effective and rapid adjustments to environmental change.

Reflexiveness is a design feature of language by which humans are capable of discussing the very communicational system in which they are carrying on the discussion. This occurs in no other animal. So far as we know, not even chimpanzees hoot at one another about hooting.

Openness or *productivity* refers to the ability of an individual to say something never before said nor heard by that person. Coining a new expression is a common occurrence in human communication. Furthermore, the new expression usually is understood by others. Communication among wild primate populations is closed; a gibbon, for example, has a number of calls but never produces a new call. We should recall, however, that the chimpanzee Washoe (Chap. 2) demonstrated the quality of openness when she invented the sign "waterbirds" for ducks.

Displacement is a feature of language rarely if ever found in other animals. It is the ability to communicate about something in the past, in the future, or far removed in space. Displacement combined with openness enables the speaker to talk about matters that are real or imagined. It empowers the human animal to engage in flights of fancy or creativity, to develop a game or a system of mathematics, or to produce a religious cult or a scientific discipline. Most importantly, it provides the basis

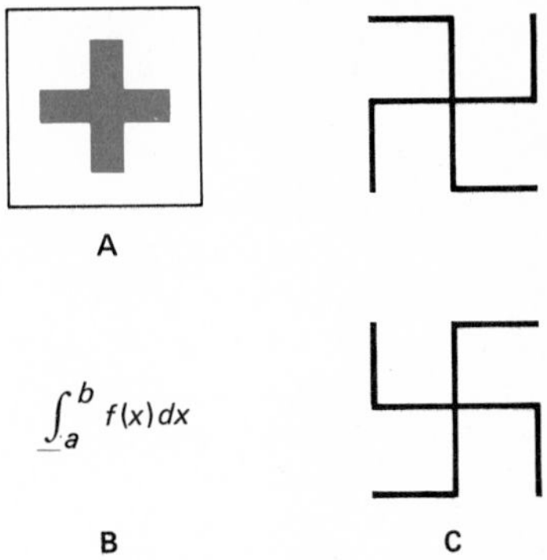

FIGURE 5-5
The arbitrary nature of symbols. (*A*) A symbol that has come to stand for help, charity, and mercy. (*B*) The symbol underlined in color in this mathematical expression has come to mean "the integral of." (*C*) A swastika, the counterclockwise form of which (*above*) was an American Indian sign for good luck, and the clockwise form of which (*below*) was the emblem of Nazi Germany.

on which man can learn from the past and plan for the future.

The language of infants: pivot grammar

When an infant first starts to talk, its speech is closed. What it says has been borrowed (modeled) from an adult and learned as a whole. Before an infant has mastered all of the sounds of its language, however, openness usually begins to develop. At this point and for several months thereafter, the early open system of the child has a characteristic grammatical pattern, *regardless of the language spoken.* This pattern is called *pivot grammar.*[11]

Pivot grammar consists of two parts, *pivots* and *names.* Names include a number of forms that refer to things, people, or impressions, such as *boat, car, milk, Mommy, Daddy, boy, hot,* and *hurt.* Pivots include a smaller number of forms that act as qualifying comments about that which is named, such as *bye-bye, hi,*

---

[10] Ronald Wardhaugh, *Introduction to Linguistics,* New York: McGraw-Hill Book Company, 1972, p. 24.

[11] Hockett, op. cit., pp. 115–117.

night-night, my, all-gone, and *more.* In talking, the child may utter the name (subject) first, followed by the pivot (comment), or vice versa. For example, if a friend leaves, the child may say *boy all gone,* or *all-gone boy.* As a child is carried off to bed, it may turn to a toy and say *night-night car,* or *car night-night.*

At this point the experiments with Washoe and other chimpanzees once again become relevant. Hockett observes:

> *In eleven months Washoe had acquired and was freely using thirty-odd gestures, and was putting them together into composite messages just as do human users of the system. Moreover, she was producing composite messages to which she had not been exposed, and these were intelligible to her human mentors. . . . Her degree of flexibility had become almost an exact match of that of a human child in the pivot-grammar stage. She may or may not pass beyond that stage, but that is already much more than has traditionally been expected from any nonhuman animal. . . .*
>
> *In pivot grammar, thus, we seem to have found a limited variety of openness much older than human language, an inherited kernel on which our cousins the chimpanzees may never have built, but on which all human languages have elaborated and with which each individual human being begins his linguistic life history.*[12]

SOCIAL BEHAVIOR

Now that a foundation has been laid in early emotional development and the ways in which the human species learns and communicates, we are in a position to investigate some of the more important aspects of human social behavior. We will focus specifically on aggression and sociosexual behavior.

[12] Ibid., p. 117.

Aggression[13]

Aggression means many things to many people. The car salesman and his "hard sell" is thought to be aggressive by some, but not by others. There is disagreement as to which of a variety of human behaviors can properly be considered aggressive. We will therefore adopt a narrow definition of aggression, about which few would disagree: human behavior is aggressive if it is directed toward harming others. We will further restrict our definition to the behavior that people direct toward other people; we will not include predation against other species.

Defining human aggression in terms of its intended consequences—that is, harming others—by no means resolves all the complexities of discussing aggressive behavior. Individuals can harm one another in a variety of social contexts. For example, aggressive behavior can be caused by anger or by fear; it is also shown during parental discipline. A study on animals suggests that these and other types of aggression differ not only in the environmental stimuli that trigger them but also in the hormones and the parts of the brain involved.[14] In short, behaviors that have a common consequence may have a variety of causes. Furthermore, when we say behavior that harms others, we must recognize that there are subtle and diverse ways in which, for example, one may inflict physical injury on another. We must also bear in mind that a person may be harmed psychologically as well as physically. No matter how it is defined, aggressive behavior should be viewed as a complex phenomenon.

The adaptive value of aggression

No less complex is the question of the adaptive value of aggression to man and to society. Some argue that aggressive behavior is a part of man's

[13] Much of the source material in this section comes from Hinde, op. cit., pp. 249–254, 272–279, 288–292.
[14] K. E. Moyer, "Kinds of Aggression and Their Physiological Basis," *Communications in Behavioral Biology,* vol. 2, 1968, pp. 65–87.

evolutionary heritage and therefore must be adaptive. Certainly there are societies today in which those who would commit violence stand a better chance of achieving their goals than those who would not. Such behavior, however, is usually harmful to the society in which it occurs.

Some contend that aggression is necessary to maintain social stability — law and order. Society must be based on a hierarchical structure maintained by force or the threat of force. It can, of course, be argued that force might not be necessary if aggressive behavior did not exist. It might also be argued that social stability exists in spite of aggression rather than because of it.

The adaptive value of human aggressiveness is a controversial issue. In today's world of terror groups and mob violence, aggressiveness often is maladaptive and self-defeating (Fig. 5-6). Aggressive behavior undoubtedly has been a powerful biologic asset during the long evolutionary history of hominids. From relatively obscure beginnings 15 or more million years ago, the hominid family has produced a creature who now is the dominant animal all over the earth. Long-range survival at this point, however, may well hinge not on conquest and aggression, but on stability and cooperation. This is a complex issue which will be addressed in greater detail in Section II when we investigate hominid evolution, and in Section III, which deals with the major ecologic problems of our time.

The causes of aggression

The causes of human aggression are undoubtedly related to fear, pain, and frustration brought about both by environmental situations and the physiologic state of the individual (blood-sugar level, state of health, etc.).

The environmental circumstances that provoke aggression are varied and complex. Fear and frustration may arise from what someone has said or is thought to have said;

they may indeed have no basis in fact whatsoever. Whether a frustrated person becomes aggressive depends upon many factors; what that individual thinks of its chances of "getting even" apparently is one of them. There is little doubt, however, that frustration can lead to aggression. As a case in point, a study of the number of lynchings in the southeastern United States from 1882 to 1930 showed that the number tended to rise during periods of economic depression and to fall during periods of economic recovery. The investigators interpreted this as redirected aggression, stemming from frustration caused by economic depression and leveled at victims who could not retaliate.[15] The reader will recall that redirected aggression was discussed in Chap. 3 with respect to dominance among male baboons.

The development of aggression in the child

The specific acts of physical aggression, such as hitting, kicking, biting, and hair-pulling, undoubtedly are learned during play behavior as they are in other primates. These physical acts become associated with aggressiveness — that is, directed toward harming someone — in a complex interaction between the child and its social environment. These interactions foster, in one way or another, the fear, pain, and frustration that lie at the roots of aggression.

Although much has yet to be learned in this area, there are certain social influences which seem to encourage the development of aggressiveness in a child. Lack of parental care and affection are among them. Often aggressive children are the products of families in which arguments, fights, and the infliction of punishment are common occurrences. It also has been found that boys who received minimal restraint and supervision from their parents tend to be more aggressive than boys who are

[15] C. I. Hovland and R. R. Sears, "Minor Studies in Aggression. VI. Correlation of Lynchings with Economic Indices," *Journal of Personality*, vol. 9, 1940, pp. 301–310.

more closely supervised and protected. We saw similar responses among infant rhesus monkeys in Chap. 3.

Overprotection, on the other hand, also may contribute to aggression. If the aggressive behavior of a frustrated child is immediately and consistently rewarded by parental attention and fondling, such behavior is likely to be encouraged through reinforcement. The effectiveness of resorting to the opposite extreme, physical punishment, is uncertain. It appears that punishment tends to reduce aggression against

FIGURE 5-6
Human violence is commonly reflected in the intense rage displayed toward social authority. [*Photograph by Dennis Connor, United Press International, Inc.*]

the punisher but to increase aggressive behavior in general. Aggressiveness probably is best suppressed by rewarding the child for its nonaggressive responses to frustrating situations.

It is quite likely that a child acquires aggressiveness through watching others who are behaving aggressively, particularly if they are liked and respected by the child. The controversial issue of television violence is relevant here, especially the glamorized variety in which killing is shown as an act of heroism, with the gory details and agony removed. There is evidence that viewers may be profoundly influenced by this through observational learning (modeling).[16]

The nature of human aggression

It is commonly contended that the human species is highly aggressive; occasionally we are said to have an "aggressive drive." We tend to forget that by far the greater part of our interpersonal relationships are fundamentally cooperative; such behavior is undramatic and commonplace.

Signs of human submission can be seen on innumerable occasions daily in any part of the world. In its extreme form it is expressed by screaming and crouching. The latter has been stylized in modern society in various forms of greeting, but they share the common effect of reducing the apparent size of the greeter. Kneeling, bowing, curtsying, tipping the hat, saluting (stylized hat removal), and lowering the head and eyes in a kind of anti-stare are common examples. In the huge cities in which we live, we are forced into frequent close contact with countless strangers daily (Fig. 5-7). We suppress aggression by not staring at them and by quickly apologizing when they are accidentally touched.

Human aggression is basically similar to aggressive behavior in other animals. The human capacity for learning and language, however, has enabled man to use aggression in

unusually complicated ways to attain specific social or economic goals. We see this in children, for example, who use aggression as a means of gaining the attention of other children or adults.

A distinctive form of human aggression, rarely, if ever, observed in other animals, involves men acting cooperatively as a group, committing aggression against other men or a group of men. This form of aggression may be divided into two types: mob violence and warfare.

Mob violence   Mob aggression commonly involves a group of individuals who have grown up under frustrating circumstances, such as poverty and inadequate parental care and affection. The cause of frustration may at times be more imagined than real. The incident that triggers violence may be insignificant but usually it symbolizes the real or imagined source of stress.

Once violence erupts, it is not a form of generalized mayhem. Contrary to what is commonly believed, mob violence is aimed at specific objectives which relate to the cause of frustration. Commonly, communication is the primary goal of mob aggression, and selective destruction or threat of destruction is the means to that end. A case in point are the black riots that began to occur in many American cities in 1965.

Within the mob itself, members tend to be united through their common aggressiveness toward outsiders. Aggressive behavior is rewarded by group approval. As a result, group leaders usually become increasingly aggressive and those less aggressive individuals are swept up in the trend. Aggression, in effect, feeds on itself, and the standard of behavior in the mob becomes more violent.

Warfare   Human warfare—that is, a state of open hostile conflict between tribes, states, or nations—has no biologic counterpart. Many animals will attack members of their own species that are strangers. A rat, for example, that enters the wrong nest may be killed. But only

[16] S. Feshbach and R. D. Singer, *Television and Aggression.* San Francisco: Jossey-Bass, Inc., Publishers, 1971.

man unites in a group for the purpose of fighting and killing members of his own kind in another group.

Unlike mob violence, the aggression of warring groups is usually not the result of frustration. Strangely enough, war depends to an important degree upon group loyalty and self-sacrifice.[17] When we humans identify with a group, we tend to be loyal to our fellows and cooperate in the fulfillment of our mutual interests. Any other group that poses a real, or imagined, threat to ours may be attacked. That attack is usually not motivated so much by frustration as it is by a sense of personal commitment to preserving the social order of which we are a part. This by no means reduces the violence and brutality of war. Acts of extreme cruelty and barbarism may be inflicted on men, women, and children. It may be done impersonally by a bomber pilot 9000 meters (about 30,000 feet) in the air. Or it can be done interpersonally by torturing prisoners in concentration camps and gunning down villagers as they flee through the streets.

Sociosexual behavior

As we noted in Chap. 4, the human pair bond is secured by three integrating factors: a high degree of sexual attraction, an almost constant sexual appetite, and highly motivating copulatory rewards. To these three biological features, we should add one more of a social nature, namely, the repressing of human sexuality in public situations.

Clothing is worn, not only because it is climatically suitable but also because it conceals critical erotic regions—the genital area in particular. Physical contact with a stranger in a crowded place is considered rude unless followed by an hasty apology. Sexual arousal from scent glands is prevented by frequent bathing and the use of deodorants. Actions which might stimulate sex interest outside the pair bond are

"just not done," "impolite," "improper," and "in poor taste." The kiss of social greeting is an indifferent peck.

There is a limit to which sexual restraint can be pressed, however. Our highly sexed biological nature rebels at excessive sexual suppression and gives vent to sharply contradictory behavior. Although the female breasts are covered in Western societies, their form is emphasized by low-cut garments, brassieres, and even wax or latex injections. High-heeled shoes exaggerate hip-swinging in the feminine gait. Lipstick conspicuously advertises the sexual attraction of feminine lips. Although women bathe regularly to remove their own sexual scents, they use comparable attractants (musks) secreted by other animals as a base for perfumes. In effect, perfumes overpower the natural product with one borrowed from another creature.

Such behavior in today's crowded world is not surprising. Technological progress has concentrated people in more and more urban centers of ever-increasing size. Countless numbers of individuals are forced to live and move about in close physical proximity to one another. This poses a distinct challenge to a species that is as sexually motivated as we are. Social and economic changes have occurred which have released increasing numbers of women into the work force. Labor-saving devices in the home, the growing awareness that birth control is essential to continued survival, and the ever-burgeoning cost of living have not only freed women for work but often have also required that they work in order to financially support the pair bond.

Our species did not evolve in response to the environment of overcrowded cities, but rather to that of a relatively small tribal unit. Our high degree of sexuality was presumably an adaptation for sustaining the pair bond in relatively small groups that occupied extensive areas. Considered in relationship to the complex heterosexual social contacts of modern society, the continuous expression demanded by human sexuality may be expected to yield

[17] Alison Jolly, *The Evolution of Primate Behavior*, New York: The Macmillan Company, 1972, pp. 271–272.

FIGURE 5-7
Urban dwellers live in close contact with countless strangers, as is shown on this day of leisure at Coney Island. [*Wide World Photos.*]

contradictory results at times. Beyond that, sexual stimulation may be purposefully used by human females as a means of suppressing aggression among males with whom they work.[18] Being sexually attractive not only tends to quench male aggression but also is readily exploitable into improved social status and economic gain without any necessity for promiscuous sexual affairs. There are, of course, varying responses among men and women to this sociosexual interplay, and pair bonds are not uncommonly subjected to great stress in the process. The stereotypes of the buxom secretary, the lecherous boss, and the jealous wife

[18] Desmond Morris, *The Naked Ape,* New York: McGraw-Hill Book Company, pp. 88–91.

are not without foundation in real life.

Excessive sexual stimulation is a natural by-product of the heterosexual contacts of crowded urban living. The pair bond is not fully capable of accommodating this situation, as the high rate of divorce at least partially attests. On the other hand, the record is not all negative. More than 80 percent of all persons over the age of 18 are married, and most copulatory activity still occurs within established pair bonds, either legally sanctioned or otherwise. There is considerable premarital sexual activity but a significant portion of this is between partners who will later become pair-bonded anyway.[19] The pair bond usually prevails, but not without challenge from a society that is overburdened with numbers and the heightened sexual climate it fosters. Surplus sexual stimulation must somehow find outlets whereby it may be drained away safely. The history of sexual suppression is full of psychological disorders and psychopathic crimes.

The drain-off of excessive sexual arousal

An effective relief valve is the indirect sex involvement provided by such communicative media as television, radio, theater, motion pictures, periodicals, novels, and art. Pornography, however that may be defined, apparently runs the gamut from viewing scantily clad persons of the opposite sex to simulated sex acts. The evidence indicates, contrary to popular assumption, that pornography is not associated with an increase in sexual promiscuity or sex crimes. On the contrary, it appears to be beneficial in that it releases sexual "steam" without involving an individual in an extramarital affair. Placing restrictions on viewing the human form also tends to support a widespread belief among Western societies that the human body and sexual behavior are somehow dirty, lewd, and obscene. This archaic notion is a serious obstruction to creating the kind of sympathetic

understanding that is required in developing and preserving a healthy pair bond.

Prostitution is a sexual outlet with a long history. Kinsey's studies purported to show that about 69 percent of the white American male population had patronized a prostitute at least once. Many of these men, however, had done so only once or twice. Although the pros and cons of sex for hire are argued strenuously, prostitution continues to flourish, whether it is legal or not, in every community of any size.

Kinsey estimated that by the age of 40, 50 percent of married males and 26 percent of married females had been involved in extramarital intercourse. Some sociologists today believe that Kinsey's figure for men has not changed but that the figure for married women may now run as high as 40 percent. In some cases, extramarital sex occurs by mutual assent of both spouses and even may strengthen the pair bond between them. The majority of occurrences are in secret and when discovered are a common cause of divorce.

Though our knowledge of heterosexual behavior is far from complete, it greatly exceeds our knowledge of homosexual behavior. Some recent researchers feel that the Kinsey data reflect frequencies that are too high for men and too low for women. It must be granted, as Kinsey and his coworkers were aware, that homosexuality is not absolute but relative. Young adolescent boys and girls are sexually inquisitive and commonly engage in both heterosexual and homosexual exploratory activities. Many adolescent as well as mature mammals behave similarly. Even as adults, our sexual behavior cannot always be clearly divided. There are people whose responses are both homosexual and heterosexual at the same time or at different times in their lives. Among the women interviewed who were 45 years old, Kinsey's data indicated that one or more homosexual experiences were had by (1) 26 percent of those who were single, (2) 3 percent of those married, prior to their marriage, and (3) 10 percent of those previously married, during

---

[19] According to Kinsey's studies, 46 percent of married women had premarital intercourse with their fiancés only. See Kinsey, *Sexual Behavior in the Human Female*, p. 331.

their postmarital life. Among the males questioned, homosexual experiences to the point of one or more orgasms were reported for (1) at least 37 percent of all males between adolescence and old age, and (2) almost 50 percent of those who remained unmarried until age 35, between adolescence and 35. Four percent of the white males in the United States were considered to be exclusively homosexual after adolescence.

The changing sociosexual environment

Human sociosexual behavior in many societies may be in the process of undergoing some rather basic changes. Increasing numbers of women feel — justly so — that the female can be as productive outside the home as the male. Many of the traditional divisions of labor between the sexes are breaking down both inside and outside the home. In short, many of the social factors contributing to behavioral differences between the sexes are disappearing or losing their effectiveness.[20] Insofar as behavior is concerned, we may speculate that this could ultimately lead to an increase in the "masculinity" of women and the "feminimity" of men.

Man's overriding problem today is numbers. As we shall see in Section III, overpopulation breeds not only economic bankruptcy, misery, and starvation but stress and aggression as well. We should begin achieving the same reduction in births that we have in deaths. Curtailing the reproductive capacity of the pair bond undoubtedly will require some modification in our sexual attitudes. Whatever these modifications may be, they probably will not be successful if they try to suppress or effectively diminish our innate and irrepressible sexual urges. Neither are they likely to succeed if they permit the outlets of sexual expression to swamp the social unit which our sexual behavior has evolved to protect, namely a viable family unit and pair-bond relationship. That, of course, is part of the population problem.

SOCIAL ORGANIZATION

Every society, whether it be the Ngatatjara people, or the people of the United States, of Kenya, or of China is composed of groups. A family is a group. So is a Ngatatjara hunting party, a Boy Scout troop, a Sunday school class, a church, General Motors, a college sorority, a football team, or two people playing tennis. Society itself is a group. The number of groups in a complex industrialized society probably exceeds the number of people in the society because the great majority of individuals are members of several groups. A woman may be wife and mother in a family, an active alumna in her college sorority, a member of the Parent-Teacher Association, a participant on a bowling team, a member of the legal profession, politically active in the Democratic party, and a citizen of the United States. Obviously, she is also female. We have listed eight groups to which this woman belongs. If we add that she is also red-headed, however, that does not place her in another group. What, then, does the sociologist mean when the term *group* is used?

A social group is not merely an aggregation of people like the occupants of a subway car, nor is it a category that can be defined solely by some physical trait such as hair color. A social group is an aggregation whose members act together in a joint effort to satisfy certain common needs, and who share a sense of common identity.[21] Even as United States citizens we are members of a national group. We act together in political campaigns, the payment of taxes, and obedience to law. And we share a sense of common identity, symbolized by our flag and national anthem, which sets us apart from the citizens of other countries.

The concept of the social group is not merely a convenient device for analyzing and categorizing human social organization. The

---

[20] Hinde, op. cit., pp. 308–309.

[21] G. Lenski and J. Lenski, *Human Societies,* 2d ed., New York: McGraw-Hill Book Company, 1974, pp. 40–41.

social group is an essential part of the socio-biological environment of man. Human behavior is controlled by group experience to a very significant degree. Studies of the behavior of soldiers under combat conditions give powerful testimony of this. For example, during World War II, units of German soldiers continued to resist long after their cause had become hopeless. Group loyalty and self-sacrifice sustained them until they were physically overpowered and separated from the remaining members of their combat unit.[22]

Major types of groups

In-groups and out-groups

In-groups are any groups to which "we" belong, such as our family or our church. Groups to which we do not belong are *out-groups;* these are the groups to which "they" belong. We are more deeply involved in some in-groups than in others. We may be staunch Catholics but indifferent Republicans. We also may not feel equally removed from all our out-groups; as Catholics we would probably find Episcopalians less alien than Buddhists. In some instances, on the other hand, we might have trouble distinguishing strangers from enemies.

Human behavior is strongly influenced by the interaction between members of in-groups and out-groups. In-group members expect one another to be loyal and helpful. From an out-group we may expect anything from indifference to hostility. A threat from an out-group, whether imagined or real, tends to intensify the solidarity of an in-group and may set the stage for conflict.

Members of out-groups are generally stereotyped as a class rather than considered as individuals. They may be viewed as "untrustworthy," "aggressive," "not very bright," or even "something less than human." Consequently, in case of conflict, otherwise kind and

compassionate people may be moved to acts of brutality.

Primary and secondary groups

A *primary group* consists of people whom we know intimately. A family and a clique (circle of close friends) are primary groups. Such groups are characterized by informality, strong emotional ties, and a sense of belonging. It is in the primary group that the human animal can satisfy its need for social interaction. As a consequence, these groups are very influential in shaping our character and behavior. We generally develop an intense loyalty for our primary groups and their members, even to the point of sacrificing our lives, if necessary, to secure their welfare.

Secondary groups, on the other hand, are formal and impersonal; they are focused on serving a particular function or achieving a specific goal. The corporations and bureaucracies of business, industry, and government as well as their subsidiary divisions, and the countless smaller agencies that service them, are all secondary groups (Fig. 5-8). Many of these groups—all of them, in the long view of human evolutionary history—have developed from primary groups. The consolidated school district of a large city had its beginnings in the "little red schoolhouse" where an intimate group of a few children and one teacher remained together for years.

The rise of modern industrialized societies has been distinguished by an enormous increase in the number, size, and complexity of secondary groups. Despite this, however, the two major primary groups, the clique and the family, seem to be stronger than ever.[23] Almost every secondary group harbors a number of cliques—small intimate groups of people who work together and share similar needs and hopes. And, with abundant leisure time and a high standard of living, the modern family is becoming more of a companionship group.

---

[22] P. B. Horton and C. L. Hunt, *Sociology,* 3d ed., New York: McGraw-Hill Book Company, 1972, pp. 157–160.

[23] Ibid., pp. 168–170.

The family

In one form or another, the family is found in every human society. It is the foundation on which human culture rests. In order to better explore the significance of the family, we consider first its structure and then its functions.

The structure of the family

Types of families Families are of two basic types, the *nuclear* and the *extended*. A nuclear family consists of a man, his wife (or wives), and their unmarried children. The married adults are the core (nucleus) of the family. An extended family is commonly composed of a group of sisters and their offspring (the matrilineal form) or a group of brothers and their offspring (the patrilineal form). A group of brothers and sisters (sibs) is the core of an extended family (Fig. 5-9).

The nuclear family is characteristic of our own as well as other highly industrialized societies where great family mobility is required. The extended family is found in relatively nonindustrialized or partially industrialized farming or hunting societies. It provides, among other things, the labor force for the family farm or hunting territory.

Forms of marriage All societies enforce a definite set of rules whereby two or more persons establish a family and direct its course. Every society, for example, requires that one's mate be chosen from outside one's own group. This is known as *exogamy*. In our own society, we may not marry close relatives such as a brother, sister, or first cousin. In some societies one must marry outside one's village or tribe. The mating of individuals within such groups is called *incest* and every society has restrictions — *incest taboos* — against the mating or marriage of such individuals.

The majority of societies also advocate that mates belong *to* a certain group (*endogamy*). One's mate should be chosen within the tribe, within a certain social caste, from the membership of a particular religious sect, and so on.

Exogamy and endogamy may be interwoven in a great variety of ways, depending upon the culture. Among Ngatatjara people, for example, a member of a nuclear family is compelled to marry someone from another nuclear family, and the married couple must live in the territory of the husband's group. Each nuclear family is, therefore, a part of a larger extended family. A system of exchange prevails by which a man usually marries a granddaughter of his mother's uncle; his own sisters marry his wife's brothers. In this way different groups are united by kinship ties but the individual unions are exogamous.

Societies also specify what shall be sanctioned insofar as *monogamy* and *polygamy* are concerned. Monogamy is a union in which a man can be married to only one woman at any given time and vice versa. Polygamy is a union involving several husbands or several wives. *Polygyny* is a polygamous marriage of one husband to several wives; *polyandry* is a polygamous marriage of several men to one woman, and occurs only rarely. Of all societies in the world today, 16 percent restrict marriages to monogamous unions, and 84 percent either sanction (44 percent) or permit (40 percent) polygynous unions.[24] Even in polygynous cultures, however, most marriages are monogamous. Only relatively successful males are generally able to afford more than one wife at a time.

Functions of the family

In any discussion of family functions, however brief, it should be understood that the family usually does not stand alone. Religious, educational, and governmental institutions are directly or indirectly involved in many familial activities. The state prescribes innumerable controls over the family which affect the marriage contract, the marriageable age, the obligations of family members to one another, the conditions for divorce, and so on. Nonetheless

[24] Hoebel, *Anthropology*, p. 429.

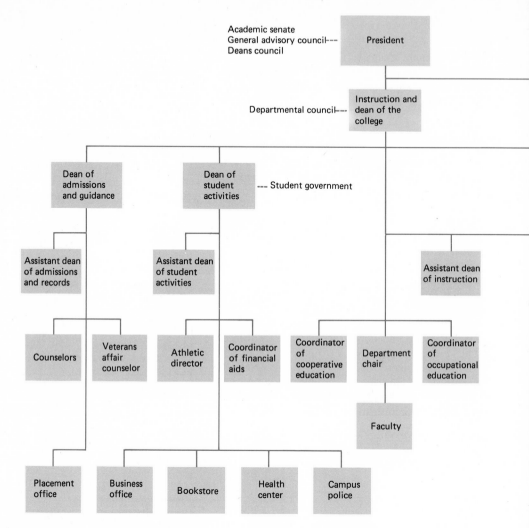

FIGURE 5-8
A college is a secondary group which, in turn, is composed of many smaller secondary groups. This fact is reflected in the organization chart of a community college in California. The faculty consists of an instructional staff of 306 in 23 departments.

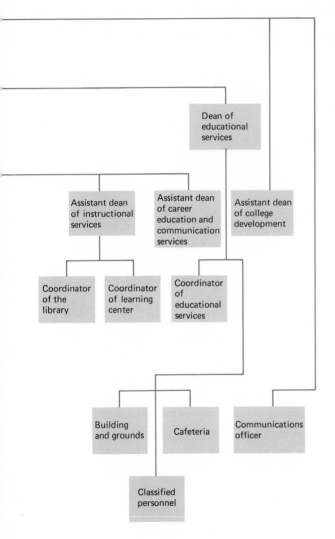

Dean of educational services

Assistant dean of instructional services

Assistant dean of career education and communication services

Assistant dean of college development

Coordinator of the library

Coordinator of learning center

Coordinator of educational services

Building and grounds

Cafeteria

Communications officer

Classified personnel

there are a number of functions that are effectively realized only through the agency of the human family. It is the center of action where certain essential social tasks are performed. We can arbitrarily divide them into five categories: (1) sexual regulation; (2) reproduction; (3) cultural transmission; (4) protection, support, and behavioral development; and (5) status and social recognition. In technologically simple societies the family also has an important economic function. Family members act as a work force on a farm, or as hunter-gatherers like the Ngatatjara, sharing in the products of their labor.

Sexual regulation   Every culture has a system of procedures to accommodate the satisfaction of sexual desires as well as to control sexual activities. Most cultures, for example, encourage premarital intercourse as preparation for marriage. Family structure is generally so designed that children born out of wedlock pose no problem for family or child. Some societies —especially many of the so-called "primitive" ones—provide sexual outlets for virtually all adults. A widow may automatically become the wife of her dead husband's brother. Similarly, a widowed or even unmarried man occasionally is allowed to have intercourse with his brother's wife. Western societies generally have made no socially acceptable provisions for the sexual gratification of the widowed and unmarried.[25]

Reproduction   All societies depend upon the family for the production of children. It is also within the family as a social institution that a legal father is established for every woman's child and a legal mother for every man's child. As a result, social responsibility becomes fixed on both the production and rearing of children.

Cultural transmission   The transmission of learned behavior from one generation to the next begins in the family. The child first learns

[25] Horton and Hunt, op. cit., p. 205.

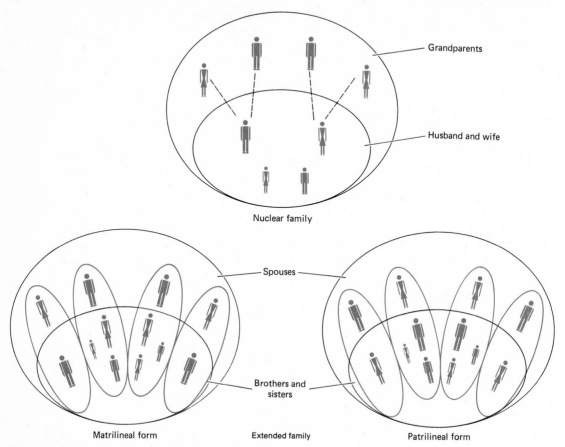

FIGURE 5-9
Types of human families. The *nuclear* family consists of a husband and his wife (or wives) and their children. The core (nucleus) of the family is the husband and wife (or wives). An *extended* family consists of brothers and sisters (sibs) and their children. The core of the extended family is the brothers and sisters. There are two types of extended family: the *matrilineal* form consists of brothers and sisters, and the children of the sisters, whereas the *patrilineal* form consists of brothers and sisters, and the children of the brothers.

how to talk from its parents. It learns how to use eating utensils, how to dress, how to greet people, how mothers and fathers behave, how to tell right from wrong, and many more of the myriad "hows," "whats," and "whys" that make up a culture. Once the child is in school, the environment of the home continues to be instrumental in determining the effectiveness of the learning process.

Protection, support, and behavioral development Between birth and maturity, human young have a prolonged period during which they are dependent upon their parents. With the increase in complexity of society, this period of dependency becomes prolonged even more. Throughout this period the child needs protection from the many hazards that might harm it. It also requires adequate food, shelter, clothing, and health care as well as a stimulating social relationship both with its parents and its peers. With these requirements met, the child stands a good chance of reaching maturity and doing so with minimal exposure to fear, pain, and frustration from which aggressive behavior springs. The human family seems to have demonstrated itself better able to meet these requirements than any other social institution.

Status and social recognition   A family may be characterized by a number of status rankings. In our society, for example, a family may be white, middle-class, Protestant, and Democrat, with both spouses college-educated and both white-collar workers. A child of that family bears the family name and is socially recognized in terms of the statuses that distinguish the family. It is through belonging to a family that we first gain social identification and recognition.

It would be difficult indeed to overstate the significance of the family in human life and society. It is the foundation on which human culture rests.

CULTURE

Culture was discussed briefly in Chap. 1. At this point we should consider it once again because most of what we have covered in this chapter deals with various facets of culture. Much of learning, virtually everything there is to language, most of social behavior, and everything we have mentioned about social organization are important aspects of culture.

In order to further clarify what is meant by culture, we should perhaps consider what it is commonly but mistakenly thought to be. Culture often is incorrectly used in the sense that it has something to do with the amount of one's formal education, one's personal refinement, or one's appreciation of the fine arts. Societies often are similarly evaluated in these terms. A given society may be considered "uncultured" because it provides little if any formal education for its members and has no written literature. Culture is not a level of sophistication nor is it something that some people have and others do not. All societies have a culture and all persons, except perhaps some of the insane, are "cultured."

Culture refers to everything that is socially learned and shared by the people in a society.[26] It consists of a social heritage comprised of both material and nonmaterial elements. *Material culture* includes the objects and physical conditions which man makes or contributes to, such as bridges, books, houses, backgammon sets, snowmobiles, and air pollution. *Nonmaterial culture* consists of the way people behave, how they think, what they believe and know, and how they feel about right and wrong, justice, beauty, and "the good life." And finally, human culture holds yet another ingredient, namely, that our material and nonmaterial cultures are both dependent upon the use of symbols and language.[27] Almost all of everything that is socially learned and shared by members of a society is passed from individual to individual and from generation to generation by means of symbol and language. Building a bridge depends upon the knowledge of how to build a bridge, and that knowledge is communicated by symbols.

Culture is the one thing that most clearly sets the human animal apart from other creatures. In the next section we will investigate human evolution and speculate about how the cultured animal came to be.

[26] Ibid., p. 48.
[27] Lenski and Lenski, op. cit., pp. 16–17.

SUGGESTED READINGS

GREENOUGH, W. T. (ed.): *The Nature and Nurture of Behavior: Developmental Psychobiology.* San Francisco: W. H. Freeman and Company, 1973. Readings from *Scientific American* on factors influencing the development of human behavior.

HINDE, R. A.: *Biological Bases of Human Social Behavior,* New York: McGraw-Hill Book Company, 1974. The cause and development of diverse behaviors in fish, birds, nonhuman primates, and man are covered, including discussions on motivation, communication, aggression, sociosexual behavior and group structure.

HOEBEL, E. A.: *Anthropology: The Study of Man,* 4th ed., New York: McGraw-Hill Book Company, 1972. A textbook of general anthropology, most of which deals with the nature of culture, social structure, and symbolic expression.

HORTON, P. B., and C. L. HUNT: *Sociology,* 3d ed., New York: McGraw-Hill Book Company, 1972. A clearly written text on the nature of culture, social organization, social interaction and social change.

MONTAGU, M. F. ASHLEY (ed.): *Culture: Man's Adaptive Dimension,* New York: Oxford University Press, 1968. Nine essays on culture as a biological adaptation.

MORGAN, C. T., and R. A. KING: *Introduction to Psychology,* 4th ed., New York: McGraw-Hill Book Company, 1975. A popular psychology text devoted to the development of behavior, learning, language and thought, motivation, emotion, perception, social processes, and individual differences (intelligence, personality, and behavior disorders).

WARDHAUGH, R.: *Introduction to Linguistics,* New York: McGraw-Hill Book Company, 1972. This small book is addressed to beginning students interested in the nature of language.

WILSON, E. O.: *Sociobiology: The New Synthesis,* Cambridge, Mass.: Harvard University Press, 1975. An outstanding book that deals comprehensively with the biologic (genetic and evolutionary) basis of all social behavior. Although diverse animal species are considered, the human animal receives a great deal of attention.

REVIEW QUESTIONS

1 The human infant is born into the world with many behavioral predispositions. Name ten.

2 According to van Hooff, what is the evolutionary origin of the human smile and human laughter?

3 Human beings have a remarkable capacity for learning. Three basic types of learning are generally recognized. Identify them and briefly describe each.

4 Hockett has shown that human language has certain design features. List eight of them and describe three which are not found in any other form of animal communication.

5 What is pivot grammar? Of what significance is it to human language?

6 Cite what are believed to be three basic causes of human aggression, and give three examples of different social influences which seem to encourage the development of aggressiveness in children.

7 In what respects is warfare an unusual form of aggression?

8 Critically evaluate the social value of two of the following: pornography, prostitution, extramarital intercourse.

9 Why is it difficult to make a clear distinction between homosexuality and heterosexuality?

10 Distinguish between the following: (*a*) in-groups and out-groups; (*b*) primary groups and secondary groups.

11 A number of important social functions are performed only through the agency of the human family. Identify five of these functions and discuss three of them in some detail.

12 Write a short essay on the nature of culture, what it means, and what it includes and consists of.

The past is but the beginning of a beginning,
and all that is and has been
is but the twilight of the dawn   H. G. WELLS

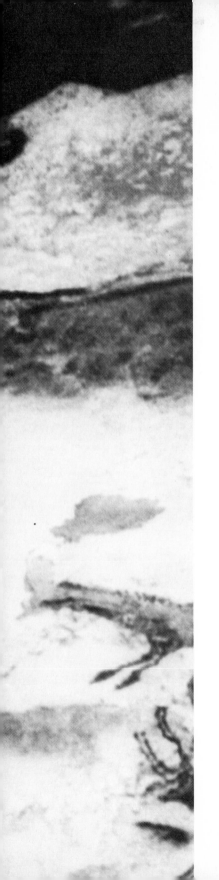

SECTION II

Twenty-five thousand years ago the earliest known paintings first appeared on the walls of caves in what is now southern France. These paintings, famous for their artistry as much as for their age, signal both a beginning and an end in the long evolutionary history of life on earth: They announce with stunning clarity the advent of *modern man, Homo sapiens.* Between the first entry of modern man into the fossil record about 100,000 years ago and the appearance of cave paintings, our species produced no artifact so distinctively and characteristically human as these first representations of animals. Today, 1,000 generations later, they remain immediately recognizable to other humans.

As such they are truly the beginning of a beginning, the twilight of a dawn that has seen in the past 5,000 years an almost explosively rapid development of human culture and technology. It may well be that this development is itself only a beginning and that, in H. G. Well's words, "A day will come when beings who are now latent in our thoughts and hidden in our loins . . . shall laugh and reach out their hands amid the stars."

But every beginning has a past which has given rise to that beginning. It is the past of *Homo sapiens* that we will be concerned with in this section — what is our biological past and how did it give rise to our species? The first two chapters of the section deal with our biological past: Chapter 6 is an account of hominid evolutionary history from early primates to the earliest members of the genus *Homo;* Chapter 7 continues the evolutionary narrative to modern *Homo sapiens* in the twentieth century.

The last three chapters deal with the evolutionary mechanisms and processes that gave rise not only to humans but to all living forms. Evolution depends upon the capacity of organisms to vary. Chapter 8 discusses this evolutionary prerequisite and provides an introduction to the basic principles of genetics, i.e., of heredity. The nature of evolutionary processes is considered in Chapter 9. Chapter 10 concludes the section and is devoted to evolutionary outcomes. The consequences of evolution are either extinction or adaptation. Accordingly, the chapter ends with a discussion of human adaptiveness.

HUMAN EVOLUTION

SIX

HOMINID EVOLUTIONARY HISTORY I:
From Early Primate to Early *Homo*

To this point we have addressed the question: Who are we? In doing so, we have placed the human species in context with other living things as one of many different primate mammals. Our status as a primate is not an arbitrary assignment made for convenience but a genuine relationship determined by common descent. We have seen what some of our living relatives are like, and we have portrayed in broad perspective the essential qualities that set us apart as a unique species.

We shall now turn our attention to the historical problem of our origin and evolutionary background: Where did we come from? What are the pathways of common descent that link us with our primate relations? We will attempt to answer these questions in two stages. In this chapter we will confine ourselves to the record of hominid evolution from early primate to early *Homo*. In the next chapter we will investigate the hominid evolutionary record from early hominid to modern man.

INTRODUCTORY CONCEPTS

The record of these events is to be found in the fossil remains of organisms preserved in the rocks. The most impressive feature of this record is the unimaginable time span that it encompasses. The oldest primate fossil yet discovered is that of a prosimian found in a geologic layer which also held the remains of one of the last dinosaurs, *Triceratops*. This deposit is of Upper Cretaceous age (Fig. 2-13), approximately 80 million years old. Perhaps we can best appreciate such an immense period of time by a calendar-and-clock time analogy. Suppose we let January 1 of one year to January 1 of the following year represent 80,000,000 years. On this scale, the oldest known fossil of *Homo sapiens* (about 250,000 years old) would appear on our calendar and clock at 8:38 P.M., December 29 and the first Egyptian dynasty (about 3300 B.C.) would be a little past 11:25 P.M. December 31, less than 35 minutes before the end of the year. A human lifetime of 75 years would be over in less than 30 seconds. It is with this perspective that the chronicle we are about to relate must be viewed.

The nature of fossils

Another significant feature of the fossil record is the nature of the fossils themselves and the rocks in which they are found. The remains or traces of ancient primates can take several forms. The skeleton and teeth are, with few exceptions, the only body structures that are found fossilized. Isolated teeth, jaws or portions of jaws with teeth, and skulls or skull fragments are the most common, probably because these parts are least often consumed by predators and scavengers. Teeth are the most useful diagnostic structures a paleontologist has in classifying a fossil specimen. Biologists who classify living mammals consider dentition one of their most reliable anatomical clues. It is sometimes possible to identify a genus and even a species on the basis of a single tooth, with the aid of computerized multivariate analysis.[1] The teeth of an animal, and the way their surfaces are worn down, also reveals much about dietary habits.

The inner surface of the braincase or the cranial portions of skulls reflect the size, configuration, and major surface features of the brain. Casts known as *endocasts* can be prepared from these surfaces to simulate the brain that was housed inside (Fig. 6-1). Heavy crests and ridges on the outside of the skull or other skeletal elements indicate the attaching sites of especially powerful muscles. Occasionally bones of the trunk and appendages are preserved. These may throw light on body size and proportion, arm-length to leg-length ratios, and locomotor behavior. Fossil footprints have been discovered in at least one instance which indicated they were made by fully erect adolescent hominids who may have been engaged in a ritualistic dance.

Fossil feces (*coprolites*) as well as ancient living sites commonly contain fossil pollen. Plant species usually can be identified from the pollen they produce. Knowledge of the plant species that lived in an area reveals a great deal about climate and habitat. Often, fossil pollen can establish whether a given area was a frigid tundra, an arid savanna, a temperate woodland, or a tropical rain forest countless millennia in the past. An inventory of all the animal fossils found with the remains of a fossil primate contributes further to an understanding of the kind of environment the primate lived in. If the skeletal remains of some of these animals are found on ancient living floors in association with primitive stone tools, one may reasonably assume that these animals were being eaten by a manlike creature, especially if some of the bones had been broken open so as to expose the edible marrow.

---

[1] A computer analysis in which every significant dimension of an unclassified object (e.g., fossil tooth) is compared with corresponding dimensions of similar classified objects (e.g., teeth of known species); often millions of mathematical comparisons are made.

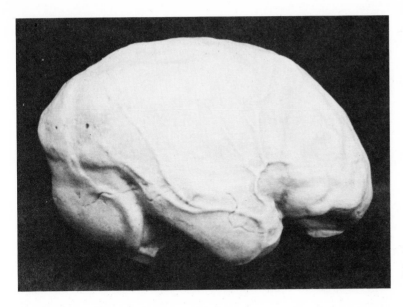

FIGURE 6-1
A plaster endocast of the brain of a fossil hominid prepared from the inner surface of the skull's braincase.

The sedimentary rock layers (*strata*) which contain primate fossils also carry clues about climate and habitat. The physical qualities of rock particles and crystals, their chemical characteristics, and the kinds of fossils entombed in the rock will indicate how the original sediments which comprise the rock accumulated in the first place. They could have been (1) laid down as ash from volcanic eruption, (2) carried and deposited by wind under arid conditions, or (3) deposited by water along the margins of a swamp, the banks of a river, the shores of a lake, or an ocean beach. Fossil shellfish such as clams can even tell us the temperature of the water when they were alive. Depending upon the temperature, shellfish have been found to show a preference for a chemical "cousin" (*isotope*) of oxygen, oxygen 18. Since molluscan shells, and many others for that matter, are composed of oxygen-containing carbonates, an analysis can be made of the relative amounts of oxygen isotopes in the shell. The technique is accurate within 1°C of water temperature.

Gathering and analyzing these kinds of evidence requires the painstaking collaborative efforts of many individuals from a variety of scientific fields. Geologists, paleontologists, anthropologists, archaeologists, zoologists, botanists, comparative anatomists, chemists, and computer analysts are represented; pathologists also are helpful in diagnosing the occasional lesion found in fossil bone. Prospective sites for exploratory work require extensive planning. The actual work of excavation demands technical expertise; it is done cautiously, painstakingly, and systematically. The position of every fossil and artifact is recorded as well as photographed before it is removed from its natural resting place for shipment to the laboratory for detailed study (Fig. 6-2). It is not a job for amateur rock hounds and fossil hunters; their clumsy, haphazard diggings have ruined many potentially fruitful sites for all time.

The identification of fossil species

The end product of team-oriented paleontologic exploration and research is a knowledge of life in the past—incomplete, certainly—but detailed enough that we may gain some under-

FIGURE 6-2
The excavation of fossils and ancient living sites requires thorough preliminary planning, painstaking care, and many scientific skills. [*Courtesy of Robert Pence, Los Angeles Pierce College.*]

standing of the evolutionary history of existing species. This introduces yet another distinctive feature of the fossil record, namely, how extinct species are identified and distinguished. A living species is usually defined as the largest natural population of organisms which may interbreed to produce fully fertile offspring. Such a definition obviously is not applicable to fossils. We must describe and distinguish extinct organisms on the basis of the characteristics of their remains. In actual practice, however, most living species are also *identified* by their external and anatomical traits. Species descriptions list a number of diagnostic characteristics and indicate the range of variation found in each. Organisms that do not fall within these prescribed limits belong to another species. This pertains to fossil specimens as well. If the remains of a number of fossil individuals do not fall within the range of variation of any living species, then these fossils represent one or more species which are no longer living today. If these same fossils do not differ from one another more than living members of a similar species do, then these fossils are representatives of one extinct species. These considerations are equally applicable to higher categories in the classification hierarchy. A group of fossil specimens representing more than one species may be grouped within one genus if they do not differ from one another more than living members of a similar genus. This fossil genus may be considered to be a unique group if its members do not fall within the range of variation of a living genus.

Time-bounded species (paleospecies)

When we turn to species distinctions in the time sequence of an ancestor → descendant lineage, however, the boundary in time between an ancestral species and its modern descendant cannot be drawn accurately. If the lineage of modern man, for example, is traced back in time for several thousand generations, populations will be encountered that are progressively less like modern *Homo sapiens*. If this backtracking of our lineage is continued to populations that lived 500,000 years ago, the individ-

uals were sufficiently distinguishable from modern man that they are placed in another species, *Homo erectus*. If the lineage of this ancient species is similarly traced backward for another 2 million years, the population had changed enough that some of them at least were members of a different genus, namely *Australopithecus*.[2] Most human biologists agree that a species of *Australopithecus, Homo erectus,* and *Homo sapiens* comprise a lineage group. It is impossible, however, to set a precise boundary in time when that species of *Australopithecus* became *Homo erectus,* or when *H. erectus* became *H. sapiens* (Fig. 6-3). We are dealing with an uninterrupted sequence of successive hominid generations, perhaps more than 85,000 of them in this 2½-million-year span. Any line of demarcation which would separate an ancestral species from its descendant species would have to separate some parental generation from its offspring. Such a division could not be made accurately.

We must conclude that "boundaries" between time-successive species (*paleospecies*) are

---

[2] This is a complex issue which we will discuss more fully later in this chapter.

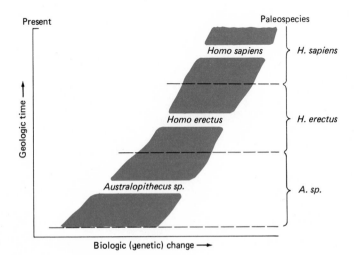

FIGURE 6-3

Biologic species and paleospecies. A biologic species is a natural population distributed in space at a given time. A paleospecies represents the successive generations of a natural population distributed over a period of geologic time. If a given paleospecies *A* gradually changed (evolved) over thousands of generations into another paleospecies *A'*, it is impossible to set a precise boundary in time when *A* became *A'*. For example, in the lineage *Australopithecus sp.* → *Homo erectus* → *Homo sapiens,* it is not possible to distinguish with any accuracy a late population of the paleospecies *H. erectus* from an early population of the paleospecies *H. sapiens.* Thus the dashed horizontal lines represent indefinite, arbitrary "boundaries." (*Australopithecus sp.* indicates a particular but unspecified species of *Australopithecus.*)

arbitrary. Usually they are placed where there is a gap in the fossil record. This works reasonably well, but only until paleontologists discover the fossils which fill the gap (as they sometimes do).

Parallel evolution

One other facet of evolutionary change should be described before we consider the chronicle of primate evolution. During the course of evolution, it is common for different kinds of primates to develop adaptations that enable them to follow similar life styles. An extinct Malagasy lemur, the modern spider monkey of the New World, and the gibbon of Asia, are (and presumably were) efficient brachiators. The ring-tailed lemur of Madagascar and the savanna baboon of Africa are adapted to semi-terrestrial living. This phenomenon is called *parallel evolution*, and results in two or more primates sharing similar adaptations. These similarities, however, do not suggest that the animals in question are necessarily closely related through common evolutionary descent. Rather, they testify to the adaptability of diverse primate families that have lived under similar environmental conditions.

With an awareness of the nature of the fossil record and some of the features of evolutionary change, we can now focus our attention on the details of primate evolution, insofar as they are known. We will begin with the origin of mammals because primates are mammals and many of the characteristics which contribute to the success of primates are shared by all creatures with a mammalian heritage.

FIGURE 6-4
Life on a Jurassic landscape 160 million years ago. Reptiles were the dominant animals, ranging from huge to small, and filling diverse ecologic niches. Mammals were small, uncommon, and of relatively few types. [*Peabody Museum, Yale University.*]

THE ORIGIN AND EVOLUTION OF MAMMALS

The first mammals evolved approximately 180 million years ago from a group of mammallike reptiles.[3] These ancient mammals were few in total numbers, lacking in species diversity, and small in size. They were to retain this status for 100 million years or more because they were born into a world dominated by reptiles (Fig. 6-4). The Mesozoic era, often called the Age of Reptiles, lasted from 230 million B.P. (years before the present) to 65 million B.P. (Fig. 6-5). It was a time in earth history during which the

[3] At about the same time, or a little later, the earliest birds arose from a group of dinosaurlike reptiles.

present continents were not separated by wide expanses of ocean but united into one large supercontinent known as *Pangea* (Fig. 6-6). High mountain ranges were lacking and moisture-laden masses of air could move far inland to distribute rainfall more or less evenly over the land surface. The climate probably was warm and varied relatively little over most of the world. Broad shallow arms of the sea spread over portions of the supercontinent. Much of the land was covered by extensive swamps and marshes. It was the kind of world to which reptiles of all types were adapted. The familiar turtles, crocodiles, and lizards of today were well represented by their ancient forebears. Their numbers were enormously augmented by reptilian species that are now long extinct: the aerial pterosaurs; the aquatic plesiosaurs, mosasaurs, and ichthyosaurs; and the terrestrial and amphibious dinosaurs. They varied from carnivorous to herbivorous and omnivorous; from huge to large, medium, and small. Some pterosaurs had an estimated wingspan of 15 meters (50 feet) and the terrestrial dinosaur *Brontosaurus* probably weighed 40 tons. On the other hand, some dinosaurs were no larger than small chickens.

For 160 million years reptiles reigned supreme. But during this time, geologic events were taking place which ultimately would bring this reign to a close. The supercontinent of Pangea began to break up into continental blocks and islands which slowly drifted away from one another (Fig. 6-6). The shallow arms of inland seas gradually retreated from the land as pressures within the earth produced land uplift and mountain building. Such changes affected the nature and course of ocean currents as well as the distribution of rainfall over continental areas. World climate was changing. Populations of land vertebrates that once had access to an entire supercontinent were being segregated and isolated on separate land masses. The scene was being set for major evolutionary changes: a new world was slowly but surely in the making.

During the Cretaceous period the nature

of this new world began to be revealed (Fig. 6-5). Increasing numbers of reptilian species were becoming extinct. Mammals, on the other hand, were gaining a new hold on life. The first placental mammals were small animals belonging to the order Insectivora. By late Cretaceous, before the rhinoceroslike dinosaur *Triceratops* had become extinct, the insectivorelike prosimians had evolved. Ecologic opportunity finally had arrived for mammals. Reptilian extinctions were leaving innumerable *ecologic niches*—habitats and food sources—vacant and available to the first vertebrate that could claim them. Apparently a major qualification for success was warm-bloodedness. From those days forward, birds have been the preeminent vertebrates of the air while mammals have commanded the land and the waters below.[4]

[4] An interesting hypothesis suggests that dinosaurs were also warm-blooded and that only the large species became extinct; the small ones were the ancestors of modern birds and, as such, still persist. See R. T. Bakker, "Dinosaur Renaissance," *Scientific American*, April 1975, pp. 58–78.

FIGURE 6-5
Divisions of geologic time during which mammals and primates evolved, with approximate time to the beginning of each in millions of years. Primates referred to in the text are listed in the column on vertebrate life. (See also Fig. 2-13.)

Era	Period	Epoch	Vertebrate life (esp. primates)
Cenozoic (65) Age of Mammals and Birds	Quaternary (2–3)	Recent (0.025)	Modern man from "the golden age of prehistory" (Upper Paleolithic cultures) to the present.
		Pleistocene (2–3)	Genus *Homo* evolved; early, middle, and late Stone Age cultures (Lower, Middle, and Upper Paleolithic industries).
	Tertiary (65)	Pliocene (12)	Early toolmaking hominids (*Australopithecus*); oldest fossil found, 5.5 million years old.
		Miocene (25)	The dryopithecine group of pongids and the earliest hominid, *Ramapithecus*.
		Oligocene (36)	Early monkeys (*Apidium, Parapithecus*); early apes (*Aegyptopithecus, Aelopithecus*).
		Eocene (58)	Early lemuroids (*Notharctos, Smilodectes*); early tarsioids (*Necrolemur*).
		Paleocene (65)	Early insectivorelike primates.
Mesozoic (230) Age of Reptiles	Cretaceous (135)		Earliest primates (*Purgatorius*). Diverse reptilian types but many became extinct by the end of the period. Mammals begin to diversify.
	Jurassic (180)		The appearance of birds. First flowering plants. A diversity of reptiles.
	Triassic (230)		Many reptilian types. First dinosaurs and mammals.

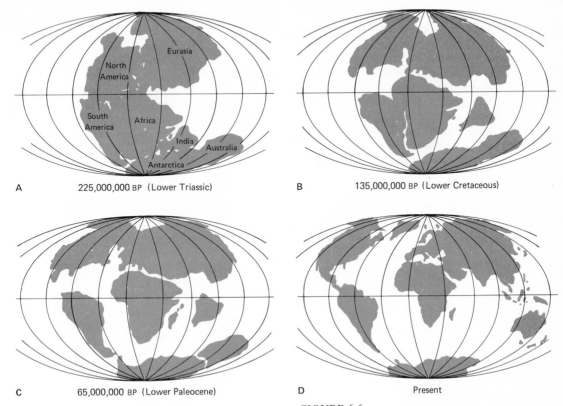

A   225,000,000 BP (Lower Triassic)

B   135,000,000 BP (Lower Cretaceous)

C   65,000,000 BP (Lower Paleocene)

D   Present

FIGURE 6-6
Continental drift and the evolution of continents. The early Mesozoic supercontinent of Pangea (*A*) broke into segments (continents) which have been drifting apart. Two continents drifting apart at an average rate of 2.5 centimeters (one inch) per year would be separated by 3750 km (2300 miles) in 150 million years. [*After Robert S. Dietz and John C. Holden, National Oceanic and Atmospheric Administration.*]

Diverse kinds of mammals evolved, adapted to almost every ecologic niche that could support a new mammalian species. With time, there were so many different species dissimilar in their biologic adaptations that they have been placed in separate orders made up of many families and genera. By the Paleocene and Eocene epochs, the ancestral stocks of all modern mammalian orders had evolved: ancient rabbits, rodents, primates, bats, whales, carnivores, hoofed animals, elephants, and others. All of these apparently trace their ultimate origin back to a Cretaceous order of placental mammals, the insectivores. This, the *adaptive radiation* of mammals in the Cenozoic era, was matched by similar radiation of reptiles that began some 200 million years earlier (Fig. 2-1).

EARLY PRIMATES

The oldest primate fossils yet discovered are those of ancient insectivorelike prosimian (*Purgatorius*) of late Cretaceous and early Paleocene age found in Montana. Of all prosimian fossils known to date, practically all those of Paleocene age and most of those of Eocene age also have been found in North America.

The Paleocene and Eocene epochs from 65 million B.P. to 36 million B.P. appear to have been the period when prosimians underwent their greatest adaptive radiation. The largest diversity of prosimian remains is found in Eocene rocks. Forty fossil genera have been identified in rocks of this age compared to only sixteen genera of prosimians alive today. During Paleocene and Eocene times, the world was apparently well suited to them. The mean annual temperature of Mexico City—about 21°C (70°F)—prevailed in what is now Seattle, London, and Paris. Tropical and subtropical forests blanketed extensive areas in almost all the Southern Hemisphere and much of the Northern (Fig. 6-7). According to geographic localities where fossils have been found, Eocene

prosimians were distributed widely in both North America and Eurasia. Early North American primates would have had access to Europe via a North Atlantic land connection and access to Asia via a land connection at the present Bering Strait (Fig. 6-6). Such migratory routes would have been open to prosimians only during the Paleocene and Eocene when these land connections had a warm climate and were covered with forests. There is little doubt that such land connections existed, at least between North America and Europe, since three genera of prosimians were common to both areas during the Paleocene and Eocene.

The nature of Paleocene-Eocene types

It is presumed that ancient primates evolved from Cretaceous insectivores because of some of the insectivorelike characteristics of the oldest prosimian fossils. Paleocene species are unlike any living prosimian in possessing these

FIGURE 6-7
The distributional limits of tropical and subtropical forests in the Eocene (heavy line) and in the present (dotted line). [*After John Napier, The Roots of Mankind, Smithsonian Institution Press, Washington, D.C., 1970.*]

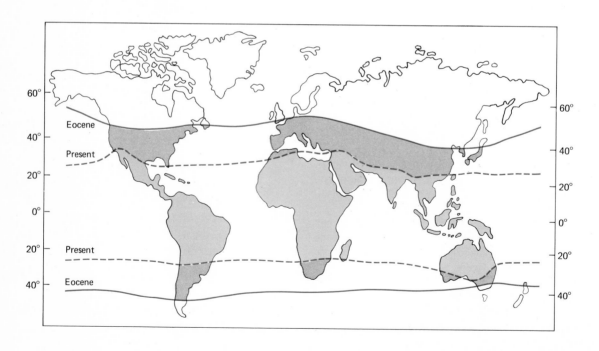

features. They are placed in four families which belong in a superfamily that has been extinct for 36 million years. Eocene prosimians, on the other hand, were largely lemuroid and tarsioid types; that is, they are classified in, or very close to, the superfamilies of Lemuroidea and Tarsiioidea (Fig. 3-1). The dentition of all these Paleocene-Eocene primates suggests that they were either arboreal or semiarboreal. Unlike their insectivorous ancestors, they probably were frugivorous (fruit-eating) and herbivorous (plant-eating). Some of the Eocene genera of both North America and Europe must have resembled modern lemurs *postcranially* (from the neck back), judging from well-preserved fossils of nearly complete skeletons (Fig. 6-8). Beautifully preserved skulls of Eocene lemuroids and tarsioids (Fig. 6-9) have yielded endocasts of relatively big brains with enlarged temporal and occipital lobes and reduced olfactory bulbs. Their brains contrasted sharply with those of contemporary hoofed animals that had brains more like those of opossums. The European tarsioid *Necrolemur* (Fig. 6-9) possessed large forwardly directed eyes and a reduced snout, both of which would favor improved depth perception. In a number of respects—the structure of the skull, brain, and hind limbs in particular—*Necrolemur* bore a significant resemblance to modern tarsiers.

The fate of Eocene prosimians

The prosimians of the early Tertiary were a successful group for 29 million years, ultimately occupying North America, Europe, and at least Eastern Asia before the Eocene drew to a close. They may have occupied an even wider area, although there is no fossil evidence as yet to support this.

    The prosimians of early Tertiary began to decline about 36 million years ago as a consequence of significant environmental changes which started to occur in early Oligocene. The continuing effects of continental drift were becoming increasingly evident with the formation of new mountain ranges. Moisture-laden air

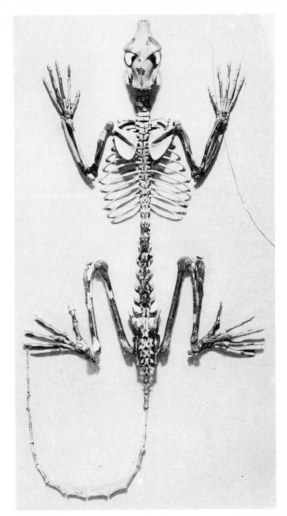

FIGURE 6-8
Skeleton of the North American Eocene lemuroid, *Notharctos*. Dark-colored bones are from one individual; light-colored portions are restored. [*American Museum of Natural History.*]

masses dumped their loads of water as they passed over these ranges, restricting the inland areas beyond to limited precipitation. The mean annual temperature in the United States and Western Europe dropped from 21 to 18°C (70 to 64°F). Increasing aridity and decreasing

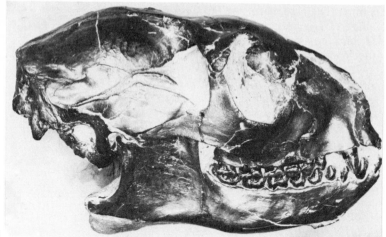

FIGURE 6-9
Eocene prosimian skulls: *A*, lemuroid skull (*Smilodectes*); *B*, tarsioid skull reconstruction (*Necrolemur*). [*A*, courtesy of F. S. Szalay; *B*, courtesy of E. L. Simons.]

A

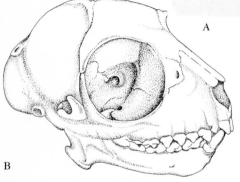

B

temperatures caused the tropical and subtropical forests to retreat from their northern limits in the Northern United States to a new line extending along the southern United States boundary. Similar changes took place elsewhere in the world. The regions vacated by tropical and subtropical forests were replaced by extensive temperate forests and grasslands. These changes alone had serious consequences on prosimian faunas, resulting in their extinction in Europe during the Oligocene and in North America during the Miocene.

But an even graver problem faced these early primates. New ecologic opportunities yielded some new competitors; monkeys and apes evolved that were better able to accommodate themselves to the new order of things.

EARLY MONKEYS AND APES

The oldest known fossils of monkeys and apes have been found in Oligocene deposits. Two of these fossils (fragmentary remains of two species of monkey) were found in South America. Over 200 primate fossils were found in the Fayum Desert near Cairo, Egypt. The great number and variety of the African fossils suggest that anthropoids were evolving in the previous Eocene epoch and that their center of origin probably was Africa. It has been suggested that South America may have been colonized by monkeys carried from the African mainland on natural rafts of floating trees and branches, while the two continents were still reasonably close together.[5]

In Oligocene times, the Fayum Desert was a dense tropical rain forest. Swamp-lined rivers cut through the forest on their lazy course to the ancient Mediterranean. Here, 35

---

[5] R. Lavocat, "The Interrelationships between the African and South American Rodents and their Bearing on the Problem of the Origin of South American Monkeys," *Journal of Human Evolution*, vol. 3, no. 4, 1974, pp. 323–326. R. Hoffstetter, "Phylogeny and Geographical Deployment of the Primates," *Journal of Human Evolution*, vol. 3, no. 4, 1974, pp. 327–350.

million years ago, the Old World monkeys and apes already had diverged as separate lines of descent. How they had evolved from earlier prosimians we do not as yet know; critical portions of the fossil record still are missing. But before the Oligocene came to a close, the rain forests that bordered the watercourses of the Fayum possessed a primate fauna that left abundant fossil remains of two genera of very small monkeys (*Apidium* and *Parapithecus*) as well as fossil specimens representing four genera of small apes. (For an orientation of fossil forms, consult Fig. 6-5.)

The dentition of one of the ape fossils resembled that of modern gibbons. The animal was about the size of a small monkey. Another of the four apes is of special interest because it may be a representative of the ancient lineage that founded both the pongid and hominid stocks. This creature, *Aegyptopithecus,* is known from several fossil remains of late Oligocene age, including a well-preserved skull (Fig. 6-10).[6] Although the size and form of both skull and brain bear certain resemblances to their earlier counterparts in Eocene prosimians, the dentition is distinctly pongid. Postcranial remains suggest that it was a monkeylike quadruped.

It would seem that *Aegyptopithecus* constitutes a well-balanced transition or connecting link between Paleocene-Eocene prosimians and certain Miocene apes which were to follow the Fayum primate by some 10 million years. The dental similarities between the Miocene forms and their predecessors from Fayum indicate a strong biologic kinship. As we are about to see, these Miocene pongids were very likely members of the lineage that led to modern chimpanzees. Since the chimpanzee is our closest living relative, it is not unreasonable to suppose that hominids trace their ultimate origin back to this same lineage.

Before we pass on to the highly significant evolutionary events of the Miocene epoch, a precautionary note about our discussion of primate evolution is in order. It is this: we should not entertain preconceived notions that the classificational status of modern primates is indicative of evolutionary descent in the past. There is no compelling reason to believe that tarsioids were ancestral to monkeys just because modern tarsiers occupy an intermediate position between other prosimians and monkeys today. Neither are we necessarily justified in the belief that apes evolved from monkeys. We may just as reasonably contend that tarsiers, monkeys, and apes are separate lines of descent that trace their origins back at various times to ancestral prosimians (Fig. 6-11). Only fossil evidence can resolve these problems, and the paleontological record is not clear, in specific cases, as to which of several possible lines of descent is correct.

On the other hand, that record is clear in a number of respects. The primate order got its start in the late Cretaceous and Paleocene with a group of ancient insectivorelike prosimians. Before the close of the Eocene, primates had become a diversified fauna of lemuroid and tarsioid types. Sometime during the Eocene, and certainly no later than the Oligocene, adaptative radiation within diverse prosimian stocks somehow gave rise, presumably in Africa, to two basic primate groups, monkeys and apes. It is believed that some of these monkeys migrated to South America, where their descendants subsequently became isolated and ultimately evolved into New World monkeys.

The record from the beginning of the Miocene on is by no means complete either, but lines of descent are a good deal clearer, probably because the evidence is progressively less ancient and consequently better preserved and more abundant.

THE AGE OF APES AND THE FIRST HOMINIDS

This segment of primate evolution was a favorable one for those anthropoids who could take

---

[6] The other two apes are *Oligopithecus* and *Propliopithecus* of early and mid-Oligocene, respectively. They are pongids of uncertain status.

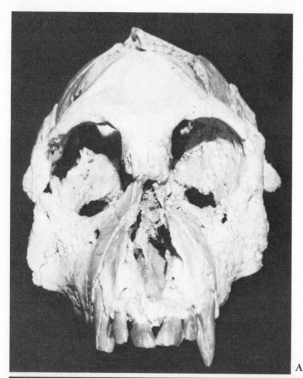

FIGURE 6-10
Aegyptopithecus from the upper Oligocene of Egypt. This monkey-sized primate was the largest of known Oligocene pongids. *A*, Front and lateral views of the skull; *B*, dentition of the upper jaw. [*Photographs by A. H. Coleman, courtesy of the Peabody Museum of Natural History. Yale University.*]

A

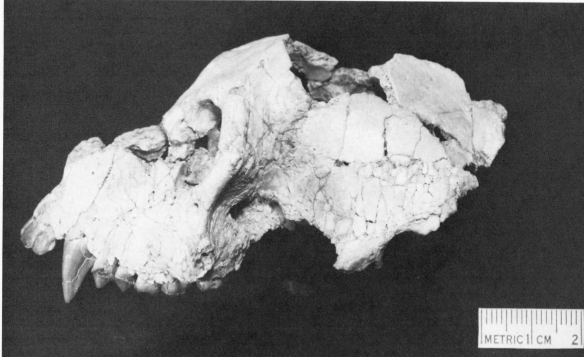

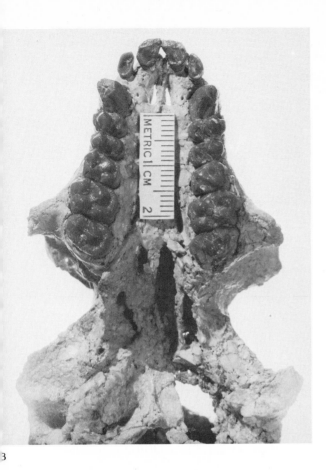

asia rammed into one another at a relative speed of perhaps 2.5 centimeters (1 inch) per year, the earth began to buckle. Long chains of mountain ranges gradually lifted lofty peaks and ridges high into the air: the Pyrenees, the Alps, the Apennines, the Carpathians, and the Caucasus. The Himalayan Range was similarly uplifted as India collided with Asia. In the Western Hemisphere, parallel events took place as a consequence of seafloor spreading. Huge plates of the earth's crust beneath the Pacific Ocean were moving eastward and bending under the western edges of the North and South American continents. The compressive effects of these collisions produced extensive folding, faulting, and volcanism, resulting in the elevation of the Andes in South America and the Coast and Cascade Ranges, the Sierra Nevada, and the Rockies in North America.

The climates and environments of early Miocene to early Pliocene

Majestic geologic events of this enormity had profound effects on climate and environments all over the world. The mean average temperature over the middle latitudes had dropped by early Pliocene to 10°C (50°F), an 8°C decrease since Oligocene times. Polar ice caps began to form. Summers were cool and winters were harsh and cold in many parts of the world. Temperatures varied significantly from season to season and from dawn to midday. Mean annual rainfall diminished in the middle latitudes and became unevenly distributed seasonally. Then, about 10 million years ago, temperatures began to oscillate in cycles that spanned tens of thousands of years. Mean annual temperatures in the mid-latitudes gradually fell from 10°C (50°F) to subfreezing cold and then rose back to about 10°C (50°F). This pattern persisted for millions of years, building up increasing depths of glacial ice which ultimately led to the Ice Age conditions of Pleistocene times.

Climatic changes of this nature and scope wrought major modifications in land vegetation. The tropical and subtropical forests of

advantage of the rapidly increasing ecologic opportunities for semiterrestrial or terrestrial life in the woodland savanna or open grassland at the forest fringe. The geologic processes of mountain building which were active in the early Tertiary gathered renewed and increased vigor in the Miocene and reached their peak in the Pliocene. As continents continued to drift, they began to collide with one another on a grand scale (Fig. 6-6). Such collisions were accompanied by tremendous pressures within the earth. Rocks became folded and faulted, bringing about widespread land uplift. The earth's crust, weakened by fissures along extensive fault zones began to belch molten masses of rock onto the earth's surface, forming islands in the sea and innumerable volcanoes and lava flows over the land. As Africa and Eur-

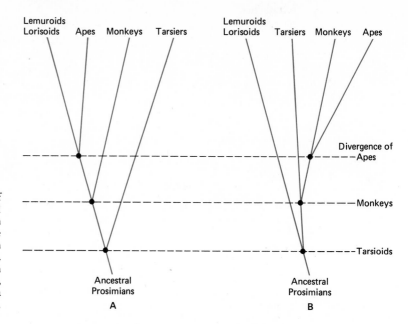

FIGURE 6-11
Two hypothetical patterns of primate evolution. *A*, hypothetical line of descent in which modern tarsiers, monkeys, and apes are collaterally related by common descent from ancestral prosimians. *B*, hypothetical line of descent in which modern tarsiers, monkeys, and apes are directly related in a tarsioid → monkey → ape lineage.

North America and Eurasia were essentially wiped out, and replaced by extensive temperate forests and expansive areas of grassland. Vast food resources of a different kind were becoming available in a new setting, open terrain, on a grandiose scale. Widespread grasslands (savannas) appeared in Africa also, but this transformation did not take place until late Pliocene or early Pleistocene. As plains continued to expand at the expense of shrinking forests, the stage was set for any woodland creature that could accommodate itself to life on open grassland.

It is in this setting that the primates of early Miocene to early Pliocene contended for survival. Events took place which foreshadowed the future of primates. Hominoids (Fig. 3-1) underwent an Oligocene-Miocene radiation of significant proportions, but suffered a sharp decline in the Pliocene as monkeys embarked on a belated but enduring adaptive radiation that has persisted to this day. Meanwhile, at the height of pongid diversity in the Miocene, a

peculiar kind of hominoid had evolved that was too extreme to be considered a pongid any longer: the earliest hominids had established a modest beginning.

The adaptive radiation of apes

The adaptive radiation of apes can be traced back to the hominoid fossils in the Oligocene deposits of Egypt. The earliest remains of a gibbonoid ape presumably are those of the small gibbonlike primate already mentioned (*Aelopithecus* of Upper Oligocene). Early pongids are known which even predate the monkey-sized *Aegyptopithecus*[7] of late Oligocene. From ancestral stocks such as these, both hylobatid and pongid hominoids (Fig. 3-1) underwent an adaptive radiation that lasted into the Pliocene. During this 28-million-year interval from early Oligocene (36 million B.P.) to mid-Pliocene (8 million B.P.), a diversity of

[7] The suffix *-pithecus* which occurs commonly in primate names is the ancient Greek word for "ape."

apes evolved. Some of these were unsuccessful after a time and became extinct. Others undoubtedly were the ancestors of modern gibbons, orangutans, chimpanzees, gorillas, and indeed, the human species itself.

The fossil remains of two genera[8] of ancient hylobatids (gibbonoids) from the Miocene and Pliocene epochs have been recovered both in Europe and Africa. These forms were not only monkey-sized but also resembled monkeys to the extent that their forelimbs were approximately the same length as their hind limbs. One genus, if not both, probably had a long tail. At least some of these ancestral gibbonoids appear to have resembled modern spider monkeys in limb structure (Fig. 3-2G). If such were the case, these "gibbons-to-be"

were quadrupeds that were very likely capable brachiators. The New World spider monkey is a very able brachiator. Comparisons of this nature suggest that the gibbon and the spider monkey may be products of parallel evolution in two different anthropoid lineages.

Dryopithecus: common ancestor of the great apes and man?

As we have mentioned earlier, the Oligocene ape *Aegyptopithecus* bore some rather remarkable similarities in its dentition to an early Miocene pongid. This early Miocene ape was a member of a group of Miocene-Pliocene pongids belonging in the genus *Dryopithecus*. Since the species is known from the many fossil specimens collected in East Africa, it was aptly named *Dryopithecus africanus* (Fig. 6-12).[9]

---

[8] *Pliopithecus* and *Limnopithecus*.

[9] Formerly called *Proconsul africanus*.

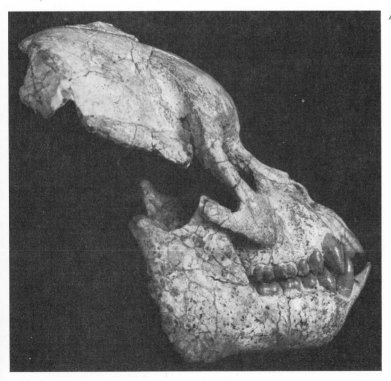

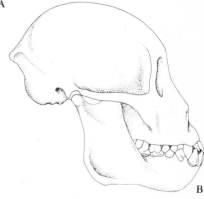

FIGURE 6-12
Dryopithecus africanus skull from Miocene deposits in Kenya (*A*). Restoration of entire skull (*B*). [*British Museum of Natural History.*]

Dryopithecus africanus was more monkey-like than modern apes, possibly reflecting its greater proximity in time to some kind of common ancestry with monkeys back in the Eocene. Individuals weighed perhaps 14 to 18 kilograms (30 to 40 pounds) and resembled modern chimpanzees in a number of respects, such as the structure of the forelimbs and the finger and toe bones. They may, in fact, have been ancestral to the chimpanzee; their more generalized structure would be expected in an ancestral form 23 million years ago.

Another member of the genus in Africa, mid-Miocene *D. major,*[10] was a considerably larger ape. Of the numerous fossil finds of this species, the jaws bore a close resemblance to those of the gorilla, as did a fossil lumbar vertebra and ankle bone (talus). The possibility that this species is in the direct lineage of gorillas is further strengthened by the fact that *D. major* fossils represent either the predominant or the only ape remains that have been recovered high on the slopes of East African volcanoes. These mountains were blanketed with rain forests in mid-Miocene, the same kind of environment inhabited by the mountain gorilla in Central Africa today.

The fossil remains of a number of other species of *Dryopithecus* have been found widely distributed throughout the Old World, including Africa, Europe, the Near East, India, China, and Russia. The African fossils have been recovered from deposits of early to mid-Miocene age, approximately 23 to 16 million years old. The Eurasian forms, on the other hand, have been discovered in deposits ranging from about 18 to 12 million years in age (mid-Miocene to early Pliocene). The younger age of the Eurasian specimens tends to confirm the belief that the genus had its origin in Africa and dispersed from that center of origin into Europe and Asia. This is corroborated further by the notable similarities between *Aegyptopithecus* of the Egyptian Oligocene and *Dryopithecus* of early

Miocene in East Africa. Most authorities place these two genera into one subfamily of pongids, called the *dryopithecines,* because of their apparent biologic relationship. It is quite probable that the dryopithecines are of African origin, and that they embrace not only the most ancient pongids known but also possibly one or more of the ancestors of the modern orangutan, chimpanzee, gorilla, and man. It is believed that *Aegyptopithecus* and *D. africanus* are in the direct line of descent leading to modern chimpanzees. Similarly, it is probable that *D. major* is a direct ancestor of the gorilla. If such is the case, the chimpanzee and gorilla lineages are between 17 and 23 million years old. The dryopithecine that was ancestral to the orangutan is not yet known but may well have lived before both *D. africanus* and *D. major.* Although the dryopithecine forebear of the hominid lineage also is obscure at the present time, it is known that hominids diverged from their pongid ancestors at least 15 million years ago, as we will see shortly.

The dryopithecine apes as a group The dryopithecines of Miocene to early Pliocene were a moderately diverse group. Probably they were arboreal, or essentially so, and thrived basically on fruits. Taken collectively, they lived in temperate, subtropical, or tropical climates and inhabited woodland savannas, temperate forests, or rain forests. Most ranged in weight from 14 to 23 kilograms (30 to 50 pounds), although some were larger and at least one species in India may have been bigger than a gorilla. Their arms and legs were about the same length, and their chests apparently were broad and shallow. Very likely, they were capable brachiators and were distinctly quadrupedal on the ground. Some, or perhaps all, of them may have engaged in knuckle-walking at least some of the time. Being fairly large animals was an obvious advantage insofar as added protection against predation was concerned. Large size undoubtedly restricted ease of travel in the trees but enabled the apes to travel with relative safety

---

[10] Once a generic name appears, it is conventional to abbreviate it in successive references that follow.

and economy of effort on the ground in much the same way that chimpanzees do today. Since large animals need a good deal more food than small animals do, they must cover a larger area to increase the volume of their bill of fare. Combined arboreal and terrestrial foraging over a wide terrain would accomplish this. It also would expose the dryopithecine ape to richer and more varied environmental experiences with which it would have to cope. Adapting to this enriched, more complex environment would have required a keen intelligence. It is probably no coincidence that the modern ape has four times the cortical area tucked away into the convoluted folds of its brain than does a monkey. The end result of dryopithecine evolution during the Miocene appears to have been a group of intelligent ape species that were not only very capable arboreal specialists but also were adapted in varying degrees to traveling and foraging in fringes and patches of open terrain. The open land that was available to them was in narrow strips that bordered forests, lakes, and watercourses, and in the interspersed areas of open ground in the woodland savanna.

Dryopithecine destiny and fate Climates and environments over the earth were changing, however, as we have noted, and the rate of change accelerated noticeably during the Pliocene. Increasing aridity and decreasing temperatures were significantly reducing the areas on the earth's surface capable of sustaining tropical, subtropical, and even temperate forests. Grasslands and woodland savannas invaded much of the land vacated by forests. Under the persistent onslaught of these trends, the arboreal dryopithecines fared rather badly and went into a sharp decline. Monkeys, which had not been nearly as common as apes among Miocene fossil primates, began to expand in both numbers and diversity. Having smaller bodies, the monkeys required less food than the larger pongids. Arboreal monkeys consequently began to provide stiff competition for the arboreal apes in this stage

of declining tropical and subtropical forests. The competition was to be heightened further as semiterrestrial monkeys arrived on the evolutionary scene to capitalize on the ecologic opportunities in the grassland and woodland savannas. The dryopithecines were not to be written off entirely, however, as the continuing chronicle of evolutionary events seems to show.

By late Miocene and early Pliocene, some distinctly different pongids had evolved in response to the drastic environmental changes that were occurring.

The Abominable Coal Man (Oreopithecus)
One of these has been called the "Abominable Coal Man" (Fig. 6-13) because its fossil remains, including a nearly complete skeleton, have been recovered from beds of coal. Almost 200 fossil specimens have been collected in Europe and East Africa in deposits of late Miocene age. This peculiar hominoid possessed humanlike traits, in its relatively short canines, broad shallow chest, short lumbar vertebral segment, and manlike pelvis. Its premolar and molar teeth, however, definitely were not those of a hominid. Furthermore, the arms were longer than the legs and the hind limb was apparently quite mobile. The "coal man" may have resembled an orangutan superficially in its body proportions and manner of locomotion. Its dentition suggests that it was a forest-dwelling herbivore. The coal in which its remains were entombed substantiates this since coal deposits presumably accumulated in swamp forests. This hominoid may have foraged in swamps, living perhaps on the roots, stems, and seeds of water lilies and the starchy roots of rushes and reeds—like some human hunters and gatherers today. In any case, the "Abominable Coal Man" was not a man. In fact even as an ape it was highly unusual and may belong in a family of its own.

The giant of the apes (Gigantopithecus)
In mid-Pliocene deposits located in the Siwalik Hills of northwestern India, an expedition headed by E. L. Simons recovered a nearly

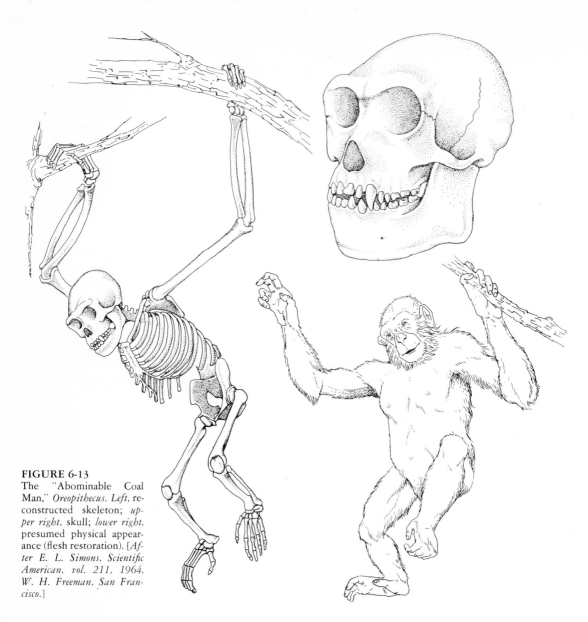

FIGURE 6-13
The "Abominable Coal Man," *Oreopithecus. Left*, reconstructed skeleton; *upper right*, skull; *lower right*, presumed physical appearance (flesh restoration). [*After E. L. Simons, Scientific American, vol. 211, 1964, W. H. Freeman, San Francisco.*]

complete mandible of what appears to have been a giant pongid. This specimen belongs to a fossil genus which has been appropriately named *Gigantopithecus*. The ancestral history of this creature is not altogether clear but

there is some evidence suggesting that it evolved from a species of *Dryopithecus*, probably *D. indicus*, that has been found in deposits of late Miocene and early Pliocene age in India. We have already referred to this dryopithecine as an Indian species that may have been larger than a gorilla. The paleospecies of *Gigantopithecus* represented by the mid-Pliocene remains in India seems to have been ancestral to a later paleospecies discovered in China. The Chinese fossils include a number of lower jaws and teeth of Pleistocene age between 500,000 and 1 million years old.

The significance of the *Gigantopithecus* finds lies in the strong possibility that these unique pongids were exclusively terrestrial inhabitants of open-country grassland. Their large size presumably was their major protection against predators. If we can assume that the relative proportions of total body size to jaw and tooth size were the same as those in a gorilla, these giant apes were much larger than wild gorillas. When standing erect, they probably reached nearly 2.5 meters (8 feet) and weighed about 270 kilograms (600 pounds).[11] Their relatively short but massive jaw was equipped with small incisors but large premolars and molars, suggesting that their diet consisted of considerable quantities of small but tough plant foods such as grass blades, roots, and rootstalks. The dentition was superficially hominidlike both in tooth proportions and in the failure of the canines to project beyond the premolars. Nonprojecting canines allowed lateral chewing movements and further aided in the grinding of tough plant foods. Although the canines were small, they were worn down to broad, flat chewing surfaces, indicating that they were used as an extra pair of premolars. Hominid canines differ significantly in that they are employed as sharp, incisorlike, cutting teeth.

Nonetheless, it is intriguing to consider the parallels between *Gigantopithecus* and hominids because these huge pongids and some of our early ancestors were not only contemporaries in the same part of the world, but they also were adapted to a similar feeding habit. Some unusual pongids and early hominids had been outfitted for comparable ecologic niches.

[11] E. L. Simons, *Primate Evolution*, New York: The Macmillan Company, 1972, p. 254.

If ever they were forced into serious competition, the handwriting clearly was on the wall. There is reason to believe that such competition may have arisen ultimately. One of the presumed competitors stumbled down the path of oblivion between 500,000 and 1 million years ago, possibly with the help of contemporary populations of *Homo erectus*.

The first hominids

By middle Miocene time, 18 to 20 million years ago, the dryopithecine apes were distributed widely over Eurasia and Africa living in a diversity of environments. In more temperate areas where plants bore their fruits only seasonally, pongids may have resorted to other food sources, perhaps shifting their feeding and foraging habits more and more toward the ground. It is not improbable that the first hominids trace their ancestry back to such a group of dryopithecines. Possibly they were forest-dwelling arm-swingers similar to the modern pygmy chimpanzees, except that their legs and arms very likely were about the same length. In any event, a semiterrestrial ground-feeding primate appears to have evolved in late Miocene. Its dentition was unquestionably hominidlike and suggests that the animal may have lived on tough plant foods and perhaps even raw meat and bones on occasion. Its name is *Ramapithecus*. Although it occupies an intermediate position between dryopithecines and the earliest toolmaking hominids, its fundamental relationship is with the hominids.

Ramapithecus

The fossil remains range in age from about 15 million to 10 million years and include a number of upper and lower jaws, teeth, and part of the lower face. They have been recovered from late Miocene to early Pliocene deposits in East Africa, Germany, West Pakistan, northwestern India, and southeastern China. Found with the *Ramapithecus* remains were fossils of forest-dwelling pongids, lesser apes, monkeys, and rodents together with such grassland types as antelopes and rhinoceros. During the late Miocene there apparently was a broad forested region that encompassed East Africa, the Arabian land mass, and northwestern India. Most probably, *Ramapithecus* originated in Africa and dispersed over this forested region into Eurasia, frequenting the forest-grassland edges.

Ramapithecus may have looked something like the modern pygmy chimpanzee: perhaps 20 to 35 kilograms (40 to 80 pounds) in weight and 90 to 110 centimeters (3 to 3½ feet) tall. The face was short and probably did not project as much as those of apes. The dental arch resembled the parabolic curve of hominids rather than the rectangular tooth row of pongids (Fig. 1-12). The incisors and canines were small and the canines were nonprojecting and incisorlike. The premolars and molars were large, broad, closely spaced teeth with a thick layer of enamel. The dentition was more hominid than pongid both structurally and functionally.

The dentition also reveals that *Rama-*

pithecus had a relatively longer period of childhood than apes. In pongids and hominids the permanent molars erupt in a time sequence: molar 1 → molar 2 → molar 3. The third molar appears at the time of skeletal maturity. Since pongids mature in little more than half the time that man does, their molars follow one another in a shorter time interval. The difference in wear is consequently slight between the first molar (M1) and third molar (M3). In man, on the other hand, M1 erupts at 6 years of age, M2 at 12, and M3 at about 19. The degree of wear decreases from M1 to M3 and is quite noticeable. A similar wear differential is seen in *Ramapithecus* molars (Fig. 6-14), implying that this creature also had a relatively long period of childhood and adolescence.[12]

Ramapithecus's dentition suggests that this hominid was a ground-feeding herbivore that lived on small tough morsels of food, such as seeds, grass blades, stems, roots, rootstalks, and possibly even raw meat and bones. The

[12] Ibid., p. 273.

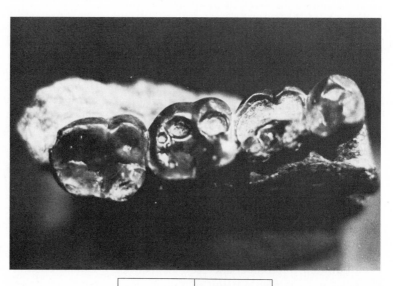

FIGURE 6-14
A lower jaw fragment of *Ramapithecus* containing the second premolar and three molars. Notice the difference in wear between the first, second, and third molars. The thick surface enamel of the first molar has been worn completely through except at the edges, exposing an extensive area of dentine (white). The third molar has but a tiny area of dentine exposed. [*Courtesy of E. L. Simons and the Peabody Museum of Natural History, Yale University.*]

0 cm   1   2

short canines would permit lateral chewing movements to expedite the grinding of tough foods. The particularly thick enamel of the grinding teeth would be similarly suited to crushing hard seed coats and tough resistant plant fiber. The associated fossil species found with the *Ramapithecus* remains indicate that these early hominids lived at the forest fringe, around lakes and along watercourses. Only grasses and grasslike plants can tolerate the intermittent flooding that occurs along the banks and perimeters of rivers and lakes. *Ramapithecus* presumably fed in such areas, spending the night in forest trees. Nothing is known of the postcranial skeleton, but it is presumed that the animal was an arm-swinger and hanger, with arms and legs of approximately the same length. On the ground, it was most likely quadrupedal and may have been a knuckle-walker. Like the chimpanzee, it may have walked bipedally at times and made a few simple tools out of twigs and leaves. No tools of any kind have been found, however, nor is there reason to suspect that the animal's toolmaking ability exceeded that of the chimpanzee to any significant degree.

The earliest hominids, as exemplified by *Ramapithecus,* may well have retained these basic biologic features for several million years.[13] But that situation was to change in some later descendants.

Hominid evolution after Ramapithecus

We know very little of the history of hominids between 5 and 10 million years ago. Only one fossil has, as yet, been retrieved from this time segment but that meager clue is a tantalizing one. It is a second upper molar dated at 9 million years that was found in northern Kenya. This tooth is intermediate between its counterpart in *Ramapithecus* and that of another hominid (*Australopithecus*) who appeared at least 5.5 million years ago and was making stone tools at least 2.5 million years ago in northern Kenya.

[13] David Pilbeam, *The Ascent of Man,* New York: The Macmillan Company, 1972, pp. 99.

From early to late Pliocene, grasslands continued their relentless expansion as forested areas shrank. It is estimated that the forested habitat once available to *Ramapithecus* in late Miocene had been reduced by 13 million square kilometers (5 million square miles), or half the area of North America, in late Pliocene. It is believed that hominids gradually moved from these ever-dwindling forests out into the grasslands between 10 and 5 million years ago (early to late Pliocene). As they did so, they shifted from the diet of vegetarian foragers to that of hunter-gatherers. Although this new diet still included large amounts of plant foods, it was distinguished by an increased consumption of meat. The change was a far-reaching one because it was the first introduction of a hominid to what was to become the human way of life.

As hunter-gatherers in open terrain, these early hominids were confronted with some serious problems. They could be preyed upon themselves by the many formidable carnivores of the grassland savannas. They had to scavenge, hunt, and gather sufficient food in a habitat that was not nearly as fruitful in its production as the borders and fringes of tropical and subtropical forests. As a result, they had to cover a greater area. This new habitat and diet would have a profound effect on cranial and locomotor anatomy because a high premium would be placed on any evolutionary adaptations that would favor habitual bipedal locomotion. A fairly large primate that stands bipedally, especially with arms upraised, presents a larger image than quadrupeds many times its size. The value of this as a protective threat against predators is considerable. Erect posture also increases the range of vision, permitting the detection of both predator and prey more readily. Hands, no longer encumbered by locomotion, are free to carry foods, transport infants, throw objects, and, above all, to make and use tools. The capability of making tools could create a simple arsenal of objects wielded as clubs or thrown as missiles which early hominids could use against predators. It could also provide a tool kit by which the scavenging and hunting of meat and the gathering of plant food would become more productive enterprises. All these activities in turn would be maximally effective only if they were undertaken as a cooperative effort on the part of all available individuals capable of performing productively. The stage was being set for a bipedal hominid hunter with the necessary intelligence to survive on the open savanna by fashioning useful tools and maximizing their employment within the framework of a unique social order.

That these changes did in fact occur is testified to by hominids who lived several million years ago. They were named *Australopithecus* (Latin *auster,* "south"; Greek *pithecus,* "ape") because the first fossils were found in South Africa and generally were considered for some time to be those of apes. Their hominid status has been fully established, however. Furthermore their fossils have been found along with primitive tools of stone and bone.[14] They lived as long as 5.5 million years ago because remains of that age have been found in northern Kenya.

THE AUSTRALOPITH HOMINIDS

Fossil evidence of *Australopithecus* has been increasing steadily over the years. It now embraces a respectable portion of the entire skeleton. Several fairly complete skulls, skull fragments, jaws and portions of jaws, innumerable teeth, a few vertebrae, several hip bones, a number of arm, hand, leg, and foot bones, and even footprints have been discovered in East and South Africa. One jawbone fragment has been recovered in Java which possibly may belong to *Australopithecus.* The fossil evidence is augmented further by the finding of living or occupation sites (living

floors)[15] in East Africa containing tools known to be associated with *Australopithecus* fossils. Significant discoveries of fossil remains, stone tools, and living floors have been made in East Africa at Olduvai Gorge in Tanzania, in an area east of Lake Rudolf in northern Kenya, and in the Omo River Valley in southwestern Ethiopia. Many fossils, including those first discovered, also have been found at five localities in the Republic of South Africa.[16]

The East African fossils vary in age from 5.5 million (Fig. 6-15) to about 1.5 million B.P. (late Pliocene to early Pleistocene). Tools discovered in southwestern Ethiopia and in northern Kenya date as far back as 2 to 2.6 million years ago. The South African remains are thought to be in the 2 to 3 million year range.

Anatomy of *Australopithecus*

Australopithecus remains resemble those of later hominids in many important respects. Cranial capacities are estimated to have ranged between about 430 and 530 cubic centimeters, although no species of *Australopithecus* appears to have weighed more than 68 to 90 kilograms (150 to 200 pounds), and one weighed only about 32 kilograms (70 pounds). This compares well with brain size in wild gorillas who weigh up to 180 kilograms (400 pounds). There also is evidence of internal reorganization in the brain. A natural endocast of an infant's brain shows enlarged parietal association areas (Fig. 6-16). This region includes the master association area which is thought to be involved in the development of language. Another specimen indicates that the external anatomy of the cerebellum was more

---

[14] Ibid., pp. 107 and 109.

[15] A living floor is a former land surface preserved in sedimentary rock that was once occupied by a hominid; it contains tools, the fossil remains of food items (e.g., bones), coprolites (fossil feces), or even hominid fossils themselves.

[16] Makapansgat, Sterkfontein, Swartkrans, Kromdraai, and Taung.

FIGURE 6-15
Oldest *Australopithecus* fossil known, dated at 5.5 million years. This specimen was found southwest of Lake Rudolf in Northern Kenya and appears to resemble *A. africanus* most closely. *Top,* fossil jawbone fragment with molar tooth (cast); *bottom,* sketch of modern lower jaw showing relative location of fragment. [*Top, by permission of R. E. Leakey, National Museum of Kenya and the Wenner-Gren Foundation for Anthropological Research.*]

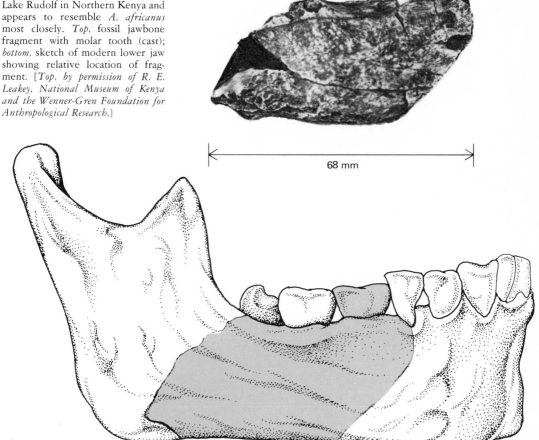

68 mm

humanlike than apelike. The vertebral column joined the undersurface of the skull at a more forward position than it does in apes, but not as far forward as in later hominids. Consequently, the spinal cord joined the brain in a position more characteristic of large-brained bipedal hominids (Fig. 1-16).

In profile, the skull had a low forehead and large projecting upper and lower jaws (Figs. 6-16 and 6-18). The canine teeth were nonprojecting and, aided by a humanlike jaw joint, permitted a lateral and rotational chewing motion. The incisors were broad and, together with the canines, functioned as chisellike slicers. The cheek teeth (premolars and molars) were larger than those of modern man and had a thick enamel layer for crushing and grinding foods. The tooth row followed the

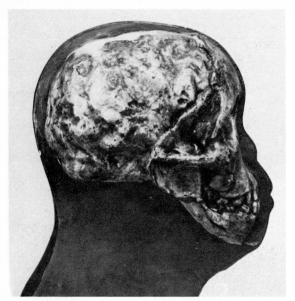

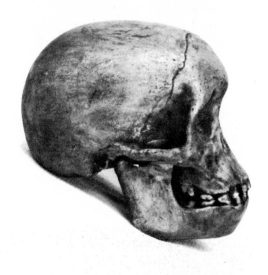

FIGURE 6-16

A   B

A six-year-old infant *Australopithecus africanus* skull from Taung, South Africa. *A,* Cast of fossil with flesh restoration (outer black margin) by R. A. Dart. All the milk teeth are intact, as are the first permanent molars. Most of the brain is preserved as a natural limestone endocast. The parietal association areas are expanded, a typically human trait. *B,* Restored skull, side view (cast). *C,* Restored skull, front view (cast).

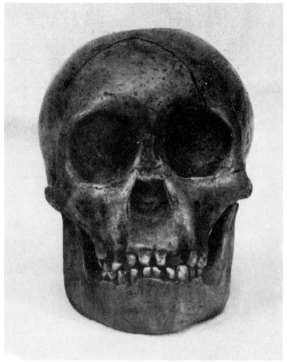

parabolic dental arch so characteristic of hominids. Differential tooth wear and the age at which the first molars erupted (Fig. 6-16) indicate that the period of australopithecine infancy and adolescence closely paralleled that of modern man.

The clavicle (collar bone) was relatively thick, suggesting that the arms and shoulders of these creatures were somewhat more powerfully built than those in people today. Their thumb was shorter and less mobile than ours. Although their fingertips were broad and flat, their fingers were stout and somewhat curved rather than slender and straight. Thus, their hands were less dextrous than ours and probably better adapted for power than for precision work.

C

The pelvis and foot definitely were those of a bipedal hominid (Fig. 6-17). The foot possessed a strongly built nonopposable big toe and three arches. Except for certain slight differences in its lower (ischial and pubic) portions, the pelvis was quite similar to that of modern man.

Australopithecine types

Although australopithecine species shared in varying degrees the generic features we have just described, there were obvious specific differences among them. We are, after all, discussing a genus of hominids who occupied perhaps much of the vast continent of Africa over a period of 4 million years or longer.

Altogether, at least three species of *Australopithecus* usually are recognized: *A. africanus, A. robustus,* and *A. boisei.* These three commonly are divided into two groups, the gracile form (*A. africanus*) and the robust form (*A. robustus* and *A. boisei*). The latter two very likely represent a lineage of paleospecies with *A. robustus* as the ancestral type: *A. robustus* → *A. boisei.* The gracile form, *A. africanus,* presumably was a contemporary of *A. robustus.*

The gracile and robust types differed in a number of ways. Gracile individuals were much smaller, standing 120 to 140 centimeters (4 to 4½ feet) tall and weighing perhaps 25 to 35 kilograms (60 to 80 pounds). On the other hand, robust australopiths were 30 centimeters (1 foot) or more taller and probably weighed 60 to 90 kilograms (135 to 200 pounds). The skull of the robust forms also had a flatter face and was more massively con-

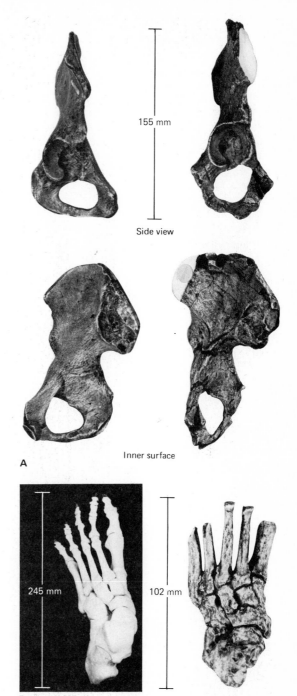

155 mm

Side view

Inner surface

A

245 mm

102 mm

B

FIGURE 6-17
Pelvis and foot of modern and early Pleistocene hominids. *A,* right pelvis of modern human pygmy (*left*) and *Australopithecus africanus* from Sterkfontein, South Africa (*right*); *B,* the foot bones of modern man (*left*) and early hominid ("*Homo habilis*") from Olduvai Gorge in Tanzania (*right*). All but the modern foot are casts. [*Courtesy of Dr. M. D. Leakey and the Wenner-Gren Foundation for Anthropological Research.*]

structed, with strong bony crests and buttresses for the attachment of powerful chewing muscles (Figs. 6-18 and 6-19). It has been suggested that rather than being different species, the gracile forms may have been the females and the robust forms the males of but one species. Sexual dimorphism, however, could scarcely account for the significant differences in dentition between the two types. The cheek teeth of the robust australopithecines were quite large and contrasted sharply with their relatively small incisors and canines. The cheek teeth of the gracile group were smaller and the incisors and canines were not disproportionately small by comparison. Furthermore, both male and female skulls of the robust type have now been found in the East Lake Rudolf area of Kenya.

A fourth hominid of controversial status

Additional hominid fossil material has been discovered in Olduvai Gorge, Tanzania, and the East Lake Rudolf area of Kenya which has been named *Homo habilis* (Greek, *Homo*,

"man"; Latin *habilis,* "able"). The designation "able, or handy, man" refers to the belief that this species rather than australopiths was primarily responsible for the first stone tools.

One skull, that of a juvenile found at Olduvai, was dated at 1.85 million years B.P. and had an estimated cranial capacity of 657 cubic centimeters. This is well beyond the australopith range of 430 to 530 cubic centimeters. An adult skull discovered in the East Lake Rudolf area in 1972 had an estimated cranial capacity of 775 cubic centimeters and is dated at 2.6 million B.P. This skull resembles that of *H. erectus* in a number of significant features, as shown in Fig. 6-20.

What is the relationship of the large-brained *"Homo habilis"* to the australopiths we have described who lived in the same time frame?

The relationship of Australopithecus to Homo

Expert opinion is divided on this issue. Some feel that the three australopith species we have

FIGURE 6-18
Skulls of *Australopithecus africanus* (*left*) and *A. robustus* (*right*). Skull of *A. africanus* is a cast. See Fig. 4-4 for comparison with skulls of modern man and gorilla. [*A. robustus courtesy of E. L. Simons.*]

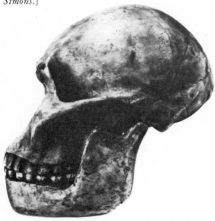
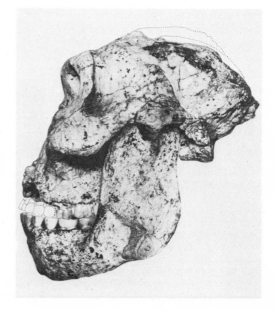

described were basically vegetarian hominids and represented a lineage that eventually became extinct without leaving any descendants. *Homo sapiens* traces its origin back to *H. habilis,* a hunter-gatherer, who in turn evolved from some, at present, unidentified australopith.[17]

Another hypothesis holds that the three australopithecine species as well a's *H. habilis* constitute a single complex lineage of paleospecies from which *H. erectus* subsequently evolved.[18]

Still a third view interprets the robust australopiths as a lineage of vegetarian hominids who became extinct without issue. The gracile form, *A. africanus,* was a hunter-gatherer who ultimately evolved into *H. erectus.*[19]

Despite their obvious differences, these three hypotheses share common ground. First, an australopithecine is the ultimate ancestor of the genus *Homo* in all of them. And second, when one is considering a lineage in which the ancestral paleospecies is an australopith and the descendant is *H. erectus,* what one calls the final transitional form can be arbitrary. The distinction between "advanced australopith," "*Homo habilis,*" and "early *Homo erectus,*" may have little real meaning.

Hominid life 2 to 3 million B.P.

South African australopithecines lived in open habitats most of which were drier than they are now. The gradual decline in rainfall which characterized mid-Tertiary times had continued unabated into the late Pliocene and early Pleistocene. Increasing aridity had not only led to more extensive grasslands but also to diminished forage production and reduced food resources. It was possibly during this time that

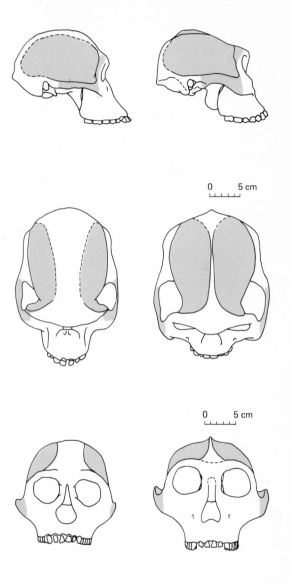

FIGURE 6-19
Side, top, and front views of skulls of *Australopithecus africanus* (*left*) and *A. robustus* (*right*). Note the larger cheek teeth in *A. robustus.* Flatter face and better development of bony crests and buttresses accommodate heavier chewing musculature, apparently to serve powerful grinding function of the cheek teeth in the *robustus* lineage. Areas for the attachment of chewing muscles (temporal and masseter) are colored. [*After P. V. Tobias, Olduvai Gorge, vol. 2, Cambridge University Press, Cambridge, 1967.*]

[17] D. Pilbeam and S. J. Gould, "Size and Scaling in Human Evolution," *Science,* vol. 186, Dec. 6, 1974, pp. 892–901.
[18] M. H. Wolpoff and C. L. Brace, "Allometry and Early Hominids," *Science,* vol. 189, July 4, 1975, pp. 61–63.
[19] J. T. Robinson, "Variation and the Taxonomy of the Early Hominid," in *Background for Man,* P. Dolhinow and V. Sarich (eds.), Boston: Little, Brown and Company, 1971, pp. 123–155.

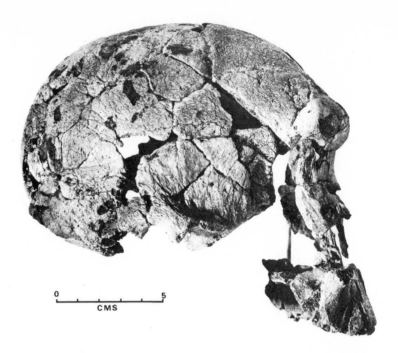

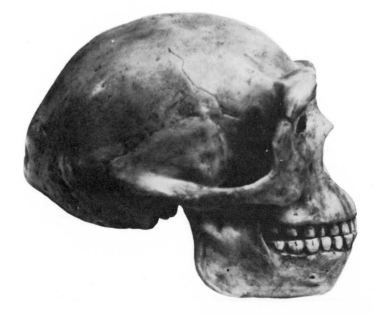

FIGURE 6-20
Unusual fossil find from Northern Kenya. *Top*, skull designated ER 1470 (ER = East Rudolf) is dated at 2.6 million years old. Its cranial capacity of 775 cubic centimeters falls within the range of *Homo erectus* skulls found in Asia (*bottom*) that were 2 million years younger. [*ER 1470 by permission of the National Museum of Kenya.*]

FIGURE 6-21
A hypothetical reconstruction of early Pleistocene hominids who have claimed the disemboweled carcass of a lion kill. They are fighting off other scavengers with whom they had to compete, such as hyenas, jackals, and vultures. The carcass is that of the large, horned sivathere (*Sivatherium*), an extinct relative of the giraffe.

early hominids developed the family unit as an effective means of exploiting restricted food supplies. When food is scarce, a small group can exist where a larger one cannot. This is illustrated today by Bushmen and baboons alike; both will break into smaller groups during periods of food scarcity.

At Olduvai Gorge the associated fossils found with hominid remains and living sites of the earliest Pleistocene indicate that these hominids inhabited open grassland near the edge of a lake. Elephants, giraffes, wild pigs, several species of antelope, rabbits, baboons, and hyenas roamed the area along with lizards,

tortoises, and birds such as the pheasantlike spurfowl. Of these, hominids hunted lizards, tortoises, spurfowl, rodents, rabbits, young pigs, and young antelope, and caught fish from the nearby lake. They also probably scavenged what they could from the carcasses of larger animals killed by lions (Fig. 6-21). Old living-floor sites testify to the existence of home bases as long as 2 million years ago. One site contained a variety of stone tools and a pile of rocks arranged in a semicircle as though it might have formed a windbreak. Another had unworked stones of lava and quartz that had been carried in from 5 kilometers (3 miles) away, presumably to hurl at animals or to serve as raw stock for toolmaking. Still another covered 316 square meters (3,400 square feet) and was strewn with different kinds of tools and a large number of bones, the large ones of which were split open as if to expose the edible marrow. The use of fire was evidently unknown because none of these living floors showed any suggestion of a hearth. This meant that hominids very likely were not yet habitual cave-dwellers since fire probably was necessary to drive large cave-inhabiting predators from their lairs.

Tools

Altogether, these living sites have yielded 11 different kinds of stone tools, including choppers, notched tools, flakes, chisels, scrapers, and gouging and engraving tools (Fig. 6-22). They range from the size of tennis balls (choppers) down to walnut-sized artifacts which could be held only in a precision grip (some flakes and scrapers). These tools, collectively

FIGURE 6-22
Oldowan chopping tool (*left*) and the forerunner of a "hand ax" (*right*). Sometimes called "pebble tools," implements like these were used by man's ancestors between 1 and 2½ or more million years ago. [*After Francois Bordes, The Old Stone Age, McGraw-Hill, New York, 1968.*]

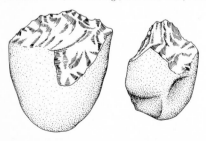

known as the *Oldowan industry* (for Olduvai Gorge), were by no means crude. The late L. S. B. Leakey demonstrated that an Oldowan tool is quite adequate for skinning out an entire antelope. Oldowan tools have also been found in association with australopithecine remains in South Africa and in a living floor in the east Lake Rudolf area dated at 2.6 million B.P. which contains a variety of them.

It would seem that the Oldowan tool kit was used, at least in part, for hunting, butchering, and food preparation. Undoubtedly, it would have been necessary to prepare bone or wooden clubs and to gather rock missiles to protect a kill from large scavengers like hyenas. Tools also may have been utilized to fashion bones or branches into digging tools to obtain edible roots, tubers, bulbs, and insect larvae from the ground. Even with an omnivorous diet, the food available to a hunter-gatherer-scavenger of small game was sufficiently scarce that early hominids would have had to maintain a low population density over a relatively large territory. Habitual bipedalism would have been a virtual necessity for such creatures because it would not only facilitate the making of tools but also the transport of raw materials to be used in toolmaking, weapon-carrying, weapon use, and the transport of game back to the home base.

Social organization

Hunting as a livelihood certainly would put a premium on greater intelligence and a larger brain because of toolmaking and the need for increased interpersonal cooperation and for language. Females would require larger pelvises to give birth to infants with bigger brains, and this in turn would reduce the efficiency of female bipedalism. Diminished female mobility, coupled with the necessity for carrying an infant whose period of dependency was prolonged, established the need for a home base and a division of labor between the sexes. Females would care for the young and gather plant foods in the vicinity of the home base while the males traveled considerable distances in search of small game and the leftovers of lion kills. It is indeed probable that all these adaptations made their first appearance among australopithecines, including the pair bond and its entrenchment in heterosexual love. A strong mother-infant bond undoubtedly existed also which, together with the pair bond, established the human family unit. Social integration was further enhanced by the necessity for cooperation between males collaborating with one another in the hunting effort. It is quite possible that the close association among hunting males, dependent as it would be upon mutual assistance and protection, carried with it a potential for homosexual love.

Language
It is difficult to believe that such a life-style could have existed even in a primitive form without language. It would seem that a brain capable of directing the manufacture of a tool kit 2.5 million years ago would be capable of designing at least a rudimentary language. Some form of symbolic communication would have been essential in a functional home base where adult males and females collaborated in butchering, food preparation, food-sharing, care of the young, resting, and looking after those who were sick or injured. Hunting strategies would have been most fruitful when they were prepared in advance. The making of tools would have been a wasteful labor were it not organized around the needs of the group. It would have been desirable for the pair-bond partners to plan their family functions at the home base and to integrate food gathering and hunting activities. Incest taboos would have had to be created and communicated to protect the pair bond as well as to enforce the perpetuation of kinship ties. The establishment and preservation of intergroup alliances based on exogamy and kinship would have given added strength and stability to the participating groups. And above all, language would have made it possible to reinforce and reward all these nonaggressive, cooperative behaviors through expressions of personal gratification and the honor of public recognition in ceremony and ritual.

From all the evidence and what can be inferred from it, it would appear that at least some early hominids 2 to 3 million years ago were cast in the mold of a human way of life, primordial though it may have been. It is only natural to wonder what may have happened to them and to any of those who may have been cast in a different mold.

The hominids win some and lose some

Early Pleistocene hominids probably began to disperse from Africa at least 2 million years ago. Most likely, they followed the rift valley system northward which would have taken them from East Africa via the Nile River basin into Egypt and thence into Israel. From here, some may have moved eastward through Iraq, Iran, India, and on into southeast Asia. The australopithecine jaw fragment in Java may represent a remnant of such a population. Others may have proceeded northward from Israel through Syria, Turkey, and across what was then dry ground at the Dardanelles to enter Europe (Fig. 6-23).

These migrations from Africa presumably took place between 2 and 1 million years ago. Undoubtedly they progressed slowly, perhaps no more than 1½ kilometers (1 mile) a year, and they may have required several thousand years. What caused them or why they occurred at that time is not known. They may have come about as a result of the dramatic oscillations in temperature that began about 10 million years ago, which we described previously. By early Pleistocene time, a more or less stable frequency of about 70,000 years had been reached in the cold-warm-cold weather cycle. A cold, or *glacial*, period was marked by an advance of glacial ice southward in the more northerly latitudes. During a warm or interglacial period the front of glacial ice would retreat northward. In Africa, glacial and interglacial climates could be contrasted as cooler and wetter versus

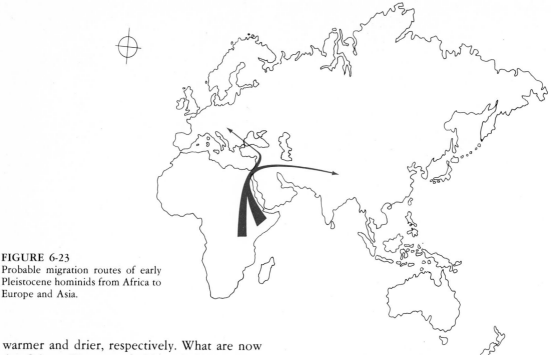

FIGURE 6-23
Probable migration routes of early
Pleistocene hominids from Africa to
Europe and Asia.

warmer and drier, respectively. What are now
the Sahara Desert and Olduvai Gorge were
well-watered plains dotted with lakes during
glacial times but were deserts during the remainder of the cycle. Segments of the early
hominid population in East Africa may have
moved northward during interglacial periods
because of the attractiveness of the wetter,
more productive environments in the temperate latitudes at that time.

In any case, certain early Pleistocene
hominids preserved their life-style and evolved
further. As they evolved, they became taller,
their brains became larger, and they began to
hunt big game. In short, some hominids—call
them "advanced gracile australopiths," "*Homo
habilis,*" or "pre-*Homo erectus*" as you will—became *H. erectus.* When, during the 50,000 generations between 2 and 1 million years ago, the
ancestor became different enough to be called
descendant is strictly an arbitrary distinction.
However, by 1 million years ago, or perhaps a
little earlier, *H. erectus* had made its debut not
only in Africa but in Europe and Asia as well.

The robust australopithecines did not fare
as well. At Olduvai, *A. boisei* persisted into mid-
Pleistocene times to become a contemporary of
H. erectus, but finally fell to extinction about
600,000 B.P. The cause of extinction could have
been one or a combination of factors. If, as
some believe, the robust australopiths were
vegetarians, they may have been unable to compete with their omnivorous relatives during
interglacial periods when the productivity of
food plants was low. They may, on the other
hand, have been unable to survive these dry
periods even in the absence of competition
from other hominids. They were good-sized
creatures and would have required a large volume of plant food which has considerably less
energy value per kilogram than meat. Finally,
it is not inconceivable that the robust species
may have been killed off by the hunter-
gatherers. Certainly it was within the capacity
of *H. erectus* to do so because no land mammal,

not even the elephant, could claim immunity from the skill of this early big-game hunter.

Our narrative of hominid evolution will begin with these creatures in the following chapter.

SUGGESTED READINGS

CLARK, W. E. LE GROS: *Man-Apes or Ape-Men?: The Story of Discoveries in Africa,* New York: Holt, Rinehart and Winston, Inc., 1967. An account of the australopith discoveries in Africa.

COLBERT, E. H.: *Wandering Lands and Animals,* New York: E. P. Dutton & Co., Inc., 1973. A good account of continental drift and its effect on animal distribution.

EDEY, M. A.: *The Emergence of Man: The Missing Link,* New York: Time-Life Books, 1972. A nicely illustrated survey of the australopiths.

MCALESTER, A. L.: *The History of Life,* Englewood Cliffs, N. J.: Prentice-Hall, Inc., 1968. A brief survey of the kinds of life that flourished during the earth's history from the origin of life to the appearance of *Homo sapiens.*

PFEIFFER, J. E.: *The Emergence of Man,* New York: Harper & Row, Publishers, Incorporated, 1972. A lively and well-written account of hominid evolution from its earliest beginnings in archaic prosimians to the invention of agriculture.

PILBEAM, DAVID: *The Ascent of Man: An Introduction to Human Evolution,* New York: The Macmillan Company, 1972. A survey of hominoid fossils from late Miocene *Ramapithecus* to the earliest known appearance of modern *Homo sapiens* in late Pleistocene; Pliocene-Pleistocene australopiths are stressed.

RAUP, D. M., and S. M. STANLEY: *Principles of Paleontology,* San Francisco: W. H. Freeman and Company, 1971. An Introductory textbook that deals with the nature of fossil evidence and its interpretation, and with the description and classification of fossil organisms.

SIMONS, E. L.: *Primate Evolution: An Introduction to Man's Place in Nature,* New York: The Macmillan Company, 1972. A comprehensive survey of Tertiary fossil primates from archaic prosimians to the earliest known hominid, *Ramapithecus.*

REVIEW QUESTIONS

1 List five different kinds of paleontological evidence which throw light on the nature, behavior, and habitat of fossil organisms. In each case indicate the kind of conclusions a given type of evidence might justify.

2 What considerations are taken into account in determining whether a group of fossils represents an extinct species?

3 The oldest known primate fossil was found in rocks of what geologic age? Compare the primates of Paleocene and Eocene time.

4 Give the geographic area and the geologic age of the deposits which contained the oldest known monkey and ape fossils.

One of these fossils may represent the ancient lineage that gave rise to both the pongid and hominid stocks. What is its name? Insofar as the fossil evidence reveals, how would you describe this creature?

5 Show how geologic processes in the Tertiary period led to profound changes in world climates and environments between late Eocene and Pliocene.

6 Largely in response to great environmental changes, adaptive radiation in apes had produced some distinctly different pongids by late Miocene and early Pliocene. Identify two of these and indicate the type of environment to which each was adapted.

7 What is the scientific name and geologic age of the oldest known hominid fossils? What is the nature of the fossil evidence which suggests that these ancient hominids had a relatively long period of childhood and adolescence?

8 Describe five characteristics which distinguish the skull of *Australopithecus* from that of modern man.

9 How many types of australopithecines were there, and what were they? Indicate three traits by which these types could be distinguished.

10 Cite three different hypotheses concerning the evolutionary relationship between *Australopithecus* and *Homo*.

11 Basing your conclusions strictly on fossil evidence and ancient living-floor sites, how would you describe hominid life 2 to 3 million years ago?

SEVEN

HOMINID EVOLUTIONARY HISTORY II:
From *Homo erectus* to Modern Man

THE FIRST BIG-GAME HUNTERS

From about 1.25 million to 300,000 years ago, *Homo erectus* occupied much of the Old World (Fig. 7-1). East Africa, North Africa (Algeria), southern France, and western Czechoslovakia have yielded fossil materials, tools, and camp-sites which indicate that these hominids were living there a million or more years ago. Indeed, if the large-brained early hominid shown in Fig. 6-20 is considered to be an *H. erectus,* this species was living in Africa 2.6 million years ago. The fossil remains of over 40 individuals dating from 500,000 to 1 million B.P. have been collected in northern China and southeast Asia (Java). Fossils, tools, and living sites have been discovered in North Africa (Morocco), northern Spain, southern Germany, and northern Hungary ranging from 300,000 to 500,000 years old.

FIGURE 7-1
Old World locations in which fossils,
tools, or living sites of *Homo erectus*
have been found.

A species with such wide distribution would be expected to show considerable geographic variation. Inasmuch as it flourished over a period of a million years or more, some variation within that time span would be anticipated also. The estimated average brain volume of the earliest forms was 940 cubic centimeters. Later forms of 300,000 to 500,000 years ago had an average cranial capacity of about 1,000 cubic centimeters. For the species as a whole, fossil skulls reflect a brain volume range from 775 to 1300 cubic centimeters.

The brain was broad and long but relatively flat; the frontal, temporal, and parietal lobes, as well as the cerebellum, were expanded (Fig. 7-2). It is believed that the improvement in both the size and internal organization of the brain may have been the result of big-game hunting and the necessity for more complex tool kits and more sophisticated levels of collaborative social behavior.

Homo erectus was a large hominid who stood 150 to 170 centimeters (5 to 5½ feet) tall. Its locomotor anatomy was that of a true strider. Undoubtedly, both these characteristics were associated with the extensive territory which a hunter of big game is obliged to cover. The postcranial skeleton was very similar to modern man's, but the cranial anatomy differed significantly (Fig. 7-3). The brain was smaller—1,000 cubic centimeters versus about 1350 cubic centimeters average for modern man—and the skull bones were much thicker. The skull was long and flat with a low cranial vault, and the occipital region was angular or pointed rather than rounded and full. The forehead was short, browridges were prominent, and both upper and lower jaws were fairly massive and bore relatively large teeth. A chin eminence was lacking.

That *H. erectus* was a hunter of large animals and represented a new high in hominid

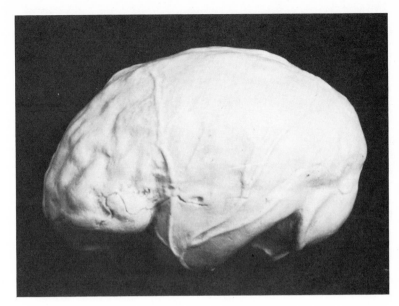

FIGURE 7-2
Endocranial cast of *Homo erectus*, left side.

technology and social integration is verified by the contents of a number of campsites and living floors which were discovered in Europe and Asia.

The life of *Homo erectus*

One of the oldest campsites of *H. erectus* was found in Vallonet Cave near Monte Carlo in southeastern France. This site is a million or more years old and contains the fossil bones of rhinoceroses, elephants, horses, and whales. Undoubtedly, the latter came from animals that had beached along the shore of the Mediterranean. Several bones appear to have been deliberately fractured and shattered, suggesting that a carcass had been butchered and marrow extracted from its bones. Scattered about the campsite were a number of stone tools including four flakes and five pebble tools (Fig. 6-22), two of which were Oldowanlike choppers. To the west, near Marseilles, relatively undisturbed living floors almost as old as the Vallonet campsite were discovered in the back chambers

of a buried cave. Excavations in this, the Escale Cave, furnished some fossil bones and the earliest conclusive evidence for the use of fire. Traces of charcoal and ash, fire-cracked stones, and reddened patches up to a meter (3 feet) in diameter on the ancient cave floor gave unmistakable proof of five hearth sites. No human fossils have yet been found in either of these caves.

Near Peking, China the skeletal remains, hearths, and Oldowanlike tools of *H. erectus* ("Peking Man") have been discovered in cave deposits between 500,000 and 800,000 years old. The deepest layers in the floor of these caves contained the fossil bones of large carnivores, like the saber-toothed tiger and giant hyena, and their prey. In the later upper layers, the bones of such creatures were gradually replaced by human remains and artifacts. It would appear that Peking Man eventually drove the large carnivores out of the caves and became the sole occupant himself. His use of fire may well have proved instrumental in making this possible. Most likely fire was also

FIGURE 7-3
Comparison of the restored skull of *Homo erectus* ("Peking Man") and modern *Homo sapiens* (the "old man of Cro-Magnon," Upper Pleistocene, France). *Left,* front view; *middle,* lateral view; *right,* rear view (cranium only). Skulls are casts.

Homo erectus

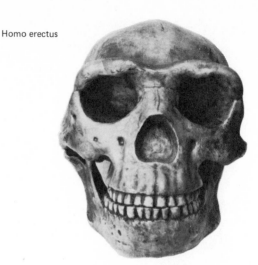

Front view

Homo sapiens

used for its warmth and to cook and tenderize meat. The charred bones of two species of deer have been recovered from these hearths as well as hackberry seeds, suggesting that Peking Man was not exclusively carnivorous. Two authorities on human paleontology, F. Clark Howell and J. D. Clark, believe that as much as 75 percent of the diet of *H. erectus* may have been vegetarian.

The appearance of a new toolmaking technology (industry)

As we move forward in time to about 300,000 years ago, hominids in Southern Europe apparently had increased their number over the earlier, sparser population of 1 million B.P., and a new technology had come into existence. Replacing the Oldowan tools and toolmaking technology (*industry*), a new tool assemblage made of stone and bone, known as the *Acheulian industry,* appeared (Fig. 7-4).

Large implements included heavy wedge-shaped cleavers which served as powerful choppers. Somewhat smaller, almond-shaped hand axes probably were not used for chopping but for skinning and slicing meat and perhaps even for shaping wooden spears and digging sticks. Among the smaller tools were various scrapers, blades, borers, engravers, and several different notched tools. Taken collectively, these implements indicate that fairly complex activities were taking place at the campsite and the home base.

Near the village of Torralba in northern Spain, such a tool kit was found in a relatively small area associated with the remains of at least 30 elephants, 25 horses, 25 deer, 10 wild cattle, and 6 rhinoceroses. Apparently the area had served as a butchering site; many bones

had been moved about and some of them had been shattered. Fossil pollen indicate the general locality had been swampland with dense stands of reeds, sedges, and bulrushes bordering a sluggish stream.

Howell collected bits of charcoal and carbon at this ancient slaughtering site, but rather than being concentrated in a few places as they

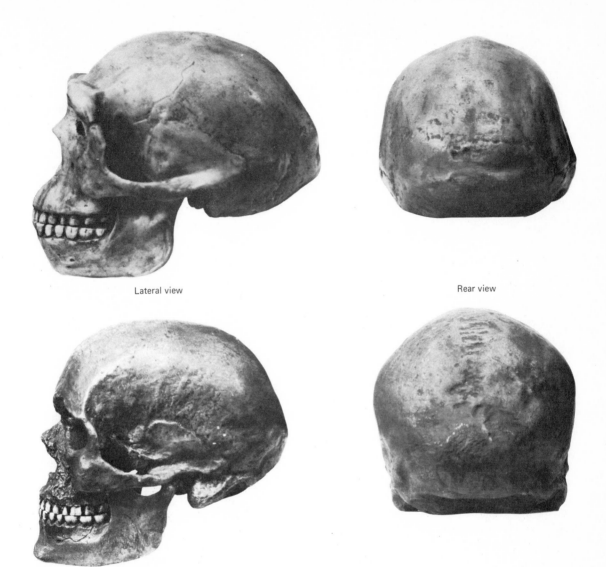

Lateral view   Rear view

would be if they represented hearth ash, they were scattered widely and thinly. Although these bits of carbon may have been hearth residue dispersed by wind, Howell suggests that hunters may have set fire to vegetation over large areas to stampede big-game animals into the swamp where they became mired down and immobilized. It is an interesting suggestion that receives additional support from an almost identical site just 3 kilometers away. Some 40 to 50 large mammals, predominantly elephants, with horses, deer, and wild cattle, were found concentrated, along with cleavers and other tools, in a deposit which had once been swampland; scattered about were bits and thin clusters of charcoal and ash, as if the same

194

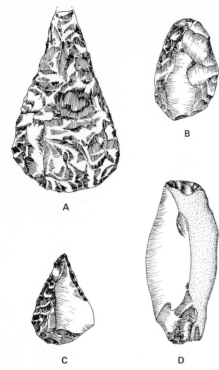

FIGURE 7-4
Acheulian tool kit: (A) hand ax, (B) side scraper, (C) point, and (D) end scraper. Compare with the Oldowan pebble tools in Fig. 6-22. [*After Francois Bordes, The Old Stone Age, McGraw-Hill, New York, 1968.*]

stratagem had been employed here as at Torralba, perhaps by the same hunters.

In any case, evidence of this nature indicates that hominid hunters somehow were capable of conducting big-game drives. Such activities required careful study of the habits of large mammals and entailed a high degree of planning and cooperation. As we will see, these hunters lived in bands of perhaps 15 to 20 individuals, women and children included. Several such bands would be required to provide the number of adult males necessary to conduct the highly organized hunt at Torralba.[1]

[1] F. Clark Howell, "Observations on the Earlier Phases of the European Lower Paleolithic," *Recent Studies in Paleontology,* American Anthropologist special publication, April 1966, pp. 111–140.

Social organization

For evidence throwing light on the size of *H. erectus* bands and the nature of the home base, we are indebted to the discovery by Henry DeLumley of the 400,000-year-old Terra Amata site in Nice, France. Evidently, substantial dwellings were being constructed at this time. The outlines of several temporary shelters were marked by the remains of postholes along an oval wall of stones. These oval dwellings were about 4.5 meters (15 feet) wide by 9 meters (30 feet) or more long and presumably were covered by branches or hides supported on sturdy poles (Fig. 7-5). The shelters contained hearths and the skeletal remains of deer, elephant, and wild boar. Also present were flat limestone blocks which may have served as seats or as flat surfaces on which meat was cut and bones broken. Pieces of a wooden bowl, the oldest container yet discovered, also were found. Located near the bowl were lumps of a natural pigment known as *red ocher* which were pointed at one end like a pencil as if they might have been used to mark the body or face for some rite or ceremony. Altogether about 20 successive living floors have been discovered at Terra Amata, each a thin layer resting on the one below, suggesting that the site was revisited regularly by one hominid band and its descendants. Judging from the dimensions of the oval huts and their contents, the size of the band was around 15 to 20 individuals and probably consisted of two or three nuclear families. The hunters visited the site in late spring because their fossil feces (coprolites) were found to contain the pollen of plants which blossom in late spring and early summer.[2]

If primitive hunter-gatherers like the Bushmen and Ngatatjara today provide relevant clues to the past, we can presume that an *H. erectus* band of 15 to 20 had a hunting territory of 1,300 to 3,900 square kilometers (500

[2] Henry DeLumley, "A Paleolithic Camp at Nice," *Scientific American,* May 1969, pp. 42–50.

FIGURE 7-5
Reconstruction of a Terra Amata
hut: interior (*above*) and exterior
(*below*), showing chimney and entrance. [*Courtesy of Henry de Lumley,
Professeur à l'Université de Provence.*]

to 1,500 square miles). Following large animals from their summer to their winter ranges and back again often necessitates extensive migrations by a hunting band. Such treks, no matter how arduous, are feasible to a hominid hunter because having a home base where rest and care are available transforms fevers and sprained ankles from fatal diseases to minor ailments. From the available evidence and what can be inferred from it, an *H. erectus* band must have utilized a home base usually for a few days if not for several weeks at a time.

Basic incest taboos must have been developed for the protection of the pair bond and the preservation of the family unit. The practice of finding one's mate from another band (exogamy) was probably encouraged, if not de-

manded, by rite and tradition. The exchange of mates between neighboring groups meant kinship ties and friendly relations among hominid bands whose territories may have overlapped within the broad region they shared. Interband collaboration suppresses needless fighting over territorial boundaries which not only wastes the energy of the hunters but also disturbs the game as well. Beyond that, big-game drives usually required the manpower that could only be provided by several cooperating groups.

The development of moral codes

Survival had become critically dependent upon social control, cooperative behavior, and the inhibition of unrestrained personal desires. The stage was set for the evolution of moral codes and ethical systems. The golden rule had become a biological necessity of life. Trivers has shown through a mathematical analysis of group behavior that the general practice of mutually acting to protect the interests of others—what he terms *reciprocal altruism*—would indeed have enhanced the survival potential of our hunting forebears.[3] The mark of success of a group whose existence depends upon mutual assistance is the capability and willingness of any member to act in the interest of the group, even at the risk of personal danger. Group preservation must have priority over self-preservation to an even greater extent than it does in most other animals. Moral indignation and feelings of guilt and shame tend to enforce the social system by discouraging irresponsible behavior. The expression of friendship, gratitude, and sympathy perform the same function positively by encouraging and rewarding responsible behavior.[4]

The significance of "domesticating" fire

Whatever social and ethical advances *H. erectus* had made over its early hominid ancestors were accompanied by a technological breakthrough of the greatest significance: the use of fire. Animals' natural fear of fire made it possible to drive predators from their dens in caves making these favored shelters available to hominids. As we have seen, fire also could be used to stampede animals into bogs or over cliffs. It provided warmth during the cold of the night and the winter, illuminated the dark cave-home, and extended the day beyond nightfall for evening relaxation, convivial conversation, and the laying of plans for the next day. Meat and vegetables cooked over the hearth not only were tenderized, but unquestionably fire also led to a major increase in the kinds of food that could be eaten safely.

Adequate cooking kills parasites in meat, such as trichinella or tapeworm larvae in pig

muscle, which might endanger the human consumer. Cooking also destroys a great variety of toxic substances found in plants which are otherwise nutritious; enzyme inhibitors, physiological irritants, allergenic substances, hormone-altering compounds, and vitamin antagonists are known to occur among legumes, cereals, and members of the potato and cabbage families. Detoxifying these substances by cooking may have added enormously to the list of plants on the human bill of fare.[5]

Homo erectus may even have used fire for religious and ritualistic purposes as did our ancestors 30,000 years ago, but there is no evidence to suggest this occurred. In sum, the control of fire was a giant step in the making of an unusual animal: a hominid whose biologic future would be marked not so much by its capacity to adapt to the environment as by its capacity to modify the environment to suit its needs—or what it presumes its needs to be.

Homo erectus in transition

To maintain such a position effectively demands the kind of power that comes only through the wholehearted collaborative effort of hominid groups acting in concert. Even this effort would be wasted unless it is directed intelligently and based upon a thorough knowledge of the hunting territories involved. Technologically primitive tribes today like the Bushmen or the Ngatatjara know their territories in meticulous detail; they are familiar with every bush, hill, ravine, and water hole over hundreds of square kilometers, not to mention the myriad places where various roots, tubers, nuts, berries, insects, reptiles, birds and their eggs, and mammals may be found at any time of the year. If this knowledge were to be printed in book form, it would require dozens of volumes. *Homo erectus* indisputably did not have the same keen perception or depth of understanding as that of modern hunter-gatherers. Such qualities, however, were be-

[3] Robert L. Trivers, "The Evolution of Reciprocal Altruism," *Quarterly Review of Biology*, vol. 46, no. 4, 1971, pp. 35–57.
[4] E. O. Wilson, *Sociobiology*, Cambridge, Mass.: Harvard University Press, 1975, pp. 120–121; 562–564.

[5] A. C. Leopold and R. Ardrey, "Toxic Substances in Plants and the Food Habits of Early Man," *Science*, vol. 176, May 5, 1972, pp. 512–513.

coming increasingly necessary in the world that hominids were cutting out for themselves about 300,000 years ago. This was beginning to be reflected by the slight but significant increase in average cranial capacity between early *H. erectus* skulls (940 cubic centimeters) and those of 300,000 to 500,000 years ago (1,000 cubic centimeters). The growing complexity of hominid life was placing a higher and higher premium on intelligence.

Near Budapest, Hungary, at Vertesszollos, the occipital bone of a hominid skull was found in association with some teeth, Oldowan tools, and hearths that are between 250,000 and 450,000 years old. The bone resembles that of modern man, and a cranial capacity of about 1,400 cubic centimeters has been established from it. Fossil remains as fragmentary as this cannot yield accurate estimates of brain volume. On the other hand, the shape of the bone indicates that the occipital region of the skull was rounded rather than angular suggesting that the remains may be those of an advanced form of *H. erectus*.

Hominids definitely were in a transitional evolutionary stage at this time because the remains of primitive forms of *Homo sapiens* have been discovered in European sites ranging from 200,000 to 250,000 years ago.

The first appearance of archaic man (*H. sapiens*)

The discovery and analysis of two fossil skulls in Europe have thrown considerable light on the ancestor-descendant relationship of *H. erectus* and *H. sapiens* (Fig. 7-6).

One specimen, the Swanscombe skull, consists of an occipital and two parietal bones which were found along with Acheulian hand axes and flakes in a gravel deposit east of London in southeastern England. The river gravels containing these remains were deposited in late middle Pleistocene time, toward the end of the great interglacial period of that epoch about 250,000 years ago. At some distance from this location, northeast of London at Clacton-on-Sea in Essex, a 38 centimeter (15-inch) spear point of about the same age was discovered. It is the oldest spear point yet found anywhere. That hominids might have reached England from the European mainland at, or prior to, this time was not at all improb-

FIGURE 7-6
Steinheim and Swanscombe skulls. The Steinheim skull (*left*) was found in southern Germany and is about 200,000 years old. The Swanscombe skull (*right*), about 250,000 years old, was found in southeastern England. Both represent an early, archaic form of *Homo sapiens*. Both skulls are casts.

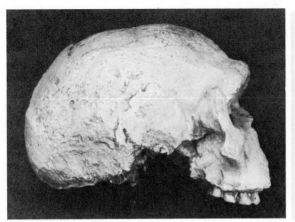

able, since sea levels were very low during glacial periods and during the early and late stages of interglacial periods. The bottom of the English Channel was above sea level, and the British Isles were a part of the European land mass during many of these intervals (see Fig. 2-16).

The other skull was an essentially complete specimen except that its left side was crushed. Known as the *Steinheim skull,* it was discovered near Stuttgart in southern West Germany and is of about the same geologic age as the Swanscombe skull, perhaps a little younger.

Comparative analysis of Swanscombe and Steinheim skulls

The Swanscombe and Steinheim skulls are of particular significance because of their intermediate position between *H. erectus* and *H. sapiens.* The evolution of *H. erectus* during middle Pleistocene time had resulted in a hominid with a bigger brain and postcranial adaptations for bipedal striding. The major changes that were made in the evolution of *H. sapiens* from late middle through late Pleistocene (some 250,000 years) were confined to the head: (1) average brain volume increased from 1,000 to about 1,350 cubic centimeters; (2) the size of the face, jaws, and teeth decreased; (3) browridges became less robust; (4) the occipital region of the skull became rounded, and the skull lost its flatness by having a higher cranial vault and a taller, more vertical forehead; and (5) the bones of the skull decreased in thickness (Fig. 7-3).

The Steinheim skull has a cranial capacity of about 1,200 cubic centimeters while that from Swanscombe is estimated to have been a little over 1,300 cubic centimeters. Insofar as points (2) to (5) above are concerned, the two skulls are generally intermediate between *H. sapiens* and *H. erectus* (compare Figs. 7-3, 7-6, and 7-7). All in all, the Steinheim and Swanscombe fossils seem to meet the specifications for an archaic form of *H. sapiens* (Latin, *sapiens,* "wise").

Despite the fact that the Swanscombe specimen lacks both forehead and face, it has been shown to bear a very close resemblance to the Steinheim skull. This has been demonstrated in a painstaking study in which a variety of anatomically critical measurements were made of the Swanscombe skull. Comparable measurements were made of several hundred modern skulls and ten fossil skulls, one of which was the Steinheim specimen. These voluminous data were subjected to computer-

FIGURE 7-7
A reconstruction of the archaic *Homo sapiens* from Steinheim. *Below,* reconstructed skull; *right,* parts of skull to which muscles attach serve as guide for reconstructing muscles; *far right,* reconstructed muscles and cranial features provide basic contours for rebuilding the skin surface, and bust is completed. [*Courtesy of Dr. Zbigniew Rajchel.*]

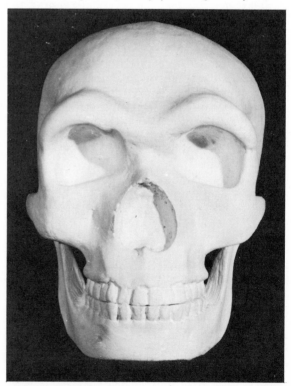

ized multivariate analysis[6] which showed that the two skulls were not only quite similar but also resembled a group of later sapient hominids known as the *Neanderthals*.[7] It is distinctly possible that some of the ancient populations represented by the Steinheim and Swanscombe fossils were ancestral to the Neanderthal peoples of 100,000 years ago.

Evolutionary increase in brain size

In retracing the evolution of the hominid family from its beginnings in the Miocene, it would seem that as far back as 200,000 years ago, the human lineage had come a long way (Fig. 7-8).

---

[6] See footnote 1, Chap. 6.
[7] Bernard Campbell, "Quantitive Taxonomy and Human Evolution," *Classification and Human Evolution*. S. L. Washburn (ed.), Chicago: Aldine Publishing Company, 1963, pp. 57–59.

Evolution apparently resulted in progressive improvement among hominids in their technological proficiency, communication, social cohesiveness, and capacity for understanding and manipulating the environment around them. Since these qualities are intimately associated with intelligence, we might expect that such manifestations of intellectual growth would be reflected in an increase in brain size. Figure 7-9 reveals that this had been the case. Increase in brain volume was pronounced, persistent, and rapid from the australopithecine stages through *H. erectus* to the archaic *H. sapiens* of Swanscombe and Steinheim. Although early *H. sapiens* probably was considerably less than twice as heavy as *"H. habilis"* (early *H. erectus?*), its brain volume was almost twice as large. This is especially significant in

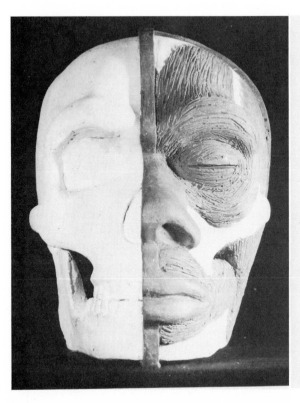
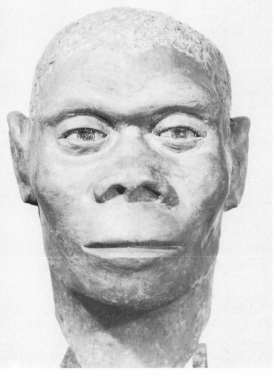

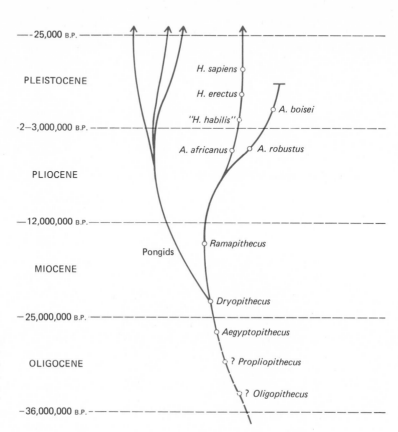

RECENT

−25,000 B.P.

PLEISTOCENE

H. sapiens

H. erectus

A. boisei

-2−3,000,000 B.P.

"H. habilis"

A. africanus   A. robustus

PLIOCENE

−12,000,000 B.P.

Ramapithecus

Pongids

MIOCENE

−25,000,000 B.P.

Dryopithecus

FIGURE 7-8
An interpretation of the hominid lineage in relation to its Miocene ancestors, the dryopithecine apes (*Dryopithecus* and *Aegyptopithecus*). It is possible that *"H. habilis"* is either an early form of *H. erectus* or an advanced australopith.

Aegyptopithecus

OLIGOCENE

? *Propliopithecus*

? *Oligopithecus*

−36,000,000 B.P.

view of the fact that small species usually have larger brains per kilogram of body weight than related larger species. The mouse lemur, for example, has a bigger brain with respect to its body weight than does modern man. The brain volume of early populations of *H. sapiens* also may have averaged a little more than the 1,260 cubic centimeters figure in the tabulation since both Steinheim and Swanscombe skulls were those of females about 20 years old. Females usually have a slightly smaller brain than males. In any case, the brain volumes of both these fossil skulls, estimated at 1,200 and 1,325 cubic

centimeters, respectively, fall well within the range of variation of modern man (1,000 to 2,000 cubic centimeters) and close to its mean of 1,350 cubic centimeters.

To this point, 200,000 to 250,000 years ago, and continuing until about 100,000 B.P., hominid technologies and ways of life are classified as early Stone Age, or *Lower Paleolithic* cultures. From such Lower Paleolithic beginnings, our ancient predecessors struck out on an evolutionary course that led to "The golden age of prehistory" and ultimately to agricultural and industrial civilizations.

THE RISE OF MODERN MAN

The history of archaic man was not confined to Europe. Many more remains have come from there simply because this is where most students of human prehistory have worked; European fossil sites are easily found and are readily accessible. Africa had the richest hunting grounds in the world, and very likely supported a human population at least five times that of Europe. During glacial periods, Europe probably harbored no more than 5 percent of the total world population because of its harsh living conditions during those times. By the same token, technological evolution appears to have been slower in Africa because favorable climates and abundant game offered less incentive for increased efficiency and creativity.

Therefore, it is not surprising that most of the record of archaic man and his technological advance comes from Europe and the eastern Mediterranean area. Deposits of early Upper Pleistocene age have yielded a wealth of evidence on the technological progress of early *H. sapiens* populations in this region. A more advanced type of tool technology (industry) and life-style had evolved which was a notch or two above the older Paleolithic cultures of the past. The human species was elevating itself to what has come to be known as the *Middle Paleolithic* level of cultural development.

Archaic man in transition

A rock shelter site[8] in the Dordogne Valley of France (Combe Grenal) chronicles much of this cultural history. The earliest record of human occupation in this ancient rock shelter comes from its lowermost deposits which were laid down some 125,000 to 150,000 years ago. Although the first occupants left none of their skeletal remains, they did leave a number of Acheulian tools like those found at Swanscombe. Numerous animal bones, predominantly reindeer, were found among the tools.

Lying directly above these Acheulian deposits is a series of sediments containing an almost unbroken record of human occupation from about 90,000 to 40,000 years ago. A group of up to 40 individuals lived at the site generation after generation for 50,000 years, except for a few small gaps in time when the

[8] A rock shelter site is one at the base of a large vertical rock face such as a cliff or steep canyon wall.

FIGURE 7-9
Progressive increase in brain size during hominid evolution from *Ramapithecus* to Swanscombe-Steinheim *Homo sapiens*. The estimated brain volumes of the Swanscombe and Steinheim specimens fall within the range of variation of modern man (1,000 to 2,000 cubic centimeters). They are close to the modern mean of 1,350 cubic centimeters since both fossil skulls were those of females about 20 years old. Females have a slightly smaller brain than males. In comparing the rate of brain volume increase, it should be remembered that small species have larger brains per kilogram of body weight than larger species of the same general kind.

Hominid species	Approximate age in millions of years	Estimated average brain volume, cubic centimeters	Estimated total body weight, kilograms*	Average estimated rate of brain volume increase from preceding hominid in cc/million years
Ramapithecus	15	300?	25	
A. africanus	5	450	to	15
"*H. habilis*"	2	657+	35	69+
H. erectus	0.5	1,000	55	229
			to	
H. sapiens (Swanscombe-Steinheim)	0.2	1,260	60	867

* 1 kilogram = 2.2 pounds.

climate may have become too harsh. The occupants left a rich array of Middle Paleolithic tools belonging to what is called the *Mousterian industry,* of which some 19,000 already have been collected. These, together with hundreds of thousands of others found in the Dordogne Valley area, have been classified into more than 60 different kinds of tools, including blades, borers, spear points, a variety of scrapers, numerous notched or toothed tools, and hand axes (Fig. 7-10).

The Mousterian industry

The Middle Paleolithic Mousterian[9] industry differed from those of the Lower Paleolithic by a great increase in the variety of flake tools designed for a specific purpose; it placed less reliance on the general-purpose hand ax. Flake tools (Fig. 7-10, no. 2) are made by striking chips (flakes) from the surface of a suitable rock. A hand ax (Fig. 7-10, no. 7) is a core tool — what is left of a suitable rock after it has been shaped by chipping.

S. R. and L. R. Binford have conducted a detailed statistical analysis of these tools to determine if particular tool types tended to occur together as specialized functional units. The Combe Grenal site lent itself beautifully to

[9] Like the Lower Paleolithic Acheulian industry, the Mousterian derives its name from the geographic location in France where tools of these types were first discovered and classified.

such a study. Voluminous records were prepared reconstructing the relationship between each tool and the other tools, hearths, and animal bones in a given living floor. The Binfords subjected their records to multivariate analysis, which revealed 14 distinct tool kits or groupings. These tool kits fell into one of two broad categories: (1) those used for such maintenance functions as the preparation and consumption of food, and the manufacture of tools around a home base, and (2) those used for specific tasks, such as at killing and butchering sites, or at quarries for the extraction of flint for toolmaking in temporary work camps.

Home base camps are selected because they afford protection from the elements, provide adequate living space, and are centrally located with respect to game, water, and toolmaking materials. Archaeologically they often can be identified by abundant traces of fire. Many of the occupational layers (living floors) at Combe Grenal indicate that the shelter was used as a base camp for long periods. Maintenance tool kits included borers, engravers, scrapers, and notched or toothed tools which may have been used for sawing, shredding, cutting, shaping, or smoothing bone or wood. The products of these endeavors might have been digging sticks, handles, spear shafts, tent pegs, and various items derived from worked animal hides, such as leather thongs, clothing,

FIGURE 7-10
Some Mousterian tool types. *A,* Notched or toothed (denticulate) tools: 1, notched tool; 2, toothed tool; 3, borer. *B,* Scrapers and blades: 4, transverse scraper; 5, backed knife on a blade. *C,* Points, 6. *D,* Hand ax, 7. [*After Francois Bordes, The Old Stone Age, McGraw-Hill, New York, 1968.*]

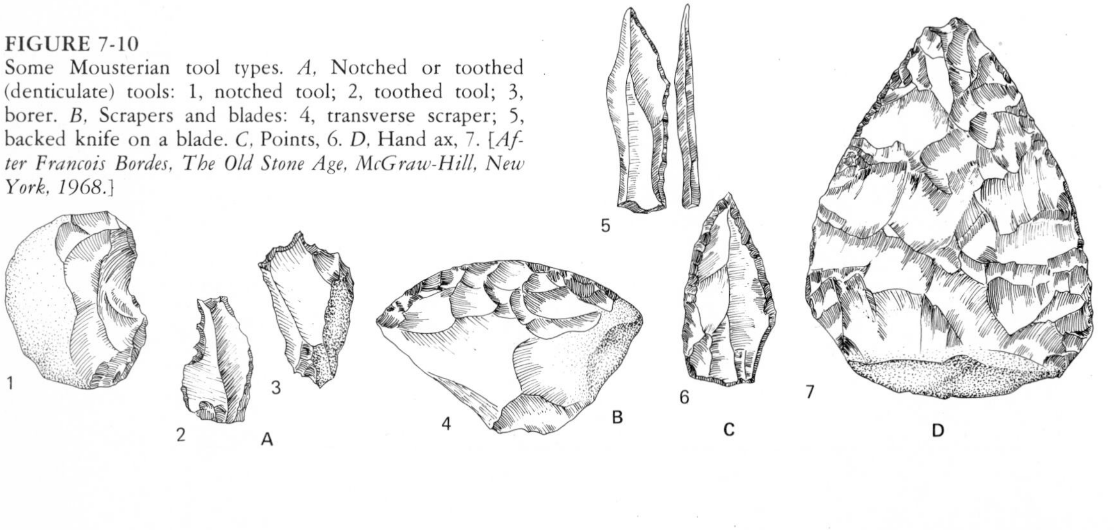

and tent covers. Numerous tools seem to have been made to prepare meat for eating. Knives apparently were used for heavy-duty cutting whereas flakes were employed for trimming and carving.

The remaining occupation layers at Combe Grenal suggest that the site was being used as a temporary station for some specialized activity during those periods. Some of these layers contain spear points and a large variety of scrapers—tool-kit items thought to be associated with killing and butchering.[10]

From this sketchy reconstruction of human activity, it is clear that the ancient inhabitants of Combe Grenal were living rather complex lives. Fourteen kinds of tool kits suggest a broad range of specialized activities. Each major function, whether it was food processing, hide preparation, toolmaking, woodworking, killing and butchering, or quarrying, very likely had more than one assemblage of special tools for dealing with different kinds of foods, hides, tools, etc. This was the character of Middle Paleolithic technology. It also was the technical culture of our early Upper Pleistocene forebears, the Neanderthals.

The Neanderthals

One of the first fossils of mid-Paleolithic man was found in 1856 in the Neander Valley of West Germany; it is from this specimen that the name *Neanderthal* was derived. We use the term here to refer to all human populations who lived from about 100,000 to 40,000 years ago during early Upper Pleistocene times.

Neanderthal *Homo sapiens* left an impressive record of fossil remains, artifacts, and cultural activities. The skeletal remains of some 150 individuals have been recovered from 70 sites in the Old World, including locations in Spain, France, Belgium, Germany, Italy, Greece, Yugoslavia, southern Russia (Crimea), Iraq, Israel, North Africa, South Africa, south central Asia (Uzbeck), southern

China, and Java. Based both on skeletal and cultural remains, the distribution of Neanderthal peoples probably approached that shown in Fig. 7-11.

During the first half of their 60,000-year span the climate of temperate Eurasia generally was mild; the world was in the midst of an interglacial period. The final half encompassed the first glacial advance of the last great glaciation of Pleistocene time; Europe became a land of subarctic cold, populated by reindeer and now-extinct wooly rhinoceros, cave bear, and mammoth.

Nonmaterial culture: ritual and altruism
The peoples of Middle Paleolithic Eurasia were culturally distinguished from their Lower Paleolithic forebears by more than technological differences. Neanderthal sites have furnished strong evidence of ritualistic practices and a religious belief in life after death. A bear cult, for example, apparently flourished in Europe. In order to reside in caves, people often had to drive out the cave bears who lived there. Commonly, the bears were killed in considerable number and eaten; but evidently they were involved in a kind of sacrificial rite as well. One of several sites which support this belief is a cave in eastern Austria. Well inside the cave and close to a rock-ringed hearth, a rectangular stone vault about 1 meter (about 3 feet) high was covered with a single limestone slab. Within the vault were seven carefully placed cave bear skulls with their snouts pointing toward the cave entrance.

Many other sites testify to the practice of human ceremonial burial. In the Dordogne Valley (Le Moustier) a shallow grave was discovered below a rock shelter. It contained the body of a youth about 15 years old who had been carefully laid to rest on his right side, his head resting on his right forearm. A hand ax lay at his side and a pile of flint chippings surrounded his head. Wild cattle bones, many of them burned, also were present. Presumably, roasted meat had been placed in the grave to sustain the departed in the hereafter.

[10] S. R. and L. R. Binford, "Stone Tools and Human Behavior," *Scientific American*, April 1969, pp. 70–84.

FIGURE 7-11
The distribution of Neanderthal *Homo sapiens* indicated by skeletal and cultural remains.

On occasion, human burial was embellished by an animal ritual. More than 50,000 years ago, a cave in Central Asia (Uzbeck) was the site for the burial of an eight- or nine-year-old youth. Over the shallow grave, some six pairs of wild goat (ibex) horns encircled the youth's head, thrust into the ground with their pointed ends downward. More than 50,000 years later, an ibex cult still persists in this region.

One of the most revealing testimonies to Neanderthalian humanity took place about 60,000 years ago in the Shanidar Cave in Iraq. A man whose head evidently had been crushed by falling rock was buried there. Fossil pollen collected at the burial site indicated that the deceased had been laid on a bed of freshly picked flowers, the wild ancestors of blue grape hyacinths, golden ragwort, bachelor's buttons, and hollyhocks. This same individual had been born with a withered right arm which

later had been successfully amputated above the elbow. The man had survived this misfortune until his head was crushed many years later, suggesting that these people not only cared for disabled members of their band but also were reasonably skilled in doing so.[11]

Cannibalism and warfare   On the basis of such evidence, it is plausible that the Neanderthal peoples may have been responsible for the development of animal cults, religion, and a certain expertise as well as concern in furthering human welfare. On the other hand, it is equally possible that they also may have played an important role in the development of warfare. A number of Old World sites suggest that men were violently killing other men. The pelvis of one fossil bears a spear hole; a spear

[11] R. S. Solecki, *Shanidar: The First Flower People*, New York: Alfred A. Knopf, Inc., 1971, pp. 195–196.

point has been found in the rib cage of another. A campsite in Java contained 11 skulls but, with the exception of two shinbones, no other skeletal parts. All the skulls were damaged and were without faces, jaws, or teeth. The site has been interpreted, not unreasonably, as a temporary headhunter's camp. Another mass killing may have taken place in north-western Yugoslavia (Krapina) and seems to have ended in a cannibalistic feast. A cave hearth was found to contain over 500 bone fragments belonging to at least a dozen individuals. Many of the broken bones were burned and the arm and leg bones had been cracked open their full length.

Neanderthals and the emergence of modern man

As we noted, Neanderthal populations occupied a large portion of the Old World (Fig. 7-11). The inhabitants of this vast region today are by no means similar in appearance or body build. We would expect Middle Paleolithic populations to show at least as much biologic variation as do their modern counterparts, particularly since Neanderthals occupied the area for 60,000 years. Moreover, during this time the climate in temperate latitudes at first was mild in the interglacial phase, but it turned to bitter cold in the final 30 millennia.

Since variation is the hallmark of every population, one must guard against the easy creation of separate species or lineages just because of the existence of differences between local groups. Unless these differences are as great as those which separate two related living species, it must be assumed that this diversity merely reflects normal variation in a species which inhabits varied habitats.

Fossil hominids ranging from 70,000 to 100,000 years old have been collected in France, Germany, and Italy which are intermediate types between the Swanscombe and Steinheim fossils and Neanderthal specimens of 40,000 years ago. The Neanderthals themselves were undoubtedly a diverse group. Even so, their cranial capacities and postcranial

skeletons fall well within the range of variation found in modern man. All these people were fully erect, striding bipeds who, contrary to many of their former characterizations, were neither brutish nor subhuman in appearance.

The first Neanderthal skulls found in Western Europe were relatively long and low, with sloping foreheads and a projecting, often bun-shaped, occipital region. Faces tended to jut forward beneath well-developed browridges (Fig. 7-12A). Skulls with these features were said to be "classic" Neanderthals. Even the "classic" Neanderthal, however, was probably not exceptional in appearance (Fig. 7-13). Furthermore, subsequent fossil finds indicate that West European Neanderthals were more varied than once believed. Forms more like modern man coexisted with the "classic" type.

The disappearance of Neanderthals and their culture About 40,000 years ago a change began to occur in the toolmaking traditions in Europe. A new level of industry, the *Upper Paleolithic,* began to emerge in Western and Central Europe associated with the remains of fully modern types of man. As these changes occurred, the archaic Neanderthal types seemed to disappear along with their mid-Paleolithic cultural traditions.

Its much more frequent use of the *blade* separates the Upper Paleolithic industry from Middle Paleolithic. A blade is a flake tool with roughly parallel sides (Fig. 7-10, no. 5). In the Upper Paleolithic these tools were made by a punched-blade technique (Fig. 7-14). From a flint core which had been especially prepared in advance, large numbers of flakes (blades) could be struck off by means of a sharpened bone or antler punch. Many more tools could be made from a single core than by older, mid-Paleolithic methods. Combination tools were introduced as well as a variety of new implements, including combination engravers and scrapers, many different chisels (burins), and saws (Fig. 7-15). New kinds of hunting instruments came into being fashioned of sinew, bone, antler, ivory, or wood; a spear-

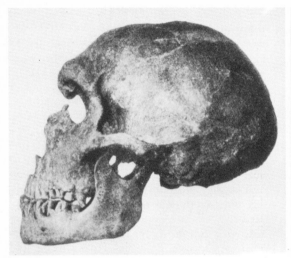

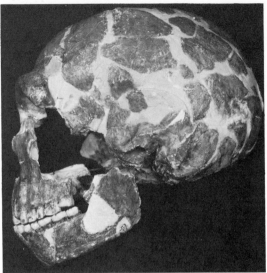

FIGURE 7-12   A

Homo sapiens skulls found in association with Mousterian cultural remains, age approximately 40,000 to 60,000 B.P. (*A*) La Ferrassie, France; (*B*) Tabun I, Israel (right side reversed); and (*C*) Skhūl V, Israel. *C* is a cast. [*A, Courtesy of the Museum of Man, Paris; B, Courtesy of the British Museum (Natural History).*]

B

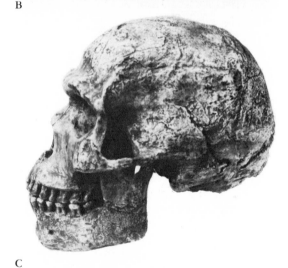

C

shaft straightener was developed and the bow and arrow, spear-thrower, and harpoon were invented. These implements commonly were decorated with engraved abstract designs or the figures of game animals.

Modern man's origin   Some persons believe that the Upper Paleolithic industry and more modern types of *Homo sapiens* appeared suddenly, replacing the mid-Paleolithic Mousterian industry and the Neanderthals who practiced it. They suggest that Neanderthals were wiped out by invading migrations of more advanced types of man. Growing evidence, however, indicates that the Neanderthals were the ancestors of modern man.[12]

In those sites where there is an uninter-

rupted sequence of living floors spanning the period from 40,000 to 25,000 years ago, there is a gradual transition from a mid-Paleolithic to an Upper Paleolithic culture. Furthermore, the Neanderthal populations of 40,000 to 100,000 years ago were represented by a large variety of types.

A series of hominid fossils recovered in Iraq (Shanidar) and Israel (Tabun and Skhūl,

[12] D. S. Brose and M. H. Wolpoff, "Early Upper Paleolithic Man and Late Middle Paleolithic Tools," *American Anthropologist,* vol. 73, 1971, pp. 1156–1194.

Fig. 7-12) reflect some of the gradations from modernlike (Shanidar, Tabun) to modern (Skhūl) among fossil skulls ranging in age from 40,000 to 60,000 or more years. All these remains were associated with a Mousterian culture. A similar gradation is illustrated in skulls collected in Kenya and Ethiopia which are 90,000 to 100,000 years old. One of these has a modern aspect comparable to the Skhūl skulls. In all these skulls, one or more advanced features are shown in varying degrees of development: (1) a shorter skull with a higher vault, (2) a more rounded occipital region, (3) more moderate browridges, (4) a less projecting facial skeleton, and (5) smaller jaws and teeth, and the development of a chin eminence.

It would appear that human populations of 100,000 to 40,000 years ago comprised a spectrum of types from the "classic" Neanderthals to forms in East Africa and the Middle East which differed little from modern man.

How, from such diverse mid-Paleolithic peoples, could modern *Homo sapiens* emerge with an Upper Paleolithic culture? It is suggested by S. R. Binford that the origin of modern man was due to changes in social organization and behavior brought about by a shift in hunting patterns. According to her, there was an apparent change, near the end of the Mousterian cultural phase, from generalized big-game hunting of individual animals to the systematic pursuit of wild cattle herds and other large herd animals. Presumably, this necessitated the formation of much larger social units by unifying formerly self-sufficient small bands through exogamous mating systems. Corresponding improvements in the economy and efficiency of tool manufacture would also be called for to implement the organized hunting of large herd animals en masse. Such a hunting economy, efficiently managed, could support a larger human population and require further advances and refinements in social organization.[13]

<hr/>

[13] S. R. Binford, "Early Upper Pleistocene Adaptations in the Levant," *American Anthropologist*, vol. 70, 1968, pp. 707–717.

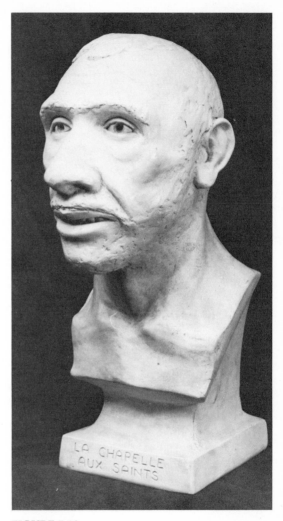

FIGURE 7-13
Flesh restoration of "classic" Neanderthal. Restoration by C. S. Coon of the skull from La Chapelle aux Saints, France (also illustrated in Fig. 2-15).

The Golden Age of Prehistory

In Europe, the transition from mid-Paleolithic Neanderthal to Upper Paleolithic modern forms of *H. sapiens* took place between about 40,000 and 25,000 years ago. The record left by European Upper Paleolithic communities

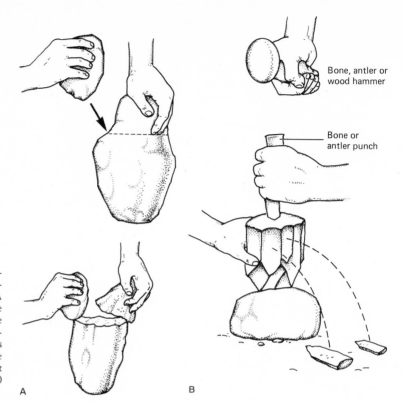

Bone, antler or
wood hammer

Bone or
antler punch

FIGURE 7-14
The prepared-core and punched-blade technique of Upper Paleolithic stone-tool manufacture. *A*, A core from which many blades can be made is prepared by breaking a large flint nodule in two with a hammer-stone. *B*, From this a series of blades can be struck off by means of a bone or antler punch. A 1-kilogram (about 2 pounds) core will yield 40 to 50 blade tools.

A   B

from 25,000 to about 12,000 years ago has been abundantly preserved and thoroughly studied in three more or less contiguous regions: a section along the northern coast of Spain, the French Pyrenees south of Toulouse and, especially, the Dordogne Valley in the general vicinity of Les Eyzies, France. It is a record complete with artistic masterpieces of sculpture and painting, the oldest of which were at least 400 centuries younger than the earliest known religious rites of mid-Paleolithic burial. It is also a record of people who were reorganizing social structure by associating bands into tribal units.

Community structure
At Les Eyzies, an early Upper Paleolithic site was excavated beneath the limestone cliff

that overlooks the town. The remains of a long house were exposed, with a row of hearths extending almost its full length. Apparently about 23,000 years ago, the structure had harbored a small community of several families shielding its occupants from the bitter cold of glacial winters. Some 10,000 years later, a much larger community thrived several kilometers down river. This was a late Upper Paleolithic site consisting of shelters known as "row houses" which were laid out side by side along a 3-kilometer (2-mile) stretch bordering the Dordogne River. This settlement is estimated to have housed between 400 and 600 persons. Upstream about 30 kilometers (20 miles), a similar settlement of the same age occupied a hundred meters or more of river bank.

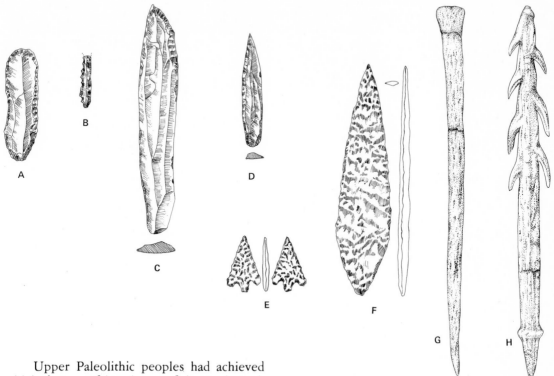

Upper Paleolithic peoples had achieved a high degree of hunting proficiency through their collaborative, community-oriented efforts. River salmon and herds of reindeer, bison, horses, and mammoth were exploited not only as food but also as sources of sinew and hides to make clothing and tent covers. These peoples used bone, antler, and ivory for manufacturing tools, tent poles (from mammoth tusks), bone whistles, clothes fasteners, necklaces, amulets, sculpted figurines, and possibly even lunar calendars (Figs. 7-16 and 7-17).

Shared traditions and rituals

The social forces which integrated community life evidently involved more than a unification of bands through intermarriage. Shared traditions and rituals seem to have played a strong role also. A wealth of art objects attest to this — statuettes, figurines, and cave paintings, engravings, and bas-relief sculpture (Figs. 7-17 and 7-18).

FIGURE 7-15
Upper Paleolithic tools of stone, bone, and antler. *A,* End scraper on retouched blade; *B,* toothed (denticulate) bladelet; *C,* retouched blade; *D,* gravette point; *E,* barbed point; *F,* laurel leaf point; *G,* bone awl; *H,* harpoon made of reindeer antler. [*After Francois Bordes, The Old Stone Age, McGraw-Hill, New York, 1968.*]

Many statuettes of the human female figure have been found, like the Venus of Willendorf (Fig. 7-17*A*); often they were much more stylized than this. Commonly, emphasis was given to the genital area, and always to the breasts, whereas the face, arms, and legs were only suggested if shown at all. The hair was stylized on some and at least one depicted clothing on the body. Some European anthropologists have interpreted Venuses as fetishes or magic talismans for ensuring fertility.

FIGURE 7-16
This Upper Paleolithic artifact from Hungary may be a lunar calendar. Diagrammatic sketch below suggests interpretation in terms of lunar cycle. The object, a flat disk of carved limestone, is one of various objects and painted notations with comparable markings. [By permission of Dr. Ilona Kovrig, National Museum of Hungary.]

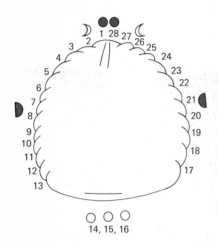

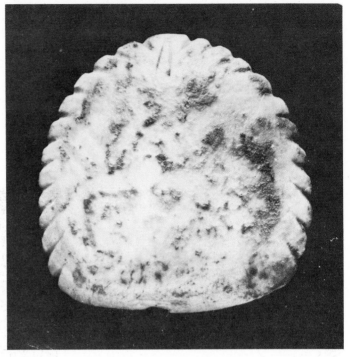

Magic hunting rituals   One does not have to look far for other evidence of ritual and cults based on magic. Animal figurines have been found which are carved from antler or ivory; some were even modeled in ceramic material and baked in a primitive kiln. The site of an Upper Paleolithic encampment in Czechoslovakia (Vestonice) has produced ceramic figurines of a variety of animals as well as the remains of a primitive clay-lined kiln surrounded by partly formed figures and lumps of modeling material bearing the sculptor's fingerprints. The ceramic material was composed of animal bone and clay, probably kneaded together with fat. Many mutilated animal figurines have been found in the encampment, suggesting the possibility of some magic hunting ceremony. It has been theorized that a tribal "sorcerer" or priest broke these animal figures as part of a pre-hunting ritual

in which the destruction of the image was believed to result in the death of the living model. It is a superstition commonly held today, especially among technologically primitive people.

Probably Upper Paleolithic people did have the equivalent of a tribal or community witch doctor, sorcerer, or priest. A number of cave paintings and engravings, such as that shown in Fig. 7-18A, are difficult to interpret in any other way. In this instance the figure of a man is revealed, dressed in an animal skin that terminates in a horse's tail and human genitalia. The head is adorned with a full beard below and reindeer antlers above, while in between a pair of glaring eyes are fixed on the viewer. The image depicted corresponds closely to the witch doctors who lead hunting rituals in hunter-gatherer tribes today.

Upper Paleolithic cave art itself very

likely attests to religious ceremonies centered around a hunting magic, at least those paintings, engravings, and bas-relief sculptures that grace cave walls and ceilings. The hunting theme overshadows all else in these art forms, many of which were exquisitely drawn with great attention to accurate anatomical detail (Fig. 7-18*B,C*). Others were done impressionistically, with a sensitive awareness of line, motion, and psychological impact.

During the late Upper Paleolithic, polychrome (multicolored) painting developed, using rich as well as gently shaded reds, yellows, and blacks made by mixing ground ochers and manganese oxide derived from local rock. With few exceptions only animals are shown, and these are almost exclusively those that were hunted, namely reindeer, wild cattle, bison, wild horse, hairy rhinoceros, mammoth, wild goat, wild boar, and cave bear. Occasionally trapping techniques were illustrated. Only seldom were people drawn, and usually they appear as diagrammatic caricatures with little regard for human form or proportion. Apparently, landscapes were not done at all. Numerous dots, lines, rectangles, and other geometric marks and signs are common, but their meanings are obscure. As noted, some may have been calendars.

Most cave art is located within relatively

A

B

FIGURE 7-17
Upper Paleolithic statuettes and figurines. *A,* Venus of Willendorf (Austria), carved from limestone, about 10 centimeters (4 inches) high; *B,* a horse carved from ivory, about 7.5 centimeters (3 inches) long (Grotte de Lourdes, France). [*A, American Museum of Natural History; B, drawing by H. Breuil, 1909, after E. Piette, 1895.*]

inaccessible recesses of the cave and along walls or ceilings that often are difficult to reach. Commonly, the animal figures have arrows or spears sticking into them. Particularly striking is the degree to which pictures are super-imposed over other pictures. There is a strong suggestion that certain parts of a cave were considered sacred, where the magic power was the strongest. Such a case would not be without precedent; aborigines in Northern Australia as late as the 1960s prepared for a hunt by first painting the animals they wanted to kill in certain sacred locations.

Polychrome art: portraiture of prayer? Most of the famous polychrome paintings were products of very late Paleolithic times when big-game herds were in a serious decline. It is as if these late Paleolithic hunters were making a special effort to restore the abundance they once had known. Vast herds of large mammals previously had populated the land, averaging perhaps 10 or more tons of meat per

A

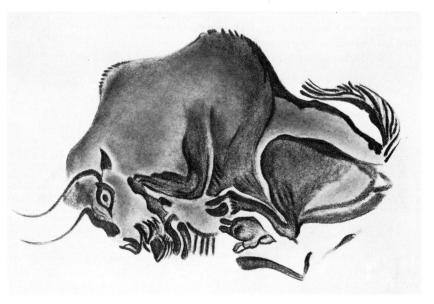

B

square kilometer (25 tons per square mile). But these animals had been systematically hunted, sometimes on a large scale, by the world's most formidable predator. Mute testimony of this lies at the foot of a high rock cliff in southern France. A layer of wild horse bones up to 245 centimeters (8 feet) thick was discovered over an extensive area along the cliff base. It is estimated that the deposit contained the remains of at least 40,000 horses which had been stampeded over the precipice by late Paleolithic hunters, presumably by setting grass fires. Large mammal herds could well find it difficult to maintain their numbers against onslaughts like this, especially since evidence for such mass slaughter comes from widely scattered quarters of the Old World—to say nothing of the mass slaughter of bison and other large mammals in the New World by Paleo-Indians.[14]

Population explosion

The skill with which man could stock his larder enabled our species to increase its numbers dramatically. The opportunity for population expansion was enhanced further by an improvement in the weather conditions between 20,000 and 16,000 B.P. The last great glaciers retreated at this time, raising sea levels 75 to 150 meters (250 to 500 feet). Vast areas of continental shelf were reflooded, contributing to the development of rich coastal marine faunas and a new food supply. Upper Paleolithic peoples, moreover, had learned the knack of living in large year-round settlements, and nomadic season-to-season movements were no

[14] P. S. Martin, "The Discovery of America," *Science,* vol. 179, Mar. 9, 1973, pp. 969–974.

FIGURE 7-18
Upper Paleolithic cave art. *A,* painting of a man (0.75 meters high) dressed in animal skin with horse's tail and stag antlers, thought to represent a "sorcerer" or "priest" in a hunting ritual (Les Trois Freres, France); *B.* a female bison from Altamira Caves, Spain; *C,* a reindeer from Font-de-Gaume Cave, Dordogne Valley, France, painted in black manganese oxide and red and yellow ochre. [*American Museum of Natural History.*]

C

longer required. Women, therefore, had no reason to limit the number of their offspring through infanticide or other means. All these factors combined to produce the first human population explosion. From an estimated world population of perhaps 1 to 3 million for archaic man, the population may have risen to 5 — and some think as high as 10 — million between 30,000 and 12,000 years ago.

The long-range effects of a milder climate and the mass harvesting of big game differed sharply from their immediate rewards. Warmer climates forced the movement of cold-adapted animals like reindeer and mammoth further and further northward. Mass-slaughter techniques may have been the chief agent in bringing about the worldwide extinction of mastodons and mammoths and the elimination of horses from North America and Europe. The human species was about to force itself out of the hunting business. Polychrome paintings would not restore the hunts of former times, but they were to become a memorial to the waning days of the world's most powerful hunter.

HUNTERS WITHOUT PREY

Homo sapiens had arrived at a major crossroad in its evolutionary journey. The hunter-gatherer economy, which had been exploited to the point where it supported large communities of people, was beginning to falter and crumble because of milder climates and excessive hunting pressure. Throughout Europe and the Near East, the vast big-game herds of the past no longer were in evidence and, with the exception of wild cattle, had been replaced by smaller, more elusive creatures such as deer, wild boar, sheep, and goats. Fewer areas of abundance were available to the hunter and the remaining submarginal lands were not productive enough to support him in the manner to which he had become accustomed. An economic change of

conspicuous proportions would be required to keep human populations from outrunning their food supplies and lapsing back into the more primitive life styles of Middle or Lower Paleolithic cultures. Such an economic revolution did occur. Since wild foods were in short supply, our hunting forebears presumably followed the path of least resistance. Through plant and animal domestication they deliberately extended the distribution of favored food species into marginal, less productive areas.

The agricultural revolution

Agriculture developed independently in Central America and the Near East, and possibly in Southeast Asia. Present evidence points to the Near East as the region where farming first was practiced. Many late Paleolithic sites along the Nile Valley in Egypt suggest that milled grain was utilized for food as early as 15,000 B.P. Numerous, heavily worn grinding stones have been found in this area along with botanical evidence for the presence of wheat rust, a fungal parasite of modern domestic wheats.[15] Domestic sheep were present in Iraq almost 11,000 years ago.[16] The region in which early agricultural settlements were located in the Near East bordered the eastern shores of the Mediterranean (Fig. 7-19).

Plant and animal domestication

Prior to the development of agricultural practices, human populations in the area were making intensive use of plant resources, as evidenced by the milling stones mentioned above. The region was predominantly an open oak woodland providing a variety of food sources — game mammals, waterfowl, and fish, as well as wild wheat, barley, peas, and lentils. These four native plants proved ideal for domestication because their seeds were easy to store and highly nutritious. They also complemented one another since wheat and barley are good

[15] Fred Wendorf et al., "Egyptian Prehistory." *Science,* vol. 169, Sept. 18, 1970, p. 1161.
[16] S. Vokonyi et al., "Earliest Animal Domestication Dated." *Science,* vol. 179, Dec. 14, 1973, p. 1161.

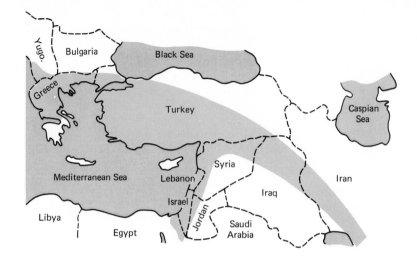

FIGURE 7-19
Area occupied by early agricultural settlements in the Near East and southeastern Europe. This region apparently was the earliest center of plant and animal domestication. It also was the general locale for the first metallurgy.

sources of starch while peas and lentils are high in protein.[17]

   Probably as early as 9000 B.P. localities in the Middle East also had domesticated a number of animal species in addition to the four plants. Cattle, sheep, goats, pigs, and dogs would be listed among these. On the other hand, horses were not; evidently they were first domesticated in the steppes of the Ukraine about 6000 B.P., perhaps earlier.[18]

Early villages
Thus, hunting and gathering ended its long reign as the basic way of life. Late Paleolithic cultures gave way to the more productive agricultural technologies of the *Neolithic*—the age of village life. By controlling the growth of domesticated plant and animal crops and by being able to store quantities of cereal grains and pulses, it was now possible to support one individual on only 10 hectares (25 acres). This surpassed the economy of late Paleolithic hunters by at least 25 times and was hundreds

of times more productive than the economy of early hunters.

   More people could now live in a smaller area. Villages developed as self-sufficient communities of individuals who tended the farm lands and herds around them.

   Increased food supplies contributed to continuing population growth and villages became larger. It also became possible to exchange food surpluses with neighboring agricultural areas. Farming communities began to change from villages in which each man participated in the food production of the community to cities, many of whose inhabitants were dependent upon food imported from elsewhere.

Cities and civilizations
Such changes started to occur in the Middle East about 8500 B.P. and by about 5000 B.P. had produced the first cities and the earliest civilization, that of Babylonian Sumer. The term *civilization* refers to a degree of cultural complexity: a society is civilized if it practices agriculture and is organized around one or more cities. Social organization embraces many dimensions, including diverse technical spe-

[17] D. Zohary and M. Hopf, "Domestication of Pulses in the Old World," *Science,* vol. 182, Nov. 30, 1973, pp. 887–894.
[18] R. Protsch and R. Berger, "Earliest Radiocarbon Dates for Domesticated Animals," *Science,* vol. 179, Jan. 19, 1973, pp. 235–239.

cialties such as metallurgy; monumental public works, such as irrigation systems, roads, temples, and palaces; codes of law; political and religious hierarchies; organized trade and commerce; a written language; highly developed art forms; a strong scientific community (mathematics, astronomy, etc.); and an effective military establishment.[19]

Opportunity for intensified conflict and warfare was increasing as expanding populations competed for productive land and resources. Trade and commerce both within and between communities was reaching impressive proportions because the human species now was dealing in a wide diversity of products and services as well as utilizing a great variety of raw materials.

Metallurgy

Living things were not the only natural resource first subjected to human manipulation and control in the Near East. The invention of metallurgy and its gradual diffusion from one creative population center to another was taking place in the Near East and Southeastern Europe between 9000 and 6000 B.P. While domesticable plants and animals were being moved into new areas, men were discovering the possibilities of metal—an interest that probably grew out of an earlier interest in stones. Neolithic societies carried on an active trade in volcanic glass (obsidian), chert, turquoise, lapis lazuli, and soapstone. It is likely that a heightened search for these stones led to the discovery of native copper, which was being hammered and annealed as early as 9000 B.P. The growth of agricultural production and the increasing importance of the cooking hearth was a major impetus to metallurgical development.

Probably no later than 8000 to 7000 B.P., man was able to build a fire hot enough to cast copper (1082°C). At that point smelting and casting became possible, first with copper followed by lead, silver, and iron. A variety of

artifacts made of these four metals have been found, dating between 7000 and 6000 B.P.; among them are implements made of copper or iron which include a number of chisels and axes, an adze, and a knife. Metallurgy already was beginning to make important contributions to the revolution in food production. The discovery of a 7,000-year-old copper mace-head testified to yet another major role that metallurgy was to play in human history.[20]

The rise and fall of civilizations

All these activities plus many others combined to fashion the ancient civilizations of the Near East. Agricultural production continued to grow and diversify with the development of elaborate irrigation systems of dams and canals. Industrial pursuits began to flourish, chief among which were quarrying, metallurgy, shipbuilding, and the manufacture of pottery, glass, and textiles. Trade and commerce with outlying civilizations grew steadily, punctuated by invasion and conquest between well-organized and well-equipped armies. Centers of civilization spread throughout the world with each passing millennium, and the human population continued to soar as more and more land was put into agricultural production. Natural food supplies no longer restrained population size (Fig. 7-20).

There are, of course, limits to which the exploitation of natural resources can be carried in the service of short-term production. These limits have been reached and exceeded on numerous occasions throughout history. Nations have been guilty of clearing too much of their forests and overcutting that which re-

[20] T. A. Wertime, "The Beginnings of Metallurgy: A New Look," *Science*, vol. 182, Nov. 30, 1973, pp. 875–887.

FIGURE 7-20
Some of the excavated remains of the ancient city of Mohenjo-Daro in southern West Pakistan. Located near the banks of the Indus River, this city housed between 20,000 and 50,000 people about 2300 B.C. [*Courtesy of Josephine Powell.*]

[19] E. A. Hoebel, *Anthropology,* 4th ed., New York: McGraw-Hill Book Company, 1972, pp. 76; 219–220.

mained. Agricultural soils have been drained of their nutrients, and pasture lands overgrazed. Excessive clearing and thinning of forested watersheds led to floods on cultivated hillsides, and overcropped rangeland was washed into rivers or blown away. Any region which has fallen victim to such calamities will suffer a serious curtailment both in its agricultural productivity and in the size of the population it can support. There is evidence that some of the great civilizations which flourished in Mesopotamia (Iraq), Palestine, Greece, Italy, China, and Mexico were subject to this fate.

Population growth, cities, and disease

But there were always new lands to be conquered and exploited. With each conquest the list of agricultural crops and products grew as new species were added to the inventory of domesticated varieties.

The sole remaining brake against runaway population growth was disease. The ravages of pestilence were made more destructive because increasingly people were being concentrated in urban centers. Cities were growing both in number and size under the influence of expanding trade and commerce. The bubonic plague, for example, periodically decimated urban communities in Europe, the Near East, and Far East from the fifth century B.C. into the nineteenth century. In A.D. 543, 10,000 residents were reported to have died in Constantinople during a single day. One-third to one-half the inhabitants of England were wiped out by the Black Death in one year (1348); two and a half centuries later, it almost depopulated China.

The industrial revolution

The agricultural revolution which had its birth in the Middle East was to be followed by another major event that began among civilizations of the Western world. More and more of mankind's affairs were being founded on reason and belief in a world governed by natural, rather than supernatural, law. Human curiosity was being freed to inquire into all manner of

things. The intellectual revolution which occurred during the seventeenth and eighteenth centuries bore fruit in many ways. Chief among these was the industrial revolution, which began around 1760 and is still going on. It followed on the heels of a long series of important scientific discoveries and inventions; its effects upon every aspect of human life were marked. Among many significant results were increased *urbanization*,[21] steady improvement in living standards, and, within the restrictions of a finite planet, an unlimited potential for population expansion — all of which will be discussed in depth in Section III.

The last consequence may be overstated in view of the possibility that the human species, like many other creatures, may demonstrate inborn mechanisms to regulate its numbers once a maximum population density is reached. Indeed, the high rate of crime, social stress, and psychotic disturbance in densely populated urban centers may be the outward symptoms of just such mechanisms at work. We will address this problem later. There is no hard evidence as yet, however, for the existence of biologically programmed, regulatory mechanisms that control population density in our species.

In any case, the industrial revolution has contributed to explosive increases in human numbers on two fronts: it created a second agricultural revolution, and it removed the only remaining check on population increase — disease — with discoveries in medicine and public health.

Agricultural revolution

Agriculture began to assume some of the characteristics of industry. New and improved plant crops were developed and more efficient breeds of livestock were introduced. Agricultural chemistry produced artificial fertilizers and a variety of pesticides. Enormous improvements in seedbed preparation, seeding, and harvesting were made through mechanization:

---

[21] Urbanization refers to an increase in the proportion of people living in cities compared to those who are rural.

improved plows and harrows, the invention of the threshing machine and the mechanical reaper, as well as hosts of others. All these implements and machines soon were to be powered by the internal combustion engine which would further enhance their output. Total food production in the agricultural sector of the new industrialized society far surpassed that of a simple agricultural economy. The distribution and use of this production was implemented by better transportation facilities with the advent of steamships, railroads, and ultimately air transport, trucking, and refrigeration.

Public health and medical technology

Advances in medicine and public health were no less impressive. Edward Jenner developed a safe technique of vaccination against smallpox. Crawford Long demonstrated the value of ether as a general anesthetic during surgery. Joseph Lister proved the importance of antisepsis in preventing infection as Pasteur and Koch established the germ theory of disease. The isolation of tuberculosis, cholera, bubonic plague, diphtheria, and lockjaw microorganisms was followed by innumerable others. Immunization techniques, antibiotics, and various other drugs have been developed for the prevention or treatment of some of man's most dreaded diseases. These and many more accomplishments in both medicine and hygiene have reduced the destructiveness of disease to relatively small percentages of people, at least in those societies capable of supporting adequate medical and hygienic facilities.

As a consequence of these advances in agriculture and medical technology, human population growth has assumed the proportions of an explosion. The world now teems with some 4 billion souls, twice the population of 1930 and quadruple that of 1830. A goodly, but minor, percentage enjoys the highest standard of living ever experienced in the history of our species, while most of the world's inhabitants are malnourished and a large percentage of them are starving. Vast multitudes are packed into overcrowded cities where living conditions are far from optimal or even de-

sirable. Unlike the days of ancient Mesopotamia and Greece, however, there are no more new lands to conquer and exploit.

Homo sapiens finally has come face to face with permanent residency.

SUGGESTED READINGS

BRACE, C. LORING: *The Stages of Human Evolution: Human and Cultural Origins,* Englewood Cliffs, N.J.: Prentice-Hall, Inc., 1967. A discussion of hominid evolution in four stages: australopithecine, pithecanthropine (*Homo erectus*), Neanderthal, and modern.

BURNS, E. M.: *Western Civilizations: Their History and Culture,* New York: W. W. Norton & Company, Inc., 1973. A classic, comprehensive, well-organized, and clearly written history of the Western world.

CHARD, C. S.: *Man in Prehistory,* New York: McGraw-Hill Book Company, 1969. A general account of Paleolithic peoples and their culture.

CLARK, J. G.: *Aspects of Prehistory,* Berkeley, Calif.: University of California Press, 1970. This and Mellaart's book discuss the background and development of early cities and civilizations.

HOWELL, F. CLARK, and EDITORS of LIFE: *Early Man (Life Nature Library),* New York: Time-Life Books, 1965. A beautifully illustrated book on the lives and cultures of hominids from australopiths to late Paleolithic peoples, with a chapter on modern aborigines; also includes discussions on paleontological and archaeological field and laboratory techniques.

MELLAART, J.: *Earliest Civilizations of the Near East,* New York: McGraw-Hill Book Company, 1966.

PFEIFFER, J. E.: *The Emergence of Man,* New York: Harper and Row, Publishers, Incorporated, 1972. A well-written account of the lives and cultures of hominids from the australopiths to the beginning of agriculture.

SOLECKI, R. S.: *Shanidar: The First Flower People,* New York: Alfred A. Knopf, Inc., 1971. The story of the discovery and excavation of Neanderthal man in Iraq.

TIME-LIFE EDITORS, *The Emergence of Man: The First Men,* New York: Time-Life Books, 1973. A richly illustrated book devoted to *Homo erectus.*

REVIEW QUESTIONS

1 Give the time span and geographic range of *Homo erectus.* Describe the general appearance and cranial anatomy of this hominid.

2 Briefly discuss the home base, hunting technology, and social organization of *Homo erectus* in Southern Europe 300,000 to 400,000 years ago. What paleontological evidence supports these conclusions?

3 Show how each of the following might have contributed importantly to the survival of *H. erectus:* (*a*) incest taboos, (*b*) exogamy, (*c*) reciprocal altruism.

4 Write a short essay on the significance of the use of fire to human evolution.

5 The major changes in hominid evolution between *H. erectus* and modern *H. sapiens* were confined to the head. Identify five of these changes. Name two fossils which represent the oldest known specimens of *H. sapiens* and give their geologic age.

6 Give a detailed account of the material culture of Neanderthal *H. sapiens.*

7 Describe in some detail the nonmaterial culture of Neanderthal *H. sapiens.* Cite five fossil sites or specimens to document your description.

8 Considerable controversy has long surrounded the relationship of the Neanderthal peoples and their mid-Paleolithic
culture to modern types of *H. sapiens* who practiced an Upper
Paleolithic culture and apparently replaced the Neanderthals.
How does S. R. Binford explain this relationship?

9 Shared traditions and rituals appear to have played important
roles in integrating Upper Paleolithic community life. Substantiate this by citing four specific examples of different types
of archaeological evidence. Indicate the conclusion that can be
drawn or inferred from each example cited.

10 The hunter-gatherer economy of Upper Paleolithic communities was gradually replaced by an agricultural economy. Offer
two reasons for the decline of the hunter-gatherer economy.
What conditions in the Near East proved ideal for plant and
animal domestication? What was the effect of the new economy
on community life?

11 What does the term *civilization* mean? What common fate be-
fell a number of great civilizations during the period from
5000 B.C. to A.D. 1600?

12 What was the industrial revolution? What were its major
accomplishments? To date, what has been its net effect on
human civilization and the human condition?

EIGHT

THE EVOLUTIONARY PREREQUISITE:
Life's Inborn Capacity for Change

In the two previous chapters we have discussed our evolutionary background and history. No attempt has been made, however, to inquire *how* these events came about. Now that the narrative has been told, the "how" question can be pursued. It will be the aim of this chapter and the next to investigate how a given population or species of organism adapts, or fails to adapt, to the environmental changes that occur over long periods of time.

We have noted that life is characterized by great variety; no two organisms ever are *exactly* identical. This variety enables living organisms to respond, *at the populational level,* in an adaptive way to their environment. Those individuals which, for one reason or another, are less able to withstand the challenges of their environment ultimately will perish and fail to reproduce. Their particular hereditary recipes for organism-making will be discarded. On the other hand, those individuals who can effectively cope with environmental change will survive and reproduce their kind; their hereditary recipes for organism-making will have been tested and found not to be wanting. In this way a species is molded and directed over a period of time by environmental changes that restrict or permit the survival and reproduction of different individuals comprising a population. In short, the environment *selects* those who will survive and leave offspring, if any.

Given sufficient time, a new species of organism ultimately results. Each species is a product of a succession of populations. Members of these populations serve as testing grounds in which biologic design is, in effect, kept abreast of current environmental conditions. Throughout the seemingly endless pattern of generation following upon generation, individuals die, populations die, and species become extinct. But in its turn, each may give rise to new individuals, a new population, and a new species.

The capacity of organisms for variety and change at the populational level is an indispensable prerequisite for organic evolution. Survival, modification, and the origin of adaptation and new species all are dependent upon populations sufficiently diverse that their individual members reflect degrees of fitness and unfitness to all kinds of situations. Variety is not only the spice of life; it is the raw material out of which evolving creatures are sculptured.

Our examination of biologic variability will involve us in an introduction to *genetics,* the scientific study of heredity, which embraces the mechanisms of biologic inheritance and the sources of hereditary variation.

PRINCIPLES OF MENDELIAN GENETICS

An Austrian monk, Gregor Mendel, first threw light on basic hereditary principles more than 100 years ago. Although he worked with plants, Mendel's discoveries apply equally well to animal genetics.

In conducting breeding tests with common garden pea plants, Mendel was impressed by the fact that this species possessed a number of characteristics (traits) that were expressed in two contrasting forms. Figure 8-1 lists four of these. The contrasting expressions of a trait, such as flower color, did not intergrade from one flower to another; flowers either were red or white and plants were either tall or short. Traits of this nature can be identified more accurately since one need not distinguish between degrees of redness, tallness, etc.

Mendel first developed true-breeding strains by breeding plants with the same trait (e.g., red flowers) together for many generations. He then crossed (interbred) strain pairs as shown in Figure 8-1. The offspring (progeny) in every case resembled one parent only. For example, in the cross between true-breeding plants that bore red flowers only and true-breeding plants that bore white flowers only, all the offspring produced red blossoms exclusively. Such plants are called *hybrids* because they result from crosses between parents that are genetically unlike. The red-flowered hybrid, for example, differed from its true-breeding parents in having one parent that bore flowers unlike its own. Mendel called the characteristic shown by the hybrid a *dominant trait* (e.g., red flowers) and that which did not appear a recessive trait (e.g., white flowers). Red flowers, long stems, and round and yellow seeds are dominant among the four pairs of traits listed.

The hybrid offspring of these crosses were then allowed to self-pollinate, yielding a second generation of plants. The recessive characteristics reappeared in this population in the ratio of about three dominants to one recessive. Since there was no blending of dominant and recessive traits—no pink flowers or medium-length stems—Mendel concluded that hereditary factors are separate and distinct entities which maintain their individuality unchanged as they pass from one generation to another. He further reasoned that each pea plant has two hereditary factors for each characteristic. These factors become segregated during sex-cell (gamete) formation; each sex cell receives just one factor for each trait—a phenomenon known as the *principle of segregation*. Consequently, offspring receive one such factor from each of their parents.

The principle of segregation

Certain techniques and terms will prove helpful at this point. It is much easier to refer to a hereditary factor, or *gene* as they are now called, by a letter than by a name. A gene set (two genes, one from each parent) can be represented by a letter which is capitalized for the dominant and in lower case for the recessive gene. Thus, *R* could signify the gene for red and *r* the gene for white flowers. The alternative members of a gene pair, such as *R* and *r*, are called *alleles*. These alleles may exist in one of three possible combinations: *RR, rr,* or *Rr*. Of the three gene combinations, or *genotypes*, two carry a double dose of the same allele (*RR* and *rr*). They are said to be *homozygous* genotypes: *RR* is homozygous dominant and *rr* homozygous recessive. *Rr*, with one of each allele, is *heterozygous*. These genotypes produce two kinds of pea plants insofar as their physical appearance or *phenotype* is concerned: (1) red-flowered plants (*RR* and *Rr*), and (2) white-flowered plants (*rr*).

With this vocabulary to assist us, let us now examine the genetic events in Mendel's red-flowered by white-flowered crosses (Fig. 8-2). Homozygous (true-breeding) red-flowered plants, *RR,* are crossed with homozygous white-flowered plants, *rr*. Since the gametes of one parent can carry only an *R* allele and those of the other only an *r* allele, all the offspring will be heterozygous (*Rr*). The dominant allele for red flowers expresses itself despite the presence of the recessive allele for white flowers, and the hybrids are red-flowered.

These hybrids, however, can produce gametes of two kinds. Because of genetic segregation, half the gametes will have an *R* allele and half will have an *r* allele. During fertilization one or the other of the two kinds of male gametes will unite with one or the other kinds of female gametes at random. The resulting genotypes are readily calculated by the checkerboard method shown in Fig. 8-2. Three gene combinations are possible: *RR, Rr,* and *rr*. The *Rr* genotype occurs twice as frequently as either *RR* or *rr*, however, because it results from not one but two combinations: (1) *R* from the male and *r* from the female gamete, or (2) *r* from the

FIGURE 8-1
Data on four of Mendel's crosses. Parent plants differing in one trait, for which they bred true, were crossed. The offspring of these crosses were then allowed to self-pollinate, yielding a second generation of plants.

Parents	First generation offspring	Second generation offspring	
		Census	Ratio
1 Red × white flowers	All plants red	705 red 224 white	3.15:1
2 Long × short stems	All plants long	787 long 277 short	2.84:1
3 Round × wrinkled seeds	All plants round	5,474 round 1,850 wrinkled	2.96:1
4 Yellow × green seeds	All plants yellow	6,022 yellow 2,011 green	3.01:1
	Totals	12,988:4,352	2.98:1

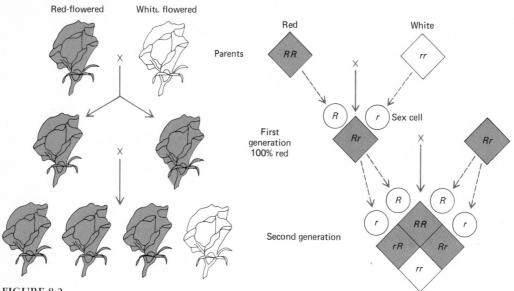

FIGURE 8-2
A homozygous red-flowered by homozygous white-flowered cross produces heterozygous offspring with red
flowers because of red-flower dominance. The second
generation exhibits a 3:1 ratio of red-flowered to white-
flowered plants since every combination of grandparental
alleles is possible among these offspring. R = red flowers;
r = white flowers.

male and R from the female gamete. As a consequence, the genotypic ratio in this second
generation is 1 *RR* : 2 *Rr* : 1 *rr*. Since three-
quarters of this population should have at least
one *R* allele and one-quarter is presumably *rr*,
the *phenotypic ratio* in the second generation
should be 3 red-flowered : 1 white-flowered. As
can be seen in Fig. 8-1, Mendel's results of 705
red to 224 white (3.15:1) came close to these
predicted values.

Note that we said "should be" and "is
presumably" above. We did so because all
these events are determined by chance, a fact
that should be stressed. When half the male
and female gametes of the first generation
hybrids are about equally divided between
those with *R* and *r*, there are four different

combinations possible during fertilization.
Either one of two kinds of male gamete may
unite with either one of two kinds of female
gamete. Since there are four possible combinations, the chance of getting any one of them,
say *RR*, would be one in four. These events are
governed by the same laws of probability that
pertain to throwing dice and flipping coins.
Expected probabilities can be depended upon
when one is dealing with large numbers, but
they can be unreliable when the number is
small. One can reasonably expect a ratio very
close to 50 percent heads and 50 percent tails
in 10,000 tosses of a coin. In 10 tosses, the
probability of getting such a distribution drops
significantly. Mendel's results demonstrate this
nicely (Fig. 8-1).

Between 7,000 and 8,000 second-genera-
tion offspring were produced in each of the two
crosses involving seed type. The phenotypic
ratios of 2.96:1 and 3.01:1 in these populations
came quite close to the expected 3:1. Each of
the test crosses on flower color and plant height,
on the other hand, yielded only about 1,000

progeny in the second generation, and the deviation from the 3:1 ratio was appreciably greater (3.15:1 and 2.84:1).

The principle of independent assortment

Mendel also studied crosses in which combinations of traits were being transmitted. One of these, illustrated in Fig. 8-3, involved crossing true-breeding (homozygous) red-flowered, tall plants with homozygous white-flowered dwarfs. The hybrid offspring were all red-flowered and tall. When the hybrids were crossed, the second generation offspring fell into four groups: red-flowered, tall; red-flowered, dwarf; white-flowered, tall; and white flowered, dwarf, in a ratio of $9/16$: $3/16$: $3/16$: $1/16$ respectively.

From such results, Mendel concluded that the hereditary factors (genes) for different traits are assorted independently. The inheritance of flower color is unrelated to plant stature and vice versa. Today the principle of independent assortment commonly is referred to as *genetic reassortment*.

Inheritance with dominance lacking or modified

There are many genetic situations in which the alternative alleles of a gene set are neither strictly dominant nor recessive. One such case involving four-o'clock plants apparently was known to Mendel. When homozygous red-flowered plants are crossed with homozygous white-flowered ones, the hybrid offspring have pink flowers. When these pink-flowered hybrids are crossed with one another, the second generation consists of plants one-fourth of which are red-flowered (homozygous red), two-fourths, or one-half, are pink-flowered (heterozygous) and one-fourth are white-flowered (homozygous white).

An example similar but not identical to this kind of inheritance can be cited for our own species. Individuals are said to have type

FIGURE 8-3

The independent assortment of two gene pairs. The second generation descendants of grandparents that were homozygous red-flowered, tall (*RRTT*) and homozygous white-flowered, dwarf (*rrtt*) show every combination of traits in the ratio of $9/16$ red-flowered, tall to $3/16$ red-flowered, dwarf to $3/16$ white-flowered, tall to $1/16$ white-flowered, dwarf.

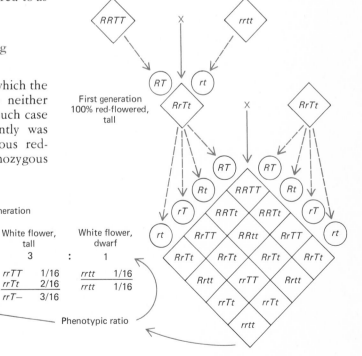

Second generation						
Red-flower, tall		Red-flower, dwarf		White flower, tall		White flower, dwarf
9	:	3	:	3	:	1
RRTT 1/16		*RRtt* 1/16		*rrTT* 1/16		*rrtt* 1/16
RrTT 2/16		*Rrtt* 2/16		*rrTt* 2/16		*rrtt* 1/16
RRTt 2/16		*R—tt* 3/16		*rrT—* 3/16		
RrTt 4/16						
R—T— 9/16						

Phenotypic ratio

M, type N, or type MN blood, depending on whether their red blood cells contain one, the other, or both of two substances called the M and N antigens.[1] There are two alleles, *M* and *N*, which are responsible for the production of these antigens. People who have the homozygous *MM* genotype have blood type M; those who are homozygous *NN* have blood type N, whereas those who are heterozygous *MN* have blood type MN. Children, both of whose parents are heterozygous *MN*, are type M, type MN and type N in the ratio of ¼: ½: ¼ respectively (Fig. 8-4). The separate identities of the *M* and *N* alleles are preserved intact, but since neither allele is dominant to the other, heterozygous individuals are intermediate in character because of the phenotypic influence

---

[1] An antigen is any substance which, if it contacts appropriate tissues in an animal body, stimulates the production of antibodies; these antibodies neutralize the antigen.

FIGURE 8-4
The *M* and *N* alleles for the M and N antigens in human blood exhibit codominance. Since neither allele is dominant to the other, they appear to blend in the first generation, but the second generation demonstrates that each allele has maintained its separate identity.

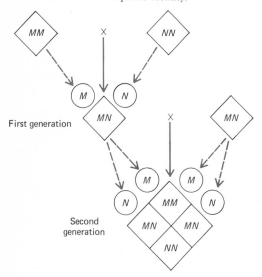

of both alleles. Cases of this kind exhibit *codominance* rather than dominance.

OTHER PATTERNS OF INHERITANCE

Multiple alleles

The patterns of inheritance examined thus far have involved only two alleles in a gene set. In many instances, however, more than two alleles may affect the same genetic trait. Any one individual can be some combination of two of these alleles.

ABO blood-type system
The human ABO blood groups are an example of inheritance resulting from such *multiple alleles* (Fig. 8-5). These blood groups are classified by the presence or absence of two antigens (see footnote 1) found in red blood cells and designated by the letters A and B. Antigen A is under the control of an allele (I^A) that is codominant with another allele (I^B) responsible for the B antigen. A third allele (*i*) produces neither of the two antigens and is recessive to both codominant alleles. Six combinations of two of the three alleles are possible, resulting in four blood groups: (1) type O with neither antigen A nor B; (2) type A with antigen A; (3) type B with antigen B; and (4) type AB with both antigens. These phenotypes are further distinguished by the presence or absence in the blood of two *antibodies*. One of these, the anti-A antibody, causes red blood cells containing antigen A to clump together in a reaction known as *agglutination*. The other, the anti-B antibody, causes agglutination in blood cells with antigen B. Each blood type possesses antibodies for those antigens, if any, that it does *not* have. Type O blood, consequently, carries both these antibodies whereas type AB blood has neither. Type A blood has anti-B antibody and B blood contains anti-A.

The transfusion of blood between individuals of different blood types can kill the receiver (recipient) because of possible agglutination between antibody and antigen. A person with type A blood, for example, cannot receive blood from a type B donor because the B antigen of the donor will be agglutinated by the anti-B antibody of the recipient as it enters the latter's bloodstream. This same incompatibility can exist between a pregnant woman and her developing embryo. The anti-A and anti-B antibodies of a type O woman, for example, can penetrate the placental barrier and attack the blood cells of a type A, B, or AB embryo with possibly severe consequences in the embryo.

Some individuals reflect their ABO blood group by the secretion of water-soluble forms of the A and/or B antigen(s) in the saliva and other body fluids. These people are called *secretors*. Others, who do not secrete these antigens in a water-soluble form, are called *nonsecretors*. The secretor and nonsecretor phenotypes result from a pair of genes that are independent of the ABO alleles. The allele for secretor (*Se*) is dominant to that for nonsecretor (*se*). They are mentioned here because they will concern us in a later discussion.

RH blood-type system

The Rh antigens, so called because they were identified first in rhesus monkeys, also may be the products of multiple alleles. The mode of inheritance of these antigens, however, has not been fully resolved. Apparently, there are three different Rh antigens.[2] Only one of these appears to be responsible for the great majority of complications described below that may arise between individuals of differing Rh type.

For the sake of simplicity, we will therefore assume that Rh blood type is determined by a pair of genes that are inherited independently of the ABO alleles. The dominant allele is responsible for producing the Rh antigen; the recessive allele, when homozygous, prevents the production of Rh antigen. Those who lack Rh antigen—the people who are homozygous recessive—are said to be *Rh negative*. Those who have Rh antigen—the people who are homozygous dominant or heterozygous—are said to be *Rh positive*.

Unlike the ABO system, the Rh blood groups do not normally carry antibodies against specific antigens. An Rh-negative person, however, can become sensitized to Rh antigen by receiving Rh-positive blood transfusions. In such cases, a kind of immune response develops in which antibodies against the antigen are pro-

[2] Commonly, they are designated C, D, and E. The D antigen is responsible for most Rh complications.

A

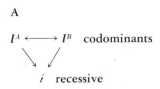

$I^A \longleftrightarrow I^B$ codominants

i recessive

B

Genotype	Phenotype	Antigen in red blood cells	Antibody in blood plasma
ii	Type O blood	None	Anti-A and anti-B
$I^A I^A$ $I^A i$	Type A blood	A	Anti-B
$I^B I^B$ $I^B i$	Type B blood	B	Anti-A
$I^A I^B$	Type AB blood	A and B	None

FIGURE 8-5
The ABO blood groups of man. Classification is based upon the presence or absence of two red blood cell antigens, A and B. (*A*) Three alleles determine blood type, I^A controlling the development of antigen A, and its codominant allele, I^B, controlling antigen B. A third allele, *i*, produces neither antigen and is recessive to both codominants. (*B*) Four phenotypes result from six possible genotypes, based upon which antigens, if any, are present. Antibodies exist in the blood plasma for those antigens not present. For example, type A blood carries anti-B antibody, whereas type O has both anti-A and anti-B antibodies.

duced and carried in the blood plasma. A subsequent transfusion of positive blood will be accompanied by widespread destruction of the transfused blood cells by these antibodies.

An Rh-negative woman can be similarly sensitized during pregnancy to an Rh-positive fetus. Although fetal blood does not mix with maternal blood, it does so at birth. The rupture of blood vessels at that time permits fetal blood to enter the mother's bloodstream. Antibodies normally do not develop sufficiently to pose a threat to the fetus until the mother has had two or three pregnancies. During the third and subsequent births, antibodies which come in contact with the fetal blood stream can cause destruction of fetal blood cells (*fetal erythroblastosis*). Usually this is fatal to the child unless it is given several blood transfusions. An Rh-negative woman usually can be prevented from producing antibodies by injecting her with serum containing Rh antibodies right after the birth of an Rh-positive child. This prevents her from producing them and thereby protects any future Rh-positive child.

Single genes with multiple effects

Genes function at the biochemical level in controlling the production of enzymes, blood-group antigens, and carrier molecules like oxygen-transporting hemoglobin. Great numbers of biochemical reactions, speeded and regulated by enzymes—which in turn are controlled by genes—produce various end products. Different end products, such as a skin pigment, a hormone, or a blood-clotting agent, commonly share segments of their biochemical development or depend upon some of the same "raw materials." It will be recalled from Chap. 2 that only 20 different amino acids are utilized in the synthesis of an astronomical array of diverse protein molecules.

Referring to Fig. 8-6, we might assume that substance *C* is one of the amino acids needed for the synthesis of both end products *F* and *J*. We might further assume that substance

B is another amino acid which is converted by enzyme number two into amino acid *C*. If this were the case, the gene controlling the synthesis of enzyme number two would not only govern the production of amino acid *C* but would also affect the production of end products *F* and *J*. It is in this fashion that a single gene may have several phenotypic effects. In fact, it is quite possible that most genes control the development of more than one trait.

Numerous examples of this are found in man. A hereditary disease, *phenylketonuria,* or PKU, is caused by the absence of an enzyme that converts one amino acid, phenylalanine, into another, tyrosine. This deficiency results from a recessive allele which, when homozygous, brings about high concentrations of phenylalanine and its metabolic by-products in body tissues. The toxicity of some of these by-products, coupled with a blockage in at least one biochemical pathway leading to tyrosine synthesis, is responsible for (1) a tendency toward epileptic seizures, (2) extreme mental retardation, and (3) failure to produce normal amounts of skin pigment. Fortunately, the disease can be diagnosed almost immediately after birth by a urinalysis. Restricting the dietary intake of phenylalanine and replacing it with substitutes early in life can largely, if not entirely, correct the symptoms of this genetic malfunction. The phenotypic influence of this recessive allele therefore is quite varied. Depending upon diet, the phenotype may be affected in several ways or not at all.

Multiple genes with a single effect

It is evident from Fig. 8-6 that a given biochemical (metabolic) end product such as *J* depends upon many preparatory reactions. Each prerequisite reaction depends upon an enzyme which, in turn, is controlled by a gene. Obviously the development of a given phenotypic trait (*J*) is the product of many genes interacting in concert. Instances of *genetic interaction* are legion. Modes of inheritance in this cate-

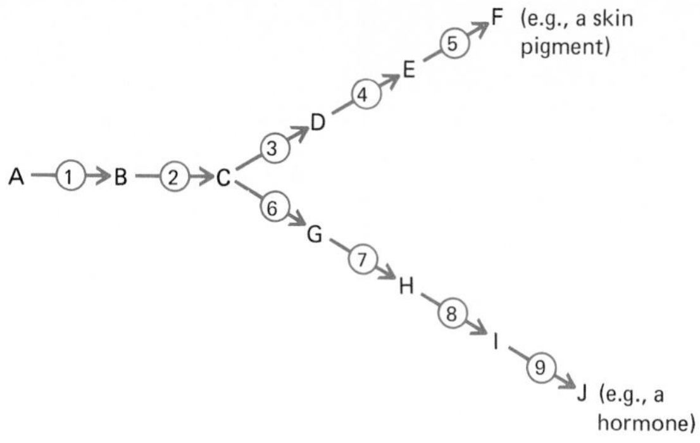

FIGURE 8-6
A schematic diagram showing how two hypothetical phenotypic traits (*F* and *J*) develop biochemically and genetically. "Raw material" *A* is converted into substance *B* by enzyme number 1. A different enzyme (2) converts *B* molecules into *C* molecules, and so on. Two different biochemical (metabolic) sequences ending in *F* and *J* use substance *C* as a raw material. Each successive reaction in the sequence is under the control of a different enzyme, and each enzyme is under the control of a specific gene (not shown).

gory are varied, often complex, and seldom understood fully, at least insofar as human phenotypes are concerned. We will cite three examples that span the gap between relatively simple and extremely complex.

Human deafness

A form of human deafness apparently is inherited through the interaction of two pairs of genes that are inherited independently. The hearing mechanism is sufficiently complex that great numbers of different genes are very likely involved; in theory there could be many different genetic ways for being deaf. We are concerned here with two of these. Normal hearing results from any genotype that has at least one dominant *D* allele and one dominant *E* allele (*D-E-*),[3] as shown in Fig. 8-7. Any genotype that is homozygous recessive for one (*ddE-*), the other (*D-ee*), or both (*ddee*) these genes will be phenotypically deaf. Unexpected results commonly occur in marriages between two genetically deaf spouses. If the father is *DDee* and the mother *ddEE,* all the children will be normal (*DdEe*). The offspring of normal parents who are doubly heterozygous, however, will be born in the theoretical ratio of nine normal to seven deaf.

Human skin pigmentation

Many pairs of genes are believed to be involved

[3] *D-E-* includes the genotypes *DDEE, DdEE, DDEe,* and *DdEe; ddE-* includes *ddEE* and *ddEe.*

in skin pigmentation. Multiple-gene traits of this nature, unlike *qualitative* characters such as type A and B blood, do not fall into distinct phenotypic groups. People are not black or white but vary gradually and continuously from very dark to very light. Pigmentation is a *quantitative* rather than qualitative characteristic.

For the sake of simplicity, we will assume that there are three pairs of independently assorting codominant genes responsible for skin color (*A,a; B,b;* and *C,c*) as shown in Fig. 8-8. Each *A,B,* or *C* allele contributes one unit of pigment (■) whereas each *a,b,* or *c* allele contributes none (□). (It is assumed that the minimal pigment possessed by very light people to form freckles is the product of another gene set.) On the basis of this hypothetical model, the offspring of very dark and very light parents would be intermediate in color. The progeny of such intermediate parents would range from very dark to very light in seven groups that differed by one unit of pigment. Over 75 percent ($^{50}/_{64}$) of this second generation, however, would be light intermediate to dark intermediate in color, with the dark and light extremes trailing off at either end of the preponderant middle group.

If the effects of environment are superimposed on such a phenotypic distribution, the distinction between color groups would become even more difficult. Individuals of a given genotype will be darker when exposed to the

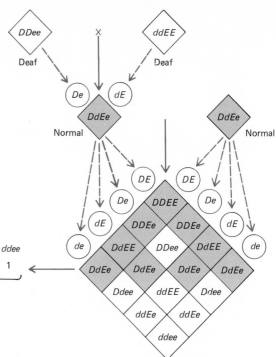

FIGURE 8-7

The presumed inheritance of a form of deafness in man. (*A*) Each of two independent dominant alleles *D* and *E* are required for normal hearing. Homozygous recessive combinations of either or both of these genes produce deafness. (*B*) Marriages between deaf parents who are *DDee* and *ddEE* produce normal offspring (*DdEe*). If this generation intermarries, the second generation would be born in the ratio of about 9 normal to 7 deaf.

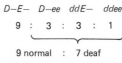

sun than when they are not. If we now add to this the likelihood that many more than three pairs of genes are involved, and therefore many more than seven genetic groups, it is easy to understand the continuous variation that is seen in quantitative traits like skin color. If we convert the hypothetical phenotypic ratio of Fig. 8-8 to a bar graph and curve, as illustrated in Fig. 8-9, it compares remarkably well with a similar graph and curve depicting height distribution in a population of men. Height and skin color both are multiple-gene traits.

Human intelligence

Knowledge of how human intelligence develops is complicated by three issues: (1) intelligence itself is difficult to define; (2) great numbers of genes undoubtedly are involved; and (3) environment plays a significant role.

Many lists of the supposed abilities related to intelligence have been proposed. One such list includes the abilities:

1 to understand words and to use them fluently
2 to think mathematically and to visualize relationships in space

3 to memorize, and to recall that which has been memorized
4 to perceive differences and similarities among objects
5 to discover rules for solving problems[4]

Psychologists have devised intelligence (IQ) tests by means of which an individual receives an IQ score which presumes to measure whatever abilities the test was designed to evaluate.

[4] C. T. Morgan and R. A. King, *Introduction to Psychology,* 4th ed., New York: McGraw-Hill Book Company, 1975, p. 43.

FIGURE 8-8

The inheritance of human skin pigmentation. This hypothetical model assumes that three pairs of codominant, independently assorting genes are involved. Each *A*, *B*, or *C* allele contributes one unit of pigment (■). Each *a*, *b*, or *c* allele contributes none (□).

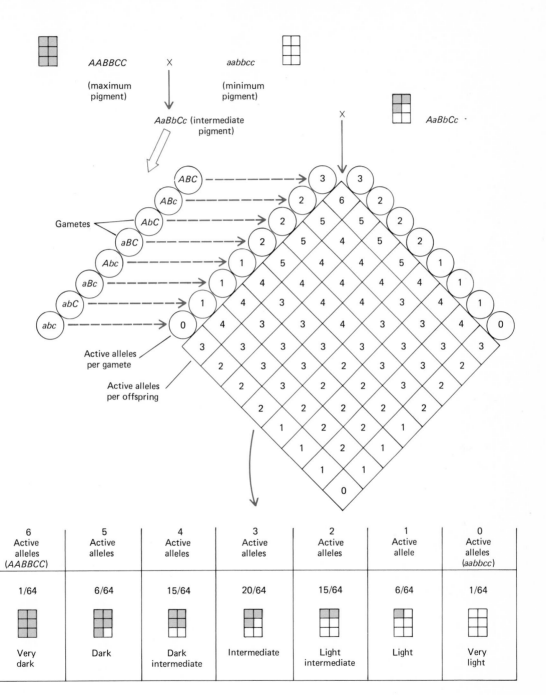

6 Active alleles (*AABBCC*)	5 Active alleles	4 Active alleles	3 Active alleles	2 Active alleles	1 Active allele	0 Active alleles (*aabbcc*)
1/64	6/64	15/64	20/64	15/64	6/64	1/64
Very dark	Dark	Dark intermediate	Intermediate	Light intermediate	Light	Very light

FIGURE 8-9
The variation in multiple-gene traits follows a normal curve of variation, particularly when consideration is given to environmental influences. (*A*) A bar graph and curve of skin color variation based on the hypothetical phenotypic ratio in the second generation of Fig. 8-8. The phenotype bars are separated to allow for environmental gradations caused by varying exposure to the sun. (*B*) A bar graph and curve approximating height variation in a random sample of 1,000 adult white males (United States). Human height, like skin color, is a multiple-gene trait.

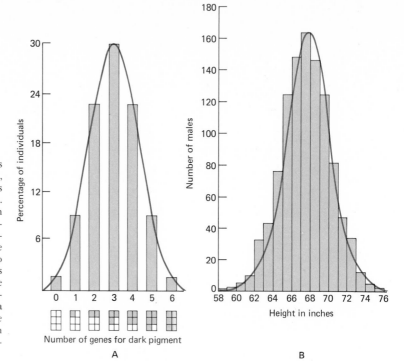

Genetic studies of intelligence have involved comparing the IQ scores of pairs of individuals with varying degrees of relationship — from none (unrelated people) to 100 percent (one-egg, or identical, twins), as shown in Fig. 8-10.[5] The extent to which members of a pair obtain similar IQ scores is expressed by a *correlation coefficient*. A correlation of 1.0 reflects perfect agreement between the paired individuals. A correlation of .00 indicates no agreement. Correlations of .80 or .90 are high whereas those between .40 and .60 may be considered moderate and those between .20 and .30 generally low.

Figure 8-11 summarizes the results of many correlational studies made on pairs of individuals in 10 different categories. These categories reflect a range of varying degrees of genetic relationship in which environmental factors were relatively constant (individuals raised together) as well as varied (individuals raised apart).

The influence of heredity in the determination of intelligence is shown by the high correlation (.87) of one-egg twins raised together. With environmental factors relatively constant (pairs raised together), the correlation drops to .53 for fraternal twins and .23 for unrelated persons. Strong support for the importance of genetic factors also is seen in comparing the correlation of identical twins raised apart (.75) with that of foster parents and their foster children living together (.20).

The data in Fig. 8-11 also point to the importance of environment in the development of intelligence. The correlations of children raised apart in different environments are significantly smaller than those raised together, whether

---

[5] One-egg, or identical, twins develop from the same fertilized egg and therefore have the same genotype. Two-egg, or fraternal, twins develop from different fertilized eggs; they are no more closely related than ordinary brothers and sisters.

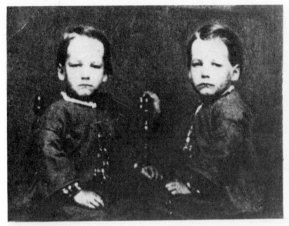

FIGURE 8-10
Identical twins develop from the same fertilized egg and are consequently identical genetically. These identical twins are shown at four different periods during their life. [*Courtesy of Dr. Lissy F. Jarvik.*]

they be identical twins, siblings, or unrelated individuals. Intelligence is affected to an important degree by educational opportunity or the lack of it, good health or bad, and stimulating or suppressive parent and peer relationships early in life.

The phenotype expressed, whatever it is, is a product of *both* heredity *and* environment. Available data are inadequate to evaluate the relative importance of either factor.

With the present state of knowledge, the often-asked question of whether there are racial differences in intelligence would appear to be unanswerable. We have no basis for assessing the role of the large environmental and cultural differences between racial and ethnic groups. That obviously leaves the contribution of genetic differences, if indeed there are any, in limbo.

Interaction of genes and hormones

Certain characteristics are inherited in a manner that is said to be sex-influenced. The baldness that commonly starts to occur in men between the ages of 30 and 40 — called *pattern baldness* — is such a trait. Baldness is controlled by a gene

Family relationship, if any, between pairs compared		Environmental conditions	Genetic relationship	Correlation of IQ test scores
Unrelated persons		Reared apart	0.00	−0.01
		Reared together	0.00	0.23
Foster parent and child		Living together	0.00	0.20
Parent and child		Living together	0.50	0.50
Siblings (brothers and sisters)		Reared apart	0.50	0.40
		Reared together	0.50	0.49
Two-egg (fraternal) twins	Same sex	Reared together	0.50	0.53
	Oppo-site sex	Reared together	0.50	0.53
One-egg (identical) twins		Reared apart	1.00	0.75
		Reared together	1.00	0.87

FIGURE 8-11
Correlations of IQ test scores for pairs of people with varying hereditary and environmental relationships. The statistical coefficients of correlation in the right-hand column are averages of a number of different studies. [*Modified from C. T. Morgan and R. A. King, Introduction to Psychology, 5th ed., McGraw-Hill, New York, 1975.*]

that behaves like a dominant allele in males and a recessive allele in females. There is one alternate allele for "not bald." Heterozygous males are bald but heterozygous females are not. The only genotype that produces baldness in both sexes is homozygous for the "bald" allele. It is believed that the primary cause for the difference in phenotypic expression in the two sexes lies in biochemical interactions involving this gene pair and the sex hormones. Recent studies have shown that female sex hormones (*estrogen* and *progesterone*) have a pronounced effect upon enzyme production. The hormones apparently facilitate those biochemical events that take place in the synthesis of gene-controlled enzymes. Consequently, enzyme synthesis is speeded up.[6] Although it is not known how this mechanism functions in the inheritance of

[6] B. W. O'Malley and A. R. Means, "Female Steroid Hormones and Target Cell Nuclei," *Science*, vol. 183, Feb. 15, 1974, pp. 610–619.

pattern baldness, we can at least draw up a hypothetical model to show the kind of phenomenon that may be operative here.

In addition to the many genes responsible for head hair growth, let us assume that there is a particular gene pair that influences the maintenance of head hair after the onset of sexual maturity. One of these alleles controls the synthesis of an enzyme that somehow interferes with normal functioning of scalp hair follicles where hair develops and grows. People homozygous for this allele become bald. Heterozygous genotypes, on the other hand, have only one allele for enzyme production and cannot produce enough of the inhibiting enzyme unless male sex hormone (*testosterone*) is present in sufficient quantity to facilitate enzyme synthesis. The other allele controls the synthesis of enzyme that encourages the growth of scalp hair. People homozygous for this other allele will have hair but heterozygous individuals escape baldness only if adequate amounts of female sex hormone are available to facilitate the synthesis of enzyme. In such a model, sex hormone could tip the balance in favor of hair growth or baldness in heterozygous individuals; the allele for baldness would appear to be dominant in males and recessive in females.

The importance of sex hormones at the biochemical level of genetic mechanisms is only beginning to be understood. When we consider the results of recent studies which suggest that the brains of men and women may be organized along somewhat different lines,[7] together with the many anatomical and physiological differences between the two sexes, we can begin to appreciate the significance of sex-influenced and other sex-related modes of inheritance in the developing human being.

Increasingly, we are made aware that genes control the synthesis of enzymes and other substances by somehow regulating biochemical reactions. How do they do this? What is a gene anyway? To answer these questions, we will turn our attention to the study of living cells.

CELLULAR GENETICS

Cells are the microscopic units of both structure and function in the living organism. A cell is enclosed by a cell membrane and contains within its mass a roundish body called a *nucleus* (Fig. 8-12). When a cell divides into two cells, rod-shaped structures called *chromosomes* (Greek *chroma*, "color"; Greek *soma*, "body") become visible in the nucleus. Genes are carried on these structures. Chromosomes actually occur in pairs, and the number for any given species is constant. In man the chromosome number is 46 (23 pairs). The members of a pair are similar

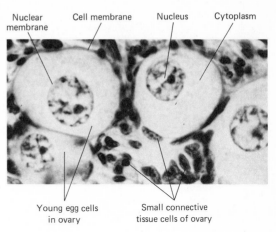

FIGURE 8-12
Stained animal cells as seen under the microscope.

in size and structure — with one exception to be discussed shortly — and are called *homologous chromosomes*.

Chromosomes and cell division (mitosis)

Chromosomes possessed by various species differ in structure as well as in number. Two or more species can have the same chromosome number, yet their chromosome sets (*karyotypes*) are unique because of structural differences in their respective chromosomes.

Chromosomes can be distinguished in any given species on the basis of their size and the position of their *centromeres*. The centromere is a clear, constricted area that may be located near the middle, toward the end, or essentially at the end of a chromosome (Fig. 8-13). These features are most easily observed in cells when they are undergoing division.

When a cell divides into two cells, its chromosomes divide also, producing two daughter cells with the same chromosome number as the parent cell from which they came. The highlights of this process, called *mitosis*, are shown in Figure 8-14A–F. For simplicity, only one pair of chromosomes is shown, one of

---

[7] Females, for example, tend to have greater verbal fluency than males, whereas males tend to have better space perception than females. See D. Kimura, "The Asymmetry of the Human Brain," *Scientific American*, March 1973, p. 78.

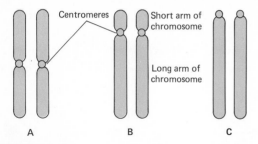

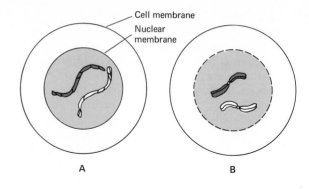

FIGURE 8-13
Chromosome types based on relative position of the centromere. Three types are shown depending upon whether the centromere is near the middle (*A*), toward the end (*B*), or essentially at the end (*C*) of the chromosome. The chromosome in *B* is said to have a long arm and a short arm.

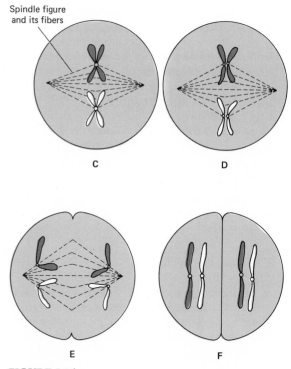

which is colored so that the fate of each member of the pair can be followed. Each chromosome replicates (duplicates) itself and the nuclear membrane disappears (*A–B*). A spindle-shaped structure composed of fibers develops, and the replicated chromosome moves to the center (equator) of the spindle, the centromere attached to spindle fibers (*C*). The centromere divides and each daughter chromosome now has its own centromere (*D*). Replicated daughter chromosomes now move to opposite ends of the dividing cell as if they were being pulled by the spindle fibers (*E*). The resulting daughter cells each contain a replica of the chromosome pair in the parent cell (*F*).

Figure 8-14*C* illustrates the stage at which chromosomes can be photographed and classified most readily. From such microscope photographs, all the chromosome sets or pairs may be arranged selectively in a series starting with the longest and progressing toward the shortest. Regardless of size, the last two chromosomes are the pair that determine sex: the **XX** chromosomes in the female and the **XY** chromosomes in the male. The Y chromosome always is much smaller than the X. Within any one size grouping, the chromosomes are subdivided further on the basis of the position of the centromere (Fig. 8-13). The result is the karyotype for a

FIGURE 8-14
Chromosome changes during mitosis. Each member of a chromosome pair replicates itself and the nuclear membrane disappears (*A* and *B*); chromosomes become aligned along the equator of a spindle-shaped figure, their centromeres attached to spindle fibers (*C*); centromeres divide (*D*) and spindle fibers appear to pull replicated daughter chromosomes to opposite poles of cell (*E*), as cell divides (*E* and *F*). One member of chromosome pair is colored so that the fate of each chromosome can be followed.

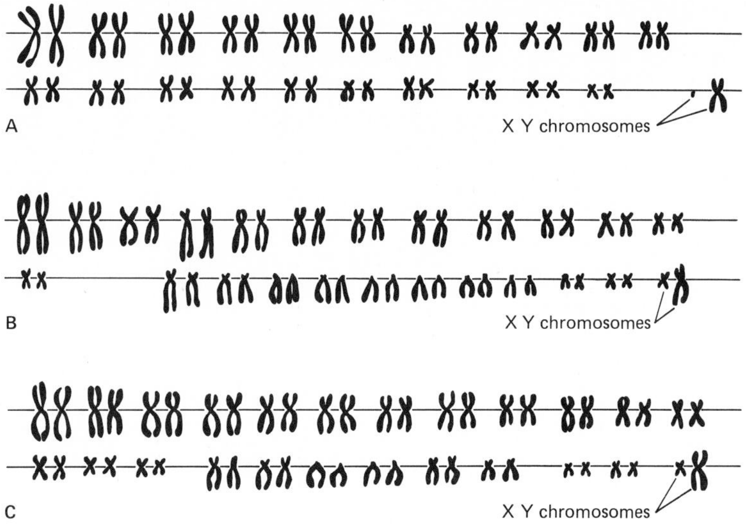

A

X Y chromosomes

B

X Y chromosomes

C

X Y chromosomes

FIGURE 8-15
Hominoid karyotypes. *A*, The gibbon, *Hylobates lar* (44 chromosomes); *B*, the orangutan, *Pongo pygmaeus* (48 chromosomes); and *C*, the gorilla, *Gorilla gorilla* (48 chromosomes). (Chromosomes are in stage *C*, Fig. 8-14.) [*After J. Buettner-Janusch, Origins of Man, Wiley, New York, 1966.*]

given species: the number, sizes, and shapes of all the chromosome pairs in a typical cell. Since genes are carried on chromosomes, the karyotype is associated closely with the genetic constitution of the species.

The karyotype of a gibbon (44 chromosomes), orangutan (48 chromosomes), and gorilla (48 chromosomes) are illustrated in Fig. 8-15.

Chromosomes and sex-cell formation (meiosis)

Chromosome behavior during sex-cell formation is the cellular foundation of genetic mechanisms.

A human being develops from a fertilized egg or *zygote* that contained 23 pairs of chromosomes. Since every zygote comes from a union of a sperm (male) cell and an egg (female) cell, the *sum* of the chromosomes carried by the two sex cells equals 23 pairs. We might expect, therefore, that each kind of sex cell or *gamete* would carry one each of the 23 different chromosomes that the zygote carries in pairs. The human sperm and ovum each have 23 different

chromosomes; their union in fertilization produces a zygote with the normal chromosome number of 23 pairs. This outcome—the production of a zygote whose number of chromosome *pairs* is equal to the number of *individual* chromosomes in a sex cell—is the case in any species, regardless of its chromosome count. The paired-number characteristic of the fertilized egg is said to be the *diploid* number whereas the unpaired number found in gametes is called the *haploid*.

The mechanism by which the chromosome number is reduced in sex cells from diploid to haploid is called *meiosis*. It is similar to mitosis (Fig. 8-14) in some respects, but it also is different, as is evident in Fig. 8-16.

In the formation of mature gametes, two consecutive cell divisions occur which are called the *first and second meiotic divisions*. At the beginning of the first meiotic division, the two members of each pair of homologous chromosomes become attached to one another along their entire length. (For simplicity's sake, only one pair of chromosomes is shown in the illustration.) Each chromosome then replicates it-

FIGURE 8-16

Meiosis shown schematically in a cell with one pair of chromosomes (one member colored, the other white). The nuclear membrane is not shown. Meiosis I (*A* to *E*): chromosomes shorten and thicken, become attached to one another and duplicate themselves, each forming two identical chromatids joined by a centromere (*A* and *B*); chromosome pair, now represented by two joined chromatid doublets called a tetrad, moves onto equatorial plane of division spindle (*C*); chromatid doublets move toward opposite poles of spindle. (*D*); cell divides, daughter cells having one chromatid doublet each (*E*). Meiosis II (*F* to *H*): centromere with its chromatids in each daughter cell moves onto equatorial plane of spindle and replicates itself (*F*); chromatids in each daughter cell separate as each cell divides, forming four sex cells with one chromosome each (*G* and *H*).

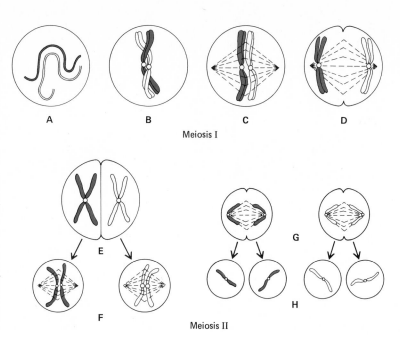

self, forming identical duplicates which are called *chromatids*. Each of the original chromosomes are represented by two identical chromatids joined by a common centromere, and the original chromosome pair now comprises a tightly knit cluster of four chromatids known as a *tetrad* (Fig. 8-16*B*).

The tetrad now moves into the equatorial plane of the spindle figure that has been forming in the cell, and the centromere connecting two chromatids attaches to a spindle fiber (*C*). One centromere with its doublet of chromatids then moves towards one pole of the spindle while the second centromere moves toward the other (*D*). Cell division follows, producing two cells each of which has a single chromosome consisting of two identical chromatids (*E*). One of these daughter cells contains the chromatid doublet that represents the original paternal member of the chromosome pair (color). The paternal member of a chromosome pair is the one that came from the sperm of the father. The other daughter cell has the maternal doublet

(white), representing the original maternal member of the chromosome pair that came from the egg of the mother.

The second meiotic division resembles mitosis. The centromere moves onto the equatorial plane of the spindle figure, becomes attached to a spindle fiber, and duplicates itself (*F*). Each chromatid now goes to opposite poles of the spindle and the cell divides. Four sex cells result from this second division, each one bearing the haploid chromosome number (*G–H*). Of the four, two have one paternal chromosome each (color) and the other two carry one maternal chromosome (white).

The hereditary consequences of meiosis

Since genes are carried on chromosomes, the distribution of hereditary material among offspring will depend upon the manner in which chromosomes were assorted in the sex cells that produced the offspring. We do not know how many genes human beings have; there may be 1 million or more. Even if this number turns out to be extravagant, it is certain that each of the 46 human chromosomes bears hundreds, if not thousands, of genes. There also is strong evidence for the belief that each of these genes has its own specific location on a particular chromosome, and that all the genes on a given chromosome are arranged in a precise linear order from one end of the chromosome to the other.

As a consequence of the nature of meiosis and the relationship of genes to chromosomes, the hereditary material is reordered and re-shuffled in two ways: the independent assortment of chromosomes and their genes—the cellular basis for Mendel's principle of independent assortment—and the recombination of genes on the same chromosome.

The independent assortment of chromosomes and their genes

Figure 8-17 illustrates a simple case of meiosis involving two pairs of chromosomes. For simplicity's sake, they are shown in a schematic end view. One pair is round and the other square. When two (or more) chromosome sets align themselves on the spindle figure, they do so independently of one another; their relative alignment is strictly random. The paternal chromosome (black) of each set may be on the same, or on different, sides of the spindle equator. With two pairs of chromosomes the tetrads can be arranged in only two possible ways.

Because of the independent alignment of tetrads on the division spindle, meiosis can produce every possible haploid combination of paternal and maternal chromosomes, in this case four. The chance of any one combination taking part in fertilization would be 1 in 4. If we had considered three pairs of chromosomes instead of two, eight combinations would be possible ($2 \times 2 \times 2$, or 2^3). With 23 pairs, as in man, the number of possible arrangements runs into the millions (2^{23}).

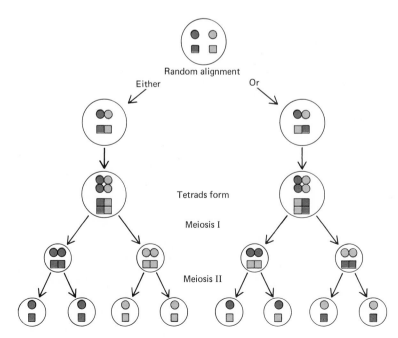

FIGURE 8-17
A diagrammatic representation of the random assortment of chromosomes during meiosis. Two pairs of chromosomes are illustrated, one represented by two circles and the other by two squares. Paternal chromosomes are black, maternal colored. Different sets of homologous chromosomes align themselves independently of one another on the equatorial plane. With two pairs of chromosomes, four combinations of maternal and paternal chromosomes are possible in mature sex cells. This is the chromosomal basis for Mendel's principle of independent assortment (Fig. 8-3).

We can now see the cellular basis for Mendel's principle of independent assortment by comparing Fig. 8-3 (cross between red-flowered, tall and white-flowered, dwarf plants) with Fig. 8-17. Let us suppose that Fig. 8-17 illustrates the two pairs of chromosomes that carry the genes for flower color and plant height in the hybrid, first-generation offspring of Fig. 8-3. Let us also assume that the gene set for flower color is located on the round chromosome and that the paternal (black) chromosome carries the gene for red color and that the maternal (colored) chromosome carries the gene for white. Let us further assume that the paternal (black) square chromosome bears the gene for tallness and the maternal (colored) square chromosome bears the gene for dwarfness. Since these genes will go wherever their chromosomes carry them, there can be four gene combinations in the sex cells produced: (1) red-flowered, tall; (2) white-flowered, dwarf; (3) red-flowered, dwarf; and (4) white-flowered, tall. These are the same gene combinations shown in the gametes of Fig. 8-3 and represent every possible assortment of the four genes. Which particular one might participate in a specific act of fertilization would be a matter of chance alone.

The recombination of genes on the same chromosome

Since chromosomes pass from cell to cell as whole units, one might assume that the genes on a given chromosome would always go together as a package. This is not necessarily so. Two chromosomes in a tetrad commonly break and exchange broken parts while the chromatids are intimately attached to, and often are intertwined around, one another. This process, called *crossover*, may occur at random along the length of any two chromatids in a tetrad. Figure 8-18 shows a crossover, indicated by the arrow, between a paternal (black) and maternal (colored) chromatid. Two genes are located on each chromosome as points of reference, *a* and *B* on one paternal member and *A* and *b*, their counterparts, on the maternal

member. Crossover is shown between these gene locations on two chromatids but not on the other two. As a result, gene *A* or *a* can become linked with *B* or *b* in all possible combinations, forming four different sex cells, two by crossover (*A-B* and *a-b*) and two without crossover (*a-B* and *A-b*).

Several examples of genes being located on the same chromosome (gene linkage) have been observed in man. A gene set for normal vision versus red color blindness is located on the same chromosome with another pair of genes for normal blood clotting versus defective clotting (*hemophilia A*). Because of gametes (sex cells) formed both with and without crossover, each of the four haploid combinations of these genes is possible: (1) normal-sighted, non-bleeder; (2) color-blind, bleeder; (3) normal-sighted, bleeder; and (4) color-blind, non-bleeder. Or, put in terms of the arbitrary letter designations above: (1) *AB;* (2) *ab;* (3) *Ab;* and (4) *aB.*

In summary, we may say that biological diversity is generated both through the independent assortment of genes on different chromosomes as well as the recombination of genes on the same chromosome. The different genetic combinations possible between two mating individuals is a staggering figure — over 70 trillion possible combinations of chromosomes, *not counting crossover.* The combinations possible in a *population* of mating individuals is quite beyond comprehension.

Sex determination and gene linkage

One chromosome pair determines the sex of an individual. In females, the members of the pair are similar and designated **XX**, whereas in males the X member is paired with a much smaller Y chromosome (Fig. 8-15). The X chromosome carries many genes, the vast majority of which are lacking on the Y.

The chromosomal basis for sex determination is shown schematically in Fig. 8-19. Since the 22 pairs of nonsex chromosomes, or *autosomes,* are not normally involved in sex determination, they are not shown. All eggs possess but one kind of sex chromosomes, the X. When sperm are formed, however, half will receive an X chromosome and half will receive a Y. The chance that fertilization will be by one or the other of the two kinds of sperm will therefore be about the same. If an X-bearing sperm fertilizes the egg, the zygote will develop into a female (XX) whereas fertilization by a Y-bearing sperm will produce a zygote that will become a male (XY).

Sex-linked genes   Since only a relatively few genes are located on the Y chromosome of the male, most of the genes on the X chromosome lack matching alleles. In females, these genes occur in their normal diploid number. As a result, we should expect the inheritance of traits governed by these genes to follow a different pattern in the two sexes. Red blindness, for example, referred to earlier, is caused by a recessive allele located on the X, but not the Y, chromosome. Although women do have this trait, it is much more common in men (Fig. 8-20 illustrates the reason). A male will be color-blind if he inherits only one recessive allele (*b*) from his mother. He could not receive it from his father. On the other hand, a female must receive a recessive allele from her mother as well as from her father to be color-blind. In other words, color-blind females can be born only to fathers who are color-blind and mothers who have at least one recessive allele. Genes of this kind that are carried on one sex chromosome but not the other are said to be *sex-linked*.

Another trait we have mentioned, that of classic hemophilia (hemophilia A), also is the product of a recessive allele (*h*) located only on the X chromosome. Here again, the phenotype is much more common among men than women, as evidenced by the occurrence of this disease in the descendants of Queen Victoria (Fig. 8-21). Victoria was not hemophilic herself, but she was a heterozygous carrier of the allele (*Hh*). Of the 10 known hemophiliacs among her children, grandchildren, and great-grandchildren, all were males (Fig. 8-22). The

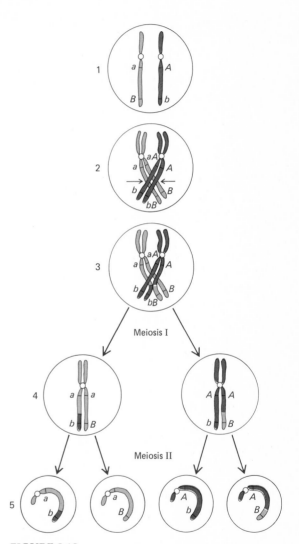

FIGURE 8-18
Recombination of genes on the same chromosome through crossover (arrow). For reference, two gene locations are shown on each chromosome: *a* and *B* on the paternal chromosome (black) and their alternative counterparts *A* and *b* on the maternal chromosome (colored). 1 to 4 are stages of first meiotic division; 4 and 5 of second meiotic division.

FIGURE 8-19
Sex is determined by a pair of sex chromosomes. *A,* In the male (♂), the pair is called XY because the chromosomes are dissimilar. In the female (♀), they are similar (**XX**). The remaining 22 pairs of nonsex chromosomes in man, called autosomes, are not shown. *B,* Sex determination of offspring depends upon which sex chromosome the fertilizing sperm carries.

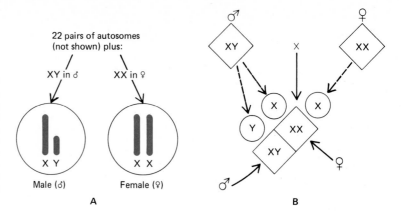

rarity of hemophilic women is not due solely to sex-linkage, however. They must be the children of a hemophilic father and a mother who is at least a carrier; such marriages are rare because of premature death in so many hemophilic boys.

The phenotypic results of genetic recombination Now that we are familiar with the inheritance of two traits whose genes are located on the same chromosome, we are in a position to examine how such traits may be inherited with respect to one another. How does the recombination of genes through crossover differ in its phenotypic results from the reassortment of genes that are located on

different chromosomes?

Since crossover depends on a break occurring someplace along the length of a chromosome, there is a greater likelihood that such a break will appear between two widely separated genes on the chromosome than between two which are relatively close together. The percentage of breaks (crossovers) that occurs between any two genes, therefore, reflects with a fair degree of accuracy the relative distance that separates those genes on the chromosome. This distance, in fact, is measured by geneticists in terms of a chromosome *map unit* that is defined as the distance within which crossover occurs 1 percent of the time.

FIGURE 8-20
Red color blindness is caused by a recessive allele *b* carried on the X but not the Y chromosome. Normal vision results from dominant allele *B*. One recessive allele causes color blindness in men (*A* and *B*) whereas color-blind women must have both recessives (*B*).

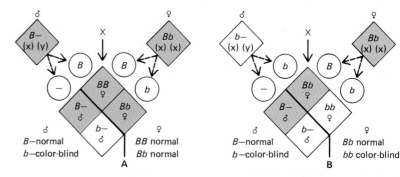

FIGURE 8-21
Queen Victoria with son Edward VII, grandson George V, and great-grandson Edward VIII (Duke of Windsor). [*Underwood and Underwood.*]

Studies of human genealogies indicate that the map distance between the genes for classic hemophilia and red blindness is 12 — that is to say, crossover occurs between these two genes in 12 percent of the sex cells. This means, of course, that it does *not* occur in 88 percent of the sex cells. In order to show how crossover affects phenotypic ratios, let us consider a hypothetical case involving the offspring of matings between hemophilic, color-blind men and doubly heterozygous normal women.

In order to demonstrate the difference between gene reassortment and gene recombination, let us first consider what would happen if these genes were located on different chromosomes (which, of course, they are not). Let us assume that hemophilia is sex-linked but color blindness is not. The genotype of hemophilic, color-blind men would then be

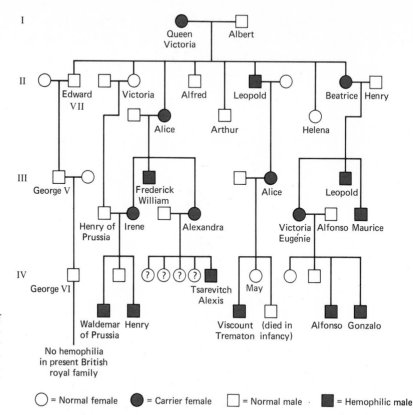

FIGURE 8-22
Hemophilia in the descendants of Queen Victoria. One of the daughters (Louise) as well as many of the grandchildren and great-grandchildren have been omitted because they did not receive the recessive allele. Generations are numbered I to IV.

h-bb, the hyphen (-) referring to the lack of a gene on the Y chromosome. The genotype of doubly heterozygous normal women would be *HhBb.* In this event, the offspring of our hypothetical matings would be distributed equally among four phenotypes: (1) nonbleeder, normal sighted; (2) nonbleeder, color-blind; (3) hemophilic, normal sighted; and (4) hemophilic, color-blind (Fig. 8-23).

Considering the case as it really is, the genotype of hemophilic, color-blind men is *hb/* —. Genes *h* and *b* are on the X chromosome and the Y chromosome lacks both. The genotype of doubly heterozygous women is *Hb/hB;*

genes *H* and *b* are on one X chromosome and genes *h* and *B* on the other (Fig. 8-24). Crossover does not occur between XY chromosomes because they are dissimilar and do not become intimately attached to one another like other chromosomes (Fig. 8-18). Crossover between X-linked genes occurs only among egg cells. Consequently, the females of our hypothetical matings will produce eggs, 88 percent of which do not involve crossover ((Hb) and (hB)) and 12 percent that do ((HB) and (hb)). The males will produce only two kinds of sperm, in equal numbers ((hb) and (—)). As can be seen, the phenotypic ratio among the progeny differs

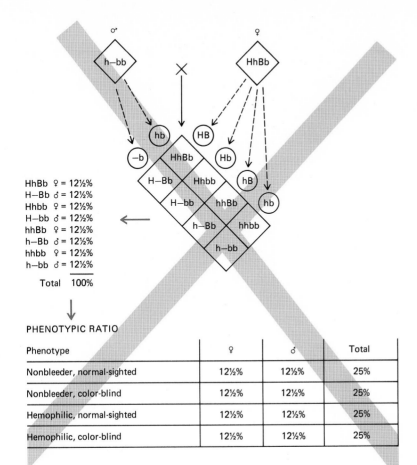

HhBb ♀ = 12½%
H—Bb ♂ = 12½%
Hhbb ♀ = 12½%
H—bb ♂ = 12½%
hhBb ♀ = 12½%
h—Bb ♂ = 12½%
hhbb ♀ = 12½%
h—bb ♂ = 12½%

Total   100%

PHENOTYPIC RATIO

Phenotype	♀	♂	Total
Nonbleeder, normal-sighted	12½%	12½%	25%
Nonbleeder, color-blind	12½%	12½%	25%
Hemophilic, normal-sighted	12½%	12½%	25%
Hemophilic, color-blind	12½%	12½%	25%

FIGURE 8-23
If we assume that hemophilia is sex-linked but color blindness is not, the mating of hemophilic color-blind males with heterozygous non-bleeder normal-sighted females would produce young with a phenotypic ratio, disregarding sex, of 1:1:1:1, as shown. *This is not the case.*

considerably from that in Fig. 8-23. Eighty-eight percent are equally apportioned between nonbleeder, color-blind and hemophilic, normal-sighted. These are the phenotypes in which crossover did not occur. The crossover phenotypes total 12 percent, equally distributed between nonbleeder, normal-sighted and hemophilic, color-blind.

Crossover also can occur in non-sex-linked genes, that is, those that are common to one of the 22 pairs of autosomes.

CHEMICAL GENETICS

To this point we have shown the relationship of chromosomes to the mechanisms of inheritance. We still have not addressed the questions of what a gene really is and how it controls the synthesis of enzymes and other substances. To answer such questions we must investigate the chemical nature of genes.

Genes have been shown to consist of nucleic acid molecules called *DNA*: deoxy-

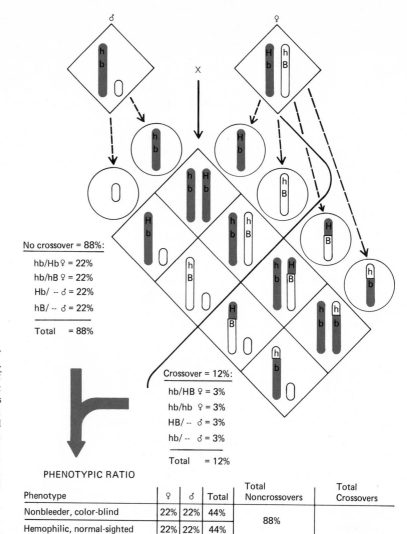

No crossover = 88%:

hb/Hb ♀ = 22%

hb/hB ♀ = 22%

Hb/ -- ♂ = 22%

hB/ -- ♂ = 22%

_____

Total   = 88%

FIGURE 8-24
Genes for hemophilia and color blindness are both sex-linked. Crossover occurs in 12 percent of all egg cells. Crossover does not occur between XY chromosomes (see text). Heterozygous normal females of genotype *Hb/hB* will produce eggs 88 percent of which do not involve crossover ((Hb) and (hB)) and 12 percent that do ((HB) and - (hb)). If such females had children by hemophilic color-blind males (*hb/* –), the offspring would have a phenotypic ratio, disregarding sex, of 44:44:6:6, as shown above. (Note how this differs from the phenotypic ratio in Fig. 8-23.) Relative location of genes on X chromosome is hypothetical.

Crossover = 12%:

hb/HB ♀ = 3%

hb/hb ♀ = 3%

HB/ -- ♂ = 3%

hb/ -- ♂ = 3%

_____

Total   = 12%

PHENOTYPIC RATIO

Phenotype	♀	♂	Total	Total Noncrossovers	Total Crossovers
Nonbleeder, color-blind	22%	22%	44%	88%	
Hemophilic, normal-sighted	22%	22%	44%		
Nonbleeder, normal-sighted	3%	3%	6%		12%
Hemophilic, color-blind	3%	3%	6%		

ribonucleic acid. They are the largest of all macromolecules, with molecular weights[8] ranging from the tens of thousands into the hundreds of millions. Despite their size, however, their structure is relatively simple.

A DNA molecule can be likened to a ladder that has been twisted upon itself to form a double helix (Fig. 8-25). Each of the two long supports, or strands, bears regularly

[8] Molecular weight is the sum of the atomic weights of all the atoms in a molecule. Table salt (sodium chloride) has a molecular weight of 58.

spaced projections called *bases*. Bases along one strand establish a chemical bond with bases along the complementary strand, forming the rungs, or steps, of the ladder. There are four kinds of bases, designated A, T, G, and C (adenine, thymine, guanine, and cytosine). A's pair only with T's and G's pair only with C's in making these rungs. A DNA molecule contains thousands, or even millions, of A-T pairs and G-C pairs.

The sequence of bases along one strand of the DNA helix constitutes a chemical language which we have heretofore referred to as a *gene*. Three consecutive bases make up a code "word" that specifies some particular amino acid. *AAC* and *GTC,* for example, code for two different amino acids (leucine and glutamine). The 18 bases along one strand of the DNA molecule shown in Fig. 8-25 code for six amino acids. An average gene includes a sequence of perhaps 1,000 bases. A gene, therefore, is a chemical language or blueprint for making a specific kind of protein molecule, such as an enzyme. It indicates not only the kinds of amino acids needed, but their precise arrangement in the macromolecule as well.

We have already discussed the complex biochemical reactions by which gene-controlled enzymes bring about the development of phenotypic traits (Fig. 8-6). We shall not attempt to describe the biochemical processes by which the chemical language of the gene is translated into the synthesis of specific enzyme molecules, since that penetrates deeper into these matters than is necessary for our purposes here. Suffice it to say that a DNA molecule is capable of transcribing a complementary copy of itself in the form of another kind of nucleic acid known as *RNA* (ribonucleic acid). The transcribed RNA molecule is, in effect, a "working copy" of the original DNA "blueprint," from which the protein manufacturing sites in the cell synthesize enzymes, antibodies, hemoglobin molecules, and so on, to specifications.

When a cell divides, the genes as well as the chromosomes replicate themselves. The

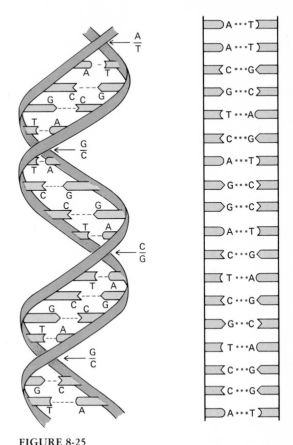

FIGURE 8-25
The DNA molecule is like a ladder twisted on itself to form a double helix (left). The two long supports or strands are the backbone of the molecule, to which are attached paired bases (A's with T's and G's with C's). These paired bases are held together by chemical bonds which comprise the rungs or steps of the ladder. The diagram on the right indicates how the helical structure would look if it were untwisted and flattened. (See text.)

double-stranded helix of DNA replicates itself by a chemical process in which the chemical bonds between the paired bases are progressively broken, somewhat like a zipper as it is being unzipped (Fig. 8-26). Each separated strand then assembles a new strand complementary to itself from available unattached bases in the vicinity within the cell (Fig. 8-26).

FIGURE 8-26
DNA replicates itself by unzipping the chemical bonds between its paired bases. Each separated strand then assembles a new strand complementary to itself (lighter color) from available unattached bases in the chemical vicinity within the cell.

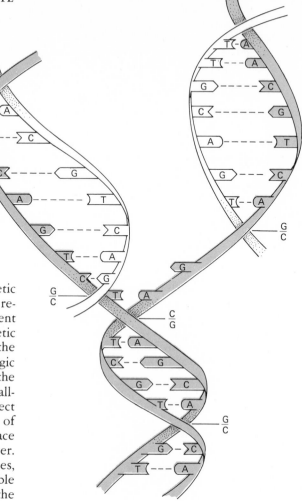

MUTATION: SOURCE OF BIOLOGIC NOVELTY

We have reviewed some of the genetic mechanisms by which diverse phenotypic results are obtained through the reassortment and recombination of genes. Shuffling a genetic deck of cards, however enormous though the deck may be, is not the sole cause of biologic novelty. The genetic "card deck" is itself the product of a genetic phenomenon whose hallmark is continuous change. Genes are subject to change and are themselves the products of change. Fundamental alterations also take place in both chromosome structure and number. These modifications in chromosomes and genes, called *mutations,* are believed to be responsible for the karyotype (Fig. 8-15) as well as all the genes of any given species. Although mutations usually are rare among individuals, they constitute a powerful ever-present force for biologic innovation when considered in the context of the large populations in which they occur.

The mutation of a specific gene may occur only once in 25,000 sex cells. A population of 500,000 breeding individuals would yield 20 mutations of this specific gene in each generation. When one considers the countless numbers of *different* genes which are subject to mutation, this population would produce many thousands of mutant individuals in every generation.

Types of mutations

These genetic changes entail modifications both in the karyotype (*chromosomal mutations*) and in the genes themselves (*gene* or *point mutations*). Chromosomal mutations fall into two groups: (1) changes in chromosome number, and (2) abnormal rearrangements caused by random chromosome breakage.

Changes in chromosome number
During meiosis, chromosome behavior occasionally is abnormal. In one such case, called

nondisjunction, the members of a chromosome pair do not move to opposite poles of the cell but remain together and pass into one of the daughter cells (Fig. 8-27). Consequently, one of the daughter cells has an extra chromosome, while the other has one less than it should. If these were human egg cells, one would have 24 chromosomes and the other 22; their fertilization by normal sperm would produce two zygotes with 47 and 45 chromosomes, respectively.

Numerous cases of this kind have been recorded. Among males, about 5 in every 2,000 are born with an extra X chromosome, giving them 47 chromosomes. Instances of this nature, in which a chromosome set is represented by three rather than two chromosomes, are called *trisomy;* in this case the karyotype is designated *trisomy XXY.* Although normal as boys, these individuals develop what is known as *Klinefelter's syndrome,* as adults. They are eunuch-like in appearance, sterile, and often mentally retarded. *Turner's syndrome,* on the other hand, involves individuals who have but one sex chromosome, the X, and bear only 45 chromosomes. Persons with this XO karyotype occur about once in every 5,000 births and develop as sterile female dwarfs.

Nondisjunction is not confined to the sex chromosomes. A familiar abnormality called *Down's syndrome* (formerly known as *mongolian idiocy*) is the result of trisomy in chromosome number 21 (see Fig. 8-28). The victims of trisomy 21 are phenotypically distinguished by their eye fold, sagging mouth, fleshiness, happy disposition, and idiot mentality; their life expectancy is about 12 years. Although they occur about once in every 600 to 700 births, their frequency rises sharply with the increasing age of the prospective mother. This may be due to the fact that all the potential egg cells in the human ovary have passed through the first but not the second meiotic division. The second division is not completed until the egg has been released and penetrated by a sperm. It may be that the prolonged delay between the first and the second

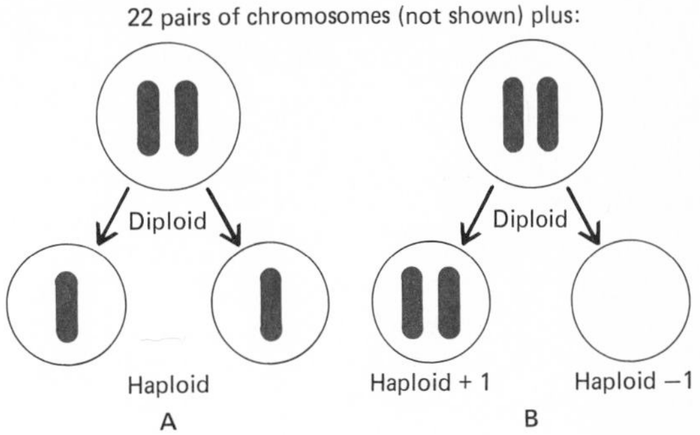

FIGURE 8-27

Normal meiosis (*A*) compared to an abnormal form of meiosis, nondisjunction (*B*). On rare occasions a chromosome set is not apportioned between daughter cells, producing gametes half of which have an extra chromosome (haploid plus one) and half of which lack one chromosome (haploid less one). More than one chromosome set may be involved in this, increasing and decreasing haploid numbers proportionately.

divisions in women who bear children later in life somehow encourages nondisjunction of chromosome 21, which is quite small in size.

Karyotypes also are possible in which more than one chromosome set is trisomic. Several individuals have been described who were XXY males as well as trisomic for chromosome 21. It is even possible for an individual to have a chromosome set represented by four chromosomes (*tetrasomy*) or five chromosomes (*pentasomy*); an XXXX female and an XXXXY male have been reported.

In this regard, it is interesting to note the remarkable similarities between the karyotypes of the chimpanzee and man (Fig. 8-28). Although there are some minor differences in several chromosomes, the major difference lies in the extra chromosome pair of the chimp (48 chromosomes versus 46). The extra chromosome set may be number 16, the last set in a group of four (numbers 13, 14, 15, and 16). In man this chromosome group has only three sets, numbers 13, 14, and 15.

The ultimate in extra chromosomes occurs when the entire chromosome set is increased by some multiple of the haploid chromosome number. This phenomenon is known as *polyploidy*. One extra chromosome of each kind, for example, would produce a *triploid* individual with 69 chromosomes (46 plus 23); two extra chromosomes per set would produce a *tetraploid* with 92 chromosomes (46 plus 46). The first human polyploid to be reported was a triploid male infant (XXY plus 66 autosomes) described in 1960. The child was obese and showed abnormal brain development; it also had small jaws, and its fingers and toes were fused or webbed.[9]

Polyploidy could result from a meiotic division that was so abnormal that all chromosomes were distributed to but one daughter cell. This would produce a diploid rather than a haploid sex cell. The same result also could be obtained if, during a meiotic division, the chromosomes behaved normally but the cell itself failed to divide. The fertilization of a diploid gamete by a normal haploid gamete

[9] Maurice Whittinghill, *Human Genetics,* New York: Reinhold Publishing Corporation, 1965, pp. 306–307.

would yield a triploid zygote. If both gametes were diploid, the zygote would be tetraploid. There are, as yet, no recorded births of a human tetraploid.

Abnormal chromosome rearrangements

Chromosomes break on occasion in a random, abnormal manner, and their fragments may become reattached in unusual ways (Fig. 8-29). These chromosomal realignments may involve the same chromosome set, as in *duplication, deletion,* and *inversion,* or they may entail a rearrangement between different chromosome pairs known as *translocation.*

Various phenotypic modifications accompany mutations of this kind. A normal egg fertilized by a sperm with a chromosome deletion would produce a zygote that would be haploid for all the genes not supplied by the sperm. In Fig. 8-29, this would be gene 3 and all its close neighbors on both sides. All these alleles contributed by the egg would express themselves phenotypically whether they were dominant or recessive, just as the sex-linked genes in males. If the zygote was homozygous for this deletion, it would probably not de-

FIGURE 8-28
Karyotypes of (*A*) man (46 chromosomes) and (*B*) the chimpanzee, *Pan troglodytes* (48 chromosomes). The extra chromosome pair of the chimpanzee may be set number 16. [*After J. Buettner-Janusch, Origins of Man, Wiley, New York, 1966.*]

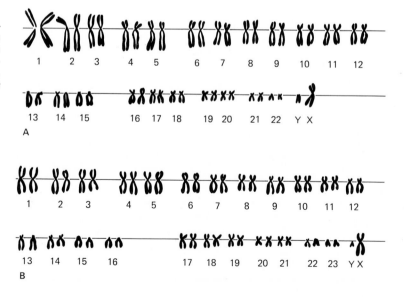

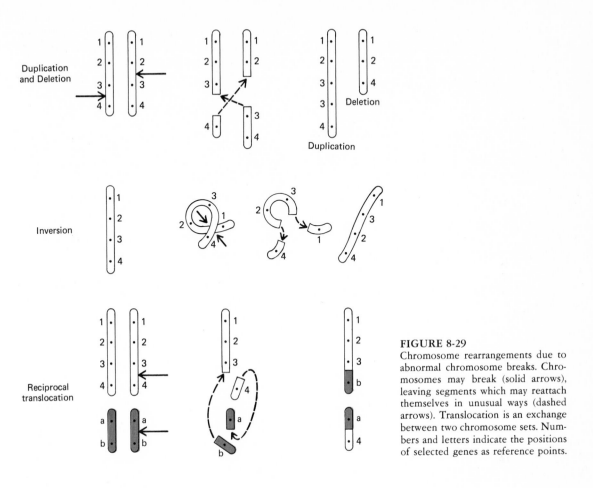

FIGURE 8-29
Chromosome rearrangements due to abnormal chromosome breaks. Chromosomes may break (solid arrows), leaving segments which may reattach themselves in unusual ways (dashed arrows). Translocation is an exchange between two chromosome sets. Numbers and letters indicate the positions of selected genes as reference points.

velop because of the absence of essential genetic information.

Translocation may mimic the phenotypic effects of trisomy. Several instances are known in which Down's syndrome resulted from the translocation of the long arm[10] of chromosome 21 onto the small arm of another chromosome. A translocation also reassociates certain genes from two different chromosome sets into a new linkage group, as in the linkage of genes *a* and 4 in Fig. 8-29. As a consequence, genes that

ordinarily are inherited through independent assortment would now recombine only through crossover.

Inversions are phenotypically significant because they modify crossover frequencies. An individual homozygous for the inversion chromosome in Fig. 8-29 would produce gametes with fewer crossovers between genes 1 and 3 than would be the case with noninverted chromosomes. This sort of thing can have important evolutionary consequences; let us see how.

The phenotypic expression of a particular gene may be influenced either favorably or

[10] When the centromere is not in the middle of a chromosome, the chromosome is said to have a long and a short arm.

unfavorably by genes lying close to it. This phenomenon is known as the *position effect*. If genes 1 and 3, as close chromosome neighbors, influence one another favorably—for example, by facilitating the production of some enzyme controlled by gene 1—individuals homozygous for the inversion would have a survival advantage. A modification of this same principle can also apply to translocations. Two genes located on different chromosomes can become neighbors on the same chromosome, as in the case of genes 3 and *b* in Fig. 8-29.

Gene (point) mutations

The occurrence of a newly mutated gene clearly is evident in the progeny of Queen Victoria and Prince Albert (Fig. 8-22). Three of the children, Alice, Leopold, and Beatrice, received the gene for hemophilia. Since the gene is sex-linked, Albert could not have transmitted it to his son, Leopold. The chances are excellent that Victoria alone supplied the hemophilic allele, but there is no record of hemophilia in any of her ancestors. It is highly unlikely that this mutation was duplicated on

three separate occasions in the egg cells of the queen herself. It is therefore most probable that the hemophilic allele was a new mutation contributed by either her mother or father. Such a mutation (change) in a single gene is called a *gene*, or *point mutation*.

Undoubtedly, changes in genes are brought about in many ways. Known mechanisms include the addition, deletion, or substitution of one or more chemical bases in the DNA molecule (Fig. 8-25). Figure 8-30 indicates how genetic information may be significantly altered by the deletion of a single base.

All the alternative alleles that make up a gene set are the products of gene mutations. A dominant gene *A,* for example, may mutate to a recessive allele *a*. Mutations of this sort which proceed from the so-called normal, or wild-type, gene (in this case *A*) to the mutant are called *direct mutations. Reverse mutations* also take place; it is possible for mutant allele *a* to revert back to the normal, dominant *A*. It should not be assumed, however, that the normal gene always is dominant. It is quite possible for the normal to be recessive, in which case a direct mutation could result in a mutant dominant allele such as that described below.

The rate at which a given gene mutates is generally constant, but the rate of mutation varies between different genes. The rate of direct mutation usually is much higher than that of reverse mutation. Normal genes are a great deal more mutable than their mutant alleles. Mutation rates for specific genes gen-

FIGURE 8-30
Gene mutation by removal (arrow) of a base (T) from a single strand of DNA. By removing (deleting) base T from the sequence of DNA bases in a normal gene, the sequence of bases beyond the deletion is shifted up one position in the new mutant gene. This results in a different sequence of base triplets or code words which would specify a different sequence of amino acids for protein synthesis. Amino acids are identified by a number. Note that the genetic language has synonyms for some amino acids (2, 4, and 8 below).

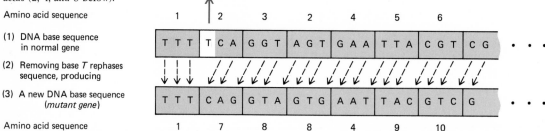

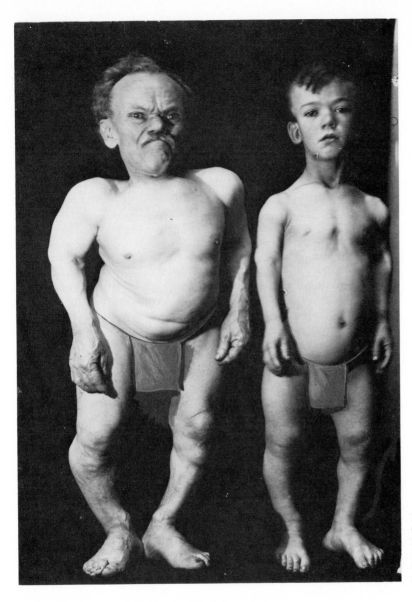

FIGURE 8-31
Chondrodystrophic dwarfism, the result of a dominant mutant gene. Photo is of father and son. [*Courtesy of Dr. E. T. Morch and the American Genetics Association.*]

erally fall between 1 and 100 mutations per million sex cells. Human *chondrodystrophy*, for example, is the result of a dominant mutant that occurs about once in every 20,000 gametes. Chondrodystrophy is a familiar type of dwarfism in which the individual has a normal-sized trunk but the arms and legs usually are short (Fig. 8-31). Chondrodystrophics almost always are born to normal parents; very few chondrodystrophic men, and even fewer women, have children.

Causes of mutation

Any agent that contributes to mutation or to an increase in the mutation rate is called a *mutagenic agent* or *mutagen.* Mutations may occur as a result of various synthetic mutagens such as chemicals (*induced mutations*) or as a result of natural causes (*spontaneous mutations*).

A variety of mutagens are known, including mustard gas, formaldehyde, sulfur dioxide, antibiotics, and even caffeine, which will increase the mutation rate in such organisms as insects, molds, and bacteria. Whether these substances are mutagenic to mammals is not known. Ionizing radiation of all kinds is mutagenic to any organism, including ourselves. Ionizing radiation includes ultraviolet light, x-rays, cosmic rays, and the radiation from radioactive wastes and atomic bomb fallout.

It was once thought that the natural sources of background radiation (cosmic radiation, ultraviolet, and others) were responsible for spontaneous mutation in man. This is no longer believed since the amount of this kind of radiation that reaches the reproductive cells falls considerably short of that required to account for known mutation rates in man and other mammals.

Whatever mutagenic agencies are involved, their effects accumulate with time. Older parents transmit more mutations to their offspring than do younger parents. A study in Denmark revealed that the frequency of chondrodystrophic dwarfism is six times higher in the children of mothers over 40 than in those whose mothers were under 25 at the time of birth.[11] At least some of this increased risk is very likely the result of x-ray exposure for purposes of medical and dental diagnosis. We will discuss this issue in greater depth in Section III.

Man-primate relationships at the molecular level of the gene

Techniques have been developed which demonstrate the genetic relatedness of different species at the molecular level of the

gene. These techniques utilize the principle that a single strand of DNA will "recognize" a complementary base sequence and combine, or hybridize, with it to form the double-stranded structure. For example, a single-strand sequence of A—A—C—G—T—C will hybridize with a strand sequence of T—T—G—C—A—G, forming the double-stranded structure:

$$
\begin{array}{cccccc}
A & A & C & G & T & C \\
| & | & | & | & | & | \\
T & T & G & C & A & G
\end{array}
$$

The DNA base sequences of different animal species can be compared by the degree to which they will combine with one another. The procedure involves treating the DNA of several species chemically and converting it into separate, single strands. For example, a preparation of single-stranded human DNA may be placed in each of five containers. To the first of these, single-stranded chimpanzee DNA may be added, to the second, single strands of gibbon DNA. The third, fourth, and fifth containers may receive single-stranded DNA from an Old World (rhesus) monkey, a New World (capuchin) monkey, and a prosimian (*Galago*), respectively. After a period of time, the degree of molecular combination between the human DNA and the DNA of each of these five primates can be measured chemically. Those preparations which show a high percentage of combination with the human DNA demonstrate strong similarities in their base sequences and a corresponding resemblance in their hereditary constitutions.

As may be seen in Fig. 8-32, such studies show a remarkable degree of base-pair matching or hybridization between man and the chimpanzees (97.5 percent). There is a progressive decrease in this percentage in the gibbon, Old World (rhesus) monkey, New World (capuchin) monkey, and prosimian (*Galago*). Even the 46 percent of base-pair matching which we share with the galago, however, is more than twice the 20 percent we share with non-primate mammals in general.

[11] A. M. Winchester, *Genetics.* Boston: Houghton Mifflin Company, 1972, pp. 455–456.

The evolutionary significance of mutation

In reviewing the types of chromosomal and gene mutations we have discussed, one is struck by the fact that usually they are harmful. Many cause the death of the embryo or the newborn. Since these mutations are caused by random changes in the karyotype and its genes, the damaging effects of most mutant alleles should not be surprising. Life has existed on this planet for about 3½ billion years. The hominid family has resided here for 15 million years. Environmental (natural) selection has had ample time to eliminate unsuccessful phenotypes and thereby preserve those genes and karyotypes that are of biologic value to their possessors. Changing these genes and karyotypes in haphazard ways usually, *but not always,* will have undesirable effects.

Advantageous mutations do occur over long periods of time. Often genes which are undesirable in one environment can be beneficial in another. An excellent example is a human mutant allele which specifies an abnormal type of hemoglobin. Individuals homozygous for this allele generally die of sickle-cell anemia (Fig. 8-33). Heterozygous genotypes, on the other hand, are healthy and suffer much less from malaria than individuals who are homozygous for normal hemoglobin. In West Africa, where malaria is a common killer and crippler, the frequency of sickle-cell anemia may reach 4 percent. In that part of the world, people homozygous for normal hemoglobin risk death or disability from malaria whereas those homozygous for sickling hemoglobin risk death from anemia. Populations supporting genotypes of both kinds, however, produce heterozygous individuals who are protected from both afflictions. We will discuss this matter in greater detail in the next chapter.

It is only when one considers entire populations of individuals that one begins to see and appreciate the evolutionary mechanisms by which biologic diversity serves the cause of adaptive change. Organic evolution is a populational phenomenon because it is dependent upon the almost limitless variety that is found among aggregations of breeding individuals. We have examined the potential for biologic change. It now remains to investigate how evolution takes place and how its course is guided.

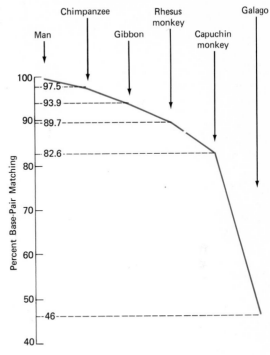

FIGURE 8-32
Approximate percentage of base-pair matching (DNA hybridization) between man and representative primates.

SUGGESTED READINGS

BEADLE, G. W., and M. BEADLE: *The Language of Life.* Garden City, N.Y., Doubleday & Company, Inc., 1966. This book, Levine's book, and the book by Srb et al. are good basic introductions to general genetics.

FIGURE 8-33
Normal and sickle-cell red blood cells. *Left,* normal cells. *Right,* cells from patient with sickle-cell anemia. Cells with sickling hemoglobin assume odd, often sicklelike shapes when deprived of oxygen. × 3000. [*Courtesy of Marion I. Barnhart, Ph.D.*]

CAVALLI-SFORZA, L. L.: *Elements of Human Genetics,* Reading, Mass.: Addison-Wesley Publishing Company, Inc., Module in Biology No. 2, 1973. This and Stern's book are introductory textbooks of human genetics.

LEVINE, R. P.: *Genetics,* New York: Holt, Rinehart and Winston, Inc., 1968.

MARKERT, C. L. and H. URSPRUNG: *Developmental Genetics,* Englewood Cliffs, N.J.: Prentice-Hall, Inc., 1971. An excellent account of how genes control embryologic development.

SRB, A. M., et al.: *General Genetics,* San Francisco: W. H. Freeman and Company, 1965.

STANBURY, J. B., et al.: *The Metabolic Basis of Inherited Disease,* 3rd ed., New York: McGraw-Hill Book Company, 1972. A clearly written book on how genetic mutations bring about errors in physiologic processes (inherited diseases).

STERN, CURT: *Principles of Human Genetics,* 3rd ed., San Francisco: W. H. Freeman and Company, 1973.

WATSON, J. D.: *Molecular Biology of the Gene,* 3rd ed., New York: W. A. Benjamin, Inc., 1976. An excellent discussion of molecular genetics by the codiscoverer of the structure of DNA.

REVIEW QUESTIONS

1 A woman with blood type N is married to a man with type MN. List all the possible blood types their natural children could have.

2 Insofar as ABO and Rh blood groups are concerned, what phenotypes could appear in the children of parents both of whom are heterozygous for blood types A and Rh positive?

3 Genes function at the biochemical level in controlling the production of enzymes. Show how it is possible at the biochemical level for one gene to have several phenotypic effects. Give an example of such a gene in man and list three of its phenotypic effects.

4 Show how it is possible at the biochemical level for a phenotypic trait to be the product of more than one set of genes. Give an example of this kind of inheritance in humans that involves two pairs of genes, and indicate how the trait is inherited.

5 Knowledge of how human intelligence develops is complicated by three issues. What are they? What major problem is inherent in the question of whether there are genetically controlled racial differences in intelligence?

6 Give an example of an inherited human trait in which the gene controlling it is influenced by sex hormones. How is the trait inherited?

7 How does the process of meiosis tend to confirm Mendel's principles of segregation and independent assortment?

8 How may genes located on the same chromosome be recombined? Cite two human traits that are controlled by genes on the same chromosome. Indicate the manner in which these genes and their traits may be recombined.

9 Suppose a normal-sighted woman whose father is red color-blind marries a normal-sighted man. What is the probability of their daughters being red color-blind? Of their sons being red color-blind?

10 Genetic mutations can occur in a number of ways. How do changes in chromosome number take place? Describe two ways in which random chromosome breakage results in abnormal chromosomal rearrangements. Explain a gene (point) mutation in terms of the molecular structure of the gene and its genetic code.

11 Discuss in detail the remarkable similarities between chimpanzees and humans as revealed by (a) karyotype studies and (b) DNA base-pair hybridization studies.

12 Write a short essay on the causes and evolutionary significance of mutation.

NINE

ORGANIC EVOLUTION I:
Its Nature and Course

Populations of organisms, specifically *Mendelian populations,* are the basic units in which evolution takes place. A Mendelian population is a group of interbreeding organisms such as a species, race, or breed that inhabits a specific geographic area. Evolution is a cumulative product of many generations of offspring produced by such populations as they interact with their environments over long periods of time.

The development of domesticated varie-

ties and breeds of plants and animals is an example of evolution in miniature. In developing breeds of dairy and beef cattle, for example, animal breeders have relied on the genetic variability in cattle populations. Some cattle had bodies which yielded more and better quality meat than others. Female meat types, however, tended to produce less milk than other females. The cows that produced the most milk generally were less desirable meat types. Just as Mendel did in developing true-breeding strains of red-flowered pea plants, animal breeders have bred like to like to obtain relatively true-breeding strains of beef and dairy cattle. By *selecting* the best meat types from cattle populations and breeding them together generation after generation, superior breeds of beef cattle have been developed. Similarly, by *selecting* the cows that produced the most milk and breeding them to bulls whose female offspring produced the most milk, superior breeds of dairy cattle have been developed.

These breeds, like any other domestic breed or variety, are the products of two factors which are essential to evolution at any level: (1) genetic variability among individuals in a population, and (2) selection. The first factor was discussed in some detail in the preceding chapter. The second will be the focus of this chapter along with some related considerations.

Selection in the example just cited is called *artificial selection* because it is controlled by man. Selection in natural populations (*natural selection*) involves complex interactions between the individuals of a species population and the environment in which the population resides. A species is the largest of all natural populations; members are potentially capable of interbreeding successfully among themselves but do not do so with members of another species. Such large species populations have diverse phenotypes, some of which have difficulty surviving while others not only have high survival rates but high reproductive rates as well. The latter phenotypes tend to pass their genes and their traits on to succeeding generations. Under the environmental conditions in which such phenotypes are *reproductively successful*, we say they are the products of natural selection.

In order to understand how a natural population changes genetically (evolves), we will first observe what a population is like that does not evolve at all.

A HYPOTHETICAL CASE OF NO EVOLUTION: THE HARDY-WEINBERG EQUILIBRIUM

Let us consider a hypothetical population of people from the standpoint of how many individuals have type M, MN, and N blood (Fig. 8-4). Examine the population of people illustrated in Fig. 9-1. Of the 100 individuals shown, 4 are type N, 32 are type MN, and 64 are type M. The 64 type M persons can produce gametes carrying only an *M* allele. Half the gametes from the 32 type MN people also will possess the *M* allele. As a result, all the gametes produced by 64 percent of the population, plus half the gametes produced by 32 percent of the population, carry the *M* allele. In short, 80 percent of all sex cells ($0.64 + 0.16 = 0.80$) will bear the *M* allele. Of the total number of alleles in this population of MN blood groups (the *MN gene pool*), the relative proportion, or *gene frequency,* of blood-antigen alleles is 80 percent for *M* and 20 percent for *N* ($0.04 + 0.16 = 0.20$).

One might think that type N people gradually would be eliminated from this population. But as Fig. 9-2 reveals, this is not the case as long as mating is entirely at random. The second generation will possess the same genotypic composition as the parental generation. There is a 20 percent chance that a sperm will contain an *N* allele. There also is a 20 percent chance that an egg will bear an *N* allele. Since the probability of these two sex cells joining in fertilization is the product of their separate probabilities ($0.2 \times 0.2 = 0.04$), 4 percent of the second generation also will be type N. Similarly the proportion of type M individuals will still be 64 percent ($0.8 \times 0.8 = 0.64$). The remaining 32 percent will be type MN ($2 \times 0.8 \times 0.2 = 0.32$). The product of these gene frequencies is multiplied by two because the genotype can be obtained in two ways: (1) *M* from the sperm and *N* from the egg ($0.8 \times$

0.2 = 0.16), and (2) N from the sperm and M from the egg (0.2 × 0.8 = 0.16).

The genetic equilibrium that would prevail in such stable, randomly breeding, populations generation after generation is called the *Hardy-Weinberg equilibrium.* It can be stated broadly in algebraic form: if the frequency of a given gene is represented by the letter p and the frequency of its single allele by the letter q, the percentage of each genotype in the next generation can be determined from the expression:

$$p^2 + 2pq + q^2$$

or

$$(p \times p) + (2 \times p \times q) + (q \times q)$$

This mathematical approach has two advantages over the checkerboard method used in Fig. 9-2: (1) it is not as cumbersome, and (2) it can be worked backward as well as forward.

Suppose we wanted to calculate the frequency of the sickle-cell allele in an African population in which 4 percent of the community had sickling anemia (q^2). Assuming the population is in genetic equilibrium, the frequency of the sickling allele (q) must be that percentage which, multiplied by itself, gives a product of 4 percent (q^2). That percentage would be 20 percent ($\sqrt{0.04} = 0.2$). Since $p + q$ must always equal 1.0 in a gene set composed of only two alleles,[1] the frequency of the gene for normal hemoglobin (p) must be 80 percent. At this point, we can draw a significant conclusion: a population which might lose 4 percent

[1] In a gene set composed of only two alleles, the frequency of one (p) plus the frequency of the other (q) must equal 1.0 (100 percent) because there are no other alleles.

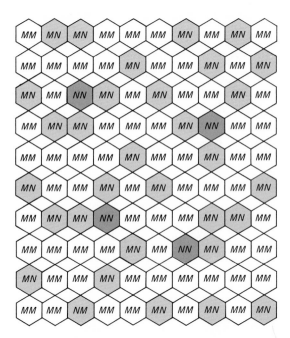

FIGURE 9-1

In a population of 100 people in which 4 have blood type N (genotype *NN*), 32 have blood type MN (genotype *MN*) and 64 have blood type M (genotype *MM*), the *gene pool* of the population consists of alleles 20 percent of which are for antigen N and 80 percent of which are for antigen M. The proportion these alleles bear to each other in the gene pool is their *gene frequency.*

| A | B | | C | |
| Percent of people in each phenotype | Percent of gametes in each phenotype carrying | | Percent each phenotype contributes to total alleles produced by all individuals (A × B) | |
	M	*N*	*M*	*N*
4 NN	0	100	0	4
32 MN	50	50	16	16
64 MM	100	0	64	0

Gene frequency = 80%   20%

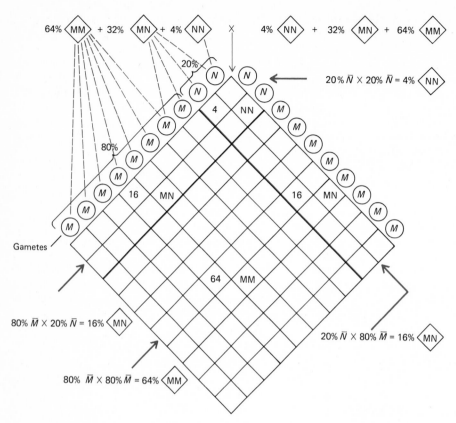

Proportion of MM in population	Proportion of MN in population	Proportion of NN in population
$\bar{M} \times \bar{M} = \bar{M}^2$	$2 \times \bar{M} \times \bar{N} = 2\,\overline{MN}$	$\bar{N} \times \bar{N} = \bar{N}^2$
80% × 80% = 64%	2 × 80% × 20% = 32%	20% × 20% = 4%

FIGURE 9-2
Even though the type N individuals in Fig. 9-1 made up only 4 percent of the total population, their number remains unchanged in the next generation. This tendency for gene frequencies to remain constant from generation to generation when mating is random is known as the Hardy-Weinberg equilibrium. The symbols $\bar{M}$ and $\bar{N}$ represent the gene frequencies of alleles M and N respectively.

of its members to sickling anemia, protects 32 percent of its members (the heterozygotes) from both malaria and anemia (2pq, or 2 × 0.8 × 0.2 = 0.32).

If no changes occurred in the gene pool of a breeding population, a state of genetic equilibrium would exist. Great numbers of genes, many with low frequencies, would be faithfully preserved from generation to generation whether they were dominant, codominant, or recessive. However, a situation in which a gene pool is not subject to some kind of disturbance is seldom, if ever, encountered. No population is ever likely to be in a completely stable genetic state for any appreciable period of time. Changes in gene frequencies and genotypic composition occur because the conditions required to sustain a Hardy-Weinberg equilibrium are disrupted by several natural phenomena.

A population could be in genetic equilibrium only when the following conditions prevailed:

1 The population must be large enough for genetic events to have a reasonable chance of occurring according to their expected probabilities.
2 The gene pool must not be added to by immigration or diminished by nonrandom emigration.
3 Reverse and direct mutations in every gene set must occur at the same rate.
4 No phenotype can have higher survival and reproductive rates than another.

But these prerequisites for genetic equilibria are effectively opposed on four corresponding fronts:

1 Populations often are so small that the occurrences of genetic events deviate significantly from their expected probabilities, resulting in *genetic drift*.
2 Immigration and/or emigration commonly occur in most populations, bringing about *gene flow*.
3 Reverse mutations are much less frequent than direct mutations, creating a *mutation pressure* favoring the less mutable, mutant allele.
4 Members of a population reflect varying survival and reproductive rates for a variety of conditions, so that a given phenotype succeeds or fails depending upon the extent to which natural selection (*selection pressure*) is exerted against it.

Were it not for these four disruptive phenomena—genetic drift, gene flow, mutation pressure, and selection pressure—organic evolution could never occur. All populations would perpetuate themselves indefinitely as static, stable aggregations of individuals. By disrupting genetic equilibria, these four processes ensure that evolution will take place.

GENETIC DRIFT

As we noted in the previous chapter, the expected frequencies of various gene combinations are less apt to be realized in small populations than in larger ones (see Fig. 8-1). The loss of just a few individuals through accident or disease could eliminate an allele from the gene pool if the population were small but would have little, if any, effect on gene frequencies in a large population. In all cases where the breeding population is small, the chances are good that the frequency of some genes will be reduced unpredictably, thereby increasing the frequency of their alternative alleles. If the genes so reduced had already been relatively uncommon, the number of homozygous individuals would increase at the expense of the heterozygotes, thus restricting variability in the population (Fig. 9-3). For example, a population with a gene frequency of 90 percent for blood-group allele M (p in Fig. 9-3) and 10 percent for allele N (q in Fig. 9-3) would have 81 percent type M blood, 18 percent type MN, and 1 percent N. It would be possible for allele N to be removed entirely from the gene pool through genetic drift resulting finally in a population that would be 100 percent type M.

Small relatively isolated populations (*population isolates*) also tend to become more homozygous because of their size. The prospect of intermarriage between people with similar or related genotypes is much better in a small population than in a large one. This in itself contributes to homozygosity and the fixation of traits. Phenotypic standardization may be enhanced further by *positive assortative mating*; that is, the tendency of people to mate with individuals similar to themselves. Men and women who are tall, or athletically inclined,

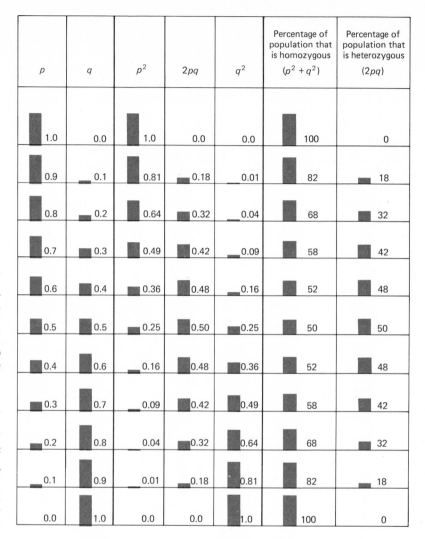

p	q	p^2	$2pq$	q^2	Percentage of population that is homozygous ($p^2 + q^2$)	Percentage of population that is heterozygous ($2pq$)
1.0	0.0	1.0	0.0	0.0	100	0
0.9	0.1	0.81	0.18	0.01	82	18
0.8	0.2	0.64	0.32	0.04	68	32
0.7	0.3	0.49	0.42	0.09	58	42
0.6	0.4	0.36	0.48	0.16	52	48
0.5	0.5	0.25	0.50	0.25	50	50
0.4	0.6	0.16	0.48	0.36	52	48
0.3	0.7	0.09	0.42	0.49	58	42
0.2	0.8	0.04	0.32	0.64	68	32
0.1	0.9	0.01	0.18	0.81	82	18
0.0	1.0	0.0	0.0	1.0	100	0

FIGURE 9-3
The effect of genetic drift on homozygosity (trait-fixing) and heterozygosity (population variability). As the frequency of a given gene (p) or its allele (q) decreases from 50 to 0 percent, the percentage of heterozygous individuals decreases from 50 to 0 percent and the percentage of homozygotes increases from 50 to 100 percent. For example, a population with a gene frequency of 90 percent for blood group allele M (p above) and 10 percent for allele N (q above) would be 81 percent type M, 18 percent type MN and 1 percent type N. Allele N could be removed through genetic drift, resulting finally in a population that was 100 percent type M.

or who are college-educated, tend to intermarry. Contrary to the popular adage, opposites do not usually attract, at least for long.

The role of genetic drift in evolution

In the species as a whole, genetic drift clearly contributes to greater genetic diversity. Every small population isolate is a distinctive aggregate of genotypes. A species like our own is composed of innumerable, partially isolated populations. Such populations demonstrate *intergroup differences (polytypism)* that far surpass the variety that could be generated in one large hypothetical population of freely interbreeding individuals. The individuality of these smaller populations generally involves phenotypic differences that have little, if any, effect on survival and reproductive success. It is possible that chance variations could result in a slight decrease in reproductive success. It is just this unpredictable quality, however, that contributes to the evolutionary process. A physiological trait that slightly handicapped a people living in a warm interglacial climate might prove beneficial many generations later during a glacial period. On the other hand, it might also prove to be an insurmountable handicap and contribute to the extinction of the population. Nonetheless, by producing a variety of populations of slightly different genetic constitutions, genetic drift tends to provide a hedge against unpredictable environmental changes.

Random genetic drift has been observed and reported for numerous small human breeding groups. A religious sect, the Dunkers (German Baptist Brethren), illustrates drift in ABO blood groups. These people generally have been *endogamous,* that is, they married only within their group since the sect was founded in West Germany early in the eighteenth century. Because of religious persecution, nearly all the Brethren had emigrated to the Eastern United States by the mid-eighteenth century. Genetic studies have shown that 59 percent of these people have blood type A, whereas type A blood is found in 45 percent of the German population in the area from which the Dunkers emigrated. The incidence of type A blood among Americans of European descent is 43 percent.

The founder principle

A phenomenon related to genetic drift is called the *founder effect,* or *principle.* Populations often have been established by small groups who wandered far from their native land and founded new communities that later expanded. Such a migrant group is a small sample of the original population and may be genetically unrepresentative of the homeland people. The inhabitants of Pitcairn Island in the Pacific are descendants of seven mutineers from the British ship *Bounty* and eight or nine Tahitian women. They are a hardy, industrious people despite the almost total absence of gene flow since the island's colonization in 1790. Therefore, this little colony is not only a good example of the founder principle but is also a strong rebuttal to the belief that inbreeding always is detrimental.

A situation genetically similar to the founder effect can develop in a population that has become greatly reduced in size. The group remaining from such a *population bottleneck* most likely will not be typical of the original population. Future population growth would continue to reflect this atypical character.

Situations are common in which both the founder principle and genetic drift have been, and are, at work. The Hutterites, a religious sect that has been endogamous for many generations, illustrates such an episode (Fig. 9-4). According to a study by A. O. Martin,[2] 91 founding individuals who settled in the United States and Canada are represented today by some 15,000 descendants living in over 100 separate communities. As a result of genetic drift, gene frequencies for several blood groups vary between these communities, and between each community and the non-Hutterite population that surrounds it.

GENE FLOW

The stability of a gene pool may be disturbed if genes are introduced through an influx of individuals from another population. This may occur between two or more populations which, because of their relative isolation from one another, have developed distinctly different gene pools. If or when migrants are enabled to cross whatever barriers isolate the groups in

[2] A. O. Martin, "The Founder Effect in a Human Isolate: Evolutionary Implications," *American Journal of Physical Anthropology,* 32, 1970, pp. 351–368.

FIGURE 9-4
A group of Hutterite children. The Hutterites, an endogamous religious sect living in over 100 separate communities in the United States and Canada, show the effects of genetic drift. [*National Film Board of Canada*]

question, gene flow is said to occur.

The human species is composed of innumerable populations that are partially isolated from one another by a variety of isolating mechanisms. These mechanisms range from geographic barriers, such as physical distance, to those that are sociocultural in nature. Language, economic status, physical and psychological characteristics, social tradition, educational background, and religious affiliation all tend to segment populations into groups and to restrict breeding between them. Most West European Gypsies, for example, formerly lived in Hungary for a considerable period of time. Both their language and their ABO blood-group frequencies, however, contrast sharply with those of native Hungarians, but strongly resemble those of Asiatic Indians with whom the Gypsies claim a strong kinship. Sociocultural tradition, the nomadic life style, and the economic practices of the Gypsies apparently were effective barriers between these people and the Hungarians who surrounded them.

Language has preserved ethnic identities in a number of instances. The Basque people who live in the western Pyrenees of France and Spain have a language that appears to be unrelated to any other. Although they share the same religion and occupations with their neighbors, it is their language that unites them. They are distinguished by a number of features including broad foreheads, narrow jaws, and certain blood-group characteristics, chief among which is a very high incidence of Rh negative blood. In North America a comparable situation exists with Athapaskan-speaking Indian tribes. Whether one chooses a tribe in Canada or in the Southwestern United States, these people have a greater variety of Rh blood types, a lower percentage of blood type N, and a higher frequency of blood type A than their neighbors.

We have already cited two cases, the Dunkers and Hutterites, in which religious restrictions have acted as a barrier to gene flow.

There can be no doubt that a variety of cultural differences can restrict gene flow and thereby foster genetic diversity. It is equally true, however, that barriers to human gene flow are not absolute nor are they consistently effective or permanent. Man is a mobile species and the very mobility of his populations pushes aside the barricades that divide and isolate. Breeding groups form, only to intermingle, disappear, and form again into new units of different dimensions and number.

The movements and migrations of people bring about a flow of genes between the partially isolated subunits of larger populations. The unique products of genetic drift and natural selection in one population isolate are combined with those of other population isolates. In this fashion, new and possibly adaptive traits may spread from one area to another, thereby contributing to the adaptability and reproductive success of the species as a whole.

Presumably as a result of several centuries of European expansion and conquest, the frequency of blondness and light skin color has increased greatly in many parts of the world. Certainly this has occurred in the Western Hemisphere where the aboriginal Indian inhabitants were dark-haired and had skins of intermediate pigmentation. The people of the New World received significant contributions from gene pools in Asia and Africa also. The end product of these episodes of gene flow is a continental population of great genetic diversity. It is regrettable, both on humanitarian and genetic grounds, that it was accomplished at the cost of reducing many vigorous Indian populations virtually, if not actually, to the point of extinction. Such a price undoubtedly has been paid in many human conquests both historic and prehistoric.

MUTATION PRESSURE

We have just observed that a population cannot be in genetic equilibrium if genes are being added to its gene pool from outside sources through gene flow. It is also true that genetic equilibria may be disrupted by the addition of genes from within the gene pool through mutation pressure. As stated in the last chapter, the mutation of a normal wild-type gene to a mutant allele (*direct mutation*) generally occurs at

a much higher frequency than that at which a mutant allele mutates back to the normal gene (*reverse mutation*). Consequently, there is a mutation pressure that tends to increase the frequency of mutant alleles at the expense of normal wild-type genes. That is to say, mutation pressure tends to increase the frequency of hemophilia, chondrodystrophic dwarfism, and diabetes at the expense of normal bodies.

Since most mutant alleles are biologically disadvantageous, selection pressure counteracts mutation pressure to the degree that a given mutant allele handicaps its possessor. Mutant alleles that are lethal have no opportunity to increase in frequency if they are dominant and cause death anytime prior to reproductive maturity. Recessive alleles that are lethal can increase in frequency because, unlike the dominant, they can remain hidden in heterozygous individuals. Many mutant alleles, however, are disadvantageous in varying degrees short of being lethal. The frequency of such mutant alleles depends largely on the degree to which they are disadvantageous. Those that are only slightly so could be expected to have a relatively high frequency in a population; as the degree of disadvantage increases, the frequency would be lowered. These sensitive interrelationships between the degree of harmfulness of a mutant gene and its frequency in a population are borne out by the inherited metabolic disorder, *diabetes*.

Diabetes is caused by insufficient secretion of insulin, a hormone produced in the pancreas by about a million cellular aggregates called the *pancreatic islets*. The disease exists in two forms. The juvenile type, apparently caused by a recessive allele in the homozygous state, is a serious disorder in which the individual must almost always be given insulin. The adult variant seems to be controlled by a dominant allele, which results in a milder form of diabetes that usually can be treated by dietary management or drugs that stimulate insulin secretion. Both forms of the disease are fatal if not treated — the selection pressure against untreated diabetes is 100 percent. The use of insulin in treatment, coupled with improvements in diet management and the development of drugs to stimulate islet activity have markedly increased the life expectancy of diabetics. Selection pressure against the diabetic phenotype has, in effect, diminished greatly under the influence of modern medical therapy.

As a result the number of diabetics has risen steadily in this country. Between 1950 and 1975 the number grew from 1.2 to 5 million, more than a 300 percent increase, while the population had grown only about 50 percent. A good portion of this increase undoubtedly is due to mutation pressure that has been freed from heavy selection pressure against the mutant phenotype.[3] We may expect the diabetic phenotype to continue to increase until such time that the number of mutant alleles entering the population through mutation pressure equals the number of mutant alleles eliminated from the population through selection pressure (diabetic death and reproductive failure). Even though modern medicine has greatly improved the survival rate of diabetics, diabetes still is the fifth leading cause of death by disease in the United States. The degree of selective advantage that the nondiabetic holds will determine in large measure the ultimate frequency of diabetics. Continued medical advances can be reasonably expected to lower selection pressures further and to increase the mutant phenotype correspondingly. In any case, the point at which a genetic equilibrium might be reached would be many centuries away.

Medicogenetic phenomena of this kind often are viewed with alarm and labeled by such ominous expressions as "genetic decay." The life of modern man, however, is a far cry from the lives of Paleolithic peoples; physical brawn and stamina are not prerequisites for

survival in modern technological society. Among diabetics, as among nondiabetics, there are many fine artists, statesmen, craftsmen, scientists, economists, and philosophers, not to mention athletes. Were we somehow to remove diabetics from the gene pool, undoubtedly we also would eliminate great numbers of genes for many traits that are of premium importance in modern society.

SELECTION PRESSURE: THE MECHANISM OF NATURAL SELECTION

Because nondiabetic phenotypes have lower mortality and higher fertility than diabetic phenotypes, the nondiabetic is said to have greater biologic *fitness*. Fitness is a measure of how well a phenotype or group of phenotypes is *adapted* to living in a particular environment. Were it not for medical treatment, diabetes would be much less common than it is because of intense selection pressure against it.

This, in essence, is the manner in which evolution takes place through natural selection. Selection pressures reduce or eliminate those phenotypes that are unadaptive and retain those that are adaptive. As a result, gene frequency changes are brought about that tend to ensure the production of adaptive phenotypes in ensuing generations. As noted earlier, natural selection is a matter of reproductive success. The adapted, biologically fit phenotypes are those that are more successful than others in passing their genes on to the next generation.

In the present state of our knowledge, it is difficult to evaluate the overall fitness of human genotypes. One source of this difficulty lies in their enormous number. For example, there are over 100 billion possible genotypic combinations of genes that control 17 known blood groups and 6 blood disorders. Even if we could identify and appraise the astronomical diversity of human genotypes, we could make no abso-

---

[3] Recent studies suggest that some viral infections (e.g., mumps and German measles) may cause pancreatic damage in persons carrying genes for diabetes. See T. H. Maugh II, "Diabetes," *Science*, vol. 188, Apr. 25, 1975, pp. 347–351.

lute judgment of their survival value because what might be adaptive in one part of the world could be unadaptive in another.

Natural selection can be seen at work in human populations, however, in what are known as *balanced genetic polymorphisms.* This phenomenon occurs in populations where selection pressure favors a heterozygous genotype over both homozygotes. The genotype *Aa,* for example, displays *hybrid vigor* or *heterosis,* and is better adapted than either *AA* or *aa.* In maintaining the more fit heterozygotes in a population, each of the less fit homozygotes is preserved. Under such circumstances natural selection tends to adjust ("balance") the frequency of gene *A* and its allele *a* at values that produce a population with the highest *average* fitness possible. Since different homozygotes, such as *AA* and *aa,* seldom, if ever, have the same survival rates, gene frequencies will tend to be balanced at levels which reflect the relative degree of unfitness of each homozygote. Sometimes the difference is large indeed and optimum population fitness can be obtained only at the cost of maintaining a lethal gene in the gene pool. We have referred to one such case, namely the incidence of the sickling gene in malarial Africa. Let us now give it a closer look.

Natural selection in action I: sickle-cell polymorphism

The development and spread of agriculture in Africa is believed to have introduced certain environmental changes which had the effect of increasing the incidence of malaria there. The *Anopheles* mosquito which transmits the malarial parasite is not a normal inhabitant of tropical forests. It requires quiet pools of water in which to rear its young, and this habitat usually is encountered in open areas. When man began clearing the tropical rain forest in order to grow his crops, he also was creating additional breeding areas for mosquitoes. Augmented food supplies from agricultural production fostered population growth which, in turn, provided more bodies on which mosquitoes could feed. Under such conditions the frequency of the disease should be expected to increase. We also would anticipate an increase in frequency of any gene, such as the sickling allele, which confers some resistance to malaria. Such an event would be adaptive in that it would not only enhance survival in existing populations but it would also permit further exploitation of the rain forest environment.

A fairly close association can be seen between the geographic distributions of falciparum malaria in the Old World and the gene for sickling anemia (Fig. 9-5). Over this broad area the intensity of malarial infection and sickling anemia vary greatly. As A. C. Allison noted more than 20 years ago, the sickling gene (Hb^S)[4] usually has its highest frequency (over 20 percent) in those populations where the risk from virulent forms of malarial parasites is the greatest.[5] The lowest gene frequencies tend to be found in areas where the incidence of malaria is relatively low.

Allison conducted a number of studies which support the belief that the heterozygous sickler genotype, $Hb^A Hb^S$, is more resistant to falciparum malaria than the normal homozygote, $Hb^A Hb^A$. He observed that the number of malarial parasites is lower among infected sicklers than among infected nonsicklers. He also inoculated both sicklers and nonsicklers with malaria in certain regions where malaria was virtually universal, and then treated those individuals in whom the disease developed. He found that the heterozygotes were less susceptible to infection than the homozygotes. Other studies have supported Allison's findings.

In sustaining the better adapted heterozygotes in a population, it is necessary to maintain certain numbers of both homozygotes, each of which is selected against. The proportion of

---

[4] The gene for normal hemoglobin A is designated Hb^A. The sickling gene is designated Hb^S because it specifies a mutant hemoglobin, hemoglobin S.

[5] A. C. Allison, "Protection Afforded by Sickle-Cell Trait Against Subtertian Malarial Infection," *British Medical Journal,* 1954, I, pp. 290–294.

FIGURE 9-5
The distribution of falciparum malaria (gray) and the sickling allele (color) in the Old World. [*After A. G. Motulsky, Human Biology, vol. 32.1, Wayne State University Press, Detroit, 1960.*]

homozygous sicklers dying from anemia is not the same as the proportion of normal homozygotes dying from malaria.[6] The degree of difference between the two selection pressures will depend greatly upon the prevalence and virulence of malaria. Optimum populational fitness will require relatively high frequencies of the Hb^S allele only when malarial risk is high.

A population in which 90 percent of all normal homozygotes survived malaria would not be benefited by a gene frequency (q) of 20 percent for the Hb^S allele (Fig. 9-6). If only 80 percent of all normal homozygotes survived malaria, however, populational fitness would be

enhanced at this gene frequency. Conversely, net populational fitness will depend on a very low frequency of the Hb^S allele when the incidence of malarial deaths is low. If 95 percent of all $Hb^A Hb^A$ individuals survived malaria, a gene frequency (q) of 5 percent for the Hb^S allele would permit 95.2 percent of the population to survive both malaria and sickling anemia.

The current use of insecticides in mosquito abatement programs over the world at large, together with improved malarial treatment, reduces, if not eliminates, the adaptiveness of the heterozygous phenotype. Consequently, we should expect the frequency of the sickling allele to decline with time. In the meantime, the incidence of sickling anemia provides a clear-cut example of the sensitive manner in which selection pressure adjusts gene frequencies to optimize biologic fitness in populations living in varying environmental conditions.

---

[6] Sickle-cell anemia ($Hb^S Hb^S$) usually is lethal. Certain foods in many African diets (such as cassava, yams, sorghum, and millet), however, contain thiocyanate which inhibits sickling and may reduce mortality greatly. See R. G. Houston, "Sickle-cell Anemia and Dietary Precursors of Cyanate," *The American Journal of Clinical Nutrition*, vol. 26, November 1973, pp. 1261–1264.

Homozygous normal ($Hb^A Hb^A$) to survive malaria, %	Allele frequency Hb^A (p)	Allele frequency Hb^S (q)	$Hb^A Hb^A$ genotype, %	$Hb^A Hb^S$ genotype, %	$Hb^S Hb^S$ genotype (lethal), %	Total survivors ($Hb^A Hb^A$ + $Hb^A Hb^S$), %
90	1.0	0.0	100	0	0	90
	0.8	0.2	64	32	4	89.6
80	1.0	0.0	100	0	0	80
	0.8	0.2	64	32	4	83.2
70	1.0	0.0	100	0	0	70
	0.8	0.2	64	32	4	76.8
60	1.0	0.0	100	0	0	60
	0.8	0.2	64	32	4	70.4

FIGURE 9-6

Adaptedness of the allele for sickling hemoglobin (Hb^S) on the basis of arbitrarily assumed values of malarial deaths among individuals homozygous for normal hemoglobin ($Hb^A Hb^A$). Four homozygote survival rates are shown (90, 80, 70, and 60 percent). In each of these, two populations are compared: in one, the gene frequency (p) of Hb^A is 100 percent and the gene frequency (q) of Hb^S is 0 percent; in the other, the two frequencies are 80 and 20 percent, respectively. Total survivors in each of the eight populations are the percentage of surviving normal homozygotes plus the percentage of heterozygotes. For example, with 90 percent of normal homozygotes surviving malaria in a population where p is 0.8 and q is 0.2, total survivors equal 89.6 percent, that is, 90 percent of 64 percent (57.6 percent) plus 32 percent. Homozygous sicklers ($Hb^S Hb^S$) are assumed not to survive. A gene frequency (q) of 0.2 for Hb^S demonstrates adaptive value in 3 of the 4 assumed survival percentages (60, 70, and 80 percent).

Natural selection in action II: ABO blood-group polymorphism

The notion that ABO blood groups are more or less neutral traits unaffected by selection pressure was effectively laid to rest by Alice Brues in a study of the world distribution of blood groups (Fig. 9-7). Although chance deviations resulting from genetic drift undoubtedly are at work in many populations, it is clear that natural selection strongly influences the establishment of balanced polymorphisms. Of all the possible combinations of ABO gene frequencies, only 12 percent are represented in the 218 widely scattered populations studied by Brues. The distribution of ABO blood groups is such that the frequency of the I^A allele ranges from 0 to 55 percent, the I^B allele from 0 to 35 percent, and the i allele rarely below 50 percent but commonly as high as 100 percent. Most of the populations tend to converge around a gene frequency of about 25 percent I^A, 15 percent I^B, and 60 percent i.

What selection pressures operate to restrict these gene frequencies within such a relatively narrow spectrum? We do not know for sure. We would expect these selection pressures, whatever they may be, to vary in intensity from region to region as they do with sickle-cell polymorphisms. Evidence that such is the case is reflected in the geographic distributions of populations with high frequencies of blood types A and B. The highest frequency of the I^B allele is found in India and Asia. As one progresses westward from Asia toward Europe, there is a gradual decline in I^B frequency and a corresponding increase in the frequency of the I^A allele. The latter gene has a high frequency among most European populations, whereas the I^B allele is relatively rare.

Two selective agencies have been suggested which may account, at least in part, for the establishment and maintenance of genetic equilibria among the ABO blood groups. They are (1) ABO-Rh complementarity, and (2) disease.

ABO-Rh complementarity

There appears to be a phenotypic interaction between ABO and Rh blood groups that affects the outcome of Rh incompatibility between mother and fetus. Fetal erythroblastosis (discussed in Chap. 8) occurs less often when the parents belong to incompatible ABO blood groups. The physiological basis for this peculiar interrelationship is as follows: an Rh-negative mother (rr) begins to be sensitized to her Rh-positive child (Rr) when fetal blood cells enter her bloodstream during birth. If, because of ABO incompatibility between the parents,

these fetal cells are incompatible with those of the mother, her ABO antibody very likely will destroy the fetal cells before Rh sensitization could take place. That is, the cells would be destroyed before the mother could start producing the Rh antibodies that cause erythroblastosis. For example, if the mother is type O, Rh negative ($iirr$), and her husband is homozygous for both type A and Rh positive ($I^A I^A RR$), the child will be type A, Rh positive ($I^A iRr$). The mother's anti-A antibody probably would destroy any type A, Rh-positive fetal cells that entered her bloodstream before her body had a chance to start producing Rh antibody. Fetal erythroblastosis would thereby be prevented.

There are two selection pressures at work

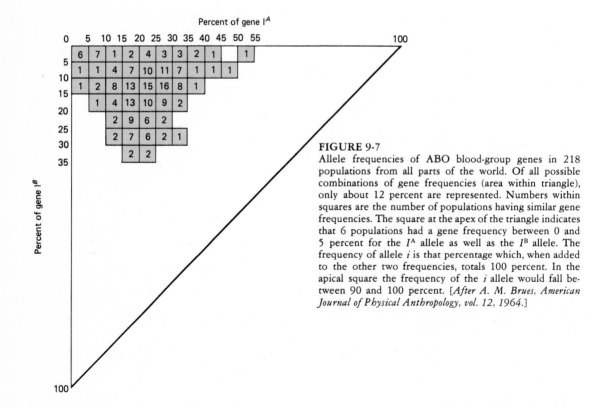

FIGURE 9-7
Allele frequencies of ABO blood-group genes in 218 populations from all parts of the world. Of all possible combinations of gene frequencies (area within triangle), only about 12 percent are represented. Numbers within squares are the number of populations having similar gene frequencies. The square at the apex of the triangle indicates that 6 populations had a gene frequency between 0 and 5 percent for the I^A allele as well as the I^B allele. The frequency of allele i is that percentage which, when added to the other two frequencies, totals 100 percent. In the apical square the frequency of the i allele would fall between 90 and 100 percent. [*After A. M. Brues, American Journal of Physical Anthropology, vol. 12, 1964.*]

here. One operates through erythroblastosis against Rh incompatibility, and the other operates through another form of hemolytic disease against ABO incompatibility. In our example above, if the mother's anti-A antibody passed into the fetal circulation, the child might well be stillborn. As with sickle-cell polymorphisms, a genetic equilibrium would be achieved in a population at that point where the opposing selection pressures were in balance. Of the two, selection against ABO incompatibility is probably the higher.

Disease

For the past two decades, statistical correlations between ABO blood groups and specific disease susceptibilities have been noted by numerous, mostly European, investigators. Ulcers of the stomach, for example, appear to be more common among persons with type O blood than among those of any other ABO blood group. Duodenal ulcers, incidentally, are much more common among people who are nonsecretors of the ABO blood-group substances than among secretors. Cancer of the stomach and pernicious anemia, on the other hand, are more likely to develop among type A than among type O individuals.

Whether these diseases actually affect ABO gene frequencies to a significant degree is questionable. They are disorders which occur during middle age or later and are not likely to influence the number of children produced. Natural selection therefore would have little effect in molding ABO polymorphisms through these channels.

Livingstone has suggested a more plausible hypothesis by which disease might be responsible for establishing ABO polymorphisms. Until fairly recently there were a number of infectious diseases responsible for high mortality rates among children throughout the world. Chief among these were cholera, diphtheria, pneumonia, smallpox, and typhoid fever. If, as Livingstone suggests, there may be varying sus-

ceptibilities and resistances to these diseases among ABO blood groups, one could reasonably expect selection to account for ABO polymorphism.[7] A study showing that *Anopheles* mosquitoes prefer hosts with type O blood certainly supports this contention.[8]

THE NATURE OF EVOLUTIONARY PROCESSES

We have observed that populations do not attain complete genetic stability. They are subject to changes in gene frequency and genotypic composition due to the disruptive influences of genetic drift, gene flow, and mutation pressure. These essentially unpredictable modifications in the gene pool confer upon members of a population varying degrees of fitness and unfitness for a variety of environmental circumstances. If environmental conditions change significantly, the criteria for survival may be correspondingly altered and some of the fit and unfit may trade places. Environment, after all, sets the standards for biologic fitness. Those genotypes that are able, or better able, to cope with their surroundings will be more successful than the unable or less able in passing their genes on to future generations. A population that continues to reproduce itself in this manner will remain adapted to its surroundings. Which populations, if any, succeed in doing this will depend largely on two limitations. One of these is the preservation of sufficient genetic diversity to accommodate environmental change. The other is the possibility that environmental change might occur too rapidly for biologic adaptation to keep pace. The rapid ex-

[7] F. B. Livingstone, "Natural Selection, Disease, and Ongoing Human Evolution, as Illustrated by the ABO Blood Groups," *Human Biology*, vol. 32, 1960, pp. 17–27.

[8] C. S. Wood, "A Relationship Between ABO Polymorphisms and Malaria Vectors," *Human Biology*, vol. 46, 1974, pp. 385–404.

tinction of prey species, for example, may bring about quick extinction of their predators. A case in point: when late Paleolithic hunters killed off the mammoth and mastodon, the great saber-toothed cats were deprived of prey and became extinct also.

In this synopsis, it is clear that organic evolution is a matter of population dynamics. Just as the cell is the unit of structural biology, so is population the unit of evolutionary biology.

Human populations: their nature and classification

Considered in its broadest sense, a population encompasses the species itself. In this context, a population may be distributed over a large area — in the case of man, the entire planet — and may embrace a great variety of phenotypes. In its narrowest sense, a population is a strictly local group called a *deme,* made up of individuals who live together in a common habitat and who usually choose their mates from their own numbers. Commonly, groups of demes occupy similar, adjoining habitats. Because of their generally similar environments, and the prevalence of gene flow between them, these deme clusters often are spoken of as *races,* or *subspecies.* Individuals within a race, and especially within a deme, tend to resemble one another more than members of other groups because they interbreed among themselves more and share a common habitat.

Many attempts have been made to distinguish racial groups in the human species. Because of a general lack of agreement as to the kinds of criteria to be used, the result has been almost as many classificational schemes as there were classifiers who championed them. It was once proposed that there are three human races or ethnic divisions, the Caucasoid, Mongoloid, and Negroid. This idea of a racial trinity is widely held by the general public, but there is little biological justification for the belief that the diverse human populations of our planet can be so simply classified.

Garn's classification of human races

Stanley Garn has proposed a classification which is worthy of consideration because it is founded, with some major exceptions to be noted later, on reasonable biological grounds. Garn divides mankind into *large geographic races,* based on the observation that people native to one large geographic region tend to resemble one another more than those native to another major geographic region. Gene flow does occur more within major geographic realms than between them, so that the inhabitants of one major region, say Latin America, would tend to share more genes with one another than with the inhabitants of some other continent such as Africa or Australia.

Nine geographic races are envisioned by Garn, designated and distributed as follows:

1 African (sub-Saharan Africa)
2 Amerindian (North, Central, and South America)
3 Asiatic (Eastern continental Asia and adjoining islands)
4 Australian
5 European (Europe, Great Britain, Scandinavia, West Asia, the Middle East, and North Africa)
6 Indian (India, from the Himalayas south)
7 Melanesian (New Guinea and adjacent islands)
8 Micronesian (Marshall Islands, Gilbert Islands, and environs)
9 Polynesian

Each of these large geographic races he divides into a number of partially isolated *local races.* Amerindians, for example, include the North American, Central American, and South American Indians, the Ladinos, and the Fuegians.[9]

Local races also show considerable genetic variation, particularly the larger ones. These are subdivided further into *microraces.* Each of these units, of which there would be countless thousands over the world, would approximate the size of a deme if they could be identified with sufficient accuracy. Each microrace represents

[9] S. M. Garn, *Human Races,* 2d ed., Springfield, Ill.: Charles C Thomas, Publisher, 1965, pp. 7–9.

a community, the rough dimensions of which would be determined by the distance most inhabitants travel to find a mate.

The existence of such communities is demonstrated in a study by R. S. Spielman et al. of the Yanomama Indians of Venezuela and Brazil (Fig. 9-8). These Indians are an isolated group distinct from other South American tribes on the basis of several genetic polymorphisms, culture, and language. The latter is not identifiable with any of the principle language families of South America. The Yanomama speak a particular dialect depending upon their home village; seven dialects were identified, designated A, B, C, D, E, F, and G. The same dialect is spoken in villages that are relatively close together, as shown in the illustration. The investigators also were able to show that this linguistic differentiation was paralleled by ge-

netic differences as well. The frequencies of 11 different genes were determined, based on blood samples taken in 50 villages. Spielman and his associates presented evidence suggesting that the Yanomama language may have originated about 2,000 years ago, and that the seven biolinguistic microraces may have been diverging for perhaps the last thousand years.[10]

Figure 9-9 illustrates microracial communities that have been identified by statistical variations in the frequency of a blood-group allele. In this case, the varying frequencies of allele i (ABO system) are shown in the provinces of Italy, Sardinia, and Sicily. These provinces are a patchwork of different genetic

[10] R. S. Spielman et al., "Regional Linguistic and Genetic Differences Among Yanomama Indians," *Science*, vol. 184, May 10, 1974, pp. 637–644.

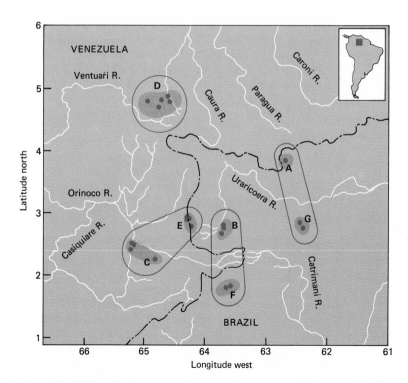

FIGURE 9-8
Locations of Yanomama Indian villages (colored dots) comprising seven dialect areas (lighter color, labeled *A–G*) studied by R. S. Spielman and associates. The Yanomama live in heavy jungle and have had permanent contact with the outside world only during the last 20 odd years. They occupy 150 or more villages over an area about 500 by 300 kilometers (310 by 185 miles) near the equator. The seven dialects group into four related Yanomama languages (colored lines) as follows: *A* and *G*, *B* and *F*, *C* and *E*, and *D*. Inset indicates relative location in South America. [*After Spielman et al., Science, vol. 184, May 10, 1974, © American Association for the Advancement of Science.*]

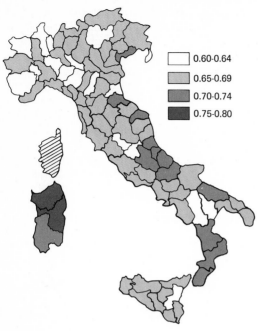

FIGURE 9-9
Variations in the frequency of blood-group allele *i* (ABO system) in the provinces of Italy, Sicily, and Sardinia. [*After G. Morganti, in Medical Biology and Etruscan Origins, G. E. W. Wolstenholme and C. M. O'Connor (eds.), Little, Brown, Boston, 1959.*]

populations. The boundaries between actual biologic communities are not indicated. It is not possible to bound human breeding groups with any degree of certainty when dealing with large, adjoining populations of this kind.

Problems with human racial classifications
Herein lies one of the major difficulties of the Garn, or any other, classification system. Human populations are not distinctly bounded breeding isolates. As one moves westward through Asia toward Europe, the frequency of the I^A allele progressively increases as I^B frequency decreases. Distinct or abrupt changes are absent. Populations merge one into the other along a gradient known as a *cline* and consequently have indefinite boundaries.

Another problem confronting racial classi-

fication lies in the fact that human populations are dynamic and everchanging. Barriers that separate people invariably are impermanent and even when they are operative do not isolate populations completely. Barriers rise and fall, and rise again in new patterns. Groups which have differentiated through genetic drift and natural selection ultimately may interbreed with other groups. They redifferentiate along new lines, as fresh barriers arise to repartition the population into semi-isolated breeding groups.

The Ladino race, for example, presumably arose as a result of a relatively few invading conquerors from Spain and Portugal interbreeding with local Latin American Indians. Africans imported as slaves also made a small contribution to the gene pool. Gene flow did not stop at that point in South American history, however. The Spanish-speaking Ladino people still are subject to significant amounts of gene flow, particularly from Afro-American groups. Allele frequencies cannot become stable under such conditions, and these conditions prevail among almost all human populations in varying degrees.

The terms *deme, microrace,* and *local race* are useful concepts and undoubtedly have some relevance to human populations. But they should not be used as if they represented static, easily identified, and readily located units. On the contrary, their number is indefinite, the characteristics by which we know them are incomplete, their distributions are imprecise, and all of these dimensions are tentative and subject to change.

Degrees of relatedness among populations

As stated earlier, a species is a population that usually consists of a number of smaller populations or races. Although gene flow occurs between these smaller populations, the species as a whole is reproductively isolated from other species. The amount of gene flow between racial groups may vary considerably. Certainly little, if any, interbreeding currently is taking place between the Ngatatjara of Australia and the Bushmen of Africa. On the other hand, there has been extensive gene flow between the people of East Asia and the Polynesians of Hawaii. We may assume that the members of these pairs of populations are not equally related to one another. Their degree of relatedness is at least partially reflected by the extent to which gene flow occurs between them.

Human populations also may vary in their relative relatedness to one another because of selection pressure. Two tribes of North American Indians who occupied adjacent hunting territories undoubtedly would be more closely allied genetically than to any tribe of South American Indians. Disregarding the gene flow that would occur between the two North American groups, the selection pressures operating against them very likely would be similar, and significantly different from those common to a Latin American habitat.

Degrees of relatedness among species

All populations, even those of different species, are related genetically to one another in varying degrees. It is true that the members of one species do not interbreed under natural conditions with those of another species except in rare instances. Under artificial conditions, however, it has been found that a number of species can be interbred with complete fertility, including various species of fish, the pheasant and the chicken, the dog and the wolf, and many others. Such species are closely related because they are completely interfertile and their offspring also are fertile. Other hybrid crosses suggest more distant relationships. Mating a donkey with a horse produces mule offspring which, with only rare exceptions, are sterile. Breeding a Hereford cow to an American bison not only produces sterile offspring but also is accompanied by a high rate of unsuccessful pregnancies. The fact that births occur at all indicates a definite relationship between the species. Going one step further, attempts to hybridize two more distantly related bovids, such as sheep and goats, have failed to produce any offspring. It is clear from these examples that degrees of relatedness exist between species just as they do between subspecific and racial populations.

Barriers to gene flow between species

One may wonder why interbreeding usually does not take place between related species under natural conditions. It does not because several kinds of mechanisms have evolved which act as barriers to gene flow, and, as we shall see shortly, it is these very devices that are responsible for the origin of new species. In many cases, related species occupy distinct, nonoverlapping territories. Such *allopatric species,* as they are called, fail to interbreed because they do not come in contact with one another. Gene flow also is effectively blocked in various ways between *sympatric species* — those related forms that inhabit identical or broadly overlapping ranges. Two such species, for example, may be reproductively isolated because they live in different habitats; one may occupy grasslands, while the other inhabits neighboring woodlands. Reproductive isolation can be equally effective when the breeding seasons of the two species are at different times of the year.

Often closely related species choose members of their own species for mates on the basis of specific courtship behaviors and sexual signals, such as ritualistic dances, vocalizations, color markings, and odoriferous chemical secretions. The signaling devices of one species attract and stimulate only members of that species. The call of a bull moose and the bugling of a male elk attract separate female audiences.

Finally there are mechanisms which result in reproductive isolation even when members of two species mate. Often sperm fail to survive in the genital tracts of alien females. If fertilization does occur the embryos die, or (as in most horse-donkey progeny) they develop and are born as sterile or otherwise defective offspring.

To recapitulate: it is clear that demes, races, and species represent intergradations of populational units that differ in size and the amount of gene flow between them. Closely related, moderately related, and distantly related, are labels that pertain to all of them. A cluster of *related demes* may be called a *race*. A group of *related races* may comprise a *species*. Several *related species* make up a *genus*.

Since all these entities merely are names for dynamic, living populations, we may pose a crucial question: two distantly related populations of the same species ultimately might achieve total and permanent reproductive isolation. In what respect would these two populations differ from closely related species?

Speciation: the origin of species

As a species increases its numbers, its subpopulations become dispersed over a larger and larger area. Certain peripheral groups tend to be placed in contact with new surroundings hitherto untried by the species. Those phenotypes capable of utilizing these new resources will hold an advantage over those unable or less able to do so. The successful phenotypes will benefit by lowered competition from other members of their species. As a consequence, natural selection and genetic drift may interact to produce a diversity of types in response to these new environments.

An excellent example is provided by the leopard frog, a common amphibian distributed virtually over the entire United States, from deserts to mountain peaks. Many geographic races have been identified, four of which are pictured in Fig. 9-10. Frogs from races that live in adjacent territories can be hybridized readily and produce healthy young. When frogs from such separated areas as Florida and Vermont are interbred, however, abnormal embryos develop, very few of which survive. Apparently, because of differences in winter length and severity in these areas, there is a difference between the two races in their rates of development. The hybrid embryos presumably receive conflicting genetic instructions and develop abnormally. The two races could be classified as

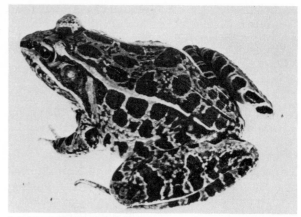

related species were it not for one fact. They are bridged by a continuous chain of intervening populations, along which gene flow can occur between adjoining groups (Fig. 9-10). If the intervening populations separating the two races were to be wiped out—or if both races were somehow able to occupy the same territory—they would become different species. Gene flow between them would be prevented because of their genetic (physiologic) incompatibility, and the process of speciation would be essentially complete.

A

B

FIGURE 9-10
Geographic variation and gene flow in the leopard frog (*Rana pipiens*). *A,* Four of many different geographic races. *B,* Neighboring races of this frog in the eastern United States can interbreed and produce normal young (curved arrows). Crosses between New England and Florida races yield few young that survive (long arrow with X). [*A, Courtesy of John A. Moore.*]

The difficulty in making absolute distinctions between distantly related races and closely related species is inherent in the evolutionary process. Theodosius Dobzhansky has described the matter clearly by likening a species and its many subpopulations to a cable composed of many strands (Fig. 9-11).[11] The species (cable) consists of a number of subpopulations (strands) ranging in size from demes to races. Some of these strands have branched from other strands,

[11] T. Dobzhansky, *Evolution, Genetics, and Man,* New York: John Wiley & Sons, Inc., 1955, pp. 182–183.

denoting populations that were derived by the splitting of an ancestral population. Other strands join one another, indicating subpopulations that merged. Still others end blindly, marking those groups that became extinct. Any given species is viewed by an observer at a particular time in its evolutionary history, for example, level A in the illustration. At this time, the species consists of a group of related subpopulations of varying size. At time level B, the species consists of two separate distributions of population groups, joined by a few intervening populations. One would be justified in calling these two major clusters distantly related racial groups, or *incipient species.* Some gene flow is still possible, however, by way of the intermediate subpopulations. It would be theoretically possible for some genes to pass from one incipient species to the other, just as some frog genes might possibly be transferred, population by

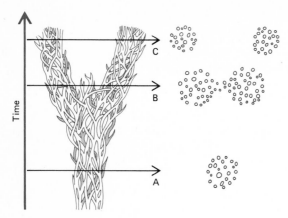

FIGURE 9-11
Diagrammatic representation of an ancestral species (time *A*) splitting into two descendant species (time *C*). Each species (cablelike bundle) consists of numerous subpopulations (individual strands). Branching strands indicate populations that divided into two or more populations, merging strands populations that fused, and dead-ending strands populations that became extinct. Sections shown at the right denote subpopulational or racial groups existing at three successive time levels, *A, B,* and *C.* [*From T. Dobzhansky, Evolution, Genetics, and Man, Wiley, New York, 1955.*]

population, all the way from Florida to Vermont. At time level C, the distantly related racial clusters, or incipient species, have become completely isolated, full-fledged species.

It is in this context that one observes living things at any given time. Some species are isolated entities in state A. Others, in state B, are populations in transition between different racial clusters and new descendant species. Still others have gone all the way to state C, where they are observed as groups of related species.

In the following chapter we will consider the factors that determine the directions taken by evolutionary change and the biologic consequences that ensue from such change.

SUGGESTED READINGS

DOBZHANSKY, T.: *Genetics of the Evolutionary Process,* New York: Columbia University Press, 1970. This book and the books by Dunn, Lerner, Mayr, and Wilson and Bossert have good introductory discussions of population genetics and evolutionary mechanisms.

DUNN, L. C.: *Heredity and Evolution in Human Populations,* New York: Atheneum Press, 1970.

GARN, S. M.: *Human Races,* Springfield, Ill.: Charles C Thomas, Publisher, 1971. A well-written book by a long-standing authority on human races.

LERNER, I. M.: *Heredity, Evolution, and Society,* San Francisco: W. H. Freeman and Company, 1968.

MAYR, E.: *Population, Species and Evolution,* Cambridge, Mass.: Harvard University Press, 1970.

MEAD, M., et al. (eds.): *Science and the Concept of Race,* New York: Columbia University Press, 1968. This and Osborne's book are a collection of essays on race.

OSBORNE, R. H. (ed.), *The Biological and Social Meaning of Race,* San Francisco: W. H. Freeman and Company, 1971.

WILSON, E. O. and W. BOSSERT: *A Primer of Population Biology,* Stamford, Conn.: Sinauer Associates, 1971.

REVIEW QUESTIONS

1 Describe the principle of natural selection.

2 What is meant by a Hardy-Weinberg equilibrium? How is it expressed mathematically? What four conditions must be met for such an equilibrium to exist?

3 What is genetic drift and how does it contribute to the evolutionary process? Cite an example of genetic drift in a human population.

4 How does the founder effect differ from genetic drift? Show how the Hutterite sect in the United States and Canada illustrates both genetic drift and the founder effect.

5 Identify five different kinds of barriers to gene flow (other than geographic barriers) among human populations. In each of two of these give an example of a human population isolated by that barrier and state some of the known genetic effects of isolation. In broad terms, what is the overall effectiveness of gene flow barriers and how does gene flow contribute to human evolution?

6 What is mutation pressure and how are its effects modified by selection pressure? Demonstrate the interrelationships of mutation pressure and selection pressure among United States diabetics and nondiabetics.

7 What is meant by a balanced genetic polymorphism? How does the incidence of sickling anemia in Africa illustrate this phenomenon?

8 What are the essential criteria of Garn's classification of human races? In what respects can such a classification be criticized?

9 Discuss degrees of relatedness among demes, races, and species. What determines the degree of relatedness between two demes of the same race? Two races of the same species? Two different species?

10 List five ways in which gene flow is prevented between different species.

11 Write a short essay on the origin of species.

TEN

ORGANIC EVOLUTION II:
Direction and Outcome

OPPORTUNISM AND
EVOLUTIONARY DIRECTION

A species tends to disperse over a larger area
as its numbers increase. This places portions of
the population in contact with new environments. In the process of meeting the requirements for survival in different surroundings,
new species may evolve. Whether this happens
depends upon how accessible the new environment is to the species in question and whether
that species can survive there. The prospect

of satisfying these conditions is strictly a matter
of chance and hinges upon certain opportunities which may or may not be open to exploitation. George Gaylord Simpson classifies these
opportunities into three categories: *physical*,
constitutional, and *ecological*. The combination
of physical, constitutional, and ecological opportunities that are open to a species determine
the direction of evolution.[1] Rather than restricting evolution to a single direction and the

[1] G. G. Simpson and W. S. Beck, *Life*, New York: Harcourt, Brace
& World Inc., 1969, pp. 286 and 291.

production of a new species, these opportunities result in evolution in many directions and the production of diverse species, such as the adaptive radiation of apes described in Chap. 6.

Physical opportunity

A species must first have physical access to a new habitat. Monkeys in the rain forests of Latin America lack the *physical opportunity* to invade the rain forests of Africa. Any potential that New World monkeys may have for evolutionary development on the African continent consequently could not be realized. Some Latin American animals, on the other hand, are much more likely to disperse over long distances. The ancestors of one of these, a small seed-eating ground finch, is believed to have colonized a group of islands, the Galápagos, that lie some 965 kilometers (600 miles) off the coast of Ecuador. The Galápagos archipelago was formed in the Miocene or Pliocene by volcanic action and never has been connected with the Latin American mainland. Today, most of the small land birds on the island chain trace their ancestry to the early pioneers from the mainland. First studied by Charles Darwin in 1832, they are known as *Darwin's finches* and consist of 14 distinct species that are found nowhere else in the world.

Constitutional opportunity

Gaining access to a new environment is one thing. Living in it is another. In order to gain a foothold in a new habitat, a species must be equipped with at least those minimum adaptations that will enable it to survive in the new surroundings. If it does not have the biologic constitution to survive and reproduce, it will never have the chance to evolve one. In addition to physical opportunity, a species also must have *constitutional opportunity* if it is to colonize a new area successfully.

Some Latin American monkeys undoubtedly have the constitutional opportunity to live in African rain forests. The adaptations they have evolved for living in New World forests would enable them to maintain a pioneer African population because the two environments are similar in many ways.[2] Their lack of physical opportunity prevents the establishment of such a foothold in the first place.

Constitutional opportunity and *preadaptation* are expressions that mean the same thing. By becoming better adapted to the environment in which they live, organisms may coincidentally develop biologic traits which could be used as stopgap measures in a new mode of life. An invading population may improve on its makeshift preadaptations through natural selection, and evolve into new forms. In effect, this is what happens in the evolution of all new animal species.

The conquest of land by vertebrates provides a clear case of making the most out of a constitutional opportunity. It began with a group of freshwater fishes called the *lobe-fins* that lived 400 million years ago in the Devonian period (Fig. 2-13). They were distinguished by having muscular, fleshy fins and by having lungs as well as gills. These features enabled the fish to live in ponds and streams where water levels fluctuated greatly from season to season, and where the water often became stagnant and devoid of oxygen. It is believed that fleshy lobed fins acted as body props by which the fish could wiggle or crawl along a stream bed to a new pond before the one they were in dried up completely. Having lungs allowed the fish to avail themselves of atmospheric oxygen, a necessity both for land-crawling and for living in stagnant, oxygen-depleted water. The modern lungfishes, incidentally, also live in water that is low in oxygen. A pair of lungs and two pairs of appendages which acted both as fins and body props were adaptations that permitted fishes to continue to live as fishes.

They also produced a vertebrate with a newfound environment, the land. Primitive

[2] Old World monkeys have the constitutional opportunity to live in New World forests. A colony of rhesus monkeys introduced by man on an island in the West Indies that had no native monkeys has thrived for almost 40 years.

amphibians gradually evolved from the lobe-fins as body-propping fins were modified into legs (Fig. 10-1). Some of these ancient amphibians, in turn, ultimately gave rise to early reptiles whose main claim to fame was an egg that would develop away from water. Even this accomplishment probably was an aquatic adaptation because the first eggs were laid by amphibious fish-eating reptiles. By producing an egg that was no longer at the mercy of transient streams and ponds, a creature had evolved whose semiaquatic existence was assured during its developmental as well as its adult stages.

After a few million years, the evolution of land plants began to open up rich ecological opportunities for terrestrial animals. Reptiles were constitutionally equipped to take advantage of them. The result was one of the most majestic adaptive radiations of all time: the evolution of 50 families (16 orders) of reptiles, some of which were the ancestors of all modern reptiles, birds, and mammals (Fig. 6-4).

Ecological opportunity

A third kind of opportunity must be open to a species before it can invade a new area. A given species A, for example, may have both physical and constitutional access to a certain environment. If this habitat harbors a native species B that would offer serious competition to A, invasion by the latter might be prevented for want of *ecological opportunity*. Even if our Latin American monkeys could gain physical access to tropical Africa, their adaptations for life in rain forests would not ensure a successful residence. A great many kinds of Old World monkeys are firmly entrenched in a variety of monkey habitats. Intensive competition from successful natives is a formidable barrier to many invaders because most of them tend to be weakly adapted.

The Galápagos Islands mentioned previously offered easy ecological access to any South American species, like the ancestral ground finch, that reached the island chain and was able to live there. Once vegetation had become established on the islands ecological opportunity would have been wide open. With a variety of food resources, no competition to thwart their utilization, and very few predators, early ground finch colonizers were provided with every opportunity for subsequent speciation. The evolutionary potential was additionally reinforced by the strong influence that genetic drift could have on populations scattered among 16 islands and the relative ease with which barriers to gene flow might develop between them. Under the force of natural selection, the stage was set for an adaptive radiation that culminated in the evolution of a unique family of birds.

Darwin's finches comprise a family of 4 genera and 14 species. One genus and species is found on Cocos Island, about 965 kilometers (600 miles) northeast of the Galápagos. The remaining 3 genera and 13 species are native to the Galápagos chain and distinguished chiefly by their size and the form of their beak (Fig. 10-2). One genus (*Geospiza*) embraces six species of ground finches, each one occupying separate but slightly overlapping ecologic niches. One lives on large seeds, another on medium-sized seeds, and another on small seeds (1, 2, and 3 in Fig. 10-2). Still another scratches among the leaves on the forest floor (4). Two live on cactus flowers, seeds, and fruits, and on cactus pulp (5, 6).

A second genus (*Camarhynchus*) consists of six species that have diversified to the extent that all of them live and forage in trees, and all but one of them feed on insects. The vegetarian tree finch (7) feeds on buds, fruits, and leaves. Three of them are omnivorous in varying degrees (8, 9, 10). The remaining two feed primarily on wood-boring insects. One of these, the remarkable woodpecker finch (12) chisels into a tree trunk with its beak, breaks off a cactus spine or a twig, and uses it as a probe to extract insects from the hole it excavated. The third genus (*Certhidia*) has radiated so far from the ancestral form that its lone species (13) resembles a warbler more than a finch. The

FIGURE 10-1
Top, the lobe-fin fish of 400 million years ago had lungs as well as gills and used two pairs of their muscular fins both for crawling and swimming. *Bottom,* in some of the descendants of the lobe-fins, body-propping fins had become modified into legs, resulting in primitive amphibians like these forms of 350 million years ago. [*American Museum of Natural History.*]

warbler finch commonly is seen catching small insects on the wing, a very unfinchlike behavior.

The Galápagos Islands are a fine exhibit of evolutionary processes at work. An ancestral ground finch, dispersing outward from its native territory, colonized the island chain because the prerequisite opportunities for such an event were available to the invaders. The new arrivals found a region of great ecologic opportunity, with a variety of ecologic niches open for exploitation. The strong selection pressures of their homeland, imposed by the heavy competition that results from increasing numbers, were relaxed in the new land. Phenotypes formerly selected against on the mainland could thrive, giving rise to increasingly diverse populations of finches. The evolution of geographic races, adapted through natural selection to this or that ecologic niche, was assured. The subsequent reproductive isolation of these populations converted races into full-fledged species, and the adaptive radiation of Darwin's finches became an accomplished fact.

EVOLUTIONARY CONSEQUENCES AND OUTCOMES

Just as one must rise above the level of the trees to gain a proper perspective of the forest, so also must one go beyond a mere detailing of mechanisms and processes to comprehend the nature of evolution. Perceived in broad perspective, the full sweep of evolution's course is best considered from the standpoint of its consequences and outcomes. There are four of major significance: (1) the increasing diversity of species, (2) the inevitable toll of extinction, (3) the uniqueness of evolutionary change, and (4) the convergence of diversified forms.

The increasing diversity of species

The evolution of Darwin's finches and, on a grander scale, the evolution of land vertebrates suggest that the course of evolutionary history leads in the direction of increasing biologic diversity. This divergence, or radiation, from one ancestral form is what is meant by *adaptive radiation.* It is elegantly demonstrated in the many transformations that have occurred in the evolution of the vertebrate limb (Fig. 2-4). The history of life as revealed in the fossil record has shown a persistent tendency toward more and more kinds of organisms. Indeed, the evolution of our own species is one of the products of an adaptive radiation that apparently began with *Aegyptopithecus* in early Oligocene (Fig. 7-8).

It will be recalled from Chap. 6 that climates and environments over the earth were changing gradually, but profoundly, during the Miocene and Pliocene. Forests of all kinds were giving way to grasslands and woodland savannas. New ecologic opportunities were opening up on a vast scale and environments were becoming increasingly varied. Several species of *Dryopithecus* evolved during the Miocene and Pliocene, two of which may be ancestral to the gorilla and chimpanzee. Terrestrial *Gigantopithecus* and *Ramapithecus* presumably descended from two others. There is strong evidence that a dryopithecine stock was undergoing adaptive radiation. A variety of species were evolving which spanned a range from arboreal, semiarboreal, and terrestrial pongids to early, presumably semiterrestrial, hominids.

The tendency of an evolving population to radiate in several directions is a response to diverse ecologic niches which become available for exploitation. The changing world gives rise to different habitats and ecologic niches. This or that population has prevailed to harvest these new resources because each had the potential to do so by reason of its genetic diversity and each was under pressure to do so because of competition. Any species that failed in this evolutionary enterprise was automatically doomed to extinction, and left no descendants. Those that succeeded perpetuated a lineage from which different species emerged, each one

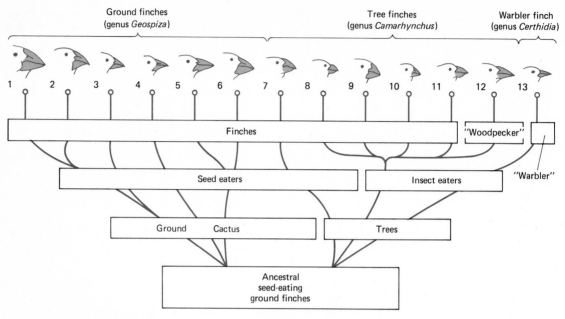

FIGURE 10-2

Adaptive radiation of Darwin's finches. Thirteen species are shown belonging to three genera (*Geospiza, Cama-rhynchus,* and *Certhidia*). A fourteenth species in a fourth genus (*Pinaroloxias*) is found on Cocos Island, about 965 kilometers northeast of the Galapagos. [*Modified from David Lack, Darwin's Finches, Cambridge University Press. Cambridge, 1947.*]

1. Large, seed-eating ground finch
2. Medium, seed-eating ground finch
3. Small, seed-eating ground finch
4. Sharp-beaked ground finch
5. Cactus ground finch
6. Large cactus ground finch
7. Vegetarian tree finch
8. Large Charles Island tree finch
9. Large Central Islands tree finch
10. Small tree finch
11. Mangrove tree finch
12. Woodpecker finch
13. Warbler finch

adapted to a particular ecologic niche. The processes that are responsible for speciation and diversity are the same processes that are responsible for adaptation and survival; diversity and adaptation are but different aspects of the same thing.

In addition to divergent evolution, new species also arise along a time sequence within one lineage, a phenomenon previously described in the context of paleospecies (Fig. 6-3). A lineage may successfully meet the chal-

lenges of environmental change and still maintain its adaptiveness to an ecologic niche that has changed relatively little. Adaptive changes occurring in a single evolutionary line are called *anagenetic,* in distinction to the *clado-genetic* modifications in divergent lines. The presumptive line of descent from *Australo-pithecus sp.* → *Homo erectus* → *H. sapiens* (Fig. 6-3) was a continuous lineage of successive adaptations. All were unique yet their temporal boundaries are impossible to establish precisely.

The inevitable toll of extinction

Despite the genetic variety found in many populations, no species is capable of sustaining its adaptiveness indefinitely. Anagenetic lineages are no exception and tend to disappear sooner or later, as apparently occurred in the *Australopithecus robustus* → *A. boisei* lineage (Fig. 7-8). Of the 2,500 families of animals whose fossil remains have been identified, only about one-third still are living and their roster of species is quite different from what it was 5 to 10 million years ago. A few of the extinct families evolved into new groups, but the majority passed into oblivion without leaving any descendants.

Causes of extinction

Extinction probably is caused in one of two ways. First, a species may lack adequate genetic diversity to meet the challenges of environmental change. This is a common plight faced by specialized species adapted to very restricted ecologic niches. Relatively slight ecological changes can prove to be catastrophic in such cases. The great saber-toothed cat of the Pleistocene (*Smilodon*), for example, apparently was a specialist in preying on thick-skinned mastodons and mammoths (Fig. 10-3). When their elephantine prey became extinct, the big lumbering cats were left with fleet-footed, wary herbivores like deer and antelope which were too elusive for them. Had the sabertooth been a more generalized hunter like man or the cougar, it would not have been dependent on such a limited resource, and might be alive today.

There is a second reason for extinction and the sabertooth fell victim to that one also. There are times in the evolutionary history of a species when environmental change occurs so rapidly that natural selection cannot keep pace even in a highly adaptable species. The lineage of saber-toothed cats was a successful one for a long-time—from the Oligocene to late Pleistocene. So were the lineages of many other large mammals: mastodons and mammoths, camels, horses, giant ground sloths, and many others (Fig. 10-3). Over 50 genera of these large mammals became extinct in late Pleistocene, yet in that same relatively short period there were comparatively few extinc-

tions among plants or smaller animals. There appears to be but one probable agent capable of inflicting mass extinction upon such a selective group over so short a time. That would be Paleolithic herd-hunters.

According to Paul S. Martin the extinction of large mammals was particularly cataclysmic in the New World. Invading Paleo-Indians found a mammalian fauna that was both abundant and naive in the ways of man. This situation may well have triggered the first human population explosion in the Western Hemisphere. Martin believes that 31 genera of large American mammals, including those already mentioned, were destroyed within 1,000 years because they lacked sufficient time to acquire defensive behaviors (Fig. 10-4).[3]

Ecologic replacement

Since extinction has been the ultimate fate of every species, one may wonder how evolution has more or less consistently produced an increasing number of different kinds of organisms. This has been brought about largely through what is called *ecologic replacement*. As one or more species gradually decline in numbers prior to their actual extinction, the ecologic niches they vacate are opened up for exploitation by other groups. Some of these other groups may be more adaptable species with a greater potential for genetic differentiation. In refilling the abandoned niches, they commonly do so more efficiently than the former occupants, sometimes establishing two or more niches where there was only one before. For example, during the late Cretaceous when the reign of the dinosaurs and several other reptilian groups came to a close, mammals and birds underwent incredible radiations, utilizing environmental resources much more fully and by many more species than their predecessors. Evolution through natural selection generally tends to move toward fuller

[3] P. S. Martin, "The Discovery of America," *Science*, vol. 179, Mar. 9, 1973, pp. 969–974.

Wooly
Mammoth
(*Mammuthus*)

Giant
ground sloth
(*Megatherium*)

Sabertooth cat
(*Smilodon*)

FIGURE 10-3
Some of the large mammals of the Western Hemisphere
which became extinct in late Pleistocene. Evidence suggests these extinctions may have been caused directly or
indirectly by Paleo-Indian hunters.

utilization of any resource capable of supporting life.

The uniqueness of evolutionary change

Evolutionary opportunity is nonreplicable
The setting in which a species evolves is as unique as the species itself. As we have stated, that setting consists of three interdependent opportunities—physical, constitutional, and ecological—each of which is a singular circumstance. Each derives a distinctive character because it is peculiar to a particular place at a specific time. It is incomprehensible that these opportunities could ever be duplicated at any other time or place because of their unimaginable complexity and specificity. To imagine that two environments separated by time or space would happen to be the same is to imagine that their physical characteristics such as terrain, latitude, elevation, water, climate, and soil are equivalent; that they both share the same thousands of ecologic niches; that these niches are occupied by the same species of plants, herbivores, carnivores, parasites, scavengers, and decomposers; that these organisms have the same population densities; and that the entire complex in both areas is subject to identical climatic, geologic, and biologic changes over significant periods of time.

Since organisms evolve in response to the particular environment in which they live, every species is a unique, unimitated creature in time and space. Our own origins trace back through a chain of circumstances that began with some fleshy-finned fishes confronted with the particular challenges of a Devonian climate. Had those circumstances been altered to a significant degree at any point among those 400 million years, the world today could have been any one of a million others, and we might have lived in none of them. It is possible, indeed probable, that life is a common phenomenon in the universe. Granting this, it is entirely possible that intelligent life exists on planets in other solar systems. There is no reason to believe, however, that these sapient beings would resemble us, or one another.

The irreversibility of evolution

The principle of biologic uniqueness means that a major or significant evolutionary step, once taken, can never be duplicated. Another principle follows from this: a major evolutionary step, once made, can never be reversed. An evolutionary sequence cannot be duplicated either forward or backward.

Thus, chimpanzees could not evolve into people. The modern chimp is a specialized creature who occupies the niche of a semi-

arborealist in tropical Africa. Man is a generalized terrestrial species. After millions of years of natural selection, chimpanzee phenotypes have been channeled and narrowed for semi-arboreal living. Genes for terrestrial life have been selected against. The ape simply lacks the genetic resources, the constitutional opportunity, to become the kind of near-terrestrial ancestor the hominid lineage evolved from. Beyond that, the absence of ecologic opportunity is even more prohibitive. Chimps today are receiving intensive competition in their own niche from monkeys. Life on the ground would

FIGURE 10-4
An artist's conception of Paleo-Indians hunting camels near Tule Springs, Nevada. [*Painting by Jay Matternes, courtesy of the National Geographic Society.*]

be intolerable for them, even if man were not present, because of competition from monkeys, especially baboons. In short, modern terrestrial environments are a far cry from those

of late Miocene time when the hominid line was differentiating. The physical, constitutional, and ecological opportunities of that time are nonrepeatable.

Porpoises and penguins appear to have put evolution into reverse. All that glitters, however, is not gold. Nor are all that look like and live like fishes, fishes.

The convergence of diversified forms

As distantly related groups of animals undergo adaptive radiation into diverse environments, some of their descendant species become residents of habitats that are very much alike. The divergent evolution of reptiles, birds,

FIGURE 10-5
Evolutionary divergence and convergence compared. The ancient stem-reptiles were semiaquatic creatures from which the ancestors of birds and mammals as well as later reptiles evolved through divergence. Further radiation within reptiles, birds, and mammals led to various animals adapted to sea, land, and air. Organisms that evolve in response to a common environment tend to resemble one another even though they are distantly related. Such adaptive convergence is reflected here in aerial forms (gull, extinct pterodactyl, and bat) and aquatic forms (penguin, extinct ichthyosaur, porpoise, shark, and squid).

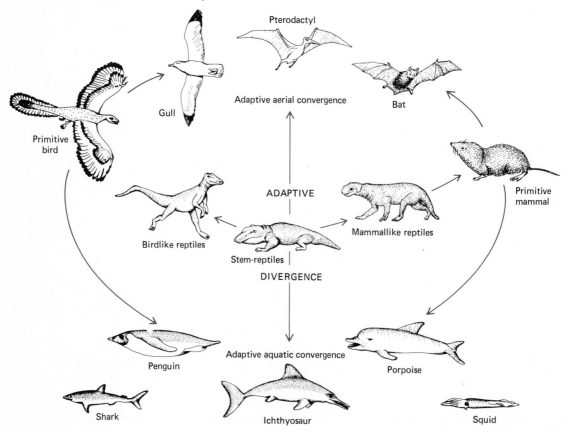

and mammals, for instance, embraced conquests of the land, sea, and air (Fig. 10-5). Those that took to life in the sea, like the extinct ichthyosaurs, the penguins, and the porpoises, bear a superficial resemblance to one another and to other active marine swimmers, such as sharks and squids. To the extent that they share a similar habitat and mode of life, all these organisms were subjected to certain selection pressures common to their survival. One of these was the necessity for being streamlined. Water is a denser medium than air, and greater streamlining is needed in water if an animal is to move fast enough to catch a meal or avoid being one. As a result, a group of distantly related forms has come to look somewhat alike through what is called *convergent evolution.*

A classic example of convergence is illustrated by the marsupial mammals of Australia and placental mammals elsewhere in the world. Although both groups have undergone independent adaptive radiations, the correspondence between species occupying comparable ecologic niches is striking (Fig. 10-6). These similarities are especially impressive when one realizes that each of the placental species in the illustration is more closely related to a blue whale than it is to its ecologic counterpart in Australia.

Parallelism

Fairly closely related species sometimes follow an evolutionary course known as *parallelism,* or *parallel evolution,* that resembles convergence. In such a case, two evolutionary lineages are related by a relatively recent ancestor rather than a geologically ancient one. If the two descendant lineages lived in similar environments and adopted comparable lifestyles, they would tend to develop common phenotypic traits and follow parallel evolutionary paths. This matter was discussed early in Chap. 6, where we considered the identification of fossil species.

New and Old World monkeys illustrate parallel evolution clearly. Having arisen from a common prosimian ancestry in Eocene time, these two groups have independently evolved a number of common adaptations which make it appear that they are more closely related than they really are. Parallel evolution, in fact, has occurred on innumerable occasions among primates, some of which were mentioned in Chap. 6. Ring-tailed lemurs and savanna

FIGURE 10-6
Convergence between two placental mammals and their marsupial counterparts from Australia. Placental mammals are more closely related to a blue whale than to their marsupial equivalents. [*After A. E. Brehms, 1912.*]

MARSUPIALS

Tasmanian
wolf
(*Thylacinus*)

Mouse
(*Dasycercus*)

PLACENTALS

Wolf
(*Canis*)

Mouse
(*Mus*)

baboons, for example (Figs. 3-2*B* and 3-4), exhibit parallelism in their anatomical and behavioral adaptations for semiterrestrial living. The spider monkey of the New World and the gibbon of Asia have similarly developed parallel adaptations for brachiation (Fig. 3-2*G* and *I*). The absence of a tail in diverging lines of hominoids probably was another case of parallelism, in which taillessness was an adaptation for brachiation and terrestrial life in apes and hominids respectively.

THE OUTCOME OF HOMINID EVOLUTION: HUMAN DIVERSITY AND ADAPTATION

Evolution through natural selection is oriented toward adaptation; the only alternative is extinction. We have already pointed out that *diversity* and *adaptation* are terms that refer to the same thing. The evolution of diverse species in filling varied ecologic niches *has been* an adaptation to many different environments. Thus far in our overview, we have stressed divergence; now we will consider the other face of the coin and lay emphasis on the adaptive aspects of evolution, with particular reference to our own species.

In the preceding two chapters, 2 inherited physical traits, 1 behavioral trait, 4 blood groups, and 10 genetic diseases and anomalies have been considered which contribute to human variability (Fig. 10-7). Within this small cluster of traits, some idea of the potential for human diversity is reflected in the calculation that there are over 100 billion possible genotypic combinations of genes controlling known blood groups and blood disorders. How these sources of human variability contribute to adaptation were discussed in the last chapter in the context of sickle-cell and ABO blood-group polymorphisms.

Chapter 4 was devoted to some of the myriad adaptations which characterize man

EXTERNAL TRAITS

1 Baldness
2 Skin pigmentation

BEHAVIORAL TRAITS

3 Intelligence

BLOOD GROUPS

4 ABO
5 MN
6 Rh
7 Secretor-nonsecretor

DISEASES AND DEFICIENCIES (PHYSICAL, PHYSIOLOGICAL, BEHAVIORAL)

8 Chondrodystrophy
9 Color blindness, red-green
10 Deafness
11 Diabetes
12 Down's syndrome (mongolian idiocy)
13 Hemophilia A
14 Klinefelter's syndrome (XXY)
15 PKU (phenylketonuria)
16 Sickle-cell anemia
17 Turner's syndrome (XO)

FIGURE 10-7
Human variation. These inherited characteristics were discussed in Chaps. 8 and 9. Skin pigmentation was also discussed in Chap. 4.

as a unique species. Theoretical consideration, however, also was given to the adaptive significance of variations in lip form and in skin pigmentation. We noted Desmond Morris' suggestion that the contrast of full red lips against a light skin acts as a sexual attractant; the lips of dark-skinned people tend to be strongly everted, sustaining this contrast. We also noted some hypotheses concerning the adaptiveness of variations in skin color. Evidence was presented suggesting that vitamin D synthesis and protection from frostbite might be involved. Dark-skinned people tend to be native to exposed habitats like deserts and grasslands in equatorial latitudes, where their greater pigmentation protects them from dangerously excessive vitamin D synthesis (hypervitaminosis D). People native to temperate latitudes and less open, forested regions usually are lighter-skinned and tend to avoid the risk of subnormal vitamin D synthesis and rickets. Such people also live in the colder latitudes where their lighter pigmentation appears to make them less susceptible to frostbite.

Variation is observed in a great many other physical traits, in which it is logical to believe that some adaptive function might be served. The color of head hair and whether it is straight, wavy, or tightly curled would be included among these, as well as relative body hairiness, ear form and size, and the absence or degree of development of an extra (*epicanthic*) fold of skin over the inner corner of the upper eyelid. These and many others are prominent features in human variation. Unfortunately nothing of a factual nature is known about the adaptive function of the great majority of these distinguishing traits. There are, however, two exceptions: body build and nose form.

Body build

Among warm-blooded vertebrates, there is a tendency within a species or in closely related species for individuals to be progressively larger the farther they live from the equator. This generalization, known as *Bergmann's principle,* or *rule,* has many exceptions. But body size among related animals generally is smaller in the warm parts of the group's range and larger in the cold portions of that range. The Arctic fox is a good deal larger animal than the little desert kit fox. A comparable difference is seen between Arctic hares and desert jackrabbits.

One does not have to look far to find a reason for this. The ratio of skin surface to body bulk is a critical one in warm-blooded animals because they produce heat in direct proportion to their total metabolically active mass, and they lose heat in direct porportion to their total radiative skin surface. Animals living in a cold climate have the problem of heat *retention* or conservation; they require optimal heat-producing mass and minimal heat-losing skin surface. The problem of animals living in hot climates is heat *loss*; they require maximal skin surface per unit of heat-producing mass (weight).

Thus, the surface-to-volume ratios of small, versus large, bodies become significant. It is common knowledge that large boulders hold their heat longer than small rocks. Small objects have more surface per unit of volume (mass) than large objects. Figure 10-8 compares the surface-to-volume ratios of three cubes. The largest cube has only $1/24$ as much radiating surface per unit of volume as the smallest cube. When the dimensions of an object increase or decrease, the change in surface area of that object varies by the *square* of the change in dimension, whereas the volume changes by the *cube.* Consequently, volume increases or decreases at a much faster rate than surface area.

There is also a tendency for warm-blooded animals of the same or related species to vary in the degree to which projecting body parts like ears and legs are elongated. Individuals who live in warm climates generally have longer ears or legs than those who live in cold climates. The ears of the Arctic fox and hare, for example, are smaller than those of their counterparts living in the desert. This observation, commonly referred to as *Allen's rule,* also is related to surface-to-volume ratios. As may be seen from Fig. 10-9, compact shapes have less surface per unit enclosed than thinned shapes of the same volume.

Discounting local variations and numerous exceptions, Bergmann's and Allen's rules apply fairly well to human populations generally. From northerly regions to the equator, both in North America and Eurasia, there tends to be a populational gradient (cline) from larger average size in the north to smaller average size in the south (Fig. 10-10). According to Eugene Schreider, Chinese males range from an

FIGURE 10-8

The effect of size on surface area. Exposed surface area, per unit of volume enclosed, increases as the volume is diminished. When the dimensions of an object increase or decrease, the change in surface area of that object varies by the *square* of the change in dimension whereas the volume changes by the *cube*. Volume consequently increases or decreases at a much faster rate than surface area. Warm-blooded animals in cold regions are generally larger than related species in warm regions; large bodies have less skin surface per kilogram from which heat can be lost than small bodies.

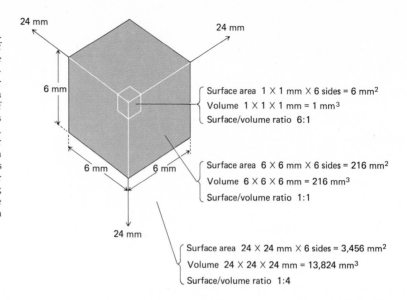

24 mm

24 mm

6 mm

6 mm   6 mm

24 mm

Surface area 1 X 1 mm X 6 sides = 6 mm²
Volume 1 X 1 X 1 mm = 1 mm³
Surface/volume ratio 6:1

Surface area 6 X 6 mm X 6 sides = 216 mm²
Volume 6 X 6 X 6 mm = 216 mm³
Surface/volume ratio 1:1

Surface area 24 X 24 mm X 6 sides = 3,456 mm²
Volume 24 X 24 X 24 mm = 13,824 mm³
Surface/volume ratio 1:4

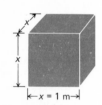

Area: 1 m X 1 m X 6 sides = 6 m³
Volume: 1 m X 1 m X 1 m = 1 m³
Ratio: 6 m² per m³

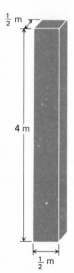

Area: $\frac{1}{2}$ m X 4 m X 4 sides = 8 m²
$\Big\}$ 8$\frac{1}{2}$ m²
$\frac{1}{2}$ m X $\frac{1}{2}$ m X 2 ends = $\frac{1}{2}$ m²
Volume: $\frac{1}{2}$ m X $\frac{1}{2}$ m X 4 m = 1 m³
Ratio: 8$\frac{1}{2}$ m² per m³

FIGURE 10-9

The effect of shape on surface area. Surface per unit volume enclosed is higher in an elongated shape (below) than in a compact shape (above) of the same volume. Warm-blooded mammals in cold regions generally have shorter ears and shorter legs than related species in warm regions; projecting body parts which are short have less skin surface per kilogram from which heat can be lost than elongated parts.

average of 36.02 kilograms per square meter of body surface in the north of China to 30.90 in the south. Similarly, North European males in Finland average 38.23 kilograms per square meter whereas the mean is 36.11 among males in northwestern Egypt.[4]

The Eskimos and the Nilotes of East Africa are clear-cut examples of the Allen principle (Fig. 10-11). The Eskimo peoples with squat, stocky bodies and short limbs present minimal surface for heat loss. The Nilotes, on the other hand, have linear bodies and exceptionally elongated limbs, enabling them to endure equally well the opposing problem of excessive heat.

Nose form

The human nasal passages perform an accessory but important respiratory function in that they sample, filter, warm, and moisten air before it reaches the delicate membranes in the

[4] E. Schreider, "Variations Morphologiques et Differences Climatiques," *Biometrie Humaine,* vol. 6, 1971, pp. 46–49.

 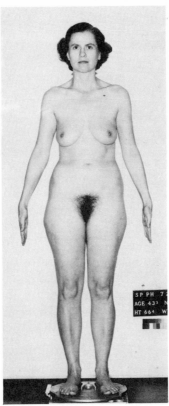

FIGURE 10-10
Body size in relation to climate. The small woman on the left is from tropical New Guinea. The larger woman on the right is a North European. [*Left, courtesy of Wide World Photos.*]

lungs where gas exchange takes place. The exchange of carbon dioxide for oxygen is facilitated greatly when the incoming air has been properly warmed and moistened. Gases diffuse faster when they are warm, and the respiratory membranes perform best when they are kept moist.

It is not surprising, therefore, that nose form, as measured by the average ratio of nose width to length (*nasal index*), correlates well with climate in populations throughout the world. Narrow noses are characteristic of cold, dry climates whereas broad noses are the rule in hot, humid regions. Wolpoff has observed gradations in nose form among both Eskimos and Australian aborigines, in which the narrow-

est noses were found in populations living in the coldest, driest climates.[5]

Theoretically, narrow noses should be associated with narrow nasal passages in which there would be maximal opportunity for the warming and moistening of inhaled air. In hot, humid climates, on the other hand, broad noses and wide nasal passages presumably are adaptive in that they permit less body heating from the breathing of hot air. The warming and moistening functions of the respiratory passages are of little to no value when breathing tropical air.

[5] M. H. Wolpoff, "Climatic Influence on the Skeletal Nasal Aperture," *American Journal of Physical Anthropology*, new series, vol. 29, 1968, pp. 405–423.

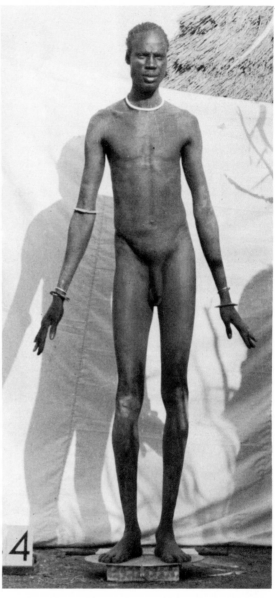

FIGURE 10-11
The compact, short-limbed body of the Eskimo (*left*) and
the linear, long-limbed body of the Nilote (*right*) clearly
reflect adaptations to cold and to heat. [*Left, courtesy of the
American Museum of Natural History; right, courtesy of D. F.
Roberts.*]

Somatogenetic adaptability: acclimatization

Human variation and adaptation are not confined to the genetic modification of specific traits like body build and nose form. Human adaptedness also is shown in the relative degree to which *individuals* can acclimatize themselves to different conditions over varying periods of time. The spanned time may be a few days, or it may encompass the entire period of development from infancy to adulthood. The capacity of an individual to adapt to varying conditions is under genetic control. Those persons capable of accustoming themselves to relatively wide-ranging conditions presumably possess genotypes of great flexibility. This kind of adaptiveness confers upon the species the constitutional opportunity to keep abreast of changing environments.

One might expect to find instances where human adaptiveness to some environmental condition occurred both as a result of acclimatization (individual adaptability) and as a result of a specific trait developed in a particular population through natural selection.

Human adaptation to altitude and to diet appears to demonstrate both types of adaptiveness.

Adaptation to altitude

As one proceeds from sea level to higher elevations, atmospheric pressure is gradually reduced because of the decreasing thickness of the air layer above. Oxygen pressure drops correspondingly and we speak of the air being thinner. At altitudes of 2,500 to 4,000 meters (8,000 to 13,000 feet), we respond to the reduction in oxygen pressure with a more rapid pulse and faster breathing to muscular activities which would have been essentially effortless at lower elevations. Indeed, there are some individuals who cannot survive at these altitudes. Most heterozygous carriers of the sickling gene cannot, for example; half their hemoglobin is the sickling type and the oxygen-carrying capacity of their red blood cells is impaired as a consequence.

Among the many individuals who can accommodate themselves to higher altitudes, chemical changes usually take place in the red blood cells within 24 hours. These changes significantly increase the oxygen-holding capability of hemoglobin. Within a few days to two weeks, the red blood cell (RBC) population in such persons also increases. At 3,660 meters (12,000 feet), for example, the RBC count of a visitor from sea level may increase from around 5 million per cubic millimeter to about 5.4 million.

Visitors to high altitudes, from sea-level areas, usually encounter difficulties with physical activity, sooner or later. Families attempting a permanent adjustment will have more miscarriages, abnormal children, and higher infant mortality than resident families. Nonresidents from lower elevations who are introduced to the higher altitude at an early age and raised there stand a better chance of becoming adapted than do the nonresident adults.

The native-born, however, fare the best apparently because they come from a genetically adapted population. The RBC count of populations native to 3,660 meters (12,000 feet) commonly ranges around 7.5 million, more than 2 million higher than the partially acclimatized visitor. Frisancho has found that Indians living high in the Andes of Peru develop a bigger chest and greater lung capacity than coastal dwellers. The right ventricle of the heart (Fig. 1-4) which pumps blood to the lungs also is more muscular than that found in lowland peoples.[6]

Nutritional adaptation

There have been episodes in the lives of countless human beings everywhere when food intake has been barely adequate to inadequate for short periods of time. Famine has befallen various peoples on repeated occasions throughout recorded history. There can be little doubt that human populations generally are suffi-

[6] A. R. Frisancho, "Human Growth and Pulmonary Function of a High Altitude Peruvian Quechua Population," *Human Biology*, vol. 41, 1969, pp. 365–379.

ciently adaptive to withstand periods of great nutritional stress.

Malnourished people everywhere, whether they are in some part of Africa, India, Mexico, or the United States, grow more slowly and attain smaller adult size than their counterparts who receive adequate, balanced diets. Their rate of metabolism also tends to be substantially lower. If their dietary standards are improved either through local change or by emigration, usually they produce children who become taller and larger than themselves. For example, since World War II the availability of more food in greater variety was responsible, at least in part, for an average height increase of about 5 centimeters (2 inches) among the Japanese. It also has been observed that the children of Mexican immigrants to the United States usually are larger and taller than their parents.

The people of any society tend to grow more slowly, to attain smaller adult size, and to have lower metabolic rates on marginal than on optimal levels of nutrition. It has been found, however, that certain populations can tolerate low food intake better than others.[7] Some of these, in fact, have adapted to diets whose caloric value is so low that other populations could not survive on them. It becomes clear then, that although there is a great deal of genetic flexibility among all people to nutritional stress, there also are genetic differences between populations in their capacity to meet dietary challenges. An excellent example of the latter involves milk.

The ability to digest milk is a straightforward case of natural selection bringing about a nutritional adaptation. Contrary to what many Americans seem to believe, most of the world's adults cannot digest milk. When they attempt to do so, their digestive tracts respond with stomach cramps, gas production, and diarrhea. The majority of people over the world lose their ability to digest milk between

the age of 2 to 4 years. Those people who can digest milk as adults trace their origins to societies in which dairying has played a major role in food production for a long time. Specifically, these people are native to or have come from Northern Europe, certain pastoral tribes in Africa, and a few other places where it has been common practice for adults to consume milk.

The major problem in milk digestion is the digestibility of milk sugar, or *lactose*. The enzyme *lactase* digests milk sugar in all normal babies the world over. This enzyme, however, is lacking or deficient among human adults, with the exception of the dairying societies mentioned. It is theorized that the presence of lactase in adults is the result of a mutant allele.[8] Such a mutant gene would have had no adaptive value among hunters and gatherers or in any society, for that matter, that did not practice dairying. But when dairy husbandry developed in certain areas many millennia ago, those adults who could tolerate milk would have had a distinct survival advantage over those who could not. Selection pressure under such conditions would have contributed to steady and substantial increases in the frequency of the mutant gene for adult lactase synthesis.

The critical adaptation: cultural accommodation

In its capacity to communicate learning to others, and to transmit this learning from generation to generation, the human species has become a singular animal. To a degree quite unmatched by any other species, we can pass information useful for our survival along two routes to succeeding generations, one of them genetic, the other cultural.[9] Our natural in-

---

[7] M. T. Newman, "Biological Adaptation of Man to His Environment: Heat, Cold, Altitude, and Nutrition," *Annals of the New York Academy of Science,* vol. 91, 1961, pp. 617–633.

[8] R. D. McCracken, "Lactase Deficiency: An Example of Dietary Evolution," *Current Anthropology,* vol. 12, 1971, pp. 479–517. N. Kretchmer, "Lactose and Lactase," *Scientific American,* October 1972, pp. 70–78.

[9] Simple, basic forms of cultural behavior (protoculture) are found in certain monkeys and especially apes, as described in Chap. 3.

clination and capacity for culture have genetic foundations in the human genotype. The human potential for language alone is powerfully influenced by adaptations in the throat and voice box (Fig. 4-5) and the master association area of the brain (Fig. 4-6); such features undoubtedly are under the control of great numbers of genes. It is also true that *man's cultural heritage is the most effective force molding his total genotype.* Ever since the beginnings of technology and the sociobehavioral innovations that made it possible, culture has been the most powerful adaptive agency supporting hominid survival.

The major attributes that enable Eskimos to live in the Arctic are their technological prowess which they developed to provide themselves with adequate shelter, clothing, and food obtained from local resources, and the social and behavioral patterns they have developed to assist one another and to make life not only bearable but also enjoyable. The same can be said for the Kalahari Bushmen, the Australian Ngatatjara, the American suburbanite, or indeed any people anywhere. The enormous dimensions of man's cultural inventory enables us to visit the highest mountain peaks as well as the hottest deserts. We can descend into the ocean depths in bathyscaphes and travel to and from the moon in rocket ships. We have the widest distribution of any living thing and can live for protracted periods where no other organism, not even a bacterium, is able to survive. We can do this because our survival no longer requires that we be biologically adapted to every environment we wish to inhabit. Through culture, we can control the environment in which we live on a scale quite unmatched by any other creature.

The adaptive nature of culture
The cultural heritage of a given society has evolved as a means of perpetuating that society and safeguarding the lives and life styles of its members. The culture of a people has become, in essence, a common medium in which every member is immersed. Each society's culture is an environment unto itself to which people respond in specific, standardized ways. Each society is distinctively adorned by its forms of artistic expression, its concept of beauty, and its prescriptions for personal dress, deportment, and manners. Concepts of personal beauty vary: many people believe that attractiveness is attained by altering physical appearance in some way. The face or body is powdered, painted, tattooed, and marked by scratches or cuts; ear lobes, lips, and the nose are pierced to support rings or other ornaments; head shape is modified by placing boards against infants' heads; and so on (Fig. 10-12). Accepted artificial embellishments of the face and head enhance the sexual attractiveness of even the unattractive. Also, modifications of this kind may be used to denote social status or the attainment of higher rank, such as in puberty rites. Culturally imposed traits that distinguish peoples by their dress, their physical appearance, their behavior, and their modes of life develop in response to the traditions and social institutions of the particular society.

The manner in which people walk, the way they communicate with one another and how they use their hands and bodies when they do, the etiquette of eating, the conventions of courtship, even the resting positions they find comfortable—all these and many others vary from society to society. Culture determines how we learn and how we think, how we view the world around us, and how we perceive ourselves in relationship to that world both individually and collectively.

Every society is set apart in some way by its moral code, its concepts of law and justice, its religious dogmas, and its philosophical perspectives. Equally characteristic are systems of economics and government. Means of making a living vary from hunting and gathering to agriculture, commerce, industry, or some combination of these. The basic patterns of economic livelihood and degrees of technological sophistication combine with the other societal dimensions we have listed to produce an economic system. The economic system of a people, aside from certain common adjustments made to other societies with whom one does business, is equally distinctive. Government, acting as the agent of society, also is the product of social history. It bears its mark on the cultural characteristics of a people not only because it is vested with the power to do so but also because it is itself a result of the socio-

FIGURE 10-12
Modifications of the face and head for aesthetic purposes. *A,* Masai dancers in Kenya, East Africa, with painted faces and perforated, stretched ear lobes; *B,* North American-European woman with rings in her ears, painting her face; *C,* North American Indian woman with flattened head. [*A, Courtesy of Marjorie Marshall; C, Courtesy of Smithsonian Institution.*]

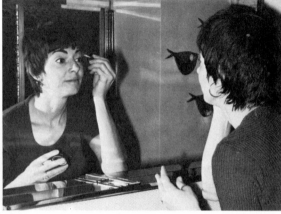

B

A

C

cultural development of the group.

Societal traditions and institutions have developed as a means of providing a variety of essential biosocial services. Social cohesion is served by a sense of identification and belonging among persons whose appearance, bearing, and modes of communication are similar. Interpersonal cooperation and collaborative efforts between groups are stimulated by codes of behavior, concepts of justice, and the legal and economic systems. Government provides safeguards against strife from within and aggression from without. Religion offers justification, if not motivation as well, for the course of sociopolitical action. And the art of a people, their music, their dances and their recreational games inject drama and excitement into rites and ceremonies of a social, political, and religious nature. They also give vent to pent-up tensions and promote the emotional well-being and contentment of all.

Maladaptive features of culture

The culture of man so completely encompasses him that it has become in itself the major environment to which man responds. The human species lives in an environment largely of its own making. The problem of human survival is not a matter of having to adapt to changes in the natural environment. Human survival depends on how well we manage our environmental manipulations. All our biologic challenges spring from this source. The vexing problems of air, water, and soil pollution—of self-contamination by harmful pharmaceutical preparations—of overexploited resources—of too many people—all these and many more have little to do with the *natural* environment and everything to do with human culture.

Our cultural superstructure has become so complex and our numbers so vast that the all-important functions of coordination and purpose are sometimes missing. Employees of bureaucracies, public and private, sometimes lose sight of the organization's avowed purpose and devote themselves to procedures which become ends in themselves. A social case-worker, for example, may follow all the agency's procedures to the letter and, in doing so, sometimes unnecessarily rules out the possibility of helping needy clients. Culture becomes something that people serve, and the all-important reciprocal function of people being served by culture becomes lost in complexity.

Man the hunter has been perennially plagued by his own proficiency. He became so skillful as a hunter that he eliminated most of the desirable prey species. Having become a hunter without prey, his creative genius answered the challenge with animal and plant domestication. The success of this agricultural revolution was marked by a significant increase in world population. More lands had to be tilled as food consumption increased and soils became depleted. Larger and larger areas and more and more regions were subject to agricultural exploitation as a result of continually expanding populations and the growing impoverishment of older croplands. Crop failures frequently resulted in disastrous famines; disease ravaged urban populations everywhere. Once again the challenge was met, this time with the industrial revolution and the rise of modern medicine and public health measures. As a consequence, disease has been reduced to a social inconvenience insofar as the survival of a society is concerned, and our capacity to produce and transport food has reached astronomical dimensions. But once again man's own proficiency is plaguing him: his agricultural feats are exceeded by his capacity to reproduce —and thereby consume the food faster than he can produce it.

The most recent exercise in human genius, like the others, carries its burdens of perplexities. Chief among these is that we hunters without prey have achieved a new station in life. We have attained the status of permanent residents. No longer can we abandon our mistakes and move on to virgin land. Now we must be very careful about the mistakes we make: we have no other option than to live with them.

SUGGESTED READINGS

BAKER, P. T., and J. S. WEINER (eds.): *The Biology of Human Adaptability,* London: Oxford University Press, 1966. This and the following four works are a collection of essays on human adaptation.

BEJEMA, C. J. (ed.): *Natural Selection in Human Populations,* New York: John Wiley & Sons, Inc., 1971.

COHEN, Y. A. (ed.): *Man In Adaptation: The Biosocial Background,* Chicago: Aldine Publishing Company, 1968.

COHEN, Y. A. (ed.): *Man In Adaptation: The Cultural Present,* Chicago: Aldine Publishing Company, 1968.

MONTAGU, M. F. A. (ed.): *Culture: Man's Adaptive Dimension,* New York: Oxford University Press, 1968.

RENSCH, B.: *Evolution Above the Species Level,* New York: Columbia University Press, 1959. This book and the following three books tend to view evolution broadly from the standpoint of direction and outcome and have become classics in this area.

SIMPSON, G. G.: *Major Features of Evolution,* New York: Columbia University Press, 1953.

SIMPSON, G. G.: *The Meaning of Evolution,* New Haven, Conn.: Yale University Press, 1967.

TAX, SOL (ed.): *The Evolution of Life: Its Origin, History, and Future,* vol. I of *Evolution After Darwin,* Chicago: University of Chicago Press, 1960. This volume is a collection of essays.

WALLACE, B., and A. SRB: *Adaptation,* Englewood Cliffs, N.J.: Prentice-Hall, Inc., 1964. An attractive small book on the nature of adaptation, giving diverse examples of how species are adapted to their environment and the evolutionary mechanisms responsible for these adaptations.

REVIEW QUESTIONS

1 The evolution of new species is strictly a matter of chance and opportunity. Name and explain three types of opportunity that must be open to the evolution of any new species. Cite an example of two of these.

2 What is meant by adaptive radiation? Explain the mechanisms responsible for adaptive radiation. Trace an adaptive radiation that began in the Oligocene from which the hominid line evolved.

3 Sooner or later all species become extinct. Give two probable causes for extinction and illustrate each with an example. Since extinction is the ultimate fate of every species, how do you account for the fact that evolution seems to produce an increasing variety of organisms?

4 Why is it that once a major evolutionary step has been made it cannot be duplicated and it cannot be reversed?

5 What is convergent evolution and what brings it about? Compare and contrast convergence and parallelism and give an example of each.

6 Critically evaluate and discuss the following statement: "Biological diversity and adaptation are terms that refer to the same thing."

7 Show how variations in human body build appear to be adapted to climate in two different ways. Cite examples for each.

8 Variations in human nose form correlate well with climatic differences throughout the world. What kinds of noses appear to be characteristic of what kinds of climate? Theoretically, how is each nose form adaptive to a particular climate?

9 What is meant by somatogenetic adaptability or acclimatization? Describe a human adaptation involving both acclimatization and specific traits developed through natural selection. Point out evidence documenting both forms of adaptation.

10 Write a brief essay on the adaptive nature of human culture.

11 Write a brief essay on the maladaptive features of human culture.

I could see that the Wasichus did not care for each other
  the way our people did before the nation's hoop was broken.
They would take everything from each other if they could,
  and so there were some who had more of everything than they could use,
  while crowds of people had nothing at all and maybe were starving.
They had forgotten that the earth was their mother.

BLACK ELK

SECTION III

The words are those of an Oglala Sioux medicine man recalling, near the end of his life, his first encounter with what is now the distinguishing feature of the civilization that had destroyed his people—the great city. Reading them in the context of today's crises of population, resources, and environment, we can see that Black Elk's words are deceptively simple. Throughout history, urbanization and technological development have, with few exceptions, been inseparable processes, each nurturing the other. In the century and a half since the beginning of the industrial revolution, they have created a civilization of previously unimaginable wealth and power. At the same time, they have brought with them problems of previously unimaginable complexity and danger to our survival—economic, political, moral, biologic. These problems are not limited to the *Wasichus,* the white men that destroyed Black Elk's nation. They are now the burden, in varying degrees, of all the nations of the earth. And ultimately they involve the relationship of our species to the earth that gave it life.

But what are the major problems that confront us and threaten our future as a species? This is the last of the three questions that this book sets out to answer.

The question is an ecological one in that it involves our interrelationships with our environment. Chapter 11 introduces the principles and concepts of ecology, providing a frame of reference against which human ecological problems can be viewed. Chapters 12 and 13 focus directly on the most pressing of human ecological problems, overpopulation; first from the standpoint of the nature of human population and its growth, and then from the standpoint of what overpopulation is, what its consequences are in human suffering, and how it may be prevented. The last two chapters are devoted to the major environmental problems which have arisen as a result of overpopulation and the growth economy it nurtures. Chapter 14 considers the problem of resource depletion and waste. Chapter 15 deals with pollution and concludes the section, and the book, with a discussion of how humanity may resolve its ecological crises.

HUMAN ECOLOGY

ELEVEN

ECOLOGY:
Basic Concepts and Principles

In Section I we focused on the question, Who are we? In doing so, we considered our biologic relationships with other primates and described in broad perspective the essential qualities that set us apart as a unique species. In Section II we addressed the question, Whence did we come and how did it happen? There we discussed the evolutionary history of hominids and showed how intimately that history was linked to the evolution of primates in general. We also considered the mechanisms of evolu-tion and their ultimate outcomes. Since the consequences of evolution are either extinc-tion or adaptation, we discussed the status of human adaptiveness. We noted that our species' basic adaptation for survival has been its cul-ture.

As pointed out at the end of the last chapter, herein lies the great irony of human-kind's present condition. As a result of cul-ture, the human species lives in an environ-ment largely of its own making. The problem of human survival is no longer a matter of adapting through organic or cultural evolution to changes in the *natural* environment. At this point in human evolution, survival depends primarily upon humanity's ability to meet the challenges of the cultural environment it has created: overpopulation, pollution, and the excessive exploitation of natural resources. Culture, which evolved as the human species' good servant and friend, is fast becoming its master and enemy. It is our master in the sense that it is served *by* us to a greater extent than it serves us. Often it creates more problems than it solves. Many of these problems are not only beginning to threaten our well-being but also the future of our species and that of many others. Indeed, as we shall see, a great many species have already become extinct as a result of human technology. In this sense, culture is becoming not only an unprotective master but an enemy as well.

As we learned in Section II, however, this is not the first time that our species has been confronted with a cultural crisis. Upper Paleolithic herd-hunters created an environmental crisis by bringing about the extinction of most of the large mammalian species that were the favored source of meat. This predicament was finally resolved by the agricultural revolution which, in turn, ultimately led to other environmental crises in the form of overpopulation, famine, disease, and the abuse of natural resources. Solutions to many of these problems were found during the industrial revolution, but this, in its turn, has left our species once again suffering from a culture that is becoming maladaptive. A study of human evolution teaches us that we are creatures of crisis. The human species creates cultures from which problems ultimately spring. Solutions to these problems have been found in cultural change. This pattern of our past does not necessarily mean that the human animal will successfully resolve its present crisis, but it gives cause for hope rather than despair.

Hope resides in the determination of humanity to find solutions to its cultural crisis.

This determination will depend — as it probably always has — upon understanding. In this instance, the human species must learn that a culture is successful only if it is built on an understanding and appreciation of how it relates to and depends upon the larger world environment of which it is an interacting part. Inasmuch as this understanding is crucial to continued human existence, we will concentrate our attention on those intricate day-to-day interrelationships of the human animal and its total environment. The study of these interrelationships is called *human ecology*. It is with the challenging field of human ecology that we will be concerned in the remaining chapters of this book.

In this chapter we shall consider the nature of ecological relationships in general. In the following four chapters we will examine some of the ecological problems humans have made for themselves and other forms of life. Equipped with this knowledge we should be in a position to suggest some remedies for these problems. Such remedies will hold promise to the extent that they are based upon a keen appreciation of the kind of creature we are. As we saw in Section I, much remains to be learned about human social behavior. Our ability to make intelligent judgments in our approach to cultural problems will depend greatly on having a better understanding of human motivation, the extent of human needs both biological and social, and the nature of altruistic, sociosexual, and aggressive behavior.

Since our concern in these final chapters will center on the interrelationships of the human animal with its surroundings, we must clarify what is meant by the nebulous term *environment*. This is done best by introducing the concept of the *ecosystem*, a term used by ecologists to represent functional units among the vast assemblages of living populations over the earth. An ecosystem includes all the organisms in a given area together with the physical environment in which they live. The diverse populations of organisms in that area, known as the *biotic community*, interact with one another and with their nonliving environment as an ecological system or ecosystem.

THE ECOSYSTEM

The life of every organism is closely associated with its surroundings. This association is so intimate that the physical environment itself is influenced by the life it supports, often profoundly. In the terrestrial biotic communities frequented by man, green plants both large and small affect the amount of sunlight that reaches the ground surface and the moisture in the soil below. They bind the soil against erosion, prevent excessive runoff and flooding, break the force of the wind, and temper the climate of woodlands. Their roots facilitate soil building by breaking rocks into smaller pieces. The excreta of animals and the dead remains of all organisms contribute organic matter to the soil. Burrowing animals till and aerate the earth, and bacteria convert the nitrogen of soil air into plant nutrient (nitrates). Examples could be added endlessly. The physical environment is as much affected by the life it supports as the biotic community is influenced by its physical surroundings.

We should also stress the importance of the biologic environment to members of a biotic community. Every species in an ecosystem has interrelationships either directly or indirectly with every other species in the community. Many of these associations are quite intimate, resulting in biologic interdependencies of an extremely complex nature as we will soon see.

Therefore, it is with good reason that ecologists speak of an ecosystem as the unit of ecological interaction. A marine estuary, a stream, a meadow, a pine forest, a woodland-savanna, or a desert are ecosystems. Each is distinguished by certain physical conditions. Each also is characterized by a biologic community of plants and animals that live there. The physical surroundings have an important

bearing on the kinds of species in the community just as that community, in turn, modifies in significant ways the character of the physical setting and materially influences its own species composition.

In short, an ecosystem is a feedback system of interdependent, interacting physical and biological components. This is shown by the manner in which energy, captured by green plants from sunlight, flows through the community, and by the processes whereby inorganic nutrients required by those plants are continuously recycled through the community in a sequence of use and reuse.

Community energy flow

All organisms process energy. Animals get this energy either by eating green plants or by eating other animals. The green plant captures energy from sunlight. By means of photosynthesis, it uses the energy it has collected to drive a series of chemical reactions whose end products are the energy-rich compounds like sugars and fats that it requires for survival. In other words, photosynthetic plants convert solar energy to chemical energy locked in organic compounds and use some of this energy for their own requirements. Green plants also store the energy that will be available for community support. A host of animals uses this energy either directly or indirectly. Green plants, therefore, are called *producers*.[1] One way or another, all other community members are *consumers*.

The herbivores that prey on green plants are, in turn, preyed upon by carnivores; omnivores feed on both (and on green plants), and parasites feed on all of these as well as on one another. Scavengers dine on dead carcasses and what they do not eat joins the accumulating bulk of fallen leaves, dead vegetation, and animal excrement. Even this does not go uncon-

---

[1] Certain (chemotrophic) bacteria are able to synthesize organic compounds by using the energy released in the oxidation of iron compounds, hydrogen sulfide, and ammonia. Their role is quite minor in total organic synthesis.

sumed for it supports a host of *decomposers:* molds, toadstools, and other fungi; invertebrate animals such as termites and earthworms; and vast multitudes of bacteria which convert organic matter to nitrates, phosphates, and a variety of other inorganic nutrients. Finally, bringing the chain of interdependencies full circle, these inorganic nutrients may be taken up by the roots of green plants and incorporated into the energy-rich compounds upon which the entire community depends.

At every level in this enormous cycle of "consume and be consumed"—whether it be the herbivores, the carnivores, the parasites, the scavengers, or the decomposers—competition within and between species tends to assure efficiency of the energy harvest. The energy captured by the producers flows down a descending cascade from prey to predator to decomposer until it has been drained away. All the while the producers continue to reinvest in more solar energy. As long as community balance is not disturbed, a steady state is maintained by the mutual interdependencies of the consumers and the consumed.

The flow of energy (food) from producers to consumers follows a *food chain,* that is, a specific sequence of species that fill the roles of producer, consumer, and decomposer. It is in a simple food chain that community energy flow can best be understood.

The energy dynamics of food chains

The classic example of a sinple food chain is illustrated in Fig. 11-1. Grass, the producer, is eaten by grasshoppers, the primary consumers. Grasshoppers are fed upon by frogs, the secondary consumers which, in turn, are prey for snakes, the tertiary consumers. At the top of the chain is the hawk which, as the quaternary consumer, dines on snakes.

This sequence of species from grass to hawk represents one food chain. Many parasitic consumers are found all along this chain as well as hosts of decomposers; none of these are indicated in the illustration since they represent a web of additional interrelated food chains.

Energy flow through a community involves numerous interrelated food chains and may be quite complex (Fig. 11-2). Regardless of complexity, however, community food chains can be segregated into their respective nutritional or *trophic levels.* Trophic level 1 includes all the producers; trophic level 2, all the herbivores (primary consumers); trophic level 3, the predators which prey on herbivores (secondary consumers); trophic level 4, the predators who live on level-3 predators (tertiary consumers), and so on, depending on the community.

In any transformation of energy from one form to another, as in the use of energy to perform work there always is a loss of useful energy which usually escapes as heat.[2] Automobiles lose a great deal of the potential chemical energy in gasoline through the loss of heat into the walls of the combustion chamber, not to mention the frictional heat produced by moving parts. The energy driving the car forward is a fraction of the total energy in the fuel used. Similarly, there is a progressive loss of energy from the community as energy is transformed from each trophic level to the next. The energy driving the metabolic "machinery" of grasshoppers also is only a fraction of the total energy in the grass these insects eat.

When we apply this principle to a food chain, we arrive at some surprising results. If frogs are to meet their minimal energy needs, they must consume many times that minimum as chemical energy in the form of grasshopper bodies. The same principle applies to the snakes that eat frogs and the hawks that prey on the snakes. Although predator-prey relationships vary as to the exact amount of energy lost to the predator, a 90 percent loss figure is typical. In other words, if we equate energy in terms of weight, about 10 kilograms (22 pounds) of grass are required to produce 1 kilogram of grasshoppers. Similarly, 10 kilograms of grasshoppers would be needed to produce 1 kilogram of frogs. To generate 1 kilogram of hawk, therefore, would require 10 kilograms

---

[2] This principle is known as the *Second Law of Thermodynamics.*

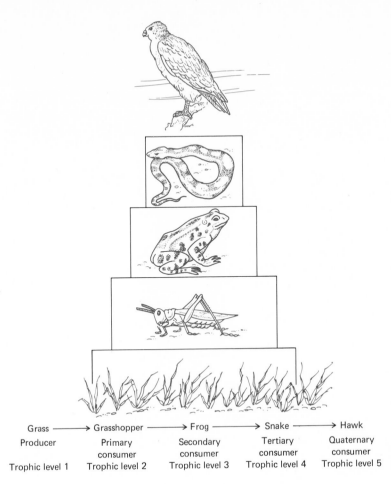

Grass ——→ Grasshopper ——→ Frog ——→ Snake ——→ Hawk

| Producer | Primary consumer | Secondary consumer | Tertiary consumer | Quaternary consumer |

Trophic level 1   Trophic level 2   Trophic level 3   Trophic level 4   Trophic level 5

FIGURE 11-1
A single food chain from grass to hawk. The pyramidal shape indicates the loss of energy at each successive trophic level.

of snakes, 100 kilograms of frogs, 1,000 kilograms of grasshoppers, and 10,000 kilograms of grass. The energy loss is so great because only 10 percent of food energy passes from one trophic level to the next and there are four trophic levels between the hawk and the producer (grass). That means that only one-hundredth of 1 percent of the energy in the grass reaches the hawk ($0.1 \times 0.1 \times 0.1 \times 0.1 = 0.0001$).

It is because of this decrease in usable energy from one trophic level to the next that Fig. 11-1 is shaped like a pyramid. Every food chain and every community is characterized by what is called a *pyramid of energy*. This is illustrated in Fig. 11-3 for two different ecosystems.

The secondary consumers of a lake ecosystem in Minnesota represented less than 2 percent of the energy equivalent of the producers. Measuring energy indirectly in terms of mass, the total bulk of tertiary consumers in an eel-grass community in the North Sea was just a little over six-hundredths of 1 percent of the total mass of producers.

Because of man's omnivorous diet, these considerations are particularly relevant to human populations. Usually we can participate at several levels along most food chains capable of supporting a large animal as is shown by the diet of Australian aborigines in Fig. 11-4. We will derive the greatest amount of energy from our food sources when we play the role of pri-

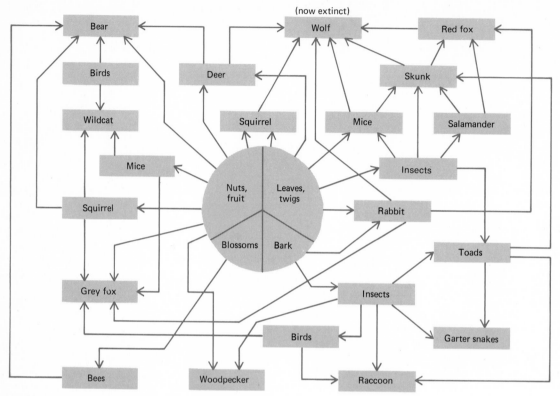

FIGURE 11-2
Community food chains in a deciduous forest in Illinois.
Interrelated community food chains are called a food web.
[*After V. E. Shelford, Ecological Monographs, vol. 21, copyright*
© *Ecological Society of America, Duke University Press,*
Durham, N. C., 1951.]

mary consumer. Eating too much meat is not only unsound from the standpoint of health but is also wasteful of food resources. The people of the Netherlands turned this knowledge to their benefit during the second World War when they were suffering from food shortages. They reduced their poultry flocks, which were fed largely on grain, by 75 percent. The grain that would have gone into raising these excess birds went directly for human consumption, supporting about 10 times as many lives as it would have, had it been diverted through

chickens to the consumer.

This same principle applies to the use of energy for any purpose. A human community, for example, that drives its electric generators by natural gas, wastes energy when it elects to cook its meals on electric rather than gas stoves.

The cycling of inorganic materials

Organisms are known to require at least 25 different chemical elements to sustain life. Some of these, like calcium, carbon, and nitrogen, are used in large amounts; others, such as iodine, iron, and manganese, are needed only in minute quantities. In fact, some of them, like copper and selenium, are poisonous if taken in by organisms in any but minute quantities. All

Energy in gram-calories per square centimeter

Trophic level 3	(Consumer 2)	1.3
Trophic level 2	(Consumer 1)	7.0
Trophic level 1	Producers	70.3

A Pyramid of energy in a Minnesota lake community

Mass in thousands of tons

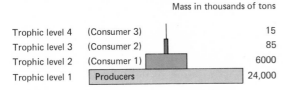

Trophic level 4	(Consumer 3)	15
Trophic level 3	(Consumer 2)	85
Trophic level 2	(Consumer 1)	6000
Trophic level 1	Producers	24,000

B Pyramid of mass in a North Sea eelgrass community

FIGURE 11-3
Pyramids of energy (*A*) and mass (*B*). In (*A*), the energy stored in a given trophic level is measured as the total gram-calories per square centimeter of lake surface in all the organisms in that trophic level (a gram-calorie is 0.001 kilogram calorie or "diet calorie"). Note that the secondary consumers of trophic level 3 had less than 2 percent of the energy stored in the producers of trophic level 1 (1.3 versus 70.3 gram-calories per square centimeter). In (*B*), trophic levels are compared on the basis of the total weight of all organisms in a given level. Consumer 2 is represented by invertebrate animals and small fish, consumer 3 by larger fish and predatory birds. [*After E. P. Odum, Fundamentals of Ecology, Saunders, Philadelphia, 1959.*]

these substances, regardless of the amounts used, are routed through the ecosystem in a continuous cycle of use and reuse. Taken from the soil, water, or air by producers, they pass through consumers and decomposers back to the medium from which they came.

The course that these materials follow through the ecosystem varies from one inorganic nutrient to another. The carbon and nitrogen cycles are representative of the general nature of their ecologic itinerary.

The carbon cycle

Producers obtain their inorganic carbon from atmospheric carbon dioxide (CO_2), as indicated in Fig. 11-5. The atmospheric supply is augmented by a vast oceanic reservoir principally in the form of bicarbonate. Some of the CO_2 carbon is converted into organic compounds—that is, chemical compounds contain-

FIGURE 11-4
The menu of Australian aborigines of the southwestern coastal region a century ago. From the ecosystems which these people occupied, all the food was gathered which could be economically extracted and prepared with the Paleolithic tools available. Food items are listed according to the trophic level of the human consumer. [*After J. B. Birdsell, The American Naturalist, vol. 87, 1953.*]

Man = Consumer 1 (herbivore)		Man = Consumer 2 (carnivore 1)		Man = Consumer 3 (carnivore 2)	
Food	Kinds	Food	Kinds	Food	Kinds
Roots	29	Kangaroos	6	Opossum	2
Fruit	4	Medium-sized marsupials	5	Dingos	1
Cycad nuts	2	Marsupial rats and mice	9	Whale	1
				Seals	2
Legume seeds	Several	Turtles	3		
				Iguanas and lizards	7
Ice plant	2	Fish	29	Snakes	8
Fungus	7	Marine mollusks	All except oysters	Frogs	11
Gum	4				
Manna	2	Freshwater mollusks	4		
Protea flowers	Several	Grubs	4		

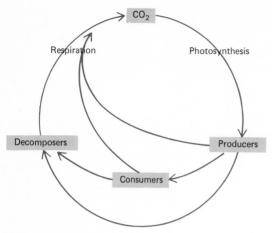

FIGURE 11-5

The carbon cycle. Producers such as green plants convert CO_2 into organic compounds by photosynthesis. Producers break down some of these compounds, releasing energy and CO_2 (respiration). Consumers (herbivores, parasites) also use (consume) some of the organic compounds synthesized by producers, releasing CO_2 through respiration. Organic compounds remaining in dead organic matter (leaf litter, animal excreta, dead bodies) is used by decomposers (bacteria, fungi). The CO_2 released by the respiration of decomposers, consumers, and producers is used again by producers in photosynthesis.

ing the element carbon—by producers.[3] These compounds serve not only the producers but also the consumers who feed on them and upon one another. The organic carbon still tied up in plant litter, animal wastes, and dead bodies is used by the decomposers. In satisfying their energy needs, the combined action of all these creatures is to reconvert high-energy organic compounds to low-energy CO_2.

This process, called *respiration,* releases the chemically bound energy in organic compounds by breaking them down into smaller compounds. One of the latter, CO_2, contains the carbon that was taken up by photosynthesis.

[3] Organic compounds, such as carbohydrates, fats, proteins, and nucleic acids, are compounds in which the element carbon is the basic "building block."

Thus, carbon is recycled to the atmosphere from which it was taken.

When the dead bodies or skeletons of organisms escape total decay, carbon is removed from the carbon cycle and stored as coal, petroleum, natural gas, limestone, etc. Modern man is now freeing the energy stored in these materials by burning fossil fuels, with the result that the percentage of CO_2 in the earth's atmosphere appears to be increasing. This may affect world climates in complex ways. In the first place, CO_2 absorbs heat more efficiently than oxygen or nitrogen, the predominant atmospheric gases. Increasing concentrations of atmospheric CO_2 might therefore have a so-called "greenhouse effect," resulting in a rise in atmospheric temperature and warmer world climates. This, in turn, could lead to accelerated melting of the polar ice caps and rising sea levels.

On the other hand, the burning of fossil fuels also increases the amount of particulate matter in the atmosphere. This would tend to counter the greenhouse effect by reducing the amount of solar radiation that reaches the earth's surface.

The nitrogen cycle

Ordinarily, we think of the atmosphere as lying above the ground surface. There is a small but significant part of the atmosphere, however, that is found between soil particles, to which we have already referred as *soil air.* Most of the atmosphere, about 79 percent, is nitrogen. Chemically it is a relatively inactive substance yet is required in large amounts by all organisms because it is an essential ingredient in proteins, nucleic acids, many fats, and a variety of other organic compounds. The only organisms capable of converting soil-air nitrogen into nitrogen-containing compounds that producers can utilize are certain soil-inhabiting bacteria and algae. Some of these bacteria live in the roots of plants belonging to the pea, or legume, family. These microorganisms convert nitrogen to ammonia, while still another group of bacteria transforms ammonia into nitrate.

From the ammonia and nitrate provided

by these microorganisms, producers synthesize proteins and other nitrogenous compounds which follow routes comparable to the carbon cycle (Fig. 11-6). The producers are fed upon by the consumers, and the dead remains of both are cycled through hosts of decomposers which, in turn, die and are decomposed by a new generation of decomposers. In this web of food chains, organically bound nitrogen is broken down into ammonia which, in turn, is converted to nitrates. At this juncture, inorganic nitrate may be recycled to the producers or transformed by certain bacteria to nitrogen gas, completing the cycle where it began.

ECOLOGIC SUCCESSION

The ecosystem is, as we have noted, a highly dynamic complex of interdependent organisms and events. The very dynamism of this system carries with it the potential for change because the community almost continuously alters its physical environment; the latter, through climatic or geologic irregularities like drought or volcanism, may also modify the community. For example, when sun-loving trees invade a mountain meadow, the shade they cast may interfere with the growth of young trees. This may permit the gradual intrusion of shade-tolerant species which, when mature, block the sun's rays to such an extent that the earlier arrivals, the sun-loving types, can no longer survive. In most ecosystems, the biologic interactions of the community so alter the physical conditions that the community itself is transformed. One community tends to clear the way for another, resulting in an *ecologic succession* of communities. Climate and soil have a great deal to do with determining the species make-up of these successional communities.

A relatively shallow mountain lake, for example, may be converted over a period of two to four centuries to a pine forest (Fig. 11-7). Sediment and the dead remains of aquatic vegetation gradually accumulate along the lake mar-

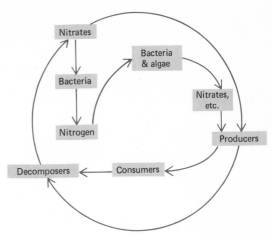

FIGURE 11-6
The nitrogen cycle.

gins, slowly transforming formerly shallow shoals into a meadowlike bog of cattails and bulrushes (*B*). The organic residue from this growth of marginal plants is added to by the remains of aquatic plants like pondweeds and pond lilies, and the bog continues to grow at the expense of the lake (*C*). Finally, the lake disappears entirely, replaced by a meadow which, in the course of time, may be invaded itself by sun-loving coniferous trees (*D*). If the area we have described were located in the Sierra Nevada Mountains of California, the pine forest community would continue as a relatively stable one unless the ecosystem were disturbed by lumbering, fire, or some other external agency. The comparative stability of such communities has earned them the name of *climax* communities, and the ecosystems of which each is a part is said to be *mature*.

Evidence of ecologic succession is visible almost everywhere. An interesting historical example is found in the New England states where stone walls, built by our pioneering forebears, extend into the thick deciduous forests of the region. At the time these walls were built, they enclosed fields and pastures. As the early farmers and ranchers abandoned their

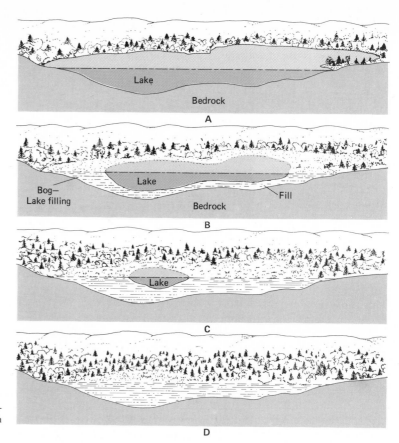

FIGURE 11-7
The conversion of a shallow mountain lake to a pine forest through ecologic succession (see text).

land, fields that had been cultivated or grazed began to undergo a secondary succession toward the community that had been there in the first place, a climax forest of beech trees and maples.

Figure 11-8 summarizes a study on the general pattern of secondary succession on abandoned farmland in the southeastern United States.[4] Bare fields are invaded by annual weeds —the pioneer species—in the first year, followed by grasses and different weeds in the second year. Grass becomes the dominant vege-

tation until about the tenth year when shrubs start to invade the area and become the dominant plant form. Over this 10-year period the soil has been progressively enriched by accumulating plant litter and increasing populations of soil microorganisms. Pine seedlings make their appearance, and eventually the shrubs are replaced by a pine forest. Pine seedlings of the southeastern United States, however, do not grow well in deep shade, and the way is now paved for the intrusion of shade-tolerant trees, which in this case happen to be hickories and oaks. In something over a century, ecologic succession progresses from bare ground to a climax hardwood forest community. Throughout

[4] Eugene P. Odum, *Ecology*, New York: Holt, Rinehart and Winston, Inc., 1963, p. 83.

FIGURE 11-8
The general pattern of ecologic succession on abandoned farmland in the southeastern United States. *Top,* plant succession; bottom, some of the accompanying changes in the perching (passerine) bird population. [*Modified from E. P. Odum, after D. W. Johnston and E. P. Odum, 1956.*]

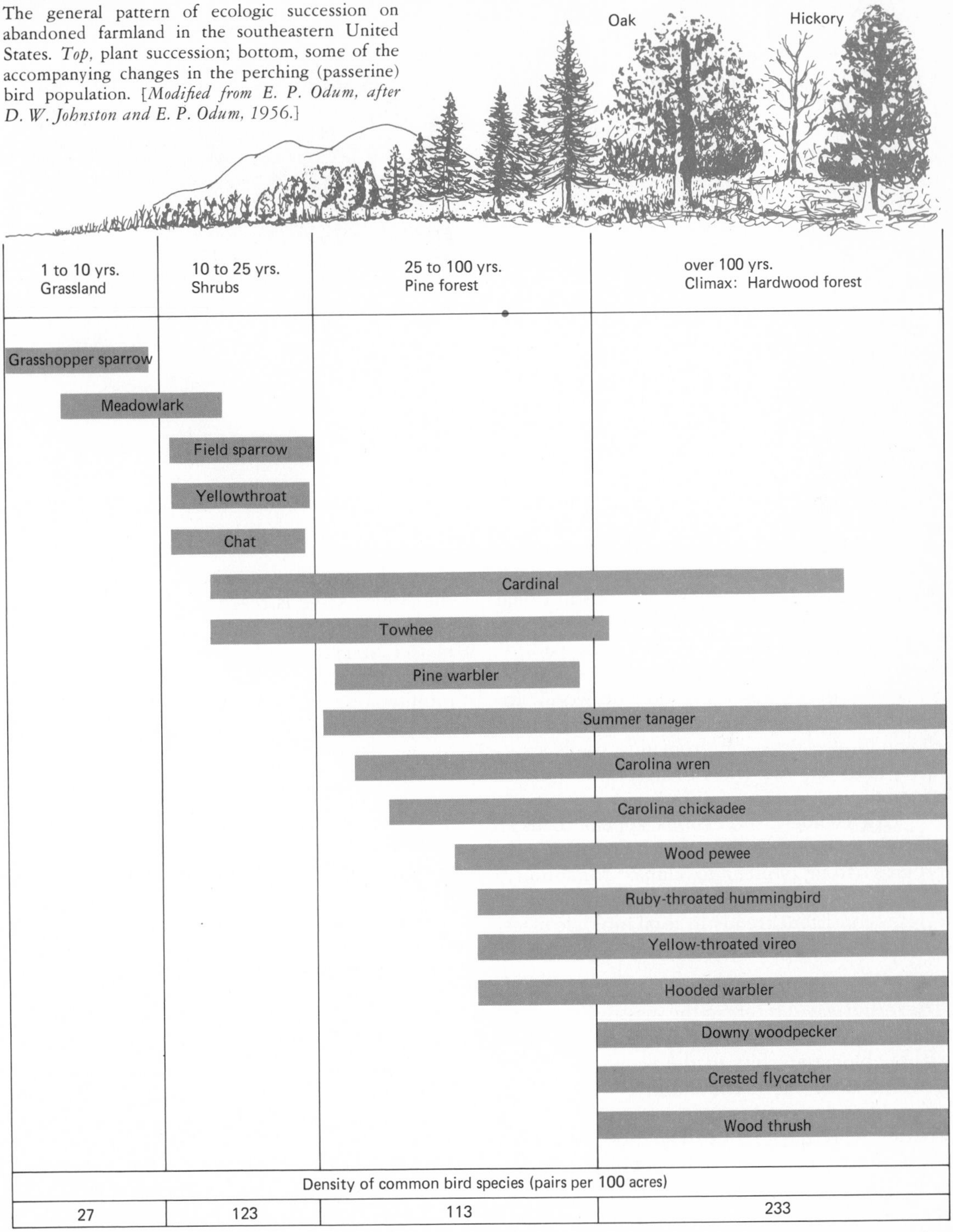

1 to 10 yrs. Grassland	10 to 25 yrs. Shrubs	25 to 100 yrs. Pine forest	over 100 yrs. Climax: Hardwood forest
Grasshopper sparrow			
Meadowlark			
	Field sparrow		
	Yellowthroat		
	Chat		
	Cardinal		
	Towhee		
	Pine warbler		
	Summer tanager		
	Carolina wren		
	Carolina chickadee		
	Wood pewee		
	Ruby-throated hummingbird		
	Yellow-throated vireo		
	Hooded warbler		
	Downy woodpecker		
	Crested flycatcher		
	Wood thrush		

Density of common bird species (pairs per 100 acres)

27	123	113	233

the entire transformation, changes occur in the animal community that parallel those taking place among plants. The successive modifications that occur among populations of perching (passerine) birds are shown in Fig. 11-8, from such pioneer species as the grasshopper sparrow to climax species like the wood thrush.

The consequence of ecologic succession

The details of ecologic succession vary from place to place and even from year to year in the same place. On the other hand, there are many consistencies in the phenomenon. Widely scattered regions of the earth with similar climatic and physiographic features, for example, tend to support climax communities whose dominant life forms are remarkably alike even though the species may be entirely different. The mature grasslands of the western United States, of Argentina, and of Northern Australia represent widely separated successions which have converged on a common constitutional type, namely grasses of some kind, as the predominant plant form. The same can be said for the rain forests, the coniferous forests, and the temperate deciduous forests of the world. Indeed, successional convergence is observable in all kinds of ecosystems from tide pools, estuaries, marshes, and lakes to deserts and arctic tundras.

All ecologic successions appear to have several operative features in common as they progress from pioneer to climax community. All successions of whatever form seem to entail certain consistent trends in total biologic mass, species diversity, and energy flow.

Total biologic mass (biomass)

The term *biomass* refers to the mass or weight of all the organisms in a given unit area; in this instance, biomass refers to the weight of all organisms in the biotic community.

As succession progresses, biomass increases. This is evident in Fig. 11-8 by the increase in the number of perching birds from 27 pairs per 40.5 hectares (100 acres) in the pioneer grassland to 233 pairs in the climax forest.

The increase in biomass continues until the climax stage is reached, at which time total biomass becomes stabilized. The dead organic matter or *detritus* of the community also continues to grow in bulk until the climax community appears.

The increase in biomass occurs as a result of the accumulation of many kinds of organic materials during succession (leaf litter, animal excreta, etc.). Growing amounts of organic matter contribute to increasing populations of soil microorganisms, larger quantities of plant nutrients, and greater photosynthetic production by plants.

Species diversity

As succession takes place, there is a tendency for the number of species to increase as one kind of community gives way to the next. This can be seen in Fig. 11-8 by counting the number of some common bird species in each of the four communities; the pioneer grassland has but 2 common species of perching birds, whereas there are 6 in the shrub community, 10 in the pine forest, and 12 in the climax community of hardwoods. As a rule, colonizing (pioneer) species are infrequent visitors to

FIGURE 11-9
The East African cattle egret, *Bubulcus ibis*, has a commensal relationship with domestic cattle and game species like the Cape buffalo, *Syncerus caffer*, shown here. The bird either rides on the herbivores or walks along beside them, eating the insects flushed up as the mammals graze.

climax communities and often are conspicuously absent. This is the case with the pioneering grasshopper sparrow and meadowlark in Fig. 11-8. Among species common to intermediate stages in a succession, occasionally some are encountered with broader ecologic niches than others, which enables them to participate in several successive communities, such as the cardinal in the illustration.

The increase in the number of species and in species diversity reflects additions to the food chains in the community. Additions to community food chains develop from the creation of new ecologic niches which arise as a result of the growing biomass during succession.

Symbiosis During late successional stages, food chains involving intimate interrelationships between participating organisms become more common. Any close association between different species is called *symbiosis* (Greek *sym*, "together"; Greek *bio*, "life"). Symbiotic relationships include three kinds of associations. *Commensalism* is a symbiotic association in which one of the participating species benefits while the other is neither benefited nor harmed. The relationship between cattle egrets

and large herbivorous mammals is a commensal one (Fig. 11-9). *Mutualism* is a symbiotic relationship in which both participating species benefit, as in the association between yellow baboons and impalas (Fig. 11-10). There is also a mutualistic relationship between humans and their intestinal bacteria. Billions of bacteria normally living among the contents of our large intestine depend upon us for their food and in return they synthesize four vitamins[5] which are absorbed into our body. *Parasitism* is an association in which one participant benefits at the other's expense, as in the case of the malarial parasite of human red blood cells discussed in Section II. Another parasite, the roundworm *Trichinella*, infects about 20 percent of the American population. This parasite, found principally in swine and man, lodges in voluntary muscle and reaches its human host through improperly processed or poorly cooked pork. Hogs are infected by being fed uncooked garbage.

Symbiotic relationships commonly are

---

[5] Vitamin K and three B vitamins (biotin, folic acid, and pantothenic acid).

not as clear-cut as our terminology would imply. A parasite that harms its host only some of the time alternates between being a commensal and a parasite, whereas a commensal that occasionally takes advantage of its associate is a part-time parasite. On the other hand, if a commensal occasionally benefits its associate, commensalism becomes part-time mutualism. Once in a great while baboons may prey upon a newborn impala infant in which case mutualism is transformed into predation. One form of symbiosis can evolve into another, but in most cases where two or more species have had a symbiotic relationship over a long period of time, it usually is one in which none of the participants are harmed appreciably and at least one of them is benefited. It is of no advantage to the parasite to kill its host.

As a consequence, the kind of symbiotic relationships commonly encountered in mature communities are like those between Indian pipes, mushrooms, and pine trees. Many mushrooms are the reproductive bodies of soil fungi whose microscopic rootlike processes permeate the soil and penetrate into the roots of other plants, like pines. The rootlike processes of the fungus greatly increase the capacity of a pine tree to absorb nutrients from the soil and, in some cases, even secrete antibiotics to protect the tree against parasites. In exchange the fungus extracts sugar from the pine roots. A colorless flowering plant known as *Indian pipe* also may be involved in the association between fungus and pine. Its roots become invaded by the fungus so that it too receives nourishment from the pine via its fungal partner. The net result of such symbiotic food chains is that the survival potential of all participants has been enhanced rather than threatened through fuller utilization of available nutrients.

Energy flow

During the early stages of succession, the photosynthetic production of plants exceeds community consumption (respiration) by a considerable margin (Fig. 11-5). As a result, organic matter and biomass increase. Pioneering com-

munities have been called young communities or "young nature";[6] species with high rates of reproduction and growth are more likely to survive in the uncrowded conditions of early succession.[7] The hallmark of young communities is productivity because the synthesis of energy-rich organic compounds by their producers exceeds community consumption (community respiration). "Young nature" is, at the same time, unstable. Its food chains are relatively simple, and its producers often cannot survive biologic competition when population densities increase.

As succession advances and organic matter and biomass continue to accumulate, new food chains come into existence and older ones are added to by an increasing number of consumers and decomposers. More and more of the energy captured by producers is passed on to the rest of the community. Meanwhile, the producers have been changing too. Selection pressures that originally favored pioneer species with high rates of growth and reproduction have changed and now favor those species that grow slowly and are adapted to crowding.[8] Throughout succession, selection pressures seem to favor those communities with the greatest biomass possible within the limits imposed by available solar radiation and soil nutrients.

By the time a mature climax community has been reached, organic matter and biomass have increased to a maximum and a relatively stable equilibrium exists between community production and respiration. The community production of energy-rich organic compounds and the community consumption of these compounds approaches a ratio of 1:1. Food chains are vast webs of symbiotic dependencies most of which have their base in community detritus. Only a minor fraction of the total photosynthetic production is consumed in the living state by

[6] Eugene P. Odum, "The Strategy of Ecosystem Development," *Science*, vol. 164, Apr. 18, 1969, p. 263.
[7] R. H. MacArthur and E. O. Wilson, *Theory of Island Biogeography*, Chap. 11, Princeton, N. J.: Princeton University Press, 1967.
[8] Ibid.

FIGURE 11-10
Baboons, impala antelope, and zebras feeding together in East Africa. The keen sense of smell and hearing of the impala combined with the excellent vision of the baboon make it virtually impossible for a predator to approach unnoticed. Each species recognizes the other's call of alarm. [*Courtesy of Irven DeVore and Anthro-Photo, Cambridge, Mass.*]

herbivores and parasites.[9] Whereas young communities are productive and unstable, mature communities are protective and stable. As much as 90 percent or more of all energy flow maintains community stability. This flow starts in community detritus and passes through a web of food chains which involve a great diversity of microorganisms, plants, and animals engaged in decomposition, scavenging, predation, parasitism, commensalism, and mutualism. It is in these symbiotic food chains that nutrients like calcium, nitrogen, and phosphorus are cycled and conserved by the community. The rich accumulation of organic detritus holds and stores water, while the entire community protects its soil from wind and water erosion and tempers its climate.

THE ECOLOGY OF SPECIFIC POPULATIONS

Now that we have clarified what environment is, we are in a position to examine how a given

9 Odum, op. cit., p. 264.

species interacts with the environment of which it is a part. Rather than viewing the ecosystem as a whole, we will focus our attention on one population of the many populations that comprise a biologic community. In this way we can see the ecosystem in a new light, from the vantage point of a participating member within the system.

Ecologically, we may define a species as a population of organisms that is adapted to fill a particular ecologic niche. Its qualifications for this biologic profession include many anatomical, physiological, and behavioral adaptations. Chief among the behavioral adaptations of many species is the tendency for individual members to join into cooperative groups. Such aggregations can reinforce reproductive efficiency by bringing prospective mates together and even ensure survival under adverse conditions. A group of ducks, for example, will keep a small area of frozen pond clear of ice by their activity and body heat. Several nursing mice will combine their litters; this distributes their milk supply more equitably among the young. Often individuals in groups collaborate for the purpose of getting food or protecting themselves from predators. The pack-hunting wild dog of Africa (*Lycaon pictus*) has more food in its belly than it would if it were a solitary hunter (Fig. 11-11). Conversely, fewer baboons wind up inside the belly of a predator because of their well-organized troop structure. Examples of this sort are legion. Primates possess a rich repertory of collaborative behaviors to ensure survival.

Running counter to the forces that bind individuals of a species into cooperative groups is the strange paradox that these same individuals are *potentially* their own worst enemies. Often, the major enemy of a species is the constitutional character of the species itself. *Intraspecific competition,* the competition that exists between members of the same species, can be the most severely restrictive force any species may face. Since all members of a species share the same ecologic niche, their requirements are essentially the same. If a population grows to the point where one or more of these shared ecologic resources are in critically short supply, the consequences usually are swift and disastrous, and may even lead to self-extinction. *The ever-present and foremost problem of any species, man included, is the regulation of population size.* As a matter of fact, the expression "balance of nature" refers precisely to the many and varied, often ingenious, procedures by which the interacting populations of a biologic community are kept in equilibrium.

Population size and its regulation

Although the reproductive rates of different species vary, the number of births per unit of time always exceeds the number of deaths from old age alone. We discussed reproductive rate and efficiency in relation to natural selection early in Chap. 9. Reproducing adults tend to be

FIGURE 11-11
The pack-hunting wild dog of Africa (*Lycaon pictus*) has more food in its belly than it would have if it were a solitary hunter.

Genera-tion	Breeding population	Number of breeding couples	Number of births	Number of deaths	Total population	Years
1	200	100	400		600	30
2	400	200	800	200	1,200	60
3	800	400	1,600	400	2,400	90
4	1,600	800	3,200	800	4,800	120
5	3,200	1,600	6,400	1,600	9,600	150
10	102,400	51,200	204,800	51,200	307,200	300
15	3,276,800	1,638,400	6,553,600	1,638,400	9,830,400	450

outnumbered by their progeny, and this relationship persists generation after generation. Since the products of population growth also grow, population increase is potentially exponential if old age is the only cause of death. For example, suppose there were a hypothetical human population composed of 100 mated couples of young adults, as illustrated in Fig. 11-12. Suppose further that each couple had four children who survived to adulthood, and that these children were born during the first 30 years of their parents' lives. If we assume that a generation is 30 years and that all adults die between their thirty-first and sixtieth year, it can be seen that this population would have grown from 200 to almost 10 million in 15 generations (450 years).

If such a reproductive potential is limited solely by death from old age, a growth curve like that on the left in Fig. 11-13 will result. No natural undisturbed population grows in this manner because of certain restraints imposed by the limited resources of the environment and the demands made on those resources by other members of the biologic community. All these restraints, or *limiting factors,* combine in the form of *environmental resistance* to the uncontrolled reproductive potential of a population. Figure 11-13 illustrates how environmental resistance modifies the potential growth rate of a population of yeast cells. In this case, available nutrient acts as the limiting factor by gradually decelerating the growth rate until the number of yeast cells levels off. The S-shaped curve that results from the interaction of re-

FIGURE 11-12
Growth in a hypothetical human population, based on the following vital statistics: (*a*) beginning population of 200 young adults comprising 100 breeding couples, (*b*) each couple has 4 children who survive to adulthood, (*c*) a generation is 30 years and (*d*) all couples reproduce during their first 30 years of life and die between their thirty-first and sixtieth year. In the second generation, for example, the 200 breeding adults of the first generation died. This means that only 400 of the total population of generation 1, that is, the offspring, will make up the breeding population of generation 2. Similarly, the breeding population of generation 3 is the progeny of generation 2, and so on. After 15 generations and 450 years the total population would have grown from 200 to 9,830,400.

FIGURE 11-13
Population growth in yeast cells.

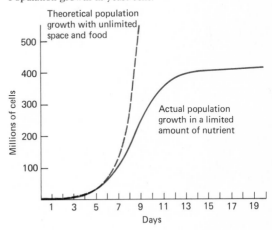

productive potential and environmental resistance is typical of population growth in an ecosystem. It is through this interaction that population size is tailored to the *environmental capacity* of an ecosystem, that is, the optimum number of individuals that the system can support indefinitely.

The nature of limiting factors

The particular nature of limiting factors varies with the species and the ecosystem. Insofar as land vertebrates are concerned, they commonly include quantity and quality of food and its apportionment throughout the year; the amount and distribution of water or succulent forage; areas for courtship, breeding, and the rearing of young; and so on. These necessities of life never are found in balanced proportions. Consequently, the weakest link or links in the long chain of requirements will be the limiting factors. A large herbivorous mammal that is part of an ecosystem which produces twice as much forage in the summer as in the winter will be limited to numbers the winter range can support. Even this number might be further reduced if the distribution of adequate watering sites rendered portions of the winter range inaccessible.

A case study in East Africa   Often, limiting factors operate in unexpected ways. A study of a grassland ecosystem in East Africa furnishes an interesting example.[10] Known as the Serengeti Ecological Unit, this ecosystem is located in Kenya and Tanzania and embraces 23,300 square kilometers (9,000 square miles)—about the area of Massachusetts (see Fig. 11-16). More than 90 percent of the mammalian biomass is composed of grazing hoofed animals; the producers are almost exclusively grasses and herbaceous plants. Three grazing species constitute the major share of primary consumers both from the standpoint of biomass and total numbers. Zebras (*Equus burchelli*), wildebeests or gnu (*Connochaetes taurinus*), and Thomson's

gazelles (*Gazella thomsoni*) have a combined population of about 700,000 and a total biomass of some 104,370 metric tons (Fig. 11-15).

One would expect that the three species compete with one another to the extent that they graze on common plant types. Competition between them, of whatever degree, would be at least one limiting factor regulating their respective populations. On the contrary, these animals do not compete with one another; the wildebeest is dependent upon the zebra for its food supply, and the little gazelle is reliant upon the wildebeest. The reasons for this have to do with digestive tracts and body size.

Wildebeests and gazelles, like cattle, are ruminants. The digestion of plant protein in such animals is very efficient, but it is also a relatively slow process. The zebra, like its close relative the horse, is a nonruminant. It extracts protein from its food at perhaps two-thirds the efficiency of a ruminant, but it does so in about one-half the time. As a result, zebras can live on forage that lacks sufficient protein to support ruminants, providing they can maintain a high food intake. Such low-protein diets exist on the Serengeti in the form of coarse vegetation, namely the stems of the taller grasses at the topmost level of the grass-herb layer (Figs. 11-14 and 11-15). Higher concentrations of protein are found in grass leaves and stems in the middle of this layer, with the highest concentration occurring at the lowermost level in the soft shoots and fruits of herbs and the tender young leaves of grass. On these higher-protein diets, the zebra's lower efficiency gives the ruminant the advantage. It is an advantage that can be exercised, however, only when grazing and trampling by zebras have made the middle level of the tall grass accessible.

The question of which ruminant is better adapted to harvest the forage layer exposed by grazing zebras involves body size. An average adult female wildebeest, at 163 kilograms (360 pounds), is about 75 percent as heavy as her zebra counterpart and at least 10 times heavier than the small female gazelle (Fig. 11-15). As a rule, metabolic rate increases as body size de-

[10] Richard H. V. Bell, "A Grazing Ecosystem in the Serengeti," *Scientific American*, July 1971, pp. 86–93.

FIGURE 11-14
The tall grass range in the northern sector of the Serengeti Ecological Unit. The car in the middleground is a Volkswagon minibus. Note giraffes in the background.

creases; the relative maintenance requirements for both protein and energy, *per unit of weight* over a given period, will be higher in a small species than in a big species. The absolute requirement *per animal* over a given time, however, will be considerably less.

These considerations have important ecological consequences. A Thomson's gazelle has two to four times the daily protein requirement of a wildebeest per unit of weight. If a grazing resource produces sufficient forage volume to support wildebeests, the small gazelle cannot compete. Such is the case in the middle level of the tall-grass layer. It is the wildebeest that harvests the forage layer left by the grazing zebras.

As wildebeests crop the grass layer shorter and shorter, they expose the relatively sparse production of the protein-rich region of small herbaceous fruits and tender young grasses. Now the absolute maintenance requirement of the small animal pays off. A Thomson's gazelle needs about one-fifth the amount of food required by a wildebeest. On a forage volume inadequate for the larger animal, the small antelope finds ample food to support a large population. Without the wildebeest, however, the gazelle would find its protein-rich fodder largely inaccessible, protected by an overlying layer of vegetation on which it could not survive.

These relationships are illustrated dramatically when these species make their seasonal migrations from the southern to the western to the northern and back to the southern sectors of the Serengeti (Fig. 11-16). Zebras always are the first to migrate. Wildebeest follow after a couple of months, and they in turn are followed, after a corresponding interval, by Thomson's gazelles.

These three grazing species are not competitors. Their coexistence in an area is not a limiting factor in curtailing population size. On the contrary, thinning of the zebra herds by disease or hunting would act as a powerful limiting factor contributing to the decline of the wildebeest population and that of the Thomson's gazelle as well.

Man also is involved in this situation in an unusual and complicated way. Undoubtedly, hominids have been a part of this ecosystem for several million years, beginning as primordial hunter-gatherers and ultimately becoming pastoral herders, farmers, and tourists. The present practice of range burning by the pastoral peoples of the Serengeti is an ancient one which apparently has tended to increase as well

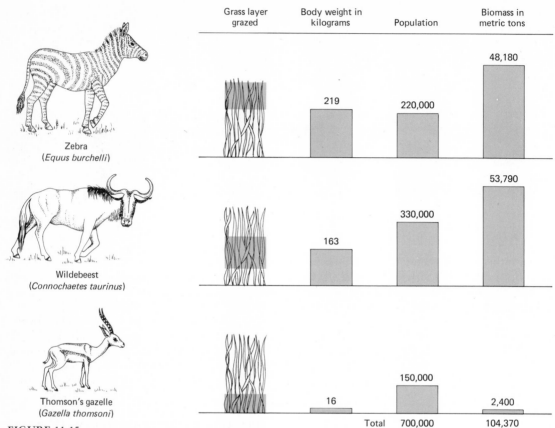

	Grass layer grazed	Body weight in kilograms	Population	Biomass in metric tons
Zebra (*Equus burchelli*)		219	220,000	48,180
Wildebeest (*Connochaetes taurinus*)		163	330,000	53,790
Thomson's gazelle (*Gazella thomsoni*)		16	150,000	2,400
		Total	700,000	104,370

FIGURE 11-15
On the basis of biomass and total numbers, the three species above constitute the major share of primary consumers on the Serengeti Ecological Unit. Over 90 percent of the mammalian biomass is made up of grazing hoofed mammals, and the producers are almost exclusively grasses and herbaceous plants. Body weight is that of an average adult female. [*Modified from R. H. V. Bell, "A Grazing Ecosystem in the Serengeti," Scientific American, July, 1971.*]

as to maintain short-grass areas. Interestingly, the largest populations of wild animals seem to be where man has grazed or is grazing domestic stock. Pastoral man has acted as a collaborating member of this ecosystem in a zebra-wildebeest-gazelle-man association. On the other hand, the plowing and fencing of more and more grassland to raise domestic crops is not only inter-

fering with the normal migratory movements of African mammals but is also reducing their population.

Now that we have some concept of the complex character of limiting factors, we are in a better position to investigate the manner in which population size is regulated in an ecosystem. Three basic agencies are operative: (1) predation and disease, (2) competition, and (3) self-regulatory devices.

Predation and disease
The interaction between predators and their prey is a sensitive interplay between their respective populations. Since this interaction

occurs at every trophic level in a biologic community, the overall effect is to regulate the size of all the interacting populations. In the simple food chain of *grass*———→*rabbit*———→*hawk,* each consumer is dependent upon its prey. If, because of abundant rainfall and a warm growing season, the grass crop is particularly luxuriant, the rabbit population can respond by an increase in the number and size of litters born.

FIGURE 11-16
The Serengeti Ecological Unit is naturally divided into three seasonal ranges: the southern sector is an expansive short grass plain with scant rainfall; the western sector has more rainfall and the grass is taller; the northern sector has the greatest rainfall and the tallest grasses. Zebras, wildebeests, and Thomson's gazelles occupy the southern sector during the wet season from March through May. At the beginning of the dry season they migrate to the western sector, grazing here from June through August. Toward the end of the dry season they migrate to the northern sector where they remain from September through February. Zebras always migrate first, followed later by wildebeests. Thomson's gazelles migrate last. [*Modified from R. H. V. Bell, "A Grazing Ecosystem in the Serengeti, Scientific American, July, 1971.*]

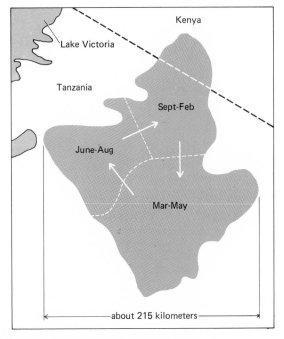

More rabbits will consume more grass. Numerous rabbits also will be more readily seen by hawks and captured with greater ease. The augmented food supply will result in more hawks just as it produced more rabbits, but the higher density of hawks also will reduce the rabbit population just as the higher concentration of rabbits depleted the forage crop. With fewer rabbits to feed on, the number of hawks declines. Lowered grazing pressure by rabbits will permit the grasses to recuperate, which in turn will provide food for a rabbit population no longer subject to heavy predation pressure. The stage will be set for a new increase in rabbits. It is in a similar manner that many populations are held in a dynamic but stable equilibrium through a repetitious cycle of population highs and lows. Figure 11-17 illustrates such a case between interacting populations of the snowshoe hare and one of its predators, the lynx.

Similar cycles often occur between parasites and their hosts. Periods of high host population density are usually the occasions when diseases strike in epidemic proportions. It is easier for parasites to be transferred to new hosts during these times, but it also appears that stress due to overcrowding may increase the susceptibility to infection in some species.

The interactions between parasites and

FIGURE 11-17
Corresponding cycles of population density between the snowshoe hare (color line) and one of its predators, the lynx (black line), as evidenced by the number of pelts sold to the Hudson's Bay Company from 1845 to 1935. [*After D. A. MacLulich, University of Toronto Studies, Biological Series No. 43, University of Toronto Press, 1937.*]

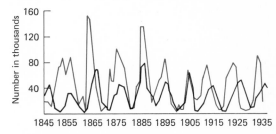

their hosts have much in common with those between predators and their prey. This was borne out in an attempt to curtail the exploding rabbit population in Australia. These mammals, originally introduced from Europe, were intentionally infected with a South American rabbit virus. The initial effects were dramatic. The first epidemic eliminated about 98 percent of the rabbit population. The second resulted in about 85 percent mortality. Successive epidemics declined in their severity until, by the sixth outbreak, fatalities had fallen to 25 percent.[11] Today the virus still takes a toll of rabbits but is of no serious concern to the future of rabbits in Australia. Natural selection has produced a population of rabbits that is more resistant to infection and a strain of virus that is less virulent. *Coevolution* between parasite and host has enabled more rabbits to survive which in turn provides that many more homes for viruses to occupy.

Competition

Competition for ecologic resources may be intraspecific, as we have noted, or *interspecific*. In the latter case, competition is between different species that have similar or overlapping requirements for food, shelter, water, or some other necessity. Usually, competition for food occurs most often. When any critical ecologic resource begins to be heavily used, interspecific and intraspecific competition becomes increasingly effective in limiting the total numbers of contestants to the environmental capacity of the ecosystem.

Because they have low population densities, the majority of species rarely are subject to the stress of competition and environmental overexploitation. In the *Origin of Species,* Charles Darwin observed that "rarity is the attribute of a vast number of species of all classes, in all countries." Typical of similar studies on a variety of animals is one reported by David Pimentel (Fig. 11-18). A random collection

[11] F. Fenner, in *The Genetics of Colonizing Species,* H. G. Baker and G. L. Stebbins (eds.), New York: Academic Press, Inc., 1965, pp. 485–499.

of nocturnal moths was taken from a single locality. Of the 240 species collected, only 35 were represented by more than 100 individuals whereas 115 species had no more than 10 and as few as 1 each.[12]

The effectiveness of predation and interspecific competition in regulating population size has been demonstrated dramatically in an often-quoted episode involving the deer herd on the Kaibab Plateau in Arizona. This episode also has shown the extent to which a species can be victimized by unbridled intraspecific competition. Prior to 1907 the environmental capacity of the Kaibab Plateau for deer was estimated to have been about 30,000 animals. Thousands of cattle and sheep also were grazing the area at that time, however, and range stock, particularly sheep, compete with deer for range forage. The deer herd, consequently, numbered about 4,000, well below the environmental capacity because of interspecific competition from livestock and the normal losses attributable to predation.

At the turn of the century, humans decided the deer needed help. Between 1889 and 1908, perhaps as many as 195,000 head of cattle and sheep that used the range for varying lengths of time during the grazing season were

[12] David S. Pimentel, "Population Regulation and Genetic Feedback," *Science,* vol. 159, Mar. 29, 1968, p. 1433.

FIGURE 11-18
Population density of nocturnal moths based on a random collection taken from one locality. A total of 240 species were represented. [*Data from David Pimentel, Science, vol. 159, March 29, 1968, p. 1433, after Fisher et al, 1943.*]

Number of species	Number of individuals collected in each species
35	1 {35 moths / 35 species}
50	2–5
30	6–10
90	11–100
35	101 or more
240 species	

removed from the area. In addition, intensive predatory-animal control measures were instigated in the mistaken belief that predators are the enemies of their prey. From 1907 to 1923, 3,000 coyotes, 674 mountain lions, and 11 wolves were killed (Fig. 11-19). By the time that control measures were terminated in 1939, wolves were extinct. Meanwhile, the deer herd, unrestrained by interspecific competition and predation pressure, responded with an explosive increase in numbers. The result was a population crash during the winters of 1924 and 1925 that reduced the deer population from 100,000 to 40,000 through death by starvation. Numbers continued to decline as heavy intraspecific competition further abused an already seriously damaged range. Insofar as it is possible to judge at this time, the environmental capacity of the Kaibab Plateau for deer has been reduced to less than one-third its former value.

Self-regulatory devices

Inasmuch as the control of population size is so basic to survival, it would seem that at least some organisms would have evolved inborn mechanisms for regulating their numbers, rather than relying on other species to do the job through predation, disease, and competition. Apparently this is the case in a large number of species, including a variety of vertebrates in all classes. Since human interference in the affairs of wild creatures has been virtually universal, the presence of subtle self-regulating mechanisms may be more widespread in the biological community than is commonly supposed.

The response of different animal species to high population density is diverse and the means of controlling population size are equally varied. Green sea turtles of the Great Barrier Reef off Australia regulate their numbers through nest destruction. Any one population of turtles digs its nests in the sand above the spring high tide mark of a particular beach. This beach can only accommodate that number of nests for which space is available. When the number of nest-digging females exceeds the available nesting space, late-arriving females

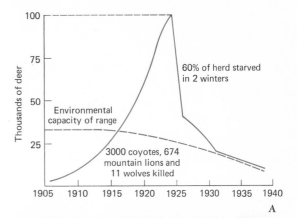

A

B

FIGURE 11-19

A, Intensive predator-control and removal of competing species (livestock) from the Kaibab Plateau in Arizona caused an explosive increase in the deer population far beyond the environmental capacity (available food). Intraspecific competition resulted in starvation, a population crash, and a reduction of the environmental capacity to less than one-third its former value. *B,* Deer do not normally browse on pine trees unless forced to by starvation, in which case the trees are denuded up to a conspicuous browse line. [*A, Modified from Aldo Leopold, Publication No. 321, Department of Natural Resources, Madison, Wis.; B, U. S. Forest Service.*]

dig up and destroy the nests of earlier females to provide space for their own eggs.[13] Unlike the early bird, it does not pay to be an early turtle.

Spacing and social dominance   Territoriality is used widely and in many ways by animals. As noted in Chap. 3, a territory is a specific area of habitat occupied by an individual, a pair of individuals, or a group belonging to the same species. The area is actively defended by the resident species against intrusion by nonresident members of the same species. If the area is not actively defended, it is called a *home range.* Among marine animals such as the elephant seal, a male defends his breeding territory from intrusion by other males. The territory in this case is a section of beach and the females that occupy it. Many birds establish territorial boundaries based upon the amount of food required to sustain a breeding pair and their progeny. This territory also is defended, usually by the male of the pair, against trespass by others of his kind, particularly males. The sound of a male bird vocalizing on a spring morning may be a song of love, but it is more likely a repetitious warning to similar males that this territory is claimed. In any case, whether the defended territory is that of a seal or a song bird, population density is controlled by limiting the number of breeding individuals and by scattering the population throughout an inhabitable area, discouraging overcrowding in one place. Territorial defense seldom is seriously injurious and rarely fatal to the contestants. Characteristically, it varies from warning or display to a relatively harmless demonstration of superior strength. Adults that fail to gain access to a breeding territory simply do not reproduce that year.

Dominance hierarchies are also important in determining who will reproduce. Studies of mammals indicate that aggression increases as population densities rise. As a result, the more dominant animals do nearly all the breeding;

the great majority of subordinates fail to reproduce.[14]

Some of the highly social primates like the baboons have a home range that is seldom defended as a territory. Each home range contains a core area where members of the troop spend most of their time. Although the home ranges of neighboring troops may overlap extensively, the members of each troop tend to avoid core areas other than their own (Fig. 3-3). Such behavior serves as an effective spacing mechanism.

Australian aborigines have a system of spacing that uses the extended patrilineal family (Fig. 5-9) as its social unit or band. These hunter-gatherers tend to arrange their band territories in such a manner as to provide reasonably reliable food for one band for all seasons of the year. If severe drought forces a band to leave its area, it seeks temporary assistance from another group, usually one with whom it has a kinship link through exogamous mating.[15]

Population density and psychophysiologic stress   In recent years, attention has turned increasingly to the effects that high population density seems to have on individual animals in species as diverse as fish, birds, shrews, monkeys, rodents, rabbits, elephants, and man. These effects may be characterized as abnormal or pathological and include both behavioral patterns and physiological processes. For example, several species of pregnant mice will abort if they smell the scent of a strange male. Presumably this is a self-regulating device to curtail reproduction in a population so overcrowded that unfamiliar males are close enough to smell.[16] Among chipmunks and gophers, litter mates at a certain age begin to fight among themselves. The mother joins in these alterca-

[13] H. R. Bustard and K. P. Tognetti, "Green Sea Turtles: A Discrete Simulation of Density-Dependent Population Regulation," *Science,* vol. 163, Feb. 28, 1969, pp. 939–941.

[14] Alison Jolly, *The Evolution of Primate Behavior,* New York: The Macmillan Company, 1972, p. 269.

[15] Joseph Birdsell, "Some Environmental and Cultural Factors Influencing the Structuring of Australian Aboriginal Populations," *The American Naturalist,* 87, 1953, pp. 171–207.

[16] R. A. Stehn and M. E. Richmond, "Male-Induced Pregnancy Termination in the Prairie Vole, *Microtus ochrogaster,*" *Science,* vol. 187, Mar. 28, 1975, pp. 1211–1213.

tions also, with the result that the family is disrupted, the young dispersed, and population concentration avoided.

Such occurrences are by no means confined to rodents, although these animals have been studied the most intensively in this regard. A study of wild monkeys by Y. Sugiyama showed that high population density resulted in deterioration of the social order, extremely aggressive behavior, and the killing of young.[17] Among elephants, fertility may be reduced when the animals are overcrowded.[18]

Two studies are particularly significant and worthy of a more detailed account. One of them, by J. B. Calhoun, compared laboratory rats living in uncrowded and overcrowded conditions. All animals were provided with sufficient food, water, and nesting materials throughout the course of the study. During the initial stages of population growth, rat behavior was normal. But as high densities were reached and the population started to stabilize in the rat pens, a number of "pathological behaviors" developed. Evidence of lowered fertility was reflected in an increase in the number of infertile females, failure to copulate, higher abortion rate, and smaller litter size. Mothers failed to prepare adequate nests and neglected the nursing and care of their young. Juveniles consequently left the nest prematurely and their mortality rates increased to more than 95 percent; many were cannibalized. Much of total rat behavior was either excessively aggressive or "psychotic." Abnormal sexual behaviors were common. Many individuals behaved as though they were sleepwalking.

Such acutely abnormal behaviors resulted in a rapid decline in numbers and the ultimate extinction of the population. It was thought that these behaviors were triggered by a stress response to individuals crowded too close together. This response entailed a modification in the delicate nervous and endocrine (hormonal) machinery responsible for all animal behavior.[19]

Genetic control of population density After Calhoun's study, Dennis Chitty discovered that the behavioral symptoms of high density among small rodent species did not appear in the generation of animals exposed to crowding but rather in their offspring. This suggested that a hereditary mechanism was involved. Chitty theorized that the stress associated with high population densities might promote the reproduction of individuals with certain genetically determined traits just as it might hamper the reproduction of others.[20]

Myers and Krebs seized upon this idea as a useful one. They were interested in learning why so many wild populations of small rodents, like lemmings and meadow mice, rise and fall in a regular cycle. They felt that predation alone was not responsible and even may be secondary to a more basic mechanism. By a series of ingenious field tests, they found that meadow mouse populations performed just as Chitty had postulated. There appear to be two genotypes of mice. One, the density-intolerant form, is distinguished by high fertility, rapid growth, and early sexual maturity. Its body size is larger than average and its survival rate is high. It makes an excellent colonizer because it is capable of exploiting a new environment quickly. The density-tolerant form, on the other hand, is marked by unusual aggressiveness and more economic use of available space. Females bear relatively few young, growth is slow, and sexual maturity is delayed. Body size is relatively small, and the survival rate, particularly among juveniles, is low. Individuals of all ages are more susceptible to the usual causes of death, such as disease, than the density-intolerant type.

Successive meadow mouse populations show a cycle of population peaks like those of the snowshoe hare in Fig. 11-17. One cycle

[17] Y. Sugiyama, "Social Organization of Hanuman Langurs," in *Social Communication Among Primates*, S. Altmann (ed.), Chicago: University of Chicago Press, 1967, pp. 221–236.

[18] R. Laws and I. Parker, in *Symposium of the Zoological Society*, London: Academic Press, Inc., 1968, pp. 319–359.

[19] J. B. Calhoun, "Population Density and Social Pathology," *Scientific American*, February 1962, pp. 139–148.

[20] Dennis Chitty, *Proceedings of the Ecological Society of Austria*, 2, 1967, p. 51.

spans three to four years and consists of three populational phases, each of which lasts for several months or more. An increase phase, marked by steadily rising numbers is followed by a peak phase in which the rate of increase reaches zero and population density is high but relatively constant. A decline phase terminates the cycle and is distinguished by a fall in population comparable to the rise of the increase phase. During such a cycle, large numbers of mice disperse to new habitats but, paradoxically, more than 50 percent of this populational loss occurs during the increase phase whereas only about 15 percent of the animals emigrate during the decline phase (Fig. 11-20).

Myers and Krebs solved this seeming dilemma by establishing that it was the quality of dispersing animals rather than their number that mattered. It was the density-intolerant genotype that was emigrating. As the population continued to grow and more of this form left, the density-tolerant genotype became progressively more abundant and better able to cope with crowded conditions of the resident habitat. The population becomes more or less stabilized at its peak at this time. When the population is overwhelmingly density-tolerant, the decline phase begins as a consequence of the lower fertility and higher mortality of the resident genotype. At this point disease and predation undoubtedly take their toll on this less vigorous form. Predation also most likely leaves its mark on the emigrants,

particularly if the new habitats being colonized are submarginal or unsuitable. The basic mechanism for population regulation, however, resides in the mice themselves. They do not passively leave the regulation of their numbers to the predators and parasites who destroy them.[21]

High density and pathological behavior among humans

The discovery that pathological behavior is associated with high population density in species as diverse as fish, birds, monkeys, rodents, and elephants poses the obvious question as to whether humans should be included on the list. A number of investigators have attempted to find the answer to this question but the problem is not a simple one. Although high density apparently has a serious suppressive effect on many species, the specific consequences are not uniform among different animals. It is possible, if not probable, that the behavioral symptoms of human overcrowding are nonuniform. There are great differences in the kind of psychological conditioning that the human animal receives among the diverse cultures in which it is reared.

Case studies in Hong Kong and Chicago

Mitchell conducted a density study in Hong Kong where virtually everyone lives in an overcrowded environment. People there lived in homes where the average floor space ranged from 6.2 to 9.3 square meters (67 to 100 square feet) or more per person. In Europe, 15.8 square meters (170 square feet) is considered to border on overcrowding, and 32.6 square meters (350 square feet) has been judged an acceptable standard in the United States by the U.S. Public Health Service. By either of these criteria, the Hong Kong population had a high density, yet Mitchell found no relationship between degree of crowding and critical emotional stress.[22]

FIGURE 11-20
Percentage of losses due to dispersal of populations of meadow mice (*Microtus pennsylvanicus*) in southern Indiana. [*After C. J. Krebs et al., Science, vol. 179, January 5, 1973, p. 38, © American Association for the Advancement of Science.*]

Population phase	Males, %	Females, %
Increase	56	69
Peak	33	25
Decline	15	12

[21] Myers and C. Krebs, "Population Cycles in Rodents," *Scientific American*, June 1974, pp. 38–46.

[22] R. E. Mitchell, "Some Social Implications of High Density Housing," *American Sociological Review*, 35, 1971, pp. 18–29.

In contrast to Mitchell's results which were based on interview records in Hong Kong, Omer R. Galle et al. found evidence for a relationship between crowding and stress from ecologic data collected in Chicago. This investigation sought to determine whether the categories of pathological behavior identified in Calhoun's study of rats applied to human populations. The categories chosen were (1) fertility, (2) mortality, (3) inadequate care of the young, (4) aggressive behavior, and (5) psychotic disorder. From raw demographic and sociologic data available to the investigators, statistical analyses were undertaken to see what correlation, if any, existed between population density and the five categories of pathological behavior. This was done for each of Chicago's 75 community areas. Population density was measured in terms of (*a*) the number of persons per room in a residential unit, (*b*) the number of rooms per residential unit, (*c*) the number of residential units per structure, and (*d*) the number of structures per hectare (1 acre = 0.405 hectare).

The analysis indicated that density may be a significant factor in the development of pathological behavior. Insofar as fertility, mortality, inadequate care of the young, and aggressive behavior were concerned, the number of persons per room was the most important measure of density. Next, but of considerably less significance, was the residential units per structure. The other two measures of density apparently were of little relevance to these four pathologies.[23] High density was associated with an increase in fertility, unlike the results of the animal studies cited. Increased fertility probably can be accounted for by the excessive sexual activity commonly associated with overcrowding in animals, as both Calhoun and Sugiyama observed in rats and monkeys. Nonhuman animals, however, can conceive only during their heat periods; higher rates of copulation do not increase the birth rate. Women, on the other hand, can be receptive at all times; the more often copulation takes place the greater the chances of additional pregnancies.

High density was similarly associated with an increased incidence of poor health and a higher death rate. Ineffectual parental care was suggested by the greater amounts of public assistance for the care and support of children without homes or from broken homes in high-density areas. Aggressive behavior as measured by juvenile delinquency and gang wars had its highest frequency in the crowded sectors of the city.

Psychotic disorders did not follow the same pattern as the other four pathologies. Psychiatric problems, as reflected by the rate of admission to mental hospitals, was most highly correlated with persons who lived alone.

In all these relationships, the investigators were careful to point out that density, socioeconomic level, and ethnic status are interrelated intimately. The correlation of pathological behavior with one or another of these human dimensions does not necessarily imply a cause-effect relationship.

In Chicago, the number of persons per room is associated with stress. Overcrowding at this personal level in which one is in almost constant contact with others was referred to by Galle and his associates as "interpersonal press." It is easy to understand how almost continuous social encounters may heighten sexual desire and contribute to promiscuity. The close proximity of persons certainly facilitates the spread of many diseases. The almost constant presence of others and the possibility that the human animal may require a certain amount of privacy might reasonably tend to make one aloof to the problems, or even the welfare, of other people. Interpersonal press is real enough that the Galle group was able to detect a relationship between it and pathological behavior.

The !Kung Bushmen On the other hand, Patricia Draper studied a population in which

[23] Omer R. Galle et al., "Population Density and Pathology: What Are The Relations For Man?" *Science*, vol. 176, Apr. 7, 1972, pp. 23–30.

interpersonal press was not associated with any of the symptoms of pathological stress. Apparently the people lived in crowded villages by choice, despite the fact that they had one of the lowest population densities in the world: about 1 person per 26 square kilometers (10 square miles). The people are the !Kung Bushmen who live at the edge of the Kalahari Desert. The group studied numbered about 150 people who lived entirely by hunting and gathering along the northern border of Botswana and Southwest Africa. This number was distributed in separate bands of 30 to 40 people which usually were separated by 24 kilometers (15 miles) or more. Membership in each band was unstable over any length of time and was organized neither according to territory nor any rigid kinship system. The size, composition, and movements of each group were determined by the availability of water and food, and the desire of individuals to visit other bands. Practically all the 150 individuals in the total population were acquainted with one another, and the few that were not usually were related to one another in some way.

The village occupied by each band was small, compact, and densely settled. It was circular in outline, ringed by small grass huts which served exclusively as storage for food, skins, and tools. Within the circle of huts the area was devoid of any vegetation which might provide shade or screen one living area from another. The family living areas, each marked by its hut and adjacent hearth, were so close together that people sitting around different hearths could pass items back and forth without getting up. From the standpoint of interpersonal press, the arrangement was equivalent to 30 or 40 people living in one room. The average density of these village camps, measured over a four-month period, was 16.8 square meters (181 square feet) per person, including hearths and storage huts (Fig. 11-21). The !Kung appeared to enjoy being close together and preferred to gather in small clusters with their bodies touching. Supposed stress-related diseases were conspicuously absent. Blood pressures were low, they did not increase with age, and blood cholesterol levels were among the lowest known anywhere.

During the day about 65 percent of the village residents remained in camp. Hunting and gathering were engaged in only by able-bodied adults, and even this effort required only about three days time each week. There was an unusually close relationship between children and adults. Unlike crowded urban populations, the children were well supervised by adults. Except for older juveniles, most youngsters confined their play activities to the camp area. Even older children did not stray far from their home. From a child's point of view, the Kalahari bush is a vast, unknown, and therefore somewhat fearsome place.[24]

Why was interpersonal press associated with stress among the Chicagoans but not among the !Kung? Draper offered some suggestions. When a !Kung individual or family experiences a personal conflict with another !Kung, a readily available option is open, that of moving to another camp. The transfer amounts to nothing more than a reassociation

[24] Patricia Draper, "Crowding Among Hunter-Gatherers: The !Kung Bushmen," *Science*, vol. 182, Oct. 19, 1973, pp. 301–303.

FIGURE 11-21
Occupation density of four !Kung Bushmen camps. The August and October data are for the same camp area. The other two entries are for different camp sites. [*After P. Draper, Science, vol. 182, October 19, 1973.*]

Date	Number of people in camp	Camp area, square feet	Area per person, square feet
July 1969	17	698	42
August 1969	28	4,419	158
September 1969	40	7,079	176
October 1969	24	8,343	348

with other friends and relatives. The economics of the urban ghetto do not permit such easy mobility. Furthermore, when urbanites move, and even when they do not, they intermingle with a great many strangers. Stranger density may be a significant element in urban stress—in hot, sweaty, jammed trains and buses at "rush hour," for example (Fig. 11-22). A !Kung, on the other hand, seldom encounters a strange face. On those rare occasions when it happens, a basis of fellowship readily develops as the parties work out their genealogical relationship. Finally, it is possible that the !Kung avoid the stress associated with

interpersonal press by the wide dispersal of their separate camps. Being a member of a tiny community in the vastness of the Kalahari bush is one thing. Being a member of a larger community in the vastness of ever-larger communities is quite another.

The regulation of human populations

From the brief survey of ways in which population size is regulated in animals, it is clear

FIGURE 11-22
A Tokyo commuter grimaces trying to keep his footing during rush-hour traffic. [*Wide World Photos.*]

that none of them are effective in controlling the size of human populations at the present stage of our history. Predation and disease in the form of pestilence, as well as competition in the form of war and starvation, have been ineffectual in curbing the world's ever-rising numbers. As for any self-regulatory devices of a biological nature, none are known to exist except for territoriality and infanticide[25] as practiced by such people as the Australian aborigines. Over most of the planet and for thousands of years, territoriality has failed to keep human numbers within the environmental capacity of occupied areas. The age-old art of organized warfare has enabled the powerful to grab up territories of others with anything but an inhibitory effect upon human numbers.

As for high population density and pathological behavior, the results of studies to date are unclear. Undoubtedly depending in large part upon the cultural environment, studies in one locality show some association while others in different places show high correlations or none at all. In no case, however, has high density been found to have the suppressive effect upon population growth that it does in the nonhuman animals that have been studied. On the contrary, the ghetto environments of the world tend to have a birth rate that more than compensates for their heavier mortality.

It is small wonder, therefore, that the human population has reached its present gargantuan proportions. Our species, through its cultural institutions and practices, has removed the natural curbs on its growth. Most authorities agree that among all the problems faced by mankind today population size is foremost.

Overpopulation is a crisis in itself as well as the major cause of environmental deterioration. The direct effects of overpopulation today are seen in densely overcrowded cities in every land and in a world population 50 percent

or more of which is *constantly* underfed if not starving. In trying to supply the requirements of enormous numbers of people, the natural resources of the world are being used at an alarming rate, resulting in environmental pollution and devastation. This environmental impact is further aggravated by the demands for higher standards of living and by economic systems that require ever-growing markets.

The following chapters will be devoted to these problems. Chapters 12 and 13 will be concerned with human population and population control. Environmental problems and their correction will be dealt with in Chaps. 14 and 15.

SUGGESTED READINGS

CHANDLER, A., and C. P. READ: *Introduction to Parasitology,* Philadelphia: W. B. Saunders Company, 1961. A classic text on parasite-host interrelationships.

EDITORS of *Scientific American: The Biosphere,* San Francisco: W. H. Freeman and Company, 1970. This and the Hazen work are a collection of articles. This book and the books by Hazen, Kormandy, and Odum and Odum deal with broad aspects of general ecology.

EDITORS of *Scientific American: Energy and Power,* San Francisco: W. H. Freeman and Company, 1971. A collection of articles on the use of energy by biotic communities and by various kinds of human communities.

HAZEN, W. (ed.): *Readings in Population and Community Ecology,* Philadelphia: W. B. Saunders Company, 1970.

KLOPFER, PETER: *Behavioral Aspects of Ecology,* Englewood Cliffs, N.J.: Prentice-Hall, Inc., 1972. A fine account of population interactions with respect to behavior.

KORMANDY, E. J.: *Concepts of Ecology,* Englewood Cliffs, N.J.: Prentice-Hall, Inc., 1969.

---

[25] See Chap. 4, *Birth and Growing Up.*

LACK, DAVID: *Natural Regulation of Animal Numbers,* New York: Oxford Book Company, Inc., 1954. A classic discussion on population control.

ODUM, E. P., and H. T. ODUM: *Fundamentals of Ecology,* Philadelphia: W. B. Saunders Company, 1971.

SCHALLER, G. B.: *The Serengeti Lion,* Chicago: University of Chicago Press, 1972. An excellent study of the interrelationships of lions, cheetahs, leopards, and wild dogs with their prey.

SHELFORD, V. E.: *The Ecology of North America,* Urbana, Ill.: University of Illinois Press, 1963. A comprehensive description of the biotic communities of North America as they are believed to have been between A.D. 1500 and 1600.

REVIEW QUESTIONS

1 What is meant by an *ecosystem?*

2 Trace the flow of energy through a biotic community. In what important way is energy flow through the community affected by the principles of energy dynamics (thermodynamics)? How is this relevant to human nutrition?

3 Show how inorganic materials are used and reused in the biotic community, employing the carbon cycle as an example. Of what significance is community respiration to community production in this cycle?

4 What is ecologic succession? Illustrate with an example and explain why succession takes place.

5 As ecologic successions progress from pioneer to climax community, important changes occur in the community. Identify three and indicate why each takes place.

6 Describe and give examples of three different types of symbiosis. In what manner do these relationships intergrade with one another? What is the net result of symbiotic food chains in community energy flow?

7 Limiting factors are of critical importance to the survival of a species by regulating population size. Compare and contrast intraspecific and interspecific competition in this regard.

8 Show, by the use of examples, how predator-prey and parasite-host interactions regulate population size. What is coevolution and how is it relevant to your answer?

9 How does territoriality regulate population size? How is population size regulated among baboon troops on their home range?

10 Briefly summarize the studies of Myers and Krebs on the genetic control of population size among meadow mice.

11 Discuss the possibility that human population size may be regulated as a result of the pathological behavior associated with high density. Cite at least two studies in support of your conclusions.

TWELVE

HUMAN POPULATION I:
Structure, Distribution, and Growth

In 1798 a British economist, Thomas Malthus, published *An Essay on the Principle of Population as It Affects the Future Improvement of Society*. In it, he observed that human populations tended to double their number about every 25 years. Croplands and pasture lands also can grow in the sense that they can be added to. But unlike population, land does not multiply. Thus, human populations grow geometrically whereas land grows arithmetically. In his words, ". . . supposing the present [world] population to be equal to a thousand millions, the human species would increase as the numbers 1, 2, 4, 8, 16, 32, 64, 128, 256, and subsistence [food production] as 1, 2, 3, 4, 5, 6, 7, 8, 9. In two centuries the population would be to the means of subsistence as 256 to 9; . . . ."

Malthus believed that human populations constantly tend to outstrip their food supplies. Starvation, disease, poverty, warfare, and other disasters keep the population within the limits of available food supply and are inevitable features of the human condition.

Malthus' views produced a storm of protest in the intellectual world and generally fell into disrepute until recent years. But the human species now finds itself caught up in many Malthusian predictions. Despite tremendous increases in food production throughout the world, starvation, disease, poverty, and warfare continue to plague mankind with growing intensity (Fig. 12-1). For example, the people of Bangladesh are crowded into a country ravaged by war, with a population density greater than the United States would have if it contained all the world's 4 billion inhabitants. In addition to starvation, disease, and poverty, for want of space many are forced to farm Ganges Delta lands which are barely above sea level; annually thousands are killed in *ordinary* storms—in 1970, 300,000 died in a severe storm.

In light of today's world, Malthusian doctrine is correct in its basic assumption that the potential for population growth vastly exceeds the capabilities of food supply. Malthus erred essentially in one particular: all populations do not grow at the same rate. Some double their number in 25 years, others in 10, and some may

FIGURE 12-1
A street scene in Calcutta, India. [*Photograph by Werner Bischof, Magnum Photos, Inc.*]

not be growing at all. Populations vary in the rate at which births are added to, and deaths subtracted from, their number.

Let us examine these matters in greater detail.

INTRODUCTION TO POPULATION DYNAMICS

The statistical study of human populations with respect to size, density, birth rate, death rate, migration, and so on is called *demography*. Whether a population is growing or declining in numbers depends upon the interrelationships between birth rate (fertility), death rate (mortality), and migration. Birth rate and immigration add to population size whereas death rate and emigration subtract from it. In most instances, demographers consider migration to be of relatively minor importance in the basic dynamics of large populations.

Birth rate usually is expressed as the number of children born per year for every thousand people at the middle of that year. Dividing the total number of births by the estimated population at the middle of the year will give the average number of children born per person. Multiplying this figure by 1,000 will give the number of children born per thousand people. For example, during the 12 months of 1970, 3,769,220 children were born in the United States. Our estimated population at midyear was 207,100,000. Therefore:

3,769,200 births ÷ 207,100,000 people = 0.0182 births per person, or 18.2 births per 1,000 people.

The *death rate* is expressed similarly. During the 12 months of 1970, 1,926,030 people died. Hence:

1,926,030 deaths ÷ 207,100,000 people = 0.0093 deaths per person or 9.3 deaths per 1,000 people.

Since the birth rate adds to a population and the death rate subtracts from it, we can determine the extent to which a population increases or decreases by subtracting its death rate from its birth rate. During 1970, for example, the *growth rate* in the United States was 8.9 persons per 1,000 because: 18.2 (birth rate) − 9.3 (death rate) = 8.9 persons per 1,000. Inasmuch as migration is not considered in the calculation, this measure of the growth rate actually is a *rate of natural increase*. Unlike birth and death rates, however, the growth rate customarily is expressed as a percentage figure, that is, the number of persons per hundred rather than per thousand. The rate of natural increase of the United States in 1970, then, was 0.89 percent (8.9 persons per 1,000 = 8.9/1000 = 0.89/100 = 0.89 percent).

In the same year, the world population was estimated at 3,632 million with a birth rate of 34 per 1,000 and a death rate of 14 per 1,000. The estimated world growth rate, therefore, was 2.0 percent in 1970 (34/1000 − 14/1000 = 20/1000, or 2 percent).

These figures begin to assume some significance when they are translated in terms of *population doubling time*. As can be seen in Fig. 12-2, if the 2 percent rate of annual growth were to remain unchanged, world population would double in 35 years. By the year 2005 the earth would be occupied by over 7 billion people. The rate at which a population doubles its numbers is much greater than might be supposed because populations grow in the

FIGURE 12-2
The time required in years for a population to double itself (*population doubling time*) for various annual growth rates.

Annual increase, %	Doubling time, years
0.5	140
1.0	70
1.5	47
2.0	35
2.5	28
3.0	24
3.5	20
4.0	17

same way that money increases when drawing compound interest. Each year the principal is augmented by the interest earned the previous year. Similarly, each year the growth rate of a population applies to a larger number because people added to the population also produce people.

Figure 12-3 illustrates this for a population of 10 million with a growth rate of 8 percent. (Kuwait in Southwest Asia had an 8.2 percent growth rate in 1970.) Within 9 years such a population would be within 54 people of having doubled itself. Had these numbers grown by simply adding 8 percent of 10 million each year, 12.5 years would have been required to double the population (800,000 × 12.5 = 10,000,000).

With this general background in population dynamics, we can now turn to the history of population growth and what significance it might have for the future.

THE HISTORY OF POPULATION GROWTH

In Chaps. 6 and 7 we traced the history of population growth in its broader aspects beginning with the australopithecines in the lower Pleistocene. Population estimates based on fossil data are inexact by nature and can be considered only as rough approximations. For millions of years hominid populations undoubtedly rose and declined, varying between slightly above and slightly below zero growth. When cultural breakthroughs occurred, they could have resulted in slight accelerations in the growth rate. The first use of fire certainly was a major accomplishment, outranked at the time only by the invention of culture itself. But even by the time archaic *Homo sapiens* had appeared, the human world population probably was no more than 1 to 3 million. The advent of herd hunting by Upper Paleolithic *H. sapiens,* however, was one of the highlights of human development. Upper Paleolithic herd hunting was responsible for what may well have been the first hominid population explosion. Between 30,000 and 12,000 years ago, the human population probably had climbed to at least 5 million, and may have reached 10 million.

The second population explosion began perhaps 10,000 years ago as the agricultural revolution was getting under way. Within 8,000 years of that time, about 2000 B.P. (roughly A.D. 1), world population very likely had reached 250 million. Growth since that time is shown in Fig. 12-4.

FIGURE 12-3

A population with an 8 percent annual growth rate will double itself in 9 years. The arithmetic of population increase is like that of money earning compound interest. People added to a population produce people just as money earned from interest earns interest. Although there is a lag for children to mature, every year more people join those already reproducing. Had these numbers grown by simply adding 8 percent of 10 million each year, 12.5 years would have been required to double the population (800,000 × 12.5 = 10,000,000). The people of Kuwait in southwest Asia had an 8.2 percent growth rate in 1970.

Year	A Population at beginning of year	B 8.0% annual growth-rate increment (column A × 8%)	C Population at end of year (column A + column B)
1	10,000,000	800,000	10,800,000
2	10,800,000	864,000	11,664,000
3	11,664,000	933,120	12,597,120
4	12,597,120	1,007,770	13,604,890
5	13,604,890	1,088,391	14,693,281
6	14,693,281	1,175,462	15,868,743
7	15,868,743	1,269,500	17,138,243
8	17,138,243	1,371,059	18,509,302
9	18,509,302	1,489,744	19,999,046

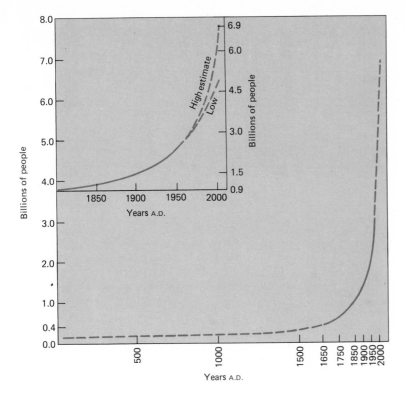

FIGURE 12-4
Estimated world population growth from A.D. 1 to 2000. [*After H. F. Dorn, Science, vol. 125, January 26, 1962, p. 284,* © *American Association for the Advancement of Science.*]

It is clear that the human population has been increasing for a very long time. This does not mean, however, that growth has been continuous in any one region or over the world at large. The history of growth in China, which has the most complete uninterrupted records of any country, testifies to fluctuations in growth rate (Fig. 12-5). Populations rise and fall but the net trend throughout most of human history has been a relatively slow rate of growth. It required 1,650 years, for example, for the world population of A.D. 1 to double itself (Fig. 12-6). The average growth rate for the entire period was only 0.04 percent per year, less than one-twentieth of that in the United States in 1970.

During all those centuries, growth rates were low because death rates were high. Human history from several centuries before the Christian era until about A.D. 1650 was marked by heavy mortality. Disease, particularly bu-

bonic plague, killed millions of people in Eurasia. Famine was widespread and frequent. No year went by that a famine was not raging somewhere in Europe or Asia.[1] Tens of millions of people lost their lives this way. Warfare also extracted its toll not only by killing people directly but also by contributing to conditions that foster pestilence and famine. The history of Western civilization is an almost continuous record of wars.

Beginning in 493 B.C. and extending to A.D. 568, mankind was engaged in constant military activity, with the Persian and Peloponnesian Wars, the conquests of Alexander the Great, and the battles and campaigns that attended the founding, spread, and ultimate decline of the Roman Empire. The Crusades from

[1] Cornelius Walford, "The Famines of the World: Past and Present," *Royal Statistical Society Journal,* 41, 1878, pp. 433–526.

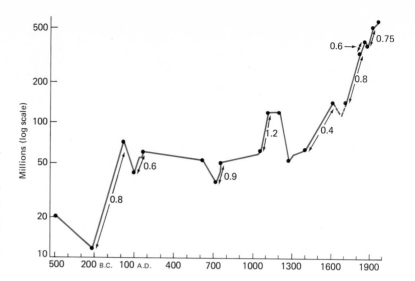

FIGURE 12-5
Estimates of the population of China from 500 B.C. to A.D. 1953. Population in millions is given on a logarithmic scale. The rate of growth, as a percentage per year, is indicated between the arrows. Highest rate of growth was 1.2 percent. [*From Colin Clark, Population Growth and Land Use, Macmillan, London, 1967.*]

1096 to 1244, the Hundred Years' War between 1337 and 1453, and the Thirty Years' War from 1618 to 1648, with the many minor battles and skirmishes in between, left little time when men were not killing other people. The carnage and plunder of the Thirty Years' War alone wrought terrible havoc in central Europe. Marauding attacks by the armies of both factions pillaged, burned, tortured, and killed to a degree that whole regions were reduced to wastelands. It has been estimated that at least one-third of the people in Germany and

Bohemia (modern Czechoslovakia and portions of Poland and Germany) either were killed outright or died from famine and disease brought about by the military devastation of human resources. In Saxony (now northeast Germany), one-third of the land was removed from agricultural production because no one was left to till it.

The era of rapid population growth

The mid-seventeenth century marked the beginning of a new trend in population dynamics. By this time the intellectual and commercial revolutions were making themselves felt in human affairs. Agriculture became more efficiently managed. International trade was stimulated and the Western Hemisphere was opened up to exploration. These changes alone reduced death rates to a substantial degree by increasing agricultural production, improving the distribution of food and other goods, and decreasing population density in Europe through emigration to the New World. The industrial revolution followed close on the heels of these major breakthroughs in the mid-eighteenth century.

FIGURE 12-6
The number of years required to double the population of the world since A.D. 1. [*Projected from United Nations estimates and the U.N. Demographic Yearbook for 1967.*]

Year (A.D.)	Population, millions	Doubling time, years
1	250	
1650	500	1,650
1850	1,171	200
1930	2,070	80
1975	4,000	45
2010	8,000?	35?

The consequences of the industrial revolution together with those of the intellectual and commercial revolutions involved significant economic, sociopolitical, and technological improvements in the human way of life. One of these was a dramatic reduction in the death rate.

As a result, growth rates began to take a sharp upturn. A world growth rate which had had an annual average of 0.04 percent for 1,650 years rose to about 0.3 percent per year between 1650 and 1750. Between 1750 and 1850 it had risen to 0.5 percent per year. These sharp increments in growth rate are reflected in Fig. 12-6 by the decrease in population doubling times. World population doubled from A.D. 1 to 1650. Between 1650 and 1850 the population doubled again in less than one-eighth the time.

This explosive increase continued to gather momentum; by the time the twentieth century was well under way, it had reached striking proportions. This is shown in Fig. 12-4 by the abrupt steepening of the curve during the past 50 years. The century from 1850 to 1950 had an average annual growth of 0.8 percent compared to 0.5 percent for the previous century. By 1970, the average annual increase had reached 2 percent. As Fig. 12-6 indicates, it took only 80 years for the 1850 population to double, whereas the 1930 population had already doubled at the end of 1975. The extent of population growth from 1930 to 1970 is illustrated in Fig. 12-7 for the six major geographic areas of the world. In that 40-year period alone, Africa and America more than doubled their population and Oceania and Asia came within 3 percent and 8 percent, respectively, of doing so.

It is clear that the decline in death rate that accompanied industrialization has had a singularly profound effect on human numbers all over the world. A close look at Fig. 12-7 reveals an interesting situation concerning 1970 growth rates. The major areas of the world seem to be divisible into two groups: those with growth rates significantly above 2.0 percent and those significantly below. The latter include Europe (0.8 percent), North America (0.9 percent), the U.S.S.R. (1.0 percent), and Oceania (1.4 percent). Japan with a 1970 growth rate of 1.2 percent also should be added. The rest of the world (Asia, Africa, and Latin America) had growth rates ranging from 2.3 percent to 2.9 percent. The members of each group have another characteristic in common. The areas with lower growth rates embrace the industrialized or developed countries of the world. The areas with the higher growth rates include the developing countries that are in the process of becoming industrialized. Apparently the demographic effects of industriali-

Major area	POPULATION, MILLIONS			Growth rate for 1970, %	Years to double population at 1970 growth rate
	1930	1950	1970		
Africa	164	222	344	2.6	27
Americas	242	329	511		
North America			228	0.9	78
Latin America			283	2.9	24
Asia	1,120	1,381	2,056	2.3	31
Europe	355	392	462	0.8	88
Oceania	10	13	19.4	1.4	50
U.S.S.R.	179	180	243	1.0	70
World total or average	2,070	2,517	3,632	2.0	35

FIGURE 12-7
Population, area, and growth rate for the major areas of the world in 1930, 1950, and 1970. Oceania includes Australia, New Zealand, Melanesia, Polynesia, and Micronesia. Growth rates are in terms of percent annual natural increase and do not include immigration. [From U.N. Demographic Yearbook for 1970.]

zation are twofold. As a country undergoes industrialization, its death rate declines. Once a country has achieved industrialization, its birth rate declines.

This phenomenon is known as the *demographic transition.*

The demographic transition

The demographic transition first began in Western Europe toward the end of the nineteenth century and continued into the twentieth. This transition is demonstrated clearly by the decreasing number of births among married women as measured by the index of marital fertility (see Fig. 12-8).[2] There was a pronounced drop in fertility among married women in Sweden, England and Wales, France, Finland, and Bulgaria beginning as early as 1850 and extending to 1930 and beyond. In 1850 the combined birthrate of Norway, Sweden, and Denmark was approximately 32 per 1,000. By 1900 it had dropped to 28 per 1,000, and by 1935 to about 16 per 1,000.

The demographic transition occurred somewhat later in North America, and more recently still in Japan. During the decade 1948 to 1958, Japan's birth rate fell abruptly and precipitously by 46 percent. At the end of that decade, her death rate actually exceeded her birth rate.

Why the demographic transition takes place in industrialized countries is not clear. Obviously it involves a commitment to birth control in some manner, but such reasoning is circular and unproductive. What encourages a commitment to birth control is the question. There are some possible causes that are at least worth theoretical consideration. The developing countries essentially are agricultural societies in which children have traditionally served two important functions: in their younger years they are a labor force on the farm, and when they are older they ensure the

[2] The index of marital fertility is the number of births of married women in a population in one year divided by the number of births these women would have had if they were reproducing at the highest birth rate for their age ever recorded in a population of substantial size. The highest value of the index is 1.0.

security of their aging parents by assuming farm operations. In the developed, industrialized societies, children do not play a useful role either on the farm or in the city. Agriculture is mechanized and is a big business member of the industrial complex. For the most part, children are economic liabilities who require health care, food, recreational opportunities, and education. Large families are not economically productive under these conditions which may account, at least in part, for the declining birth rates of industrial countries. In any case, during the late nineteenth and early twentieth centuries, there was a definite trend in Europe toward reducing the number of children in a family, as is evident in Fig. 12-8. This was accomplished in part by people marrying at an older age, thereby decreasing the reproductive years of married women. The dramatic decline in birth rate in Japan following World War II was largely the result of legalized abortions performed at an annual rate of about 1,500,000.

Various birth-control practices and devices have long been effectively used by members of industrialized nations. These will be discussed in the next chapter. Suffice it to say here that the exercise of birth control during the demographic transition is largely, but not entirely, responsible for the difference in growth rate between developed and developing countries. There is another factor that also contributes to this difference. By the end of World War II, the industrialized countries had made a series of significant advances in public health. Powerful antibiotics and insecticides were available for the treatment of diverse deadly diseases and infections and for the control of insects that transmitted them. Most importantly, it was economically feasible as well as morally desirable to export this technology to the developing countries.

The export of public health technology

This new technology had developed gradually among the industrialized nations, which had comparatively low birth rates. The effect of its relatively rapid introduction into developing

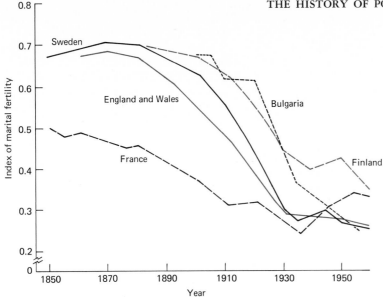

FIGURE 12-8
Demographic transition of five European countries as indicated by changes in the index of fertility of married women. The index of marital fertility is the number of births of married women in a population in one year divided by the number of births those women would have had if they were reproducing at the highest birth rate for their age ever recorded in a population of substantial size. The highest value of the index is 1.0. [*Modified from A. J. Coale, in Fertility and Family Planning, B. Berelson et al. (eds.), University of Michigan Press, Ann Arbor, 1969.*]

nations with high birth rates was predictable. Figure 12-9 illustrates the drop in death rates for several Asian nations between their 1945 to 1949 averages and those of 1960 to 1961.

The effort of Sri Lanka (formerly called Ceylon) to control the population of mosquitoes that transmit malara is a classic case in point. Malaria was the chief cause of death on the island. As a consequence, DDT was introduced in 1946 in a massive mosquito-control program. That year, the death rate in Sri Lanka was 22 per 1,000. By 1970, it had dropped to 8 per 1,000. Malaria control was primarily responsible for this marked decline.

The industrialized nations with their declining birth and death rates show decreasing growth rates. On the other hand, the developing nations have consistently sustained their high birth rates to which they have added a rapid drop in death rates. The result is an explosive increase in rate of growth.

Figure 12-10 shows the extent of this contrast between a Western industrialized country (Sweden) and a developing country (Mexico). From about 1940 to 1970, the death rate in Mexico declined precipitously whereas the birth rate varied little and remained high. As a

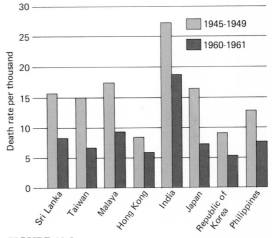

FIGURE 12-9
A comparison of the death rates of selected Asian nations between their 1945–1949 averages and those of 1960–1961. [*After Population Bulletin, vol. 20, no. 2, U.S. Population Reference Bureau.*]

consequence, the Mexican growth rate increased at a rapid pace. In 1970, with a birth rate of 43.4 per 1,000 and a death rate of 9.9 per 1,000, the growth rate was over 3.3 percent

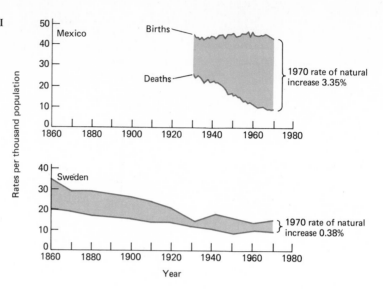

FIGURE 12-10
A comparison of birth rates, death rates, and rates of natural increase in a developed country (Sweden) and a developing country (Mexico). The 1970 birth and death rates for Mexico were 43.4 per 1,000 and 9.9 per 1,000, respectively. The 1970 birth and death rates for Sweden were 13.7 per 1,000 and 9.9 per 1,000. Colored area represents rate of natural increase. [*From the U.S. Population Reference Bureau.*]

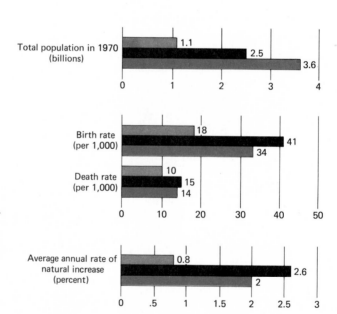

FIGURE 12-11
A comparison of the average birth rates, death rates, and growth rates (percent annual natural increase) of the developed (gray bar) versus the developing (black bar) countries in 1970. The colored bar represents world averages. [*Data from 1971 World Population Data Sheet of U.S. Population Reference Bureau and U.N. Demographic Yearbook for 1970.*]

(population doubling time of 21 years). Sweden, on the other hand, had a growth rate of about 1.4 percent in 1860. Since that time both its birth rate and death rate have gradually dropped. In 1970, its birth rate was 13.7 per 1,000 and its death rate 9.9, which meant that the annual rate of natural increase was only 0.38 percent. Nor are these exceptional ex-

amples, as Fig. 12-11 shows.

One might assume that even though a country had a growth rate as low as 0.38 percent its population would continue to grow for the simple reason that there are more births than deaths. One might also assume that native Mexicans and Swedes are about equally long-lived because they both have a death rate of

9.9 per 1,000. But neither of these assumptions is correct. If Sweden were to maintain a growth rate of 0.38 percent, its population would decrease. As for longevity, Swedish men live over 10 years longer, and Swedish women live over 12 years longer, than their Mexican counterparts. The reason for these apparent contradictions lies in population structure.

As the birth rate drops, fewer individuals in the next generation reach reproductive age. At the same time, declining death rates contribute to an increase in the percentage of older people in the population. The net result is a population which has a relatively large and growing percentage of older people, in which the risk of death is higher and a relatively small and shrinking percentage of people who are reproducing. Such a population contrasts sharply with one that has a large percentage of people at the reproductive prime of life and relatively few older people.

A knowledge of population structure is very useful in the study of human population problems. Such knowledge enables demographers to make predictions, called *population projections,* about future populations.

FORECASTING FUTURE POPULATIONS

Population structure is most easily visualized by means of age profiles like those in Fig. 12-12. A given population is divided into age-classes by increments of 5 years (0 to 4, 5 to 9, etc.). Each age-class is a horizontal bar extending on either side of a vertical center line. The segment to the left of the center line indicates the percentage of males in that age-class and the segment to the right indicates the percentage of females.

In Fig. 12-12, a developing country (India) with a high birth rate and declining death rate is compared with a developed country (Britain) having a low birth rate and low death rate. The differences are marked. The rapidly expanding population of India had a preponderance of young people. Thirty-seven percent of the population was under 15 years of age and only six percent was over 64. Most importantly, the majority of marriageable women were in the childbearing age-classes of 15 to 44. By contrast, Britain displayed a more evenly distributed age pattern. Only 23 percent were under 15, 12 percent were over 64, and marriageable women were not concentrated in the childbearing age-classes.

Two major features distinguishing these populations are their reproductive potential and the relative number of individuals in the "dependent" age-classes of under 1 to 14, and 65 and over.

India, typical of developing nations, had a much larger proportion of marriageable women in the childbearing age-classes than Britain. In addition, India had a much larger number of future child producers in the under 1 to 14 age-classes than Britain. As a consequence, India's capacity for population expansion was explosive whereas that of Britain was stationary to slow.

The proportion of people in dependent age-classes showed corresponding differences. India had 43 percent (37 percent below 15 plus 6 percent above 64). Britain had only 35 percent (23 percent below 15 plus 12 percent above 64). In short, 65 percent of the people in Britain were in working age-classes contributing to the support of the remaining 35 percent. India had 57 percent in working age-classes supporting a dependent population of 43 percent. It is of course true that India, like other developing nations, was an advanced agricultural society in which child labor is used extensively. On the other hand, it is also true that such countries are attempting to become industrialized. In making the transition, the economic burdens of education and health care alone are stifling to large populations with a high percentage of young dependents. India, for example, was faced with providing educational facilities and teachers for 20 million more children from 1961 to 1966 than she had to accommodate from 1956 to 1961.

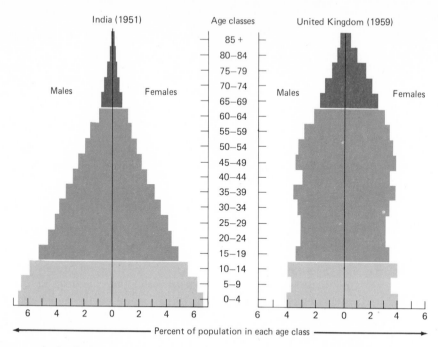

FIGURE 12-12

A comparison of the age structure of a developing country (India, 1951) and a developed country (United Kingdom, 1959). Such age profiles give age-classes in increments of 5 years (0 to 4, 5 to 9, etc.) up to 85+. The percentage of males of each age-class in the population is shown to the left of the center line and that of females to the right. The working ages (15 to 64), the young dependents (0 to 14), and elderly dependents (65 and over) are distinguished by differences in shading. Note that the rapidly growing country (India) has a preponderance of young people whereas the slow-growing United Kingdom has a more even distribution of ages. Of the entire Indian population, 37 percent was under 15 years of age and only 6 percent was over 64. The United Kingdom had 23 percent under 15 and 12 percent over 64. In 1891 the age structure of the United Kingdom was very similar to India's in 1951. [*India from Thompson and Lewis, Population Problems, 5th ed., McGraw-Hill, New York, 1965; United Kingdom, from Population Bulletin, vol. 18, no. 5 (1966), of the U. S. Population Reference Bureau.*]

In general, developing populations usually have between 40 and 50 percent of their number in the under 1 to 14 age-classes, whereas industrialized populations seldom have over 30 percent. However, developed populations have consistently higher proportions of working and elderly dependent age-classes. These distinguishing features are the products of high birth rate and declining death rate in one case and low birth and low death rate in the other.

Age structure, fertility, and population growth

We are now at a point where we can consider what may happen to a given population over time. Examine, for example, the age profile in Fig. 12-13. The 1960 profile of Japan illustrates a nation that markedly reversed its high birth rates following World War II. The Japanese accomplished this mainly through legalized abortion, which lowered the effective fertility of women. The sudden drop in the Japanese birth rate was due to a sharp reduction in the *fertility rate* and not a shortage of childbearing women. Fertility rate is a very useful demographic measure. It is defined as the number of live births per 1,000 women of childbearing

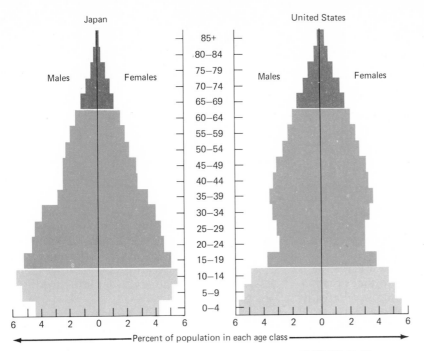

Japan

Males   Females

United States

Males   Females

85+
80—84
75—79
70—74
65—69
60—64
55—59
50—54
45—49
40—44
35—39
30—34
25—29
20—24
15—19
10—14
5—9
0—4

6   4   2   0   2   4   6   6   4   2   0   2   4   6

◀──── Percent of population in each age class ────▶

FIGURE 12-13
A comparison of two contrasting age profiles for 1960 populations, Japan (*left*) and the United States (*right*). Prior to World War II, Japan's profile resembled India's in Fig. 12-12. After the war a dramatic drop in birth rate caused a narrowing of the profile's base. The United States profile prior to the war resembled Britain's in Fig. 12-12. After the war an impressive increase in birth rate caused a broadening of the profile's base. [*After Thompson and Lewis, Population Problems, 5th ed., McGraw-Hill, New York.*]

age, which includes the 15 to 44 age-classes.

Returning to the 1960 Japanese profile, it can be seen that by 1970 females in the 5 to 9 age-class would have attained childbearing status. At this point, assuming the fertility rate had not changed significantly, the Japanese birth rate would have dropped even more sharply. By then there would be fewer births, for two reasons: lowered fertility rate and fewer childbearing women. In another five years, the effect would have been compounded further by still fewer childbearing women. It should be noted, however, that the Japanese fertility rate rose from 56.1 to 59.9 per 1,000 childbearing women between 1970 and 1971. Even so, the 1971 figure was still a low one.

The 1960 profile of the United States (Fig. 12-13) is almost a perfect opposite to that of Japan. Until the end of World War II (15 to 19 age-class), the United States age structure resembled that of Britain in 1959 (Fig. 12-12). After the war, the country underwent a rapid

rise in fertility rate, aptly called the "baby boom," which did not begin to slacken until about 1957 (Fig. 12-14). As a consequence, the United States profile has a spreading base unlike the constricted base of the Japanese profile. Rather than decreasing its number of future child producers, the United States was enlarging its inventory.

After 1960, the fertility rate in the United States dropped rapidly to 61.6 in 1970 and by 1972 had reached 59.3. These figures were about 15 per 1,000 lower than they were during the Great Depression years of 1933 to 1936.

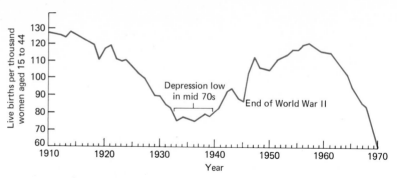

FIGURE 12-14
Fertility rate in the United States from 1910 to 1970. In 1970 it had dropped to 61.3 and by 1972 was only 59.3. [*From Population Profile, U.S. Population Reference Bureau, Mar. 1967 and U.N. Demographic Yearbooks for 1970 and 1972.*]

The 1933 to 1936 period is the narrowest portion of the United States profile below age 45, represented by age-classes 20 to 24 and 25 to 29.

Therefore, in the 1970s and early 1980s the United States is in an interesting situation. Although its fertility rate has dropped greatly, as a result of the postwar baby boom it is faced with an increasing number of women in the childbearing age group. Unless the fertility rate continues to drop sharply, or the death rate increases, birth rates should rise until the postwar baby crop matures and passes its reproductive prime. Since the majority of children are born to women in the 20 to 29 age-classes, birth rates should start to decline sometime between 1980 and 1985. The largest and last segment of the postwar baby boom, the under 1 to 4 age-class in 1960, will be 20 to 24 years old in 1980 and 25 to 29 in 1985.

Birth rates should then begin to drop, assuming fertility and death rates are somewhere near current levels. This does not mean, however, that population growth will stop. With decreasing birth rates, each generation will have fewer women of childbearing age. The resulting decline in the percentage of children, coupled with a low death rate, will produce a population in which the 65 and over age-class becomes progressively larger. As the age-class most subject to fatality increases, the death rate begins to catch up with the birth rate and a period of populational stability would theoretically be achieved. The date at which

that state may be attained, and the total population which will prevail at that time, depend upon the fertility rate and death rate in future years. As we have seen, the fertility rate can change drastically over a period of 10 years or less, so that predictions very far into the future are hazardous.

The Bureau of the Census has prepared projections of the United States population for the year 2020 based on varying rates of fertility but with mortality rates fairly close to the current value of 9.4 per 1,000. Fertility was considered in terms of the average number of children born per woman in her lifetime. The highest value was 3.1 children per woman. The lowest was a *replacement fertility level* of 2.1, that is, that level which, if continued unchanged, would *eventually* result in zero population growth.[3] All population projections assumed a net average immigration figure of 400,000 per year. Based upon these premises, the population in the United States in 2020 would range anywhere from 307.4 million (lowest estimate) to 447 million (highest estimate). Assuming a replacement fertility level and no net immigration after July, 1970, the population would be 279.5 million, or about 76 million more people than in 1970.[4]

In case A.D. 2020 seems a long way off, it is worth remembering that the postwar babies

[3] Replacement fertility level is greater than two to compensate for child mortality, infertility, and nonmarriage. Its value may vary between cultures.
[4] *Current Population Report,* Series P-25, no. 470, November 1971.

who were four years old and younger in 1960 will not have reached retirement age by that time. They will be 60 to 64 years old and some of their parents will still be living.

Projections of world population and its distribution

In 1966, the United Nations prepared a report which is a major source of data in forecasting future world populations. Four sets of estimates were employed in this report: *low, medium, high,* and *constant fertility, no migration.* These estimates represented different assumed levels of birth rates and death rates. The *constant*

fertility, no migration estimates were based upon the assumption that the high birth and declining death rates of the 1950s would remain constant and that no migration would occur between regions. These were the highest estimates and also the least likely. The most plausible projections were based on "medium" estimates because they were more in line with the history and current situation in each region. They are the estimates used here.

As might be expected, the developed and developing regions of the world (Fig. 12-15)

FIGURE 12-15
The developed and developing regions of the world for which the United Nations has prepared demographic projections. [*Map No. 1620, United Nations, October 1965.*]

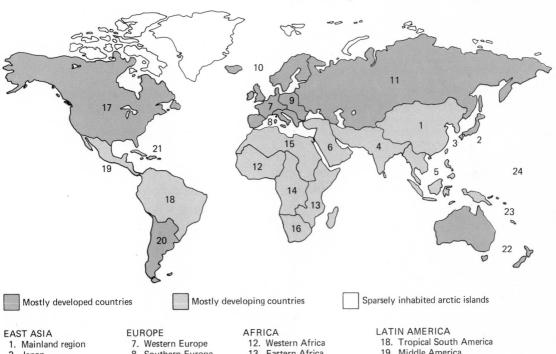

Mostly developed countries   Mostly developing countries   Sparsely inhabited arctic islands

EAST ASIA
1. Mainland region
2. Japan
3. Other East Asia

SOUTH ASIA
4. Middle South Asia
5. South-East Asia
6. South-West Asia

EUROPE
7. Western Europe
8. Southern Europe
9. Eastern Europe
10. Northern Europe

SOVIET UNION
11. Soviet Union

AFRICA
12. Western Africa
13. Eastern Africa
14. Middle Africa
15. Northern Africa
16. Southern Africa

NORTHERN AMERICA
17. Northern America

LATIN AMERICA
18. Tropical South America
19. Middle America
20. Temperate South America
21. Caribbean

OCEANIA
22. Australia and New Zealand
23. Melanesia
24. Polynesia and Micronesia

have significantly different projections. In Fig. 12-16 we can see that the developing nations harbored 67 percent of the nearly 3 billion people in the world in 1960. In A.D. 2000 they may reasonably be expected to have 76 percent of the more than 6 billion people projected for that date.

These are sobering statistics. The population of East and South Asia is projected to increase by more than 40 percent between 1980 and 2000, at which time these peoples will constitute over 56 percent of the world's population.[5] The economic burden alone of

[5] "World Population Prospects as Assessed in 1963," *Population Studies* No. 41, 1966.

FIGURE 12-16

World population growth from 1960 to 2000 segregated into developed and developing regions. These projections are based upon United Nations "medium" estimates in 1963. The developed regions include Europe, the U.S.S.R., North America, Japan, temperate South America, Australia, and New Zealand. The developing regions include East Asia less Japan, South Asia, Latin America less temperate South America, Oceania less Australia and New Zealand, and Africa. These regions are shown in Fig. 12-15. [*From "World Population Prospects as Assessed in 1963," U.N. Population Studies No. 41, 1966.*]

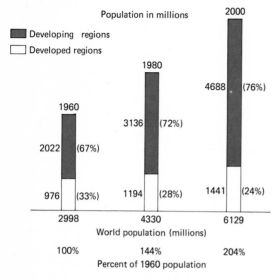

such vast numbers will be a monstrous one for any nation facing the problems of industrialization. Most importantly, even in 1976, more than half the world's population is inadequately fed and a large percentage of these are starving. The future demand for food, water, energy, raw materials, and manufactured goods will have a tremendous environmental impact.

But there is more to human population than mere numbers. How these numbers are distributed is also very important.

Human distribution: the trend toward urbanization

Obviously people are not distributed evenly over the face of the earth. The average population density of planet earth in 1970 was 27 people per square kilometer (0.386 square miles). In Mongolia the density was 1, in the United States 22, and in India 168. Even these figures convey no idea of the true extent of nonuniformity in human distribution because population density can vary widely in relatively small regions. The United Kingdom (Great Britain and Northern Ireland), for example, had a density of 228, but in England and Wales the figure was 324 and in Scotland it was 66. Many cities, on the other hand, have densities greatly in excess of these amounts. Although mainland China had an average density of 79 persons per square kilometer in 1970, that area of Hong Kong known as Victoria Town had 290,000.

While Hong Kong is an exceptionally crowded city, large urban centers are by nature relatively crowded compared to rural communities. What is significant is that human beings are distributed in precisely these two kinds of communities: thinly populated rural areas and densely populated urban centers.

Ever since the first true cities arose in ancient Mesopotamia between 4000 and 3000 B.C., there has been a worldwide trend toward urbanization. During the last half of the nineteenth century, this trend began to accelerate markedly. Although various reasons for this have been suggested, all of them undoubtedly trace their origins to the industrial revolution. The demand for labor either caused industry to locate in cities, or cities to develop around industry. Mechanization led to the feasibility of larger farms with smaller labor forces. The mechanization of farming, coupled with growth in the rural population, has caused large numbers of people to move from farming communities and small towns into large cities in search of a better life.

For whatever reasons, urbanization has been rapid over the past hundred years. In 1800 only about 7 percent of the United States population lived in towns and cities (Fig. 12-17). This figure rose to 16 percent in 1850, 39 percent in 1900, and 64 percent in 1950. By 1970, 73.5 percent of all United States residents were urban dwellers.

This same phenomenon also was occurring throughout the rest of the world; it was not

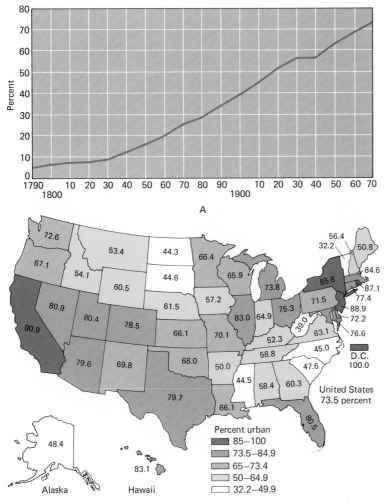

FIGURE 12-17
Urbanization in the United States, 1790 to 1970. *A,* Percentage of urban population, 1790 to 1970; *B,* percentage of urban population by states in 1970. In 1970, 73.5 percent of Americans were urban dwellers. [*From 1970 Census of Population, U.S. Summary, PC(1)-A1, December 1971.*]

confined to the more developed countries (Fig. 12-18). In 1920 there were 83 cities in the world with 500,000 or more inhabitants. Of these, 69 were located in the more developed regions and 14 in the less developed. By 1960, there were 234 such cities. The developed nations had doubled their number to 139 while the developing nations had almost septupled theirs to 95.

Figure 12-19 offers a more comprehensive summary of these changes from 1920 to 1960, and projects them to 2000. The illustration is based on United Nations data[6] in which *urban* is considered to be a city of 20,000

[6] "Growth of the World's Urban and Rural Population, 1920–2000," United Nations, 1960.

FIGURE 12-18
Urbanization levels in the major regions of the world in 1960. Urban is here considered to be that portion of population living in cities of 20,000 or more. (For legend of geographic areas see Fig. 12-15.) [*From U.N. Report, "Growth of the World's Urban and Rural Population, 1920–1960," and U.N. Maps 1620 and 1819.*]

or more. *Rural* includes farming communities and towns under 20,000. The projected figures for A.D. 2000 are based upon the United Nations "medium" estimates.

The urban population more than doubled in the developed regions between 1920 and 1960, and is predicted to double again by 2000. The urban population in the developing regions more than quadrupled between 1920 and 1960 and is projected to nearly quintuple itself by 2000.

Rural populations, on the other hand, have grown much more slowly. Among developed countries, the rural segment grew only about 11 percent from 1920 to 1960 and is forecast to grow less than 3 percent by 2000. Even in the rapidly expanding less developed countries, rural growth was only 52 percent between 1920 and 1960, with a predicted increment of less than 90 percent for A.D. 2000. Although these are large increases, they fall far short of the 450 and 462 percent increments in the urban population.

■ More than 55% Urbanized   ■ 40-55% Urbanized   ■ 25-40% Urbanized   ▢ 10-25% Urbanized   ▢ Less than 10% urbanized

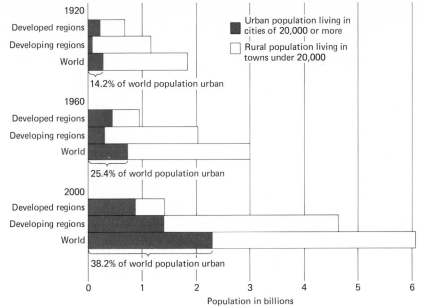

FIGURE 12-19
World population growth from 1920 to 2000. In these bar graphs, growth in developing and developed regions is further divided into that portion of the total population in each region which is urban and that which is rural. Urban populations (colored) are defined as those living in cities of 20,000 or more. These graphs are based on "medium" estimates of U.N. projections in 1969. Note increasing percentage of urban dwellers. [*Data from "Growth of the World's Urban and Rural Population, 1920–2000," United Nations, 1969.*]

If these "medium" estimates for the beginning of the next millenium prove to be reasonably accurate, the world will have changed to a remarkable degree from what it was in 1960. About 61 percent of the urban population of the world will be located in developing regions with a projected annual growth rate of 3.7 percent (Fig. 12-20). Nearly 39 percent of that population will inhabit developed regions with a projected growth rate of 1.6 percent. If the rate of urban growth among developing

nations dropped to 3.0 percent after A.D. 2000, the year 2024 would find an urban population among developing nations almost equal to the total world population of 1960. If, by chance, the rate after A.D. 2000 dropped to 1.6 percent for the entire urban population, the people living in cities in 2044 would outnumber the 1970 world population by more than 1 billion.

If these projections are reasonably accurate, the year 2000 will witness a world population of over 6 billion, possibly more. Between

	1920–1940	1940–1960	1960–1980	1980–2000
URBAN POPULATION				
Developed regions	2.2	2.0	1.9	1.6
Developing regions	3.1	4.5	4.1	3.7
RURAL POPULATION				
Developed regions	0.4	1.0	0.1	0.1
Developing regions	0.9	1.2	1.8	1.4

FIGURE 12-20
Estimated annual rates of growth (%) in urban and rural populations of developed and developing regions between 1920 and 2000. Rural population includes towns under 20,000. [*From "Growth of the World's Urban and Rural Population, 1920-2000," United Nations, 1969.*]

1960 and 2000, the number of people living in cities will have increased from 25 to 38 percent. Having considered some of the possible potentials for expansion beyond that date, the obvious question arises as to whether spaceship earth, not to mention *Homo sapiens* itself, can accommodate such numbers over the long term. What, in short, is the earth's environmental capacity[7] for its human inhabitants?

In the next chapter we will address the question of optimum population size and the problem of controlling human numbers within the limits of that optimum.

[7] See *Population size and its regulation* in Chap. 11.

SUGGESTED READINGS

BOYDEN, S. V. (ed.): *The Impact of Civilization on the Biology of Man,* Toronto: University of Toronto Press, 1970. A collection of papers from a symposium in Austria.

DALE, T., and V. CARTER: *Topsoil and Civilization,* Norman, Okla.: University of Oklahoma Press, 1955. A fascinating account of agricultural history, particularly in Europe and in the Middle East.

EDITORS of *Scientific American:* "The Human Population," *Scientific American,* September 1974. This entire issue of 11 articles is devoted to the human population, most of which deals with the subject matter of this chapter.

EHRLICH, P. R., et al.: *Human Ecology: Problems and Solutions,* San Francisco: W. H. Freeman and Company, 1973. This small book on human ecology has excellent discussions on population structure, distribution, growth, and many related topics.

SOUTHWICK, C. H.: *Ecology and the Quality of Our Environment,* New York: Van Nostrand Reinhold Company, 1972. This book and the work by Turk et al. are on general and human ecology and contain interestingly written discussions of population dynamics and many related topics.

TURK, J., et al.: *Ecosystems, Energy, Population,* Philadelphia: W. B. Saunders Company, 1975.

YOUNG, J. Z.: *An Introduction to the Study of Man,* New York: Oxford University Press, 1971. An encyclopedic account of human biology with two chapters devoted to easily understood discussions of human fertility, mortality, and population growth.

REVIEW QUESTIONS

1 What is Malthusian doctrine? To what extent is it considered valid today?

2 What demographic measures are employed and how are they used in determining and expressing the extent to which a population has grown or declined? In a growing population, what measure is used to project (predict) population growth and future population size? Define all terms used.

3 In broad outline trace the course of population growth from the time of early Neanderthal populations to the present. Indicate episodes of rapid growth (population explosions) and identify the major factors affecting growth rate and death rate levels.

4 What is the demographic transition? What are its probable causes?

5 The difference in growth rate between the developed and developing countries cannot be entirely explained in terms of the demographic transition. What other factor is involved in this difference, and explain its effects by citing a specific example.

6 In 1970 both Mexico and Sweden had a death rate of 9.9 per 1,000. Nonetheless, Swedish men live over 10 years longer and Swedish women live over 12 years longer than their Mexican counterparts. How can you account for this difference?

7 Developing countries have high birth rates and declining death rates whereas developed countries have low birth rates and low death rates. Two major demographic features distinguish these two populations insofar as population structure is concerned. What are these features and what are their economic consequences?

8 If one assumes a certain fertility rate and death rate for a given population, the future growth of that population can be projected on the basis of its age profile. Explain how this is done.

9 A population with a replacement fertility level may not stop growing for two or more generations. What conditions in addition to low fertility must be met before population growth finally stops?

10 Although there has been a worldwide trend toward urbanization ever since the first true cities arose thousands of years ago, this trend accelerated markedly after 1850. List three reasons which have been suggested for this.

11 According to United Nations population projections ("medium" estimates), what will the world population be in A.D. 2000? Approximately what percentage of this population will be distributed among the developing countries? Approximately what percentage of the world's urban population will live in developing countries? What will be the projected growth rate for the urban population in developing countries and in developed countries?

THIRTEEN

HUMAN POPULATION II:
Optimum Size and Population Control

In the previous chapter we noted the explosive nature of human population growth during the past century and forecast future population increases to and beyond A.D. 2000. Two important questions are posed by the phenomenal rise in human numbers. First, what is the optimum population size; that is, what is the earth's environmental capacity for its human inhabitants? Second, by what means can human numbers be kept within the limits of optimum population size? In this chapter, we will focus on these two questions.

OPTIMUM POPULATION SIZE

The question of optimum population size is complex and can be answered in numerous ways. In the first place, the demands that a people make on their environment is closely related to their standard of living. The world could support many more inhabitants if they lived like Chinese than it could if they lived like North Americans. In the second place, there will be many future developments in agriculture, industry, transportation, and hopefully, economic systems which may affect optimum population size. We should not expect too much of such technological and socioeconomic changes, but neither should we assume that they will be ineffectual.

Finally, there are many factors affecting the quality of human life about which very little is known at present. As we saw in Chap. 11, crowding and the lack of natural open space may affect human behavior in important ways. People of various cultures seem to respond differently to "interpersonal press." Are the residents of Hong Kong and Tokyo, for example, unaffected by it, or have they developed a culture which enables them to tolerate the discomforts of interpersonal press? There also are differences in response to crowding between socioeconomic levels of the same culture. Overcrowding in the ghettos of the world, however, is more an effect than a cause of the helpless despair that engulfs poverty-stricken people.

Despite the fact that the optimum population level is a complex issue, some reliable observations can be made about the nature of optimum population size. There is a common commitment the world over to a growth economy. "Progress," however it is defined, usually is dependent on sustaining a continuous and increasing demand for the goods and services of technology. Adherence to such an economic philosophy in the face of an ever-growing number of consumers is doomed to failure sooner or later because of the finite resources of the earth. Both economic philosophy and population must be subject to the restraints of our place of residence.

Any region is overpopulated in which (1) nonrenewable resources are being depleted rapidly, or (2) the environment is steadily deteriorating through pollution. The extent to which this already has occurred will be the subject of the next two chapters. Our planet is overpopulated now by either criterion.

Hulett calculated the degree of this overpopulation by dividing the per capita consumption of resources by United States citizens into the total world production of those resources as estimated by the United Nations. Hulett concluded that the maximum world population that could be supported by present agricultural and industrial systems was about 1 billion people living at United States' levels of affluence. Without a decrease in the standard of living, even this number would start running out of certain critical resources in a few generations.[1]

A consideration of optimal world numbers is not a simple matter of dealing with some population as a model from which projections can be made, particularly when that population is as untypical as our own. Several factors contribute to a proper understanding of optimal population levels. We will consider them in three contexts: the pressure of underdeveloped societies; population density, open space, and overpopulation; and population and food.

The pressure of underdeveloped societies

In 1970, the developing countries, with a total population more than twice that of industrialized countries, accounted for a little more than 14 percent of the world's total energy consumption. In contrast, Canada and the United States together consumed 36 percent. Although the United States musters only 5 percent of the global population, it consumes 35 percent of the world's resources.

Statistics such as these reflect the disproportionate consumption of natural resources by the United States and other developed societies compared to the rest of the world. The rest of the world, however, has a much larger population which is growing at a much faster rate; most importantly, it is now aware of the possibilities of achieving a higher standard of living. Since the wealth and the production potential of most developed countries is dependent upon resources possessed by underdeveloped nations, the handwriting clearly is on the wall. The demand for a higher living standard in developing regions will depress that

[1] H. R. Hulett, "Optimum World Population," *BioScience*, vol. 20, no. 3, 1970, pp. 160–161.

standard among industrialized people if we are to avoid the alternative of world conflict and the eventuality of nuclear warfare. The process already is in motion, as witnessed by the dramatic rise of petroleum prices in 1974 through unilateral action of Middle East oil-producing nations.

The security of industrialized societies is tied directly to the security of underdeveloped countries. The developed nations currently consume and wastefully mismanage a disproportionate share of the world's mineral resources, including phosphate, potash, and nitrogen fertilizers. Since a large and indispensable portion of these resources belong to underdeveloped societies, it is in the long-range interest of developed nations to give economic and technical assistance to underdeveloped regions in their quest for a better life. There is a strong likelihood that everyone will benefit in the process. As our own standard of living drops, we will have to forego electric hair groomers and (bite the bullet!) perhaps even electric-powered toothbrushes; automobiles built to cruise comfortably at 115 kilometers an hour (70 miles an hour) probably will become a thing of the past. We may even have to reduce our gargantuan inventory of cosmetics and useless-to-harmful nonprescription drugs. Our inalienable right to squander natural resources may become alienable after all. It is doubtful that these sacrifices would affect our mental or physical health adversely, and there is every possibility that both would improve. After all, we would be ridding ourselves of the awful cost and waste of this gadgetry—and in the process making our air a little easier to breathe and our water a little safer to drink. We also would be following the only course of action that can ever bring about the peaceful coexistence of the diverse cultures that inhabit our small planet.

Population density, open space, and overpopulation

Commonly, overpopulation is thought of in terms of too many people for the available space—that is, population density. Conversely, areas that contain large expanses of open space and relatively few people per square kilometer or square mile are considered to be underpopulated. Both these assumptions are false.

An overpopulated society usually is one that has exceeded the capacity of its available resources. Southern California, with several large cities interconnected by an almost continuous web of suburbs, is overpopulated because of a water shortage and air pollution. Vast expanses in the Mojave and Colorado deserts, on the other hand, are only sparsely settled, yet they too are overpopulated. In this case, it is due to a shortage of water and the heavy recreational pressure of off-the-road traffic by dune buggy and motorcycle riders (Fig. 13-1). Water is in short supply, in fact, for the entire continental United States.

The Netherlands often has been considered to be much more overpopulated than the United States because its density is about 18 times higher. Actually the reverse is true because Holland obtains most of its resources from vast areas beyond its borders. It imports 63 percent of its cereals and is the world's second largest importer of protein. In addition to all its cotton and 77 percent of its wool, Holland imports all its phosphate rock and potash for fertilizer. Practically all its minerals are imported as well.[2] Although Holland produces the energy equivalent of over 20 million metric tons of coal in petroleum products, its energy consumption is equivalent to over 47 million.[3]

Population and food

The most effective limiting factor for humankind is food supply. The President's Science Advisory Committee Panel on the World Food Supply estimated in 1967 that 20 percent of the population in developing countries was

[2] Holland imports all its antimony, asbestos, aluminum ore, chromium, copper, diamonds, gold, iron ore, lead, magnesium ore, manganese, mercury, molybdenum, nickel, silver, tin, tungsten, vanadium, and zinc.

[3] P. R. Ehrlich and J. P. Holdren, "Impact of Population Growth," *Science,* vol. 171, Mar. 26, 1971, pp. 1212–1217.

FIGURE 13-1
Motorcyclists on the Mojave Desert
in California. [*Bob Waterman/Photography.*]

undernourished (lacking sufficient calories per day) while 60 percent was malnourished (deficient in one or more nutrients, usually protein). This means that about 1.5 billion people were either undernourished or malnourished or both. The United Nations Food and Agriculture Organization (FAO) placed the number at 2 billion. Of these, about 500 million were habitually hungry or starving, and between 10 and 20 million die annually from either undernourishment or malnutrition. But even this is not the full picture. Additional millions die every year of tuberculosis, leprosy, diseases of the digestive tract, and animal parasites that are not included in these figures; yet malnutrition predisposes the individual to all these afflictions and impedes recovery seriously. The thousands of people in Bangladesh who are killed every year on the Ganges Delta from ordinary storms are not included either. Few would risk the hazards of living there to farm the land if Bangladesh were not so overpopulated.

The figures quoted do not include the millions of malnourished and underfed people in developed countries. Malnutrition among the poverty-stricken and those forced to live on fixed incomes has reached formidable propor-

tions in the United States. The specter of senior citizens raiding garbage cans and being obliged to eat canned pet food has become a national disgrace. Despite the fact that the United States is the richest country in the world, her wealth is distributed quite disproportionately. During 1969, which was a good year economically, the bottom 60 percent of the people on the economic ladder received 34.4 percent of the net national income while the top 20 percent took home 43 percent. When incomes this diverse are coupled with rampant inflation, large segments of people on low incomes have little opportunity to provide themselves with an adequate diet. This is compounded further to an inordinate degree by the high birth rates prevailing in the ghettos, where most of the poverty is concentrated.

There is little doubt that the statistics we have been reviewing are the symptoms of overpopulation in both industrialized and underdeveloped societies. We can, of course, look to the past to find episodes in human history when undernourishment, malnutrition, and starvation took human lives by the millions. Four million starved to death in China during 1920 to 1921. Five to ten million Russians met a similar fate in 1918 to 1922 and 1932 to 1934. Famine struck India in 1943 when between two and four million perished in West Bengal. As late as 1973, 100,000 died of starvation in Ethiopia after six years of African drought.

But these horrendous events fell short of the current world situation in several respects. Catastrophic though they were, each was restricted to a particular region for a limited period and generally was caused by weather or warfare. Today the catastrophe of malnutrition and starvation is unceasing for 2 billion or more people throughout every region because food production has not kept pace with reproduction.

The developing countries suffer the most from food deficiencies and are the least able to cope with the problem because of the economic burden of excessive overpopulation. Figure 13-2 shows clearly that the average diet per capita in underdeveloped countries is significantly lower in calories, total protein, and animal protein than that in developed countries. The consumption of animal protein is particularly low, less than one-fifth of that in developed nations. This is an especially serious problem because animal proteins contain more of the essential amino acids than plant proteins and are superior in quality. Diets low in animal protein require more total protein when it comes from plant sources to compensate for the latter's inferior quality.

Figure 13-3 shows that some progress has been made in the food production of industrialized regions since 1963. World per capita food production in 1971, for instance, was 8 percent higher than in 1963. But this increase was lim-

ited to the developed nations. Africa, Asia, and Latin America essentially were no better off in 1971 than they were in 1963, and 1963 was by no means a banner year. Even among developed nations, the improvements in food production were partly offset by inadequate food distribution: the poor did not get their proportionate share.

The prospect of per capita food increases

Formidable obstacles confront any programs that might improve the production and distribution of food sufficiently to relieve human suffering. In the practical world of capital investment and available time, these obstacles are insurmountable in the face of continued population growth. The North American Water and Power Alliance is a case in point. This was a United States proposal to route water from Canadian rivers to various locations over the United States. At an estimated cost of 100 billion dollars, this project would have increased United States water supplies by 21 percent. It would have required 20 years to complete, however, during which time the population is expected to increase by 25 percent and possibly more.

Food production might be improved in four major ways: (1) increasing agricultural lands, (2) improving crop yields, (3) increasing the harvest of the seas, and (4) developing detritus agricultural and aquacultural systems.

Increasing agricultural lands Most of the potentially arable land in the world is in Africa, South America, and Asia (Fig. 13-4). What appears to be a great opportunity, however,

	Developed countries	Developing countries
Daily consumption of calories (kilocalories) per person	2,941	2,033
Daily consumption of protein in grams	84.0	52.4
Daily consumption of animal protein in grams	38.8	7.2

FIGURE 13-2
Comparison of the average caloric and protein consumption per person per day in developed and developing countries. There are 453.6 grams in one pound. [*After D. Paarlberg, in Overcoming World Hunger, C. M. Hardin (ed.), © The American Assembly, Columbia University, 1969. By permission of Prentice-Hall International, Inc.*]

Region	1963	1965	1967	1969	1971
World (excluding China)	100	100	105	105	108
Africa	100	97	99	98	101
Asia					
Near East	100	100	103	104	102
Far East (excluding China)	100	96	97	101	101
Europe					
Eastern and U.S.S.R.	100	108	121	122	129
Western	100	100	107	108	114
Latin America	100	100	103	102	100
North America	100	101	107	105	111
Oceania	100	95	97	108	108

FIGURE 13-3
Per capita food production of the major geographic regions of the world from 1963 to 1971 in terms of the percentage of 1963 production. [*Data from the U.N. Statistical Yearbook for 1972.*]

carries heavy restrictions with it. Nearly all the land that can be farmed with the limited water and money now available is already in production. Putting new lands into production is costly and time-consuming. It involves surveys, clearing the land, building roads, developing irrigation systems, and providing large numbers of resettled people with homes, schools, and essential services. Beyond that, additional large sums are required for the purchase of fertilizers, pesticides, power for irrigation, and farm machinery, including the fuel and oil for its operation. It is conservative to say that 3 to 5 *trillion* dollars would be required to put the 5

billion acres of potentially arable lands in Africa, South America, and Asia into production.[4] It would take decades to accomplish, during which time the population would at least double and possibly quadruple. Needless to say, the major share of the economic and technical burden for such a task would have to be assumed by developed societies. And to no avail — because, as we have seen, the task would be self-defeating.

In fact, it is becoming increasingly difficult

[4] The President's Science Advisory Committee, "The World Food Problem," 1967.

FIGURE 13-4
The population and cultivated land area in the major geographic regions, compared with potentially arable (tillable) land as of 1965. Cultivated land includes areas in temporary fallow (resting land) which may include as much as one-third or more of all cultivated land in any one year. An acre is 0.405 hectares. [*From The President's Science Advisory Committee, "The World Food Problem," 1967.*]

Continent	Population in 1965 (millions of persons)	Area in billions of acres		
		Total	Potentially arable	Cultivated
Africa	310	7.46	1.81	0.39
Asia	1,855	6.76	1.55	1.28
Australia and New Zealand	14	2.03	0.38	0.04
Europe	445	1.18	0.43	0.38
North America	255	5.21	1.15	0.59
South America	197	4.33	1.68	0.19
U.S.S.R.	234	5.52	0.88	0.56
Total	3,310	32.49	7.88	3.43

even to maintain current cultivated acreages. Great quantities of electricity are used in the manufacture of agricultural chemicals. Since electricity commonly is produced in generators driven by petroleum products, the drastic rise in petroleum prices has created a worldwide shortage of nitrogen fertilizers. The high cost of petroleum also has interfered with the pumping of irrigation water in the underdeveloped countries.

Urbanization and overland transport make further inroads on existing cropland. The highways and freeways of the United States surpass the area of The Netherlands and Belgium combined. California, the richest agricultural state in the Union, is reputed to have 25 percent of its area occupied by cities, sprawling suburbs, towns, reservoirs, roads, highways and freeways, power-line rights-of-way, and firebreaks. Unfortunately, the best sites for urban development are the best sites for raising crops: level land with deep soil and plenty of available water. California and other states are losing some of their best croplands to urbanization (Fig. 13-5). According to the U.S. Department of Agriculture, over 800,000 hectares (2 million acres) of rural land are converted annually to nonagricultural use.

Improving crop yields   Much greater production can be obtained from croplands through heavier application of fertilizers and the use of new high-yield varieties of grain. These two practices have become increasingly widespread, which has given rise to the term *green revolution*. Although the most ardent advocates of the green revolution do not claim that it can keep pace with population growth, it is the only program that can reasonably be expected to increase food production in the immediate future.

Acreage planted to new grain varieties has increased markedly in Asia since 1965 (Fig. 13-6). This was responsible, at least in large measure, for India's remarkable gains in grain production from 1965 to 1971. Although its population grew by 80 million (17 percent) during that period, its wheat harvest increased by almost 89 percent (from 12.3 to 23.2 million

metric tons) and its rice harvest by 39 percent (from 46 to 64 million metric tons). These harvests contributed importantly to a total food production gain of about 20 percent over 1963 production.

But the green revolution has its limitations, particularly in developing regions. Underdeveloped economies cannot expect to equal the agricultural yields of Western technology and expertise. The tiny nation of Holland, for example, provides a large portion of Western Europe as well as itself with fruit and vegetables which it grows, for the most part, in greenhouses. Stretching as far as the eye can see, these closely packed greenhouses cover hundreds of square kilometers (Fig. 13-7). If India were to match Holland's per capita use of fertilizer, it would consume almost 50 percent of the world's output.

Other problems are inherent in the green revolution itself. High-yielding strains require heavy fertilization. The large amounts of soil nitrogen and phosphate that are needed result in increasing amounts of these nutrients being carried by runoff and streams into lakes, where they stimulate the excessive growth of algae. This process of nutrient enrichment and excessive algal growth is called *eutrophication*. As portions of the massive algal "bloom" die, the decaying mass consumes available oxygen, causing the death of multitudes of fish. Eutrophication has become a common problem and results in the loss of valuable animal protein.

High-yielding strains of grain usually are quite susceptible to pests which, like man, find them quite palatable and nutritious. This means that the green revolution requires not only the added cost of increased fertilization (and eutrophication) but also the higher cost of more extensive pesticide applications and the risk of greater soil and water pollution.

Finally, there is growing concern for the diminishing populations of plants which constitute the original genetic raw material from which new high-yielding varieties are developed. We discussed the production of domesticated varieties of plants and animals in Chap. 2 (*Applied genetics*) and Chap. 9 (*In-*

FIGURE 13-5
Prime agricultural land in Santa Clara Valley, California being overrun by urbanization. *A*, The farming community surrounding the city of Santa Clara in 1950 (top right); *B*, in 1970 most of the agricultural land shown in *A* was covered by urban sprawl. [*By permission of Air Photo Co., Inc. and the Santa Clara County Planning Department.*]

A

troduction). Some former cultivated varieties and their "wild" cousins apparently have been lost forever in the sweep of civilization and others are becoming rare. Such "genetic erosion," if allowed to continue, will seriously

FIGURE 13-6
Estimated acreages of new varieties of grain in Asia, 1964 to 1968. The 1968–1969 figure was projected. [*After Dalrymple, International Agricultural Development Service, U.S.D.A., November 1968.*]

Year	Acres
1964–1965	200
1965–1966	37,000
1966–1967	4,800,000
1967–1968	20,000,000
1968–1969	34,000,000

obstruct the continuing development of new, improved strains or even the regeneration of old ones.

Increased harvest of the seas   It is commonly assumed that the open seas of the world are a vast, largely untapped reservoir of animal protein. On the contrary, quite the opposite is true. A careful analysis by John H. Ryther of the Woods Hole Oceanographic Institution makes it clear that the open seas essentially are a "biological desert" with no significant potential for future increase in yield (Fig. 13-8). Although the open sea comprises 90 percent of the world's oceans, it yields less than 0.07 percent of the total estimated production of marine fish annually. Upwelling regions which make up some 0.1 percent of the ocean's surface (an area roughly the size of California) produce about one-half the world's

B

marine fish supply while the other half comes from coastal waters.

Ryther estimates that approximately 240 million metric tons of fish are produced annually in the sea. This does not mean, how-

FIGURE 13-7
Greenhouses in The Netherlands, between Rotterdam and the Hook of Holland. Vegetables and fruits as well as ornamental flowering plants are grown in these structures. This particular group covered an area of 6 by 15 kilometers (3.7 × 9.3 miles).

Ocean province	Percent of ocean	Fish production in metric tons of fresh weight
Open seas	90	160,000
Coastal waters and estuaries	9.9	120,000,000
Coastal upwelling areas	0.1	120,000,000
Total		240,160,000
Less that left for sustained yield, and that taken by predation		140,160,000
Potential harvest theoretically available to humans		100,000,000

FIGURE 13-8
Estimated annual world production of marine fish, and the potential harvest theoretically available to man. [*After J. H. Ryther, Science, vol. 166, October 3, 1969, p. 74, © American Association for the Advancement of Science.*]

ever, that amount can be harvested. In the first place, man is competing with other carnivores for this animal protein. It is estimated, for example, that 8 million tons of anchovies are consumed annually off the coast of Peru by such predators as guano birds, squid, tuna, and sea lions. This is almost equal to the amount

FIGURE 13-9
Some species of marine fish and mammals whose populations are stressed, declining, or on the verge of extinction because of overfishing. Overfishing has wiped out entire fishery industries, including the California sardine industry and the herring industries of Hokkaido, Japan and of Britain's east coast. [*From the Red Data Book, vol. 4, International Union for the Conservation of Nature and Natural Resources (IUCN), Switzerland.*]

Peruvian anchovy
Barents Sea cod
Newfoundland cod
Bottom fish of the Western Pacific and Eastern Atlantic
Bering Sea flatfish
North Atlantic hake
Atlanto-Scandian herring
British Columbia herring
North Sea herring
Menhaden
North Sea plaice
Northwest Pacific salmon
California sardine
East Asian sardine
Atlantic, Pacific, and Indian Ocean tunas
Antarctic blue whales
Antarctic fin whales

harvested by man. In the second place, enough fish should be left in the ocean to guarantee a maximum sustainable yield in the years ahead.

With these limitations to be considered, it is probable that the maximum sustained yield to man will not exceed 100 million tons annually.[5] The harvest in 1970 was 70 million tons. Since the fishery industry has been increasing its catch at an average rate of some 8 percent per year for the 25 years prior to 1970, it is unlikely that this expansion can continue beyond 1980.

It is, in fact, quite possible if not probable, that the marine fishery may never attain an annual catch of 100 million tons. According to FAO data, the 1973 catch was 5 million tons less than that of 1970. Overfishing has stressed and, in some cases, reduced almost to extinction the populations of numerous whale and fish species (Fig. 13-9).

There is one form of sea harvest, however, which holds some promise. Known as *marine farming,* it is based not on exploiting nature's productivity but on sharing it. As indicated in Chap. 11, young ecosystems produce a large biomass. Intertidal ecosystems like estuaries are perpetually young because they are continually disturbed as well as enriched by alternating tides. They also are naturally fertilized by the nutrients supplied them from terrestrial runoff.

[5] J. H. Ryther, "Photosynthesis and Fish Production in the Sea," *Science,* vol. 166, Oct. 3, 1969, pp. 72–76.

Japan practiced oyster farming 2,000 years ago and also has pioneered modern improvements in the technique. Oysters are filter feeders; that is, they get their food by filtering out the microscopic organisms in seawater. Miniature oysters are collected on shells which are strung together; the string of shells and their attached oysters are then suspended in water, generally by being attached to rafts (Fig. 13-10). Such suspension cultures of oysters yield 51.6 metric tons of shucked meats per hectare in the small cultivated areas of Japan's Inland Sea.[6] Experimental tests in Rhode Island indicate that the coastal waters of the Eastern United States might yield more than 56 metric tons of oyster meat per hectare of cultivated area. Mussels, also filter-feeding

[6] Gifford B. Pinchot, "Marine Farming," *Scientific American*, December 1970, pp. 15–21.

FIGURE 13-10
Seed-oyster production near Hiroshima, Japan. *Top,* general view of the area; *bottom,* detailed view of the strings of shells on which oysters are grown. Each shell (scallop shells are used here) is a platform to which a number of miniature oysters are attached. [*By permission of J. H. Ryther.*]

mollusks, are cultivated in the Bay of Vigo, Spain with even more impressive yields. The annual harvest there averages 268.9 metric tons of mussel meat per hectare, five times the oyster yield in Japan. By comparison, the best rangelands will produce about 0.28 metric tons of beef meat per hectare.

Marine farming is a form of intensive agriculture which involves, at least with present techniques, a heavy investment in labor. It would seem, however, that the economic limitation is more than compensated by the prospect of obtaining remarkably high yields *at no environmental cost.*

Detritus agricultural and aquacultural systems Another food production program which holds promise for the future is patterned after food chains found in climax biologic communities. It will be recalled from Chap. 11 that about 90 percent of all food chains in mature ecosystems have their source in the organic detritus of the community. Organic matter is continuously recycled through the community. Detritus agriculture and aquaculture — food production from land and water based upon the recycling of organic matter — are attempts to bring the same stability and economy into food production in the human community.

Biochemical and food technology have advanced to the point that the texture, appearance, taste, and smell of a great variety of food substances can be controlled and modified. This technology could certainly be extended to apply to highly nutritious substances like algae and yeasts which are now used only as additives in food preparation, if at all. Yeast has a high protein content and is rich in B vitamins. Some algae contain large amounts of protein, plant fats, and vitamins, especially A and C.

A fermenting tank seeded with 249 kilograms (500 pounds) of yeast immersed in a nutrient medium of acid-digested plant fiber and ammonium salts can reasonably be expected to produce a metric ton of yeast

every day. Algae of the type referred to have been grown in sewage processing ponds where they provide the oxygen necessary for sewage decomposition. Properly processed, prepared, and cooked these algae would be suitable for human consumption. Those who shudder at the idea might bear in mind that for generations, Americans have eaten and relished hot dogs and sausages whose skins were made of hog intestines.

One of the most striking demonstrations of the prolific harvests possible in detritus aquaculture is illustrated by fish culture programs in Indonesia. Bottom-feeding fish (the carp *Cyprinus carpio*) are confined in bamboo cages placed in rapidly flowing streams with a high sewage content. The fish, feeding on the dense carpet of worms and insect larvae in the sandy stream bed, grow rapidly to yield an annual harvest in West Java of more than 500 metric tons per hectare (220 short tons per acre). The warmth of Indonesian streams is an important factor in these high yields.[7] Even in the cold waters of Munich, however, the Bavarian Hydropower Company produces about 0.5 metric tons of carp per hectare per year in its sewage ponds — a yield 78 percent higher than beef production on the best rangelands.

The world population of fish from ponds (aquaculture) in 1967 amounted to nearly 4 percent of the total fish harvest for that year. Mainland China alone reported an annual harvest of 1.5 million metric tons of carp and carp-like fishes (Fig. 13-11). With the application of inorganic fertilizers to increase fish food growth, the production of carp in Israel, catfish in the Southern United States, and milkfish in Indonesia and Taiwan, has ranged from 2.0 to 3.4 metric tons per hectare. The use of partially processed sewage to fertilize fishponds might reduce the cost of fertilization and thereby increase aquacultural production by the more widespread use of fertilizer. Cer-

[7] J. E. Bardach, "Aquaculture," *Science,* vol. 161, Sept. 13, 1968, pp. 1098–1106.

tainly it would reduce environmental costs by saving the energy used in manufacturing chemical fertilizers and returning at least some of our organic wastes back into food production rather than abandoning them to the processes of decay in our oceans, rivers, and lakes.

Detritus agriculture and aquaculture, however, should not be expected to solve our food production problems. The products of detritus farming will be either novel or repugnant to many people. It is not easy to change habits and attitudes which are firmly entrenched by tradition. Furthermore the increased harvests that could be expected from detritus farming, combined with those from marine farming and improved crop yields, cannot accommodate the populational crises we face now and in the future.

Energy cost of the green revolution

One aspect of the population-food dilemma remains to be considered: the energy cost of the green revolution. A thoughtful analysis of United States agriculture by J. S. and C. E. Steinhart indicates that the enormous energy cost of industrialized agriculture very likely prevents its use in developing countries and ultimately may be self-defeating even among developed nations. Nonindustrialized food systems in "primitive" cultures and a few highly civilized ones have obtained 5 to 50 or more food calories (kilocalories) per calorie of energy expended. Through the use of fertilizer, gasoline, and so on, the United States' system expends at least 9, and possibly as much as 12, calories of fuel energy for each calorie of food energy on the table.

This exorbitant energy investment is required to provide power for irrigation, fuel to operate farm machinery, electricity to produce fertilizers and pesticides, power to manufacture farm machinery, energy for food processing and packaging, fuel for delivery trucks and for private automobiles on food-shopping trips, electricity and gas for refrigeration and cooking, and the proportionate energy cost of all highway construction shared by that 50 per-

FIGURE 13-11
Fish ponds in Kwan Tung Province, China. [*By permission of J. H. Ryther.*]

cent of all truck traffic which transports agricultural items.[8]

If India attempted to raise its present level of nutrition (2,000 calories per day) to the United States level of 3,000, it would need more energy than it now expends for all purposes. If the entire world were to meet such a standard, almost 80 percent of world energy use would have to be channeled into food production.

Of much greater import, however, is the fact that farm output no longer increases in proportion to energy input (Fig. 13-12). The

[8] J. S. Steinhart and C. E. Steinhart, "Energy Use in the U.S. Food System," *Science*, vol. 184, Apr. 19, 1974, pp. 307–315.

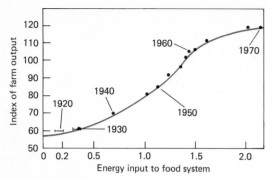

FIGURE 13-12
The relationship of farm output to energy input in the United States from 1920 through 1970. Index of farm output is based upon 1957 through 1959 output/input = 100. Energy input is measured in quadrillions (10^{15}) of kilocalories. Although energy input to the food system increased tenfold between 1920 and 1970 (0.2 to 2.0), farm output only doubled (index rise from 60 to 120). Note also S-shape of curve and leveling of output despite increased input. [*After J. S. Steinhart and C. E. Steinhart, Science, vol. 184, April 19, 1974.*]

curve of farm output with respect to energy expenditure resembles an S-shaped curve. Since 1920, energy input into high-yield agriculture has increased 10 times but farm output has only doubled. At the present time, according to the Steinharts, further increases in food production from increasing energy inputs will be harder and harder to come by.

As the world is now witnessing all too clearly, the energy pinch already has resulted in skyrocketing food prices. There is nothing to indicate that the trend will not continue. We may indeed see the day when it becomes desirable to reduce agricultural mechanization and to increase the input of farm labor into the food system. We may also hopefully see the day when out plant breeders give hardiness, disease and pest resistance, lower water requirements, and higher protein content prime importance, even if some yield is sacrificed in the process. After all there are some 80,000 species of edible plants; only about 50

species are cultivated on a large scale and 90 percent of the world's crop tonnage comes from just 12 of them.[9]

CONTROLLING POPULATION SIZE

People are dying now of respiratory diseases in Tokyo, Birmingham, and Gary, because of the 'need' for more industry. The 'need' for more food justifies overfertilization of the land, leading to eutrophication of the waters, and lessened fish production—which leads to more 'need' for food.

What will we say when the power shuts down some fine summer on our eastern seaboard and several thousand people die of heat prostration? Will we blame the weather? Or the power companies for not building enough generators? Or the econuts for insisting on pollution controls?

One thing is certain: we won't blame the deaths on overpopulation. No one ever dies of overpopulation. It is unthinkable.[10]

At this point let us review the major populational problems we have considered so far in this and the preceding chapter:

1 There are 2 billion or more people today who are undernourished or malnourished, most but by no means all of whom live in developing countries.
2 The populations of all major societies—both those that are industrialized and have low birth rates as well as those that are underdeveloped and have high birth rates—are increasing and will continue to do so for some time to come. Even if the United States does not exceed the replacement fertility rate of 2.1 children per family, our numbers will not stop increasing until the death rate catches up with the birth rate in about 50 to 60 years.
3 The capacity to feed these numbers adequately

[9] Ibid., p. 313.
[10] Garrett Hardin, "Nobody Ever Dies of Overpopulation," *Science*, vol. 171, Feb. 12, 1971, p. 527.

by the increased production and improved distribution of food is lacking; the green revolution already is resulting in resource depletion and environmental pollution.

4 Unrealistic demands on the earth's limited resources are compounded further by adherence to an economy based on growth and the desire of all people to have a standard of living like that in the industrialized world.

These are a singularly formidable battery of circumstances. The problems facing humans are not going to be solved in the near future by working towards population control measures at this late date. One thing seems certain, however. The human predicament cannot be resolved without giving first priority to a solution of the population problem. Overpopulation is the world's major and most merciless killer. Until population growth is curtailed, the human condition will continue to decline steadily.

Controlling population size is a many-sided problem. Technology is involved in the development of safe and economical contraceptive procedures by which the number of births can be regulated effectively. Social institutions and government should be concerned in educating people on the need for, and the advantages of, regulating population size as well as instructing them on the availability and use of birth-control devices. The low literacy rate in many developing countries and the large numbers of poor in all countries emphasizes the need for widespread maternal care and birth-control clinics. Societies also should foster incentive programs to encourage participation in the population-control effort. But no amount of technology or sociopolitical programming is going to resolve the population problem until certain moral issues have begun to assume the proportions of a global ethic. Moral conviction essential to population control rests in a genuine reverence for the life and dignity of *people* everywhere, and in a firm belief that the earth's limited resources are not so much owned as they are used and shared by all of us, and by our descendants as well.

Technology and birth control

Contraceptive methods and their effectiveness

Contraceptive methods vary greatly in their dependability and the extent of their possibly harmful side effects. Most of the older methods are reasonably safe (relatively harmless), but their reliability ranges from low to moderate. Some of the newer methods are quite reliable but may be accompanied by undesirable side effects, such as greater menstrual discomfort and increased risk of cancer. Still others appear to be both reliable and safe. Since research is active in this area, there are also new techniques which have not been adequately tested to establish their effectiveness, safety, or even their applicability for human use.

Least effective methods Withdrawal, the rhythm method, douching, and the use of spermicidal foams, jellies, and creams are among the least reliable contraceptive techniques.

Preventing conception by withdrawing the penis immediately prior to ejaculation has two serious limitations. The male is understandably reluctant to withdraw at the precise instant it is most natural to thrust forward. It is also common for some sperm to be discharged into the vagina prior to ejaculation.

The rhythm method depends on abstaining from intercourse during ovulation as well as a couple of days before and after that event. Usually this restricts intercourse to about 10 days following the end of the menstrual cycle since the next ovulation cannot be predicted accurately. The rhythm technique is undependable because of irregularities in the menstrual cycle of even those women who are relatively predictable.

Douching or vaginal irrigation is quite unreliable because some sperm usually have entered the uterus within a few seconds after ejaculation. Sperm-killing creams, jellies, or foams inserted with an applicator into the upper vagina are more effective than any of the above, but none of these spermicidal agents are as effective as the contraceptive methods discussed below.

Moderately effective methods   The condom is a device, usually made of thin rubber, that is designed to envelop the erect penis. It is drawn over the penis after erection but before intercourse. It is often objected to because the application of the device interrupts sexual foreplay and restricts the sensitivity of the penis. Also, care must be taken when the penis is withdrawn after intercourse that the condom does not slip off, emptying some of its semen into the vagina. On rare occasions, the condom may break during intercourse.

The diaphragm is a sturdy rubber device in the form of a shallow flexible cup that is designed to fit over the opening of the cervix (Fig. 4-9). Diaphragms come in varying sizes and should be fitted by a doctor. If properly fitted and not accidentally dislodged during intercourse, the diaphragm is a fairly reliable and satisfactory birth control device.

Most effective methods   The most effective contraceptive methods entail the oral ingestion of hormones (the "pill"), intrauterine devices (IUDs), and sterilization (vasectomy and tubal ligation).

Oral contraception is virtually 100 percent reliable in preventing pregnancy if the prescribed routine of pill-taking is adhered to. Most pills contain two female hormones, estrogen and progestogen. Estrogen works by suppressing the monthly release of an egg from the ovary while progestogen apparently maintains a mucus plug in the cervix that blocks the entrance of sperm. A dangerous complication in the form of abnormal blood clotting is responsible for the death of about 3 women per year in every 100,000 who use the pill. The maternal death rate from childbirth in this country, however, is almost 10 times that high.

The "morning after" pill has stimulated considerable interest, but its use is approved by the Food and Drug Administration (FDA) only for "emergency purposes," that is, after rape or incest. This contraceptive operates on the principle that heavy doses of estrogen speed the passage of the egg to the uterus before that organ is prepared to receive it. But the synthetic estrogen, diethylstilbestrol (DES), used for this purpose has been linked to the occurrence of a rare form of vaginal cancer in the daughters of women who took the drug when pregnant.

Intrauterine devices (IUDs) are small objects 2 to 3 centimeters (1 inch) in their long dimension which are inserted by a doctor into the cavity of the uterus. They are made of plastic or metal and come in various shapes, some of the more efficient of which are illustrated in Fig. 13-13. The three IUDs shown are from 97 percent (Lippes loop) to 99 percent (Dalkon shield) effective.[11] The IUD prevents

[11] Effectiveness is measured in woman-years of use (one woman using a device for one year = one woman-year); 99 percent effective = one pregnancy in 100 woman-years of use. See Earl L. Paar, "Contraception With Intrauterine Devices," *BioScience*, vol. 23, 1973, pp. 281–286.

FIGURE 13-13
Three of the more efficient and commonly used intrauterine devices (IUDs): Dalkon shield (*left*), copper T (*middle*), and Lippes loop (*right*). IUDs interfere with the implantation of the early embryo in the uterine wall. Copper leached from the wire wrapped around the stem of the copper T is thought to facilitate this reaction. Grid lines are 1 centimeter apart.

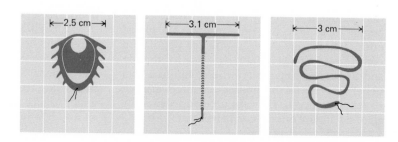

implantation of the early embryo in the uterine wall presumably because of an inflammatory reaction to the presence of a foreign body. The Dalkon shield has been the most effective IUD in general use but in those few cases where pregnancies did occur, a number of miscarriages ensued in which four women died. The main objections to all IUDs are the possibility that the device may be expelled from the uterus and the increased incidence of cramping, backache, and bleeding during the first few months after insertion.

Sterilization is the most effective contraceptive procedure, and it is accompanied by no known undesirable side effects. Contrary to widespread belief, it does not depress sexual drive and pleasure but rather tends to elevate them, perhaps because of release from worry over unwanted children. There are two main objections to current sterilization techniques: (1) surgery is required, and (2) once the procedure is completed, a reversal to the fertile state cannot be guaranteed. However, a good deal of research is going into procedures that would allow reversible sterilization.[12] The surgery involved is minor in men and does not require hospitalization. In the male, vasectomy consists in tying off, or cutting, a small section from each sperm duct (vas deferens, Fig. 4-9). Sperm continue to be formed but they are resorbed in the testis. Hormone secretion is unaffected, the prostate gland and seminal vesicles continue to produce seminal fluid, and erection and ejaculation are normal in every respect except for the absence of sperm in the ejaculate. In the female, tubal ligation is a comparable procedure in which each uterine tube (oviduct) is cut (Fig. 4-9). After surgery, ovulation, hormone production, and menstruation continue as before, with the exception that the ovulated egg cannot reach the uterus, and sperm cannot reach the egg.

Much current research is directed toward new birth-control techniques. Fertility control in the male by the oral ingestion of hormone shows some promise for the future. So also does the prospect of controlling fertility in the male by means of the immunization response. One study showed that female rabbits immunized with sperm, semen, or testis extracts of males to which they were later mated had significantly fewer pregnancies than normal.[13] Time will tell whether such research has any practical application to human birth control.

Public acceptance of birth-control technology
The National Fertility Studies by the Office of Population Research at Princeton University have included analyses of the methods of contraception used by United States married couples practicing birth control. The 1965 study showed that 37.2 percent of all couples practicing birth control used the most effective contraceptive methods. The 1970 study indicated that this figure had risen to 57.9 percent (Fig. 13-14). This increase was reflected in a 36 percent decline in unwanted pregnancies between the periods 1961–1965 and 1966–1970.

In 1970, 65 percent of all married couples practiced birth control. Sterilization was selected by a fourth of all couples in which the wives were between 30 and 44 years old. Vasectomies and tubal ligations were about evenly divided.

Of special interest is the finding that the overwhelming majority of poor persons accept the most reliable contraceptive procedures if they are given the choice. Governmentally subsidized birth-control services have shown remarkable results among populations of the poor and near poor. One begun in New Orleans in 1967 had enrolled almost two-thirds of its target population by the end of 1968. Meanwhile, the percentage of those using the most reliable contraceptive methods rose from 25 to 82 percent.[14]

---

[12] Jean L. Marx, "Birth Control: Current Technology, Future Prospect," *Science,* vol. 179, Mar. 23, 1973, p. 1224.

[13] Erwin Goldberg, "Infertility in Female Rabbits Immunized With Lactate Dehydrogenase X," *Science,* vol. 181, Aug. 3, 1973, pp. 458–459.

[14] J. D. Beasley, *Family Planning Perspectives, I,* Spring 1969.

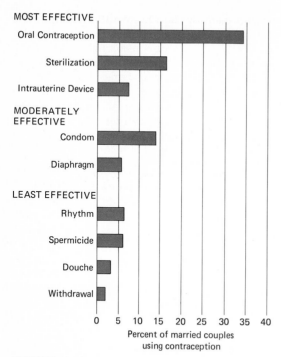

MOST EFFECTIVE
Oral Contraception
Sterilization
Intrauterine Device
MODERATELY EFFECTIVE
Condom
Diaphragm
LEAST EFFECTIVE
Rhythm
Spermicide
Douche
Withdrawal

0   5   10   15   20   25   30   35   40
Percent of married couples
using contraception

FIGURE 13-14
Methods of contraception used by United States married couples in 1970. Sterilization was selected by 25 percent of all couples in which the wives were between 30 and 44 years old. Married couples practicing birth control made up 65 percent of all married couples. [*From 1970 National Fertility Study by the Office of Population Research, Princeton University.*]

Other heartening signs are seen in the changing attitude of the average citizen toward the desirability of large families. Gallup polls conducted over the past 38 years, including early 1974, show that the proportion of Americans favoring large families has reached its lowest point. As recently as 1968, 41 percent of those polled thought four or more children was an ideal family. Today only 19 percent desire four or more whereas 49 percent prefer two or less (Fig. 13-15).

A recent study indicates that there is a widening defection of American Roman Catholic women from the 1968 papal encyclical banning all forms of contraception other than the rhythm method. By 1970, two-thirds of all Catholic women and three-fourths of those under 30 were using contraceptive methods disapproved by their church. Of particular significance is the finding that this defection has been most evident among those who receive Communion at least once a month.[15]

Birth control by abortion
It has been estimated that about 1 million women in the United States obtain induced abortions annually. (A "natural" abortion usually is called a miscarriage.) Until recently the vast majority of these were performed illegally and all too often by incompetent personnel under grossly substandard conditions. In January 1973 the United States Supreme Court legalized abortion by ruling that no state could interfere with decisions made between a woman and her doctor during the first 12 weeks of pregnancy.

When other techniques of contraception have failed, induced abortion is the only avenue left to limit family size. The operation consists of dislodging the implanted embryo from the uterine wall either by scraping the uterine lining or by using a suction device. It is a simple, safe procedure when performed by a competent doctor under antiseptic conditions, requiring only a few minutes to complete. If done within the first 12 weeks of pregnancy, it is, in fact, a good deal safer than childbirth.

Worldwide birth control
Although induced abortion is illegal in many countries, undoubtedly it is the most common method of birth control throughout the world. Estimates of the number of abortions worldwide range from 20 to 30 million annually, but such appraisals cannot be made accurately; this one may even be conservative.

Illegal abortions are particularly common in Latin America. The poor and near poor who

[15] C. F. Westoff and L. Bumpass, "The Revolution in Birth Control Practices of U.S. Roman Catholics," *Science*, vol. 179, Jan. 5, 1973, pp. 41–44.

comprise the bulk of the population in Latin America usually cannot afford reliable contraceptive methods, and so they are left little recourse but to use crude folk rituals for contraception. When these fail, which is most of the time, they practice induced abortion upon themselves. More than 40 percent of all hospital admissions in Santiago, Chile, are thought to be the result of crudely performed abortions.

More and more countries are legalizing abortion. Among these are England, the Scandinavian countries, Switzerland, the countries of Eastern Europe, the U.S.S.R., India, China, Japan, and the United States.

Today, no nation prohibits the use of effective contraceptive methods. The availability of these methods to the masses of poor and low-income families, however, is quite another matter, particularly among the developing nations where the population problem is the most acute.

China apparently has been making remarkable strides in reducing the growth rate in urban areas through a planned-birth program. This includes delaying marriage until the man is 30 and the woman is 25; encouraging the use of oral contraception, IUDs, and sterilization; and legalizing induced abortion. These measures have brought down the growth rate in urban areas to about 1 percent a year. The family-planning program has not fared so well in rural villages, however, where the traditional desire for many male children remains strong.[16]

According to polls taken by various Gallup foreign offices and affiliates, in many parts of the world there seems to be a growing disenchantment with large families (Fig. 13-16). Polls taken during the first three months of 1974 were compared with those taken in earlier years. In Canada, Great Britain, Switzerland, and Uruguay the percentage of people favoring families of four or more children decreased by 36 to 66 percent.

[16] *Studies in Family Planning,* Population Council, 1973.

A

Ideal number of children	%
None	1
One	2
Two	46
Three	22
Four	14
Five	2
Six or more	3
No opinion	10

B

Year	Percent Favoring Four or More as Ideal Number of Children
1936	34
1941	41
1945	49
1947	47
1953	41
1957	38
1960	45
1963	42
1966	35
1968	41
1971	23
1973	20
1974	19

FIGURE 13-15
Results of United States Gallup poll surveys. *A,* Ideal number of children according to a poll taken in early 1974; *B,* percent favoring four or more as an ideal number of children from selected polls during the period 1936–1974. [*Gallup Organization, Inc.*]

Population control at the sociopolitical level

Many major problems—both national and international—confront population control at the sociopolitical level. The most pressing international problem is the unwillingness of nearly all developing nations in sub-Saharan Africa and Latin America to curb population growth. Leaders in these countries view increasing numbers of people as necessary to achieve full development of their untapped resources, rather than as an economic burden

Country	Percent Favoring Four or More as Ideal Number of Children
Australia	21
Canada	23
Great Britain	14
Spain	18
Switzerland	7
United States	19
Uruguay	7

FIGURE 13-16
Results of polls taken by various Gallup foreign offices and affiliates in early 1974 compared to United States poll. Poll reflects percentage of those favoring four or more as the ideal number of children in a family. [*Gallup Organization, Inc.*]

that will hinder the realization of their goals.

Many feel, particularly in underdeveloped sub-Saharan Africa, that the Western world fears industrialization in the developing countries as a redistribution of wealth in the world. Much of sub-Saharan Africa looks upon population control as a form of economic genocide that the West is trying to foist on them. Regardless of the error in such reasoning, it is an understandable point of view among these peoples and constitutes a major obstacle to effective population control.

Within societies, problems of equal magnitude exist. The major barriers blocking progress in population control are threefold: (1) resistance to any form of reliable birth control on grounds of moral conviction or tradition, (2) reaction to governmental involvement in population control as an abridgment of human freedom, and (3) restrictions against adequate distribution and use of contraceptive methods because of economic limitations and bureaucratic inefficiency. The issue of morality will be addressed later. Relative to governmental involvement in population control, the case is clear. Overpopulation is the major biosocial problem in this nation and the world. A problem of this magnitude cannot be resolved by the discretionary judgment and

economic capability of individuals any more than murder, rape, robbery, fraud, and false advertising can. Society, in protecting itself against these evils, makes mankind more free rather than less free. Human freedom at its optimum rests on a foundation of individual responsibility and restraint.

The opponents of governmental participation in population control have argued that government has no place meddling in such affairs. The proponents have replied that in this country the government has been meddling in these affairs ever since the Great Depression by subsidizing population increase with income tax deductions and social welfare payments based on family size. To this was added, until quite recently, highly restrictive legislation against induced abortion. The precedent for governmental participation in the population problem is long standing. The problem does not lie in involvement but in the *misdirection* of that involvement.

Many programs and policies have been suggested in recent years aimed at achieving effective population control in this country and throughout the world. Some of these are drastic, perhaps too drastic, for the tastes of many. Such judgments are meaningful, however, only in terms of the problem to be solved. When a situation is left to deteriorate to the point that a crisis prevails, the most drastic measures usually are the only effective ones left. At that point, even they might fail.

The suggestions which follow in outline format have been extracted from a compilation prepared by Bernard Berelson, President of the Population Council in New York.

I *Intensified Voluntary Fertility Control*
   1 Establish village centers in the rural areas of developing countries which will provide care for pregnant women, family planning education, and birth control services.
   2 Remove legal and economic prohibitions against induced abortion everywhere.
II *Establishment of Involuntary Fertility Control*
   1 Introduce chemical fertility control agents or temporary sterilants into the water supply or into staple foods.

2 Issue licenses to have children, to be given to women in such numbers as to ensure zero population growth; licenses could be sold or exchanged.

3 Temporarily sterilize girls by time-capsule contraceptives, and all females after the birth of a child, sterilization to be terminated by certificate of approval.

4 Sterilize all men with three or more children, and require mandatory abortion for all illegitimate pregnancies.

III The Intensification of Educational Campaigns

1 Teach the implications of overpopulation, the use of contraceptives, and the nature of sexual behavior in primary and secondary schools.

2 Beam television programs on population growth and control, and family planning to TV receiver centers in all parts of the world.

IV Incentive Programs

1 Payments or prizes for child spacing, or to couples who practice contraception or accept sterilization.

2 Lottery schemes which issue tickets only to childless couples and to teenagers who avoid illegitimate childbearing.

V Tax and Welfare Programs to Discourage Childbearing

1 Withdrawal of maternity benefits and all child and family allowances after the birth of a given number (N) of children.

2 Assessment of a tax on each birth after the Nth child, with tax benefits for the unmarried and the parents of small families.

3 Limitation of governmentally sponsored medical care, housing, scholarships, loans, and the like to families with fewer than N children.

4 Governmental provision of X years of free schooling to each family, thereby giving more free schooling to each child in a small family than to each child in a large family.

5 Payment of a special social security pension to poor couples with fewer than N children.

VI Broad Changes in Socioeconomic Institutions

1 Increase the minimal age for marriage through legislation, imposing a costly marriage license fee, or rewarding delayed marriage with a special bonus or government grant.

2 Institute two kinds of marriage, one easily terminated for couples who choose to be childless, the other of greater permanence and licensed for children.

3 Encourage social and economic reforms that improve the status of women by developing socio-economic opportunities in education, government, sports, communication, agriculture, research, industry, business, and so on as alternative roles to marriage or childbearing.

VII Political Methods and Institutions

1 The application of political and economic pressure by the United States on any governments or religious institutions that obstruct progress in population control.

2 The establishment of worldwide national agencies and one international body to deal with the population problem and to promote zero population growth.

VIII Augmented Research Efforts

1 Research on socio-political techniques for achieving desired fertility goals.

2 Research on practical methods of sex determination in early embryos, permitting abortion of undesired sex and aiding family in sex planning.

3 Increased research on improved methods of contraception, particularly for the poor and illiterate.

It is probable that whatever degree of population control can be achieved will come from a combination of medical, legal, economic, and social efforts. What is done will hinge on how well people around the world appreciate the seriousness of their plight. As Berelson stated:

In the last analysis, what will be scientifically available, politically acceptable, administratively feasible, economically justified, and morally tolerated depends upon people's perception of consequences.[17]

The moral issue

The issue of morality is a many-sided one, and it penetrates deeply into the whole population problem. There can be no technological solution to family planning and population control until the matter of morality has been resolved. Reproduction among humans as in all crea-

[17] Bernard Berelson, "Beyond Family Planning," *Science,* vol. 163, February 7, 1969, pp. 533–542.

tures has been, and will continue to be, essential to survival. Throughout our evolutionary history, fertility has been something to be worshipped. The Venuses of late Paleolithic cultures (Fig. 7-17A) suggest this, as we stated in Chap. 7. Childbearing provided bands, tribes, and nations with an unceasing supply of young individuals to give vigor, imagination, and continuity to human existence. Fertility has been viewed traditionally as something that is good for the family, good for society, and good for the species. In the light of human history, the presumption that the freedom to procreate is a human right, is a natural one.

Herein lies the moral dilemma that must be resolved before effective population control becomes a reality (Fig. 13-17). In the world today, the right to reproduce interferes with other human rights, most of which have a much higher priority than the privilege of childbearing. Among these are the right to have enough to eat, the right to be free of disease, the right to enjoy life, and the right to be a contributing member of society.

Even the right of free choice in family planning is denied to millions of people, especially the poor. Untold numbers of couples are restrained from making a free choice through (1) ignorance of the availability and use of contraceptive methods, and of the consequences of high fertility for their family and country, (2) inability to pay for effective contraception, (3) anti-abortion legislation, (4) traditional mores that restrict the role of women in society to childbearing and childrearing, and (5) religious doctrine, regardless of the individual's acceptance of such dogma.

Today's world requires a fundamental shift in the traditional view. A much higher morality is served when the freedom to procreate is seen as a privilege rather than a right. Society is sharing more and more of the cost of raising, educating, and providing the recreational needs of children. More importantly, *society provides all the ecologic resources used by those children as well as their elders.* In short, only

a part of the economic cost, and none of the ecologic cost, of childrearing is borne by parents. Unbridled freedom to breed serves neither freedom nor moral justice when it saps a nation's economy without purpose, and when it pollutes and wastes the limited air, water, open space, and other resources that belong to everyone. Above all, it cannot be condoned on any grounds in regularly committing inordinate numbers of people to destinies of squalor, disease, calamity, and starvation.

The right to breed often is viewed as a kind of biologic obligation to perpetuate one's family lineage. Such biologic egoism differs little in principle from its economic counterpart which holds that one should produce X children because they are affordable financially. Both the biologic and economic egoist fail to realize that they and their children are products of a community, one distributed through time, the other in space. All that a parent actually gives a child is a random haploid set of chromosomes. Even these random chromosomes are not the same as those the parent received at conception because they have been altered by mutation. A parent is merely the temporary custodian of a haphazard sample of chromosomes that trace back through about 300 years (10 generations) to more than 1,000 ancestors. Origins can be traced to a genetic community, not to a famous or infamous ancestor. And this genetic community is only a reflection of the total society of which it is a part.

Whatever course is chosen to curb population growth, the stakes in human suffering are high and regrettably will remain so for some time to come. Society must be rescued from the assault of overbreeding. The kind of person one can become, the kind of life one can live, and the kind of freedoms one can enjoy are functions of society.

The next two chapters will deal specifically with the manner in which overpopulation affects the quality of human life and the environment in which we live.

FIGURE 13-17
The moral issue. An anti-abortion demonstration (*left*); a starving mother and child in Ethiopia (*right*). [*Left, Wide World Photos; right, Woodfin-Camp, Inc.*]

SUGGESTED READINGS

The books by P. R. Ehrlich et al., C. H. Southwick, and J. Turk et al. cited at the end of the last chapter also contain excellent discussions of the subject matter of this chapter.

BARDACH, J. E., et al.: *Aquaculture: The Farming and Husbandry of Freshwater and Marine Organisms,* New York: John Wiley & Sons, Inc., 1972. A thorough review of aquaculture techniques.

DASMANN, R. F.: *African Game Farming,* New York, Pergamon-Macmillan Press, Inc., 1964. A documentation of the evidence that native game can outproduce domestic stock with little if any environmental abuse.

DEMAREST, R. J., and J. J. SCIARRA: *Conception, Birth, and Contraception: A Visual Presentation.* New York: McGraw-Hill

Book Company, 1969. An excellent, fully illustrated review.

EBERSTADT, N.: "Myths of the Food Crisis," *The New York Review of Books,* vol. 23, no. 2, Feb. 19, 1976. A vigorous and informative criticism of the view that overpopulation and food shortages are the major causes of famine and starvation.

EDITORS of *Science:* "Food," *Science,* vol. 188, May 9, 1975. The entire issue of 24 articles is devoted to food from the standpoint of socioeconomics, nutrition, agricultural research, and basic biology.

EHRLICH, P. R.: *The Population Bomb,* New York: Ballantine Books, Inc., 1972. A dramatic portrayal of how overpopulation inevitably leads to hunger and environmental abuse.

HARDIN, GARRET (ed.): *Population, Evolution and Birth Control: A Collage of Controversial Ideas,* San Francisco: W. H. Freeman and Company, 1969. This book and the books edited by Hinrichs and by Reid and Lyon are superb collections of essays covering every aspect of the human population problem.

HINRICHS, NOEL (ed.): *Population, Environment, and People,* New York: McGraw-Hill Book Company, 1971.

NATIONAL ACADEMY OF SCIENCES: *Resources and Man,* San Francisco: W. H. Freeman and Company, 1969. A report on the problems faced by human populations insofar as food, minerals, and energy are concerned.

REID, S. T., and D. L. LYON (eds.): *Population Crisis: An Interdisciplinary Perspective,* Glenview, Ill.: Scott, Foresman and Company, 1972.

SHEPARD, P., and D. MCKINLEY (eds.): *The Subversive Science: Essays Toward an Ecology of Man,* New York: Houghton Mifflin Company, 1969. A classic collection of essays on many aspects of human ecology with emphasis on populational problems.

U. S. DEPARTMENT OF AGRICULTURE: *Contours of Change,* Yearbook for 1970. The central theme of this large volume is agricultural revolutions.

VAN VLECK, D. B.: *How and Why Not To Have A Baby,* Charlotte, Vt.: Optimum Population, Inc., 1971. A well-written 40-page essay, which is easily read and amply illustrated.

REVIEW QUESTIONS

1 A determination of optimum world numbers may be based on a model population from which projections can be made. Show how the interrelationships between developing and developed societies can have a strong influence on the characteristics of that model population.

2 Discuss the following thesis: Overpopulation is largely a matter of high population density and too little open space.

3 Formidable obstacles confront any program that might substantially improve the production and distribution of food. What are these obstacles? Cite an actual example of such a program.

4 What are the prospects of increasing agricultural lands? Indicate the problems involved and the opportunities for greater per capita food production.

5 The green revolution holds the best promise of increasing food production in the immediate future. Even this program has its limitations. What difficulties are posed by the energy cost of the green revolution? Identify three additional problems and indicate the nature of each.

6 Cite an example of marine farming and of detritus farming in which there have been exceptional harvests of animal protein. What are the advantages of such farming techniques? Of what significance are they in solving the food problem?

7 List the most effective contraceptive techniques. Describe each and evaluate its reliability and safety.

8 Write a brief summary of the evidence pointing to greater public acceptance of birth control in the United States in recent years. Prepare a similar summary for worldwide birth control.

9 There are many sociopolitical obstacles, both national and international, to population control. Describe three such problems at the national level and two at the international level.

10 Many programs and policies have been suggested in recent years to achieve population control. Identify and critically evaluate three such suggestions in each of the following categories selected from Berelson's compilation: (*a*) tax and welfare programs to discourage childbearing; (*b*) broad changes in socioeconomic institutions.

11 Discuss the historical bases for the belief that freedom to procreate is a human right. What are the interrelationships between the right to reproduce and other human rights? In what ways is the right of free choice in family planning denied to people throughout the world?

12 Write a short essay on the extent to which the welfare of society is at the mercy of unbridled individual freedom. Critically analyze the following two issues in particular: (*a*) it is morally more justifiable for rich parents to have large numbers of children than for parents of moderate or low incomes; (*b*) the right to breed is a biologic obligation to perpetuate one's family lineage.

FOURTEEN

THE HUMAN ENVIRONMENT I:
Resource Depletion and Waste

Homo sapiens has experienced three major population explosions. The first of these, triggered by herd-hunting among late Paleolithic peoples, culminated in the extinction of a number of big-game species. The second was ushered in some 10,000 years ago by the agricultural revolution, and had even more drastic consequences. The third followed on the heels of the industrial revolution and plagues us now.

THE ENVIRONMENTAL IMPACT OF OVERPOPULATION[1] IN HUMAN HISTORY

Mounting archaeological and ecological evidence supports the belief that humans played

[1] As noted in the previous chapter, an overpopulated society is one that has exceeded the capacity of its available resources.

a role in creating the great expanses of barren land and desert in the Middle East and North Africa.[2] This role was that of a catalyst: human activity intensified the climatic effects of increasing continental aridity. In so doing, it accelerated the rate and extent of desert formation.

The agricultural revolution introduced land practices that greatly accelerated soil and water loss. Deforestation, overgrazing, land clearing, and cultivation led to rapid surface runoff, soil erosion, and declining water tables. Large expanses of bare ground increase heat reflectivity. The natural vegetative cover of native forest and grassland communities protects the soil from the erosive action of rain and retards the flow of runoff waters. Without this protective cover, surface water and wind are free to remove the topsoil and carry it great distances. Plant stems, roots, and organic matter also contribute to the porosity of soil, allowing rainfall to percolate to the water table below (where it is called *groundwater*); this leaves minimal amounts of surface water for runoff. Large quantities of this groundwater are recycled back into the atmosphere through the leaves of a forest community, only to return again as rain. In fact, much of the water required by a forest is recycled by the forest community itself. Over the long run, cutting down forests over extensive areas to provide more pasture for livestock results in diminished rainfall.

The ancient civilizations of the Middle East and North Africa apparently followed such land practices. The headwaters of the Tigris and Euphrates Rivers in Mesopotamia and Sumeria were covered with forests and grasslands in 7000 B.C.[3] Domestic cattle appeared in this region around 6300 B.C.[4] Cities began to develop during the fourth millennium B.C., and the need for building material caused additional

deforestation. The increased soil erosion resulting from deforestation and overgrazing contributed an ever-growing load of silt to the Tigris and Euphrates. As a consequence, the sediment carried by these two rivers has filled in the Persian Gulf for a distance of 290 kilometers (180 miles) during the past 5,000 years. The enormous impact of such ecologic destruction on agricultural productivity undoubtedly was a major factor in the fall of the Babylonian Empire.

In the days of early Rome, much of North Africa was blanketed by cedar forests and renowned for its fertility.[5] Intensive exploitation during the growth of the Roman Empire combined with natural climatic trends to reduce vast areas of rich productive land to desolate barrens lacking both vegetation and soil (Fig. 14-1). Continued exploitation over the last few hundred years has extended the area of the Sahara Desert by 1,010,000 square kilometers (390,000 square miles).

Such episodes of environmental destruction were not limited to the Middle East and North Africa. Comparable incidences have occurred throughout the Mediterranean area, sub-Saharan Africa, India, China, and the Western Hemisphere. Needless to say, these destructive land-use practices were not restricted to ancient peoples. Forest clearing, overgrazing, and unrestrained burning have intensified wind erosion in Australia to the extent that desert lands have been expanding over the last 100 years. In the United States, great regions that once were grassland communities, have suffered serious to devastating losses of their topsoil to water and wind erosion over the past 50 years (Figs. 14-2 and 14-3). Most of the damage was inflicted by wind erosion on overstocked pasture lands and on unprotected plowed ground. Water erosion, however, also took its toll.

The impact of these errors in our recent past have cost us dearly in agricultural productivity. The continental United States, excluding

[2] C. H. Southwick, *Ecology and the Quality of Our Environment.* New York: Van Nostrand Reinhold Company, 1972, pp. 67–75.
[3] Ibid.
[4] D. Perkins, Jr., "Fauna of Catal Huyuk: Evidence for Early Cattle Domestication in Anatolia," *Science,* vol. 164, 1969, pp. 177–179.

[5] C. O. Sauer, "Theme of Plant and Animal Destruction in Economic History," *Journal of Farm Economics,* vol. 20, 1939, pp. 765–775.

FIGURE 14-1
Ancient pollen deposits indicate that this hillside was clothed in a cedar forest at the time of the early Roman Empire. The area is now devoid of both vegetation and soil. [*From C. H. Southwick, Ecology and the Quality of Our Environment, Van Nostrand Reinhold, New York, 1972.*]

mountains and deserts, embraces more than 6.9 million square kilometers (2.7 million square miles). The U.S. Soil Conservation Service estimated that some 1,214,000 square kilometers (468,750 square miles) of this has been either destroyed or severely damaged by soil erosion. Farms that were abandoned because of erosion damage (Fig. 14-3B) totaled an additional 202,344 square kilometers (78,125 square miles). Of the land remaining, 3,108,000 square kilometers (1.2 million square miles) had lost between 25 and 75 percent of its topsoil. Losses of this magnitude are unrecoverable. Many thousands of years are needed to produce fertile soils.

During recent times, numerous tech-

FIGURE 14-2
Destroying the vegetative cover through overgrazing leaves the soil vulnerable to water erosion. [*U.S. Forest Service.*]

A

FIGURE 14-3

Wind erosion. *A*, Dust storm in Colorado, 1937; *B*, the consequences of severe wind erosion in Oklahoma, 1937. A sand dune in central Oregon about 16 kilometers (10 miles) long was found to have had its origin in the farmstead of a sheep-ranching family that had operated from the one site for three generations. [*A, USDA; B. USDA. Soil Conservation Service.*]

B

FIGURE 14-4
Block cutting of old-growth Douglas fir in a national forest near Mt. Saint Helens, Washington. Seeds from uncut trees bring about forest regrowth in cutover areas. Theoretically, by the time the entire forested area has been cut, the areas first harvested will have produced marketable timber. [*U.S. Forest Service.*]

niques have been devised to correct many of the land abuses that are as old as the agricultural revolution. Timber harvesting often is done by block cutting, leaving peripheral areas of forest uncut for reseeding cutover areas (Fig. 14-4). Windbreaks of sturdy trees and shrubs are employed to curb wind erosion (Fig. 14-5). Strip-cropping and contour farming reduce water runoff and erosion (Fig. 14-6). Lands already severely damaged can be retired from agricultural production and revegetated with hardy species (Fig. 14-7). These plantings not

FIGURE 14-5
This windbreak on a farm in Kansas consists of 9 species of large trees, small trees, and shrubs distributed in 10 rows. [*USDA, Soil Conservation Service.*]

FIGURE 14-6
Contour farming and strip cropping. Growing crops in strips that follow the land contours increase infiltration of rain and reduces runoff and erosion. The small pear-shaped area is the highest elevation. Different colored strips represent different crops, one of which is often a hay crop, the other being grain or corn. [*USDA, Soil Conservation Service.*]

only control erosion but also beautify the landscape and provide habitats for wildlife.

The industrial revolution, however, introduced new sources of environmental abuse. At the present time, most of these are not subject to effective control. The problem is further compounded by a steady increase in the number of new ecologic assaults against human health and survival. These growing challenges embrace two broad categories: (1) resource depletion and waste, the subject of this chapter, and (2) environmental pollution, to which the final chapter is devoted.

A major cause of resource depletion and waste is an economic system based upon an ever-enlarging market—a growing population with increasing "needs"—supplied by ever-expanding production.

THE "GROWTH" ECONOMY

Soil and water loss

Although soil erosion on agricultural lands in the United States has been reduced materially in the past 40 years, it has been increasing as a result of urban, commercial, and industrial construction. Excessive soil and water losses are occurring through land excavation and grading in residential subdivision development, industrial expansion, highway and power-line construction, and surface mining. Bare ground left by these activities is susceptible to the accelerated runoff of surface water, causing flooding, silt-laden streams, and significant losses of both soil and water.

According to the U.S. Soil Conservation

FIGURE 14-7
Control of gully erosion on a Minnesota farm before (*top*) and five growing seasons after (*bottom*) the area was fenced off and planted with protective vegetation. The large plants are locust trees about 4.5 meters (15 feet) tall. [*USDA, Soil Conservation Service.*]

Service, this nation is still losing about 3 billion tons of soil annually from human-induced, accelerated erosion. This amounts to an average annual loss of about 3.7 tons per hectare (1.5 tons per acre).

Of the various activities contributing to erosion, the most intensive damage is inflicted by surface mining techniques: quarrying, hydraulic mining, open-pit mining, and strip-mining. Of these, strip-mining for coal has the greatest potential for destruction (Fig. 14-8).

Over 5,180 square kilometers (2,000 square miles) of coal fields have been strip-mined in the Eastern United States. Much of this area, particularly in Appalachia, has been left in a state of total desolation because required rehabilitory measures were either inadequate or not enforced. The technology for rehabilitating most of this land does exist but seldom has been applied properly, if at all. The proposal of coal and energy interests to strip-mine up to 5,960 additional square kilometers (2,300 square miles) in the northern Great Plains consequently met with active opposition from ranchers and wheat farmers in the area, but to little avail.

Several bills passed by both the Houses of Congress failed to override President Ford's persistent veto. Some of the important provisions of these bills stipulated that (1) strip-mining cannot be undertaken without the surface owner's consent, (2) strip-mining shall require a permit which shall be issued only when an acceptable plan of reclamation has been submitted by the stripper, (3) the entire cost of reclamation shall be borne by the stripper, (4) no stripping shall be permitted in agriculturally productive valley floors, and (5) no stripping shall be permitted if it affects water sources adversely. Additional provisions were made to finance the reclamation of "orphan" lands strip-mined in the past. The cost of reclamation borne by the mining operation apparently would be nominal. A committee of the National Academy of Sciences and the National Academy of Engineering concluded that reclamation costs might reach several thousand dollars per acre in some cases, but even this expenditure would represent less than 35 cents per ton on the coal removed.[6]

Wastewater losses
Vast quantities of water are used in the United States, much of it unnecessarily, to carry wastes

[6] L. J. Carter, "Strip Mining: Congress Moves Toward 'Tough Regulation,'" *Science*, vol. 186, Aug. 9, 1974, pp. 513–514; "Strip Mining Legislation—the Prospects Look Bleak," *Science*, vol. 188, June 27, 1975, p. 1287.

from homes, businesses, and industries. The sewage produced is more than 99.9 percent water. To dispose of this water into the ocean prevents its reuse and is becoming increasingly unwise, in the face of growing demand for water and the diminishing prospects of satisfying that demand. Sewage also possesses valuable soil nutrients that should be used in agricultural production rather than being wasted at sea or committed to the eutrophication of inland lakes. As noted in the previous chapter, these nutrients also can be discharged into ponds stocked with edible fish. In these ways, humankind can start recycling nutrients rather than continuously manufacturing them anew at enormous ecologic costs.

The processes by which municipal wastewater is treated are classified as *primary, secondary,* and *tertiary.* Primary treatment consists essentially of allowing suspended solids in the sewage to settle. The water is then separated from the sludge on the bottom and the scum on the top, chlorinated, and released into a stream, a lake, or ocean. This treatment removes about a third of the suspended solids and organic matter but only a small part of the soil nutrients (nitrates, phosphates). The sewage from about 40 percent of the United States population receives treatment varying from primary to none at all.

In secondary treatment the clarified wastewater (*effluent*) from the primary process is subjected to the action of microorganisms under controlled, well-aerated conditions. Most of the organic material is broken down by the microorganisms, settling out as a sediment called *activated sludge.* At this point, the clear water remaining still contains soil nutrients and varying amounts of dissolved organic compounds and suspended solids. Approximately 40 percent of the United States population gets sewage treatment of this kind.

Advanced or tertiary treatment largely is in the developmental stage and entails procedures to remove the contaminants in the effluent coming from secondary treatment. Chemical methods and soil filtration are com-

FIGURE 14-8
Strip-mining for coal in Montana. *Top,* coal seams lying close to the surface are exposed by huge power shovels holding up to 97 cubic meters (140 cubic yards). Vegetation and the entire mantle of soil are removed over extensive areas. *Bottom,* close-up view of power shovel in right midground. [*USDI, Bureau of Land Management.*]

monly employed. The chief accomplishment has been the successful removal of phosphates. Methods for the trapping of nitrogen compounds have not been very successful.

Many difficulties obstruct effective waste-water treatment. One of these is the handling of sludge, a mixture that is 5 percent solids and 95 percent water. About 50 percent of the total cost of treatment usually is expended in de-watering sludge and disposing of the solids. The solids are sold as fertilizer, buried in land fills, or incinerated.[7] Research is advancing rap-

[7] R. W. Holcomb, "Waste-Water Treatment: The Tide is Turning," *Science,* vol. 169, July 31, 1970, pp. 457–459.

idly in this area, however, and pilot programs already are producing low-sulfur crude oil and natural gas from organic wastes.[8]

A major difficulty is getting the money to incorporate thoroughly tested, proven procedures into wastewater treatment facilities. In 1970, the Federal Water Quality Administration estimated that it would cost $13.3 billion to bring domestic and industrial wastewater up to recommended standards.[9]

Undoubtedly, this figure is low because surprisingly little is known about industrial wastes (including agricultural wastes such as chemical fertilizer carried in runoff water). The volume of industrial wastewater is estimated to be over two and a half times that of domestic, yet only about one-half the volume of sewage treated in domestic plants comes from industry. A volume of industrial sewage equal to about three-quarters of that treated by domestic facilities consequently is unaccounted for. Some of this passes directly, without processing, into natural waterways. It has been estimated that one-half the phosphates in natural waters may come by direct runoff from the agricultural industry.[10]

Significant improvements are possible in the more sparing use of water by industry. Most steel mills utilize from 75,760 to 189,390 liters of water (80 to 200 tons) per ton of steel produced. One company, however, has cut this to less than 7,570 liters (2,000 gallons) through conservational measures. About 40 percent of this water is reused throughout the industry generally. Corresponding economies are possible in the cooling-water requirements of petrochemical (petroleum-processing) plants. Although the petrochemical industry probably averages about 1 liter of new water for every 3 liters used, one large facility takes only 10 percent of its 5.682-billion-liter daily requirement from outside sources.[11]

[8] T. H. Maugh II, "Fuel From Wastes: A Minor Energy Source," *Science,* vol. 178, Nov. 10, 1972, pp. 599–602.
[9] Holcomb, loc. cit.
[10] Ibid.
[11] K. E. Maxwell, *Environment of Life,* Encino, Calif.: Dickenson Publishing Company, Inc., 1973, p. 100.

The biggest problem in the handling of wastewater is the large and ever-growing number of trace contaminants against which sewage treatment is ineffective. Since routine water analyses check only for major indicators of pollution, unusual substances may be present for long periods of time before their presence becomes known. DDT and mercury are two well-known trace contaminants; the list includes viruses, chemical and biological toxins, pesticides, cancer-inducing agents *(carcinogens),* trace elements (mercury, lead, and so on), antibiotics, and hormones.[12]

Raw materials → manufactured products → solid wastes

The economy of expanding production has a history of converting raw materials into unused solid wastes. The United States generates over 1 billion tons of inorganic mineral wastes and more than 2 billion tons of organic wastes (880 million tons dry weight) every year.[13] This enormous quantity of discarded material embraces such diverse items as 8 million junked automobiles (Fig. 14-9), municipal refuse (Fig. 14-10), organic wastes from a variety of sources (Fig. 14-11), and a host of inorganic substances abandoned by industry.

The disposal of ever-increasing amounts of solid waste presents many problems. The simplest repository for waste is the open dump, but it is both unsightly and unsanitary; if it is burned regularly, it is a source of air pollution. Sanitary landfills are more desirable (Fig. 14-12) because they can be used later for parks, golf courses, or construction sites. They change the character of the land, however, and may contribute to groundwater contamination; they also are expensive and, like open dumps, wasteful of natural resources. Ocean dumping is wasteful and also contributes to pollution.

Methods for recycling solid wastes
Fortunately, thriftier methods have been de-

[12] Holcomb, loc. cit.
[13] Maugh, loc. cit.

FIGURE 14-9
Each year 8 million automobiles are junked in the United States. The salvage of such material is a welcome conservation measure. [*Wide World Photos.*]

vised for handling our solid wastes. The incineration of refuse in scientifically designed combustion chambers greatly reduces, although it does not eliminate, air pollutants caused by ordinary burning. The heat produced can be used to generate electricity. This has been a common practice in Europe for many years. The industrial salvage of scrap metal and metal products like discarded cans and junked automobiles (Fig. 14-9) is a welcome practice.

Certain new techniques involving heat in the absence of oxygen have shown great promise and may be in general use by 1980. One such process converts solid organic waste into crude oil or natural gas (methane). If the readily collectable wastes of the United States were so treated, they would have yielded 27 million cubic meters (170 million barrels) of low-sulfur oil, or 38.86 million cubic meters (1.36 billion cubic feet) of natural gas, in 1971 (Fig. 14-11).

These amounts are equal to about 3 percent of our crude-oil consumption and roughly 6 percent of our natural-gas consumption in that year. Another related process is designed for urban refuse disposal. Each ton of refuse yields nearly 160 liters (1 barrel) of oil, 63 kilograms of ferrous (iron-bearing) metals, 54 kilograms (120 pounds) of glass, 72 kilograms (160 pounds) of char (carbon) and varying amounts of low energy gas. The gas is recycled to provide the oxygen-free atmosphere, and some of it is burned, along with part of the char, to supply the heat needed. Plants embodying this pollution-free process are already in operation in several United States cities.

Type of refuse	Percent of total
RUBBISH (64%)	
Paper	42.0
Dry leaves	5.0
Grass	4.0
Street refuse	3.0
Wood and bark	2.4
Brush	1.5
Green cuttings	1.5
Household dirt	1.0
Oils and paint	0.8
Plastics	0.7
Rags	0.6
Rubber	0.6
Leather goods	0.3
Linoleum	0.1
Miscellaneous	0.5
FOOD WASTES (12%)	
Garbage	10.0
Fats	2.0
NONCOMBUSTIBLES (24%)	
Ashes	10.0
Metals	8.0
Glass and ceramics	6.0

FIGURE 14-10
Average percentage composition of municipal refuse by weight. [*After W. C. Gough, "Why Fusion," U.S. Atomic Energy Commission, 1970.*]

FIGURE 14-11
Solid organic wastes produced in the United States in 1971, in dry, ash-free weight. Much of this waste is scattered and not readily collectible. The net fuel potential of this waste by physiochemical processing is given (1 barrel = 0.159 cubic meters of oil; 1 cubic foot = 0.028 cubic meters of natural gas, methane). Total United States consumption in 1971 was 5.6 billion barrels of oil and 22.5 billion cubic feet of natural gas. [*After T. H. Maugh II, Science, vol. 178, Nov. 10, p. 599, © American Association for the Advancement of Science, 1972.*]

The necessity for recycling mineral resources

The need for recycling our mineral resources is clear. It is more obvious in the case of crude oil because of the restricted distribution of oil deposits and the recent unilateral action of the oil-producing cartel of Middle Eastern nations. Recycling is no less mandatory, however, for nonfuel minerals. Contrary to popular belief, in most cases the reclamation of mineral wastes is necessary not because minerals are nonrenewable and in limited supply but because of the form in which mineral resources are most abundant. With the exception of a few commodities like manganese, chromium, and tin, the United States has enormous quantities of minerals, including vast reserves of petroleum in the form of oil shale. One million tons of zinc and copper along with 300 million tons of aluminum and iron are contained in every cubic kilometer of average crustal rock.[14]

Seawater harbors comparable reserves. It is not a question of running out of mineral supplies but rather a matter of the economic and, more importantly, the ecologic cost of exploiting these reserves once our higher-grade stocks have been depleted. How much environmental destruction and contamination can be

[14] D. B. Brooks, "Mineral Resources, Economic Growth, and World Population," *Science*, vol. 185, July 5, 1974, pp. 13–19.

Source	Wastes generated (in millions of tons)	Readily collectible (in millions of tons)
Agricultural crops and food wastes	390	22.6
Manure	200	26.0
Urban refuse	129	71.0
Logging and wood manufacturing residues	55	5.0
Industrial wastes	44	5.2
Municipal sewage solids	12	1.5
Miscellaneous	50	5.0
Total	880	136.3
Net oil potential (millions of barrels)	1,098	170
Net methane potential (billions of cubic feet)	8.8	1.36

FIGURE 14-12
Sanitary landfill. Solid wastes are shredded or compacted and laid down in layers that alternate with layers of soil or gravel. The area is continually compacted and graded. [*DHEW, Office of Solid Waste Management Programs.*]

condoned in the name of economic growth?

Largely because of economic costs, the United States imports more than half its supply of 20 nonfuel minerals. These imports totaled $6 billion in 1971 and are expected to rise to $20 billion by 1985. A large share of these imports come from the developing nations of the Third World who are attempting to industrialize and improve their living standards. Sooner or later it is reasonable to expect the appearance of cartels among the Third World producers of nonfuel minerals. In the world of increasingly interdependent nations today, the maintenance of glaring inequalities in the distribution of wealth is becoming progressively less defensible.[15]

In the interest of conserving those resources whose exploitation causes the least environmental degradation, it is necessary for all societies, particularly the industrialized, to give ecologic costs a higher priority than economic

costs. By using and improving their domestic supplies, industrialized nations can reduce the heavy demands against the mineral resources of underdeveloped countries.

Recycling should be encouraged everywhere if unacceptable levels of environmental deterioration are to be avoided in the future. The frenzied extraction of raw materials from distant lands cannot continue to end in growing mountains of solid refuse in our cities. Despite this, however, our society perversely encourages resource depletion and discourages waste recycling in its tax policies. We grant generous tax incentives for draining off our resources in the form of depletion allowances rather than levying prohibitive penalties against resource depletion. We make it cheaper to transport a ton of iron ore than a ton of scrap iron by discriminatory interstate tariffs that

[15] Nicholas Wade, "Raw Materials: U.S. Grows More Vulnerable to Third World Cartels," *Science*, vol. 183, January 18, 1974, pp. 185–186.

should favor the transport of scrap.

Our society does this, along with all other societies committed to a growth economy, because of a bias for production and consumption. Obviously a growth economy cannot live with *reduced demand,* yet this is precisely what is needed in resource management. The growth economy must be replaced by a stabilized economy that lives within its means and is concerned with the quality of human life.

Fuel resources → expanding production → energy crisis

The history of fuel minerals differs little from that of nonfuel minerals. The use of energy has increased enormously among industrialized nations during the past century, but none, with the exception of Canada, approaches the per capita energy consumption of the United States. People in European countries use half the energy we do. Although our population is more than 5 times larger than it was a century ago, our energy consumption has increased 17 times. Our current demands for oil have been rising recently at the rate of 7 percent annually, which is more than 6 times faster than the population is growing.

At the present time, about 50 percent of our energy needs are being met by oil, 26 percent by natural gas, and 18 percent by coal with the balance falling to hydroelectric and nuclear power.[16] In 1975 our energy use was estimated at just under the crude-oil equivalent of 40 million barrels per day. Of the total energy used, about two-thirds goes to industrial processes and transportation (Fig. 14-13). The 4 million barrels of petroleum consumed by the automobile every day in 1971 accounted for about 14 percent of the nation's total energy use in that year.[17]

Our domestic production of crude oil and natural gas reached an all-time high in 1972 but

has been falling since that time. As a result, domestic fuel supplies began to fall sharply behind rising energy demands; we had a growing energy shortage that made us increasingly dependent upon overseas imports. This dependency is unlikely to lessen.

The National Academy of Sciences and the U.S. Geological Survey recently estimated the total oil and gas resources of the United States, including the outer continental shelf and Alaska's North Slope. Assuming we import 35 percent of our supplies from other oil-producing countries, these estimates indicate the United States will exhaust its oil and gas resources sometime between 1998 and 2016. If imports are cut, our reserves will be exhausted sooner.[18] It would be unrealistic economically to expect substantial production from new sources. For example, it is estimated that it would require $50 billion and 8 to 10 years to achieve a capacity of 5 million barrels per day of synthetic crude oil from coal and oil shale. As a consequence, the United States will require overseas oil imports for an indefinite period. The dependence of this nation and many others on the rich oil resources of the Middle East has made most of the industrialized world vulnerable to the actions of the cartel of oil producing and exporting countries (OPEC). Exorbitant price increases on this oil have caused world economic disruption and may have disastrous long-range consequences for the poorer, developing nations.

Although the energy crisis will not be resolved for some time, there is much that can be done to relieve it. We can reduce the demand for energy by practicing conservation and we can increase the supply of energy by developing nonconventional sources.

Energy conservation
The conservation of energy is a direct approach to the problem because it attempts to eliminate

[16] David J. Rose, "Energy Policy in the U.S.," *Scientific American,* January 1974, pp. 20–29.

[17] L. J. Carter, "Environment: A Lesson for the People of Plenty," *Science,* vol. 182, Dec. 28, 1973, p. 1324.

[18] Deborah Shapley, "Senate Study Predicts U.S. Oil Exhaustion," *Science,* vol. 187, March 21, 1975, p. 1064; Robert Gillette, "Geological Survey Lowers Its Sights," *Science,* vol. 189, July 18, 1975, p. 200.

the very causes that are responsible for energy shortages in the first place. An energy crisis exists primarily because we waste energy needlessly and because we encourage the depletion of fuel resources. Consequently energy can be conserved if we improve the efficiency of its use and discourage rather than encourage its demand through economic incentives.

Improved efficiency of energy use   The wasteful use of energy in buildings, industrial processes, and transportation is a major contributor to energy shortages in the United States. *Wasted energy* is defined here as *that which could have been saved if presently available technology had been applied.* According to Charles Berg, energy waste in buildings and industrial processes alone accounts for about 25 percent of national energy consumption.

Over 24 percent of all energy use is expended on space heating, air conditioning, and water heating in buildings (Fig. 14-13). Approximately 40 percent of the energy used for space heating and air conditioning could be saved if all buildings were insulated and sealed according to minimum standards established by the Federal Housing Authority in 1972. Recent studies indicate that the costs of upgrading existing structures that do not meet these standards could be paid off in less than five years at current fuel prices. Additional energy savings can be obtained by the diligent maintenance of heating and air conditioning equipment that was selected for its efficiency in the first place. Hot water heating can be made more efficient by using heat exchangers (heat-recovery devices) on drain pipes. The use of solar water heaters, commercially available in many countries, could cut *total* energy consumption in this country by 2 percent.

The illumination provided in office buildings in the United States surpasses that in comparable European buildings considerably, and yet there is no evidence that the increased lighting benefits the human occupants. About 1.5 percent of United States energy expenditures are on illumination.

Use	Percent of national total
RESIDENTIAL BUILDINGS	
Space heating	11.0
Water heating	2.9
Cooking	1.1
Refrigeration	1.1
Air conditioning	0.7
Clothes drying	0.3
Other	2.1
Total	19.2
COMMERCIAL BUILDINGS	
Space heating	6.9
Air conditioning	1.8
Feedstock	1.6
Refrigeration	1.1
Water heating	1.1
Cooking	0.2
Other	1.7
Total	14.4
INDUSTRIAL PROCESSES	
Process steam	16.7
Direct heat	11.5
Electric drive	7.9
Feedstock	3.6
Electrolytic process	1.2
Other	0.3
Total	41.2
TRANSPORTATION	
Fuel	24.9
Raw materials	0.3
Total	25.2
National Total	100.0

FIGURE 14-13
The distribution of energy consumption in the United States in 1968. Fossil fuels or their by-products used as raw material in manufacture are called feedstock. [*Data from Patterns of Energy Consumption in the U.S., prepared by the Stanford Research Institute, November 1971 for the Office of Science and Technology.*]

Approximately 30 percent of the energy utilized by industrial processes could be saved through the use of existing techniques, such as heat-recovery devices. Their application would not only conserve energy but, at today's fuel prices, reduce production costs as well.[19]

Since the price of fuels, until recently, has been low, high energy consumption has been designed into buildings and equipment in order to reduce initial (building) costs. With an indefinite future of high fuel prices ahead, it will be both economically and ecologically good management to give much more attention to lifetime operating costs than to building costs.

Transportation consumes about 25 percent of the total energy of this country. Automobiles used 55 percent of all transportation energy in 1970; trucks were second at 21 percent and aircraft third at 7.5 percent. Railways, buses, waterways, and pipelines made up the remaining 16 percent.[20] The persistent demand for greater speed and convenience has been

[19] C. A. Berg, "Energy Conservation through Effective Utilization," *Science,* vol. 181, July 13, 1973, pp. 128–133.
[20] G. A. Lincoln, "Energy Conservation," *Science,* vol. 180, Apr. 13, 1973, pp. 157–158.

realized at the expense of increased energy consumption.

Railroads and waterways have given way to trucks for the movement of intercity freight; buses and railroads have yielded to aircraft and automobiles for intercity passenger traffic; and buses and trains have given way to the automobile for urban passenger traffic. Every one of these exchanges has resulted in greater energy consumption (Fig. 14-14). Aircraft, automobiles, and trucks have the lowest propulsion efficiencies of any type of transport. *Partially loaded* automobiles consumed almost 8 percent of the nation's energy in urban travel in 1971.[21] Even if these vehicles had been fully loaded, mass transit systems would have carried these urbanites to the same places at one-fourth to one-sixth the energy cost, thereby conserving between 1.6 and 1.7 million barrels of petroleum per day. Even without mass-transit relief, we can realize enormous savings in fuel utilization by driving small, fuel-efficient cars. By using such vehicles, as Europeans do, our petroleum consumption could be reduced by over 1 million barrels daily.

Incentive programs Strong incentives for excessive energy utilization exist today in the form of rate structures which encourage high-

[21] Carter, loc. cit.

FIGURE 14-14
Transportation propulsion efficiency in terms of standardized gallons of fuel. [*After R. A. Rice, American Society of Mechanical Engineers Paper, 70-WA/ENER-8, 1970.*]

Passenger		Freight	
Transport type	Passenger miles per gallon	Transport type	Cargo tonmiles per gallon
Jet plane (Boeing 707)	21	One-half of a Boeing 707	8.3
Automobile (sedan)	32	40-ton trucks	50.0
Cross-country train (four 70-seat coaches, diner lounge, and baggage coach)	80	Fast 3,000-ton, 40-car freight train	97.0
Large bus (40 feet)	125	Inland tow barge, 60,000 gross tons	220.0
Suburban train, 10 cars, 160 seats per car	200	5,000-ton, 100-car freight train	250.0
		Large pipeline, 100 miles, 2 pumps	500.0
		100,000-ton supertanker	930.0

volume consumers and tax structures which stimulate resource exploitation. Reversing these incentives provides a means of fostering energy conservation.

In most states, high-volume consumers receive large discounts on the price of electricity; small users in effect subsidize large users. A study in Wisconsin indicates that the demand for electricity can be significantly reduced if power is priced in proportion to the true cost of supplying it to the consumer.[22] When large users are not rewarded, they find ways to save.

Unlike other industries, the energy producers are subsidized by a special tax system which has served to keep fuel prices unnaturally low, thereby discouraging conservation. This subsidy takes the form of at least three direct income-tax benefits: (1) a percentage depletion allowance exempts substantial amounts of crude oil profits from taxation; (2) "intangible drilling" regulations permit immediate deductions of capital expenditures which other industries must spread over several years; and (3) generous tax deductions are permitted on foreign production and profits.

Another subsidy also has fed the energy crisis, namely the heavy flow of tax monies into highway construction rather than public transportation. Cheap gasoline and highways have made it possible to live in suburbia and to drive inefficient, oversized automobiles back and forth to work and to the grocery store, laying waste to energy, open space, and rich agricultural land in one fell swoop.

Tax reform that results in higher energy prices certainly will provide an incentive for conservation. A Rand Corporation study in California in 1972 claims that the application of conservational measures could reduce projected energy demands by 50 percent. If there is incentive to do so, it may well be that the future energy needs of this country will have been grossly overestimated.[23]

Increasing the supply of energy

About two-thirds of the undiscovered oil in the United States are thought to be offshore in the outer continental shelf and in Alaska. Finding and extracting substantial amounts of this oil will be a slow process. It requires five to seven years to bring a *known* oil field into production. The Trans-Alaska pipeline eventually will carry 2 million barrels a day at peak load.[24] This is about 5 percent of our 1976 consumption.

Other than fossil fuels, our only substantial energy sources today are hydroelectric power and nuclear plants. Most hydroelectric sites already have been developed, and it will be virtually impossible to build more nuclear plants than those already planned before 1980.

It would seem that for the next decade or more, our key energy resource will be domestic and foreign fossil fuels. Over the long range, we must look to new methods of extracting and using these fuels and to different sources of energy entirely.[25]

Improving fossil-fuel production and use

The U.S. Geological Survey estimates that the United States possesses coal equivalent to 500 times our total energy consumption in 1973. Only about one-third of this reserve can be recovered by present methods at a reasonable cost. Much of this can be extracted only at the cost of miners' health or environmental damage. Enormous reserves of oil shale lay untapped for similar reasons. Research and development efforts on acceptable methods of extracting, processing, and using these resources could be rewarded richly. Several opportunities exist for increasing the supply of fossil fuels and improving the efficiency of their use.

Synthetic crude oil can be produced from coal and oil shale by a liquefying process (*liquefaction*). Deep deposits of coal can be utilized by a process known as *underground gasification* without sending men underground and with

[22] A. L. Hammond, "Energy Needs: Projected Demands and How to Reduce Them," *Science,* vol. 178, Dec. 15, 1972, p. 1187.
[23] Ibid., pp. 1187–1188.
[24] Rose, op. cit., p. 28.
[25] P. H. Abelson, "A Lost Opportunity," *Science,* vol. 184, May 3, 1974, p. 525.

minimal environmental disturbance. Two holes are drilled into the deposit. Air or oxygen is pumped down one hole, bringing about the partial oxidation of coal and the release of certain gases including hydrogen and methane. The released gases escape out the other hole and can be used to produce several natural gases as well as methanol (methyl alcohol). Methanol is a possible substitute or supplement for gasoline. Hydrogen gas, of course, has tremendous potentialities itself as a nonpolluting fuel. An engine fueled with hydrogen and oxygen produces water vapor for exhaust. Hydrogen incidentally also is *less likely* to blow up or burn than is gasoline.

Coal or fuels derived from coal also can be used as a source of MHD (magnetohydrodynamic) power. The MHD generators operate at high temperatures (2400°C) and convert heat directly into electricity. They are efficient converters of fossil-fuel energy into electricity; they also have no moving parts and contribute much less to air pollution than conventional coal-fired power plants.[26]

Underdeveloped energy sources Potential sources, other than fossil fuels, that have been suggested or are being actively developed are ocean tides, winds, nuclear reactors, geothermal energy, and solar power. Harnessing the tides could provide only a small fraction of our energy needs even if we built a dike around the entire country.[27] Batteries of giant windmills astride towers 38 meters (125 feet) high are being considered. The National Aeronautics and Space Administration (NASA) predicts that mills could supply 5 to 10 percent of our total electric power needs by the end of the century.[28] Nuclear reactors, geothermal energy, and solar power, however, hold the greatest promise of satisfying future energy requirements, with solar power the first choice.

Nuclear reactors are of two basic types: fission and fusion. The physical principles that distinguish the two processes are illustrated in the Hiroshima fission bomb of World War II and the modern hydrogen (fusion) bomb. The development of a fusion reactor is confronted with formidable problems and may not even be scientifically feasible. Fission reactors in current use and on order for future development are of the converter type that use a rare form of uranium, ^{235}U, as fuel. Another fission reactor, the breeder, uses the common form of uranium, ^{238}U, but it is still in an experimental stage of development. One of the problems with nuclear reactors is the possibility of radioactive contamination in the cooling water or exhaust gases. Faulty equipment or a nuclear accident might result in serious damage over the surrounding area. The major difficulty, however, is the problem of radioactive-waste disposal. Much of this waste will be dangerously radioactive for thousands of years.

Heat in the earth's interior (geothermal heat) is a valuable energy source because it can be extracted by means of wells. Geothermal deposits range from steam (Fig. 14-15) to hot water to hot rock; the energy they contain is used to drive turbines which generate electricity. It has been estimated that the geothermal development of steam and hot water alone could yield almost 4 percent of our projected energy needs in 1985, and this figure could rise to over 7 percent by A.D. 2000. Since dry geothermal deposits are thought to be at least 10 times more extensive than the others, this resource appears to have a strong potential for future energy production.[29] Tapping deposits of dry, hot rock entails drilling down to the thermal region which may be no more than 1 or 2 kilometers below the surface. Water is then pumped into the well, fracturing the hot rock and creating a labyrinthine "boiler" below. Another hole is drilled so that water entering the first hole can be brought to the surface after

[26] A. L. Hammond, "Magnetohydrodynamic Power: More Efficient Use of Coal," *Science*, vol. 178, Oct. 27, 1972, pp. 386–387.

[27] Rose, op. cit., p. 23.

[28] Nicholas Wade, "Windmills," *Science*, vol. 184, June 7, 1974, pp. 1055–1058; A. L. Hammond, "Artificial Tornados," *Science*, vol. 190, Oct. 17, 1975, p. 257.

[29] A. L. Hammond, "Dry Geothermal Wells," *Science*, vol. 182, Oct. 5, 1973, pp. 43–44.

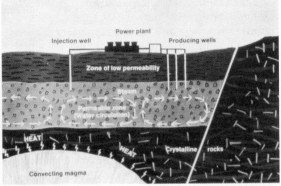

FIGURE 14-15
Geothermal energy. *Above,* molten rock (magma) may rise through a fissure in earth's crust to within 8 to 16 kilometers (5 to 10 miles) of earth's surface, heating water within fractures in near-surface rocks. Drilling into such reservoirs of heated water allows hot water and steam to flow to the surface. Steam drives turbines, which generate electricity. *Left,* part of the Pacific Gas and Electric Company's *The Geysers Power Plant* north of San Francisco. The capacity of the entire facility is 396 megawatts of electricity, enough to supply a city of 400,000. [*Pacific Gas and Electric Co., San Francisco.*]

heating. Precautions against air pollution must be taken with geothermal power plants because noxious gases, particularly hydrogen sulfide, are a common by-product of the wells. The steam geothermal plant shown in Fig. 14-15 produces electricity cheaper and costs less to build than comparable plants in California using fossil fuel or nuclear energy.

Solar energy   Of all forms of energy available to us, solar radiation is the most plentiful. Its supply is inexhaustible, and its use is accompanied by negligible to minimal pollution depending on how it is harnessed. Solar (photovoltaic) cells, such as those used to power space satellites, convert sunlight directly into electricity. Although they are nonpolluting, existing cells are relatively inefficient and much too expensive for terrestrial use. It has been suggested that electricity generated by cells carried on satellites might be converted to microwave power and transmitted to giant antennas on earth. This suggestion is not economically feasible either at the present time, and there also is the possibility that microwave radiation might harm life near the receiving antennas.

Solar energy is converted biologically into chemical energy through photosynthesis. Hydrocarbons similar to those in fossil fuels can be found in, or derived from, plants. Agricultural and forest wastes such as spoiled grain or the slash of cutover timberland can be fermented to produce methanol. Used in conjunction with what are known as *fuel cells,* this alcohol could be an effective, relatively pollution-free fuel.[30] Giant kelp (seaweed) when fermented produces methane. Current experimental work indicates that marine energy farms may be feasible, consisting of kelp beds attached to submerged rope rafts. As more is learned about the biochemistry of photosynthesis itself, it is quite possible that solar energy can be converted into hydrogen, oxygen, and electric power by imitating portions of that biologic process.[31]

The greatest potential for expanding our energy resources in the immediate future lies in the development of solar-thermal technology. Surfaces for absorbing sunlight (solar-energy collectors) already have been designed for solar-thermal equipment that could reduce conventional energy consumption for space and water heating by 50 percent. Such equipment is located where the energy will be used and is incorporated into building design. Technically it also is feasible to use solar energy for air conditioning. Expected improvements in collector efficiency and the use of modern heat-transfer technology (heat exchangers) will almost certainly lead to the development of a solar refrigeration system using ammonia as the coolant. By using solar energy in conjunction with booster equipment operated by fossil fuel or electricity, 50 percent of this nation's energy requirement for space and water heating and for air conditioning could be met by local solar-thermal sources.[32] Had such solar-thermal facilities been in operation in 1975, we would have saved the energy equivalent of more than 4.5 million barrels of petroleum per day.

The generation of electricity from solar energy collectors has possibilities but it requires the use of direct sunlight and extensive reflecting surfaces. In the southwestern United States where there is ample sunshine, a 1,000-megawatt power station capable of supplying a city of 1 million people probably would require 23 square kilometers (9 square miles) of reflecting surfaces.[33]

Solar-thermal power from the sea, however, has almost unlimited potentialities in the form of ocean temperature gradients. The Gulf Stream approaches very close to the southeastern coast of Florida. It has a flow of 2,200 cubic kilometers (523.6 cubic miles) per day and its waters are 16 to 22°C warmer than the water below. It is estimated that the thermal gradients of the Gulf Stream could generate 75 times more energy than our projected demand for 1980. Ocean thermal gradient power plants are considered to be both scientifically and economically feasible. Such a plant would be submerged at a depth of 30 to 60 meters (100 to 200 feet). Warm water flowing through a plant at, say, 25°C would pass through a heat exchanger, causing the working fluid (probably liquid ammonia) to boil. The expanding vapor would drive a turbine to produce electricity and then be condensed back to a liquid in a condenser cooled by seawater at 5°C. The electricity generated could either be transmitted to shore through underwater cables or used to convert (electrolyze) water to hydrogen and oxygen. The two gases could then be piped to shore and stored.

Ocean gradient plants would have two additional advantages. It is estimated that a 100-megawatt plant could produce 60 million gallons of fresh water a day through vacuum vaporization and condensation. The cold water brought up from the ocean depths for plant operation also is rich in nutrients and can be used for the aquaculture of clams, oysters, scallops, lobsters, and shrimp at shore stations.[34]

Research and development priorities

In its fiscal year 1976 budget, the U.S. Energy Research and Development Administration

---

[30] T. B. Reed and R. M. Lerner, "Methanol: A Versatile Fuel For Immediate Use," *Science*, vol. 182, Dec. 28, 1973, pp. 1299–1304.

[31] Melvin Calvin, "Solar Energy by Photosynthesis," *Science*, vol. 184, Apr. 19, 1974, pp. 375–381.

[32] Berg, op. cit., p. 134.

[33] A. L. Hammond, "Solar Energy," *Science*, vol. 177, Sept. 22, 1972, pp. 1088–1090; "Solar Energy Reconsidered," *Science*, vol. 189, Aug. 15, 1975, pp. 538–539.

[34] W. D. Metz, "Ocean Temperature Gradients: Solar Power From The Sea," *Science*, vol. 180, June 22, 1973, pp. 1266–1267.

(ERDA) allotted $1.68 billion for direct energy research and development programs. About 45 percent of this amount went to the breeder reactor, 25 percent to fossil fuel energy, and 16 percent to the fusion reactor. Only 4 percent was allocated for energy conservation and 5 percent for solar energy.[35]

Budgetary allotments would suggest that energy conservation and solar energy are of low priority (Fig. 14-16). Scientific and engineering evidence indicates quite the contrary. Energy conservation could reduce our energy demands by 50 percent. Solar-energy utilization is a great deal closer to realization than fusion reactors, and probably breeder reactors

[35] W. D. Metz, "Energy," *Science,* vol. 189, Aug. 1, 1975, pp. 369–370. P. M. Boffey, "Energy Research," *Science,* vol. 190, Nov. 7, 1975, pp. 535–537.

as well. Its uses would certainly be less hazardous, and it carries the potential of satisfying all our energy needs, not just a portion of them.

ECOSYSTEM DECAY

Few, if any, ecosystems on the planet have not been affected by human activity. Many of them have been and are being destroyed. Many more have been affected in different ways and over varying periods of time. All ecosystems and

FIGURE 14-16
Fiscal 1976 budgetary imbalance in U.S. energy research and development. Of its total budget, the Energy Research and Development Administration (ERDA) allocated 86 percent to the colored areas, 45 percent to breeder reactors alone. Conservation received 4 percent, solar energy 5 percent.

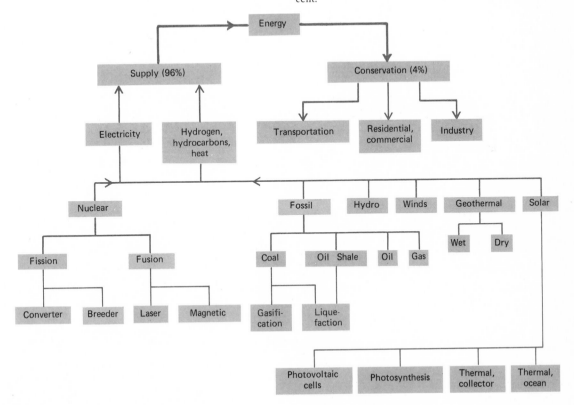

their biotic communities are products of millions of years of evolution. They embrace the great out-of-doors which contributes so powerfully to the richness and joy of being alive. They conserve our water, protect our soil, and provide us with food. They are essential to scientific research and offer unparalleled opportunities for study. They contain all that is left of the genetic resources from which our farm animals and plants are bred, and they include *all* that we have for the development of new ones. The extinction of an animal or plant may be more than biologically regrettable; it could be an economic calamity. The continued destruction of the world's ecosystems is a matter of grave concern.

Biologic communities gradually are wasting away under the steady onslaught of attacks on two fronts. In one, communities are being disrupted from within by the introduction of exotic species from other continents. In the other, members of the community are assaulted directly by hunting, trapping, and poisoning, or the ecosystem is damaged by overgrazing, plowing, lumbering, swamp drainage, eutrophication, etc. In either case the results are comparable. Diversity in the biotic community, so essential to the balance of nature,[36] is progressively reduced, leaving the ecosystem vulnerable to gradual disintegration.

The introduction of exotic species

Humans have greatly accelerated the exchange of species between continents in the past 300 years either by intention or accident. If done purposefully, the alien species usually is brought in to add variety or color to the local biota (plants and animals), to serve as game for food, or to prey on some pest. Nearly a century ago a number of societies were organized for this purpose and released hundreds of thousands of birds representing more than 100 foreign species.[37] Few of these efforts succeeded because

the species lacked either the constitutional or the ecological opportunity to become established. On the other hand, where such opportunities are open the introduced species may find an open niche with almost unlimited food and few to no competent predators, parasites, and competitors. Under these conditions a formerly well-balanced biotic community can be thrown into turmoil. The introduced species can become a pest by seriously reducing the populations of other species if not eliminating them entirely.

Examples of such disturbances are legion. Inadvertent introductions into the United States include such agricultural pests as the European corn borer insect, the Japanese beetle, Russian thistle, and the stock-poisoning Klamath weed. The Norwegian rat and the house mouse probably arrived by ship in colonial days and now plague our homes and cities from coast to coast. With the deepening of the Welland Ship Canal connecting Lakes Ontario and Erie, the lamprey eel gained access to all the Great Lakes and brought collapse to the whitefish and lake trout fisheries of the region.[38] The economic and ecologic effects of these invasions can be far-reaching.

The Amazonian peacock bass (*Cichla ocellaris*) was introduced both by chance and by intent into rivers feeding Gatun Lake in the Panama Canal Zone. Since its first introduction around 1967, this large predatory game fish now occupies most of Gatun Lake. In the area it occupies, *Cichla* has eliminated six of the eight formerly common fish species and drastically reduced another. As a consequence, there appears to be an increase in the population of malaria-carrying mosquitos because some of the fish that were eliminated lived on insects. Other top carnivores (tertiary consumers) competing with *Cichla* fare poorly because they are simply outclassed. These animals include several species of fish-eating birds (terns, herons, and kingfishers) and the tarpon, a large game fish. They

[36] See the increasing diversity of species, Chap. 10; Community energy flow and species diversity, Chap. 11.
[37] O. S. Owen, *Natural Resource Conservation*, New York: The Macmillan Company, 1971, p. 287.

[38] Lampreys were subsequently controlled by killing their larvae with a species-specific larvicide. Coho salmon introduced from the Northwest are now a successful fishery.

are found less and less frequently in areas commanded by the invader. Finally, the alien has so completely overwhelmed the entire food web that the producers (microscopic algae) may be adversely affected.[39]

The record of intentional introductions is not much better. The English sparrow was imported in 1865 followed by the European starling in 1880. Both these birds are raucous, aggressive species that have displaced more attractive natives like red-headed woodpeckers, purple martins, and bluebirds from large portions of their habitat. In the West Indies, the weasellike mongoose of India was introduced to protect sugarcane crops from rat damage. The rats were controlled, but the mongoose became a pest by turning to poultry and ground-nesting birds for its food supply.

The English colonizers of New Zealand found no native mammals on that island. By 1900 they had introduced over 200 species of vertebrates, many of them in an attempt to make the area more like England. Excluding livestock, only 55 of the 178 species of birds and mammals introduced during the nineteenth century became established. Many of these did not perform quite as planned. The red deer of Scotland and the European rabbit were introduced as game animals. An herbivorous opossum from Australia was imported as a furbearer. These three species, with the help of a North American goat, have been primarily responsible for destroying more than half the forests of New Zealand.

Not all introductions have been harmful, especially when they have been adequately researched in advance with experimental trial releases. The ring-necked pheasant and chukar partridge from Asia have proven to be admirable additions to our upland game bird fauna. German brown trout perform well in water too warm for native species. The Coho salmon of the Pacific Northwest has done well in the Great Lakes; so has the Atlantic striped bass in Pacific waters. And of course there have been innumerable exchanges of domesticated animal and plant varieties between every corner of the globe.

Habitat disruption and direct assault

The International Union for the Conservation of Nature and Natural Resources (IUCN) periodically publishes a list of species considered to be rare or endangered (the *Red Data Book*) and a list of species that have become extinct since A.D. 1600 (the *Black Data Book*). The IUCN estimates that there were 4,226 species of living mammals in 1600, of which 36 have since become extinct and 120 are in some danger of becoming so. Of the 8,684 species of birds thought to have been alive in 1600, 94 have become extinct and 187 are endangered. In 375 years, 130 species of birds and mammals have become extinct and 307 living species currently are threatened. Of the 130 extinct species, the U.S. Fish and Wildlife Service believes nearly 40 were North American species that passed into oblivion in the last 150 years. At least 60 species of birds and 27 of mammals are considered to be currently threatened in the United States, and special efforts will be required to save them.

Within the United States, the list of extinctions includes the passenger pigeon, Townsend's finch, Carolina parakeet, sea mink, Merriam's elk, and 17 races of grizzly bear. The Hawaiian goose, lesser prairie chicken, bald eagle, tule elk, polar bear, and gray whale are numbered among those with seriously reduced populations.

The probable reasons for the present rarity and past extinction of these warm-blooded vertebrates are tabulated in Fig. 14-17. It is clear that human activity causes about 75 percent of the extinctions and threatened extinctions and that hunting and habitat disruption alone account for well over 50 percent.

A case study in species extinction
The power of human destructiveness was most effectively demonstrated in the demise of the

[39] T. M. Zaret and R. T. Paine, "Species Introduction in a Tropical Lake," *Science*, vol. 182, Nov. 2, 1973, pp. 449–455.

Cause of extinction	BIRDS (percent of all extinct species)	MAMMALS (percent of all extinct species)
Natural causes	24	25
Man-caused		
Hunting	42 }57	33 }52
Habitat disruption	15	19
Introduced predators	15 }19	17 }23
Introduced parasites, competitors	4	6
	100	100

Cause of present rarity	(percent of all rare species)	(percent of all rare species)
Natural causes	32	14
Man-caused		
Hunting	24 }54	43 }72
Habitat disruption	30	29
Introduced predators	11 }14	8 }14
Introduced parasites, competitors	3	6
	100	100

FIGURE 14-17
The probable causes of extinction and present rarity of mammal and bird species, weighted according to the percentage of species falling victim to each cause. Only those extinctions since A.D. 1600 are considered. [After J. Fisher et al., Wildlife in Danger, Viking, New York, 1969.]

passenger pigeon. This animal was reputed to have been the most abundant bird on earth. Early in the nineteenth century the noted ornithologist Alexander Wilson observed a migrating flock that required hours to pass by. He estimated the flock to be 1½ kilometers (1 mile) wide, 385 kilometers (240 miles) long, and to number about 2 billion birds, roughly 10 times the population of North American waterfowl today. One century later in 1914, the last passenger pigeon died in the Cincinnati zoo at the age of 29 (Fig. 14-18).

Habitat destruction and direct assault were primarily responsible for extinction. The birds nested in beech, maple, and oak trees and fed extensively on beech nuts and acorns. These trees were cleared from millions of hectares for their wood and for land cultivation. Market hunters slaughtered the birds by every imaginable means including guns, nets, traps, clubs, fire, and dynamite. Nearly 15 million pigeons were killed at a single nesting area in northern Michigan in 1861. They were sold for 2¢ a bird to restaurants in Chicago, Boston, and New York.[40]

A case study in ecosystem disintegration
The extent of human destructiveness is currently being witnessed by the rapid disintegration of entire ecosystems. Of these, the destruction of tropical rain forests is the most distressing. No other type of ecosystem even remotely approaches the biologic diversity found in the climax evergreen forests of tropical latitudes (Fig. 14-19).

Contrary to common belief, rain forest soils are poor in nutrients because they are leached out by rainfall ranging from 200 to 760 centimeters (80 to 300 inches) per year. The biotic community recycles the nutrients that remain and is replenished only by the bacterial synthesis of nitrates from atmospheric nitrogen and the nutrient brought with rain. Food webs are of enormous complexity and are very stable. Epidemics and similar erruptive out-

[40] Owen, op. cit., pp. 281–282.

FIGURE 14-18
Martha, the last passenger pigeon on earth, in the Cincinnati Zoo. A century before, this species was reputed to be the most abundant bird in the world. In 1914, Martha died at the age of 29. [*National Audubon Society.*]

breaks simply do not occur. Identified species number in the hundreds of thousands and the actual number may run into the millions.[41] Because of the strong interdependence among members of the community, it would probably require centuries of ecologic succession to produce a climax rain forest *even if the necessary species were available.*

[41] One and a half million species of organisms have been identified over the world. Most authorities believe there are about ten million species in the world today.

Much of the existing fauna and flora of the world, including man himself, trace their evolutionary origins to the rich biologic diversity of tropical rain forests. The loss of this vast genetic resource would be one of calamitous proportions, and yet the destructive agency of human activity already is pressing toward that end (Fig. 14-20). Slash-and-burn farming is bringing about the retreat of these forests everywhere. Unless corrective measures are taken they will have dwindled to a few small

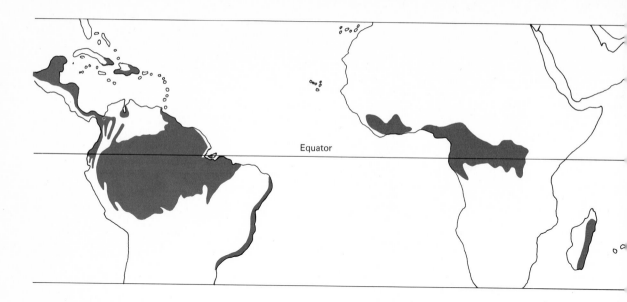

Equator

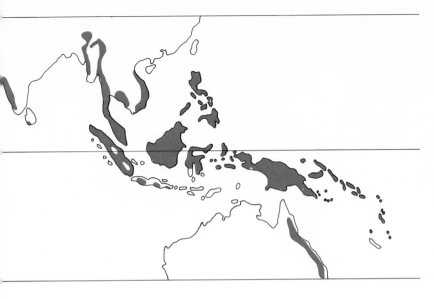

FIGURE 14-19
The distribution of tropical rain forests (colored areas). Clearing forests for raising crops, for pasture land, and for habitation has reduced rain forests of India, Sri Lanka (formerly Ceylon), and Australia to isolated blocks and patches. [*Courtesy of P. W. Richards, University College of North Wales.*]

relics by century's end. From Borneo to Africa to Costa Rica they are being transformed into pastures, croplands, and Scandinavian furniture. In Sri Lanka, India, and Australia they already have been reduced to a few small patches, robbed of their former biologic diversity.[42]

Ample natural reserves of the rain forests over the world must be set aside if we expect to preserve what is left of these rich gene pools. Zoos also must become survival and breeding centers as well as exhibitional facilities for endangered wildlife species. Our biological resources must be conserved if we wish to advance our knowledge of biology and medicine, and to continue breeding animals and plants that are useful to us. The raw material of future evolution is in our hands; we should treat it responsibly.

One major ecologic problem remains to be considered, that of environmental pollution. The final chapter will focus on the pollution issue, and will close with a discussion on the merits of a stable economy and how the human species may resolve its ecology crises.

[42] Paul W. Richards, "The Tropical Rain Forest," *Scientific American,* December 1973, pp. 58–67.

FIGURE 14-20
Slash-and-burn farming, the predominant agricultural system in the humid tropics. Tracts of forest are periodically cut down, burned, and farmed until the nutrients in the soil are exhausted. A new section of forest is then cleared and the former field lies fallow. This aerial photograph shows recently burned forest (light area in foreground) in Brazil. The central area was burned a year or two earlier and supports a crop of manioc grown by farmers in nearby village (huts left of center) near riverbank; uncut forest appears at upper right and upper left. [*Courtesy of P. W. Richards, University College of North Wales.*]

SUGGESTED READINGS

The two books by P. R. Ehrlich et al. and C. H. Southwick cited at the end of Chap. 12 deal at some length with the subject matter of this chapter.

COX, G. W. (ed.): *Readings in Conservation Ecology,* New York: Appleton-Century-Crofts, Inc., 1969. A collection of essays on wildlife populations, pest control, timber and grassland, water resources, soils, and related topics.

EHRENFELD, D. W.: *Biologic Conservation*, New York: Holt, Rinehart and Winston, Inc., 1970. This book and Mossman's book deal with much the same subject matter as the larger Owen book, but their coverage is more restricted.

ELTON, C. S.: *The Ecology of Invasions by Animals and Plants*, London, Methuen & Co., Ltd., 1958. This small book is a classic in its field and written by an outstanding ecologist.

GARVEY, G.: *Energy, Ecology, Economy*, New York: W. W. Norton & Company, Inc., 1972. An interesting treatment of the economics of the energy problem.

HAMMOND, A., et al.: *Energy and the Future*, American Association for the Advancement of Science, Washington, D.C., 1973. A survey of present and future energy sources.

HAYEMS, E.: *Soil and Civilization*, London: Thames and Hudson, 1952. An interesting account of the effects of man-induced soil loss on human history in the Western World and the Far East.

MISHAN, E. J.: *Technology and Growth; The Price We Pay*, New York: Praeger Publishers, Inc., 1970. A critical view of growth from the standpoint of its economic cost.

MOSSMAN, A. S.: *Conservation*, New York: Intext Educational Publishers, 1974.

OWEN, O. S.: *Natural Resource Conservation: An Ecological Approach*, New York: The Macmillan Company, 1975. A clearly written, beautifully illustrated, and comprehensive treatment of the conservation and management of soils, water, rangelands, timber, wildlife, and both freshwater and marine fisheries.

PACKARD, V.: *The Waste Makers*, New York: David McKay Company, Inc., 1960. The economics of planned obsolescence.

ROCKS, L., and R. P. RUNYON: *The Energy Crisis*, New York: Crown Publishers, Inc., 1972. A popular book about the energy crisis and its background.

U.S. BUREAU OF SPORTS FISHERIES AND WILDLIFE: *Rare and Endangered Fish and Wildlife of the U.S.*, Publication 34, Superintendent of Documents, Washington, D.C., 1966. The best and most up-to-date source available on American wildlife problems.

REVIEW QUESTIONS

1 Describe land practices used by ancient civilizations in the Middle East and some of their ecologic consequences. To what extent have these same land abuses recurred in the United States in the past 75 years? Identify four techniques that have been devised in recent times to correct these land abuses in the United States.

2 Explain the processes by which municipal wastewater is treated. Cite three major difficulties that impede progress in reclaiming wastewater for reuse.

3 The growth economy has a history of converting raw materials into unused solid wastes. What progress is being made in recycling such wastes? Cite two examples. Insofar as the economic interrelationships between developed and developing countries are concerned, why is solid-waste recycling absolutely imperative?

4 Compared to the rest of the industrialized world, what is the per capita energy consumption of the United States? What percentage of our energy "needs" are met by oil and gas? According to the most reliable and most recent estimates, if the United States imports 35 percent of its oil and gas from other oil-producing countries, the entire oil and gas resources of the United States will be exhausted in about how many years?

5 Show how energy can be conserved in (a) buildings, (b) industrial processes, and (c) transportation. According to a Rand Corporation study, how much would the application of such conservational measures reduce projected energy demands?

6 Energy will be conserved only if there are strong incentives for such conservation. Discuss three ways in which energy conservation can be encouraged by merely reversing present economic and political policy.

7 Describe two possible techniques for improving fossil-fuel production or use. What are the prospects of the United States increasing its supply of fossil fuels in the near future?

8 Critically evaluate the usefulness of the following as energy sources: (a) nuclear reactors, (b) geothermal wells.

9 Identify five potential and/or actual energy-source technologies based on solar radiation. Which two of these show the greatest promise either now or in the future, and what is the energy potential of each?

10 List five ways in which natural ecosystems are indispensable to human life. Unless studied carefully in advance, one of two consequences usually follows the introduction of an exotic species into an ecosystem. What are these two consequences? Illustrate each with an example.

11 Since A.D. 1600 about how many species of birds and mammals have become extinct? About how many species of birds and mammals are currently threatened? About what percentage of these extinctions and threatened extinctions is thought to be caused by habitat disruption and hunting?

12 Give an account of an actual occurrence in which habitat disruption and direct assault have resulted in the extinction of a once abundant species. Give a similar account in which a particular type of ecosystem is being destroyed on a worldwide basis.

FIFTEEN

THE HUMAN ENVIRONMENT II:
From Pollution to Resolution

In Chaps. 13 and 14 we saw some of the ways in which overpopulation and the economy of growth undermine the quality of human life and lay waste to the environment in which we live. No such discussion would be complete, however, without considering environmental pollution because it constitutes a major ecologic assault against human health and survival.

ENVIRONMENTAL POLLUTION

Human activity contributes to environmental pollution in diverse ways. A variety of substances contaminate the air (*air pollution*). Others find their way into streams, lakes, and oceans, contributing to *water pollution*. An inordinate number of artificial substances are best considered as general pollutants because of their varied avenues of dispersal; they may contaminate air, water, soil, and food, or may enter our bodies directly (*general pollution*).

Air pollution

Strictly atmospheric pollutants fall into two classes: smog and noise.

Smog

Atmospheric pollution resulting from the products of combustion is not a new problem. England enacted legislation to regulate the burning of coal at least 200 years ago. Over a thousand people died from the effects of smoke and fog in Glasgow, Scotland during the fall of 1909. Sixty people lost their lives due to smog in the industrial Meuse Valley of Belgium in December 1930, and thousands complained of respiratory ailments. A heavy smog which settled on Donora, Pennsylvania in the fall of 1948 killed 20 people and sickened over 6,000. London's black fog of December 1952 caused about 4,000 deaths, most of which were the direct or indirect result of respiratory complications.

Today, smog afflicts the inhabitants of both large and moderate-sized cities throughout the world. Although killing smogs are rare, countless millions are subjected to an almost continuous assault of airborne toxic substances that impair or endanger human health and welfare in some degree. Even remote urban centers like the capital city of Nepal in the Himalayan Mountains are no longer immune from air pollution.

The problem is being aggravated further by the current energy crisis. For example, in an attempt to improve air quality, power plants in the United States have been encouraged to change from high-sulfur coal, of which we have a plentiful supply, to low-sulfur oil, most of which must be imported. Efforts to meet present energy shortages oppose such changes, in the belief that air quality must be sacrificed to meet the country's energy needs. Such belief misses the obvious point that the energy crisis is a warning that we have already exceeded the capacity of our environment.

The nature of smog Airborne contaminants become concentrated when a temperature inversion layer of cool air forms, or moves in, under a layer of warm air. The cool dense air does not rise but remains near the ground, accumulating pollutants to form what we know as *smog* (Fig. 15-1). The chief producers of atmospheric contaminants are automobiles,

FIGURE 15-1
Smog in Denver, Colorado. [*Photograph by Charles E. Grover, Environmental Protection Agency.*]

Pollution source	Particulate matter	Sulfur oxides	Nitrogen oxides	Carbon monoxide	Hydrocarbons	Total
Vehicles	1.1	0.7	7.3	57.9	15.1	82.1
Power and heating	8.1	22.1	9.1	1.7	0.6	41.6
Industry	6.8	6.6	0.2	8.8	4.2	26.6
Refuse disposal	0.9	0.1	0.5	7.1	1.5	10.1
Evaporation: solvent and gasoline	0.0	0.0	0.0	0.0	3.9	3.9
Total	16.9	29.5	17.1	75.5	25.3	164.3

FIGURE 15-2
Atmospheric pollutants emitted in the U.S. during 1968. The figures are estimates expressed in millions of metric tons. [*Modified from G. B. Morgan et al. of the National Air Pollution Control Administration.*]

trucks, buses, aircraft, power plants, industry, and refuse disposal sites (Fig. 15-2). But the automobile is the major offender (Fig. 15-3).

Of the five emission pollutants listed in Fig. 15-2, two (nitrogen oxide and hydrocarbons) are subjected to further chemical reaction in the atmosphere by ultraviolet light. These reactions yield additional substances with irritant or toxic properties, notably ozone, peroxides, and aldehydes. The entire complex encompasses the major air pollutants in smog. Currently, it is believed that each of these major contaminants has a threshold concentration below which the pollutant has no measurable, harmful effect.

Some airborne contaminants, however, are probably harmful in any concentration. These hazardous nonthreshold substances include such toxic trace elements as mercury and lead; 10 such elements already have been

FIGURE 15-3
Automobile traffic is the major contributor to air pollution. [*U.S. Department of Housing and Urban Development.*]

identified in smog (Fig. 15-4). These materials are tolerated only in minute quantities, if at all, by most organisms, including man. Since their presence in the air usually is undetected, they constitute one of the most dangerous forms of air pollution.

Seven of the elements that are asterisked in Fig. 15-4 have been found in microscopic particles emitted from coal-fired power plants, metallurgical smelters and blast furnaces, municipal incinerators, and automobiles. Their concentration is highest in the most miniscule particles ranging below one micrometer (1/1000 of a millimeter) in diameter. Such particles are too small to be trapped by conventional smog-control equipment. When breathed, they deposit predominantly in the lung; relatively few are trapped in the nose, throat, and bronchial passages, where they might be removed by the normal flow of mucus.[1]

Smog hazards and damage   There is abundant evidence that the levels of air pollution in the

[1] D. F. S. Natusch et al., "Toxic Trace Elements: Preferential Concentration in Respirable Particles," *Science*, vol. 183, Jan. 18, 1974, pp. 202–204; D. F. S. Natusch and J. R. Wallace, "Urban Aerosol Toxicity," *Science*, vol. 186, Nov. 22, 1974, pp. 695–699.

FIGURE 15-4
Nonthreshold toxic trace elements found in smog (asbestos, a silicate of magnesium, is a compound). Asterisked elements are associated with microscopic particles emitted from high temperature combustion sources in fossil-fueled power plants, metallurgical smelters and blast furnaces, municipal incinerators, and automobiles. Their concentration is highest in particle sizes too small to be trapped by conventional control equipment.

Beryllium
Mercury
Antimony*
Arsenic*
Cadmium*
Lead*
Selenium*
Thallium*
Vanadium*
Asbestos (magnesium silicate)

major cities of the United States, Europe, and Japan pose a serious threat to human health. This is not surprising in view of the 164 million metric tons of pollutants the United States alone dumps into its atmosphere every year (Fig. 15-2). Increasing percentages of city dwellers are falling victim to pollution-related ailments ranging from minor respiratory inflammations to chronic bronchitis, asthma, emphysema, and lung cancer.

Figure 15-5 illustrates the consequences of a fivefold increase in atmospheric sulfur dioxide over a two-day period in New York. An epidemic of respiratory complaints and allied symptoms followed almost immediately. A Los Angeles study indicated a direct correlation between the frequency of automobile accidents and air pollution. Drivers with high carbon monoxide (CO) levels in their blood appeared to be more accident-prone. The CO level may reach 400 parts per million in the air over crowded freeways. Breathing only 50 parts per million will raise the CO blood-saturation level to 2 or even 5 percent, at which point both visual discrimination and hearing are impaired. High CO blood levels also show a positive correlation with mortality in patients with heart trouble.[2]

The air-quality standards of the Clean Air Act of 1971 set a CO blood saturation limit below 1.5 percent for physically active non-smokers. A study of the residents of Chicago, Milwaukee, New York, and Los Angeles from 1969 to 1972, however, indicated that a significant proportion of these populations were continuously exposed to CO concentrations exceeding air-quality standards. Some non-smokers had CO saturations as high as 5.8 percent and smokers as high as 13 percent.[3]

Numerous studies have linked air pollution and cigarette smoking to the rapidly rising incidence of lung cancer. Smoking and smog

[2] J. R. Goldsmith and S. A. Landow, "Carbon Monoxide and Human Health," *Science*, vol. 162, 1968, pp. 1352–1359.
[3] R. D. Stewart et al., "Carboxyhemoglobin Concentrations in Blood Donors in Chicago, Milwaukee, New York, and Los Angeles," *Science*, vol. 182, Dec. 28, 1973, pp. 1362–1364.

seem to have a *synergistic* effect; that is, the risk of lung cancer in people who smoke and breathe airborne pollutants is greater than the sum of the separate cancer risks in smokers who breathe nonpolluted air and nonsmokers who breathe polluted air.[4]

Knowledge of health problems associated with nonthreshold trace elements suffers from inadequate study and a lack of sufficiently sensitive monitoring techniques. Both lead and mercury are associated with irreversible mental and nervous damage. Children are particularly sensitive because of their higher respiratory rate; they may breathe two to three times as much pollutant per kilogram of body weight as an adult.

Lead and mercury have been widely distributed around the globe during the last few decades, as is witnessed by the increasing lead content in the snowpacks of Antarctica and the growing amounts of mercury in the Greenland ice sheet. It is estimated that about 3,000 metric tons of mercury are spewed into the world's atmosphere annually, largely from the burning of coal and oil and from cement manufacturing plants.[5] Over 180,000 tons of lead are injected into the air of the United States every year from automobiles, trucks, and buses.

The air in a middle-class West Side community in New York showed an average of 5.4 micrograms of lead per cubic meter of air. Two young children in the area had excessive amounts of lead in their blood. A particularly sinister finding is that lead apparently can accumulate in the human body and be passed from generation to generation. A number of newborn babies in the Bronx had lead concentrations in their blood similar to their mothers. The danger of this form of lead contamination is compounded further by an accumulation of lead in the environment. Between 1961 and 1969, airborne lead concentrations increased by as much as 32 percent in Cincinnati, 35 per-

[4] H. R. Menck et al., "Industrial Air Pollution," *Science*, vol. 183, Jan. 18, 1974, pp. 210–212.
[5] H. V. Weiss et al., "Mercury in a Greenland Ice Sheet," *Science*, vol. 174, Nov. 12, 1971, pp. 692–694.

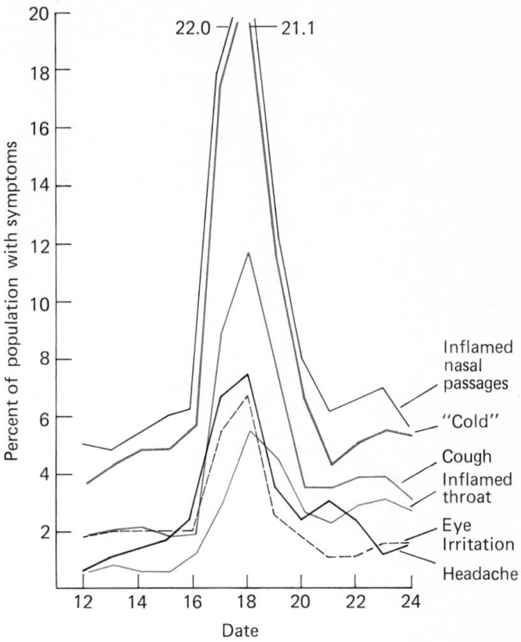

FIGURE 15-5
Outbreak of respiratory disease in New York City following increase in levels of atmospheric sulfur dioxide (SO_2). The SO_2 levels increased from less than 0.2 ppm (parts per million) to 0.8 and 0.9 ppm on December 16 and 17 in 1962. [*After J. R. McCarroll et al., American Journal of Public Health, vol. 56, no. 2, American Public Health Association, 1966.*]

cent in Philadelphia, and 64 percent in Los Angeles.[6]

In addition to its health hazards, air pollution has adverse effects on agricultural crops, natural ecosystems, property and buildings, climate, and the very quality of life itself. Crop damage alone in the United States may amount to a billion dollars annually (Fig. 15-6). Sulfur dioxide and nitrogen oxides in smog combine with moisture to form sulfuric and nitric acids. These strong acids, in combination with ozone and peroxides, corrode, oxidize, and discolor a great variety of materials, including stone,

[6] R. J. Bazell, "Lead Poisoning," *Science*, vol. 174, Nov. 5, 1971, pp. 574–576.

Trees and fruits
  Grapes
  Oranges
  Pine
  Spruce
  Several species of
    deciduous trees

Truck crops
  Green beans
  Lima beans
  Pinto beans
  Celery
  Chard
  Lettuce
  Onions
  Peanuts
  Potatoes
  Soybeans
  Spinach
  Tomatoes

Field crops
  Alfalfa
  Sweet corn
  Tobacco

Ornamental plants
  Carnation
  Chrysanthemum
  Larkspur
  Orchids
  Pansy
  Petunia
  Rose
  Snapdragon
  Zinnia

FIGURE 15-6
Some of the plants and agricultural crops that are seriously damaged by smog. Both wild and domesticated species are injured.

cement, brick, metals, paint, rubber, textiles, paper, and plastics. As a consequence, excessive waste occurs in the accelerated deterioration of buildings, equipment, storage facilities, art treasures, and miscellaneous property; extraordinary sums must be expended in maintenance and repair. It is estimated that the Parthenon in Athens has deteriorated more in the past 50 years than in the previous 2,000.

For the last 20 years, acid rain and snow have been falling in the northeastern United States, southeastern Canada, and southern Sweden. The major cause is sulfur dioxide which, in the case of Sweden, apparently is transported more than 1,000 kilometers (620 miles) from the industrial sectors of England and the Ruhr Valley in Germany. The reduction in forest growth in northern New England and in Scandinavia during the last two decades is thought to be related to this acid precipitation. Numerous rivers and lakes in Scandinavia as well as several lakes in Canada have suffered serious game-fish mortality. The acidity of these waters has increased by as much as a hundredfold and more. Damage to structures and art forms in these regions may be enormous.[7]

The climatic effects of air pollution are substantial in local areas, particularly large urban centers. The increased use of energy in large cities raises air temperature, creating an urban "heat island." The particulate matter in smog forms a haze that reduces both visibility and solar radiation. The large amount of water vapor released from auto exhausts and industrial processes adds to this haze by forming water droplets around airborne particles. Consequently, cities are foggier and cloudier than surrounding rural areas and have 10 to 30 percent more rainfall.

There is a real future possibility that these climatic changes of human origin may become more widespread and perhaps even global in extent. It is estimated that the burning of fossil fuels has increased atmospheric CO_2 over the world by 10 to 15 percent since 1860. This presumably should result in warmer world climates because of the greenhouse effect (see Chap. 11, The carbon cycle). Ever-expanding urban heat islands could contribute enormously to higher world temperatures. In fact, if the current rate at which we have been increasing energy production continues, the human species would be producing as much energy in 200 years as our planet receives from the sun. Obviously our use of energy would have to be greatly restricted long before such a point was reached.[8]

Smog control Smog control is a complex socioeconomic issue that can be approached at several levels. Many air pollutants can be technologically controlled at the pollution source by devices that either trap the offending sub-

[7] G. E. Likens and F. H. Bormann, "Acid Rain," *Science,* vol. 184, June 14, 1974, pp. 1176–1179.
[8] A. L. Weinberg, "Global Effects of Man's Production of Energy," *Science,* vol. 186, Oct. 18, 1974, p. 205.

stances in some manner or convert them into harmless products that may be released safely. Pollution also can be reduced by changing to cleaner energy sources of comparable efficiency; high-sulfur coal pollutes more than low-sulfur oil just as high-lead gasoline pollutes more than a mixture of methanol and no-lead gas. A drastic but effective measure is to eliminate the polluting instrument itself. It is inevitable, for instance, that the private gasoline-powered automobile will some day be abandoned as a major means of urban and suburban transportation, not only because it is the chief contributor to air pollution but also because its use of energy is grossly inefficient.

A major step can be taken toward solving the dual problems of air pollution and energy demand by using our energy sources to produce hydrogen. Every prime energy source lends itself to hydrogen generation. It can be generated chemically, using heat from fossil-fueled, geothermal, solar thermal, or nuclear sources. It is a natural product of coal and oil gasification, and it can be produced by the decomposition of water through electrolysis, using electricity generated by fossil-fueled, geothermal, ocean-thermal-gradient, or nuclear power plants. The hydrogen so generated could be employed safely as a nonpolluting multipurpose fuel. It will readily fulfill all the functions of natural gas, oil, and gasoline. If properly utilized the sole exhaust product is water vapor.[9]

A major problem in air-pollution control is ensuring that satisfactory air-quality standards are met. Since the atmosphere, along with public lands and waterways, belongs to everyone (society), it is owned by no one. Consequently, these resources have been regarded as free commodities. Their availability to users at no cost obviously has led to their overuse and abuse. People discharge wastes into the air free of charge, despite the social debt that is incurred by impaired health and smog damage.

Existing federal and state laws have resorted largely to a regulation-enforcement strategy, using the police power of the state to keep pollutant discharges within acceptable air-quality standards. Because of political bargaining and legal bickering, the public interest usually has not been adequately protected.

Many economists favor a different strategy which uses economic incentive to achieve control.[10] A tax or fee would be levied on wastes discharged into the air, based on the amount and harmfulness of each pollutant emitted. Such a strategy would give an economic incentive to air-pollution control as long as the social costs of pollution were significantly higher than the cost of pollution control. By avoiding the high costs of air emissions, the industry that pollutes the least could get its product on the market at the cheapest price, and the owners of those automobiles with the lowest emissions would have the cheapest private transportation.

Noise pollution

Excessive noise has characterized the industrial environment for a long time. Now, however, the general public has become a victim of noise in almost every aspect of human life. On the way to work, urban dwellers are immersed in a heavy din created by automobiles, motorcycles, buses, trucks, ambulances, fire engines, and trains. When at work or while shopping, traffic noises are a background accompaniment to overflying aircraft, jackhammers in the street below, and the monotony of canned music punctuated by the blaring of a public address system. At home we fare little better in the presence of the automatic dishwasher, food blender, garbage disposal, vacuum cleaner, and power lawn mower, reinforced by airplanes and helicopters aloft, not to mention the stereos, radios, television sets, model airplanes, and motorbikes in our households as well as our neighbors'. Even the annual vacation in the great out-of-doors offers limited relief. Earth-

[9] D. P. Gregory, "The Hydrogen Economy," *Scientific American*, January 1973, pp. 13–21.

[10] A. M. Freeman III and R. H. Haveman, "Residual Charges for Pollution Control," *Science*, vol. 177, July 28, 1972, pp. 322–329.

FIGURE 15-7

Sound sources, noise levels, and human response. The decibel is a unit of loudness measuring how much louder a given sound is than the softest audible sound. It is expressed as the logarithm of that loudness ratio, multiplied by 10. The logarithm of a number is the number of times 10 is multiplied by itself to get the number. A sound that is 10,000 times louder than the softest audible sound registers 40 decibels. The logarithm of 10,000 is 4, that is, 10 multiplied by itself 4 times. The decibel rating would therefore be 10 times that number, or 40. A 100-decibel noise is 10 billion times louder than the softest audible sound.

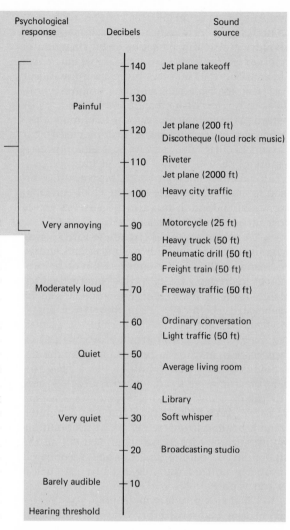

moving machinery, power saws, outboard motors, snowmobiles, diesel generators, and the omnipresent radios, motorcycles, and dune buggies are no consolation to eardrums and temperaments already overtaxed.

Noise has numerous undesirable effects. It restricts verbal communication and interferes with sleep. Prolonged exposure to noise levels of about 90 decibels and above causes hearing loss and early deafness (Fig. 15-7). Above intensities of about 120 decibels, rising sound levels cease to be louder but become increasingly painful. Protracted exposure to noise intensities of 70 decibels and above has been shown to be related to symptoms of nervous stress. Increased heart rate and blood pressure occur along with irritability, anxiety, and fatigue. Such responses would very likely contribute to impaired health, higher accident rates, and reduced job efficiency.

Noise control, like smog control, is a matter of assessing proper charges against the use of a common property resource. Although we all may wear earplugs or insulate our homes with acoustic tile, the burden of control must be placed on the users of the public's air, namely the noisemakers. The manufacturers and users of machines, airplanes, automobiles, household appliances, etc., will reduce the noise levels of their gadgetry when there is an economic incentive to do so.

Water pollution

Streams, lakes, coastal waters, and even the open sea receive pollutants, sometimes in massive quantities, as a result of human activity.

Oil pollution

It is estimated that about 6 million metric tons of oil enter the world's oceans annually, of which some 10 percent comes from natural seeps in the ocean floor. At least half of it comes via rivers and sewer outfalls from land-based sources like petroleum-refinery wastes and service-station crankcase drainings. Such contamination is not only unnecessary but wasteful; crankcase drainings can be refined for reuse. Oceangoing vessels, especially tankers, account for about 1.5 million metric tons. Large amounts of oil escape when ships collide, during loading and unloading, and particularly when the oily ballast water is discharged prior to reloading.[11] Pollution also has resulted from leaks in offshore drilling operations such as occurred during 1969 in the Santa Barbara Channel off the California coast.

The total biologic impact of such oil pollution at present is unknown. Certain chemicals in oil are toxic and some are known to be carcinogenic (cancer-causing). Large numbers of seabirds, fish, and shellfish have been killed at and near the site of contamination where the oil forms a continuous layer over the water surface. The hazard such oil presents after it has become widely distributed over the ocean's surface as "clots of oil" (pelagic tar) is another matter. Some biologists fear this diluted oil may interfere with the ability of marine organisms to communicate. Many marine creatures ranging from bacteria to lobsters communicate by means of chemical secretions (*pheromones*). Substances in petroleum are similar to some of these secretions and might have disruptive effects on reproductive cycles. This, in turn, could disturb food chains and entire ecosystems.

Sewage

The streams and lakes of the United States as well as its coastal waters annually receive many billions of liters of raw sewage, millions of tons of sewage sludge and enormous volumes of effluent from primary and secondary municipal treatment plants throughout the country. Diseases, such as typhoid, bacterial and amebic dysentery, cholera, and infectious hepatitis,

that are caused by waterborne microorganisms may become a real threat to public health. Public swimming areas in lakes and along ocean beaches often are closed because of bacterial comtamination resulting from water pollution. Millions of Americans drink water with bacteria counts exceeding U.S. Public Health Service standards; many thousands become stricken with waterborne diseases annually.

Industrial wastes add a new dimension in the form of pesticides, radioactive substances, trace elements, and various chemical by-products with toxic or carcinogenic properties. Since industrial wastes often tend to contaminate both air and water, however, they will be considered later as general pollutants.

Excessive nutrient concentration

Effluents of modern sewage-treatment plants are rich in nitrogen-containing ammonia, nitrates, nitrites, and phosphates. Although most of these substances are basic plant nutrients, their urban sources are diverse; most of the phosphates, for example, come from detergents. Such nutrient-rich wastewater is emptied into streams and lakes which, in turn, receive additional nutrient from the runoff water of adjacent farmland which has been fertilized with nitrogen and perhaps even phosphorus. A study revealed that some 55 percent of the nitrates in Lake Decatur, Illinois originated from fertilizer nitrogen in the surrounding watershed. This lake provides drinking water for a nearby city of 100,000.[12]

Waters enriched in this way undergo eutrophication[13] and may develop luxuriant growths of aquatic vegetation, notably algae. In advanced stages of eutrophication, massive algal blooms occur which produce undesirable tastes and odors. As portions of these algal masses die, their decomposition depletes the dissolved oxygen supply, killing useful organisms such as game fish and rendering the water unfit for swimming or boating (Fig. 15-8).

---

[11] Willard Bascom, "The Disposal of Waste in the Ocean," *Scientific American*, August 1974, p. 21; J. N. Butler, "Pelagic Tar," *Scientific American*, June 1975, pp. 90–97.

[12] D. H. Kohl et al., "Fertilizer Nitrogen," *Science*, vol. 174, Dec. 24, 1971, pp. 1331–1334.

[13] See Chap. 13, Improving crop yields.

Most, if not all, of the major rivers and lakes in the United States, and many of the lesser ones, are in varying states of eutrophication from early to advanced. This situation will improve, of course, only when effective steps are taken to counteract it. An experimental study of lakes in Ontario, Canada indicates that phosphorus is much more important in promoting eutrophication than nitrogen. If this is the case, a basinwide ban on detergent phosphates in the Lake Erie–Lake Ontario region would have a beneficial effect on these badly abused bodies of water.[14]

A potential health hazard may exist when drinking water has a nitrate nitrogen concentra-

[14] D. W. Schindler, "Eutrophication and Recovery in Experimental Lakes," *Science*, vol. 184, May 24, 1974, pp. 897–899.

FIGURE 15-8
The waters of Lake Minnetonka, Minnesota. Nutrients emptying into the lake from sewage treatment plants and agricultural runoff resulted in eutrophication. Dead and dying masses of algae consume available oxygen, excluding desirable forms of aquatic life such as edible fish, and destroy the recreational value of the lake. [*The Minneapolis Star and the Environmental Protection Agency.*]

tion greater than 10 parts per million. Well water in Illinois, Minnesota, and southern California has been found to exceed this limit at many locations. Nitrates become toxic under conditions in which they can be reduced to nitrites; in the presence of nitrites, hemoglobin loses its ability to transport oxygen. The stomachs of infants under four months of age apparently provide conditions appropriate to nitrite formation because numerous infant deaths have been caused by drinking water of high nitrate content.[15]

Thermal pollution

Today's technological society releases tremendous amounts of heat to the environment, particularly in large metropolitan and industrial areas. The atmosphere above cities becomes thermally polluted from the heat (thermal energy) emitted by automobiles, trucks, buses, fossil-fuel power plants, industrial processes, and residential and commercial heating. We have referred to this phenomenon previously as the *urban heat island.* Thermal or heat pollution is not confined to the atmosphere, however. Water has a much greater capacity for absorbing heat than air. As a consequence, water is used to remove all the waste heat of nuclear power plants and the major part of waste heat from fossil-fuel power plants and such industrial processes as steel manufacture. Considering current and projected energy demands, power plants are the major agencies to be contended with in avoiding whatever hazards may be associated with the thermal pollution of water.

Both nuclear and fossil-fuel power plants produce electricity from generators driven by steam turbines. Steam is reconverted to water for reheating in condensers cooled by water taken from the ocean or a nearby lake or stream. The coolant water carrying waste heat from the condensers is then returned to the source from which it came. Nuclear and fossil-fuel plants differ basically in the fuel used to generate steam and the amount of cooling

[15] I. A. Wolff and A. E. Wasserman, "Nitrates, Nitrites, and Nitrosamines," *Science*, vol. 177, July 7, 1972, pp. 15–16.

water required. Whereas fossil-fuel plants lose about 40 percent of their fuel energy value to waste heat in coolant water, atomic-powered installations lose 55 percent. As a result nuclear plants contribute more to thermal pollution than fossil-fuel facilities per kilowatt of electricity generated.

The temperature of coolant water is raised between 6 and 17°C (10 and 30°F) in the steam condensers of power plants. Returning this heated effluent to the natural water source from which it came ultimately may harm aquatic organisms, particularly in view of the planned increases in power facilities through A.D. 2000. At that time we are scheduled to have power plants, most of them nuclear, which would require the equivalent of one-third the yearly freshwater runoff of the United States for cooling purposes. During the dry summer season this requirement would equal the total flow of all rivers in the country.[16]

In order to lessen the possible risks of

[16] J. R. Clark, "Thermal Pollution and Aquatic Life," *Scientific American*, March 1969, p. 23.

thermal water pollution, cooling towers are being used as a means of eliminating waste heat (Fig. 15-9). The most common type cools by evaporation, exposing hot effluent water to air rising through the tower. The cooled effluent that escapes evaporation is collected in a basin at the base of the tower where it can be recirculated to the condensers or returned to the source from which it came. Evaporative cooling towers are objected to because of the large amount of water vapor they release into the atmosphere. Towers for a 1,000-megawatt power plant eject water equivalent to 2.5 centimeters (1 inch) of daily rainfall over a 5 square kilometer (2 square mile) area. Nonevaporative cooling towers can be built on the principle of a gigantic automobile radiator but such installations cost two and one-half to three times as much as the evaporative type.

In this era of energy crisis, one might hope that some of the waste energy released by power plants could be put to useful production. It has been suggested that power plants become centers around which certain agricultural, industrial, or commercial activities might be es-

FIGURE 15-9
The three massive cooling towers on the right will cool 2,927,000 liters (773,300 gallons) of coolant water per minute through a range of 15.3°C (27.5°F) in this Kentucky power plant. Air rising through the tower cools hot water discharged into lower part of tower by evaporation. Effluent water that evaporates escapes into the atmosphere, leaving the cooled effluent in a basin at the bottom of the tower where it can be recirculated to the condensers or returned to the source from which it came. [*Tennessee Valley Authority.*]

tablished. Steam and hot water could be used to operate hothouse complexes for the growing of fruits, vegetables, and flowers. Waste heat might also be utilized for space heating in a warehouse facility or for manufacturing processes at an industrial site. The aquaculture of fish and shellfish in artificial ponds of heated ocean water currently is under investigation. All these proposals hold some promise, but none have as yet proven to be economically feasible. In any case, sooner or later, and perhaps as soon as 30 to 50 years, the human species will have to curb its use of energy. As we noted earlier, we cannot continue adding heat to our small planet because of its adverse effects on global weather.[17]

General pollution

General pollutants encompass such diverse materials as radioactive substances, pesticides, and a miscellaneous assortment of food additives, drugs, cosmetics, household chemicals, and industrial wastes. Their actual number is unknown. There are, for example, about 1.8 million chemicals formulated in the United States. But the number grows annually by some

[17] Weinberg, op. cit., p. 205.

250,000 new compounds. Of the total number, only a few thousand have been tested for carcinogenicity, and of those tested, 1,000 have shown evidence of being carcinogenic.[18]

Radioactive pollution and hazards

Elements such as those illustrated in Fig. 15-10 are said to be radioactive because of the high-energy (ionizing) radiation emitted by their unstable atoms. Although the energy emission rate of different radioactive elements varies widely, that for a given substance is constant and is expressed in terms of its *half-life*. The half-life is the time required for half the atoms of a radioactive element to decay into stable, nonradioactive atoms. Iodine 131 has a half-life of 8 days; for strontium 90, it is 28 years, and for uranium 238 it is 4.51 billion years. Since strontium 90 loses half its radioactivity every 28 years, in 112 years (four half-lives) it would retain only 6.25 percent of its original radioactivity (Fig. 15-11).

   The potential biologic hazards of ionizing radiation are critical for several reasons. In the first place, the toxicity of radioactive emissions is vastly greater than the most virulent of non-

[18] Robert Gillette, "Cancer and the Environment," *Science*, vol. 186, Oct. 18, 1974, p. 245.

FIGURE 15-10
Sources of radioactive atmospheric pollutants.

Nuclear weapons testing
Cadmium	109
Cesium	137
Iodine	131
Iron	55
Manganese	54
Rhodium	102
Strontium	90
Tungsten	185

Reprocessing of nuclear-fuel elements
Krypton	85 (gas)

Satellite failure (April 1964)[1]
Plutonium	238

[1] Satellite with portable nuclear power plant burned up in atmosphere over southern Indian Ocean.

FIGURE 15-11
Strontium 90, a radioactive element, has a half-life of 28 years. That is, every 28 years it loses half of its remaining radioactivity.

Time	Radioactive decay, %	Radioactivity, %
0 years (0 half-life)	0	100
28 years (1 half-life)	50	50
56 years (2 half-lives)	75	25
84 years (3 half-lives)	87.5	12.5
112 years (4 half-lives)	93.75	6.25

radioactive poisons. The emissions from even minuscule amounts of a radioactive substance several meters away may prove to be fatal over a period of time. Biologic injury ultimately is traceable to the alteration or destruction of body protein, DNA, and other macromolecules by ionizing radiation. The biologic consequences vary depending upon the degree of radiation exposure; they range from deep radiation burns and immediate death to afflictions that may not occur for many years after exposure, such as leukemia and other forms of cancer, anemia, cardiovascular disease, impaired growth, premature aging, and reduced fertility.

The effects of radiation are not confined to exposed individuals. Future generations are involved because ionizing radiation is *mutagenic;* that is, it increases the mutation rate. Mutation frequency increases in direct proportion to the amount of accumulated radiation exposure and includes both gene (point) and chromosomal mutations. The amount of radiation exposure is usually expressed in *rem* units (roentgen equivalent man); the rem was devised as a standardized measure for estimating the degree of biologic injury for various types of ionizing radiation.

Additional hazards are posed by the long half-lives of many radioactive elements; some of the wastes from nuclear power plants are powerfully radioactive and will be dangerous for 200,000 years. The ease with which radioactive wastes enter the body and become concentrated in food chains also is a major concern. The radioactive form (isotope) of an element reacts chemically in the same way as its nonradioactive counterpart. Thus, an organism will use a harmful isotope, for example, iodine 131, as readily as its harmless cousin. The same principle pertains to different chemically related elements. Strontium and cesium, for example, are similar to calcium and potassium. As a result, strontium 90 can become lodged in bone or transmitted to children in milk. Since potassium is found in all body cells, cesium 137 can become widely distributed throughout the body.

A given amount of radioactive pollutant dispersed throughout an ecosystem—like any chemical pollutant—will tend to become concentrated in the top-level consumers of the biologic community. This is a natural consequence of the energy dynamics of food chains. A radioactive contaminant that has polluted trophic level 1 (the producers) will become progressively concentrated with each ascending trophic level in the pyramid of energy (Fig. 11-3). This was demonstrated in a region of Alaska where the natural forage had become contaminated from radioactive fallout with cesium 137. Caribou grazed this forage and were in turn eaten by Eskimos. Eskimos had twice as much cesium radioactivity per gram of tissue as the caribou.[19]

The real and potential sources of radioactive pollution and contamination are three: (1) nuclear power plants, (2) medical x-radiation, and (3) nuclear terrorism and warfare.

Nuclear power plants   Under properly monitored operating conditions and in the absence of serious mechanical failure, a modern nuclear power plant will release only small amounts of radioactive pollutant to the environment. Such a plant is illustrated schematically in Fig. 15-12. Very little of the radioactive fission products escape through the walls of the fuel rods into the primary coolant water. When they do, usually it is through occasional fractures or pinholes that develop in the fuel rods. Some of the solid fission products such as strontium 90 can be trapped and disposed of as nuclear waste; a small fraction of the remainder may find its way into effluent wastewater through tiny plumbing leaks. Radioactive gases such as hydrogen 3 (tritium) and krypton 85 must be continuously removed from primary coolant water. After a relatively short period of storage they are released to the atmosphere while they are still radioactive (tritium has a half-life of 12 years).

What is of particular concern today, however, is protection against the hazards of nu-

[19] G. M. Woodwell, "Toxic Substances and Ecologic Cycles," *Scientific American,* March 1967, p. 29.

FIGURE 15-12
Schematic diagram of a nuclear pressurized-water reactor (PWR). The heat source consists of thousands of hollow rods filled with pellets of radioactive fuel. Pressurized water (primary coolant water) flowing through the reactor is heated by nuclear energy and in turn converts water to steam in a steam generator. The pressurized reactor water returns to the reactor and the steam drives a turbine which powers an electric generator. The steam is converted to water as it gives up its heat to coolant water in a condenser and returns to the steam generator where it is again routed to the turbine as steam. The intensity of nuclear reactions creates very high pressures in the reactor which makes it necessary to pressurize the primary coolant water passing through the reactor. Pressurizing the water sufficiently also keeps it in a liquid state. The containment structure is a reinforced concrete housing more than 1 meter (3¼ feet) thick with a vapor-proof steel liner. The illustration is not to scale.

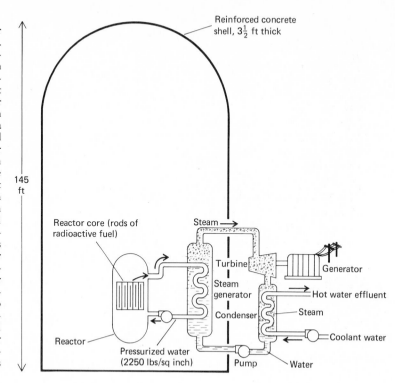

clear accidents and of nuclear-waste disposal. In several nuclear reactors of about 500 megawatt capacity, large numbers of fuel rods have been found to undergo a puzzling type of damage in which the rods become bent, crushed, and even cracked. The behavior of fuel rods weakened in this way would be virtually impossible to predict in case there was an accidental loss of primary coolant water from the reactor. Every reactor is equipped with an emergency core-cooling system to guard against the possibility that primary coolant water might be lost through a broken pipe or valve. But present indications are that these emergency systems may be less than adequate to prevent a major nuclear accident. Current evidence suggests that the demand to build 1,000-megawatt plants be withdrawn until the problem of reactor

safety is resolved.[20] Modern plants of 500 megawatt capacity are cause enough for concern as we look to the end of the century, when our nuclear energy needs are projected at 1,000,000 megawatts. A small risk in one 500-megawatt plant looms much larger in 2,000 of them.

Nuclear wastes other than those already mentioned involve the processing and ultimate disposal of spent fuel rods. These wastes make up the bulk of radioactive pollution from reactor plants. Only small amounts of reactor fuel can be used before it is contaminated by accumulated waste products. Fuel rods must then be removed and repurified in a reprocessing

[20] Robert Gillette, "Nuclear Safety," *Science,* vol. 177, July 28, 1972, pp. 330–331; "Nuclear Reactor Safety," *Science,* vol. 176, May 5, 1972, pp. 492–497; "Nuclear Critics Escalate the War of Numbers," *Science,* vol. 189, Aug. 22, 1975, p. 621.

plant. The rods are chemically freed of their radioactive contaminants, whereupon they may be used again. Large amounts of solid, liquid, and gaseous wastes remain for disposal. Much of the krypton 85 and tritium is released to the atmosphere. The remainder is buried underground. Many formidable problems confront this entire technology. How does one safely ship this material between reactor and reprocessing plant, and from the latter to burial sites? How can one be sure that some of the buried contents will not be released to the environment over the thousands of years that it may be dangerously radioactive?[21] And how does society develop social institutions with sufficient stability and permanence to protect such sites from the unwary as well as from the terrorist?

Medical x-radiation X-rays are a form of ionizing radiation that are used widely in medicine as a means of diagnosing various types of disease. According to the U.S. Public Health Service, about 130 million Americans received 650 million x-ray exposures in 1970. As may be seen from Fig. 15-13, diagnostic x-rays contribute more to human radiation exposure than all other man-made sources of ionizing radiation combined. It is estimated that 40 percent of the average human radiation exposure in this country comes from diagnostic x-rays while 56 percent is received from natural-background sources. Background radiation includes ultraviolet and cosmic rays from the sun and interstellar space, natural radioactive isotopes in the atmosphere such as carbon dioxide containing carbon 14, and radioactive elements like uranium or thorium in native rocks, soils, and building materials.

The Committee on the Biological Effects of Ionizing Radiation (National Academy of Sciences) reported in 1972 that populationwide exposure for one generation to the 1970 dosage level (0.182 rems, Fig. 15-13), could be expected to increase genetic defects and diseases

[21] P. M. Boffey, "Radioactive Waste Site Search Gets into Deep Water," *Science,* vol. 190, Oct. 24, 1975, p. 361.

by 5 percent. The Committee observed that genetic damage from diagnostic x-rays could be reduced by 50 percent through the use of improved equipment, proper shielding of ovaries and testes, and the elimination of unnecessary exposures. Such practices also would lessen the risk of cancer.

Nuclear terrorism and warfare The utter destruction and long-term pollution that would attend nuclear warfare between the world's major powers are quite beyond comprehension. Fortunately there is a strong possibility that such an event can be avoided. On a smaller scale it is easy to imagine that Iran and one or more Arab nations might barter oil for India's capability in making atomic weapons. Should this occur, the probability that nuclear warfare might be prevented on a regional scale would be less reassuring.

FIGURE 15-13
Estimated annual whole-body dose rates of ionizing radiation in the United States (1970). Total radiation from all sources is averaged on a per capita basis. (A millirem is 0.001 rem.) [*Data from the Report of the National Academy of Sciences on the Biological Effects of Ionizing Radiation, November 1972.*]

Source	Average dose rate (millirems)
Environmental	
Natural background radiation	102
Global fallout	4
Nuclear power	0.003
Subtotal	106
Medical	
Diagnostic x-ray	72
Radiopharmaceuticals	1
Subtotal	73
Occupational (x-ray technicians, etc.)	0.8
Miscellaneous	2
Subtotal	76
Total radiation, all sources	182

Even this risk is small, however, compared to the imminent dangers of terrorism. The expertise to build an atomic bomb is no longer rare. Precise instructions on how to make a nuclear weapon at home have become widely distributed. A very small inefficient bomb by modern standards could kill 100,000 people in a football stadium and endanger the lives of thousands more from radioactive fallout. All that is needed is weapons-grade radioactive waste which already is being produced by the tens of thousands of kilograms from nuclear power plants. Nuclear reprocessing plants with their enriched nuclear fuels could become prime targets for the growing number of highly organized terrorist groups.

The protection of nuclear material probably is weakest during shipment, but safeguards against theft are presently inadequate at several levels in the nuclear industry, including tactical United States' nuclear warheads stored in foreign countries.

Pesticides

Since there are few ecosystems on earth in which man has not become a conspicuous intruder, the human species finds itself in conflict with a great variety of organisms. Our plant crops have to compete with wild species (weeds), and we as consumers have to share our role with herbivores (rodents) and parasites (insects, fungus, etc.). We as well as our domestic animals are tormented by parasitic insects and insect-borne diseases. Even our homes and furnishings are subject to attack by termites, moths, and carpet beetles.

To keep these pest populations under control, large quantities of chemical compounds that destroy pest species (*pesticides*) are manufactured and distributed for use around the world. Some of these, for example, DDT, have saved millions of human lives from insect-borne diseases, such as malaria and typhus fever, and have prevented insect damage to crops and livestock that might otherwise have been catastrophic.

Paradoxically, many of these dramatic results seem to have been made at the cost of eco-system destruction and environmental pollution. The major difficulties with pesticides are twofold. They are not specific enough to control the pest species exclusively; they are damaging to other species, often to man himself. By killing beneficial predators who feed on pest species, the use of pesticides often is self-defeating. Their use may be responsible for the virulence and frequency of subsequent pest attacks. Secondly, many pesticides are not readily broken down or degradable into harmless products either in the environment or inside the animal body. Because of the relatively long time they remain in an active form, the concentration of these pesticides increases dramatically in the higher trophic levels of a biologic community just as radioactive pollutants do.

The chlorinated hydrocarbons Figure 15-14 illustrates the more common pesticides that have been in use over the past decade or more. Of the insecticides listed, the chlorinated hydrocarbon DDT has been used most widely and over the longest time, dating back to the early 1940s. Its potential for controlling almost any insect species and its apparent harmlessness to man accounted for its popularity.

Concern over the use of DDT began to grow with the discovery that it is stored in the fatty tissues of vertebrate consumers in food chains and that several months may be required to eliminate it from the body. Apprehension deepened as diverse vertebrate species throughout the world began to show DDT in their fat stores. Not even the seals and penguins of Antarctica were free of contamination. People in the United States and over most of the world showed DDT in their fatty tissues. Being fat-soluble, DDT can be carried in the butterfat of milk and transmitted to infants or end up in dairy products for general consumption.

Additional danger signals began to appear. DDT was found to be a very stable compound. Soils contaminated with DDT require 6 months to 10 years or more before the insecticide is degraded into harmless residues. During this time, the compound may be converted into the related insecticides DDE and DDD. The DDT

Chlorinated hydrocarbons (common name)	Phosphoreted hydrocarbons (common name)
INSECTICIDES	
Aldrin	Azodrin
Chlordane	Diazinon
DDT and derivatives DDE and DDD	Malathion
Dieldrin	Parathion
Endrin	Phosdrin
Heptachlor	
Lindane	
Toxaphene	

HERBICIDES

2,4-D
2,4,5-T

COLLATERAL ANIMAL TOXICANTS

PCBs (polychlorinated biphenyls), which may be formed from DDT in the environment
Dioxin, an impurity in 2,4,5-T

FIGURE 15-14
Common synthetic pesticides (pest-killing chemicals) and their associated toxicants (toxic agents). Hydrocarbons containing chlorine (chlorinated hydrocarbons) are used to control insects (insecticides) and weeds (herbicides). Hydrocarbons containing phosphorus (phosphoreted hydrocarbons or organophosphorus compounds) are also used as insecticides, acting as nerve poisons. Collateral toxicants are poisons that may be formed from pesticides in the environment or that occur as impurities in a pesticide.

content of croplands and marshes consequently accumulates with successive applications of the pesticide over a period of years. Since much of the DDT applied persists for a month or two as airborne gaseous molecules, the substance becomes widely dispersed over oceans and bodies of fresh water as well as over the land.

Under such conditions it is not surprising that high concentrations of DDT, DDE, and DDD began showing up in the top consumers of many food chains. Robins, pheasants, fish-eating birds, carnivorous fishes, and porpoises have been shown to have concentrations ranging from 200 to 3,000 parts per million in their body fat. In fact, DDE contamination equivalent to 50 to 200 parts per million fat content has been detected in the dried membranes of falcon eggshells collected from 1948 to 1950.[22]

High levels of DDT contamination were soon found to be associated with a critical de-cline in certain bird populations, notably the peregrine falcons, ospreys, and bald eagles of the Eastern United States and the brown pelicans off the coast of Southern California. Reproductive failure was primarily responsible. The pesticide upsets calcium metabolism, resulting in eggshells which are so thin that they usually break before the embryos have developed to the hatching stage. Reproductive failure also has been reported in California sea lions contaminated with DDT and PCBs (polychlorinated biphenyls); in this instance there is a higher rate of infant mortality from premature births.[23]

The interrelationship between DDT and PCBs is an intriguing one. The PCBs are industrial chemicals widely used in adhesives, paints, inks, hydraulic fluids, and many other products. Although never intended to be released into the environment, they have in some

[22] D. B. Peakall, "DDE: Its Presence in Peregrine Eggs in 1948," *Science,* vol. 183, Feb. 15, 1974, pp. 673–674.

[23] R. L. DeLong et al., "Premature Births in California Sea Lions," *Science,* vol. 181, Sept. 21, 1973, pp. 1168–1170.

unknown way become as broadly distributed as DDT. Like DDT they are stable compounds. They also are toxic to a variety of animals and have been responsible for a number of human deaths. The similarity in distribution between DDT and PCBs may not be coincidental. Laboratory research has shown that DDT vapor can be converted into PCBs by irradiation with ultraviolet light of the same kind present in the lower atmosphere.[24] Should this process occur in nature, the widespread distribution of PCBs would no longer be a mystery.

Growing evidence of the potential risks of DDT and related insecticides led to an Environmental Protection Agency (EPA) ban on almost all uses of DDT in 1972. In 1974 the further manufacture of aldrin and dieldrin also was suspended by the EPA. These were landmark decisions. None of these insecticides had done demonstrable injury to man. The EPA's Office of Hazardous Materials had found that low dosages of all three caused cancer in laboratory mice and were therefore potentially carcinogenic to humans.

As a consequence, all insecticides containing chlorinated hydrocarbons are now suspect. Even the herbicide 2,4,5-T has been banned by the EPA as a weed-control agent on most croplands. This pesticide contains a manufacturing impurity called *dioxin* which could increase significantly the incidence of human birth defects. 2,4-D also is suspected of having this property. Since all these substances are stable and can be incorporated into plant tissues, they threaten our water and food supplies.

Alternative methods of pest control   There is an obvious need for controlling the insect pests that are man's major competitors for food. The problem is to do this effectively and economically and to avoid the environmental and public health risks associated with chlorinated hydrocarbons. A number of procedures have been or are being developed which show varying degrees of promise.

[24] T. H. Maugh II, "DDT: An Unrecognized Source of Polychlorinated Biphenyls," *Science,* vol. 180, May 11, 1973, pp. 578–579.

1 *Short-lived pesticides.* The phosphoreted hydrocarbons shown in Fig. 15-14 decompose relatively quickly in the environment and do not become concentrated in food chains. They are nonselective, however, and kill beneficial as well as pest species (as DDT and other long-lived pesticides do). Malathion is mildly toxic to humans and domesticated animals, but parathion is extremely dangerous even on contact with the skin.

2 *Predators and parasites.* Insect pests often can be controlled by their natural predators and parasites. The advisability of introducing foreign predators or parasites must, of course, be checked very carefully beforehand. The Japanese beetle was accidentally introduced into the United States and became a serious agricultural pest. To control this beetle, an Asiatic wasp was brought in which preys only on this beetle. The wasp paralyzes the larva of a Japanese beetle and attaches an egg to it. When the egg hatches the wasp larva consumes its host. Most insect viruses also are specific for one or a few closely related hosts. Tussock moth virus has been used to control damage to Douglas fir trees by tussock moth larva. The virus is sprayed on the foliage as a suspension with the same equipment used for chemical insecticides.

3 *Male sterilization.* Some insect species can be controlled by the periodic release of large numbers of males that have been sterilized by exposure to ionizing radiation. Wild females that mate with these males lay eggs that do not hatch. A serious pest of livestock known as the screwworm, a flesh-eating larva of the horn fly, has been kept under control in this way.

4 *Pheromones.* Many animals and most insects secrete substances (pheromones) that influence the behavior of members of their own species (Fig. 15-15). One of these, an olfactory sex attractant produced by females, is effective in amounts so minute that one female contains enough pheromone to attract millions of males. Consequently, a sex-attractant pheromone can be used as bait to lure males into traps. It also can be distributed randomly over any area, confusing the males and thereby frustrating efforts to locate a female. Both these techniques have proven effective in controlling light infestations of several pest species.

5 *Hormones.* Two hormones secreted within the insect body regulate normal growth and

development. The secretion of one of these, the juvenile hormone (JH), must stop at a certain stage in order to allow the larva to develop into a sexually mature adult. Since the larva develops abnormally and dies if JH secretion does not stop, the hormone (or a synthetic counterpart) can be used as an insecticide. Several species of flies and mosquitos have been controlled in this manner.

The above methods are superior in many ways to pesticides containing chlorinated hydrocarbons. Phosphoreted insecticides do not build up in food chains. The remaining procedures have several additional advantages. They are much more selective and are commonly species-specific; that is, they control just one species of pest. Pests would also be less likely to build up a resistance to their predators or to their own hormones and pheromones than to chemical pesticides. Selection pressure commonly produces populations of insects that are quite resistant to chemical insecticides. Above all, these procedures use materials that have little, if any toxicity, to vertebrates, and they are effective at low, often minuscule, doses.

Miscellaneous pollutants

People in the United States are exposed to a vast assortment of substances that pollute air, water, soil, and food. Industrial wastes and by-products already have been described in this context during our discussion of wastewater treatment, air pollution (Fig. 15-4), and water pollution. Industrial products themselves are important in this regard. Between 300 and 500 new chemical compounds annually go into major commercial use in the United States. Of the total number produced each year, a great many are synthetic organic compounds, more than 9,000 of which are manufactured in amounts exceeding a half ton. Their total annual production surpasses 60 million tons. Unfortunately most of these substances have been produced commercially before they were adequately tested for possible harmful effects. The risks of such a practice are obvious, especially from cancer, which usually does not develop until 20 to 30 years after the initial exposure to a carcinogen.

FIGURE 15-15
Ants following a trail laid down by drawing a line with a stick tipped with the contents of a pheromone gland from one ant. [*Photo by Sol Mednick.*]

As a case in point, the industrial gas vinyl chloride was assumed to be biologically safe and has been used by the millions of tons in the manufacture of polyvinyl plastics. It also has been used as a propellant in aerosol cans of hair spray, deodorant, insecticide, and other consumer products. The latter use was banned in 1974 when vinyl chloride was discovered to cause a form of liver cancer in humans. About 100,000 tons of vinyl chloride are released to the environment annually in the manufacture of polyvinyl plastics. Polyvinyl plastics themselves are suspected of leaching out vinyl chloride into foods packaged in these plastics.

Organic chemicals known as chlorofluoro-carbons (compounds containing chlorine, fluor-ine, and carbon) also are used as aerosol pro-pellants and as refrigerants (Freon). Over the decade ending in 1974, the world had produced about 6 million metric tons of these substances, much of which was released into the atmo-sphere. It is believed that nearly all the chloro-fluorocarbons so released are still in the at-mosphere because the chemicals are highly volatile, relatively inert, and seem to be dis-tributed throughout the world.

This may pose a serious problem insofar as the ozone layer in the upper atmosphere (stratosphere) is concerned.[25] This ozone layer envelopes the earth and filters out more than 90 percent of all ultraviolet radiation from the sun. Chlorofluorocarbons are decomposed by ultraviolet light, producing free chlorine which destroys ozone.[26] Relatively small amounts of free chlorine can destroy large quantities of ozone. Should the destruction of this protec-tive layer occur to a significant degree, there would doubtless be an increase in skin cancer.

Food and drug contaminants   With so many chemicals being used for diverse purposes, there is an ever-present danger that foods and drugs may be unintentionally contaminated. This has occurred on numerous occasions in foods contaminated by pesticides containing lead, mercury, arsenic, and parathion. Two re-cent cases involve the use of (1) a synthetic hormone and (2) asbestos.

DES, previously described in relation to the "morning after" contraceptive pill, is a highly potent synthetic estrogen. In 1954, DES was approved as an additive to the feed of beef cattle because it makes animals fatten faster on less feed, thereby enabling the beef industry to produce meat cheaper. What seemed to be an economic breakthrough, however, proved to be hazardous to public health. An extremely rare form of vaginal cancer was found in seven young women who had been admitted to a Massachusetts hospital in 1971. The mothers of all seven had taken DES when they were preg-nant. When it was learned that government tests had repeatedly shown DES residues in meat for several years, the FDA finally placed a ban on its use in animal feed effective January 1, 1973. Meanwhile, small amounts of DES had been known to cause cancer in mice since 1964 and 22 countries already had taken steps to eliminate it from their food supply; as of August 1970, Sweden refused to import Ameri-can beef fattened with it.

Asbestos (Fig. 15-4) also is carcinogenic, causing cancer of the human lungs, digestive tract, and associated structures. It has been found as a contaminant in food, beverages, and drinking water. A mining company controlled by ARMCO and Republic Steel corporations has been dumping 67,000 tons of iron ore wastes (tailings) into Lake Superior daily for more than a decade. These tailings contain asbestos-carrying minerals which have contami-nated the municipal water supplies of Duluth, Minnesota and other North Shore communities (Fig. 15-16).[27] An insidious form of contamina-tion has come to light in the use of asbestos as a filtering material. Asbestos has been used widely for this purpose by the drug industry. Unfortunately such filters add a contaminant of their own. Drugs used for injection into muscle, the abdominal cavity, and the bloodstream have been found to contain measurable amounts of asbestos in one-third of the samples tested.[28]

Additives in foods, drugs, and cosmetics   Sev-eral thousand substances are used to process, preserve, flavor, color, and texture foods, drugs, and cosmetics. Hundreds of millions of kilo-grams of these additives are used annually in the United States. The FDA has the primary

[25] P. H. Howard and Arnold Hanchett, "Chlorofluorocarbon Sources of Environmental Contamination," *Science,* vol. 189, July 18, 1975, pp. 217–219.

[26] Nitrogen oxides from nuclear explosions or from the jet engines of supersonic transports (SSTs) have a similar effect; see F. N. Alyea et al., "Stratospheric Ozone Destruction by Aircraft-Induced Nitro-gen Oxides," *Science,* vol. 188, Apr. 11, 1975, pp. 117–121.

[27] L. J. Carter, "Pollution and Public Health," *Science,* vol. 186, Oct. 4, 1974, pp. 31–36.

[28] W. J. Nicholson et al., "Asbestos Contamination in Parenteral Drugs," *Science,* vol. 177, July 14, 1972, pp. 171–173.

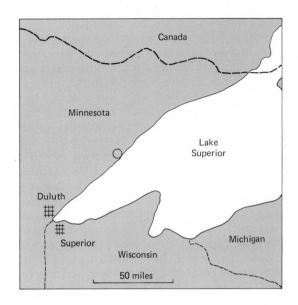

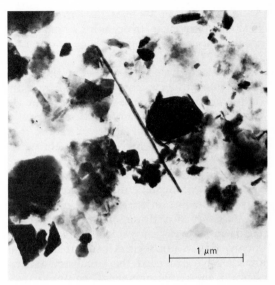

FIGURE 15-16
Asbestos contamination. *Left,* Reserve Mining Company (circle) has been dumping iron-ore wastes containing asbestos into Lake Superior for more than 12 years. *Right,* electron micrograph of asbestos fiber from Duluth, Minnesota drinking water. (1 μm = 0.001 millimeter.) [*Courtesy of Philip M. Cook and the Environmental Protection Agency.*]

responsibility for protecting the American consumer against both known and suspected harmful effects of these additives. Despite this theoretical protection, the general public has been exposed to unnecessary risks, as two examples will illustrate.

Various artificial colorings and flavorings have been used extensively before they were found to be toxic and, in some cases, even after their toxicity had been established. A dye known as FD & C Red No. 2 was used for several years in over $20 billion worth of foods, drugs, and cosmetics annually, notwithstanding studies showing that it caused birth defects and possibly cancer in mice. It was banned by the FDA in early 1976.

The processing or curing of meat and fish (e.g., ham, hot dogs, smoked fish) involves the use of nitrites. They not only act as preservatives but also give those foods a characteristic color and flavor. Nitrites also are known to react with certain organic substances found in meat (amines) to produce highly toxic nitrosamines. Animal studies have shown that nitrosamines at very low dosages are carcinogenic,

and they may be mutagenic and capable of inducing birth defects as well. It is also of some concern that a number of drugs (e.g., disulfiram) might be potential producers of nitrosamines. Since these drugs contain amines, they could prove dangerous if they were taken into the body with nitrite or with water having a high nitrate content.[29]

RESOLVING OUR ECOLOGIC CRISES: THE STABLE ECONOMY

Problems confronting man's future

Overpopulation is the foremost environmental crisis that endangers long-term human survival.

[29] Wolff and Wasserman, "Nitrates, Nitrites, and Nitrosamines," pp. 16–18.

Another major problem is the virtual world-wide commitment to an economy of expanding production and consumption. Such an economy clearly is an unrealistic one in a world of limited resources and space. Resources cannot be converted into products, consumed, and then discarded in some out-of-the-way place. They are limited commodities that often are extracted at the cost of environmental deterioration; they are used and, unless recycled, they clutter up our living space, our water and our air, and force us to tap lower-grade resources at even greater environmental costs. The growth economy would solve an energy crisis by lowering the standards of environmental quality and engaging in an orgy of fossil-fuel extraction. The energy crisis is not seen as a sign that humans already have exceeded the environmental capacity of their environment. The "productive" economy, in its zeal to stimulate the consumption of goods, proliferates new products of which many are more damaging to the environment than the products they replaced. Neither growth nor standard of living can be the measure of progress when they result in a steady decline in the quality and character of human life. Overpopulation, affluence and waste, and the technological production of harmful substances are an awesome trinity of destruction.

We have considered these matters in some detail and have pointed out corrective measures that can be or are being undertaken. These problems cannot be resolved as if they were separate issues, however. They must be considered within the framework of broad changes in our relationship to our environment. The human species, particularly those members living in industrialized societies, traditionally have looked upon the environment in terms of exploitable resources. Once a source of industrial production was located, the human animal would somehow fend for itself because it had an economic livelihood.

A stable economy, on the other hand, is based upon the quality of human life and looks upon the human-nature interrelationship with a different set of priorities. The environment is a place in which people may find optimal conditions for living in terms of food, water, and a potential for adequate recreation, education, and public health. Industry is viewed as a cultural system, whose sole function should be to support this basic aim.

Unlike the economy of expanding production, the stable economy would live within its means, conserving its nonrenewable and exploiting its renewable resources, recycling its materials, keeping its population size within the environmental capacity of the human ecosystem, and guiding its course by a sensitive awareness of the quality of human life. Should our species adopt such a socioeconomic structure, the future of *Homo sapiens* can be long and bright. To embark on such a course will require ecologic land- and water-use planning on an intensive worldwide scale.

Ecologic land- and water-use planning

Humans, no less than other creatures, are a part of, not apart from, the environment in which they live. This environment essentially is the planet's entire land- and waterscape. We must treat this habitat wisely in terms of our *long-range* interests. In order to do this, it is imperative that we develop techniques for analyzing and appraising the ecosystems in which we are participating and beneficiary members.

In broad perspective the ecosystems of which we are a part fall into five environmental categories: (1) productive, (2) protective, (3) a compromise of productive and protective, (4) commercial-industrial and (5) urban (Fig. 15-17).[30]

1 *Productive environments* include those intensively harvested agricultural and forested areas from which we get out food, cotton, wool, and wood products. They are artificial ecosystems usually devoted to a single crop such as wheat, sheep, or the planted stands of pine on a tree farm.

[30] E. P. Odum, "The Strategy of Ecosystem Development," *Science,* vol. 164, Apr. 18, 1969, pp. 266–269.

2 *Protective environments* are the mature climax ecosystems that provide us with the essential life resources we cannot produce. These environments and their biologic communities provide us with pure water, help maintain a balance between CO_2 and O_2 in the atmosphere, act as a climatic buffer, recycle essential nutrients, and harbor a vast genetic resource of animals and plants. They also add wonder and exhilaration to the dimensions of human life.

3 *Compromise* or *multiple-use environments* are both protective and productive. They include natural ecosystems that are kept in an intermediate stage of succession between youth and maturity by some more or less regular disturbances such as annual fires or recurring changes in water level. For example, in the southeastern United States, periodic light fires can maintain succession at the pine forest stage, preventing the invasion of climax hickories and oaks which are economically less desirable trees. The pine forest provides wood of high quality, protective cover against soil erosion, a home for quail and other game birds, and a pleasant place for a stroll in the woods. Such multiple use also is possible in estuaries and intertidal zones where, as we have described, oyster and mussel culture may be combined with swimming, boating, and fishing.

4 The *commercial-industrial environment* supplies an economic and technological support system for ecosystem planning and management.

5 The *urban environment* in any given region accommodates an increasingly large share of the human population. It serves as our home base while the remaining four environments encompass our territory. In a stable economy, the productive, protective, compromise, and commercial-industrial environments would be planned and managed so that they would contribute optimally to the urban environment.

If the human environment is to be intelligently programmed in this way, it is obvious that a great amount of ecological study will be required in any given region if a safe balance of environmental requirements is to be achieved. The protective and compromise environments can be particularly vulnerable to excessive

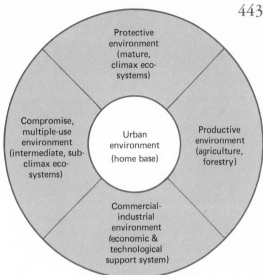

FIGURE 15-17
The human habitat in terms of its broad environmental requirements. The urban environment serves as our home base while the productive, protective, compromise and commercial-industrial environments encompass our territory. [*Modified from E. P. Odum, "The Strategy of Ecosystem Development," Science, vol. 164, April 18, 1969.*]

agricultural or mining activities. Urban sprawl and overpopulation are equally damaging to the productive environment (Figs. 13-5 and 15-18). The environmental capacity of a region must be determined in terms of its resources. Only after such a determination has been made can ecosystem development proceed in a rational manner. Since humanity has committed itself to urbanization, that development should begin in the city and extend outward.

Ecologic urban planning

Following World War II, urbanization in the United States has consisted essentially of rapidly expanding suburbs. A major cause of this suburban "explosion" was the increasing number of urban dwellers who had become dissatisfied with the quality of city life and who wanted, and could now afford, a home in suburbia. Suburbs grew and fused with others, destroying any link the central cities might have with open space (Fig. 15-18). Cities became connected by the suburbs that lay between them, forming a huge solidly urbanized region known as a *megalopolis*. One such megalopolis extends for 800 kilometers (500 miles) and includes Boston, New York, Philadelphia, Baltimore, and Washington, D.C.

Inordinate amounts of prime agricultural land have been sacrificed to suburban sprawl. Vast highway networks are required to connect the places where people work and where they live, while an automobile-oriented society has forced both cities and suburbs to sacrifice enormous amounts of space to automobile traffic, parking facilities, and the attendant pollution of private cars (Fig. 15-19).

The tragedy of the flight from the cities is that in large part it has failed to fulfill its promise of improved quality of life; suburbia has lost its real political and cultural connec-

tions with the city. So-called bedroom communities often lack the public facilities—the parks, museums, business establishments, civic centers, theaters—that cater to the public's needs; suburbanites, now neither city folk nor country folk, are isolated with their multi-bathroom, multi-garage status symbols, but still lack the clear air and water, the open countryside, and all those cultural aspects that made actual life in the city stirring and significant. For its part, the city has become the site of big commercial complexes, factories, and railroads, and the victim of noise and pollution from commuters' vehicles. The city has lost much of its resident population to suburbia. Many of those who remain are there because they lack the socioeconomic means to move away, and find ·themselves caught up in the urban blight of growing slums. Under such conditions, the role of the city as the heart of civilization and culture is compromised.

FIGURE 15-18
Urban sprawl. [*Wide World Photos.*]

FIGURE 15-19
Nearly 75 percent of the surface area of Detroit, Michigan is given over to auto traffic and parking facilities. This city of 4 million has no rapid mass transit system. [*U.S. Department of Housing and Urban Development.*]

Various urban redevelopment programs have been proposed and, in a number of instances, acted upon. The objectives of such programs differ according to the nature of the problem. They include improvements in public transportation, energy conservation and greater use of nonpolluting energy sources, and reduction of noise levels. Although high-rise buildings commonly are necessary because of space restrictions, planning proposals seek to minimize their use because of their extensive heat loss and high energy requirements (Fig. 10-9). When planned, high-rise structures are so designed and spaced as to permit ample open areas in full sunlight for shopping malls, sidewalk cafes, and parks. Wherever possible, the elimination of automobile roads and parking in the central city can free large amounts of space to accommodate parks, libraries, theaters, schools, churches, and shops; such facilities could be so planned as to be easily reached by walking or public conveyance from attractive dwelling units.

In outlying suburbs and towns, urban-planning objectives attempt to preserve the surrounding protective, productive, and compromise environments. Individual communities are so planned that population size is restricted to encourage social communication and participation in community decisions and events. Urban services such as shops, schools, hospitals, theaters, churches, a library, and community center are interspersed with parks, gardens, and landscape plantings; all these are arranged so that they are easily accessible to residential areas. To provide employment opportunities, nonpolluting light industries and businesses are usually incorporated in redevelopment planning. Rapid mass transit to the nearest metropolitan city also is included to afford additional employment plus those urban resources a small city cannot supply: major sports facilities, museums, opera, symphony orchestra, legitimate theatre, art galleries, universities, and so on.

Urban planning and redevelopment programs such as we have just described have so far taken two forms: (1) new towns and satellite towns and, (2) revitalization of the inner city and metropolis.

New towns and satellite towns

First introduced as a means of draining off excess population of burgeoning cities, the concept of "new towns" began in England. From the outset they were designed as self-sufficient planned communities with residential areas, parks, shopping centers, civic buildings, and industrial districts. Cumbernauld, near Glasgow, Scotland, is a new town designed to accommodate a projected population of 70,000.

Unlike new towns, "satellite towns" are planned suburbs. The satellite towns of Stockholm, Sweden are excellent examples (Fig. 15-20). Stockholm's satellite towns encompass numerous communities separated from each other and the city by protective environments of parklands and forests. Each community has residential areas, a town center including shopping, commercial, civic, and cultural facilities;

FIGURE 15-20
Satellite towns of Stockholm, Sweden. The aerial view (*left*) is of Salem, a town of small residences accommodating 11,000 people. Interspersed among abundant parks and forested areas are the town center, schools, churches, day nurseries, fair grounds, tennis courts, and other areas for athletic activities and public use. Auto traffic is restricted to certain areas only. The close-up view (*above*) shows the shopping center and one of the apartment buildings of Hässelby Gärd. The elevated level accommodates a high-speed transit system into central Stockholm. [*Photographs courtesy of Scandinavian National Tourist Offices, Los Angeles.*]

various recreational accommodations; and commonly an industrial center. Each is connected by a high-speed electric transit system with central Stockholm.

Revitalizing city and metropolis

Revitalizing our inner cities and laying the groundwork for the metropolises of tomorrow is a monumental task. What progress has been made is small relative to the challenge. The crisis of our inner cities, however, is not being ignored (Fig. 15-21).

To gain some insight into the kind of thinking that is going into large-scale metropolitan planning, let us consider a theoretical scheme designed by the architect-planner Victor Gruen. Likening a metropolis to an urban organism, he refers to his scheme as the cellular metropolis of tomorrow (Fig. 15-22).[31]

For illustrative purposes, the figure is quite schematic, showing urban subunits ("cells") and clusters of subunits as geometric forms and circles of equal size. In actuality, of course, the communities, towns, and cities that make up a metropolis vary both in size and shape. The colored areas represent open space devoted to protective, productive, and compromise environments (local and city recreation, and regional parks). The metropolis is

[31] Victor Gruen, *The Heart of Our Cities*, New York: Simon and Schuster, 1964, pp. 271–286.

designed for a population of 3,300,000 people. The dimensions and population densities shown or implied are based upon actual data from established communities. Each of the 10 cities making up the metropolis has a population of 280,000 and the core of the metropolis (metro core) accommodates 500,000. A detailed census is given in the figure.

Such a metropolis would occupy 1,800 square kilometers (690 square miles), more than half of which would be devoted to easily accessible open space represented by parks, orchards, forests, lakes, and recreational facilities. By comparison, metropolitan Boston with 80 percent as many people occupies 50 percent more land none of which includes accessible expanses of open space. Los Angeles with over twice the population occupies seven times the land area, very little of which is accessible open space.

To accomplish these undertakings in ecologic planning will require our best expertise, great care and forethought, much time, and enormous amounts of money. But the effort, overwhelming as it is, is dwarfed by the urgency of the task. In the words of the late Adlai Stevenson:

We travel together, passengers on a little spaceship; dependent on its vulnerable reserve of air and soil; all committed for our safety to its security and peace; preserved from annihilation only by the care, the work, and the love we give to our craft.

FIGURE 15-21
This pleasant pedestrian mall in Burbank, California, was once a busy city street congested with automobile traffic.

448

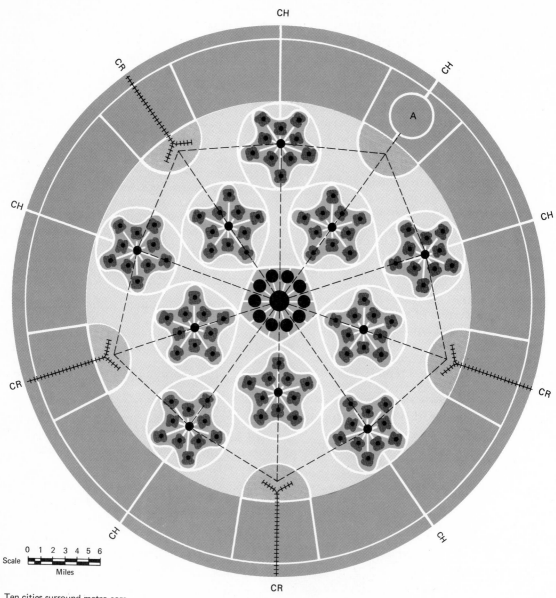

Ten cities surround metro core
consisting of ten core frame units
and metro center.

The metropolis of tomorrow

Scale 0 1 2 3 4 5 6
Miles

Population:

Each of 10 cities	= 280,000 × 10	=	2,800,000
Each of 10 core frame units	= 25,000 × 10	=	250,000
Metro center	= 250,000 × 1	=	250,000
		Total	= 3,300,000

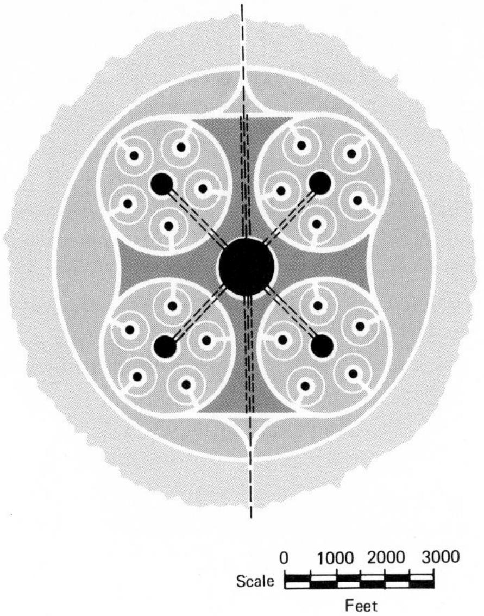
0 1000 2000 3000
Scale
Feet

Legend

A	Airport
++++++	Railroad
	Industrial Area
----	Rapid Transit
	Regional Parks
	City Recreation
	Local Recreation
●	Urban Centers
CR	Connections with National Railroad-Network
CH	Connections with National Highway-Network

Detail of a typical town
It consists of a town center around which four communities are placed. Each community consists of one community center and five neighborhoods.

Population:

Town center	= 3400 × 1 =	3,400
Each of 4 community centers	= 900 × 4 =	3,600
Each of 20 neighborhoods	= 900 × 20 =	18,000
	Total	25,000

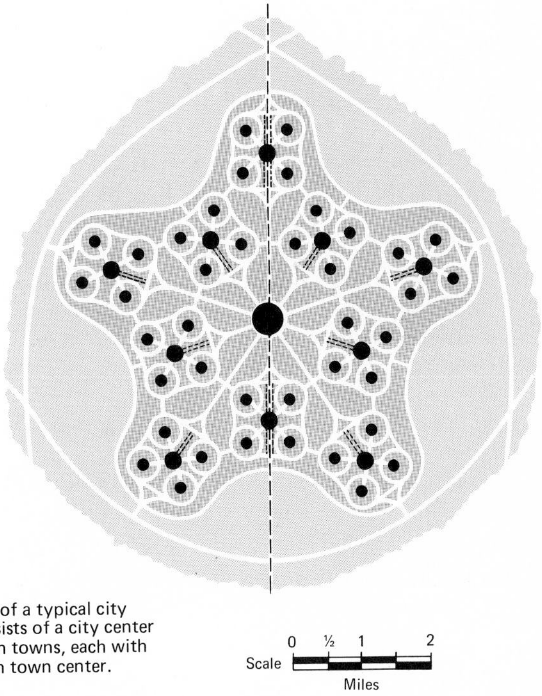
0 ½ 1 2
Scale
Miles

Detail of a typical city
It consists of a city center and ten towns, each with its own town center.

Population:

Each of 10 towns	= 25,000 × 10 =	250,000
City center	= 30,000 × 1 =	30,000
	Total	280,000

FIGURE 15-22
The cellular metropolis of tomorrow, designed by Victor Gruen, a preeminent environmental architect. The metropolis accommodates 3,300,000 people and occupies 1,800 square kilometers (690 square miles), more than half of which is easily accessible open space. The dimensions and population densities shown or implied are based upon actual data from established communities. For illustrative purposes, the figure is quite schematic. [*From Victor Gruen, The Heart of Our Cities, Simon and Schuster, New York, 1964.*]

SUGGESTED READINGS

CROCKER, T. D., and A. J. ROGERS III, *Environmental Economics,* Hinsdale, Ill.: The Dryden Press, Inc., 1971. A wise and witty analysis of how an acceptable level of environmental quality may be achieved within the context of this country's economic system.

EHRLICH, P. R., et al.: *Human Ecology: Problems and Solutions,* San Francisco: W. H. Freeman and Company, 1973. A wide-ranging account of diverse aspects of human ecology, including environmental pollution and the economic, social, and political means by which man may bring his ecological problems under control.

ESPOSITO, J. C.: *Vanishing Air,* New York: Grossman Publishers, 1970. A report by Ralph Nader's Study Group on air pollution.

GRAHAM, F., JR.: *Since Silent Spring,* Boston: Houghton Mifflin Company, 1970. A sequel to Rachel Carson's book (1962) on the environmental effects of pesticides.

HARTE, J., and R. H. SOCOLOW (eds.): *Patient Earth,* New York: Holt, Rinehart and Winston, Inc., 1971. An unusually stimulating collection of articles, including ten cases of studies of contemporary environmental problems in the United States where positive accomplishments have been made and six articles devoted to the stable (nongrowth) society.

HELLER, A.: *The California Tomorrow Plan,* Los Altos, Calif.: William Kaufman, Inc., 1972. A rational state development plan is outlined and compared to what probably will take place.

NOVICK, S.: *The Careless Atom:* Boston: Houghton Mifflin Company, 1969. A discussion of the risks involved in nuclear power plants.

STILL, H.: *In Quest of Quiet,* Harrisburg, Pa.: Stackpole Books, 1970. A popular but thorough account of noise pollution.

TOFFLER, ALVIN (ed.): *The Futurists,* New York: Random House, Inc., 1972. A fascinating selection of essays by outstanding social critics, scientists, philosophers, and planners whose major activity concerns the study of the future.

TUNNARD, C., and B. PUSHKAREV: *Man-made America: Chaos or Control?* New Haven, Conn.: Yale University Press, 1963. A beautifully illustrated book on urbanization and its effect on the environment.

TURNER, J. S.: *The Chemical Feast,* New York: Grossman Publishers, 1970. A report by Ralph Nader's Study Group on food additives in the American diet.

WARREN, C. E.: *Biology and Water Pollution Control,* Philadelphia: W. B. Saunders Company, 1971. A comprehensive treatment of water pollution and its control.

REVIEW QUESTIONS

1 Discuss the nature of smog. Include atmospheric conditions required, chief producers of atmospheric contaminants, the chemical identity of pollutants, and their relative toxicity.

2 Cite two specific instances in which smog has been shown to be damaging to each of the following: (*a*) human health; (*b*) agricultural crops, (*c*) natural ecosystems, (*d*) property and buildings. Insofar as air pollution control is concerned, compare and contrast the regulation-enforcement strategy with that based on economic incentive.

3 List five ways in which noise affects human health adversely.

4 The effluent from sewage plants and runoff from fertilized farmland are major contributors to water pollution. Describe three different ways in which pollution from these sources causes ecologic damage and hazards to health.

5 If most of our projected power plants in A.D. 2000 are nuclear powered, as is currently planned, about what percentage of the total freshwater runoff in the United States will be required to cool them?

6 Cite four ways in which radioactive substances and ionizing radiation are hazardous to organisms. In what ways do nuclear power plants present risks of radioactive pollution? To what extent does the average United States citizen receive excessive radiation from diagnostic x-rays? Indicate the nature and potential risk of a nuclear catastrophe from terrorists.

7 What characteristics of DDT led to concern over its use as an insecticide? (List three different attributes and document each with ecologic data.) What crucial finding finally led to an EPA ban on the use of DDT?

8 A number of alternative methods of pest control are available or are being developed which do not rely on chlorinated hydrocarbons. Describe five of these, illustrating each, and indicating the advantages, disadvantages, and relative effectiveness of the method.

9 United States industry releases thousands of inadequately tested substances into the environment annually, many of which have proven to be potentially hazardous to human life. Substantiate this statement by citing an example in some detail of each of the following: (*a*) the release of a harmful synthetic organic compound into air, water, soil, and food; (*b*) the unintentional contamination of food or drugs; (*c*) the addition of a substance to preserve, flavor, color, or texture foods or drugs or cosmetics.

10 Distinguish between a growth economy and a stable economy. Compare and contrast these two economies from the standpoint of their ecologic relationships and commitments.

11 Write a short essay on what land-use planning would entail and what ecosystem management would mean in a hypothetical stable economy.

12 The following three questions are to be answered both with respect to (*a*) suburbia and (*b*) the inner city or metropolis. (1) Discuss the cultural and ecologic effects of urban sprawl. (2) What are the objectives of ecologic urban planning? (3) Describe an actual example of ecologic urban planning.

GLOSSARY

Abortion (induced) Operation in which the implanted embryo is dislodged from the uterine wall by use of a suction device or by scraping the uterine lining; preferably done within the first 12 weeks of pregnancy.

Acclimatization (somatogenetic adaptability) Biologic adaptation involving individuals being able to accustom themselves to different conditions over a period of time.

Adaptation A particular structure, physiologic function, or behavior which enables an organism to live in a specific environment.

Adaptive radiation Production of a variety of species adapted to diverse ecologic niches by an evolutionary lineage stemming from a common ancestor, as in the adaptive radiation of pongids and hominids from a presumed *Aegyptopithecus*-like ancestor in the Oligocene. (See Fig. 7-8.)

Aegyptopithecus An Egyptian fossil of late Oligocene age that may represent the ancestral stock from which pongids and hominids evolved.

Aggressive behavior Behavior directed by a member or members of a species toward harming other members of that same species.

Allele One of two or more alternative forms in a gene set; the genotypes *AA, Aa,* and *aa* possess two alleles: *A* and *a.* (See *gene.*)

Allen's rule The tendency among warm-blooded vertebrates for individuals within a species or in closely related species to have projecting body parts, like ears and legs, progressively shorter the farther such individuals live from the equator. (See *Bergmann's principle,* and Figs. 10-9 and 10-11.)

Allopatric Pertains to two or more related species which occupy separate, nonoverlapping areas. (See *sympatric.*)

Altruistic behavior Behavior in which an animal risks its life to benefit another; behavior in which individuals mutually act to protect the interests of one another is called *reciprocal altruism.*

Anagenetic Adaptive changes within a single evolutionary lineage in which adaptedness to a particular ecologic niche changes but little. (See *paleospecies, cladogenetic.*)

Anthropoidea One of two suborders of Primates, which includes monkeys, apes, and humans. (See Fig. 3-1.)

Antibody A protein manufactured by an animal body that renders a foreign substance harmless. (See *antigen.*)

Antigen Any substance which, if it contacts appropriate tissues in an animal body, stimulates the production of antibodies in that animal. (See *antibody.*)

Aquaculture Food production in water.

Arboreal adaptations Modifications of an organism enabling it to live in trees, such as the grasping hands and feet of primates.

Australopith A member of the genus *Australopithecus* (family Hominidae) of Pliocene and early Pleistocene; divided into two groups: the gracile form (*A. africanus*) and the robust form (*A. robustus* and *A. boisei*).

Balanced genetic polymorphism The tendency of natural selection to preserve, when the heterozygote *Aa* is better adapted than either *AA* or *aa,* each of the less fit homozygotes in such a proportion as to produce a population with the highest *average* fitness possible. (See Fig. 9-6.)

Behavior Any observable action or activity performed by an animal.

Bergmann's principle The tendency among warm-blooded vertebrates for individuals within a species or in closely related species to be progressively larger the farther they live from the equator. (See *Allen's rule,* and Figs. 10-8 and 10-10.)

Biogeography Study of the geographic distribution of living things over the earth.

Biomass Weight of all the organisms in a given area; also may refer to total weight of a species or a group of species in a given area.

Biotic community See *ecosystem.*

Bipedalism Locomotion in which the animal characteristically walks on two legs, as in man.

Birth rate The number of children born per year for every thousand people at the middle of that year.

Brachiation A specialized form of arboreal locomotion in which the animal is propelled from branch to branch by hand-over-hand arm-swinging. Gibbons are *true brachiators* because this is their major method of locomotion. Chimpanzees who move quadrupedally on the ground but may brachiate in the trees are called *semibrachiators.*

Cambrian period Earliest of the six periods in the Paleozoic era, lasting from 600 to 500 million years ago. (See Fig. 2-13.)

Carboniferous period One of six periods in the Paleozoic era; between the Devonian and Permian periods; it lasted from 345 to 280 million years ago. (See Fig. 2-13.)

Carcinogen Agent that induces the development of cancer.

Carnivorous Feeding on animals.

Ceboidea One of three superfamilies of anthropoids, and includes all New World monkeys (marmosets, squirrel monkey, spider monkey, etc.). (See Fig. 3-1.)

Cell The basic unit of structure in all living things; the smallest structural unit capable of carrying on all living functions.

Cenozoic era One of the major subdivisions of geologic time, lasting from 65 million years ago to the present. (See Figs. 2-13 and 6-5.)

Cercopithecoidea One of three superfamilies of anthropoids, which includes all Old World monkeys (langurs, macaques, baboons, etc.). (See Fig. 3-1.)

Chlorinated hydrocarbons Compounds containing carbon, hydrogen, and chlorine; used widely as pesticides. (See Fig. 15-14.)

Chromosome A structure in the nucleus of a cell that contains the hereditary material (genes). (See Figs. 8-12 to 8-16.)

City A community of individuals having a division of labor involving many specialized occupations, a system of trade and commerce, and a social organization based upon occupation and social class rather than kinship. (See *village.*)

Civilization A society with a high degree of cultural complexity, organized around one or more cities, and having a written language.

Cladogenetic Pertains to adaptive changes within a divergent evolutionary lineage which result in various species, each adapted to a different ecologic niche. (See *adaptive radiation.*)

Class One of the principal divisions of a phylum, and consisting of one or more orders, such as the class Mammalia (mammals).

Classical conditioning (learning) Learning that occurs when a conditioned stimulus (CS) is associated with an unconditioned stimulus (UCS); for example, if a light is shined (CS) into a person's eye, the pupils contract. If the light is accompanied by the ring of a bell (UCS), the pupils eventually contract at the sound of the bell alone. (See *operant conditioning.*)

Climax community The final biotic community in an ecologic succession, relatively stable and self-perpetuating unless disturbed by an external agency; an ecosystem with a climax community is said to be mature. (See Figs. 11-7 and 11-8.)

Cline Gradual and continuous change in a trait or the frequency of a trait in a series of geographically adjacent populations; a character gradient.

Coal gasification Process for producing natural gases (e.g., methane) from coal desposits.

Codominant genes Genes in which both alleles of a pair are fully expressed in the heterozygous genotype, as in blood type AB (genotype $I^A I^B$).

Coevolution Evolution in two or more species of organisms that have a close interrelationship, resulting in mutual adaptations for living together, as in zebras, wildebeests, and Thomson's gazelles (Fig. 11-15).

Cognitive learning Altering the meaning of previous learning through the accumulation of new information and experience. Sometimes called *latent learning* because it may not be put to immediate use, as in reading a book. *Modeling* (learning by imitation) is also a form of cognitive learning.

Commensalism A symbiotic association in which one of the participating species benefits while the other is neither benefited nor harmed, as in cattle egrets and Cape buffalo (Fig. 11-9).

Competition A relationship common to organisms that are sharing resources which are in limited supply; of two types: *intraspecific,* between members of the same species; *interspecific,* between members of different species.

Computerized multivariate analysis A computer analysis in which every significant dimension of an unclassified object (e.g., fossil tooth) is compared with corresponding dimensions of similar classified objects (e.g., teeth of known species); often millions of mathematical comparisons are made.

Consumers Organisms who feed on other organisms, including primary consumers (herbivores and plant parasites), secondary consumers (carnivores and parasites that feed on herbivores and plant parasites), and so on.

Continental drift, theory of The belief that the continents of the earth move (drift) about 1 to 2 centimeters per year, gradually changing their distances from one another. (See Fig. 6-6.)

Convergent evolution The superficial resemblance of dis-

tantly related organisms which have evolved as residents in a common environment and have shared a similar habitat and mode of life (e.g., porpoise and shark). (See Figs. 10-5 and 10-6, and *parallel evolution.*)

Cretaceous period The youngest of three periods in the Mesozoic era, lasting from 135 to 65 million years ago. (See Figs. 2-13 and 6-5.)

Crossover See *genetic recombination.*

Culture Learned behavior that is transmitted from individual to individual and from generation to generation; human culture is distinguished by language and divisible into *material culture* (objects and physical conditions) and *nonmaterial culture* (behavior, belief, and understanding).

Death rate The number of deaths per year for every thousand people at the middle of that year.

Decomposers Organisms (bacteria, fungi, etc.) which convert dead organic matter into inorganic materials.

Deme A strictly local Mendelian population composed of individuals who live together in a common habitat and who usually choose their mates from their own numbers.

Demographic transition Decline of the death rate, as a country undergoes industrialization, followed by decline of the birth rate when industrialization has been achieved.

Demography The statistical study of populations.

Dental formula A system of numbers expressing the numbers and kinds of teeth in mammals. The dental formula of man is $\dfrac{2.1.2.3}{2.1.2.3}$, indicating that one half of the upper and lower jaws contains two incisors, one canine, two premolars, and three molars.

Dentition The kinds of teeth in an animal, their number, arrangement, and form. Mammals have four kinds: incisors, canines, premolars, and molars.

Design features (language) The basic characteristics of human language, such as arbitrariness, duality of patterning, and openness; some are not found in nonhuman animal communication.

Detritus Dead organic matter.

Detritus farming Food production in which recycled organic waste (e.g., processed sewage) is used as fertilizer.

Devonian period One of six periods in the Paleozoic era; between the Silurian and Carboniferous periods, it lasted from 405 to 345 million years ago. (See Fig. 2-13.)

Diploid Cells in which the chromosomes occur in homologous pairs; in man such cells have 23 pairs of chromosomes (46). (See *haploid.*)

Displacement activity Behavior that is not relevant to a situation, usually seen in animals that are uneasy or frustrated; a chimp so disturbed may scratch its side or its arm.

Diurnal Active during the day in distinction to nocturnal (active at night).

Divergent evolution See *adaptive radiation.*

Dominance hierarchy A system of social ranking among members of a group of animals; rank may vary in different kinds of social situations.

Dominant gene A gene that expresses its full phenotypic effect in both homozygous and heterozygous genotypes.

Dryopithecines A subfamily of ancient pongids, including *Aegyptopithecus* of the Egyptian Oligocene and several species of early Miocene to early Pliocene apes (genus *Dryopithecus*) whose fossil remains have been found widely distributed in Africa and Eurasia; believed to include one or more ancestors of the orangutan, chimpanzee, gorilla, and man.

Ecologic niche The specific relationship an organism has with reference to both the physical environment and the biotic community in an ecosystem, especially in regard to the way the organism obtains food or nutrient.

Ecologic replacement The filling of ecologic niches by other species as the one or more species which held these niches decline in numbers prior to their actual extinction.

Ecologic succession The progression of biotic communities in a particular area over a period of time, from initial colonization until a relatively stable climax community is reached. (See Figs. 11-7 and 11-8.)

Ecology The study of the interrelationships of organisms with one another and with their physical environment.

Ecosystem All the organisms in a given area (the *biotic community*) and the physical environment in which they live as an interacting system.

Effluent Waste emitted by industrial processing, either waterborne or airborne from tall smokestacks.

Endocrine gland An organ or a cluster of cells producing a secretion (hormone) that is emptied directly into the blood, such as the thyroid gland.

Endogamy (*a*) marriage or mating between persons belonging to the same social group as prescribed by law or custom; (*b*) a mating between two organisms that are closely related (e.g., first cousins). (See *exogamy*.)

Energy, geothermal Energy derived from heat in the earth's interior; extracted by wells (see Fig. 14-15).

Energy, nuclear Energy derived from a nuclear reactor. (See Fig. 15-12.)

Energy, solar Energy derived directly or indirectly from solar radiation through (*a*) solar (photovoltaic) cells, (*b*) fermentation of natural organic waste materials, (*c*) solar energy collectors, and (*d*) ocean thermal-gradient power plants.

Energy flow, community The capture, use, and transport of energy in the biotic community from producers to consumers to decomposers.

Environmental capacity The optimum number of individuals in any one species that an ecosystem can support indefinitely without damage to the ecosystem; a number determined by the interaction of reproduction potential and environmental resistance.

Environmental resistance See *limiting factor*.

Enzyme A protein substance which serves as a catalyst, that is, a substance that speeds a chemical reaction.

Eocene epoch One of five epochs in the Tertiary period; between the Paleocene and Oligocene epochs, it lasted from 58 to 36 million years ago. (See Figs. 2-13 and 6-5.)

Erythroblastosis (fetal) A blood disease affecting unborn or newborn infants caused by an Rh incompatibility between mother and child.

Eutrophication The process of nutrient enrichment and excessive algal growth in streams and lakes, caused by fertilizers and other chemical agents.

Evolution (organic) Descent with modification; change in the gene pool of a population through time.

Exogamy (*a*) Marriage or mating between persons belonging to different social groups as prescribed by law or custom; (*b*) a mating between two organisms that are not closely related. (See *endogamy*.)

Exploratory drive Motivation, active striving, or need to explore a new environment.

Family (*a*) One of the principal divisions of an order, and consisting of one or more genera, such as the family Pongidae to which orangutans, chimpanzees, and gorillas belong. (*b*) In terms of human social organization, families are of two types: a *nuclear family* consisting of a man, his wife (or wives), and their unmarried children; an *extended family* composed of a group of sisters and their offspring (the matrilineal form) or a group of brothers and their offspring (the patrilineal form). (See Fig. 5-9.)

Fertility rate The number of live births per thousand women of childbearing age (15 to 44 age-classes).

Food chain A specific sequence of species that fills the roles of producer, consumer, and decomposer, such as grass-grasshoppers-frogs-snakes-hawks (decomposer unspecified). (See Figs. 11-1 and 11-2.)

Fossil fuels Petroleum products, natural gas, and coal.

Fossils The remains or traces of organisms that lived in past geologic ages.

Founder effect Establishment of a new population by a small number of migrants (founders) whose genetic make-up may be unrepresentative of the gene pool in the homeland.

Frugivorous Feeding on fruits.

Gamete A sex cell (sperm or ovum).

Gene A hereditary factor; the functional unit of heredity occupying a specific location in a particular chromosome.

Gene flow The movement of genes into or out of a Mendelian population through immigration and emigration.

Gene linkage Genes located on the same chromosome.

Genetic drift Random changes in gene frequency due to sampling error; particularly marked in small populations.

Genetic reassortment See *independent assortment, principle of*.

Genetic recombination The rearrangement of alleles in a homologous chromosome pair through a chromosome break and an exchange of broken parts (*crossover*). (See Fig. 8-18.)

Genetics The scientific study of heredity and the sources of hereditary variation.

Genotype The genetic make-up of an individual; *AA, Aa,* and *aa* are three genotypes (homozygous dominant, heterozygous, and homozygous recessive).

Genus (plural, genera) One of the principal divisions of a family, and consisting of one or more species, such as the genus *Pan,* which includes two species (*P. troglodytes,* the common chimpanzee and *P. paniscus,* the pygmy chimpanzee).

Green revolution Increased production from croplands through heavier application of fertilizers, increased irrigation, and the use of high-yield plant varieties.

Grooming Cleaning the coat and skin, removing parasites and foreign matter; an important part of primate behavior and social life.

Growth rate (rate of natural increase) The death rate subtracted from the birth rate, expressed as a percentage.

Half-life (radioactive) The time required for half the atoms of a radioactive element to decay into stable, non-radioactive atoms (28 years for strontium 90, 4.5 billion years for uranium 238).

Haploid The chromosome number found in mature sex cells (one of each of the different chromosomes); in man such cells have 23 chromosomes. (See *diploid*.)

Hardy-Weinberg principle A law of population genetics which states that gene frequencies will remain constant generation after generation in a large, randomly interbreeding population in which selection pressure, mutation pressure, and gene flow are absent.

Herbivorous Feeding on plants.

Heterozygous A genotype having two different alleles in the same gene set (for example, *Aa*).

Home range See *territory*.

Hominidae Family of Primates to which humans belong, represented today by but one species, *Homo sapiens*. *Ramapithecus* (late Miocene to early Pliocene) and *Australopithecus* (Pliocene to early Pleistocene) were also hominids. (See Fig. 3-1.)

Hominoidea One of three superfamilies of anthropoids which includes apes and humans. (See Fig. 3-1.)

Homozygous A genotype having identical alleles of the same gene set (for example, *AA* or *aa*).

Hormone A substance secreted by cells which has specific effects on the activity of other cells, to which it is transported by the bloodstream, such as insulin or estrogen.

Hylobatidae Family of Primates consisting of the Lesser Apes: gibbons and siamangs. (See Fig. 3-1.)

Hypothesis A plausible explanation which lacks adequate testing or substantiation.

Incest taboo A cultural restriction against marriage or mating between certain types of relatives, usually those considered too closely related.

Independent assortment, principle of Different traits are inherited independently of each other; for example, in pea plants, flower color is inherited independently of plant stature. Also called *genetic reassortment*. (See Fig. 8-3.)

In-groups Groups to which one belongs, such as one's family or church. (See *out-group*.)

Innate (inborn) behavior Behavioral patterns present at birth and determined basically by hereditary mechanisms, such as human infants blind from birth who smile at voices and turn their eyes toward the sound.

Insectivora An order of placental mammals that includes shrews, moles, and hedgehogs.

Insectivorous Feeding on insects.

Intelligence (IQ) test A test which presumes to measure whatever abilities the test was designed to evaluate, based on the assumption that certain specified abilities are related to native intelligence.

Interpersonal press Human overcrowding in which one is in almost constant contact with others most of the time (term coined by O. R. Galle et al.).

Ionizing radiation High-energy radiation, such as ultra-violet (black) light, cosmic rays, x-rays, and the radiation from nuclear reactors, nuclear explosions, and radioactive elements (strontium 90, plutonium, etc.).

Jurassic period The middle of three periods in the Mesozoic era, lasting from 180 to 135 million years ago. (See Figs. 2-13 and 6-5.)

Karyotype The number and kinds of chromosomes in a cell, usually shown by microscope photographs of metaphase chromosomes arranged in a standard sequence. (See Figs. 8-15 and 8-28.)

Kingdom One of the principal divisions of living organisms, such as the animal kingdom and the plant kingdom.

Knuckle-walking Semi-erect quadrupedal locomotion, as in chimpanzees and gorillas, where the weight on the forelegs is borne on the knuckles rather than on the palm.

Language Communication by use of a system of symbols; not to be confused with animal communication by vocalizations (calls), scents, facial expressions, gestures, and postures.

Learning Any relatively permanent change in behavior as a result of practice or experience.

Lemuriformes One of three infraorders of prosimians that includes lemurs and sifakas (superfamily Lemuroidea) and the aye-aye (superfamily Daubentonioidea). (See Fig. 3-1.)

Limiting factor (biotic) Any factor in the physical environment (e.g., water) or the biotic environment (e.g., interspecific competition) that restricts the population growth or distribution of a species; all limiting factors of a species = the *environmental resistance* to that species.

Liquefaction (coal and oil shale) Process for making crude oil by liquefying coal or oil shale.

Living floor A former land surface preserved in sedimentary rock that was once occupied by a hominid; it contains tools, the fossil remains of food (e.g., bones), coprolites (fossil feces), or even hominid fossils themselves; also called occupational layer.

Lorisiformes One of three infraorders of prosimians that includes the lorises and bushbabies (superfamily Lorisoidea). (See Fig. 3-1.)

Macromolecule A giant molecule; protein molecules (e.g., hemoglobin) and nucleic acid molecules (for example, DNA) are macromolecules.

Malnutrition A deficiency in one or more nutrients, usually protein. (See *undernourishment*.)

Malthusian Refers to the doctrine of Thomas Malthus (1766–1834) that human populations constantly tend to outstrip their food supplies.

Mammal A class of vertebrate animals; they are warm-blooded, possess hair, have teeth differentiated into different types (incisors, canines, premolars, molars), and nourish their young with milk.

Marital fertility, index of The number of births of married women in a population in one year divided by the number of births these women would have had if they were reproducing at the highest birth rate for their age ever recorded in a population of substantial size.

Master association area A well-developed association

center in the human cerebrum, poorly if at all developed in other primates; it is located near the body-sense, visual, and auditory areas and is thought to be involved in the development of language.

Mature ecosystem See *climax community.*

Meiosis A type of cell division which occurs in maturing sex cells; two successive divisions result in daughter cells that are haploid. (See Fig. 8-16.)

Menopause The period when menstruation permanently ceases in the human female, usually at 45 to 50 years old.

Mesozoic era One of the major subdivisions of geologic time, lasting from 230 to 65 million years ago. (See Figs. 2-13 and 6-5.)

Miocene epoch One of five epochs in the Tertiary period; between the Oligocene and the Pliocene, it lasted from 25 to 12 million years ago. (See Figs. 2-13 and 6-5.)

Mitosis A type of cell division in which the daughter cells are diploid; occurs in all cells of the body during growth or cell replacement. (See Fig. 8-14.)

Monogamy Marriage to only one person at a time.

Motivation State within an animal that drives behavior toward some goal or "need," such as the basic drives of hunger, self-preservation, sex, and exploration; may also be learned, as in the drive to earn money or gain social status.

Mutagenic agent (mutagen) Any agent that contributes to mutation or to an increase in the mutation rate (e.g., radioactive substances, ionizing radiation).

Mutation Any genetic change involving the alteration of a gene, an abnormal break in a chromosome, or a change in chromosome number. (See Figs. 8-27, 8-29, and 8-30; also see *mutation pressure.*)

Mutation pressure The difference between the mutation rate of a wild-type gene, *A*, to a mutant allele, *a* (*direct mutation*), and the mutation rate of the mutant allele, *a,* back to the normal gene, *A* (*reverse mutation*); since the direct mutation rate is much the higher of the two, mutation pressure favors higher frequencies of the mutant allele.

Mutualism A symbiotic relationship in which both participating species benefit, as in the association between yellow baboons and impalas (Fig. 11-10).

Natural selection The process by which certain phenotypes with high survival rates in a population tend to pass their genes and their traits on to succeeding generations; differential reproductive success.

Neanderthal peoples All human populations (*Homo sapiens*) who lived from about 100,000 to 40,000 years ago.

Neolithic The New Stone Age; the first agricultural technologies and the age of village life; the most primitive agricultural societies today.

New towns Cities designated as self-sufficient, planned communities with residential areas, parks, shopping centers, civic buildings, and industrial districts (e.g., Cumbernauld, Scotland).

Olfactory Pertaining to smell.

Oligocene epoch One of five epochs in the Tertiary period; between the Eocene and Miocene epochs, it lasted from 36 to 25 million years ago. (See Figs. 2-13 and 6-5.)

Omnivorous Feeding on plants and animals.

Operant conditioning (learning) Learning to make a specific response to obtain positive reinforcement (reward) or to avoid a painful stimulus; also called "trial and error" learning. (See *classical conditioning.*)

Opportunity, constitutional (in evolution) Opportunity for the evolution of a new species from an ancestral species because the ancestral species possesses the minimum adaptations to survive in a new environment; also called *preadaptation.*

Opportunity, ecological (in evolution) Opportunity for the evolution of a new species from an ancestral species because a new environment, open to colonization by the ancestral species, possesses native species against which the ancestral species could compete.

Opportunity, physical (in evolution) Opportunity for the evolution of a new species from an ancestral species because the ancestral species has physical access to a new environment.

Opposable thumb or big toe The fleshy tip of the thumb or toe squarely meets the corresponding tips of the other four digits.

Ordovician period One of the six periods in the Paleozoic era; between the Cambrian and Silurian periods, it lasted from 500 to 425 million years ago. (See Fig. 2-13.)

Order One of the principal divisions of a class, and consisting of one or more families, such as the order Primates to which man belongs.

Organic compounds Chemical compounds containing the element carbon; includes carbohydrates, fats, proteins, nucleic acids, and many others.

Out-groups Groups to which we do not belong; groups to which "they" belong. (See *in-groups.*)

Paleocene epoch The earliest of five epochs in the Tertiary period, lasting from 65 to 58 million years ago. (See Figs. 2-13 and 6-5.)

Paleolithic The Old Stone Age cultures of early Recent, Pleistocene, and possibly late Pliocene epochs. A hunter-gatherer economy featuring stone tools made by chipping and flaking and the absence of cultivated plants and domesticated animals; divided into Lower, Middle, and Upper Paleolithic cultures. (See Fig. 6-5.)

Paleontology The study of the remains or traces (fossils) of ancient organisms preserved in the rocks.

Paleospecies Species distinguished by a time sequence separating an ancestral species from its descendant species; *Homo erectus* 300,000 years ago and its descendant species *H. sapiens* 250,000 years ago are paleospecies, one having gradually evolved into the other. Such changes in a single evolutionary line are called *anagenetic.*

Paleozoic era One of the major subdivisions of geologic time, lasting from 600 million to 230 million years ago. (See Fig. 2-13.)

Parallel evolution The evolution of similar forms in separate but related biological lineages, as in the New World spider monkey and the gibbon of Asia (Fig. 3-2*G* and *I*). See *convergent evolution.*

Parasitism A symbiotic association in which one participant (the parasite) benefits and the other (the host) is usually harmed, as in the malarial parasite and its human host.

Permian period The youngest of the six periods in the Paleozoic era, lasting from 280 to 230 million years ago.

Pesticide A chemical agent that kills pests, for example, insecticides and herbicides. (See Fig. 15-14.)

Phenotype The physical appearance or performance of an organism in contrast to its genetic make-up (genotype); red-flowered and white-flowered pea plants are two phenotypes.

Pheromone A substance produced by an animal that influences the behavior of other members of the same species.

Photosynthesis The process by which green plants, algae, and certain bacteria produce carbohydrates and other organic compounds from carbon dioxide and water in the presence of light and chlorophyll.

Phylum (plural, phyla) One of the principal divisions of a kingdom and consisting of one or more classes, such as the phylum Chordates which includes sea squirts, lancelets, and all vertebrate animals. (See Fig. 2-1.)

Pivot grammar Characteristic grammatical pattern of infant language regardless of the language spoken; consists of two parts, pivots (qualifying comments) and names (things, people, impressions).

Placenta A structure formed by the union of embryonic membranes and the uterine lining, by means of which the embryo receives nutrients and oxygen and eliminates its wastes.

Pleistocene epoch The earlier of two epochs in the Quaternary period, lasting from $2\frac{1}{2}$ million to 25,000 years ago. (See Figs. 2-13 and 6-5.)

Pliocene epoch The youngest of five epochs in the Tertiary period, lasting from 12 to $2\frac{1}{2}$ million years ago. (See Figs. 2-13 and 6-5).

Polyandry A polygamous marriage of one wife to several husbands (occurs rarely).

Polygamy Marriages involving several husbands or several wives. (See *polygyny* and *polyandry*.)

Polygyny A polygamous marriage of one husband to several wives.

Pongidae Family of Primates consisting of the Great Apes: orangutans, chimpanzees, and gorillas. (See Fig. 3-1.)

Population bottleneck The gene pool of a population that has become greatly reduced in size may be atypical of the original gene pool; a variation of the founder effect.

Population, Mendelian A group of interbreeding organisms such as a species, race, or deme that inhabits a specific geographic area.

Population structure (age profile) The proportionate division of a population into age classes by sex; age classes are represented in increments of five years as horizontal bars extending on either side of a vertical center line (left of center line = males, right = females). (See Figs. 12-11 and 12-12.)

Positive assortative mating The tendency of people with similar constitutions, backgrounds, and interests to mate.

Power grip A grip in which the object held is between the undersurfaces of the fingers and the palm, as in holding a hammer.

Preadaptation See *opportunity, constitutional.*

Precision grip A grip in which the object held is between the tip of a finger, usually the index finger, and the tip of the thumb, as in holding a toothpick.

Predation The act of killing and consuming another animal for food; predatory behavior.

Primary group One that consists of people who know one another intimately, as in a family or a clique (circle of close friends). (See *secondary group* and *social group*.)

Primary, secondary, and tertiary consumers See *consumers.*

Primates An order of mammals which includes humans, apes, monkeys, and prosimians.

Producers Essentially the green plants that capture solar energy and transform that energy into energy-rich organic compounds. (See *photosynthesis*.)

Production, community The manufacture of high-energy organic compounds by the producers of a biotic community. (See *respiration, community*.)

Pronation Rotating the palm to face downward. (See *supination*.)

Prosimii (Prosimians) One of two suborders of Primates that includes lemurs, lorises, bushbabies, and tarsiers. (See Fig. 3-1.)

Protein A macromolecule composed of a long chain of smaller molecules called amino acids; albumin and hemoglobin are proteins.

Pyramid of energy Large amounts of energy are lost as energy passes from one trophic level to the next in a biotic community; the energy content of trophic levels decreases progressively above level 1, being the least at the topmost level. (See Fig. 11-3.)

Quantitative character. A trait determined by the cumulative action of many genes which shows gradual, continuous variation in a population between two extremes, as in human skin pigmentation, height, and intelligence.

Quaternary period The younger of two periods in the Cenozoic era, spanning the past $2\frac{1}{2}$ million years. (See Figs. 2-13 and 6-5.)

Race A Mendelian population composed of a cluster of demes between which gene flow occurs; although distinguished from other races by differences in gene frequencies, racial interbreeding may take place.

Ramapithecus The earliest known hominid in the fossil record; fossils range from late Miocene (about 15 million years ago) to early Pliocene.

Recent epoch The younger of two epochs in the Quaternary period, spanning the past 25,000 years; also called the Holocene epoch. (See Figs. 2-13 and 6-5.)

Recessive gene One that expresses its phenotypic effect only in a homozygous genotype.

Redirected aggression The transfer of threat or aggression to an uninvolved individual or inanimate object, such as the man who yells at his wife, who then scolds her child, who in turn kicks the cat.

Replacement fertility level That fertility level which, if continued unchanged, would eventually result in zero population growth, measured by the average number of children born per woman in her lifetime; is slightly greater than two to compensate for child mortality, infertility, and nonmarriage.

Reproductive potential The reproductive capacity of a

species if death occurred solely from old age.

Respiration, community The processes whereby the producers, consumers, and decomposers in a biotic community convert the high-energy compounds manufactured by producers to low-energy CO_2. (See *production, community.*)

Satellite towns Planned suburbs around a large metropolitan center, for example, Salem and Hässelby Gärd near Stockholm, Sweden (Fig. 15-20).

Secondary group A formal, impersonal group devoted to a particular function or goal, as in a corporation or bureaucracy, its subsidiary divisions, and the countless small agencies that serve it. (See *primary group* and *social group.*)

Secondary sexual characteristics Traits that distinguish the two sexes but which play no direct part in reproduction, such as the deeper voice, greater size, and beard in men.

Segregation, principle of In the formation of sex cells in one individual, the paired alleles of a gene set separate, producing sex cells with one or the other allele but not both.

Selection pressure The pressure exerted by environmental factors in eliminating phenotypes that are unadaptive and poorly adapted, and in perpetuating those that are adaptive.

Sex chromosomes The X and Y chromosomes (XX = female; XY = male), which are found in all mammals and many other animals.

Sex-linked genes Genes that are carried on one sex chromosome (for example, X) but not the other (Y).

Sexual dimorphism A significant difference in the body structure of the two sexes other than in the sexual organs themselves.

Sexual response cycle The physiologic changes that occur in both sexes during sexual intercourse; divided into four phases: (*a*) excitement, (*b*) plateau, (*c*) orgasmic, and (*d*) resolution.

Sickle-cell anemia A hereditary disease caused by an abnormal form of hemoglobin; red blood cells take on a sickle-shape in homozygous individuals when blood oxygen levels are low (see Fig. 8-33).

Silurian period One of the six periods in the Paleozoic era; between the Ordovician and Devonian periods, it lasted from 425 to 405 million years ago. (See Fig. 2-13.)

Social group An aggregation whose members act together in a joint effort to satisfy common needs, and who share a sense of common identity. (See *primary* and *secondary groups* and *in-groups.*)

Speciation The origin of a new species.

Species Largest Mendelian population, the members of which interbreed (or have the potential to do so) but are reproductively isolated from all other Mendelian populations; the basic unit of biological classification, designating a particular kind of organism.

Supination Rotating the palm to face upward. (See *pronation.*)

Symbiosis A general term used for all types of intimate interrelationships between different species; includes commensalism, mutualism, and parasitism.

Symbol A sound, visual form, or tactile surface that has been arbitrarily chosen to represent something else, as in the sound or appearance of the word *book*.

Sympatric Pertains to two or more related species which inhabit identical or broadly overlapping areas.

Tactile Pertaining to touch.

Tarsiiformes One of three infraorders of prosimians that includes the tarsiers (superfamily Tarsiioidea). (See Fig. 3-1.)

Territory A specific area or habitat occupied by an individual, a pair of individuals, or a group belonging to the same species. The area is defended by the resident species against intrusion by nonresident members of the same species. If the area is not defended, it is called a *home range*.

Tertiary period The earlier of two periods in the Cenozoic era, lasting from 65 to $2\frac{1}{2}$ million years ago. (See Figs. 2-13 and 6-5.)

Theory An hypothesis supported by an impressive body of scientific evidence and which has withstood repeated attempts to disprove it.

Thermal pollution Heat pollution by releasing heat into the air over cities (See *urban heat island*) or into oceans, streams, and lakes by the coolant water effluent from power plants and other industrial processes.

Thinking The mental manipulation and use of memories and images of past experiences.

Tree shrews A controversial group of small, active mammals (family Tupaiidae) which some biologists place in the order Insectivora and others in the order Primates.

Triassic period The earliest of the three periods in the Mesozoic era, lasting from 230 to 180 million years ago. (See Figs. 2-13 and 6-5.)

Trophic level One of the successive levels of nutrition in community energy flow; trophic level 1 = producers, level 2 = primary consumers (herbivores and plant parasites), level 3 = secondary consumers (carnivores and parasites that feed on herbivores and plant parasites), and so on.

Tubal ligation Female sterilization; consists surgically of tying off, or cutting, a small section of each uterine tube (oviduct, Fig. 4-9). (See *vasectomy.*)

Twins, one-egg Twins which develop from the same fertilized egg and therefore have the same genotype; also called identical twins.

Twins, two-egg Twins which develop from different fertilized eggs; also called fraternal twins.

Undernourishment Lacking sufficient calories per day. (See *malnutrition.*)

Urban heat island The higher air temperatures around a city caused by the increased use of energy.

Urbanization Increase in the proportion of people living in cities.

Vasectomy Male sterilization; consists surgically of tying off, or cutting, a small section from each sperm duct (vas deferens, Fig. 4-9). (See *tubal ligation.*)

Vertebrate Animals possessing a backbone (vertebrae); includes fishes, amphibians, reptiles, birds, and mammals.

Vestigial organ Structure of reduced size with no apparent function, such as the ear muscles of man.

Village A farming community in which each individual participates in food production, and social organization is based on kinship and the family unit. (See *city.*)

Young ecosystem An ecosystem with a biotic community that is in a relatively early stage of ecologic succession.

INDEX